MW01104045

EDWARD TETZ
ED WILSON
DANIEL A. LAUER

MCSE
TRAINING GUIDE

WINDOWS 95

MCSE Training Guide: Windows 95

Library of Congress Catalog No.: 97-81213

ISBN: 0-56205-880-0

01 00 99 98 4 3 2

Interpretation of the printing code: the rightmost double-digit number is the year of the book's printing; the rightmost single-digit number, the number of the book's printing. For example, a printing code of 98-1 shows that the first printing of the book occurred in 1998.

Screen reproductions in this book were created using Collage Plus from Inner Media, Inc., Hollis, NH.

Executive Editor
Mary Foote

Acquisitions Editor
Nancy Maragioglio

Development Editors
Ami Frank
Robyn Holtzman

Technical Editors
Dave Bixler
Walter Glenn

Managing Editor
Sarah Kearns

Project Editor
Mike La Bonne

Copy Editors
Keith Cline
Gayle Johnson
Daryl Kessler
Amy Lepore

Indexer
Kevin Fulcher

Cover Designer
Jay Corpus

Book Designer
Ruth Harvey

Production Team
Cyndi Davis-Hubler
Terri Edwards
Kelly Maish
Donna Martin

About the Authors

Edward Tetz graduated from Saint Lawrence College in Cornwall, Ontario, with a diploma in business administration in 1990. He spent a short time in computer sales, which turned into a computer support position. He has spent the last seven years performing system and LAN support for small and large organizations. In 1994, he added training to his repertoire. He is both a Microsoft Certified Trainer and a Microsoft Certified Systems Engineer. He has experience with Apple Macintosh, IBM OS/2, and all Microsoft operating systems. He is currently an information technology coordinator and an instructor for PBSC Computer Training Centres, delivering certified training in most Microsoft products.

Ed Wilson is a senior networking specialist with Full Service Networking, a Microsoft Solution Provider Partner, in Cincinnati, Ohio. A former naval officer, he holds degrees from the University of Mississippi and Maysville Community College. He is actively involved in teaching Windows-based classes in the adult education program and is currently working on developing A+ certification classes with Maysville Community College. Ed, who holds both the MCSE and A+ certifications, has been working with computers for nearly 15 years and worked with both Novell and Windows NT networks for the last five years. He lives in Hamilton, Ohio, with his wife Teresa and can be reached on the Internet at **Ewilson@One.Net**.

Daniel A. Lauer currently works as a support specialist in the Teaching and Learning Information Technologies division at Indiana University, Bloomington. His main duties involve providing LAN administration and workstation support to the University Information Technology Services offices. He also helps teach the official Microsoft Certified Professional courses through the IU AATP program. Before becoming a computing professional, Dan was pursuing graduate studies in Astrophysics at IU. He now lives in Bloomington, Indiana.

Acknowledgments

From Dan Lauer

I thank **Sean Angus** and **Ami Frank** at Macmillan Computer Publishing, and **Jeff Cook** for pointing them to me.

Dedications

From Edward Tetz

This book is dedicated to my wife, **Sharon**, and children, **Emily**, and **Mackenzie**. If not for their support and understanding, I would not have the time or ability to write.

From Ed Wilson

Ed dedicates this to his **mom**, who taught him to love books; his **dad**, who taught him to love troubleshooting; and his **wife**, who taught him everything else. He also dedicates this to **Dennis Van Pelt**, who gave him his first networking job, and to **Robbie Graves** and **Terry Paisly**, who taught him his first computer classes.

We'd Like to Hear from You!

As part of our continuing effort to produce books of the highest possible quality, MCP would like to hear your comments. To stay competitive, we really want you, as a computer book reader and user, to let us know what you like or dislike most about this book or other Macmillan products.

You can mail comments, ideas, or suggestions for improving future editions to the following address below or email us at **networking@mcp.com**. The address of our Internet site is **http://www.mcp.com** (World Wide Web).

Thanks in advance—your comments help us to continue publishing the best books available on computer topics in today's market.

Although we cannot provide general technical support, we're happy to help you resolve problems you encounter related to our books, disks, or other products. If you need such assistance, please contact our Tech Support department at 800-545-5914 ext. 3833.

Contents at a Glance

Table of Contents

Part II: Exam Practice

Part III: Appendixes

Introduction

If you're an advanced end-user, service technician, or network administrator, *MCSE Training Guide: Windows 95* is designed to get you certified as a Microsoft Certified Systems Engineer (MCSE). This exam (Exam 70-064): Implementing and Supporting Windows 95, measures your ability to implement, administer, and troubleshoot information systems that incorporate Windows 95, as well as your ability to provide technical support to users of that operating system.

Who Should Read This Book

This book is designed to help prepare you for Microsoft's Implementing and Supporting Windows 95 test (Exam 70-064).

This book is your one-stop shop. Everything you need to know to pass the exam is in here, and Microsoft has approved it as study material. You do not *need* to take a class in addition to buying this book to pass the exam. However, depending on your personal study habits or learning style, you could benefit from taking a class in addition to buying the book, or buying this book in addition to attending a class.

This book also can help advanced users and administrators who are not studying for the exam but are looking for a single-volume reference on Windows 95.

How This Book Helps You

This book covers all the areas covered by the Windows 95 exam and teaches you the specific skills you need to achieve your MCSE certification. You'll also find helpful hints, tips, real-world examples, exercises, and references to additional study materials. Specifically, this book is set up to help you in the following ways:

- **Organization.** This book is organized by major exam topics and individual exam objectives. Every objective you need to know for the Implementing and Supporting Windows 95 exam is covered in this book; we've included a margin icon like the one here to help you quickly locate these objectives as they are addressed in the chapters. This information is also conveniently condensed in the tear card at the front of this book.
- **Time-management advice.** Quizzes appear at the beginning of each chapter to test your knowledge of the objectives contained within that chapter. If you already know the answers to some or all of these questions, you can make a time-management decision accordingly, adjusting the amount of time you spend on a given topic.
- **Extensive practice test options.** Plenty of questions appear at the end of each chapter, as well, to test your comprehension of material covered within that chapter. An answer list follows the questions so you can check yourself. These review questions will help you determine what you understand thoroughly and what topics require further review on your part.

You'll also get a chance to practice for the certification exams by using the TestPrep test engine on the accompanying CD-ROM. The questions on the CD-ROM provide a more thorough and comprehensive look at what the certification exams are like.

For a complete description of New Riders' newly developed test engine, please see Appendix F, "All About TestPrep."

For a complete description of what you can find on the CD-ROM, see Appendix E, "What's on the CD-ROM."

For more information about the exam or the certification process, contact Microsoft:

Microsoft Education: (800) 636-7544

Internet: ftp://ftp.microsoft.com/Services/MSEdCert

World Wide Web: http://www.microsoft.com/train_cert/default.htm

CompuServe Forum: GO MSEDCERT

Understanding What the Implementing and Supporting Windows 95 Exam (70-064) Covers

The Implementing and Supporting Windows 95 exam (70-064) covers the six main topic areas represented by the conceptual groupings of the test objectives. Each chapter represents one of the following main topic areas.

Planning

- Develop an appropriate implementation model for specific requirements. Considerations include choosing a workgroup configuration or joining an existing domain.
- Develop a security strategy. Strategies include system policies, profiles, and file and print sharing.

Installation and Configuration

- Install Windows 95. Installations include the following:

  Automated Windows Setup
  New
  Upgrade
  Uninstall
  Dual boot combination with Microsoft Windows NT

- Install and configure the network components of a client computer and server.

- Install and configure network protocols. Protocols include the following:

  NetBEUI
  IPX/SPX
  TCP/IP
  Data Link Control (DLC)
  PPTP/VPN

- Install and configure hardware devices. Hardware devices include Modems and Printers.

- Configure system services. Services include Browser.

- Install and configure backup hardware and software. Hardware and software include tape drives and the backup application.

Configuring and Managing Resource Access

- Assign permissions for shared folders. Methods include passwords, user permissions, and group permissions.

- Create, share, and monitor resources. Resources include the following:

  Remote
  Network Printers
  Shared fax/modem
  Unimodem/V

- Set up user environments by using profiles and system policies.

- Back up data and restore data.

- Manage hard disks. Tasks include disk compression and partitioning.

- Establish application environments for Microsoft MS-DOS applications.

Integration and Interoperabilty

- Configure a Windows 95 computer as a client in a Windows NT network.
- Configure a Windows 95 computer as a client in a NetWare network.
- Configure a Windows 95 computer to access the Internet.
- Configure a client computer to use Dial-Up Networking for remote access.

Monitoring and Optimization

- Monitor system performance. Tools include Net Watcher and System Monitor.
- Tune and optimize the system. Tools include the following:

  Disk Defragmenter
  ScanDisk
  Compression Utility

Troubleshooting

- Diagnose and resolve installation failures.
- Diagnose and resolve boot process failures.
- Diagnose and resolve connectivity problems. Tools include the following:

  WinIPCfg
  Net Watcher
  Troubleshooting Wizards

- Diagnose and resolve printing problems.
- Diagnose and resolve file system problems.

- Diagnose and resolve resource access problems.
- Diagnose and resolve hardware device and device driver problems. Tools include MSD and Add/Remove Hardware Wizard.
- Perform direct modification of the Registry as appropriate by using Regedit.

Hardware and Software Needed

As a self-paced study guide, this book was designed with the expectation that you will use Windows 95 as you follow along through the exercises while you learn. Microsoft designed Windows 95 to operate in a wide range of actual situations, and the exercises in this book encompass that range. Your computer should meet the following criteria:

- On the Microsoft Hardware Compatibility List
- 486DX2 66-Mhz (or better) processor for Windows NT Server
- Minimum of 32 MB of RAM; 48 MB of RAM is required if SQL Server is installed on the same computer
- 340-MB (or larger) hard disk for Windows NT Server, 100 MB free and formatted as NTFS
- 3.5-inch 1.44-MB floppy drive
- VGA (or Super VGA) video adapter
- VGA (or Super VGA) monitor
- Mouse or equivalent pointing device
- Two-speed (or faster) CD-ROM drive (optional)
- Network Interface Card (NIC)
- Presence on an existing network, or use of a 2-port (or more) mini-port hub to create a test network

- MS-DOS 5.0 or 6.*x* and Microsoft Windows for Workgroups 3.*x* pre-installed
- Microsoft Windows 95
- Microsoft Windows NT Server version 3.51 with service pack 3 or later, or Windows NT Server version 4.0 (CD-ROM version)

It can be somewhat easier to obtain access to the necessary computer hardware and software in a corporate business environment. It can be difficult, however, to allocate enough time within the busy workday to complete a self-study program. Most of your study time should occur after normal working hours, away from the everyday interruptions and pressures of your regular job.

Tips for the Exam

Remember the following tips as you prepare for the certification exams:

- **Read all the material.** Microsoft has been known to include material not expressly specified in the objectives. This course has included additional information not required by the objectives in an effort to give you the best possible preparation for the examination, and for the real-world network experiences to come.
- **Complete the exercises in each chapter.** They will help you gain experience using the Microsoft product. All Microsoft exams are experience-based and require you to have used the Microsoft product in a real networking environment. Exercises for each objective are placed toward the end of each chapter.
- **Take each pre-chapter quiz to evaluate how well you know the topic of the chapter.** Each chapter opens with at least one short answer/essay question per exam objective covered in the chapter. At the very end of the chapter you will find the quiz answers and pointers to where in the chapter that specific objective is covered.

- **Complete all the review questions.** Complete the questions at the end of each chapter—they help you remember key points. The questions are fairly simple, but be warned: Some questions require more than one answer.
- **Review the exam objectives.** Develop your own questions for each topic listed. If you can create and answer several questions for each topic, you should not find it difficult to pass the exam.

Although this book is designed to prepare you to take and pass the Implementing and Supporting Windows 95 certification exam, there are no guarantees. Read this book, work through the questions and exercises, and when you feel confident, take a practice assessment exam by using the TestPrep test engine. This should identify whether you are ready for the real thing.

When taking the actual certification exam, make sure you answer all the questions before your time limit expires. Do not spend too much time on any one question. If you are unsure about an answer, answer the question as best you can and mark it for later review, when you have finished the rest of the questions.

Remember, the primary objective is not to pass the exam—it is to understand the material. After you understand the material, passing the exam should be simple. Knowledge is a pyramid; to build upward, you need a solid foundation. The Microsoft Certified Professional programs are designed to ensure that you have that solid foundation.

Good luck!

New Riders Publishing

The staff of New Riders Publishing is committed to bringing you the very best in computer reference material. Each New Riders book is the result of months of work by authors and staff who research and refine the information contained within its covers.

As part of this commitment to you, the NRP reader, New Riders invites your input. Please let us know if you enjoy this book, if you have trouble with the information or examples presented, or if you have a suggestion for the next edition.

Please note, however, that New Riders staff cannot serve as a technical resource during your preparation for the Microsoft certification exams or for questions about software- or hardware-related problems. Please refer instead to the documentation that accompanies Windows 95 or to the applications' Help systems.

If you have a question or comment about any New Riders book, there are several ways to contact New Riders Publishing. We will respond to as many readers as we can. Your name, address, or phone number will never become part of a mailing list or be used for any purpose other than to help us continue to bring you the best books possible. You can write to us at the following address:

New Riders Publishing
Attn: Publisher
201 W. 103rd Street
Indianapolis, IN 46290

If you prefer, you can fax New Riders Publishing at (317) 817-7448.

You also can send e-mail to New Riders at the following Internet address:

certification@mcp.com

NRP is an imprint of Macmillan Computer Publishing. To obtain a catalog or information, or to purchase any Macmillan Computer Publishing book, call (800) 428-5331.

Thank you for selecting *MCSE Training Guide: Windows 95*!

Part 1

Exam Preparation

Chapter 1

Planning

This chapter helps prepare you for the exam by covering the following objectives:

- Develop an appropriate implementation model for specific requirements in a Microsoft environment and a mixed Microsoft and NetWare environment. Considerations include the following:
  - Choosing a workgroup configuration or joining an existing domain
- Develop a security strategy in a Microsoft environment and a mixed Microsoft and NetWare environment. Strategies include the following:
  - System policies
  - Profiles
  - File and print sharing

Test Yourself! Before reading this chapter, test yourself to determine how much study time you will need to devote to this section.

1. When opening the Network Neighborhood, what icons should you see?
2. Do all servers support long filenames? If not, what types of servers do not?
3. What are some of the factors that you should consider before moving a network over to Windows 95?
4. What is the relationship between User Profiles and System policies?
5. What are some tasks that can be accomplished through remote administration?
6. How must a computer be configured for remote registry editing to take place?
7. What is the name of the answer file for the Windows 95 setup executable?
8. What file is replaced or copied for every user who maintains a User Profile on a computer, and in what directory is it stored?
9. What is the name of the default template file that ships with the System Policy Editor, and what program do you use to edit the template file?
10. What is required to be on a computer that will be using File and Print Sharing for NetWare Networks?

Answers are located at the end of the chapter...

"An ounce of prevention is worth a pound of cure," is often used to describe the benefits of pre-planning anything you do in life. Installing Microsoft Windows 95 is no different, whether it is a single installation or a nation-wide installation on thousands of computers. This chapter examines some of the questions you should consider before you start the first installation. The actual installation will be covered in Chapter 3, "Installation and Configuration, Part 2: Network Components."

- Understanding the new features of Windows 95
- Choosing between Windows 95 and Windows NT Workstation
- Steps in planning and conducting a Windows 95 rollout or implementation, including the following:
  - Inventory of current hardware and software to mark equipment for upgrades
  - Deciding on a version of Windows 95
  - Installation and distribution of software issues
  - Configuring Windows 95 in a workgroup or domain environment
  - Browsing networks or workgroups and how the browsing service works
  - Supporting long filenames in your environment
  - Assembling a distribution team
  - Setting up a representative test lab
  - Conducting a test rollout
  - Documenting and finalizing
  - Performing the rollout

- Developing a security strategy in a Microsoft environment and a mixed Microsoft and Netware environment, including the following:
    - File and Print services and the differences in sharing methods between the two services that Microsoft supplies
    - System policies created with the System Policy Editor
    - User Profiles for separate local settings or for network stored profiles that will follow users around the network
    - Remote registry editing and system monitoring
    - Remote Administration of local file systems: How file and Print Sharing settings modify remote administration settings
- Web services and Internet connectivity

Most of the topics in the preceding list require a trip out to a person's computer to install or configure an additional component if you have not already performed this task. This can lead to many additional hours of time (possibly triple or more for repeated trips). The goal of planning is to eliminate the inconvenience and cost of these repeated trips to the desktop by getting it right the first time.

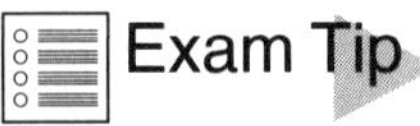

You are likely to be tested on the following:

- Your knowledge of what can be done with System policies, and using policies to solve the most common support issues. Know how to solve the top five support problems, which include the following:
    - Changes in video settings or display adapter type, so the display will not work
    - Changes to the network settings, such as the removal of required protocols or clients or the addition of conflicting components, causing network access to fail

  - Installation of unsupported or untested software that is now causing problems with required applications
  - Removal of required applications
  - Modification to or deletion of required configuration files, such as CONFIG.SYS
- What must be configured for Remote registry editing to take place
- What can be accomplished through Remote Administration and how it is configured
- Where profiles are stored in a network environment and what is part of a User Profile and what is part of a System policy
- What can solve browse failures

Microsoft Windows 95 Key Features

Before you actually plan a Windows 95 rollout, it's important to familiarize yourself with the features of the operating system. Although this might not be specifically tested, the test assumes you know this. If you already do, proceed to Exercise 1.1, "Choosing Between Windows 95 and Windows NT."

In Windows 95, there are significant improvements. It is now a true operating system, combining elements of DOS and Windows 3.x. Designed to become the desktop standard, Windows 95 is tuned to deliver the best performance from personal and business applications in either standalone computers or networked workstations. With millions of previously installed MS-DOS and Windows 3.x platforms existing today, Windows 95 is ideally suited as an upgrade product. The following sections describe key features of Windows 95 that explain why someone should upgrade.

A Better, More Intuitive User Interface

Microsoft conducted usability studies to improve the ease-of-use aspects of Windows 95. The *user interface* (UI) in Windows 95 had to meet certain requirements: It should be easy to set up, intuitively simple to learn, quick to use, and much better to manage and support. This simplicity should exist for both the novice or experienced user alike. Not only are the interface icons different, but the layout of the Desktop makes it easy to find and use resources.

32-Bit Operating-System Architecture

The 32-bit architecture and superior resource handling within Windows 95 produce a more stable operating-system environment. The 32-bit, protected-mode subsystems built into Windows 95 are more crash resistant. A bad application, whether 16-bit or 32-bit, is less likely to stop the operating system. Even though the architecture is 32-bit, Windows 95 uses a combination of 32-bit and 16-bit code. The 32-bit code maximizes the performance of the system. The 16-bit code helps maintain compatibility with existing applications and drivers.

Preemptive Multitasking

The previous versions of Windows 3.x use cooperative multitasking, whereas Windows 95 uses preemptive multitasking. To the end user, the difference is subtle. Cooperative multitasking means the operating system is relying on each application under Windows 3.x to cooperate in giving up control and system resources while running. *Preemptive multitasking* means that the Windows 95 operating system is tracking and preemptively allocating system resources. This feature enables Windows 95 users to carry on several simultaneous computing tasks more smoothly than ever before.

Plug-and-Play Technology

Windows 95 is compatible with the Plug-and-Play (PnP) technology specification. Hardware devices written to this specification can identify themselves and their settings to Windows 95. When these hardware devices are added or reconfigured, Windows 95 adjusts the computer's hardware configuration automatically to operate with those hardware device changes. It is a design philosophy that enables installation and configuration of new devices without any intervention by the user.

Integrated Networking Support

For most network administrators, Windows 95 is the perfect client workstation. Windows 95 comes with 32-bit networking components that enable it to work with all major networks, including Microsoft, Novell, and Banyan. These networking components include the redirector, the protocol, the network adapter, and various network services, such as File and Print Sharing. They are written for the multitasking environment, take up no real-mode memory, and offer fast, stable networking support.

Centralized Security and System Policies

Windows 95 supports "pass-through," server-based security for both Microsoft Windows NT and Novell NetWare networks. Users can be required to *log on* (Windows NT) or *log in* (NetWare) before they can use Windows 95 in a networked environment. This enables increased system security and control (over Widows 3.1), which enables the network administrator to use existing user-based security rules to manage access rights. The use of System policies (new with Windows 95) enables further control over user access to the network. System policies also can be used to restrict a user's Windows 95 Desktop functionality. An administrator, for example, can set up a System policy so that a user cannot save changes made to the Desktop, such as wallpaper or color scheme changes. This way, each time the user starts Windows 95, the default Desktop appears.

Built-In Support for Mail, Fax, and Telecommunications Functions

Mail, fax, and telecommunications functions are part of the Windows 95 operating system. A universal inbox is provided for all messaging services that support the *Messaging Application Programming Interface* (MAPI). Users need only go to one location to retrieve email and fax information. The Microsoft Network and Internet Explorer provide users easy access to online services and the Internet.

Support for Mobile Services and Remote Access

Windows 95 supports the use of PCMCIA (PC Card) adapters as well as "hot" docking and undocking. This means users can add or remove a device, such as a PC card, while the computer is running. The computer automatically detects the change and adjusts the system settings accordingly. Windows 95 helps mobile computing by supporting dial-up network remote access and file synchronization.

Compatibility for Devices and Applications

Windows 95 was designed with backward compatibility in mind. Much of the existing hardware and software in use today will work with the new operating system. Windows 95 supports 32-bit applications and remains backward compatible with existing DOS-based and 16-bit Windows-based applications.

Multimedia Capability

Windows 95 expanded the existing Windows multimedia capabilities, including built-in audio and video drivers and applications. No additional software is required to use most business and entertainment multimedia programs.

The video playback engine (Video for Windows) and CD-ROM file system (CDFS) are new 32-bit components of Windows 95 that deliver smoother video and sound reproduction.

Long Filenames

A Windows 95 filename can be a total of 255 characters long. Windows 95 uses a new *Virtual File Allocation Table* (VFAT) system that enables filenames with up to 255 mixed-case characters and spaces. Completely compatible with MS-DOS and Windows 3.1, VFAT writes two filenames to disk for each file saved on a VFAT volume: One is an 8.3 short filename (an example would be bananas.doc for a Word document called bananas), also referred to as an *alias*, and the other a long filename. By creating two filenames, the VFAT system enables users to create files with long filenames using 32-bit Windows applications. Windows 95 opens files using the 8.3 filename in 16-bit Windows and DOS applications. Chapter 6, "Monitoring and Optimization," discusses long filenames in detail.

New Tutorial and Help Files

Windows 95 includes a new tutorial called the "Windows Tour" as well as a new task-based help file. Very little written documentation comes with Windows 95. The hope is that using Windows 95 is very easy—so easy, in fact, that between the new tutorial and the help file, little training is required for new users.

Now that you are well-versed in the features of Windows 95, you are more qualified to choose between Windows 95 and Windows NT Workstation.

How to Determine When to Use Windows 95 and When to Use Windows NT Workstation

When should you use Windows 95 over Windows NT Workstation? The best answer at this time is: "It depends on what you're trying to do with the computer." Microsoft has published a white paper on the subject, a copy of which is included on the CD-ROM. (An updated version for Windows NT 4.0 is available on the WWW at **http://www.microsoft.com/windows/common/aa2699.htm**.) However, the criteria for determining when to use one instead of the other are simplified into several essential differences, discussed in the following sections.

Windows 95

The following points address when to use Windows 95 instead of Windows NT Workstation:

- Windows 95 makes computing easier for anyone using a wide range of personal and business applications on desktop and portable computers. To protect their current investments, these Windows 95 users require the highest level of backward compatibility with today's applications and device drivers (32-bit Windows, 16-bit Windows, and MS-DOS).
- Windows 95 runs on an Intel 386 or better platform, 4MB or more RAM (Microsoft now recommends 8MB of RAM), and 40MB or more hard drive space. This represents a lower hardware requirement than Windows NT 4.0.
- Windows 95 uses a new Windows (Next Generation) user interface, which is now also present in Windows NT 4.0.
- Windows 95 provides PnP technology support.

Windows NT Workstation

The following points address when to use Windows NT Workstation instead of Windows 95:

- Windows NT Workstation provides the most powerful desktop operating system for solving complex business needs. It delivers the highest level of performance to support the most demanding business applications for developers; technical, engineering, and financial users; and for critical line-of-business applications.

- NT Workstation will run some MS-DOS applications, 16-bit and 32-bit Windows applications, POSIX, and OS/2 1.x applications but supports only 32-bit Windows device drivers. The limitation on running MS-DOS and 16-bit Windows applications is that the applications cannot make any direct hardware calls.
- It will run on Intel 486 and better platforms, as well as PowerPC, MIPS, and DEC Alpha-based RISC systems with 12–16MB RAM, 90–110MB hard drive space.
- Windows NT Workstation supports symmetric multiprocessor (SMP) configurations for scalable performance without changing the operating system or applications.
- Windows NT Workstation offers C-2 certifiable user-level security access to a standalone workstation. Files, folders, and applications on both the desktop and the server computers can be restricted to specific users.
- Windows NT Workstation currently has limited Power Management Support.
- Windows NT 4.0 is a pure 32-bit operating system that uses a protected environment for each application. This provides a very stable, crash-proof operating system.

Now that you are sure Windows 95 is the right operating system for you, there are some issues you will need to consider when planning a Windows 95 rollout. The next section takes you through those steps.

Conducting a Windows 95 Rollout

This section will look at the planning that must, or a least should, go into a rollout of Windows 95 in any organization. The goal of this section is not to tell you what decisions should be made, but rather to present you with the different options that are available to you to allow you to make the appropriate decisions for yourself. The decisions that you make will lead to developing a final implementation model that is right for your particular situation. There will be points that are too large to discuss as part of the implementation model, such as File and Print sharing and System policies, so they will be discussed later in this chapter. The Windows 95 rollout has been broken into several small sections:

- Taking an inventory of current equipment and software
- Choosing a Windows 95 version
- Choosing a software distribution method
- Choosing a workgroup name in workgroup or domain environments
- Using long filenames
- Assembling a distribution team
- Setting up a test lab
- Conducting a test rollout
- Documenting the problems and solutions
- Conducting the final rollout

This is a minimum number of steps that you should follow when preparing for a Windows 95 rollout. The following sections will discuss each point in depth. Most corporate sites begin planning their Windows 95 installations a year in advance to provide themselves time to perform the listed pre-planning steps and to fit into their annual budgets any costs that will be associated with the installation.

Step 1: Taking a Current Inventory

Before any other planning for the installation, you must take a thorough inventory of all hardware and software that your organization is currently using. This is vital, as it gives you the base that you will be starting with. From this base you will cull any items that are excessively old or otherwise incompatible with Windows 95. You will also be able to determine what upgrades are necessary. You can get a copy of the Windows 95 Hardware Compatibility List (HCL) from Microsoft's Web site. From the new short list of hardware, you now have the foundation and can start building.

You might have to target some users who will be getting new computers.

For the same reason, the software currently installed on the system should be identified, and a list of software then built, detailing items that should be replaced or upgraded. This process can help to determine applications that might be incompatible with Windows 95. Some of these applications might work if certain Windows 95 settings have been changed or if a special installation procedure is followed. If there are special procedures that must be followed, they must be built into the general installation procedure for Windows.

Step 2: Choosing a Version of Windows 95

Microsoft has two official versions of Windows 95: the Retail (or Upgrade) version and OSR2 (Original Equipment Manufacturer Service Release Two). The only place that OSR2 is available from is with the shipment of new computers. If you buy a version of Windows 95, it will be the retail version. If you happen to have both versions on your network, you should attempt to standardize on one or the other. This will require an analysis of the features and benefits of OSR2 to see if it should be installed rather than the retail version.

Some of the reasons why you might want to consider OSR2 are as follows:

- Support for large hard drive partitions (larger than 2GB) in the form of FAT 32
- System Agent task scheduler (also available in the Windows 95 Plus Pack)
- DriveSpace 3 disk compression (also available in the Windows 95 Plus Pack)
- Includes drivers for newer hardware, without your having to supply driver disks
- Comes pre-loaded, so there is less installation work to perform

Some of the reasons why you might want to use the retail version are as follows:

- Upgrade existing copies of Windows.
- Dual boot with DOS 6.x and Windows 3.1 or Windows for Workgroups 3.11.
- Does not support FAT 32, so all other local operating systems can always read all of the disk partitions. FAT 32 is not required when using OSR2, but on larger networks, you will often find that some computers will be incorrectly configured.
- Offers more compatibility with older software and hardware. OSR2 might not work with all.

Some of the most important features of OSR2, with the exception of FAT 32, are available as options for the Retail version of Windows 95. Many are available in the form of the Windows 95 Plus Pack or from Microsoft's web site at **http://www.microsoft.com/windows95**.

Step 3: Installing and Distributing the Software

First, you have to ask yourself how you plan to get Windows 95 out to all of your computers. There are several options that you might want to consider. The three largest are Push installations with packages such as Microsoft's System Management Server (SMS), Pull or Automatic installation, and Disk Images. Push and Pull installations both run a standard scripted installation of Windows 95, which is the cleanest (and recommended) way of deploying Windows 95.

Push installs are initiated at a remote server and sent to the workstation through a login script or other application. If you are using a network management package such as SMS, the server actually moves your source files to a location of your choice. On a Wide Area Network (WAN), the server you choose would be a server on the user's side of the WAN link to speed up the actual installation. SMS then sends the installation command to the workstation. The workstation then starts the installation of Windows 95 by using a setup information (*.INF) file that ships with SMS or one that you have created yourself.

Pull installations also use a setup INF file that you have created, but the installation is initiated at the client workstation and pulled down from the server. The INF file can automate the actual installation, but this differs from the Push installation in that the command to perform the installation starts at the workstation, not at the server. Both the Push and Pull installations offer the capability to include automated installation of applications, as well.

Disk Images offers advantages over the previous two methods in that the entire hard drive can be configured with multiple applications after the Windows 95 installation has been completed. This fully configured hard drive can now be copied to single file through a special application. The process is then reversed to copy the contents of the file back to a hard drive. The destination hard drive should be in a computer that is identical in hardware configuration to the original, or source computer. Be aware, though, that you will run into any number of difficulties if you try to put the drive into a computer that has been configured differently or is a different type. Microsoft does not fully support or recommend this method of installation of Windows 95.

You can use any of these methods to deploy Windows 95 to a large number of computers. Each has benefits and drawbacks. Scripts (*.INF) are clean but often require several different versions to get Windows 95 and all applications installed. Images are easier to install but are not as clean because they are hardware specific.

Automatic installation through script files is covered in Chapter 2, "Installation and Configuration, Part 1."

Step 4: Choosing a Workgroup Name in Workgroup or Domain Environments

Objective

When configuring a workgroup name for Windows 95, you should take some care in choosing the name. If the name is different from the workgroup names used by any servers on your network, then you will not be able to browse network resources without knowing the names of the servers that you want to visit. The term *server* refers to any computer on your network that shares resources, so it encompasses Windows for Workgroups, Windows 95, and Windows NT. If your computer has the File and Print Sharing service installed, then your computer is a server for your workgroup. As a server for your workgroup, you must keep a list of servers in your workgroup, as well as a list of other workgroups on the network.

If you have installed File and Print Sharing Services for NetWare Networks, then you will not be able to name your computer with the name of an existing NetWare server. If the only protocol you have installed is the IPX/SPX Compatible protocol, and you have not installed NetBIOS support, then you will be able to use duplicate computer name on your network. The Windows 95 computer names are NetBIOS name, and without the NetBIOS support, they will not be able to find duplicate names on the network.

If you decide to make your workgroup name the same as your domain name, then your computer will appear to have joined the domain in the Network Neighborhood. The benefit you receive from this is seeing your domain servers as soon as you open the Network Neighborhood (see Figure 1.1), which makes navigating your server's unmapped drives much easier. The drawback occurs when most computers on your network have File and Print Sharing enabled, as they will all show up as servers, possibly making the list unwieldy to use.

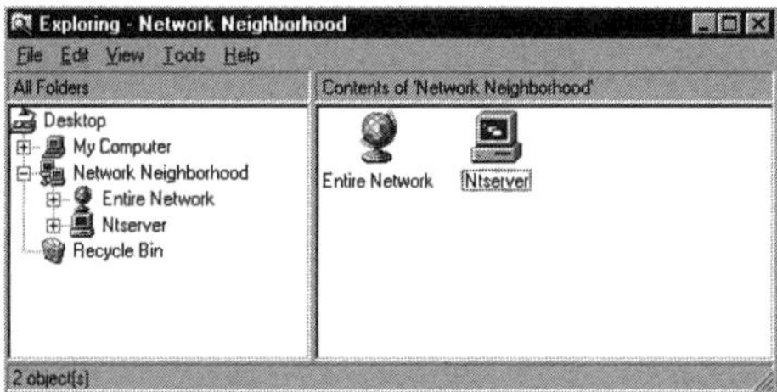

Figure 1.1

When you open the Network Neighborhood, you will see the contents of your current workgroup.

If you have installed the Client for NetWare Networks, then you will see all the NetWare servers when you open the Network Neighborhood. Workgroup names will only affect locating Microsoft servers on your network.

Windows 95 can never be anything other than a part of a workgroup on your network. The only operating system that can be a part of a Windows NT domain is Windows NT. If you set a Windows 95 workgroup name to that of a Windows NT domain name that is currently in use, both computers will share a list of resources. The Windows 95 computers will also appear listed in Windows NT administration tools, such as Server Manager. This appearance is a bit of an illusion, as the Windows 95 computers are not a part of the domain.

If you choose a name for your workgroup that is different from your domain name, then you will have a shorter server list in that domain, but people will have to locate those servers through the Entire Network icon of the Network Neighborhood (see Figure 1.2). If they regularly have to browse for network resources, this can quickly become an annoyance.

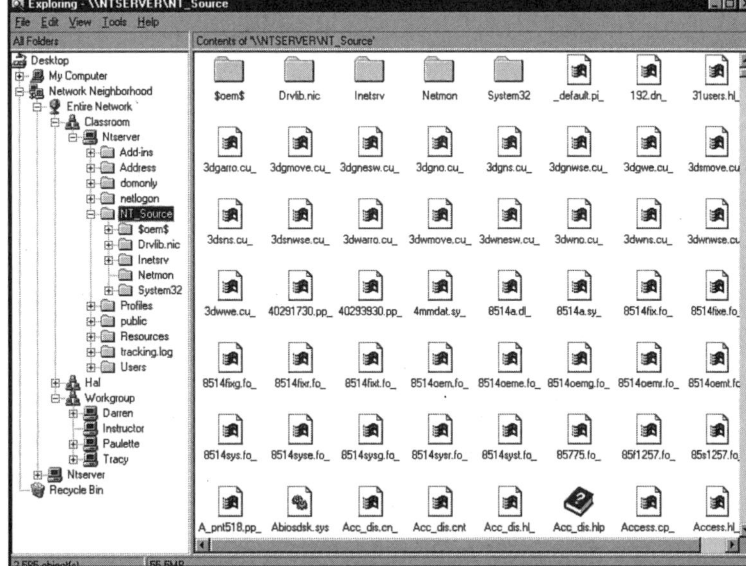

Figure 1.2

When browsing for a domain, you might have to take a long trip to your server.

If you choose a workgroup name that differs from your domain name, then at least one computer in that workgroup must have File and Print Sharing installed. By installing File and Print Sharing, the computer will maintain a list of servers in the workgroup, as well as a list of other workgroups or domains that exist on the network. If you do not have this list, you will receive an "Unable to Browse the Network" error message when attempting to access the Entire Network icon of the Network Neighborhood.

Workgroup configurations are discussed further in Chapter 3.

Step 5: Preparing to Support Long Filenames

Windows 95 supports filenames up to 255 characters, but all the computers on your network might not be running Windows 95. For the computers that are not running Windows 95, your filenames will have to conform to other standards, and those computers might have problems dealing with the Windows 95 filenames. Some of your network servers might not support long filenames, so you could run into problems with some configurations.

You must consider some things when deciding how to handle this. You might decide that additional computers should be upgraded to Windows 95 immediately or at the same time as others. You might also decide to upgrade to newer versions of your server software or migrate the servers to another operating system altogether, such as Windows NT 4.0. If you are in an environment in which the other computers cannot be modified to support long filenames, then you must train the Windows 95 users to refrain from using long filenames in situations in which they will cause problems for others.

For more information on long filenames, see Chapter 4, "Configuring and Managing Resource Access."

Step 6: Assembling a Distribution Team

"Many hands make light work." Having other people work with you as you roll out Windows 95 will make the whole process move more smoothly. If you choose people who can represent a number of departments or areas, then your rollout can address many of the concerns that are held by people in each of the departments.

Because the conversion to Window 95 will affect every employee in your company in all of your organizational units, you should try to choose people from each unit. For example, the people in your human resources department will have different concerns and work with different applications than the people in your Engineering department. By choosing people from each department, you will be aware of how the departments operate and how Windows 95 will affect both the way the department operates and the applications that they use. By being aware of how the change will affect the departments, you can address and prevent problems before they occur.

In many environments, employees are cross-trained to perform many jobs, possibly even jobs from other departments. These cross-trained individuals are the most valuable on your deployment team, as they have the largest base of experience to draw upon. They can also be made responsible for testing their applications for compatibility with Windows 95.

If you fail to get representation from a department, you will find that during the rollout of Windows 95, that department encounters more errors or has more problems than the other departments. Being forewarned is the best way to prevent problems from occurring.

Step 7: Setting Up a Test Lab

After taking a thorough inventory, steps should be taken to get a representative sample of the various pieces of hardware and software that are in use on the network. This will enable you to test whether everything will work with Windows 95. The computers in the test lab are used to develop the installation script files (*.INF), as well as the installation procedure.

Windows 95 is compatible with a very wide range of hardware, but there are often times when certain pieces of hardware will not function properly together. Occasionally you will find information about incompatibilities listed in the installation documentation or on the web site for the hardware. You might also need updated drivers for the hardware before it will work properly with Windows 95. Just because two pieces of hardware work with Windows 95 does not mean that they work together. For example, you might find that a particular sound card does not support CD-ROM drives from a certain manufacturer.

By choosing a full cross-section of all your hardware, you will be able to find out what does work, what doesn't work, and what doesn't work together. You will also be able to assemble a set of drivers that do not ship with Windows 95 but that are required for installation of Windows 95. There will always be "one of" pieces of hardware, that you will be able to test only when performing the actual installations. You can prepare for these "one of" installations by reading the latest documentation and by getting a copy of the latest drivers.

The importance of the test lab is like that of the distribution team. By choosing wisely, you will limit the number of surprises that will occur during the actual deployment.

Step 8: Conducting a Test Rollout

After performing thorough testing of software and hardware, you are ready to conduct a test or pilot rollout. This rollout should be limited in scope so that problems can be given a proper amount of attention and time. After resolving all problems, you should conduct a second, third, and fourth pilot rollout until you no longer have any problems with the deployment. You might limit the scope of the rollout by testing only one department or even just a handful of people in a department.

The test rollout provides a shakedown test of your installation procedure that you developed through testing. When testing one computer at a time, there are circumstances that might be overlooked, such as the load that 10 concurrent installations will put on the server. This also lets you see what changes should be made to the installation procedure to keep some of the problems from arising again. If there are any problems with the test rollout, because the number of computers has been kept relatively small, you may be able to revert them back to their original state.

Step 9: Documenting the Problems and Solutions

Documentation is one of the keys to a successful rollout. "Those that do not remember their history are doomed to repeat it." Any problems you have during your pilot rollouts should be documented and added to a database. This database can be referred to and added to during the rollout. Document the steps required to perform the setup of each computer so that your distribution team will not have to perform ad hoc installs.

Step 10: Conducting the Final Rollout

With all of the preceding steps completed, your rollout should go smoothly. You should plan to perform upgrades in synchronization with a training schedule for the users. Ideally their computers will be upgraded the day they are in training. The training should cover the changes to their operating system, as well as any changes to the applications that they use. Windows 95 enables users to be more productive, but productivity will drop during the orientation phase. By delivering timely training, this drop in productivity will be minimized.

The final rollout should be scheduled in order to convert users in a logical order. This order should be determined by how one user's upgrade will affect the other users who have not been upgraded. What happens if one person is using the newer version of the software, while everyone else still has the old version? You might decide that upgrading by branch or department makes the most sense in your situation. You might also decide that because sections of two departments communicate regularly, they should be upgraded together. If you have a number of branches, you will likely upgrade them one at a time; but you might start with the head office, because it communicates with all the branches.

Whatever order you decide on for the upgrades, you should educate all of the users, upgraded or not, on how the temporary mixed environment will affect the way they work. For example, now that the Windows 95 users are allowed to use long filenames, they should avoid them, as it is difficult to use them on computers that have not been upgraded; conversely, the users who have not been upgraded should be told how to deal with long filenames when they encounter them.

Throughout this whole process, you should refer to the deployment database for solutions to previous problems, as well as posting new problems and solutions.

With your deployment strategy in hand, you might feel as though you are ready to run out and start the installations. You should hold off just a little bit, as there is still a large issue at hand: Your deployment plan covers compatibility and logistics, but you have not created a secure network yet. The next major section prepares you to develop a security strategy.

Developing a Security Strategy

There are components of the Windows 95 operating system that behave as a double-edged sword in that they offer indispensable benefits but also unwanted problems. A perfect example of an indispensable and unwanted item that you use is the telephone. Most people would say that they could not live without phones; phones enable them to communicate with the outside world and gather required information. Along with these benefits, however, you leave yourself open to receiving unwanted telephone solicitation and abuse of the tool. Even in the face of this downfall, most people still opt for use of the telephone. Likewise, Windows 95 has several components that you will find indispensable but that offer definite security problems for users and LAN administrators. There are also utilities that we would rely on heavily if only we knew that they existed. These are the components that you will consider in this section. They include the following:

- File and Print Sharing services
- System policies

- User Profiles
- Remote registry editing and remote system monitoring
- Remote Administration

Understanding File and Print Services

File and Print Sharing services can represent a major security problem on your network, and this is something you must consider before conducting your installations. If you decide to remove File and Print Sharing services after the users on your network have gotten used to the local power, you might have a political problem within your organization when removing this privilege from your users.

There are many LAN administrators who flinch at the mention of "Personal File and Print Sharing"—this author included. The reason that they flinch is almost exclusively because it takes control away from the central security, which is usually the administrator. They are not there to be a scolding mother telling you that you can't do this, that, and the other thing; their job is to keep your files safe and sound. This section elaborates on the purpose and use of File and Print services, as well as the differences in sharing methods between the two services that Microsoft supplies.

Files are kept safe, and information is kept hidden most effectiveley, if the files reside on a central server where a central security authority can control access to them. This is not to say that there are not administrators that take control to absurd levels. With the files in this central location, administrators can control who is on the list of users who have access and the level of access that they have. On the point of safe files, most sites have implemented procedures to regularly back up the contents of the servers, daily or less.

When files are kept on local hard drives, security is compromised. People who are not even users on the network can obtain local access to files by pressing cancel at the network login dialog. By ignoring the network login dialog box, you will gain access to all local files with total control, unless some type of local security has been implemented (which is usually not the case). Local files are also usually not part of a regular and systematic backup procedure. This is a problem because some people will back up a few files faithfully, whereas most will not back up any files. One reason for not backing up these files is the size of the backup. With multi-gigabyte hard drives in most new computers, backups are also becoming multi-gigabyte backups, which are far too large to accomplish without a proper tape backup device. If security and safety do not convince you to keep files on a central server, then enabling users to share local files with others increases the risk to the files.

When network users have access to, or are allowed to share, files with other network users, they will usually accomplish sharing through the Microsoft's File and Print Sharing for Microsoft Networks. It is usually implemented with the default system security—Share-level Access Control. With Share-level Access Control, users are asked for either a Read-only password, a Full Access password, or both (see Figure 1.3). Either password can be left blank, which can leave the shared folder open to Full Access with no check in place (see Figure 1.4). This security breach is impossible to control if each user is responsible for his or her own file sharing.

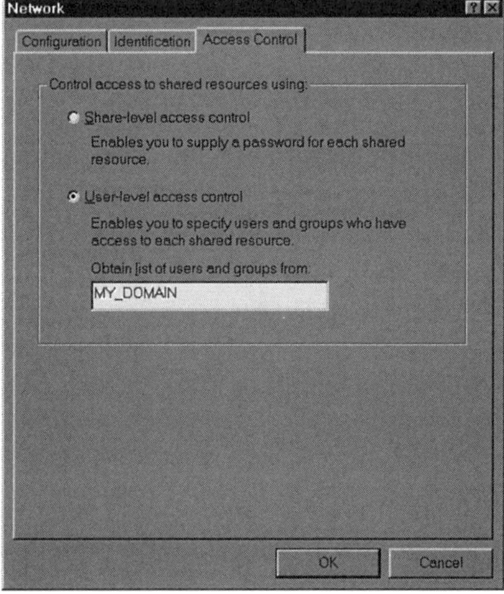

Figure 1.3

When using the File and Print sharing for Microsoft Networks, you have two security levels.

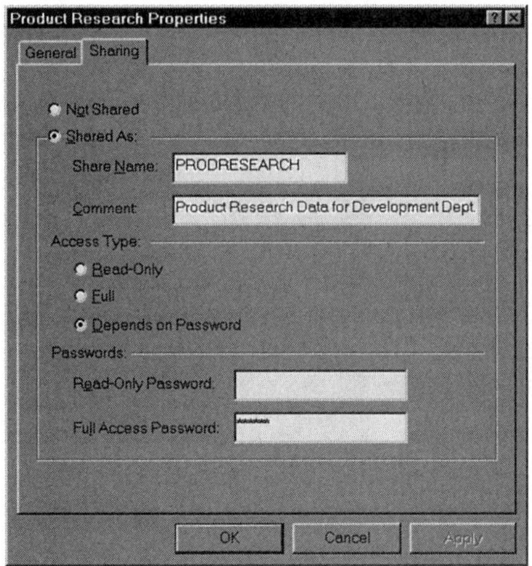

Figure 1.4
When implementing Share-level Access Control, your security is based on one or two passwords.

Rather than implement Share-level Access Control, you might choose to implement the other type of security: User-level Access Control. This method provides substantially better security, but it does have some restrictions. You must log in by using a username and password that is valid on a Windows NT Domain, a Windows NT Server, a Windows NT Workstation, or a Novell NetWare server (3.x or 4.x). In addition, when you choose User-level Access Security on the Access tab of the Network control panel, you must supply the name of server or domain where your account is from. This enables you to grant access to your system to users who are registered on a controlled server. It also means that you do not have to distribute a list of passwords out to people accessing your computer, because all that they need are their usernames and passwords from the main server. This whole process does nothing to prevent users from giving too much access of their system to others on the network or sharing data that they shouldn't; it does, however, enable the data to be accessed only by users registered on the network.

When using Microsoft's File and Print Sharing Service for NetWare (see Figure 1.5), the only security option is User-level Access Control, and the Security provider must be a Novell NetWare server.

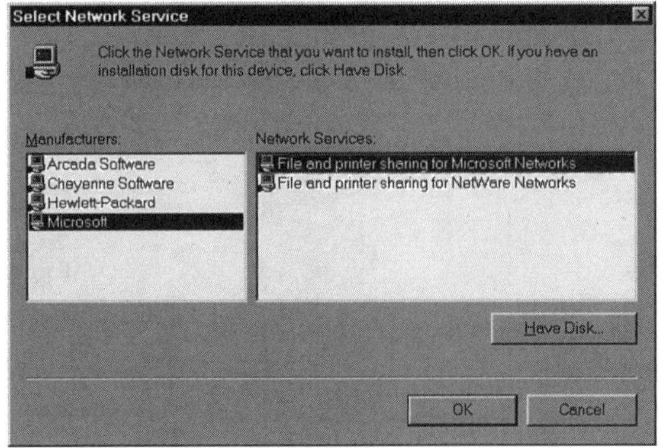

Figure 1.5
File and Print Services are available for both Microsoft and Novell Networks.

If File and Print Sharing represents a potential security problem on a client's workstation, the next section represents the fix for that problem. Unfortunately, an overzealous administrator can cause as many problems as he can prevent through System policies.

Understanding System Policies

A *System policy* is a single file on a server that is processed when users log on to your network. This file contains a list of settings or restrictions that are to be applied to the users at logon. System policies work in conjunction with *User Profiles* (customized settings maintained for each user) to restrict or control access to components of the Windows 95 operating system or to configure an environment for the user. Much of the security that Windows 95 is capable of can be implemented through System policies, which are created with the System Policy Editor. In this section you will do the following:

- Read the installation overview of the System Policy Editor
- Examine the user settings of a policy file
- Examine the computer settings of a policy file
- Create policies for specific users, groups, and computers
- Create policy Template files

Installation Overview of System Policy Editor

> The complete System Policy Editor installation and policy file creation will be performed in Chapter 4, "Configuring and Managing Resource Acess." A brief summary is presented in this chapter for planning purposes.

The System Policy Editor is not installed as one of the default applications with Windows 95. The application will have to be installed from the ADMIN\APPTOOLS\POLEDIT directory of the Windows 95 CD-ROM. From this location, you are able to install both the System Policy Editor and Group policies on your computer. You have to install the System Policy Editor only on the machine that you will be using to create the System policy. If you plan to assign the policy to users based on the server groups to which they belong, you must install the Group policies on every machine on your network.

After the System Policy Editor is installed, you can create a Policy file (*.POL). The default policy file that Windows 95 looks for is CONFIG.POL, which is expected to be in one of the following locations:

- Windows NT Domain, in the NetLogon directory of domain controllers, which is <win_root>\SYSTEM32\REPL\IMPORT\SCRIPTS\
- Novell NetWare 3.x, or 4.x server on the SYS volume in the PUBLIC directory

To work with the Policy Editor, select it from the Start menu, under Programs, Accessories, System Tools, System Policy Editor. To create a policy file, select New from the File menu. This leaves you with two icons: Default User and Default Computer (see Figure 1.6). You also have the capability to use the System Policy Editor to edit the local registry by choosing Open Registry from the File menu. If you open the Registry by mistake, the two icons in the Policy editor read Local User and Local Computer (see Figure 1.7).

Figure 1.6
System Policy Editor working on a policy file.

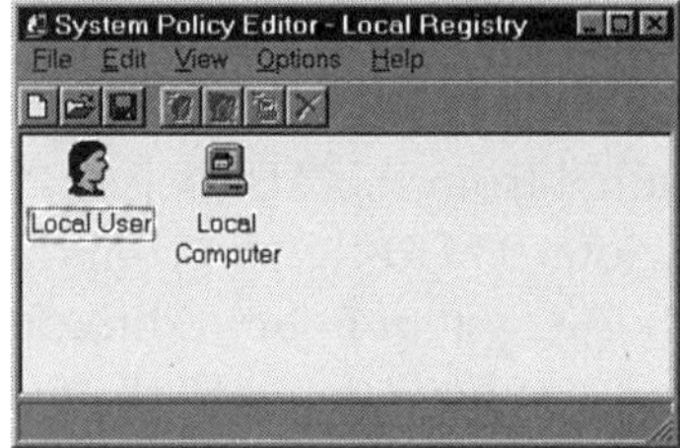

Figure 1.7
System Policy Editor working on a local registry.

When using the Policy Editor to make a policy file, each check box in the settings windows has three settings: On, Off, and Neutral (see Figure 1.8). When you use the Policy Editor to edit the local registry, there are only two settings: On and Off.

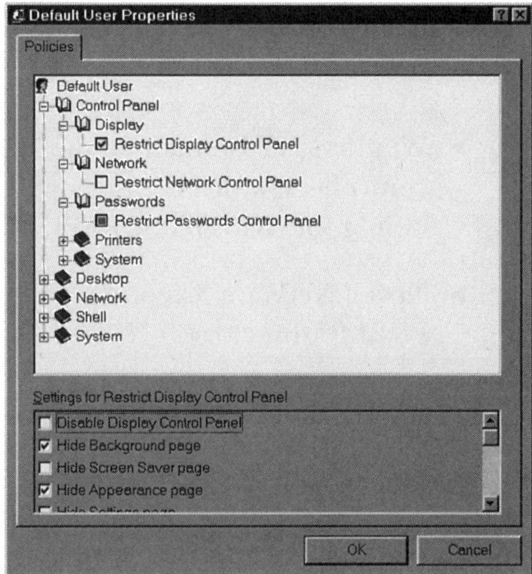

Figure 1.8
Each check box in the Policy Editor has three settings; the gray box is a neutral setting.

User Settings in the Policy File

The following list examines the settings that can be adjusted or enforced in a System policy. To access this screen, double-click on Default User or Local User in the System Policy Editor. The user settings are applied for each user regardless of what computer they have logged on to, and the changes that are implemented are stored in the user's USER.DAT file. You will now cover the following topics:

- *Control panel settings* Enable you to disable or restrict sections of certain control panels or disable the entire control panel. Many of the settings that end users will inadvertently change are changed through the control panels. You will be able to control the following panels, which help you in the following ways:
    - *Display* Prevents users from changing the current display adapter or the screen resolution.
    - *Network* Prevents users from changing their workgroup name, which can cause problems when they are browsing the network. This also prevents them from changing the network adapter, protocol, or network client settings.
    - *Passwords* Prevents users from modifying Remote Administration or User Profile settings.
    - *Printers* Prevents users from modifying printer settings and adding or removing printers.
    - *System* Prevents users from changing most of the settings in the system control panel, such as the device manager, hardware profiles, and virtual memory settings.
- *Desktop settings* Does not restrict the desktop, but rather enforces settings for both wallpaper and color schemes.
- *File and Print Sharing settings* Enables you to disable the capability to share folders or printers.
- *Windows Explorer Shell settings* Enables you to control the entire Start menu and to remove from the menu whatever commands you want.
- *Application restrictions* Enables you to specify additional restrictions on the way in which applications will run on the workstation.

Computer Settings in the Policy File

The next list examines the settings that you can adjust or enforce in a computer section of a policy. To access this screen, double-click on Default Computer or Local Computer in the System Policy Editor (see Figure 1.9). The computer settings are applied to the computer regardless of any user who has logged on to the computer, and the changes that are implemented are stored in the computer's SYSTEM.DAT file.

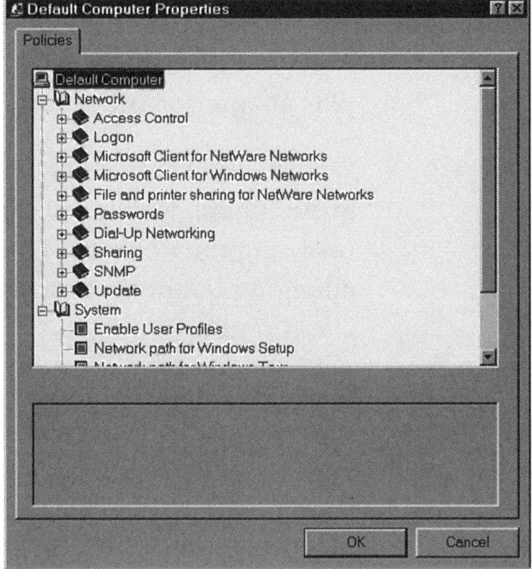

Figure 1.9

Default Computer has settings for Network options and other System restrictions.

- *Network Settings* Enable you to configure the following settings:
  - *Access Control* Enables you to configure the type of access control used at the workstation—User-level, or Share-level. If you choose User-level, you can specify the name of the security provider.
  - *Logon* Enables you to specify a logon banner and whether or not the user must log on to gain access to Windows 95.

- *Microsoft Client for NetWare Networks* Enables you to configure settings for the NetWare Client, such as which server should be logged on to.
- *Microsoft Client for Windows Networks* Enables you to configure settings for the Microsoft Client, such as which domain should be logged on to.
- *File and Print Sharing for NetWare Networks* Enables you to broadcast your network presence as a Novell NetWare server.
- *Passwords* Gives you control over how Windows 95 maintains its passwords. This applies both to the Windows password and passwords that are applied to shared resources.
- *Dial-up Networking* Enables you to disable all dialing connections to the Windows 95 computer.
- *Sharing* Enables you to disable File and Print Sharing services on the workstations.
- *SNMP* Enables you to remotely and automatically configure all of the SNMP settings on the computers on your network, including Community names and Trap Destinations.
- *Update* Enables you to change the location of the policy file that will processed for that computer.

- *System settings* Enable you to enable User Profiles, as well as configure RUN and RUN ONCE registry keys to automatically start up applications when Windows 95 boots.

Policies for Users, Groups, and Computers

When creating a policy file for a server, you have the additional option of adding individual icons for each user group of users from your server, as well as icons for each computer on your network (see Figure 1.10). To add additional entries to your policy, choose Add User, Add Computer, or Add Group from the Edit menu. If you have configured your system for User-level Access Control, you will be able to browse a list of users, groups, and computers; otherwise, you must type the name of the user, group, or computer.

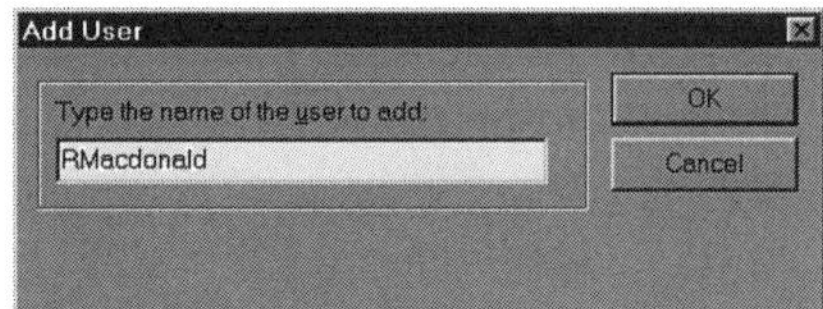

Figure 1.10
Individual policy entries can be created for users or groups from your server, as well as for computers on your network.

When applying the policies, Windows 95 first looks to see if there is an entry for the user logging in, and then applies the changes for that user. If there are no entries for that user, Windows 95 checks to see if the user is a member of any the of groups that it has entries for. If the user is not a member of any of the groups, then the entry for Default User is applied. After applying the user policy, Windows 95 then applies a computer policy. If there is an entry for your current Computer Name, then it is applied; otherwise the entry for Default Computer is applied. There is no way to create policies for groups of computers; all computers on the same domain or server will apply and use the same policy.

When working with groups in the Policy Editor, the client computers need to have Group policies installed, as described at the beginning of this section. The groups listed in the policy file are applied in a particular order, which can be seen by choosing Group Priority from the Options menu (see Figure 1.11). The policy entries are applied for each group that the user is a member of, starting from the bottom of the list and working up. This means that if any of the entries conflict with one other, the entry that is higher in the list takes precedence.

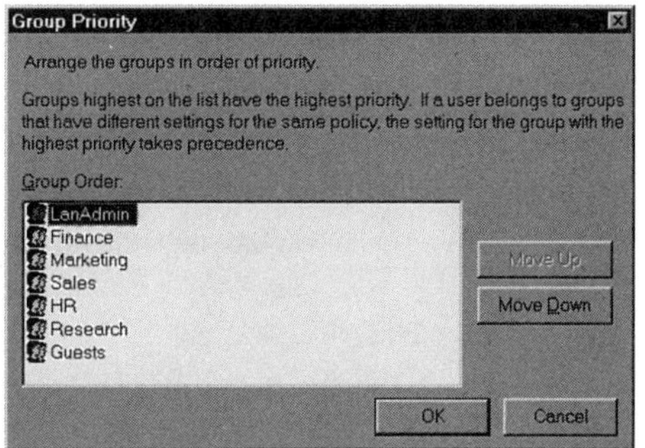

Figure 1.11

Groups are processed from the bottom up, making the items higher in the list to override lower settings.

Policy Template Files

The Policy Editor is an alternative shell to enable editing of the Windows 95 Registry. By itself, it does not know anything about the structure or form of the registry. Everything that it displays and changes is a result of the Policy Template file that is in use. The default template file is C:\WINDOWS\INF\ADMIN.ADM. To change the template file, choose Template from the Options menu. The template file is a text file with a particular structure. What follows is an excerpt from the default ADMIN.ADM file that ships with Windows 95, and Figure 1.12 shows the results of this section of the template:

```
...
CLASS USER

CATEGORY !!ControlPanel
      CATEGORY !!CPL_Display
           POLICY !!CPL_Display_Restrict
            KEYNAME Software\Microsoft\Windows\CurrentVersion\
           Policies\System
                  PART !!CPL_Display_Disable CHECKBOX
                  VALUENAME NoDispCPL
                  END PART

                  PART !!CPL_Display_HideBkgnd CHECKBOX
                  VALUENAME NoDispBackgroundPage
                  END PART

                  PART !!CPL_Display_HideScrsav CHECKBOX
                  VALUENAME NoDispScrSavPage
                  END PART
```

```
                        PART !!CPL_Display_HideAppearance CHECKBOX
                        VALUENAME NoDispAppearancePage
                        END PART

                        PART !!CPL_Display_HideSettings CHECKBOX
                        VALUENAME NoDispSettingsPage
                        END PART
                END POLICY
        END CATEGORY      ; Display
…
END CATEGORY       ; Control Panel
…
[strings]
System="System"
…
ControlPanel="Control Panel"
CPL_Display="Display"
CPL_Display_Restrict="Restrict Display Control Panel"
CPL_Display_Disable="Disable Display Control Panel"
CPL_Display_HideBkgnd="Hide Background page"
CPL_Display_HideScrsav="Hide Screen Saver page"
CPL_Display_HideAppearance="Hide Appearance page"
CPL_Display_HideSettings="Hide Settings page"
…
```

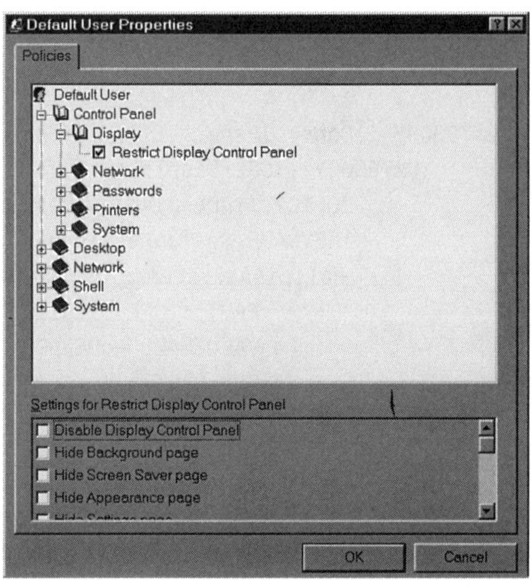

Figure 1.12

The entire structure of the System Policy Editor is based on the contents of the Policy Template file.

To learn more about the structure of the template files, see the Windows 95 Resource Kit. For more information on System policies see Chapter 4.

Understanding User Profiles

User Profiles are customized settings for each user's environment. Until this option is enabled, every person that logs on to the computer uses the same USER.DAT file and shares the same subfolders in the Windows folder. After turning on this feature, each user gets her own settings or USER.DAT file and her own folder in the Windows folder. If the servers and workstations have all been properly configured, then when you work in a network environment, these settings will follow you from computer to computer.

The Basics of User Profiles

To turn User Profiles on, you must choose the User Profiles tab in the Passwords control panel (see Figure 1.13). Switch the option button from All Users of This PC Use the Same Preferences and Desktop Settings to Users Can Customize Their Preferences and Desktop Settings. Windows switches to your personal settings whenever you log in. This enables User Profiles after your next reboot. When you reboot, Windows takes your username and creates a directory with your username in the C:\WINDOWS\PROFILES directory (see Figure 1.14).

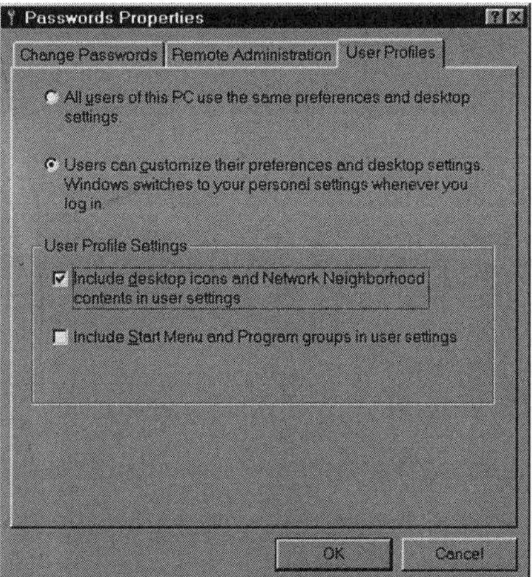

Figure 1.13
Use the Passwords control panel to enable User Profiles.

By enabling User Profiles, Windows now maintains a separate USER.DAT file for each user. The USER.DAT file contains all the personal control panel settings for a user, such as Mouse, Display, and Keyboard settings. This is especially useful if left- and right-handed people are sharing the same computer because the mouse settings will be restored as soon as the person finishes logging on or if you are sharing a computer with a person who prefers to use the High Contrast Black (extra large) color scheme for the desktop. All of these settings—and many for specific applications, such as Microsoft Office 97—are stored in the USER.DAT file.

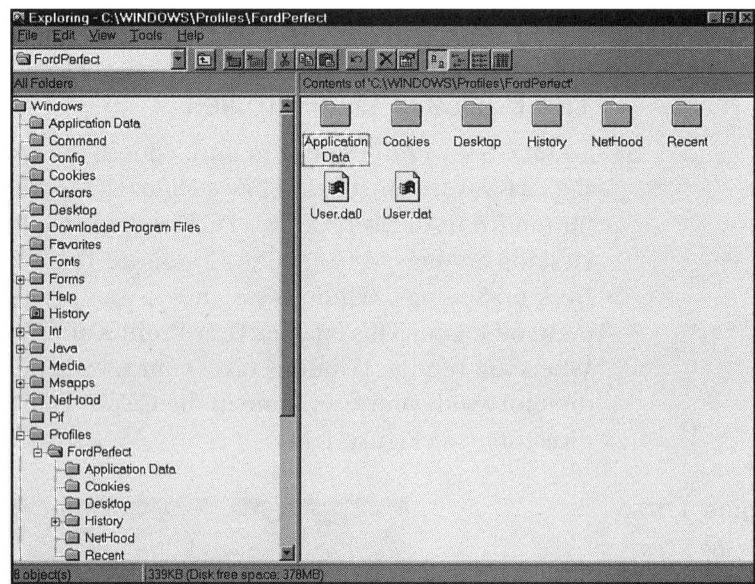

Figure 1.14

Windows 95 creates a directory for each user in the Profiles directory.

In addition to the separate USER.DAT files, by choosing the Include Desktop Icons and Network Neighborhood Contents in User Settings check box, you maintain additional settings for each user. The following folders from the Windows directory can also be duplicated for each user who logs on:

- Desktop
- NetHood
- Recent

Other applications installed on your computer can create folders that will be included in your User Profile, such as Internet Explorer 3.0.

By also selecting the Include Start Menu and Program Groups in User Settings check box, you also maintain separate Start menus and Programs folders. This option should be applied with care, however. Because each user maintains his own Start menu, applications installed by one user might not show up on the Start menu for other users. This might lead to confusion, as well as multiple installations of applications on the same computer.

If a Local Profile becomes corrupt, you can escape the logon dialog box and delete any or all of the profiles in the Profile directory. If the entire directory for a user is deleted, then fresh copies of the files and directories can be taken from the Windows directory.

User Profiles are vital to security because System policies enforce their environment changes on the user by modifying each user's profile. If User Profiles have not been implemented, it is impossible to influence or control the user's environment.

User Profiles on a Network

If you are logging on to either a Windows NT domain or a Novell NetWare 3.1x or 4.x server, your User Profile can follow you around the network, if certain conditions are met. When this occurs, you are said to have a *Roaming Profile.*

For Windows NT networks, the following conditions must be met:

- The Windows NT Network must be configured as a domain.
- The user's account must be configured for a network directory in the Home Directory section of the User Environment Profile, as shown in Figure 1.15. The user needs at least Change [RWXD] permissions to the directory.

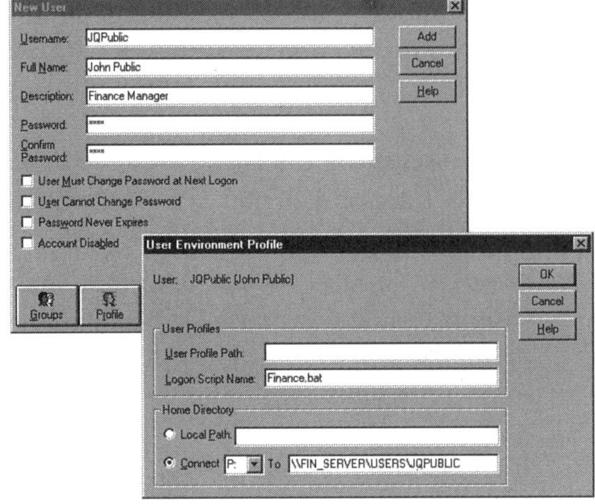

Figure 1.15

Setting a home directory for a user is set with User Manager for domains.

- The client computer must be configured to log on to the Windows NT domain. This is done through the properties of the Client for Microsoft Networks in the Network control panel, as shown in Figure 1.16.

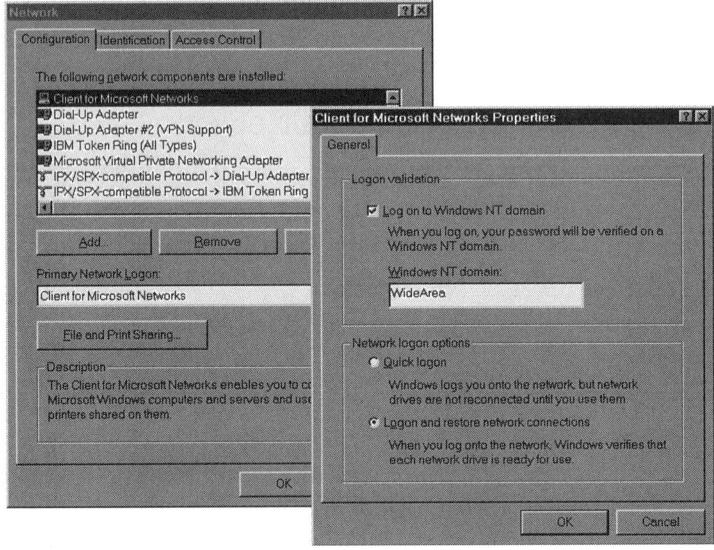

Figure 1.16

Domain logons are enabled in the Network control panel on the client.

- User Profiles must be enabled on the User Profiles tab of the Password control panel.

When the prior conditions are met, the User Profile will be activated on the next logon. During the logon process, the user will be told that he has not logged on to this computer before and is asked if he would like to retain his settings for the future (see Figure 1.17.) If you answer No, you will use the default files found in the Windows directory; if you answer Yes, these files are copied into your Local Profile directory. When you log out, your Local Profile directory is copied to your user directory on the server—this will include any shortcuts that are on your desktop. Windows 95 does not copy the files (except for USER.DAT) as part of your profile. It moves folders but will only copy the contents if they are shortcuts.

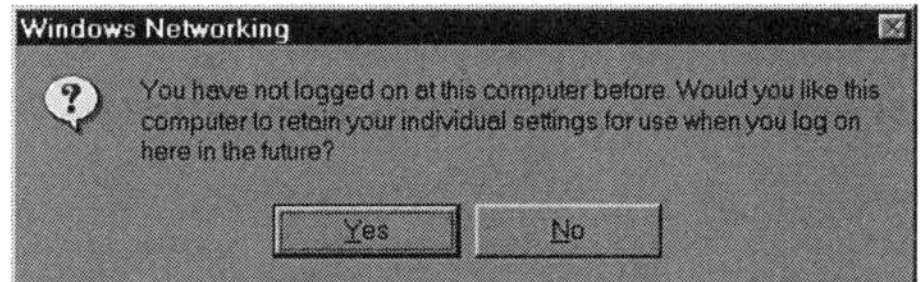

Figure 1.17
All new users are prompted to retain settings.

For NetWare 3.1x and NetWare 4.1 servers, the profile is automatically stored in the user's NetWare mail directory. If you are using a NetWare 4.1 server, then a Home directory must be configured in the User's account properties to store the user profile. In order to automatically store and retrieve your User Profile (Roaming Profile) on a NetWare server, the Client for NetWare Networks should be set as your Primary Network Logon.

When working with profiles, Windows 95 always checks in the network location to see if you already have a profile created. If Windows 95 finds one, it copies the profile down to your Local Profile directory.

If you or your network administrator renames the USER.DAT file to USER.MAN, then any desktop changes made will not be saved back to the network copy of your profile. These are referred to as Mandatory Profiles.

For more information on User Profiles, see Chapter 4.

Understanding Remote Registry Editing and System Monitoring

You will be learning how to use the Registry Editor (Chapter 7, "Troubleshooting") and System Monitor (Chapter 6) later in this book. From the planning side, if you wish to use either of these tools, there are some things you must take into consideration. To perform remote registry editing, you must meet the following criteria:

- File and Print Sharing must be installed.
- Remote Administration must be enabled (covered later in this chapter), and the person attempting remote registry editing must have administration rights.
- The remote registry editing service must be installed. This can be done through Add, Service in the Network control panel. Click the Have Disk button and specify the path <Windows_95_cd>\ADMIN\NETTOOLS\REMOTREG.

When System Monitor runs, it requires access to registry key HKEY_DYN_DATA\PERFSTATS and its sub-keys, as shown in Figure 1.18. To perform remote system monitoring, you will require access to the same registry keys on the remote machine. It is for this reason that all of the requirements for remote registry editing must also be met for remote system monitoring.

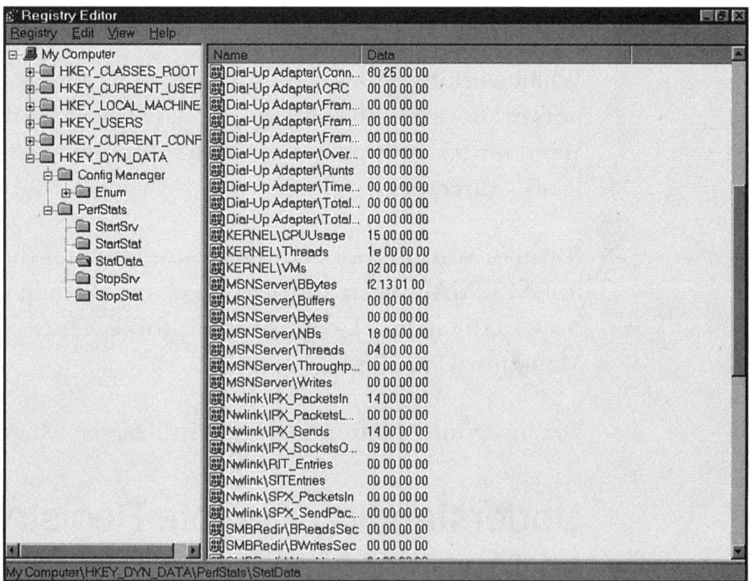

Figure 1.18
System Monitor retrieves its information from the registry.

The reason this is a planning issue is that it requires extra services to be installed on all machines, and as discussed earlier, the File and Print Sharing service can be a potential security hole. You do have the option of disabling the sharing controls for all users through a System policy, which helps the situation.

Understanding Remote Administration

Remote Administration is enabled in the Passwords control panel. The goal of Remote Administration is to give someone on the network full access to your local file system and to allow remote changes to your File and Print Sharing settings. This enables a network administrator to control the local shared resources on your computer, as well as update any files that might be corrupted or out of date.

Files and Print Sharing must be installed to implement Remote Administration. When enabling Remote Administration, the settings will look different, depending on the type of access control that you are using. If you are using Share-level Access Control, then the Remote Administration tab has a check box to enable Remote Administration and two text boxes for a password and confirmation. Anyone that knows your password will be able to perform Remote Administration on your computer. If you are using User-level Access Control, then user or group names from your security provider are granted administration rights on your computer (see Figure 1.19).

If you are logging on to a Windows NT domain or a Novell NetWare server, have installed File and Print Sharing, and are using User-level Access Control, then Remote Administration will be enabled automatically. Remote Administration rights will automatically be granted to Domain Admins, Supervisor, or Admin, depending on the type of security provider you are using. Other users can be granted the right to perform Remote Administration by adding their network account names to the list on the Remote Administration tab of the Passwords control panel.

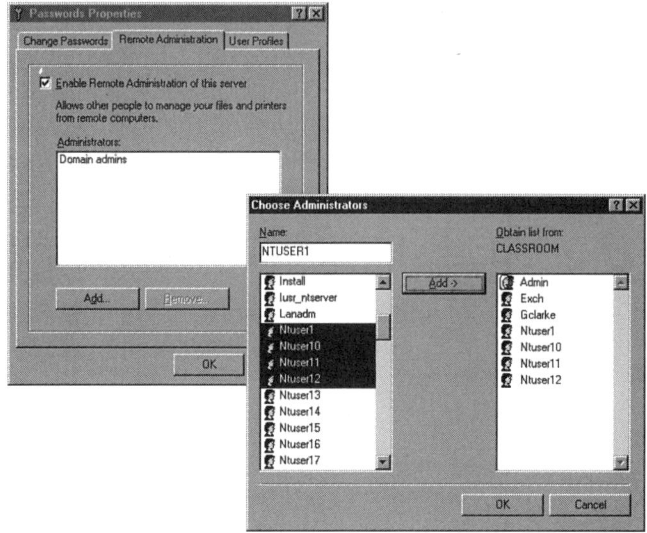

Figure 1.19

Users and groups from your security provider can be assigned administration privileges on your computer.

To perform Remote Administration on a network computer that you have Remote Administration rights on, you can browse the Network Neighborhood for a target computer and get its properties (see Figure 1.20). Choose the Administer button on the Tools tab to gain access to the local file system. You will see all fixed hard drives with dollar signs after the drive letters. These represent the hidden drive shares on the target machine. When Remote Administration is enabled, each fixed drive is automatically shared with Full Control rights for the people who have administration rights. This enables the administrator to navigate the entire directory structure and add, modify, or delete any files that are necessary (see Figure 1.21).

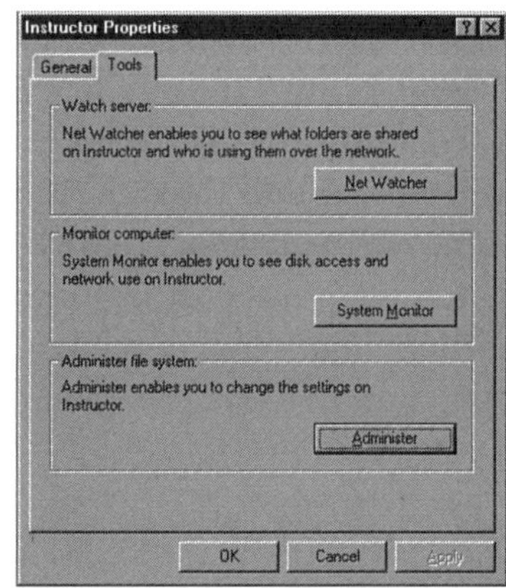

Figure 1.20

Properties of remote computers can give you access to the Remote Administration tools.

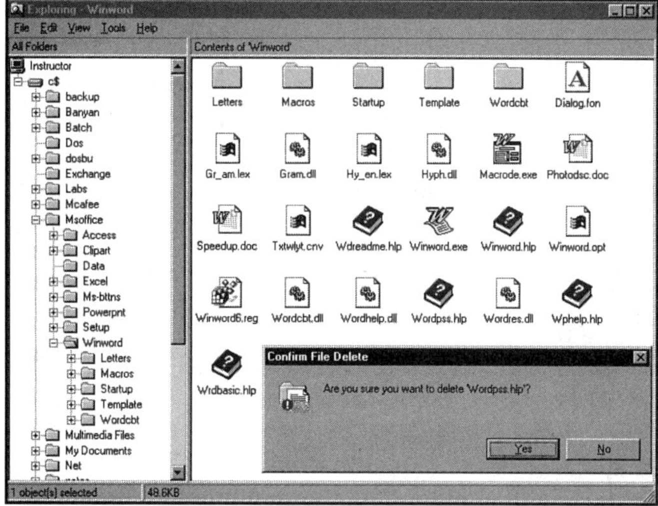

Figure 1.21
Remote Administration of a remote file system gives you full control to the drives on the target computer.

There is one additional share that is not listed when using the Administer button—ADMIN$ (see Figure 1.22), which is the hidden share for the current Windows directory.

Figure 1.22
The ADMIN$ share is a direct link to the target computer's Windows directory.

In addition to the Administer button, the Tools tab also has buttons to launch System Monitor and Net Watcher (both discussed in Chapter 6). System Monitor enables you to view utilization of system resources, whereas Net Watcher enables you to view and share resources, connected users, and open files; you are also able to modify the shared resources on the target computer. Both System Monitor and Net Watcher require that File and Print Sharing be installed on the target computer. When File and Print Sharing has been installed on a computer, care should be taken if giving that computer access to the Internet, which will be the next topic you consider.

Web Services and Internet Connectivity

Allowing people to connect to and host Internet services should be carefully considered. There are many people in the world that will attempt to cause mischief or do malicious damage to your network if there is any form of Internet connectivity. Before allowing this access, you should carefully weigh all of your options for securing your network. Most people will secure their network with a proxy or gateway server; these security methods cannot be implemented on dial-up connections through an Internet Service Provider (ISP). These servers act as "front men" for your network, performing whatever outside tasks are requested—for example, retrieving a web page from a server. To all computers on the Internet, your company has only one computer—the gateway server. If you decide that the cost of security does not outweigh the risk, or if you are using a dial-up connection to the Internet, you should be aware of the following:

- Windows 95 will respond to Window for Workgroups logon challenges. You will send an encrypted logon response to servers you are contacting, if they request it.
- People can connect to shared resources on your computer over the Internet, if they know your IP address. The IP address can easily be obtained.
- People can connect to web and FTP servers running on your computer, if they know your IP address.

The final decision to make regarding Internet connectivity influences the way Windows 95 must be set up, as well as how the rest of your network must be set up.

Summary

Planning requires a good grounding in all areas of Windows 95 to effectively come up with an implementation and configuration procedure for Windows 95. This chapter has covered installation, configuration, network structure, and LAN rollouts for Windows 95. Each of these topics will be covered in more depth in the rest of this book.

Exercises

Exercise 1.1: Choosing Between Windows 95 and Windows NT

Exercise 1.1 helps you choose between a Windows 95 or Windows NT operating system. In each of the following cases, indicate which Windows operating system should be used, either Windows 95 or Windows NT:

1. Office environment with general tasks, such as word processing, spreadsheet analysis, and email, running on an installed base of Intel-based personal computers, where management wants to maximize its existing investment

2. Engineers, scientific researchers, statisticians, and other technical users who often use processing-intensive applications for data analysis and design activities

3. Employees who spend a lot of their working hours away from the office (at a customer site, in a hotel, or out in the field) and rely on personal laptop computers to help them perform their jobs

4. Banking or defense workers who need to protect sensitive data or application files with high levels of security

5. Home-based users who find computers challenging and unfriendly, but want to be able to take advantage of new capabilities, such as multimedia and easily accessible online information services

6. Experienced computer users who require very high levels of availability and performance and cannot afford downtime, regardless of the application that they are running

The following are the answers to Exercise 1.1:

1. Windows 95, because it is compatible with a greater range of software and hardware.

2. Windows NT, because it can be installed in a multi-processor environment, which is often the type used in these fields. NT

also offers a more stable environment for some high-end applications.

3. Windows 95, because it is less intensive on hardware use, such as low RAM or hard drive space in a laptop. Both operating systems offer excellent dial-up networking capabilities.

4. Windows NT, because it offers a much higher level of security than Windows 95.

5. Windows 95, because although both Windows 95 and Windows NT support the same user interface, Windows 95 is easier to use and configure due to features such as Plug and Play.

6. Windows NT, because it is a higher performance operating system than Windows 95 is. It is also more stable when applications crash or hang.

Exercise 1.2: Choosing a Protocol

In Exercise 1.2, you select the protocol that is most appropriate for a variety of situations. In each of the following cases, determine which protocol should be used—either NetBEUI, IPX/SPX, or TCP/IP:

1. A local area network, running against both a Novell NetWare server and a Windows NT Server.

2. A small office network with Windows 95 computers, plus some Windows for Workgroup computers that have not been upgraded yet.

3. A wide area network, connecting to UNIX Servers and the Internet.

The following are the answers to Exercise 1.2:

1. IPX/SPX is the required protocol for communications with a Novell NetWare server. IPX/SPX can also be used for communications with NT Server.

continues

Exercise 1.2: Continued

2. NetBEUI is the easiest protocol to install on a small network that does not require routing.

3. TCP/IP is the required protocol for access to the Internet. It is also the most used protocol for UNIX computers.

Exercise 1.3: Selecting a Security Level

In Exercise 1.3, you choose the optimal level of security for a variety of situations. In each of the following cases, select the appropriate level of security: User-level, Share-level, or no (no File and Print Sharing) security:

1. A local area network running against both a Novell NetWare server and a Windows NT server

2. A small office network with Windows 95 computers, plus some Windows for Workgroup computers that have not been upgraded

3. A wide area network connecting to UNIX Servers and the Internet

The following are the answers to Exercise 1.3:

1. User-level, because it provides a higher level of security, and the required servers are available on the network to act as security providers

2. Share-level, because the servers that are required to act as security providers are not available

3. With access to the Internet, the best security is no File and Print Sharing

Review Questions

1. When planning to deploy Windows 95, you should do which of the following?

    A. Check all CPU types and peripherals for compatibility.

    B. Check all required business applications for compatibility.

    C. Purchase installation licenses for Windows 95.

    D. Check compatibility with current network servers.

    E. Deploy across the company at once to shorten the transition period.

    F. Book all employees into training for Windows 95 this month for next year's deployment.

2. Why do User Profiles provide a high level of security for a computer?

    A. They enforce registry settings as users log on to networks.

    B. They are stored in network locations that users have no access to, making editing and changing them secure.

    C. They do provide security.

3. Remote Administration can be enabled:

    A. On all computers on the network, regardless of whether they have File and Print Sharing services

    B. Through the Passwords control panel

    C. Through the Network control panel

    D. Through the Remote Administration control panel

    E. Only on computers using the Client for Microsoft Networks

4. The benefits of implementing User-level security include which of the following?

   A. People connecting to the computer will each require a unique, secure password.

   B. Passwords are validated at the Windows 95 computer.

   C. No additional information must be given to users; their current network usernames and passwords are used to validate when connecting.

   D. Passwords are validated through a separate server.

5. Which of the following questions should you consider before granting Internet access to users on the network? Select all that apply.

   A. Will they have local File and Print Sharing installed?

   B. Will the network have a firewall enabled?

   C. What network protocols will they have installed?

   D. Will they have dial-up or LAN access to the Internet?

   E. What web sites will they be accessing?

6. Which of the following statements about System policies is *not* true?

   A. System policy files can be stored on local hard drives.

   B. Policy files can be stored on either NetWare servers or Windows NT domain controllers.

   C. Policy files are created from template files.

   D. To fully implement policies, User Profiles must be enabled.

   E. The name that must be given to the default policy file is CONFIG.POL.

7. Which of the following need *not* be enabled for remote registry editing to be implemented?

    A. The remote registry editing service must be installed on both computers.

    B. File and Print Sharing must be installed on the target computer.

    C. Share-level security must be enabled.

    D. The editor must be on the target Remote Administration list.

Review Answers

1. A, B, C, and D. Windows 95 training should be planned to coincide with the deployment so that there is very little overlap between the two. Your deployment should be careful, with a test deployment on a small group of machines; when the system is considered to be stable, Windows 95 should be deployed across the network at a rate that ensures trouble-free operations for all concerned.

2. C. System policies provide security. User Profiles maintain user settings but do nothing to prevent the user from modifying the system.

3. B. Remote Administration is enabled on the Remote Administration tab. File and Print Sharing is required for Remote Administration to function.

4. C and D. Users do not require additional information before connecting to the Windows 95 computer, and their User credentials are verified against a security provider configured at the Windows 95 computer. The security provider can be Windows NT Workstation, Windows NT Server, Windows NT Domain, or Novell NetWare Server.

5. A, B, and D. File and Print Sharing is okay to install if you have a firewall to separate your clients from the servers they

are attempting to access. If you grant dial-up access, then you will not have a firewall, which will leave those individual computers open to attack.

6. A. System policies must be stored on a network drive. By default the location will be the NETLOGON share on Windows NT Domain controllers and the SYS:PUBLIC directory on Novell NetWare servers. User Profiles are used to restrict access on a user-by-user basis.

7. C. The computer must be set up to use User-level security.

Answers to Test Yourself Questions at Begining of Chapter

1. You should see any servers that are part of your current workgroup and the Entire Network icon.
2. No. Windows NT Servers, Novell NetWare 3.11 (patched), Novell NetWare 3.12 and 4.*x* with OS/2 name space, Novell NetWare 4.11 with Long Name space, and Banyan Vines 7.0 all support long filenames.
3. You should consider current hardware and software in operation, network OS, knowledge-level of employees and training requirements, the need for new OS, and the configuration of services.
4. User Profiles are used to maintain user settings. Multiple User Profiles can be maintained on one computer. System polices enforce specific desktop settings for users. System polices make users of User Profiles enforce their settings.
5. Remote Administration can read and write to any hard drive through hidden drive shares, as well as control shared resources on the remote machine.
6. To employ remote registry editing, both computers (the editor and target), must have File and Print Sharing installed, Remote Administration enabled, the remote registry editing service installed, and be enabled for User-level Access Control, and the Editor must be on the Remote Administration list.
7. Any answer files that are created for the Windows 95 installation have an extension of INF. If not specified in the setup command, Windows 95 looks for and uses MSBATCH.INF in the setup directory.
8. USER.DAT, which maintains user settings, is copied and individually maintained for each user on the computer in <win_root>\PROFILES\<user_name>\.
9. ADMIN.ADM is the template file for System Policy Editor. It is a text file, so NOTEPAD.EXE can edit it.
10. To use File and Print Sharing for NetWare Networks, you are required to have the IPX/SPX-compatible protocol, the Microsoft Client for NetWare Networks, and User-level Access Control enabled.

Chapter 2
Installation and Configuration, Part 1

This chapter focuses on the following exam objectives:

- Installing Windows 95. Installation options include automated setup, new, upgrade, uninstall, and dual-boot configuration with Windows NT.
- Installing and configuring hardware devices. Hardware devices include both modems and printers.
- Installing and configuring backup hardware and software. Hardware and software include tape drives and the Windows 95 backup application.

Test Yourself! Before reading this chapter, test yourself to determine how much study time you will need to devote to this section.

1. You are installing Windows 95 on a computer that currently has MS-DOS 5.0 and Windows 3.1. What is the lowest Intel processor you can have in this computer and still install Windows 95?
2. Jill uses a computer running Windows 3.11 for Workgroups, with several 16-bit applications installed. She has program groups set up for these applications. When she installs Windows 95, what is one way she can be sure that her application program groups are maintained?
3. A law office with 15 desktop computers is networked using Windows NT Server on one server. The partners want to ensure that their new operating system for the 15 desktop computers (either Windows 95 or Windows NT Workstation) provides file-level security. Which operating system should they adopt?
4. Windows 95 includes networking features to make it easier for users to connect to existing networks or to build a network from the ground up. Which three networking protocols included with Windows 95 are Plug and Play-enabled? Which two protocols are installed by default?
5. Windows 95 supports share-level and user-level security. You want to set up Windows 95 on 10 workstations on a network to share printer and file resources, but you want to make sure that pass-through authentication is used to validate users who access these resources. Which type of security must you set up?
6. Larry, a system administrator, must set up Windows 95 on 10 computers that are not connected to a network. He must perform a manual installation process on each machine, but he wants to automate the process as much as possible using a custom setup script. What is the name of the file on which he needs to base his setup scripts?
7. Windows 95's installation process is modular. Name the four logical phases of the Windows 95 installation process.

8. Missy has Windows 95 installed on her computer. When she boots her computer, it usually starts Windows 95. One day, however, Windows 95 fails to start, and her computer displays the Startup menu. Name the Startup menu option that Missy needs to select to start Windows and display each startup file line by line.

9. Windows 95 is being installed from a network server as a server-based setup. What is the name of the server-based setup program you must use to install Windows 95 source files on the network server?

10. Cindy encounters problems during the Windows 95 installation process and needs to troubleshoot the process. Name the three log files that Windows 95 created when Cindy ran the Windows 95 Setup program.

Answers are located at the end of the chapter...

The installation of Windows 95 requires careful planning, an understanding of the hardware and software requirements, an appreciation of the steps in the installation process, and the ability to troubleshoot any problems that arise. Although the Windows 95 Setup program handles most types of hardware configurations, you might be called upon to respond to many of the common problems. Experience in performing the Windows 95 installation is the best teacher.

This chapter is your guide to understanding Windows 95 installation and configuration. You will learn about the following:

- Windows 95 installation media options
- Preparing for Windows 95 installation
- Windows 95 hardware and software requirements
- Installation decisions
- The four phases of the Windows 95 installation process
- Troubleshooting the Windows 95 installation
- Installing either locally or from the network
- Installing and configuring hardware devices
- Installing and configuring tape backup devices
- Developing an effective tape backup strategy

Windows 95 is the successor to Microsoft's Disk Operating System (DOS), Windows 3.x, and Windows for Workgroups 3.x products. It is part of the Microsoft Windows operating system family, which also includes Microsoft Windows NT. Windows 95 is the standard operating system for the general-purpose user and runs only on an Intel-based computer. Windows NT (New Technology) is designed for leading-edge systems, running on Intel-based as well as RISC-based architectures.

In the preceding chapter, you learned all about Windows 95, and you have obviously chosen it as the operating system appropriate for your company. Before you embark on a large-scale rollout, you will need to prepare thoroughly.

Preparing for Installation

Some activities can be done ahead of time to ensure that the Windows 95 installation goes smoothly. The end-user of the computer can perform some of them with guidance from you. For some activities, however, inexperienced end-users might not know how to conduct proper installation preparation procedures. You might need to conduct these preparations for them or provide adequate training on these tasks. The following sections present questions that constitute a preparation checklist. Such a checklist produces several benefits:

- It forces careful consideration and planning.
- It involves the end-user in the process.
- It improves the chances of a trouble-free installation.
- It allows for easier troubleshooting and recovery in the event of installation failure.

There is plenty of material to help guide you in your planning efforts. The Windows 95 CD-ROM has a directory called Admin\Nettools that includes several useful tools to help you plan your installation. Another useful directory is Reskit, under Admin. It has some sample scripts to aid your planning. In addition to these, you might want to download the Deployment Planning Guide from Microsoft's Web site. This tool lays out a pretty detailed project plan for a Windows 95 rollout.

Is the Hardware Supported?

The Microsoft Hardware Compatibility List (HCL) details whether your computer hardware is supported. Newer computer hardware might not appear on the list. If in doubt, check with the manufacturer. These Hardware Compatibility Lists are updated periodically, so contact Microsoft to obtain the latest list. Read the Windows 95 SETUP.TXT file on the installation disk; it's a valuable source of information. If you don't see the hardware component listed in the Add New Hardware Wizard list, either select a close, emulated component or seek installation disks directly (.INF) from the manufacturer.

Does the Computer Meet the Minimum Requirements?

See Table 2.1 later in this chapter for the minimum hardware requirements to run Windows 95. One design goal for Windows 95 was to have it run on computers capable of running Windows 3.x. In reality, the minimum hardware requirement is much higher. Whereas Windows 3.1 will run on an Intel 286 computer with 2MB of RAM and an EGA monitor, Windows 95 needs more. The real published minimum hardware requirements for Windows 95 are an Intel 386DX computer, 20MHz (or higher) with 4MB of RAM, and a VGA monitor.

Now the question becomes one of economics. Is it cheaper to upgrade older computers or simply replace them with new computers? Depending on the application, you might want to consider replacing anything less than an Intel 486DX computer, 33MHz. Nonstandard hardware components also might need to be replaced to get away from having to run real-mode drivers within the CONFIG.SYS file.

There are useful utility programs that can test a computer to see if it will run Windows 95. A simple one, supplied by Microsoft, is called W95CHECK. It is available on Microsoft's Web site. This program scans a single machine for processor, memory (RAM), disk space, and applications. It does a good basic test but is not intended to serve as an all-inclusive diagnostic check for every known hardware and software compatibility issue with Windows 95.

Is Backup Completed for Important User Document Files?

Always back up your files. Network administrators harp on this theme, but most end-users don't listen. At a bare minimum, backup your key document files. Applications can always be reinstalled, but document files are difficult, if not impossible, to replace. The single question that drives home the point is: If your hard drive were to crash tomorrow, what key files would you save today?

Have TSRs and Virus Checking Been Disabled?

Terminate and Stay Resident (TSR) programs and antivirus programs are loaded in the CONFIG.SYS and AUTOEXEC.BAT files, are loaded and run from the WIN.INI file, and are found in the startup group within Windows itself. These programs should all be disabled. Those that should not be disabled include the following: any that are required for partition or hard-drive management, network drivers, video drivers, or devices (such as CD-ROMs and sound cards). The safest method, if possible, is to move both CONFIG.SYS and AUTOEXEC.BAT aside by renaming them and entering Windows without any other programs running.

Some motherboards also support BIOS antivirus checking upon bootup, which needs to be disabled. See the Windows 95 README file and SETUP.TXT on the installation disks for information on how to do this for specific antivirus software. These files are valuable sources of information on specific software products.

Can Any Unused Programs Be Removed or Uninstalled?

Hard drives tend to collect programs, applications, and data. Old applications, partially uninstalled programs, expired demos, and obsolete memos lie around on the hard drive, taking up valuable space. Instruct users to do some spring cleaning by removing anything that is no longer needed. (You might provide a list of programs that need to remain on everyone's computer, such as networking programs, email applications, and so on.) Most uninstall programs help in this effort by tracking down all the various pieces of an application. Newer programs often include an uninstall program, but many older programs don't. Reclaim some of that space on the hard drive.

Is the Hard Drive Scanned and Defragmented?

Windows 95 will do a cursory ScanDisk during the installation to check the integrity of the hard drive where Windows 95 will be installed. A better plan is to run a thorough scan with the version of the program that shipped with MS-DOS 6.2x before the Windows 95 installation and then disable the scan during the installation using the setup `/is` switch.

In addition, it's a good idea to run the Defrag utility to defragment the hard drive. Over time, a hard drive's performance can deteriorate as the files stored on the hard drive become fragmented and written to different portions of the hard drive.

Are All the Key System Files Backed Up?

Several key system files should be backed up as a precaution. You might want to instruct all end-users to make backup copies of these files or perform these backups yourself on all computers. The files are as follows:

- All initialization (.INI) files in the Windows directory
- All Program Manager group (.GRP) files in the Windows directory
- The Registry (.DAT) files in the Windows directory
- All password (.PWL) files in the Windows directory
- The CONFIG.SYS and AUTOEXEC.BAT files in the root directory

- Any critical hardware drivers and support programs listed in either the CONFIG.SYS or AUTOEXEC.BAT files
- Any batch files called from AUTOEXEC.BAT
- All network configuration (NET.CFG) files (programs to connect with the network)

You can easily back up these files by using a batch file inserted into a network login script. In fact, you could even carry it one step further and copy all .DOC, .XLS, and .PPT files as well.

Is the Network Software Working Correctly?

Make sure that network connectivity is working properly before you install Windows 95. During setup, Windows 95 uses the settings to help configure itself. If there are problems with the network wiring, interface card, configuration, security, or the like, they must be resolved prior to Windows 95 installation.

What Setup Information Is Needed?

At a minimum, three pieces of information are needed for a successful Windows 95 installation. The Windows 95 Setup program can automatically detect nearly everything else, including the current computer's hardware configuration. The following three pieces of information are unique to each Windows 95 installation:

- Default username: The initial user defined to the Windows 95 computer. Usernames are limited to 15 characters with no embedded spaces and can contain any of the following special characters:

  ```
  ! @ # $ % ^ & ( ) - _ ' { } ~ .
  ```

  This name should be unique and should correspond to your rules for usernames in either the Windows NT domain environment or the Novell NetWare bindery/NDS environment.

Although Windows NT and Novell NetWare allow longer names, most usernames get no longer than eight characters. This is to allow mapping to the user's home directory on a file server.

- Computer name: The name of the particular Windows 95 computer as it is known on the network. Computer names also are limited to 15 characters, with no embedded spaces. They can contain any of the following special characters:

  ```
  ! @ # $ % ^ & ( ) - _ ' { } ~ .
  ```

  This name should be unique and should correspond to your rules for computer names for either the Windows NT domain environment or the Novell NetWare bindery/NDS environment. When you share a computer resource on the network, other users reference that shared resource by using a combination of the computer name and the share name. For example, if your computer name is JACK-PC1 and the Windows 95 install share is WIN95-INSTALL, users connect to \\JACK-PC1\WIN95-INSTALL.

  Along with the computer name, you can have an optional computer description. This description, which can be up to 48 characters long, allows the sharing of other information about the Windows 95 computer. Information such as the owner's full name, telephone number, building or room, and type of computer can be included. This description can contain embedded spaces but no commas. When users browse the Microsoft Network, both the computer name and description are available. Using a good description makes browsing easier.

- Workgroup name: The workgroup is a logical association of computers that connect to one another to share resources, data, or email. Workgroup names are limited to 15 characters, with no embedded spaces. They can contain any of the following special characters:

  ```
  ! @ # $ % ^ & ( ) - _ ' { } ~ .
  ```

The workgroup name should be unique. A Windows 95 computer can freely join any peer-to-peer workgroup by simply changing the name. In addition to a workgroup name, you might need to specify the name of a Windows NT domain and/or a Novell NetWare preferred server if they are utilized to provide user authentication.

These three pieces of information (the username, the computer name, and the workgroup name) are unique to each computer installation. Duplicate computer names can prevent the Windows 95 computer from joining the Microsoft Network. Wrong workgroup names affect the browse list generated when you open your Network Neighborhood. Incorrect or missing computer descriptions confuse users wanting to share resources or data. In a corporate environment, it is important to agree on a standard naming convention that everyone adheres to and supports. It can make administering the Windows 95 network much easier for all concerned.

The requirement for unique names stems from the way information is shared on a Microsoft-based network. If you try to bring a second computer onto a network without a unique name, it won't be able to join.

If you're doing Windows 95 installations from a network share, and the new computer won't connect due to a duplicate computer name, you could be in trouble. A short-term fix is to use a temporary computer name, complete the Windows 95 installation, and sort out the computer names later.

Standard naming conventions should allow you to keep things unique. Good computer descriptions with accurate location information will help track down duplicate computer names.

After asking, answering, and resolving all these questions, the next step is to make sure that you meet the hardware and software requirements for installation.

Understanding Hardware and Software Requirements

The hardware and software requirements for Windows 95 need to be clearly understood. These requirements are confusing, especially with older hardware and software combinations. (See the next section for specific requirements.) For example, if you have an Intel 386 computer with 4MB of RAM and at least 50MB of hard drive space, and you install Windows 95, the performance should be the same as, or even better than, Windows 3.x with the same hardware. This hardware configuration is what Microsoft labels a "minimal" computer for Windows 95. What is not said is that the performance of Windows 3.x on that minimal computer is poor in comparison to the standard Pentium computer in wide use today.

Identifying Appropriate Hardware Requirements for Installation

Table 2.1 details the minimum hardware requirements for running Windows 95 from the hard disk. Remember that Windows 95 is designed to run only on Intel-based 386DX or higher processors, such as 386, 486, Pentium, Pentium Pro, or Pentium II processors. For backward compatibility, this minimum hardware requirement is exactly the same as that recommended for Microsoft Windows for Workgroups 3.x. In reality, however, it should be considered the bare minimum. A mouse or a similar pointing device is listed as optional, but you should consider this a requirement due to the graphical nature of the Windows 95 user interface.

Table 2.1

Hardware Requirements

Component	Minimum for Windows 95
Computer	386DX 20MHz (or higher) processor
Memory	4MB (or more) of RAM, 420KB of conventional memory within Windows

Component	Minimum for Windows 95
	or 470KB conventional memory from MS-DOS (600KB total below 1MB)
Floppy and hard drive	A high-density (HD) floppy disk drive and a hard drive, if installing locally to the computer
Disk space	Approximately 10 to 87MB of hard drive space, depending on the installation options chosen, plus space for a swap file whose size is at least 14MB (minus the RAM size installed on the computer)
Video display	VGA (or better)
Optional	A mouse or similar pointing device, CD-ROM drive, modem, sound card, and Network Interface Card (NIC)

Windows 95 basically needs 14MB of memory to run. This can be divided between physical RAM and a swap file on the hard disk. For instance, if your machine has 8MB of RAM, you will need at least 6MB of free space for a swap file.

These minimum hardware requirements reflect computers that have been in broad-scale use since the late 1980s. If you purchase a new computer, you will see specifications far in excess of the minimum. A basic rule of thumb when purchasing a new computer is to purchase the best computer you can afford, because the average corporate life cycle before obsolescence is now only two to three years.

If you are shopping for a new processor, be aware that the Pentium Pro has been optimized for 32-bit operating systems, such as Windows NT. Windows 95 still contains 16-bit code and is not the ideal operating system for this processor. The Pentium II, however, with its integrated MMX technology (for multimedia applications), will run Windows 95 very well.

These minimum hardware requirements often show up as a test question, if nothing other than to drive home the point that Windows 95 will actually run on an Intel 386 with 4MB of RAM.

Identifying Appropriate Software Requirements for Installation

You can install the retail version of Windows 95 as either a new installation or an upgrade over an existing operating system. You can also install Windows 95 over a number of different Microsoft operating systems, including MS-DOS, Windows 3.x, and Windows for Workgroups 3.x. It also can be installed over Novell DR DOS (or Novell DOS), IBM PC-DOS, and as a dual-boot operating system with either IBM OS/2 or Microsoft Windows NT.

The following is the minimum operating system software required to install an upgrade version of Windows 95:

- MS-DOS version 3.2 or higher, or an equivalent version from the hardware manufacturer (such as Compaq version 3.31) that supports partitions greater than 32MB; MS-DOS version 5.0 or better is recommended
- Windows 3.x (in combination with MS-DOS)
- Windows for Workgroups 3.x (in combination with MS-DOS)
- OS/2 2.x
- Dual-boot with OS/2 (with MS-DOS installed)
- Dual-boot with Windows NT (with MS-DOS installed)

You don't need to meet all these software requirements to install the upgrade version of Windows 95. You just need a combination of either MS-DOS and Windows, or OS/2. The ability to dual-boot Windows 95 with either OS/2 or Windows NT requires you to install over a previously installed version of MS-DOS. See the section "Dual Booting with Windows NT" for more details.

> **Tip**
>
> Windows 95 Setup checks the version of DOS as well as whether there is enough disk space to complete the installation. This space requirement is based on which Windows 95 components are selected for installation. If you are installing on a computer with partitions of 32MB or less, you are better off using FDISK to delete the partitions. From that point, format the hard drive using the `FORMAT` command, and install a new copy of MS-DOS. Use Microsoft DOS version 5.0 or better, because that will make the upgrade to Windows 95 run more smoothly and allow you to boot into the older version of DOS by pressing F8 during bootup if necessary.

To check which version of DOS is installed on your computer, enter `ver` (version) at the command prompt.

To check which version of Windows is installed on your computer, enter `winver` (windows version) at the command prompt. From within Windows, choose Help | About to display the Program Manager dialog box and check the version.

After you install Windows 95, try the commands `ver` and `winver` again. Compare the difference in the results. The `ver` command under MS-DOS gives the version of MS-DOS; under Windows 95, it lists Windows 95. The `winver` command under older versions of Windows gave an MS-DOS reply of the Windows version; under Windows 95, it opens a dialog box. These differences highlight the fact that the new version of MS-DOS (version 7.0) has been incorporated directly into the Windows 95 operating system.

Many early versions of DOS were heavily modified by the Original Equipment Manufacturer to meet its specific hardware and tuning requirements. Even now, special utilities appear in the DOS directory of some laptops for such things as power management and hardware configuration. There are very subtle differences between the different companies' versions of DOS. Be aware that there might be problems with the installation because of these differences. Chapter 6 of the *Windows 95 Resource Kit* contains a Setup Technical Discussion that covers the installation of Windows 95 over different versions of DOS.

Setup Type and Hard Drive Space Requirements

Within the Windows 95 Setup, you can choose a Typical, Compact, Portable, or Custom installation. To a large degree, the choice you make will dictate the size of the Windows 95 installation on the computer. It also dictates the number of optional components installed and the amount of control you will have in customizing the installation. Table 2.2 lists the setup types.

Table 2.2

Setup Types

Setup Type	Description
Typical	The default option, which Microsoft recommends for most users with desktop computers. This option performs most installation steps automatically for a standard Windows 95 installation with minimal user action. You need to confirm only the directory where Windows 95 files are to be installed, provide user and computer identification information, and specify whether to create a startup disk.
Portable	The recommended option for mobile users with portable computers. Installs the appropriate set of files for a portable computer. This includes installing Briefcase for file synchronization and the supporting software for direct cable connections to exchange files.
Compact	The option for users who have extremely limited disk space. Installs only the minimum files required to run Windows 95.
Custom	The option for users who want to select application and network components to be installed, and confirm the configuration settings for devices. Installs the appropriate files based on user selections. This type of setup is recommended for advanced users who want to control all the various elements of Setup.

Table 2.3 compares many of the differences in the optional components installed for all four types of installation. An X means that the component is selected by default, and an O indicates that it is not selected by default but may be selected optionally. Notice that for a Custom setup, the options selected by default are the same as for a Typical setup. For a Portable setup, the preselected options are designed to assist mobile users. For a Compact setup, the only optional components that are preselected are two disk utilities. Regardless of which setup type is selected initially, you can choose to see the list of components and can then choose which to install.

Table 2.3

Optional components installed during installation.

Optional Component	Typical	Portable	Compact	Custom	Size in MB
Accessibility options	X	X	O	X	0.3
Audio compression	X	X	O	X	0.2
Backup	O	O	O	O	1.0
Briefcase	O	X	O	O	0.0
Calculator	O	O	O	O	0.1
CD Player	O	O	O	O	0.2
Character Map	O	O	O	O	0.1
Defrag	X	X	X	X	0.3
Desktop Wallpaper	O	O	O	O	0.6
Dial-Up Networking	O	X	O	O	0.4
Direct Cable Connection	O	X	O	O	0.5
Disk compression tools	X	X	X	X	1.0
Document templates	X	O	O	X	0.1
Games	O	O	O	O	0.6
HyperTerminal	X	X	O	X	0.4

continues

Table 2.3 Continued

Optional Component	Typical	Portable	Compact	Custom	Size in MB
Media Player	X	X	O	X	0.2
Microsoft Exchange	O	O	O	O	3.6
Microsoft Fax Services	O	O	O	O	1.7
Microsoft Fax Viewer	O	O	O	O	0.3
Microsoft Mail Services	O	O	O	O	0.6
Mouse pointers	O	O	O	O	0.2
Net Watcher	O	O	O	O	0.1
Online User's Guide	O	O	O	O	7.7
Paint	X	O	O	X	1.2
Phone Dialer	X	X	O	X	0.1
Quick View	X	X	O	X	1.4
Screen savers	X	X	O	X	0.1 to 0.2
Sound and video clips	O	O	O	O	0.4 to 6.5
Sound Recorder	X	X	O	X	0.2
System Monitor	O	O	O	O	0.1
The Microsoft Network	O	O	O	O	2.0
Video Compression	X	X	O	X	0.4
Volume Control	X	X	O	X	0.1
Windows 95 Tour	O	O	O	O	2.4
WordPad	X	O	O	X	1.2

Table 2.4 lists the approximate hard disk space requirements for Windows 95. This table doesn't indicate the maximum requirements, just the average requirements based on the default components installed. The actual space required depends on which options you choose to add during the Windows 95 installation. The bottom line, however, is that Windows 95 requires more space than previous versions of both MS-DOS and Windows. The operating system and all its programs are getting increasingly larger. If your hard drive is getting cluttered with unused programs and files, it might need cleaning up before the installation.

Table 2.4

Approximate Disk Space Requirements for Windows 95

Installation Base	Typical	Portable	Compact	Custom
New installation	47MB	47MB	44MB	48MB
MS-DOS upgrade	55MB	55MB	45MB	55MB
Windows 3.x upgrade	40MB	40MB	38MB	40MB
Windows for Workgroups 3.x upgrade	40MB	40MB	38MB	40MB

Setup Switches

Windows 95 Setup provides standard command-line options to control the installation process. These options, or *switches,* are specified on the command line as arguments for the setup command (such as `setup /?`). Similar to MS-DOS command arguments, the specific option is preceded by a slash character (/), not the backslash character used to specify directory mappings (\).

Setup can be run with the setup command with the switches listed in Table 2.5.

Table 2.5

Setup Switches

Switch	Description
`/?`	Provides help with the syntax and use of Setup command-line switches. Available from both MS-DOS and Windows.
	Troubleshooting Switches
`/C`	Instructs Windows 95 MS-DOS Setup not to load the SmartDrive disk cache.
`/d`	Instructs Windows 95 Setup not to use the existing version of Windows for the early phases of Setup. Use this switch if you have problems starting Setup that might be due to missing or damaged supporting DLL files within the existing version of Windows.
`/in`	Instructs Windows 95 MS-DOS Setup not to run the Network Setup module when installing Windows 95.
`/im`	Instructs Windows 95 Setup not to check for the minimum conventional memory required to install Windows 95.
`/id`	Instructs Windows 95 Setup not to check for the minimum disk space required to install Windows 95.
`/iq`	Instructs Windows 95 Setup not to perform the ScanDisk quick check when running Setup from MS-DOS. You probably want to use this switch if you use compression software other than DriveSpace or DoubleSpace. Also used from Windows in conjunction with `/is` to not perform a cross-linked hard disk check.
`/is`	Instructs Windows 95 Setup not to run the ScanDisk quick check. You probably want to use this switch if you use compression software other than DriveSpace or DoubleSpace.

Switch	Description
`/ih`	Runs ScanDisk in the foreground so that you can see the results. Use this switch if the system stalls during the ScanDisk check or if an error results.
`/l`	Loads the Logitech mouse driver. Use this option if you have a Logitech Series C mouse.
`/nostart`	Instructs Windows 95 Setup to install the required, minimal Windows 3.x DLLs used by the Windows 95 Setup, and then to exit to MS-DOS without installing Windows 95. These files are copied to the \WININST0.400 directory.
	Administrative Switches
`File.inf`	Instructs Windows 95 Setup to use settings in the specified script file to install Windows 95 automatically. For example, executing `setup mybatch.inf` specifies that the Setup program should use the settings in the MYBATCH.INF script file.
`/IW`	This new switch lets you bypass the license agreement screen. It is very useful when creating an automated script file that will run without stopping. This switch must be entered in capital letters.
`/t:tempdir`	Specifies the directory where Setup is to copy its temporary files. If the directory doesn't exist, it will be created. Be aware that any existing files in this directory will be deleted.

Hopefully, you will never need to use Setup's troubleshooting switches, but it's important to know that they are available and to know when to use them. Remember that `/a` and `/n` are no longer valid. Use the NETSETUP program instead.

Well, you're just about ready to get started on the actual installation process. First, however, you need to decide how you want to actually carry out the installation. The following section outlines the different options and helps you choose the method that is right for you and your company.

Microsoft Windows 95 Installation Options

Two versions of Windows 95 are available: a full version and an upgrade version. The upgrade version is used when the computer already contains a copy of DOS in combination with Windows 3.x or Windows for Workgroups 3.x, or when the computer contains a copy of OS/2. The full version is intended for new computers that don't already have an operating system or for installing Windows 95 on a new, unpartitioned, unformatted hard drive. Except for new computer vendors and suppliers, often called Original Equipment Manufacturers or OEMs, most Windows 95 installations will be upgrades. The cost of a full version is roughly twice the cost of an upgrade.

The upgrade version checks for the existence of specific files to validate the installation. If you get stuck with a newly formatted hard drive on a system that had both MS-DOS and Windows 3.x on it, follow these steps:

1. Format the drive with an MS-DOS 5.0 or later bootable disk using the `FORMAT` command.
2. Make the drive bootable by using the `FORMAT /S` command-line option to copy the system files after the format is completed.
3. Run the floppy disk upgrade version of the Windows 95 Setup program from MS-DOS to begin the restoration of the hard drive.

If the computer has a CD-ROM, load enough of MS-DOS to get access to the CD-ROM drive, and then run the CD-ROM version of the Windows 95 Setup program from MS-DOS to begin the restoration of the hard drive.

The Windows 95 upgrade version checks the hard drive for an existing installation. The following files are used: WINVER.EXE, USER.EXE, WIN.COM, SYSTEM.INI, and WIN.INI, plus PROTOCOL.INI in Windows for Workgroups 3.x. Version information is part of this check; false files with the same names won't work. The first three files are the key files being checked. If these files aren't found, Setup will ask for Disk 1 of a qualifying product.

You have three options by which to install Windows 95:

- CD-ROM
- Floppy disks
- Across a network

After learning to do the "floppy shuffle" with 13 to 14 floppy disks, you quickly begin to appreciate the value of a CD-ROM version. In addition, the floppy disk version leaves out some minor things, such as the Online Help Documentation (7.8MB) and the Windows 95 Tour (2.5MB). The CD-ROM version includes many useful administrative extras that can help you become certified.

Windows 95 is installed through a program called Setup, which is a Windows 3.1-based application. Setup is usually run from within Windows, although it can be launched from MS-DOS. When you start from MS-DOS, a stripped-down Windows 3.1 environment is loaded, with just enough functionality to activate the Windows portion of the installation, beginning in real mode and then switching to protected mode.

Using Floppy Disks

Windows 95 can be installed from floppy disks. The first disk (Disk 1—Setup) is used to start the installation. Be aware that Disk 2 and those following are formatted with the new Microsoft Distribution Media Format (DMF), which allows more data to be stored on one disk. This format means that MS-DOS disk commands such as `COPY` and `DISKCOPY` won't work. For the average user, there is no way to make backup copies of these disks if needed.

Although you can't use standard DOS utilities such as `COPY` and `XCOPY` to duplicate the 1.68MB DMF disks, some shareware utilities can. One such utility, WinImage, is available on the World Wide Web. One place to find it is to search ClNet's `shareware.com` page with the keyword WinImage. Once you download WinImage, you can use it to make backup copies of your Windows 95 floppy disks.

Using the CD-ROM

When you use the CD-ROM to install Windows 95, the "floppy shuffle" goes away. It is the same procedure as the floppy disk installation, but easier. As I mentioned, the CD-ROM also contains additional components, including administrative tools, that are not included with the floppy disk version. It would be worthwhile to browse the CD-ROM after your first installation to see exactly what it contains. One hidden jewel found on the CD-ROM is the Windows 95 Resource Kit help file.

Although copying the Windows 95 cab files onto the local hard drive isn't one of the official installation methods, it might be the safest one should the installation fail and either the CD-ROM or the network become unavailable. The Windows 95 installation files take up over 33MB of space on the hard drive. For you as an installer, there might not even be enough hard drive space for Windows 95, let alone a copy of the installation files. (Table 2.4 lists the approximate disk space requirements for Windows 95.)

This method of storing the Windows 95 installation files locally is very sound for laptop users, who are often disconnected from the network and can't afford to carry extra media around with them as they travel. In addition, it solves Windows 95's annoying habit of constantly requesting the setup disk whenever you make a minor change to the system.

Installation Steps Using the CD-ROM

The following steps show you how to install Windows 95 on Computer 1 using a CD-ROM drive. This is a hands-on example that requires about 60 minutes:

1. Reboot Computer 1, loading MS-DOS and Windows for Workgroups. Access the Windows 95 CD-ROM by selecting

File | Run in Program Manager, and start the Windows 95 setup.exe program.

A routine check of the system is done, followed by the preparation of the Setup Wizard.

2. The software license appears. After reading it, tab or click the Yes button to continue.
3. The Setup Wizard appears to start collecting information about your computer. Click Next to continue.
4. When prompted for a location in which to install Windows 95, take the default, which is C:\WINDOWS. Click Next to continue.
5. Windows 95 will prepare the directory, check for installed components, and check for available disk space.
6. Because you upgraded from Windows for Workgroups, you will be asked whether you want to save system files. With these files saved, you could easily uninstall Windows 95 if you wanted to. These files take up approximately 6MB of disk space. If you want to be able to cleanly uninstall Windows 95, as if it were another software application, click the Yes button, and then click Next to continue.
7. Choose the type of installation. The default is Typical. Click Next to continue.
8. For User Information, enter your full name and the name of your organization or company. Click Next to continue.
9. For Product Identification, enter the product key code from the CD-ROM cover. Setup will analyze your computer, searching for all hardware devices available.
10. If you're asked whether you want to check for specific hardware such as a CD-ROM drive or sound cards, check the appropriate boxes and then click Next to continue.

11. After hardware detection, you will see the Getting Connected dialog box. Do not select any of these components.

12. You are prompted to install the default components, as determined by your setup option. Accept the defaults, and click Next to continue.

13. Verify your network configuration, if prompted. For a standalone installation, you will not see these screens.

14. If asked to identify your computer and workgroup, enter the appropriate information. Ensure that the computer name is unique. Click Next to continue.

15. When asked whether you want to create a startup disk, accept the default of Yes, I want a startup disk. Click Next to continue.

16. The Setup Wizard begins copying files to your computer. Click Next to continue.

17. The copying process might take a while. Put in a startup disk floppy when prompted.

18. The Setup Wizard reappears to finish the Windows 95 installation on your computer. Click Finish to continue.

19. Windows 95 starts and prompts you for your name and password. The Control Panel, Start menu, and Help system will be configured.

20. When prompted for Time Zone, click your approximate location on the world map, which helps select the correct time zone. Click Close to continue.

21. **If you have a printer, ignore this setting and continue.**

22. The Welcome to Windows 95 screen appears. Click the buttons to take both the Windows 95 Tour and to see What's New in Windows 95.

The Windows 95 Setup program is very automated and modular. In most cases, very little information is required in order to install Windows 95, and the CD-ROM installation is no exception.

Using the Network

Windows 95 can be installed across a network. It can be installed from a file server such as Microsoft Windows NT Server, Novell NetWare Server, or another network-shared resource.

The initial Windows 95 administrative setup option is done with a program called NETSETUP. This option is used to place the Windows 95 files on a network server. Don't try to use the regular setup program used on the floppy disk or CD-ROM and the administrative options of `/a` or `/n` (as could be done with Windows 3.1), because they aren't available with Windows 95.

You must run NETSETUP from a Windows 95 workstation. The files will be written to a mapped network drive on which you have full security rights. During a network setup, which must be done from a CD-ROM media version of Windows 95, all the files are transferred to the mapped network drive. At this point, you now have a server-based Windows 95 installation share.

Depending on the Windows 95 installation policy option selected while running NETSETUP, you can allow users to install to the local hard drive from the network, install a "shared copy" networked Windows version, or choose between the two. In a shared installation, most of the Windows 95 system files are stored on the server. Only the essential files required to start the network are stored locally. A shared copy of Windows 95 makes network administration easier, but due to the size of the of the operation, system network performance will be somewhat degraded. Additionally, DOS mode will not work on a shared installation, due to the fact that you lose your network connection when you shut down Windows. Another limitation of a shared installation is that you can't log off and log on as another user. In order to log on as another user, you will have to restart the computer.

As an exercise in Windows 95 installation, you will do an administrative setup later in this chapter.

In a networked environment, this installation offers the best performance overall. Storing 87MB of the Windows 95 installation files on a network drive, and then making that drive readily available to all the installers, gives you the most flexibility. However, don't neglect to have some backup media ready in case you get stuck and lose network connectivity on the Windows 95 computer near the end of the Windows 95 installation. Setup reboots your computer under Windows 95 and uses network (or CD-ROM) drivers to complete the installation. If Windows 95 is unable to make a connection to the network (or to your local CD-ROM), it can't complete the installation.

If needed, you can point to alternative sources for the installation files, so keep a copy of the floppy disks handy, just in case. The Iomega ZIP drive, which can attach to the parallel port of the computer as a guest drive and provide 100MB of disk storage, provides another alternative source. All the Windows 95 installation files fit on a single Iomega ZIP disk.

Using Networked Windows

Microsoft refers to networked Windows as running a "shared copy" from a server. During this Windows 95 installation, the user simply connects to the server-based copy that the network administrator has previously created and shared. With this installation option, the network administrator might have restricted the user to install only a shared copy of Windows 95. Selecting the Server radio button during the administrative setup sets this restriction.

The networked Windows 95 option installs the minimal files required into a temporary directory on the computer and starts Setup from that temporary directory. Therefore, most of the actual code remains on the server, not on the local computer. The advantages of this option include less disk space required on the local computer and better administrative control. The disadvantages are increased network traffic, shared space (approximately 87MB) on the server, and slower load times for both Windows 95 and any shared applications.

Although technically it might be possible to run Windows 95 as a shared, networked copy, there are few compelling reasons to justify the performance degradation incurred by such an arrangement. Some ease of administration can be effected by running a shared copy, but the judicious application of policies, profiles, and scripting tools employed in ZAK (the zero administration kit) can prove just as effective in reducing administrative overhead. Network bandwidth is a critical resource, and with applications growing larger and more complex, the extra network traffic generated by running a shared, networked copy of Windows 95 is not worth the trouble. If at all possible, run local copies. Your users will thank you for it.

Upgrading from Windows 3.1

Upgrading is pretty simple. When you start to run the Setup program, it detects the existence of a Windows 3.x or Windows for Workgroups 3.x installation on the computer. Should it find one of them, it will offer to install Windows 95 in the same directory in order to upgrade the existing installation.

If you choose to install into the same directory, the Windows 95 Setup program takes the Windows 3.x or Windows for Workgroups 3.x Program Manager groups and converts them into folders in the Programs directory. It does this to display them on the Windows 95 Start menu under Programs. These folders contain shortcuts to the applications previously found within each Program Manager group. The Windows 3.x application icon converts into a Windows 95 shortcut. Setup also moves the configuration settings in SYSTEM.INI, WIN.INI, and PROTOCOL.INI, plus file associations from the Windows 3.x Registry, into the Windows 95 Registry. This allows all applications and networking settings to work automatically in the new Windows 95 environment.

If you don't want to reinstall all your applications, just upgrading the existing Windows environment to Windows 95 will save you a lot of work. This is an important exam question. Just remember, if you want to keep your old configuration, upgrade to Windows 95 on top of it.

There are several questions about this on the Microsoft Self-Assessment Windows 95 exam, so be open to other possible means of getting access to your Windows 3.1 environment.

You must choose to install Windows 95 in a new directory if you want to preserve the existing MS-DOS or Windows installation. When you do install into a new directory, you might have to reinstall most Windows-based applications before they can function properly in the new environment.

Using Automated Windows Setup

In a large corporate environment, if you can automate the Windows 95 installation by using script files, you will save yourself and your installers a lot of work. By automating routine Windows 95 installations, you are freed to focus on the real problem installations. Expect installation problems so that you won't be surprised when they occur.

The previous installation options discussed where to load the Windows 95 installation files before performing a network-based installation of Windows 95. Batch file automation offers the capability to use a batch script file to automate much, if not all, of the installation of Windows 95. A batch script file is used in either a CD-ROM, a local hard drive, or a network setup.

The administrator can predetermine most of the settings required for Windows 95 installation. In an extreme case, depending on your configuration and degree of standardization, installation could be wholly automated from start to finish. These batch script files (.INF) can be called from Setup using the filename as a command switch, without the slash (/) leading character. It's best to leave the autodetect feature on during automated installations so that Windows 95 can detect the hardware devices installed on a computer.

The automated method involves using both a customized setup script and a mandatory process for installing Windows 95 on multiple computers with the source code on a file server. Several different approaches automate installation:

- Use a login script to run a custom setup script, which activates when each user logs on to the file server.
- Use the System Management Server (SMS) to distribute a mandatory Windows 95 Installation Package that runs Setup using a custom setup script.
- Use a network management software distribution package, such as Norton Administrator for Networks (NAN), to install Windows 95, automatically running Setup using a custom setup script.
- Use Network Client Administrator in Windows NT 4.0 Server to create a network startup disk that points to an installation share.

In addition to these methods for automating setup, you can use NETSETUP from the Windows 95 CD-ROM. Just follow these steps:

1. Run NETSETUP from the ADMIN\NETTOOLS\NETSETUP directory on the Windows 95 CD-ROM. The server-based setup program can be run only from a computer already running Windows 95.
2. The Server Based Setup dialog box will appear. Click the Make Script button to specify that you want to create a batch script.
3. Select the MSBATCH.INF file from the server-based setup directory. A properties sheet will appear. Here you can graphically create a batch script file for use in automating your Windows 95 installations (see Figure 2.1).

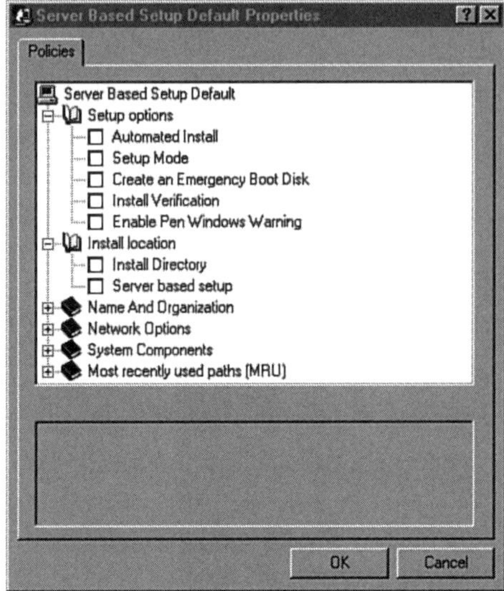

Figure 2.1

Batch file server-based setup.

4. Set a few values, save them by clicking OK, and then exit.

5. Start the Notepad application by choosing Start | Programs | Accessories | Notepad. Open the text file MSBATCH.INF in your server-based setup directory. You will see how the information gathered in the previous step translates into options, fields, and values that Setup can read and understand.

There are many ways to create a custom script file for a Windows 95 installation. As in the preceding steps, you can use the server-based setup (netsetup.exe) program. This program also lets you install source files and create machine directories for a shared network installation. A Windows-based program called Batch Setup (batch.exe) makes it easy to create custom scripts. Finally, you can use a text editor such as Notepad (notepad.exe) to directly edit the custom script file.

It's a good idea to read and understand all the basics surrounding the automated installation of Windows 95.

In the case of network drivers, especially Novell NetWare, Setup keeps any 16-bit real-mode network drivers, such as NETX or VLMs, instead of installing the 32-bit protected-mode clients. A batch file can be used to force the installation of a new device driver, regardless of what was previously installed. Network drivers are covered in greater detail in Chapter 5, "Integration and Operability."

Performing a New Installation of Windows 95

How do you load Windows 95 onto a computer's hard drive after formatting the hard disk? This is a key question that many network administrators would like to know the answer to.

Currently, there is no easy way to format a computer's hard drive and copy an "image" of another standard Windows 95 computer. When used in this context, the word "image" refers to a backup copy of an entire computer's hard drive that is stored on a network file server.

Under MS-DOS and Windows 3.x, it is possible to take a standard computer and create an image that could be downloaded on top of a newly formatted hard drive on one or more computers. As long as the computers were roughly identical, this strategy could save you a significant amount of time conducting many installations. Otherwise, you could easily take a day per computer to reinstall and test (on a clean hard drive) the operating system, Windows, and all the applications. This time estimate also assumes that you have easy access to all the license software setup disks and backups of key data files.

This same strategy of creating a Windows 95 image isn't very practical. The Registry plays a much more important role under Windows 95. Each machine's Registry entries are different. This makes creating a usable image extremely difficult. What can be done is to format the hard drive and then install Windows 95.

After Windows 95 is installed, you can use automated processes to load the rest of the applications.

There are several workable approaches to this clean Windows 95 installation process that work, and they all follow a set pattern:

1. Use a Windows 95 startup disk to boot the computer to a Windows 95 command prompt:
   - If installing from a floppy disk, continue.
   - If installing from a CD-ROM, ensure that the CD-ROM is accessible to the system by adding references to both the CONFIG.SYS and AUTOEXEC.BAT files.
   - If installing from the network, load network drivers and map the Windows 95 installation drive.
2. `fdisk` and `format` the hard drive(s), adding Windows 95 system files to the C:\ drive.
3. Access the Windows 95 Setup program and run it. If installing from the network, ensure that the network configuration is set up correctly.

The floppy version of Windows 95 that is for computers without Windows already includes a boot disk. This version runs an OEMSETUP.EXE program to accomplish the task. Upgrade versions of Windows 95 will prompt you for Disk 1 of Windows 3.x or Windows for Workgroups 3.x, or an OS/2 2.x installation disk in order to verify that you qualify for running the upgrade.

Although the procedure in the following steps installs a clean copy of Windows 95 on the computer, it still leaves the network administrator with the arduous task of reinstalling all the applications. A better approach might be to create a clean MS-DOS and Windows 3.x image with all the applications already installed, download that image, and then upgrade the computer to Windows 95.

The procedure in the following steps uses either the floppy disk or the CD-ROM version of Windows 95 to do a new installation.

Here are the steps for doing an installation with the floppy disk version. If you removed Windows 95 in the previous section, please complete this exercise as well:

1. From Computer 1, boot with the Windows 95 startup disk, format the hard drive, and add the Windows 95 system files to the boot drive (`format c: /s`).
2. Insert Disk 1 of the floppy version of the Windows 95 installation disks into the floppy drive and run setup.exe from the command prompt.
3. Complete the Windows 95 installation.

If you have only the CD-ROM version of Windows 95, you have to boot the computer with an earlier version of MS-DOS that has all the files required to access the CD-ROM drive, or create a modified Windows 95 startup disk that adds the equivalent files to allow access to the CD-ROM drive. Here are the steps for doing an installation with the CD-ROM version:

1. From Computer 1, boot with either the Windows 95 startup disk or an equivalent MS-DOS boot disk. The boot files on the disk, CONFIG.SYS and AUTOEXEC.BAT, must be able to allow access to the CD-ROM drive. Format the hard drive and add the Windows 95 system files to the boot drive (`format c: /s`).
2. Insert the CD-ROM version of the Windows 95 installation disks into the CD-ROM drive and run setup.exe from the command prompt.
3. Complete the Windows 95 installation (see Exercise 2.4).

Microsoft realizes that the essential ingredient of a successful installation of Windows 95 is the Windows 95 Setup program. It needs to handle the millions of different hardware and software combinations. It needs to look easy to users who are installing Windows 95 for the first time. It needs to be able to recover safely from most of the problems encountered during the installation. Setup uses a wonderfully complex installation process. As part of the certification process, you need to understand what is happening behind the scenes and be able to troubleshoot any Windows 95 installation problems.

The Windows 95 installation process is modular. The Windows 95 Setup program steps through this process, running only the modules either requested or needed. For example, the hardware detection phase identifies specific components on the computer, and the Setup runs only the installation modules that match. Some of the modules used by the Windows 95 Setup program are standard wizards, such as the setup for network components, modems, printers, and display monitors.

There are four logical phases to Windows 95 installation:

- Startup and information gathering
- Hardware detection
- File copy
- Final system configuration

The next few sections explore the Windows 95 installation process in detail.

Make a list of the questions you would ask in order to determine the best method of installing Windows 95 at your location, and then make a flowchart of the process. Keep these queries in mind when you take the exam. Using the CD-ROM is the best standalone method available. Using the network, along with a standard customized Setup script and a fully automated installation, is the optimum method for doing wholescale corporatewide Windows 95 installations.

From the Computer's Perspective

From the workstation's perspective, the Windows 95 Setup program performs a series of steps when installing Windows 95. The first few steps depend on where the Setup program starts.

Whether setup begins in DOS mode or Windows mode, Setup ends up running Windows in protected mode. This merge in the Windows 95 installation process occurs just before the hardware detection phase, as shown in Figure 2.2.

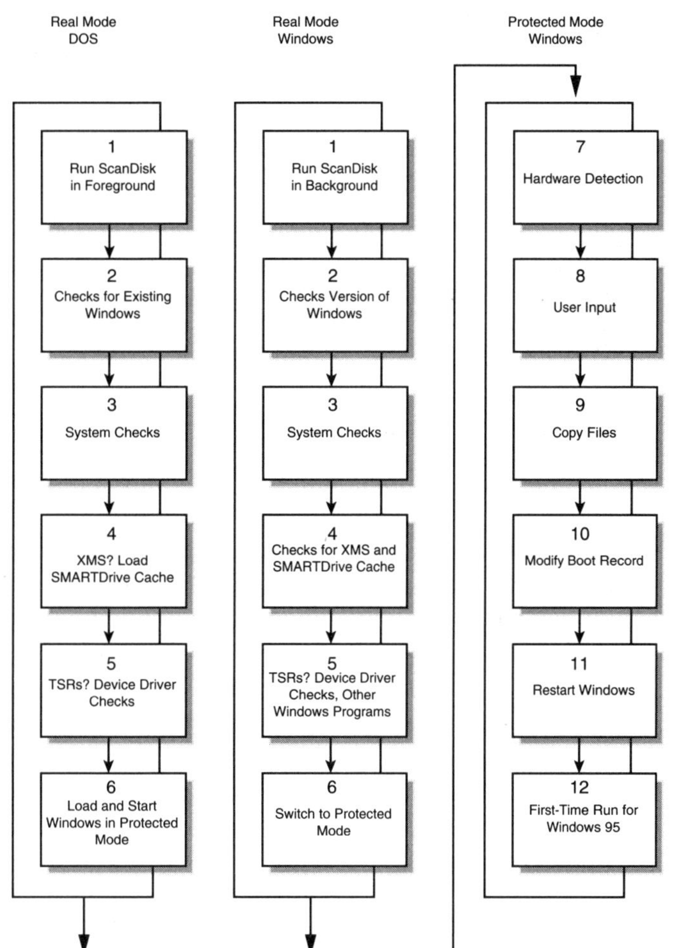

Figure 2.2

The workstation perspective on the Windows 95 installation process.

The Windows 95 Setup program automatically performs 12 steps during installation. You will not be aware that these steps are occurring; however, as an aid to troubleshooting you should understand the sequence:

1. From DOS, the Windows 95 Setup program runs ScanDisk 7.0 in the foreground.

From Windows, the Windows 95 Setup program runs ScanDisk 7.0 in the background after prompting the user to perform a routine check on the computer.

2. From DOS, the Windows 95 Setup program searches the local hard drives for Windows 3.1 or better. If it's found, Setup suggests that you start the existing version of Windows and then run the Setup program. You can bypass this suggestion and continue to run from DOS.

   From Windows, the Windows 95 Setup program checks the version number because it needs Windows 3.1 or better in order to run successfully. If you are trying to run from Windows 3.0, an error message should appear.

3. Setup checks to confirm that the computer is capable of running Windows 95. These checks provide information on the processor, the amount of RAM memory, the amount of disk space, and the version of MS-DOS on the computer. If there is a problem, Setup will halt and inform you.

4. Setup checks for extended memory (XMS) and installs an XMS provider if none is present. If disk caching is not running, Setup automatically loads SmartDrive.

5. Certain Terminate and Stay Resident (TSR) programs and device drivers can cause problems with the Windows 95 installation. Known troublemakers, if found, are either closed or unloaded. If Setup is unable to close or unload them, the installation halts and asks you to disable or close them before restarting.

   From Windows, the program checks for any other running processes and asks you to close them before continuing.

6. From DOS, the Windows 95 Setup program installs a minimal Windows 3.x environment and starts it with the `shell=setup.exe` command, running in protected mode.

From Windows, the Windows 95 Setup program switches to protected mode. At this point, a Windows graphical user interface appears. It is here that a safe recovery screen would appear if Windows 95 Setup detected a failed installation attempt.

7. From this step onward, Setup runs the same, whether started from DOS or Windows. Certain user information gets gathered, such as where to install Windows 95, what configuration to use (Typical, Portable, Compact, or Custom), user name and company, and other related information.

   Setup examines the computer for all attached hardware devices and then creates the Registry entries to contain the hardware configuration information for the computer.

8. Setup requests user input on what components to install, how to configure the network, identification information, and whether to create a Windows 95 startup disk. If setup can't determine the hardware or configuration settings, the user must provide the information.

9. The required files are copied onto the computer's hard drive, according to where Setup was instructed to install them.

10. After all files are copied, the boot records are modified. This is where the computer is changed from its previous operating system to Windows 95.

11. Windows 95 restarts the computer.

12. Several programs run when Windows 95 boots for the first time. These include the Plug and Play Hardware Configuration Wizard (if any of these hardware devices exist). Other programs perform final system configuration: They set up Control Panel, migrate existing program group settings, add programs to the Start menu, create Windows Help, create MS-DOS program settings, and set the time zone. A final reboot might be required to finalize any newly installed Plug and Play hardware devices.

From the Installer's Perspective

Much of the Windows 95 installation process is automatic. Microsoft uses a Setup Wizard to guide the installation, prompting for information and requiring some decisions throughout the process. This section covers the typical interaction seen during the Windows 95 installation.

As soon as you start the Windows 95 Setup program, a dialog box indicates the running of a routine check on the system. During this earliest phase, Setup copies several files to the local computer. ScanDisk checks the integrity of the hard disk. If successful, another dialog box appears as the Setup Wizard gets ready.

The license agreement now appears. To continue with the installation, you must agree to the licensing terms. If you don't agree to the licensing terms, Setup terminates.

If the hard drive doesn't contain a copy of the old software, you can insert a disk to verify qualification for the upgrade. Usually this doesn't happen, because a previous qualifying version of the software is already on the hard drive.

The Setup Wizard, once loaded, divides the remaining activity in the Windows 95 installation into the following three parts:

- Gathering user and computer information: Information must be provided to Setup from either a script or direct input. This phase includes the hardware detection done when analyzing your computer.
- Copying Windows 95 files: Setup copies files to the computer that are required based on the hardware configuration and the program components you have chosen to install.
- Restarting the computer and finishing Setup: Windows 95 starts up and completes the final settings needed to run properly.

The Setup Wizard initial screen, shown in Figure 2.3, and the steps that it follows to complete the Windows 95 installation reinforce this perspective. This initial screen appears again at each of the three parts of the process, with the current part highlighted in bold type and a small triangular arrow pointing to it. This allows you to follow along in the Windows 95 installation process.

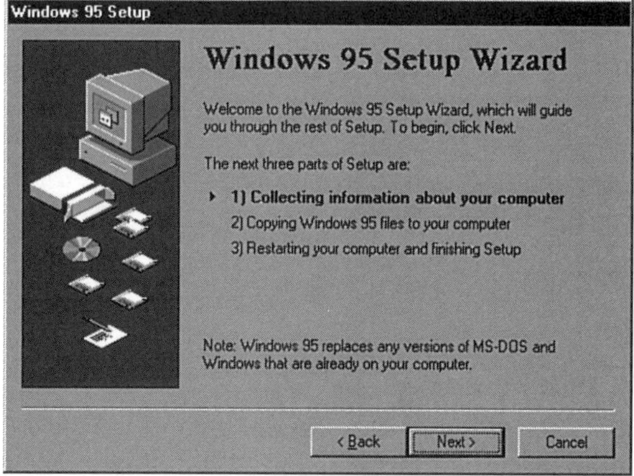

Figure 2.3

The installer's perspective on the Windows 95 setup process.

Gathering Information

The first part of the Windows 95 installation process gathers information about the computer.

This begins only after the following things have occurred:

- The startup process completes.
- A routine check runs on the system.
- The Windows 95 Setup Wizard loads.
- You approve the Microsoft Windows 95 license agreement by clicking OK.

To navigate through the Windows 95 Setup program, click the Next or Back button. Click the Next button or press Enter to accept the choices you have made on the current screen and to continue to the next screen. Click the Back button to return to the previous screen to review or make changes.

Choosing the Windows Directory

If a previous installation of Windows 3.1x or Windows for Workgroups 3.x exists, Setup asks you to confirm the directory where Windows 95 is to be installed, as shown in Figure 2.4. The directory containing the existing Windows installation is the default.

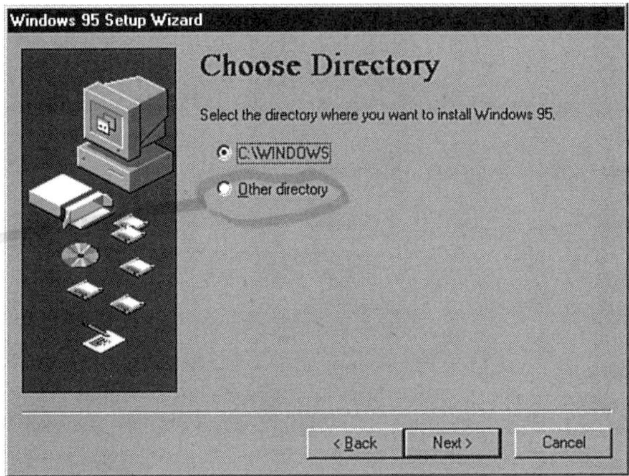

Figure 2.4

Choose the directory in which to install Windows 95.

If you choose to install Windows 95 in a new directory, you might need to reinstall some Windows-based applications. This is because Windows 95 can't migrate your old program settings to the new environment. Additionally, application support (.DLL) files normally found in the Windows 3.x System directory will be missing from the new Windows 95 directory.

Setup next checks for previous installations and for sufficient disk space on the computer. If Setup doesn't think there is enough disk space, you will get a warning. Generally, pay close attention to any warnings while running the Windows 95 installation.

Selecting the Type of Setup

The Windows 95 Setup program asks you to select the type of setup you want. For a description of these options, refer to Table 2.2. The default selection is the Typical setup option.

Figure 2.5 shows the Setup Options dialog box, where you choose the type of setup you want to install.

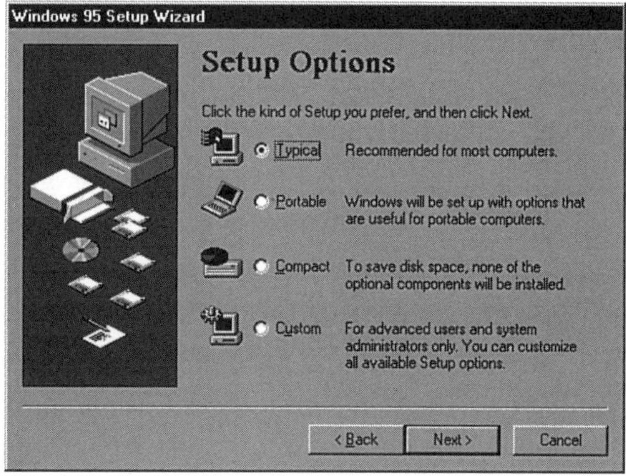

Figure 2.5

Choosing the type of setup option.

Providing User Information

Whatever setup option you choose, you will supply user information, as shown in Figure 2.6. Windows 95 uses this information to identify both the user's name and the company. This information will show up in the Windows 95 Help About dialog box and the Fax Configuration dialog box. The user name is truncated and used to populate the Computer Name and Description fields on the Computer Identification screen later in the setup process.

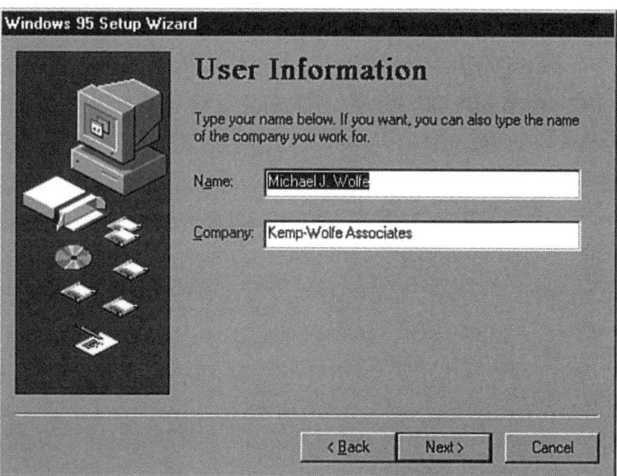

Figure 2.6

Entering user information.

You must type and verify a response in order for Setup to continue.

Setup next requests a product serial number. You must type and verify a response before Setup continues. The serial number dialog box might not appear if you're installing Windows 95 from the network, depending on the license agreement at your site. The product ID number is on the Windows 95 floppy disks, CD-ROM jacket, or Certificate of Authenticity.

Analyzing Your Computer

After you enter the user information, Setup prepares to analyze your computer. This is the hardware detection phase. Setup will automatically search for basic system components such as disk drives and controllers, display devices, pointing devices, and keyboards. The detection process involves a series of approaches to detect these hardware devices.

The first approach determines whether the computer is already running Windows 95. If so, Setup identifies any Plug and Play components.

The second approach is *safe detection mode*. This involves methodically searching the computer for software clues that can indicate the presence of certain devices. The CONFIG.SYS, AUTOEXEC.BAT, and all initialization (.INI) files are checked. Setup inspects memory locations for installed drivers as well. If these safe methods suggest the presence of a device, it is configured.

If some devices are not identified during this safe detection, you will be asked to confirm the existence of certain classes of devices, as shown in Figure 2.7. They include the following:

- CD-ROM drives (proprietary cards)
- Sound, MIDI, or video capture cards
- Network adapters
- SCSI devices

Figure 2.7

Analyzing the computer.

The third approach involves interactive query routines to spot any additional devices. This process of examining specific memory locations, testing values and return codes, and actively probing for devices can cause the computer to lock up during hardware detection. If the computer fails during this detection process, you will need to turn the machine off and restart Setup. The Setup Failure and Recovery process will avoid the trouble area and continue from that point. Troubleshooting setup issues is discussed in Chapter 7, "Troubleshooting."

Tip

Give Windows 95 hardware detection a chance to work. Just because the computer locks up during the detection phase doesn't mean that Windows 95 will be unable to detect the hardware. You might have to turn the machine off two or three times to effect detection of all the hardware. However, patience during this phase of setup will pay dividends during later setup and configuration.

For information about specific device types supported in Windows 95, see the Manufacturers and Models lists in the Add New Hardware Wizard, as well as the Windows 95 README and SETUP.TXT files.

Hardware Detection

The hardware detection process can take several minutes. The indicator bar shows the progress of the hardware detection phase, as shown in Figure 2.8. Note that this is also the point at which Setup can stall if hardware detection fails for a particular system component.

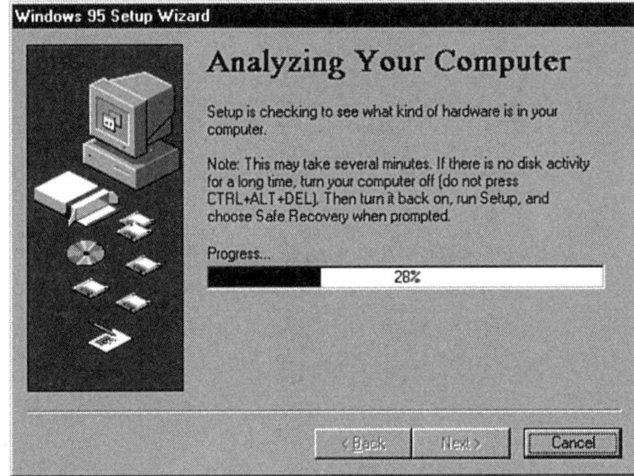

Figure 2.8

The hardware detection phase.

Getting Connected

After the hardware detection completes, Setup asks whether you want to install a variety of tools that allow you to access various services. The three choices included in the Windows 95 installation are the following (see Figure 2.9):

- The Microsoft Network: Installs files required to access the Microsoft Network (MSN). MSN is an online server run by Microsoft that enables electronic mail, bulletin board access, chat sessions online, file library information, and Internet connectivity. When you select this, you don't automatically sign up. You do that later. In order to have access, you must have a modem.

- Microsoft Mail: Installs files that enable connectivity to a Microsoft Mail Post Office running on a local area network file server. This component is only the service provider portion, as opposed to the Microsoft Exchange client application, which enables it.

- Microsoft Fax: Installs files that let you use your computer to send and receive faxes from the computer. In order to use this, you must have a fax modem.

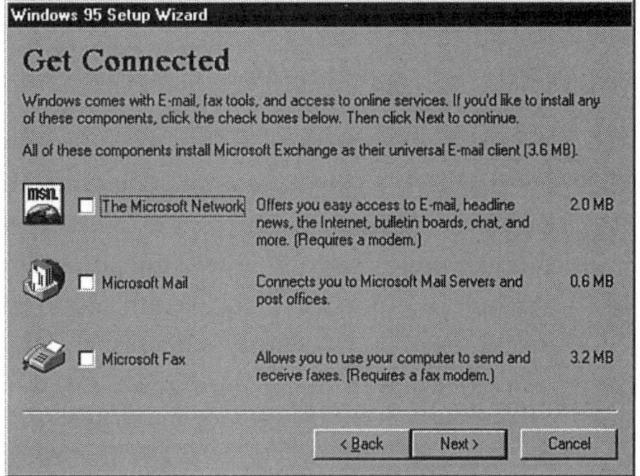

Figure 2.9

Getting connected components.

If you select any of these three choices, the Microsoft Exchange client application is installed as well. This extra component requires another 4.6MB of hard disk space, plus a minimum of 8MB of RAM to operate properly.

Windows Components

The Windows Components screen is essential. Setup asks you whether you want to install the common components. The selected setup option (Typical, Portable, Compact, or Custom) governs this phase. As I mentioned earlier, the Custom setup option gives you the most control over the Windows 95 installation process. Under the Custom setup option, you will not even see this screen. However, whatever setup option you selected, you will get a chance to choose from the various components.

If you trust the components that Microsoft has recommended for installation under each of these setup options, accept the default selection and continue. If there are optional components you want to add (refer to Table 2.3), select the Show me the list of components so I can choose radio button.

When you're making your selections, if a check box is clear, none of the items in that category will be installed. If it is grayed out, some but not all of the items in that category are selected for installation. If the box is simply checked, all items are selected.

If you choose the option for customizing the list of components to be installed, or if you selected the Custom installation, the Select Components dialog box appears, as shown in Figure 2.10. This is the one place where you will see actual information about the amount of cumulative disk space required for the Windows 95 installation. As you either select or deselect each component, the space needed by Setup changes.

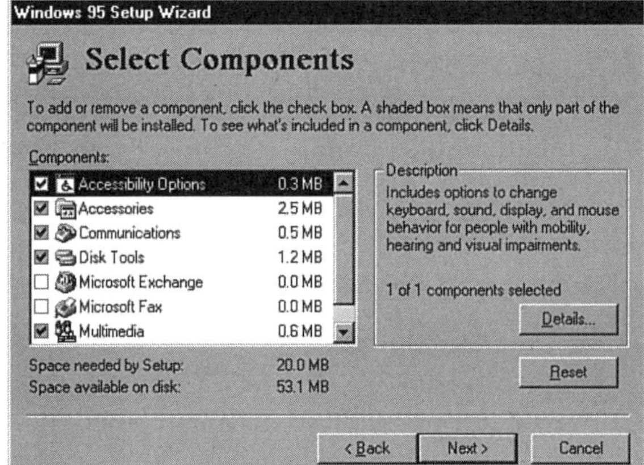

Figure 2.10

Selecting Windows components.

Within the Select Components dialog box, use the following guidelines to select or deselect components:

- From the Components list, select a component category, and then click the Details button. A dialog box appears, listing the components in the category.
- Select the component you want to install, and then click OK. To add a component, make sure that the component is checked.

- ▶ To prevent a component from installing, make sure that the component isn't checked.

You can add or remove any of these components after completing the Windows 95 installation by using the Add/Remove Programs option in Control Panel.

Network Connection

The Windows 95 Setup program lets you specify network components and settings. With a Typical installation, this happens automatically if you have a network adapter or if you choose to install Dial-Up Networking. The Network Wizard lets you configure these settings.

Setup provides appropriate settings based on the hardware and software detection for the network components running when you start Setup. You should accept the default settings unless you know that particular settings need to be changed.

Identification

After configuring network components and settings, Setup prompts you for a unique identifier for your computer. The rules for naming were covered earlier, in the section "What Setup Information Is Needed?" In the Identification screen, shown in Figure 2.11, you supply a computer name, a workgroup if you plan to use Microsoft Networks, and an optional computer description.

Creating the Startup Disk

A startup disk is a Windows 95 bootable floppy disk that contains utilities you can use to troubleshoot a malfunctioning system. The startup disk loads the operating system and presents an MS-DOS command line. You can create a Windows 95 startup disk during Setup's file copying phase, as shown in Figure 2.12. You can also create or update a disk after the Windows 95 installation by using the Add/Remove Programs option in Control Panel.

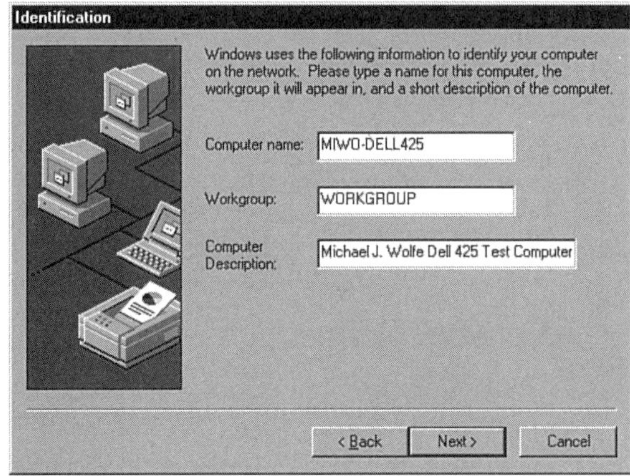

Figure 2.11

Identification for Microsoft networking.

Figure 2.12

Creating a Windows 95 startup disk.

To create a startup disk, Windows 95 formats the floppy disk in drive A and then copies files to the disk in drive A. These 16 files take up 948KB of space on a 1.44MB floppy disk. Table 2.6 describes the files that are on the disk. Other programs and files need to be added to support access to CD-ROM drives, the network, or any other special requirements.

Table 2.6

Files Found on the Startup Disk

File	Description
attrib.exe	File attribute utility
chkdsk.exe	Disk check utility
command.com	Core operating system file
debug.exe	Debug utility
drvspace.bin	Disk compression utility
ebd.sys	Utility for the startup disk
edit.com	Text editor
fdisk.exe	Disk partition utility
format.com	Disk format utility
io.sys	Core operating system file
msdos.sys	Core operating system file
regedit.exe	Real-mode Registry Editor
scandisk.exe	Disk status and repair utility
scandisk.ini	Disk status utility configuration file
sys.com	System transfer utility
uninstal.exe	Uninstall utility

For recovery purposes, you might also want to copy the following files into a subdirectory on the startup disk: **SYSTEM.DAT**, **CONFIG.SYS**, **AUTOEXEC.BAT**, **WIN.INI**, and **SYSTEM.INI**, plus any CD-ROM or other device drivers. If you don't place these files in a subdirectory, you'll have to rename them to prevent problems with the startup disk.

You should create at least one startup disk during a Windows 95 setup. If you want to create a startup disk after the installation, you can use the Add/Remove Programs option in Control Panel to create one. Because there is nothing special about a Windows 95 startup disk, you can save some time during Windows 95 installation by not creating extras.

After hardware detection is complete and Windows 95 Setup has obtained all required information, the next phase of Setup begins. During this phase, Setup copies the Windows 95 files to the destination drive and directory.

Copying Windows 95 Files

This second part of the Windows 95 installation process uses the information previously gathered to start copying all the files it needs (see Figure 2.13). The sources of these files are the Windows 95 Cabinet (CAB) files. If you are installing from floppy disks, here comes the floppy shuffle. Installing from CD-ROM or from the network is a lot faster. Depending on the speed of your computer and installation source, this part can take anywhere from 20 minutes to an hour.

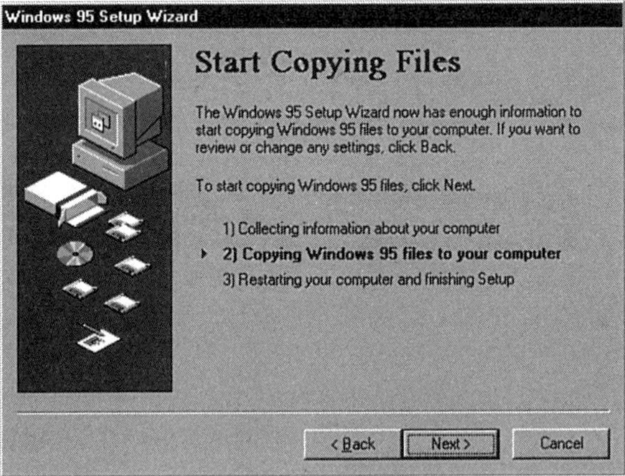

Figure 2.13
Copying Windows 95 files.

The first group of files copied is those used to create a startup disk. After about 20 percent of the elapsed time, if you elected to create a startup disk, Setup asks you to insert a floppy disk into drive A. The disk doesn't need to be formatted or empty, but the process permanently destroys any information on the disk. After you insert the disk, click OK to create the startup disk. Setup formats the disk and copies the appropriate files (refer to Table 2.6). This disk will be useful when you troubleshoot problems with Windows 95.

After copying the appropriate files, the Windows 95 Setup program updates the configuration. This process can take a couple of minutes. Finally, Setup asks you to remove any disks from the floppy disk drives. After you click Finish, the computer restarts, and the third and final part of the installation process begins, as shown in Figure 2.14.

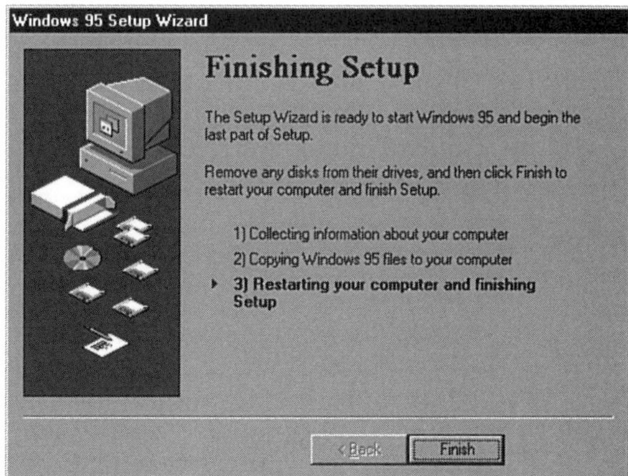

Figure 2.14

Restarting for final Windows 95 installation.

Preparing the Computer to Restart

Just before actually restarting the computer, Setup renames existing MS-DOS boot files, copies a new IO.SYS and MSDOS.SYS, and modifies the boot records and the boot track to point to the new IO.SYS file.

So far in the Windows 95 installation, your old operating system has been available in case the Windows 95 installation fails. The Safe Recovery feature of Windows 95 would allow you to restart the Windows 95 Setup program in your old operating system. Now you are running Windows 95. Beyond this point, if Setup fails, you need to restart in Windows 95 to complete the installation. In most cases, the remainder of the Windows 95 installation goes easily.

Restarting Your Computer and Completing Setup

The initial bootup of Windows 95 is called First-Time Run because it is the first time that Windows 95 has been started on this computer. The standard Windows 95 bitmap is displayed, with the lower banner indicating that this the first-time startup. This is the third and final part of the Windows 95 installation.

Windows 95 might prompt you to log on to the computer. The user ID and password are saved in a Password List (.PWL) file.

Windows 95 sets up the hardware configurations and recognizes any Plug and Play devices.

Finally, Windows 95 asks you to complete several configuration options. These are the run-once options that Windows 95 starts the first time it runs:

- Control Panel configuration: Sets up the Control Panel icons and programs.
- Programs on the Start Menu configuration: Builds the Start menu shortcut and converts old Program Manager groups into folders and menu selections.
- Windows Help file configuration: Builds the Help file index for search capability.
- MS-DOS program settings: Creates the default MS-DOS shortcut.
- Time zone configuration: You select the time zone appropriate to your location and whether the clock should automatically adjust to Daylight Savings changes. This is a nice graphic map representation where you can click a location on the map and it selects the appropriate time zone for you. You can adjust the date and time later from either the Control Panel or taskbar.
- Printer configuration: You can use the Printer Wizard to define either a local or a network printer. You can add printers later using the Printers folder located in My Computer.

This configuration option might not always appear. Previously defined printers retain their old configuration.

Completing Windows 95 Setup

Depending on which options you selected during Setup, the hardware devices you have, or the computer you have, additional run-once options might need to be completed. One example is the wizard for configuring MIDI devices. After all the run-once options are completed, the computer is ready to run Windows 95. Some hardware devices, including Plug and Play-enabled hardware devices, might require another reboot of the computer before they are fully configured.

Setup Failure Detection and Recovery

Hardware and software can cause problems during a Windows 95 installation. Therefore, Microsoft has wisely built in mechanisms for Setup to detect failure and to recover automatically. This isn't a very sophisticated process, but it does ensure a high percentage of successful Windows 95 installations.

The Windows 95 Setup program maintains a setup log (SETUPLOG.TXT) during the installation and can determine where failures have occurred. The most likely place for failure is during hardware detection. A detection log (DETLOG.TXT) keeps track of what Setup discovers during the hardware detection phase. These files are covered in Chapter 7 in the section "Troubleshooting Setup Problems."

If any previous attempt to install Windows 95 has failed, Setup gives you the option of using the Safe Recovery feature or running a full new Setup process (see Figure 2.15). If the Safe Recovery dialog box appears when you start Setup, you should always select the Use Safe Recovery option. When you select this option, Setup can use various built-in methods to avoid problems that occurred previously.

Figure 2.15

Using Safe Recovery.

The following are basic Safe Recovery rules for you to know in case a failure happens:

- Before hardware detection begins, the Windows 95 Setup program uses SETUPLOG.TXT to determine the point of failure when you restart. Setup then knows what to redo and what it can skip.
- During the hardware detection phase, Setup creates DETCRASH.LOG to keep track of identification efforts. When Setup restarts, it finds this file and uses it to determine which detection module was running at the point of failure. In a Safe Recovery mode, Setup reads the Registry to verify all the devices already detected and skips any detection modules up to the point of failure. It also skips any detection modules that caused the failure or any previously logged failure. Safe Recovery then proceeds to the next detection module. When the hardware detection phase finishes, Setup deletes DETCRASH.LOG.
- After the hardware detection phase finishes, Setup skips past this point, assuming that all the necessary hardware information is now stored in the Registry.

The Safe Recovery process depends on what point in the installation Setup reached before encountering problems. It continues from that point onward, attempting to bypass the problems.

Although this approach lets Setup complete the Windows 95 installation, it might leave these problems for you to resolve later.

To continue if Windows 95 Setup stops during hardware detection, do the following:

1. Press F3 or click the Cancel button to quit Setup.

   If the computer doesn't respond to the Cancel button, restart the computer by turning it off and then on again. Do not press Ctrl-Alt-Delete or the Reset button.

2. Run Setup again. Setup prompts you to use Safe Recovery to recover the failed Windows 95 installation.
3. Choose Use Safe Recovery (this should be the default), and then click the Next button.
4. Repeat your installation choices. Hardware detection then runs again, but Setup skips the portion that caused the initial failure.
5. If the computer stops again during the hardware detection process, repeat this procedure until the hardware detection portion of Setup completes successfully.

Your most likely point of failure will occur during the hardware detection phase. With the millions of Intel computers in use today, the countless number of hardware configurations, old legacy hardware, and the new Plug and Play hardware available, this is where you see most of the problems. Only a limited number of interrupts (IRQs), DMA channels, I/O address assignments, and upper memory space allocations are available. There might be conflicts—especially if you add multimedia capability, CD-ROMs, network interface cards, SCSI adapters, and other hardware devices to your computer.

These resource conflicts might already be resolved before you begin installing Windows 95. If your computer is running well, and you make no hardware changes, you can reasonably expect that simply upgrading to Windows 95 won't create any problems. If you upgrade the computer with new hardware devices at the same time you install Windows 95, conflicts might occur. It's much easier to resolve these conflicts after Windows 95 is installed. Safe

Recovery helps you blow past hardware detection conflicts, but it doesn't always solve them. You need to be knowledgeable about the computer configuration in order to uncover conflicts and fix them. As you install Windows 95 on a variety of platforms, you will probably get this opportunity.

If Setup fails after modifying the boot records, you simply restart Windows 95 to complete the installation. There is no need to start the Windows 95 Setup program from the beginning.

Set Up Files for Network Installation and Shared Use: Windows 95 Server-Based Setup

The following steps should be treated as a network (or server-based) installation. Run this setup from the CD-ROM on Computer 1. This process requires access to either a mapped, shared drive on Computer 2 or a new separate directory on Computer 1 if you're using only one computer. Warning: This installation requires up to 87MB of hard disk storage.

Ensure that Computer 2 is running Microsoft Networking under Windows for Workgroups and that both computers are in the same workgroup name. Each computer should be able to see the other before proceeding.

Use netsetup.exe to install Windows 95 source files on a network server and to prepare for either network installations or shared installations of Windows 95. (This tool replaces `SETUP /A`, used in earlier versions of Windows.)

It is recommended that you run NETSETUP from the CD-ROM.

For more information about server-based setup, see Chapter 4 of the *Windows 95 Resource Kit.* To execute a server-based network installation, follow these steps:

1. From Computer 1, with CD-ROM drive, start Windows 95. On Computer 2, install both DOS and Windows for Workgroups. In this case, the server-based installation can be to

either Computer 2, as a network shared drive, or to a Windows NT Server or a Novell NetWare Server.

For the purposes of this example, use Computer 2. If you have only one computer, install to a new directory.

2. Establish an Install directory share with full rights on Computer 2. If you're using a Windows NT Server or a NetWare Server, be sure to grant sufficient privileges or rights if required.
3. Run NETSETUP from the ADMIN\NETTOOLS\NETSETUP directory on Computer 1 from the Windows 95 CD-ROM. The server-based setup program can only be run from a computer that is already running Windows 95.
4. The Server Based Setup dialog box appears, as shown in Figure 2.16. Click the Set Path button to specify the server path where the Windows 95 installation files will be installed. Click OK when done. If the server path was previously defined, the button name is Change Path.
5. Click the Install button to start the installation.

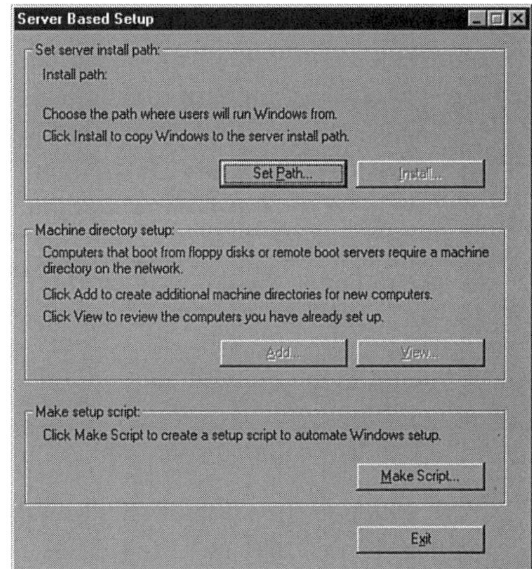

Figure 2.16

Server-based setup.

6. You will see a series of dialog boxes. They will confirm the paths to install from and to. They will also specify how the users can install Windows 95 from the server to a local hard drive as a shared copy or user's choice. Choose user's choice for the purposes of this exercise. Click OK to continue.
7. Click Don't Create Setup Batch Scripts, because you will do this in the next exercise.
8. Enter the Product Identification number when prompted. Click OK to continue.
9. You will see a dialog box when the server-based setup is complete. Click OK, but don't close the window. You will examine a batch file script in the next exercise.

The Windows 95 server-based setup program is simple, and it makes it easy to install Windows 95 on a server. With the Windows 95 installation files on a server, installations are much faster.

Dual Booting with Windows NT

Windows 95 can dual boot with other operating systems. If you install Windows 95 into a separate directory when upgrading an older version of Windows, you can boot to old Windows. But it's more likely that you want to dual boot with Windows NT. The file that makes this possible is the Windows 95 version of MSDOS.SYS. In MSDOS.SYS, you must ensure that the entry `BootMulti=1` is set properly. If it is set to 1, running multiple operating systems is enabled. If it is set to 0, it is disabled. The following are the steps to take to enable dual booting with Windows NT if Windows 95 is already installed:

1. Start Windows 95.
2. Exit to a command prompt.
3. Switch to the directory holding the Windows NT source files, and type `WINNT /w` (this will allow Windows NT Setup to run under Windows).

4. Windows NT will create a boot.ini file that will list the location of the WINNT directory, the Windows directory, and the default boot operating system.

If Windows NT is already installed, the procedure is a little more difficult. Here are the steps to follow:

1. Make sure that the NT machine will already dual boot between MS-DOS and Windows NT.
2. Start the computer under MS-DOS.
3. Run Windows 95 Setup.
4. If you run MS-DOS from a floppy disk when you install Windows 95, you will have to run the Windows NT Emergency Recovery Disk (ERD) in order to be able to start Windows NT.
5. If you want to run MS-DOS after you have installed Windows 95 in a dual-boot configuration, you will have to select MS-DOS from the boot menu and then, when the Windows 95 menu comes up, select Previous Version.

There are a few things to keep in mind when dual booting with Windows NT and Windows 95:

- If your Windows NT machine has an NTFS file system and doesn't have a FAT partition, you won't be able to dual boot Windows 95.
- If you have Windows 95 installed, and you install Windows NT on the same partition, and in the process you convert your FAT partition to NTFS, Windows 95 will no longer work.
- It works out best if you have two partitions—one FAT and one NTFS. That way, you can take advantage of the strengths of both operating systems.
- If you want to share an application (such as Office), you will have to install it twice in order to effect the appropriate

Registry entries for both operating systems. However, you can install to the same directory as long as you use the same options.

Make sure you have a good backup before you try any of this! Refer to the section "Installing and Configuring Backup Software" for assistance in this area.

Uninstalling Windows 95 from a Computer

If you upgraded from Windows 3.1x or Windows for Workgroups 3.x, you have the option of saving system files. This saves the existing MS-DOS-based and Windows-based system files and lets you easily uninstall Windows 95 from the computer if required, such as if mission-critical applications don't run properly under Windows 95. These system files you save require about 6MB of hard disk space.

The following steps work properly only if you selected Save System Files during the Windows 95 installation. Otherwise, you need to follow a longer series of steps. See Chapter 6 of the *Windows 95 Resource Kit* under "Removing Windows 95 with Your Previous Operating System."

To remove Windows 95, use the Windows 95 startup disk's Uninstall program (uninstal.exe). Follow these steps:

1. From Computer 1, place your Windows 95 startup disk in the floppy drive.
2. Choose Start | Run. Type `a:\uninstal.exe` and press Enter.
3. In the Windows 95 Uninstall dialog box, click Yes to begin the process. Windows 95 will then shut down, and the uninstallation will continue automatically.

Your previous configuration will be restored. When finally prompted, remove the Windows 95 startup disk from the floppy drive, and press Enter to reboot your computer.

The preceding steps will remove Windows 95 from the computer. To continue with the remaining exercises in this chapter, do a standard Windows 95 installation to Computer 1. Alternatively, you can do a clean Windows 95 installation to Computer 1, as outlined in the earlier section "Performing a New Installation of Windows 95."

Now that you have seen how to install Windows 95, it's time to look at configuring various hardware devices. A finely honed Windows 95 machine isn't much good if it can't communicate with others. The first device we will look at is the printer. Since Windows 95 has completely redesigned the printing structure, we'll spend some time examining the new implementation, because the understanding gleaned will be a boon to your troubleshooting efforts later.

Windows 95 Printing Features

Windows 95 includes many new printing features, including support for the following:

- Plug and Play (PnP) printers
- Extended Capabilities Ports (ECPs)
- Image Color Matching (ICM)
- A unidriver/minidriver printer driver model
- Point and Print setup
- Drag and Drop printing
- Enhanced Metafile (EMF) Spooling
- Improved conflict resolution
- Deferred printing

Plug and Play (PnP) Printers

Windows 95 can take full advantage of the automatic configuration features of Plug and Play (PnP) printers. Windows 95 automatically detects and configures devices complying with PnP standards each time the operating system initializes. Thus, when a PnP-compliant printer is plugged into a port on the computer, and Windows 95 is started, the operating system can detect the model of printer and set up the printer in the Printers folder.

The PnP setup uses bidirectional communication through the printer cable to obtain information on the printer, including the following:

- Manufacturer and model
- Memory installed
- Font cartridges installed

The printer model is reported as a device ID defined in the IEEE1284 PnP standards. If Windows 95 has a printer driver for that specific device ID, it installs the driver and creates a print queue for that printer in the Printers folder.

If Windows 95 doesn't have the exact driver for that device ID, a dialog box appears, giving the following options:

- The user can insert a floppy disk with a Windows 95 driver for the printer.
- The user can select a driver for a printer that Windows 95 has determined to be compatible.
- The user can choose not to install the printer.

Bidirectional printer capability allows printers to send unsolicited messages to Windows 95, such as being out of paper or low on toner.

To enable the bidirectional printing features of Windows 95, including PnP configuration, you must have the following:

- A printer that supports bidirectional communication
- A printer with a PnP BIOS (if PnP is to be used)
- An IEEE 1284-compliant printer cable (this has "1284" stamped on the cable)
- A port configured for two-way communication in the Windows 95 Device Manager. For example, if the port is in AT-compatible mode, change it to PS/2-compatible mode.

Extended Capabilities Port (ECP)

An Extended Capabilities Port (ECP) allows Windows 95 to use data compression to speed the data transfer to an attached printer. The improvements in printing speed are even greater if the printer is also ECP-compliant.

By default, ECP features are not enabled, although Windows 95 might have detected the ECP port. To enable ECP support, follow the next steps.

You must have an ECP printer port installed to follow these steps.

1. Determine the IRQ and DMA settings required for the ports according to the documentation for the computer or ECP card.
2. Double-click the System icon in Control Panel and select the Device Manager tab.
3. Click the plus sign (+) next to Ports to display the installed ports. Select the ECP port and click Properties.

4. Select the Resources tab to display the I/O address range that has been automatically detected for the ECP.

5. Select Basic Configuration 2 in the Settings Based On field.

6. In the Resource settings list box, select Interrupt Request and click Change Setting.

7. In the Edit Interrupt Request dialog box, type the IRQ value you noted in step 1 and click OK. The Conflict information field should report "No devices are conflicting." If it doesn't report this, you must change the IRQ setting for the conflicting device.

8. In the Resource settings list box, select Direct Memory Access and click Change Setting.

9. In the Edit Direct Memory Access dialog box, Type the DMA value you noted in step 1 and click OK. The Conflict information field should report "No devices are conflicting." If it doesn't, you must change the DMA setting for the conflicting device.

10. Shut down and restart the computer so that the changes can take effect. After restarting, you can take advantage of fast I/O capabilities offered by the ECP.

Image Color Matching (ICM)

A problem that has always been associated with color printing is that you can never be too sure what a color will look like when it's printed, or how closely it will match what you see onscreen. A traditional solution was to use hard-copy color samples, printed on the color printer so that you could see exactly what shade the red would be or how blue the blue really was. Unfortunately, this required a hard copy for each printer to be used, which could be cumbersome, especially if you were working with 64 million colors.

To solve this problem, a group of industry hardware vendors (chiefly Kodak, Microsoft, Apple Computer, Sun Microsystems, and Silicon Graphics) created a color-matching specification known as InterColor 3.0. Windows 95 implements Kodak's Image Color Matching (ICM) technology, which conforms to the InterColor 3.0 specification to ensure that the colors displayed on a monitor closely match colors printed from any ICM-supporting printer.

Each color monitor, printer, and scanner supporting ICM has a color-matching profile stored in the *systemroot*\SYSTEM\COLOR directory (where *systemroot* is WINDOWS, for example). This profile takes into account how closely the device matches various colors to the international (CIE) color reference standards. The Windows 95 operating system then takes these color-matching capabilities into account and makes any modifications necessary when displaying that color on the monitor, so what you see is as close as possible to the color that is printed.

For example, if printer A generally prints a darker red than printer B, the ICM profile for printer A tells Windows 95 to display a darker red onscreen when the driver for printer A is selected. In addition, if that document is open at another computer whose monitor displays colors slightly differently, the ICM profile for that monitor causes Windows 95 to adjust the onscreen colors so that they look the same as in the original document.

In summary, the benefits of ICM are as follows:

- The color onscreen closely matches the color of the printout if ICM devices and applications are used.
- The colors used are consistent on any ICM-compliant devices, ensuring colors that match the international standards regardless of which ICM device they are printed to or displayed on.

Printer Drivers

The Windows 95 printer driver architecture is similar to that used with Windows NT. Printing is controlled through a Microsoft-written universal driver, along with a small machine-specific minidriver supplied by the printer manufacturer. Thus, a printer manufacturer needs to write only a small amount of code to customize the driver to the particular requirements and features of that printer.

Unidrivers

Windows 95 uses two universal drivers: one for PostScript printers and one for non-PostScript printers.

Non-PostScript

The non-PostScript universal driver (unidriver) has built-in support for almost all the existing printer control languages, such as the following:

- HP PCL
- Epson ESC P/2
- Canon CaPSL
- Lexmark PPDS
- Monochrome HP-GL/2
- Most dot-matrix technologies

The non-PostScript driver also supports device-resident Intellifont and TrueType scalable fonts, as well as downloading TrueType fonts for rasterizing by the processor of a PCL printer.

PostScript Universal Driver

Unlike the Windows 3.x PostScript driver, the Windows 95 PostScript universal driver supports PostScript Level 2 commands for advanced PostScript printing support. In addition, Adobe PostScript Printer Description (PPD) files are supported for version 4.2 and older PPDs. Another new feature of the Windows 95 PostScript universal driver is the offloading of ICM processing to the printer's PostScript processor. This reduces the processor load on the computer, which improves system performance.

Minidrivers

Windows 95 includes a large number of minidrivers for the most common printers. In addition, because of the Windows 95 driver architecture, a manufacturer can create a minidriver for its printer much more quickly and easily. Furthermore, because most of the driver code is in the universal driver, the possibility of the minidrivers needing to be updated to fix programming bugs is decreased.

Point and Print Setup

A network printer serving as a Windows 95, Windows NT, or NetWare print server can be configured as a Point and Print printer. When a Windows 95 client on the network first attempts to print to the network printer or "points" to the printer by opening the print queue in Network Neighborhood, the printer driver files can be automatically copied to and installed on the Windows 95 client. In addition, if the print queue is on a Windows 95 server, such settings as printer memory, paper size, and so on can be automatically configured on the client. The Windows 95 .INF files define the files required for a particular printer.

You must have File and Print Sharing for Microsoft Networks or File and Print Sharing for NetWare Networks enabled in order for Point and Print to work.

With a print queue configured for Point and Print setup, a Windows 95 user can have the printer drivers automatically installed on the Windows 95 client, without having to worry about what the printer model is, what driver to use, and so on. The information obtained from a printer when you enable Point and Print can include the following:

- The printer driver name and file information
- Model information about the printer

- Which printer driver to retrieve from the Windows folder on a local or network computer. Printer driver files are located in the \WINDOWS\SYSTEM folder.
- The server name on which the printer files are stored

The \WINDOWS\SYSTEM folder is automatically set up as a read-only share when you share a printer under Windows 95. It uses the share name PRINTER$ and has no password. It is part of the UNC share name of the computer that shares the printer. So, if a computer named \\PEART is sharing a printer, Windows 95 automatically creates a share named \\PEART\PRINTER$. You can't see this share in Explorer because it's hidden. You can, however, map to the hidden share using the `NET USE` command. This hidden PRINTER$ share is needed for Point and Print support so that the printer driver files can be available across the network.

When a print server supports Point and Print and UNC (Universal Naming Convention) names, the remote printer doesn't have to be associated with any of the local computer's printer ports. On the other hand, if the server doesn't support UNC names, you can set up one of the local printer ports with the network printer. In fact, the printer port can be a virtual port—that is, a port that isn't physically part of the computer. This means, for example, that you can associate LPT3 up to LPT9 to a remote printer.

For information on how to configure and use a printer for Point and Print setup, refer to the section "Connecting to a Network Printer Using Point and Print Setup" later in this chapter.

Drag and Drop Printing

Do you have a document that you want to quickly send to a printer without having to manually open the document in an application? Simply click the document and keep holding down the mouse button, and then drag the document until it's over the printer icon. When you release the mouse button, the application associated with the document opens, the document is sent to the print queue, and the application then automatically closes.

Most applications support this feature. If an application doesn't support this feature, you have to open the file in the application and then print the file.

If you right-click a document and select Print from the context-sensitive menu, the same process occurs, except that the document is sent to the default printer. If you want to print to a different print queue, you can use the drag-and-drop method if the application supports printing to a nondefault printer.

Enhanced Metafile (EMF) Spooling

For non-PostScript printing, Windows 95 generates an Enhanced Metafile (EMF) instead of sending the raw data directly to the printer. Spooling to an EMF allows control to be returned to an application approximately twice as fast as if the data is sent directly to the printer. Therefore, the printing process time that makes your computer inaccessible is much shorter in Windows 95 than in Windows 3.1.

With Windows 3.1, raw printer data (such as HPPCL commands or escape codes) was sent directly to the printer driver for rendering and submission to the Print Manager queue. The application stayed busy until all the data had been rendered and sent to the Print Manager queue. During this time, the user was unable to do anything else in that application, such as work on another document.

With Windows 95, the Graphical Device Interface (GDI) generates an EMF using the document information generated by the application. The EMF is a collection of Windows 95 commands for creating an image, such as commands to draw a rectangle and put some text underneath it. The EMF print API has a command to draw a rectangle and instructions on placing the text underneath it. The EMF can be created in about half the time it would take to send the raw data directly to the printer. After the EMF is created, the application no longer is busy, and the user can continue to work in it.

The GDI in Windows 95 is the key to understanding EMF. The GDI handles most graphical I/O tasks in Windows 95. These include painting the screen, sending output to printers, and rendering graphical objects and text. The EMF file that is created when you send a print job to a printer set up for EMF contains GDI commands, a color palette, and additional data used to render the image defined by the GDI commands.

The EMF is then interpreted in the background by the 32-bit printing subsystem, which translates the EMF into raw printer data that can be sent to the printer (called *rasterizing*). EMF spooling adds an intermediate step in the print process but returns control to an application much more quickly.

A PostScript printer handles the rasterizing process itself, so EMF isn't necessary when you print to a PostScript printer. Instead of using EMF, PostScript uses page description language commands to rasterize the print job, so you might need to disable the EMF spooling on these PostScript printers.

Figure 2.17 illustrates the differences between the Windows 3.x and Windows 95 print processes.

To set the spooler settings for a printer, open the Printers folder (from My Computer or Control Panel), right-click the printer you want to examine, and choose Properties from the context menu. The Properties page for that printer appears. Click the Spool Settings button to display the Spool Settings dialog box, shown in Figure 2.18.

From this dialog box, you can turn the spooler on and off and control when the system begins printing. The following options control when printing starts:

- Start printing after last page is spooled
- Start printing after first page is spooled

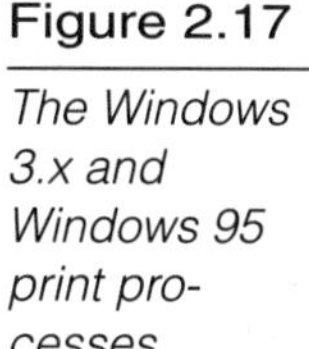

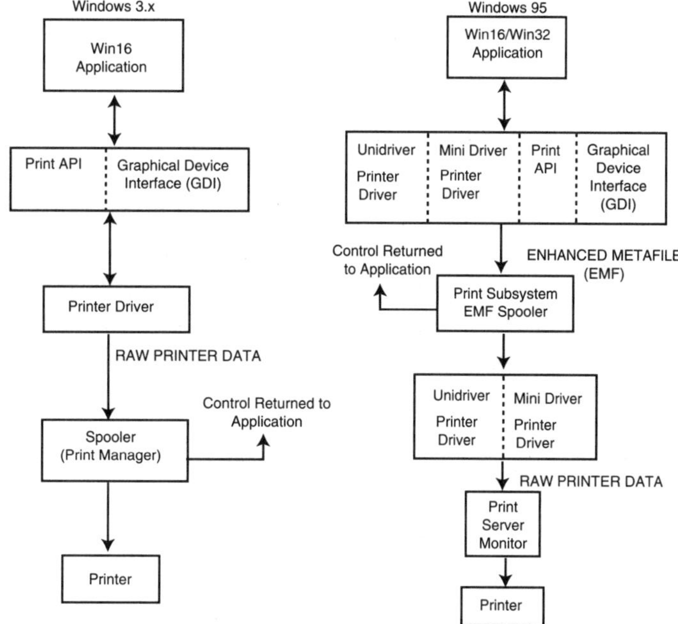

Figure 2.17

The Windows 3.x and Windows 95 print processes.

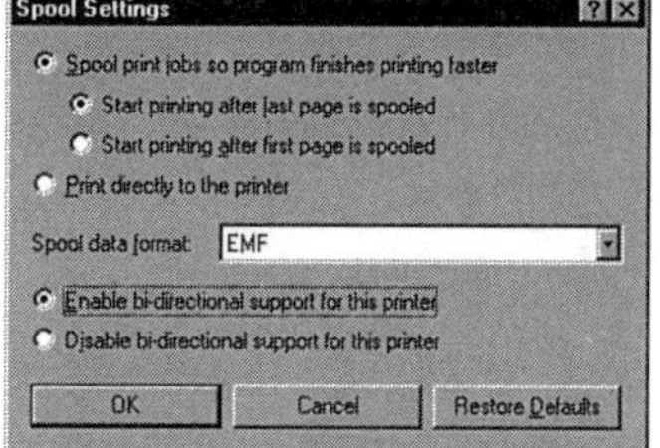

Figure 2.18

The Spool Settings dialog box.

Some options in the Spool Settings dialog box might be disabled, depending on the printer driver installed.

EMF spooling works with most Windows applications. However, some applications might be capable of printing to a driver using only raw printer data. For these applications, you might need to bypass EMF spooling. The following steps show you how to disable EMF spooling:

1. Right-click the Printer icon and select Properties. The properties sheet for the printer appears.

2. Select the Details tab and choose Spool Settings. The Spool Settings dialog box appears.

3. In the Spool Data Format list box, select RAW and click OK. Data sent to this printer no longer will be spooled to an EMF file.

In most situations, using EMF is a good idea if your system can handle the background printing. If your computer suffers in performance due to background tasks like this, you might want to follow the preceding steps to disable EMF. Also, you will see a slight decrease in free hard disk space when you send a print job to a printer using EMF. This is because the EMF file consumes disk space until the print job finishes. If you encounter a problem with EMF, run ScanDisk to check for disk integrity and free disk space. If you still experience problems after running ScanDisk, switch to RAW printing.

The following list describes instances in which EMF rendering is processed when sending a print job from Windows 95 to a network or local printer:

- Printing to a local printer: Rendering occurs on the local computer.
- Printing to a Windows 95 Server across a peer-to-peer network: Rendering occurs on the server instead of on the client computer that sends the print job.
- Printing to a Windows NT or Novell NetWare print server: Rendering occurs on the client computer that sends the print job.

DOS applications don't benefit from EMF spooling. However, as you'll see in the next section, DOS applications can use Windows 95's spooling feature so as not to encounter conflicts with other applications when sending print jobs to the printer.

Conflict Resolution

The Windows 95 printing subsystem handles conflicts between different MS-DOS and Windows applications trying to print to a printer port simultaneously. This functionality is an improvement over the Windows 3.1 printing subsystem.

In Windows 3.1, conflicts usually occurred when you tried to print from an MS-DOS-based application and a Windows-based application simultaneously, because the DOS application couldn't use the Windows 3.1 Print Manager. The Print Manager set up a spooler to spool all print jobs. Because a DOS application couldn't use the Print Manager, the DOS print job went straight to the printer, conflicting with other jobs.

Under Windows 95, however, printer spooling is automatically set up for DOS applications (in other words, the user doesn't need to manually configure this support). Now when you send a print job from a DOS application, it goes to the spooler first and then to the printer. This spooling action also has the benefit of turning control back over to the DOS application sooner under Windows 95 than under Windows 3.1.

Deferred Printing

The spooling capabilities of Windows 95 allow a job to be spooled to a print queue even if the printer is currently unavailable. For a remote user, Windows 95 automatically detects that the laptop is not connected to a local or network printer and sets the print queue to Work Offline mode. The job is still sent to the print queue, but it doesn't print until a connection to that printer is detected. For example, when the user returns to the office, attaches to the printer or the network, and starts Windows 95, the jobs can be sent to the printer as a background process.

You can also manually set a print queue to hold print jobs by right-clicking the printer icon and selecting Pause Printing. This might be useful if you want to hold the jobs until later in the day, for example. To resume sending jobs to the printer, right-click the printer icon and deselect Pause Printing.

The Windows 95 Printing Process

The printing model for Windows 95 is made up of modular components, which allow a great deal of flexibility because individual components can be substituted. For example, if a PostScript printer driver is used, the EMF component of the printing model is not used.

To illustrate the Windows 95 printing model, the following list contains the three different printing processes that can occur:

- Printing from a non-Windows application
- Printing from a Windows application to a non-PostScript printer
- Printing from a Windows application to a PostScript printer

Regardless of which print process is used, the print job is eventually formatted into raw printer data that is sent to the local print spooler on the Windows 95 computer.

Print Spooler

A *print spooler* essentially is an internal print queue where the print job data is written while the print job is being processed. Any printing done in Windows 95 uses the local print spooler on the Windows 95 client. In addition, if a Windows application prints to a non-PostScript printer, an additional spooler known as the EMF sprint spooler may be used. If the network printer is used, the local print spooler passes the print job to the spooler on the network print server.

As the print jobs are spooled, they are written to a temporary file on the hard disk. For Windows 95 computers, the print jobs are queued in *systemroot*\SPOOL\PRINTERS—for example, C:\WINDOWS\SPOOL\PRINTERS.

When a job begins to spool, it is the responsibility of the Print Monitor to decide when to send the information to the printer.

Using the default settings, and assuming that the printer is available to accept a new print job, the Print Monitor starts sending the job to the printer after the first page has spooled. To change this, choose Spool Settings from the Details tab of the properties sheet for the printer. The Print Monitor writes the spooled data to either a port (if the printer is locally connected) or a print spooler on a network print server.

After the job has printed, the Print Monitor can display a pop-up message informing the user that the job has printed.

Printing from a Non-Windows Application

For non-Windows (that is, DOS) applications, the application sends information to the printer driver, which converts the information into raw printer data using a printer control language that the printer understands. For example, to print a circle, an HP LaserJet driver would send an HPPCL command to the printer specifying the size of the circle and the location on the page. The raw data is then sent to the print spooler, and control is returned to the application after all the raw data has been submitted to the print spooler.

Printing from a Windows 95 Application to a Non-PostScript Printer

When you select a network printer in a Windows application, Windows 95 can copy the printer driver to the local directory *systemroot*\SYSTEM (for example, C:\WINDOWS\SYSTEM). If the file has already been copied, the print server driver is not copied to the local computer unless the local driver is an older version than the driver on the print server. Similarly, if a local printer is selected, the driver already is on the local computer.

When the client has the correct printer driver on the hard drive, the driver is loaded into RAM. The Windows application can then query the printer driver for the current print settings (such as page orientation) to produce a What-You-See-Is-What-You-Get (WYSIWYG) image onscreen.

To print the document, the Windows 95 GDI (which is responsible for displaying how the screen looks—for example, drawing the text in a certain font) sends a series of commands to the Windows 95 graphics engine. The Windows 95 graphics engine then translates the GDI commands into an EMF, using the EMF spooler. After the EMF has been created, control is returned to the application. The EMF spooler then processes the EMF information in the background using the printer minidriver. The minidriver converts the EMF to raw printer data, which is then spooled to the print spooler.

Printing from a Windows Application to a PostScript Printer

This process is the same as for non-PostScript printers, except that the GDI doesn't generate commands for an EMF file. Instead, to print a document, the PostScript driver generates a series of raw printer commands to tell the printer how to print the specified pages. The raw printer data (in the PostScript language) is then sent to the print spooler.

Installing a Local Printer in Windows 95

A local printer can be installed in Windows 95 using either PnP hardware detection or the Add Printer Wizard, if the printer isn't PnP-compliant.

Installing a Plug and Play Printer

If a PnP-compliant printer is connected to the Windows 95 computer at startup, the printer is detected, and the appropriate printer driver is automatically installed. If Windows 95 can't determine the proper driver to be used, it prompts the user to specify the correct driver.

Installing a Printer Using the Add Printer Wizard

The Add Printer Wizard is used to install a printer driver in Windows 95. The Add Printer Wizard can be accessed from the Printers folder. To access the Printers folder, select Start | Settings | Printers or open it after opening My Computer.

The Printers folder can be used to perform the following functions:

- Install a printer
- Share a printer on a network
- Set permissions for accessing a printer
- Connect to a network printer
- Manage printers
- Change printer properties such as page size

For an exercise testing this information, see end of chapter.

The following steps show you how to use the Add Printer Wizard to install a locally attached printer.

If you don't have an actual printer attached to your computer, you can still perform the following steps and select FILE: as the port to print to. When you print to FILE:, you are prompted for a filename and path to which to save the output. Printing to FILE: is usually used with the Generic/Text Only printer driver to create text output in a file.

1. Open the Printers folder.
2. Double-click the Add Printer Wizard and choose Next. You are asked whether the printer is attached directly to the computer or is accessed from the network.
3. Select Local Printer and click Next.

4. Select the printer manufacturer from the Manufacturers list.
5. Select the printer model from the Printers list. If you do not have an actual local printer, you may select the Generic/Text Only driver after selecting Generic as the manufacturer.
6. From the list of Available ports, select the port to which the printer is connected. For example, for a parallel port, you might need to select LPT1:. If you don't have a local printer attached, select FILE:.
7. Choose Next and assign the printer a printer name. You can accept the default name, or you can use a more descriptive name, such as LaserJet II in Room 312.
8. If you want print jobs to be sent to this printer by default, click Yes and then click Next. Otherwise, click No and then Next.
9. The Add Printer Wizard asks you whether you want to print a test page, and then it copies the files from the Windows 95 distribution media. If Windows 95 can't find these files, you are prompted for the path.
10. An icon for the printer is created in the Printers folder. To configure the printer, see the following section.

Configuring a Printer in Windows 95

The settings on a printer are controlled through the properties sheet for that printer. To access the properties sheet, right-click the printer icon and select Properties.

The properties sheet contains the following tabs:

- General
- Details
- Paper
- Graphics

- Fonts
- Device Options
- PostScript

These tabs are described in the following sections.

Selecting General Properties

On the General tab, you can specify the printer name and any additional descriptive comments. In addition, if you want to print a separator page between print jobs, this instruction can be specified here.

Setting the Details

On the Details tab, you can specify the printer driver to be used, as well as various port settings. For example, if you change the Transmission Retry setting, Windows 95 will wait that number of seconds before reporting a timeout error if the printer is not responding. This is helpful in remote printing situations. Additionally, you access the Spool Settings dialog box from the Details tab.

Choosing Paper Properties

The type of information on this tab varies depending on the printer driver used. The Paper tab may contain configuration settings for some of the following items:

- Default paper size
- Default orientation (for example, landscape or portrait)
- Paper source (for example, tractor feed or upper paper tray)
- The number of copies to print for each print job

Selecting Graphics Settings

The configurable information in this tab varies depending on the printer driver used. It may contain settings such as the following:

- Resolution: Specifies the number of dots per inch (dpi) used for printing graphics or scalable fonts.
- Dithering: Specifies how the colors are blended together for a color printer.
- Intensity: Specifies the degree of lightness or darkness of the print job.

Figure 2.19 shows an example of a typical Graphics tab on a printer's properties sheet.

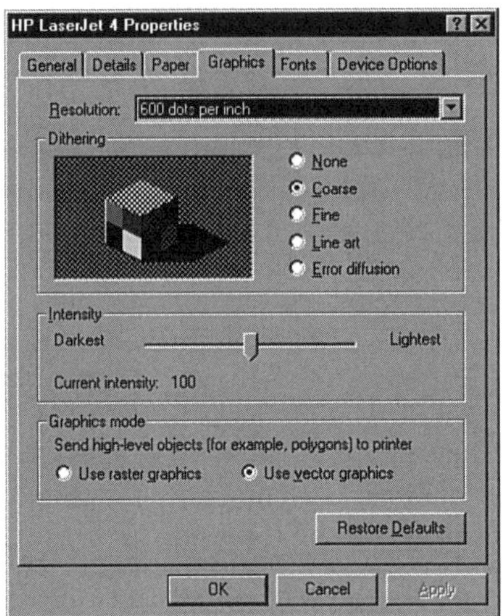

Figure 2.19

A typical Graphics tab from a printer properties sheet.

Setting Fonts Options

The Fonts tab is usually available for laser printers. If cartridges are installed on the printer, they can be specified here. In addition, you can specify whether to use TrueType fonts or built-in printer fonts. In general, the fonts built into the printer can be rendered more quickly. For PostScript printers, a font substitution table can be configured to substitute TrueType fonts for PostScript fonts.

Selecting Device Options

If this tab is available, it can be used to configure information specific to the printer. For example, the printer manufacturer might include options to specify the amount of memory installed or other printer-specific features. Figure 2.20 shows an example of the Device Options tab.

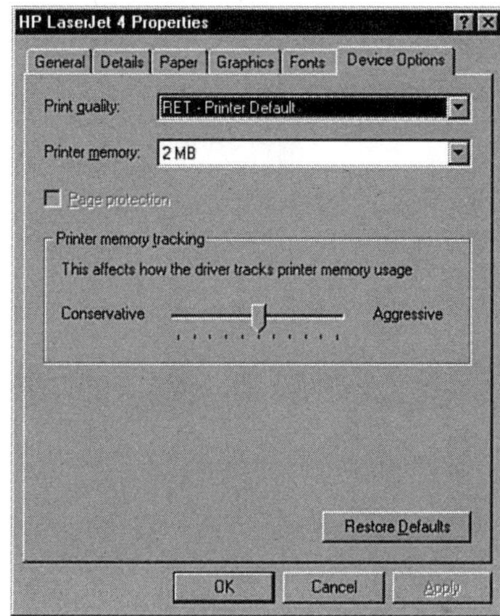

Figure 2.20

A typical printer Properties Device Options tab.

Selecting PostScript Settings

This tab is available on PostScript printers and can be used to configure the PostScript options, such as the following:

- Output format: Used for file compatibility.
- Header: By default, a PostScript header containing printer-specific configuration information is sent with each print job. If the printer is accessed only locally, you might want to change this setting so that a header need not be sent with each print job.
- Error information: Allows the printer to print error messages.

- Advanced: Additional information, such as the PostScript language level and data format, can be specified. Windows 95 supports PostScript Levels 1 and 2.

Figure 2.21 shows an example of the PostScript tab for a PostScript printer.

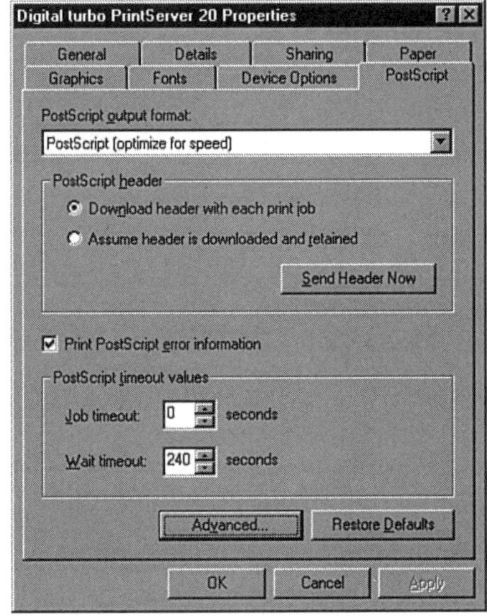

Figure 2.21

The PostScript tab for a PostScript printer.

Windows 95 Network Printing

Windows 95 network printing support includes a number of new features:

- A modular architecture, which allows for different print providers for different types of networks
- Point and Print installation, which allows printer drivers to be automatically installed over the network
- The capability to assign network permissions to print queues, which can prevent unauthorized changes to the print queues or print jobs
- Support for different network print servers, including HP JetDirect printers and DEC PrintServer printers

Architecture

The modular format of the Windows 95 printing subsystem uses a layered model. The four layers are

- Print Application Programming Interfaces (APIs)
- Print router
- Print Provider Interface
- Print providers

Print Application Programming Interfaces (APIs)

The Print Application Programming Interfaces (APIs) are used to pass information to and from the Windows application and the print router. Windows 95 includes the 16-bit Win16 API for use with WIN16 applications, as well as the 32-bit Win32 API for use with WIN32 applications. The print APIs provide such functions as opening, writing, and closing print jobs. The print APIs are also used for print queue management.

Print Router and Print Provider Interface

The print router passes printing requests from the print APIs to the proper Print Provider Interface (PPI). The PPI in turn passes this information to the correct print provider. For example, if the printing request is for a local printer, the print router sends the information through the PPI to the Windows 95 local printing print provider.

Print Providers

A print provider is a 32-bit dynamic link library (DLL) that contains code for printing and network support, as appropriate. The print providers translate requests from the PPI to the appropriate network or local printer requests.

The following print providers are included with Windows 95:

- Local Printing Print Provider
- Microsoft 32-bit Network Print Provider

- Microsoft 16-bit Network Print Provider
- NetWare Network Print Provider

In addition, third-party network vendors can supply their own print providers, which can be designed to fit in with the modular Windows 95 printing subsystem.

Local Printing Print Provider

The Local Printing Print Provider is found in the SPOOLSS.DLL file, along with the Print Router. This print provider handles the local print queue and manages print jobs that are sent to local printers (a printer directly connected to a port on the Windows 95 client).

Microsoft Network Print Provider

Two print providers for Microsoft Network printing support exist. The 32-bit print provider, known as WinNet32 Network Print Provider, is contained in the file MSPP32.DLL. The 16-bit print provider, WinNet16 Network Print Provider, is actually a part of MSPP32.DLL, which translates PPI requests into 16-bit WinNet16 requests for backward compatibility with 16-bit Microsoft Network drivers.

When a print job is submitted to a Microsoft Network printer, the PPI interacts with the Microsoft Network Print Provider (MSPP32.DLL) and the Microsoft Network support library (MSNET32.DLL if a 32-bit network client is used and MSNET16.DLL if a 16-bit network client is used). It sends the print job to the network printer using the Installable File System (IFS) Manager (IFSMGR.VXD). The IFS Manager then interacts with the network redirector (VREDIR.VXD) to send the job over the network.

For print queue management (for example, viewing a print queue), the print provider and network support library send requests directly to the network redirector.

The Registry subkey that contains information about the print provider for the Microsoft Network is as follows:

```
HKEY_LOCAL_MACHINE\System\CurrentControlSet\Control\Print\
Providers\Microsoft Networks Print Provider
```

Microsoft provides the Microsoft Remote Procedure Call (RPC) Print Provider on the Windows 95 CD-ROM. You can find the RPC in the \ADMIN\NETTOOLS\RPCPP folder on the Windows 95 CD-ROM; you can set it up from the Network icon in Control Panel. This provider improves network printing and remote administration of printers by providing Win32 APIs for Windows 95 clients to be able to administer print queues on Windows NT servers. When you install this RPC, you can use a Windows 95 client to obtain print job status information and accounting information from a Windows NT server.

NetWare Network Print Provider

Similar to the Microsoft Network Print Provider, the NetWare Network Print Provider (NWPP32.DLL) uses the IFS Manager (the IFSMGR file) to submit jobs to the network redirector. NWPP32.DLL also interacts with the NWNET32.DLL file, which is the NetWare Network Support library. For a NetWare network, the network redirector is NWREDIR.VXD.

Windows 95 currently supports bindery-based NetWare print queues, but not NetWare Directory Services (NDS)-based print queues common with NetWare 4.x servers.

The NetWare Network Print Provider can also translate print requests into 16-bit calls if a real-mode (16-bit) NetWare client is used. When a 32-bit network DLL, such as NWPP32.DLL or NWNET32.DLL, accesses a NetWare service, the file NW16.DLL provides the translation and thunking necessary for real-mode NetWare clients. NW16.DLL then sends the call to NETX or VLM via VNETWARE.386.

You can use the Microsoft Printer Server for NetWare utility (PSERVER) with Windows 95 to despool print jobs from NetWare queues to Windows 95 printers. You can connect a Windows 95 printer directly to a NetWare print queue using the NetWare queue configuration. After you share the printer on the Windows 95 network, any NetWare print queue can use it.

The Registry subkey that contains information about the print provider for NetWare is as follows:

```
HKEY_LOCAL_MACHINE\System\CurrentControlSet\Control\
Print\Providers\Microsoft Print Provider for NetWare
```

Third-Party Network Print Providers

Third-party network vendors can write their own print provider and print provider interface that communicates with their own network redirector software. A third-party network print provider can be installed using the Control Panel Network applet.

Printing to a Network Printer

To connect to a network printer, you must first install, configure, and share the printer on the network server. For information on installing and configuring the driver on the network server, refer to the preceding sections on local printer installation and configuration.

After the Windows 95 printer driver has been configured on the network print server attached to the printer, the printer must be shared to allow other users to access it. To share a printer in Windows 95, the network print server must be running a 32-bit protected-mode client, and a file and printer sharing service must be enabled. The following steps demonstrate how to share a network printer:

1. Right-click the Printer icon and select Properties to open the properties sheet.

2. Select the Sharing tab to display the Sharing configuration settings, shown in Figure 2.22.

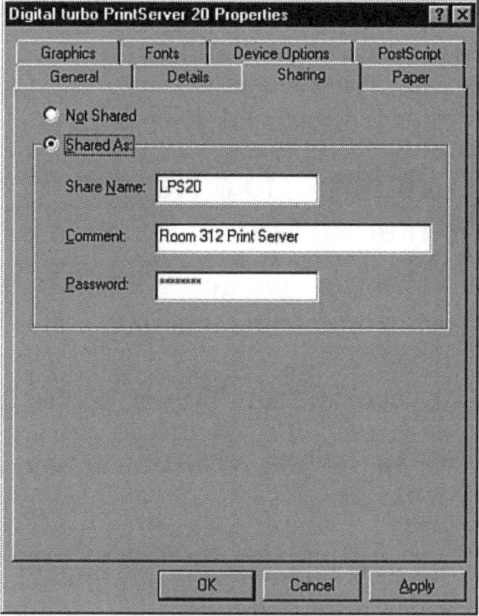

Figure 2.22

The printer Sharing tab.

3. Select Shared As and enter a share name and an optional descriptive comment for the printer. Windows 95 doesn't allow a share name to contain invalid characters, including spaces. The share name also must not exceed 12 characters.

4. You also must grant permissions to access this printer. If share-level permissions are used, you must assign a password to the printer. To access the print queue, users must supply the correct password. If user-level permissions are used, you must add the users who will be granted access to this print queue. For example, to allow everyone to print to the print queue, you would add the Everyone group and give it the print access right.

5. Click OK to share the printer. The printer icon now appears as a hand holding or sharing the printer with others. Remote users with the correct permissions can now access the print queue after setting up the correct printer driver on their computers.

When the printer has been configured and shared on the network print server, a Windows 95 client can be configured to connect to the print server and print to the printer over the network. This configuration can be done either manually with the Add Printer Wizard or by configuring the network printer for Point and Print setup.

Connecting to a Network Printer Using the Add Printer Wizard

To manually configure a Windows 95 client to print to the network printer using the Add Printer Wizard, follow these steps:

For an exercise testing this information, see end of chapter.

1. Start the Add Printer Wizard from the Printers folder.
2. In the Printer Type field, select Network Printer and click Next.
3. Enter the Universal Naming Convention (UNC) path of the network printer—for example, \\SARAH\HP4.
4. If you won't be using MS-DOS applications to print to this printer, you can select No under Do you print from MS-DOS—based programs?. To have the printer be associated with a printer port, such as LPT1:, you should select Yes for this option. Click Next.
5. If you have specified that you will print to this printer using MS-DOS—based applications, you are prompted to select the desired port from the Capture Printer Port dialog box. Click OK to continue.
6. Click Next and select the printer manufacturer and model from the Manufacturers and Printers lists.
7. Enter a name for the printer—for example, HP4 in Room 11.
8. If you want to see whether you can print properly to the network printer, click Send Test Page. Click Finish to have Windows 95 begin copying the printer driver files to the hard drive if the latest drivers aren't already on the hard

drive. If Windows 95 can't find the files, you are prompted to enter the path to the Windows 95 distribution files.

9. An icon for the network printer is created in the Printers folder. If desired, you can drag a copy of this icon to the Desktop to create a shortcut.

Connecting to a Network Printer Using Point and Print Setup

To connect to a network printer that is *not* configured for Point and Print setup, a client must know the correct printer driver to be used. In addition, the client must know other information, such as the share name and network server name. However, after a network printer has been configured to enable Point and Print setup, the printer driver installation on the client is greatly simplified. The Point and Print printer supplies the client with information such as the UNC path and the printer driver to be used.

To install the printer drivers for the Point and Print printer on a Windows 95 client, locate the icon for the printer in Network Neighborhood. Next, drag the printer icon onto the Desktop. Alternatively, you can right-click the network Printer icon and select Install.

In Network Neighborhood, if you double-click the name of a network printer not set up on your computer, Windows 95 displays a Printers message asking if you want to set up the printer now. Click Yes to start the Add Printer Wizard and walk through the wizard to set up the printer.

In addition, if you try to drag and drop a document onto the network printer icon, the printer driver will be installed on the Windows 95 client if it hasn't already been installed. If the driver version on the network printer is more recent than the version on the client, the later printer driver version will be copied to the client.

A Point and Print printer can be configured on any of the following servers:

- Windows 95 server
- Windows NT server (including both Windows NT Server and Windows NT Workstation servers)
- NetWare bindery-based server

Windows 95 Server

A Windows 95 server is simply a computer running Windows 95 that has a file and printer sharing service enabled. Any printers directly connected to the Windows 95 server are automatically enabled for Point and Print setup. No further configuration is required.

When you use Point and Print over a Windows 95 server, printer information is communicated between the client (the computer sending the print job) and the server (the computer to which the printer is attached) using VREDIR and VSERVER drivers. VREDIR initiates a request for Point and Print printer setup. VSERVER replies to VREDIR with the name of the printer. Then the following events take place:

1. The Windows 95 client displays the name to the user.
2. VSERVER receives a message from VREDIR, asking which files are needed on the client machine and where those files are located.
3. In response, VSERVER tells VREDIR the name of the files and that they are in the \\server_computername\PRINTER$ folder.
4. VREDIR connects to the *server_computername*\PRINTER$ folder and makes copies of the necessary printer files. If the client machine already has a printer driver or other software that matches the files in *server_computername*\PRINTER$, Windows 95 asks the user if she wants to keep the existing files. The user should respond Yes to make sure that the latest files are copied to the client computer.

5. VREDIR terminates the connection to the *server_computername*\PRINTER$ folder.

6. A new icon pointing to the network printer displays in the Printers folder on the client computer.

Any settings that have been configured for the server printer (such as memory) are also copied to the Windows 95 client.

Understanding Modems and Data Communications

Before you begin using the remote access features of Windows 95, you need an understanding of the key piece of hardware used to connect your local computer to a remote system—the modem. A *modem* is a special piece of computer hardware that converts the data coming from your computer to a signal that can be transmitted through normal telephone lines. This process is called *modulation.* The modem also converts signals from the phone line into data that your computer can understand through a process called *demodulation.* From these two processes (modulation and demodulation) comes the term *modem.*

Most computers now come with modems already installed. If your computer doesn't already have a modem, however, you can purchase one separately. Many brands and varieties of modems are available today, although most fall into one of these categories: internal, external, PCMCIA format (for notebook computers), and portable.

Modems also have a variety of attributes and features, such as error correction, compression, and flow control. Perhaps the most important attribute, however, is the speed with which the modem can transfer data over the telephone line. This speed is measured in bytes per second (bps, commonly referred to as baud). As might be expected, a faster transfer rate is generally better. As recently as five years ago, 1200bps was considered standard, and 2400bps was fast. Currently, 28800bps, 33600bps, and 56000bps are standard. However, the sender and receiver, as well as the physical phone lines, must support 56KB.

Windows 95's Dial-Up Networking supports modems supported by the miniport driver. This includes modems that use the standardized set of modem commands, called the AT command set. Some of the advanced modem features that Dial-Up Networking supports include MNP/5 and v.42bis compression and error controls, as well as RTX/CTS and XON/XOFF software follow control.

To find out if a modem you have or intend to purchase is supported by Windows 95, read the Windows 95 Hardware Compatibility List. You can find this on the Windows 95 CD-ROM in the \DRIVERS folder. The filename is HCL95.HLP; it is a Windows Help file. You can display it by double-clicking the file in Windows Explorer. You can obtain the most recent version of the Windows 95 Hardware Compatibility List, HCL95.EXE, and the most recent versions of the Windows 95 Driver Library drivers, from the following site: `ftp://ftp.microsoft.com/kb/softlib`.

As mentioned in the preceding paragraph, Windows 95 supports v.42bis and MNP/5 compression and v.42 error correction. Flow control, which regulates data traffic between communication devices, is a key component of implementing data compression and error correction in modem devices.

In Windows for Workgroups 3.11, Windows NT clients, and Windows NT Server, flow control is supported. However, MS-DOS RAS client software doesn't support flow control or software compression.

Installing and Configuring Modems Under Windows 95

Windows 95 makes installing and configuring your modem a simple process. If you have a modem installed in your computer, for example, the Windows 95 Setup program will attempt to detect the modem brand and speed and then install the proper driver files.

If you want to change your modem or install a new modem after you're already running Windows 95, you can install and configure the modem yourself from the Windows 95 Control Panel. You can also reconfigure an existing modem. To display the Modem properties sheet, which you use to add, remove, or modify a modem, follow these steps:

1. Select Start | Settings | Control Panel.

2. Double-click the Modems icon to display a general Modems properties sheet, shown in Figure 2.23.

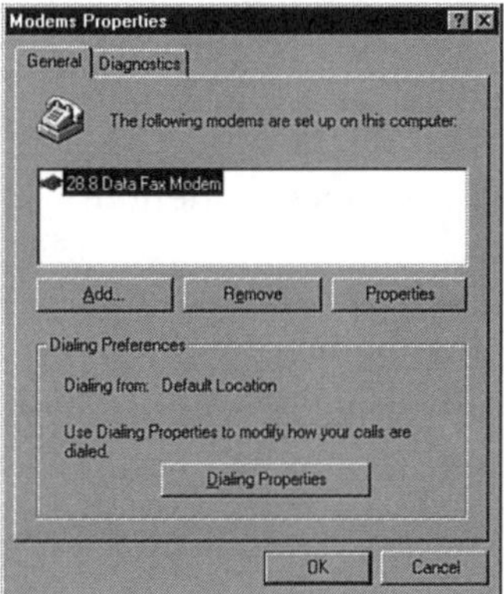

Figure 2.23

The Modems properties sheet.

To reconfigure an existing modem from this sheet, follow these steps:

1. Click the Properties button to display the properties sheet for the selected modem, as shown in Figure 2.24.

2. To change the connection settings for a modem, click the Connection tab. Some of the connection settings you can change include stop bits, parity, and data bits.

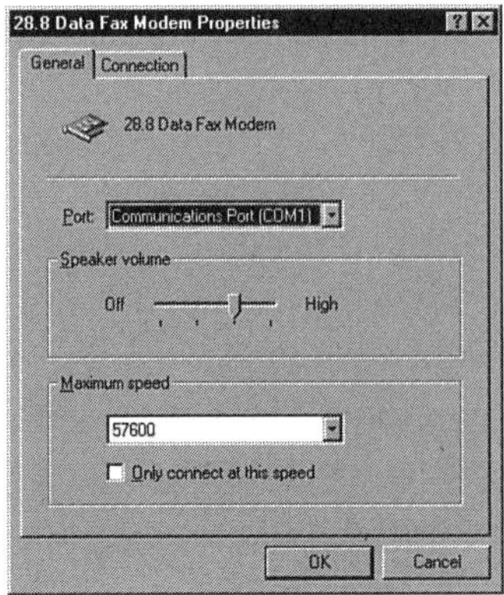

Figure 2.24

A specific modem's properties sheet.

Installing a new modem is just as easy:

1. Click the Add button on the Modems properties sheet (refer to Figure 2.23). A Windows 95 wizard guides you through the process of installing the new modem.

2. Specify the modem's manufacturer and name (which installs the proper modem drivers).

3. Select the port number and other information. After installing the new modem, you can, if necessary, change its properties using the information in the preceding numbered list.

Examining COM Ports

Modems are configured to transfer data to and from your computer through connections called COM ports (communication ports). COM ports are connected to your computer's main motherboard and allow communications devices to pass data into and out of the computer.

The Windows 95 Setup program automatically detects your COM ports and attempts to configure any devices (such as modems) attached to those ports. Alternatively, you can select a specific COM port for your modem from the Connections tab of a modem's properties sheet. Windows 95 attempts to communicate with the COM port and creates the computer files and connections necessary to allow data to flow from the computer to the device.

To manually configure a COM port (without a modem attached), open the Control Panel, double-click the System icon, and select the Device Manager tab. You see a list of all the computer devices in your computer.

Double-click the COM port you want to configure. You see a Communications Port properties sheet with several tabs, as shown in Figure 2.25.

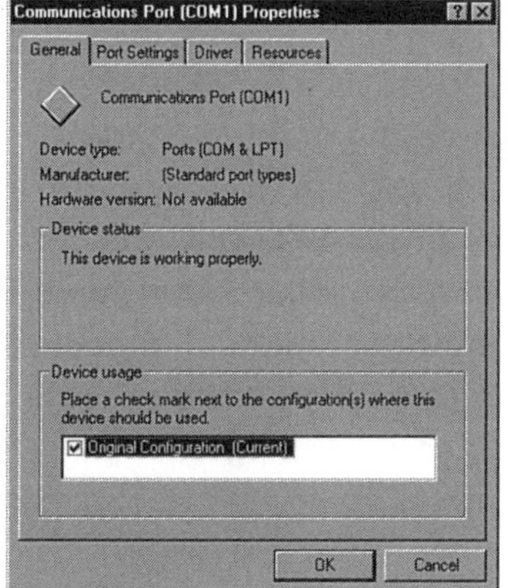

Figure 2.25

The Communications Port properties sheet.

From this properties sheet, you can configure the port to any specifications you need. These settings include port settings, device driver setup, and resource allocation information.

You can run the Modem Diagnostics tool in Windows 95 to identify and solve modem problems. Open the Modems properties sheet and click the Diagnostics tab. Next, choose the modem you want to troubleshoot and click More Info. Windows displays a message letting you know that this process might take a few minutes. After the Modem Diagnostics tool runs, you see a window with information about your modem, including the port it uses, resources, highest speed, and command set configured for it. However, note that you can't run this utility while you're using the modem.

Installing and Configuring Backup Software

To ensure that data on the system isn't lost due to power failures or other forms of corruption, Windows 95 includes a Backup utility that lets users make a copy of the data on their hard drives and store it on alternative media. You need to make several decisions regarding backup procedures; these are discussed in the following sections.

The Windows 95 Backup program supports backup to three locations: tape, floppy, and networked drive. With PC drives approaching 5 and 6 gigabytes in size, floppy is impractical except for archiving relatively small amounts of data. Backing up to a remote network location can be useful if, for example, a network administrator wants all users to back up their files to one central location on the network to simplify his management tasks. This works basically the same way as backup to tape, and since that is the most common kind of backup, we will focus on it for the remainder of our discussion.

Installing Backup for Windows 95

By default, Backup for Windows 95 is not installed. To install it, you need to go to Add and Remove Programs in Control Panel. Select Disk Tools and make sure that there is a check mark in the box beside Backup (see Figure 2.26).

Backup Types

Windows 95 backup can perform two basic kinds of backups: full and incremental. In a full backup, all selected files are backed up. An incremental backup copies only those files that have changed since the last backup. The files' time/date stamps determine which files these are. Suppose you do a full backup on Monday. On Tuesday, you do an incremental backup. All the files that have changed since Monday are backed up. On Wednesday, you do another incremental backup. This time, all the files that have changed since Tuesday are backed up. Typically, incremental backups are used to maintain archives without unnecessarily backing up files that have not changed since the last backup, thus conserving disk space at the backup destination.

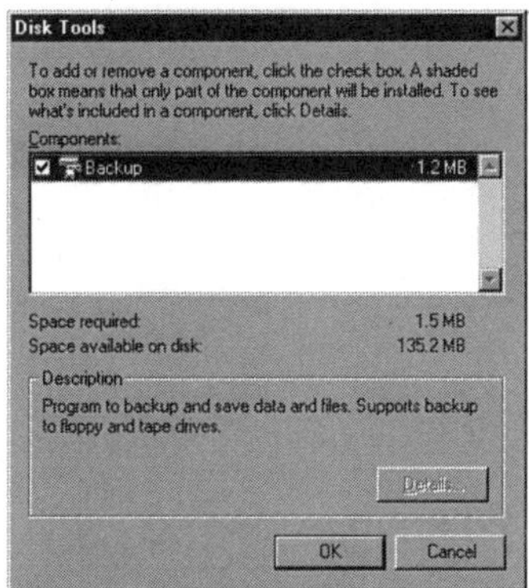

Figure 2.26

To install Windows 95, go to Control Panel, choose Add and Remove Programs, and select Disk Tools.

> **Tip** For recovery purposes, you want a collection of both kinds of backups. You will need your full backup to restore program and system files, and then you would restore the incremental backups to recover data that had changed since the last full backup. However, if you have only one full backup and 20 incremental backups, you would have to first restore the full backup and then restore each incremental backup in order to effect a full restore. For this reason, network administrators generally do a full backup at least once a week. In addition, you might consider off-site storage of a full backup and make arrangements to rotate this tape with your other backup tapes.

Backup Sets and File Sets

A *backup set* is a collection of files that have been backed up. A backup set is created during each backup procedure and contains not only the actual files, but also the parameters that were set for the backup (for example, which file types to include in the backup). When you first start Windows 95 Backup, it creates a full backup set for you. This is called "Full System Backup.Set." You can customize other backup sets as well, as shown in Figure 2.27.

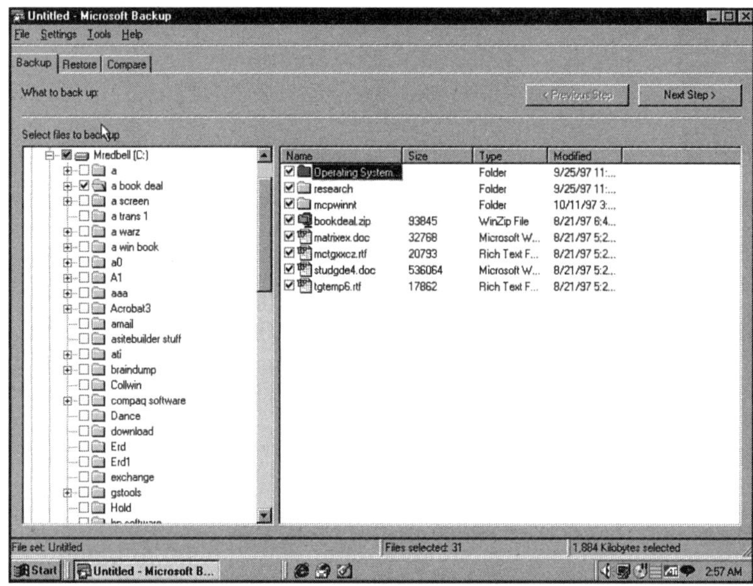

Figure 2.27

To create a custom backup set, you first select the drive and directory you want to back up.

You select the directories and files you want to back up. Follow these steps:

1. Check or clear the check in the box beside the directory or file in the list.
2. Select the files inside the directory you want to back up.
3. Click the Next button to choose the destination for the backup.
4. Select your tape device (or network drive or floppy).
5. Choose File | Save and give the file a name ending in .set.

A *file set* is a list of files you want to back up (see Figure 2.28). You can save file sets so that you don't have to select the files for backup every time you perform the backup.

In order to restore from tape, you simply reverse the order (see Figure 2.29):

1. Select the Restore tab.
2. Choose the restore from location (either tape, floppy, or network drive).

3. Select the directories or files to be restored.

4. Click Next and select the destination.

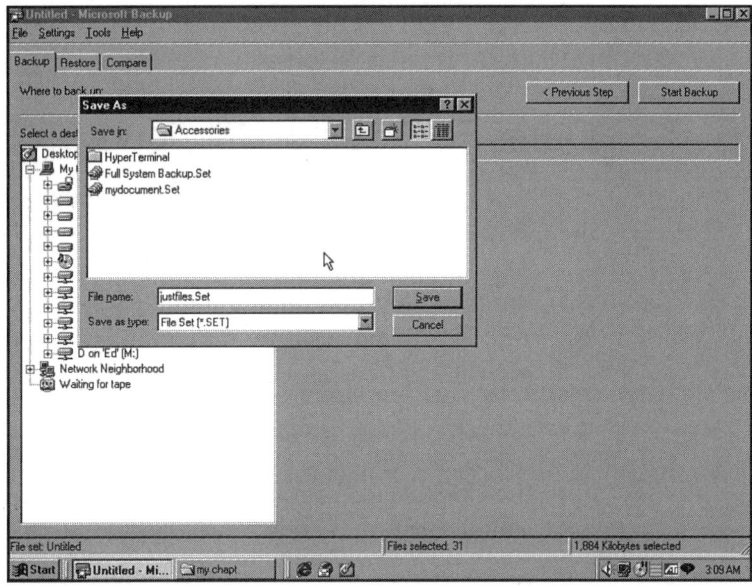

Figure 2.28

By creating a custom file set, you can simplify the backup of critical data.

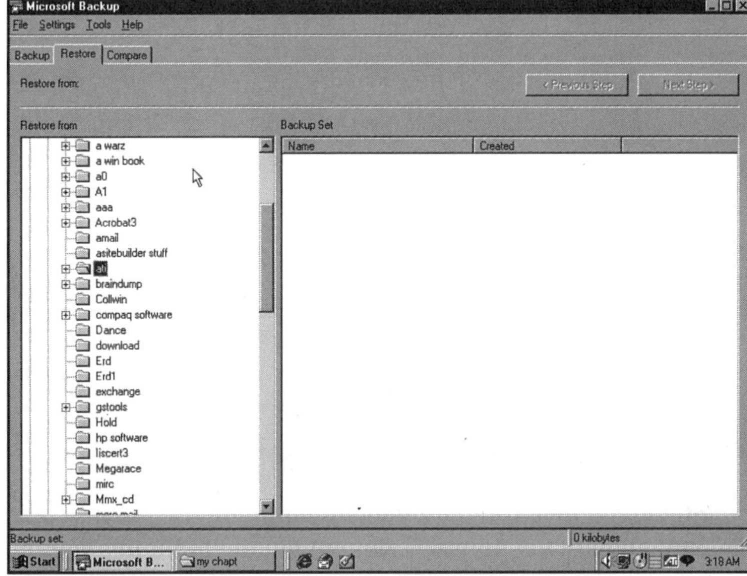

Figure 2.29

To restore a file or directory, reverse the process of backing up.

It is vitally important to ensure that your backups are in good shape. In order to do this, you should periodically test them by performing restorations. One way to do this is to create a junk file, back it up, delete it from your machine, and then restore it.

Other Features of Windows 95 Backup

Windows 95 contains a number of additional features, including the following:

- It is possible to perform a comparison between a backup set and the directories from which it was backed up to determine any differences between the two.
- Long filenames are fully supported.
- It is possible to drag and drop backup sets onto a backup icon to restore the set.
- During a full system backup, Windows 95 also backs up the Registry by copying it to a temporary file. When the backup set is restored, the Registry files are merged back into the existing Registry.
- Backup allows the filtering of file types for inclusion or exclusion from a file set.

MS-DOS 6.2 and Windows 3.1 backup sets can't be restored using the Windows 95 Backup utility due to incompatibility issues with long filenames in MS-DOS 6.2 and earlier.

Configuring Tape Drives

Once you have Backup installed, you have to tell it what kind of tape drive you have (see Figure 2.30). Just select Tools | Redetect Tape Drive.

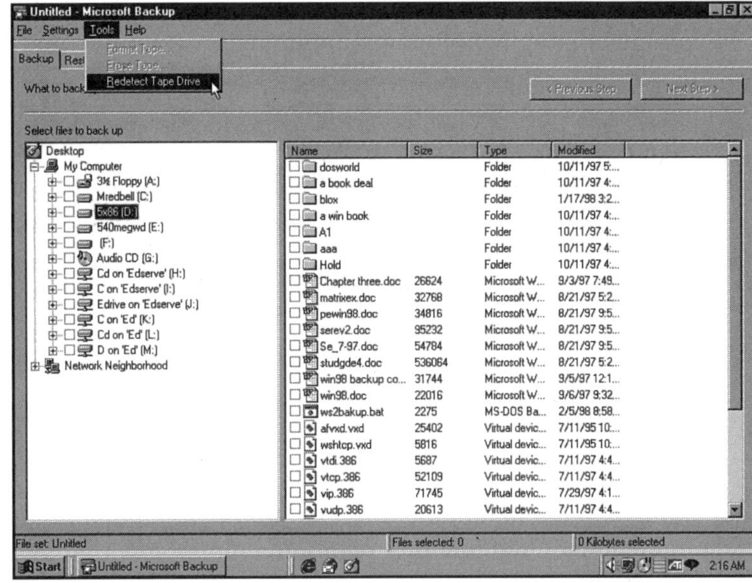

Figure 2.30

To tell Backup what kind of tape drive you have, select Tools / Redetect Tape Drive.

The capability to back up to a tape drive is new to the Windows 95 version of Backup (previous MS-DOS versions supported only floppy backups). The type of tape media that is supported is called Quarter-Inch Cartridge (QIC). It comes in various specifications:

- QIC 40, QIC 80, and QIC 3010 tape drives connected through the primary floppy disk controller (various manufacturers)
- QIC 40, QIC 80, and QIC 3010 tape drives connected to a parallel port (Colorado Memory Systems only)

SCSI tape backup units aren't supported by Windows 95 Backup.

Windows 95 should be able to detect any supported tape drives automatically. If it can't detect a tape drive, a message to that effect appears when you start Backup, and a number of troubleshooting suggestions are listed.

Exercises

Exercise 2.1: Choosing a Protocol

In this exercise, you will select the protocol that is most appropriate for a variety of situations. In each of the following cases, determine which protocol should be used—NetBEUI, IPX/SPX, or TCP/IP:

1. A local area network, running against both a Novell NetWare Server and a Windows NT Server
2. A small office network with only Windows 95 computers, plus some Windows for Workgroup computers that have not been upgraded yet
3. A wide area network, connecting to UNIX servers and the Internet

Here are the correct responses:

1. IPX/SPX to access the Novell server, and in addition, maybe TCP/IP to access the NT server if it is NT 4.0 and not running NWLINK (Microsoft IPX/SPX). If the NT server is running NWLINK, you can skip the TCP/IP on the Windows 95 workstations.
2. This one is easy. Install NetBEUI. NetBEUI is small, fast, and ideal for a small workgroup.
3. This one is also easy. TCP/IP is the perfect solution for a heterogeneous environment.

Exercise 2.2: Choosing an Installation Method

This exercise is aimed at helping you determine the appropriate installation method to use for certain installations. For each of the cases listed, choose from the following list the letter that corresponds to the correct response:

a. Set up from MS-DOS

b. Set up from Windows 3.x

c. Typical, Compact, or Custom setup type

d. Portable setup type

e. Local Windows

f. Shared Windows

g. Manual installation

h. Customized Setup Script installation

i. Automated installation

j. Repair installation

k. Maintenance applications

1. A key Windows 95 system file has become corrupted. How would you fix it?

2. A computer with MS-DOS 5.0 and Windows 3.0 needs to be updated to Windows 95. Where would you start the setup?

3. If a computer is running Windows 95 from its local hard drive, it is said to be running what kind of Windows?

4. What setup type of Windows 95 installation should you use to heavily customize both components and settings during installation?

5. An installation of a home computer without a CD-ROM drive that needs to be updated to Windows 95 is an example of which kind of installation?

6. If a computer with MS-DOS 6.22 and Windows for Workgroups 3.11 needs to be updated to Windows 95, where do you start the setup?

7. What setup type of Windows 95 installation should you use for a laptop computer on which you want to run Windows 95 mobile computing components?

continues

Exercise 2.2: Continued

8. A computer running Windows 95 from a file server rather than its local hard drive is running which kind of Windows?

9. A batch file, such as MSBATCH.INF, that is used to preselect Windows 95 installation settings is an example of which kind of installation?

10. If a Windows 95 component is not installed during the Windows 95 installation, how might you add it later?

11. A Windows 95 installation program that can be set for a mandatory start during the network logon is an example of which kind of installation?

The correct responses are as follows:

1. j
2. a
3. e
4. c
5. g
6. b
7. d
8. f
9. h
10. k
11. i

Exercise 2.3: Determining the Hard Disk Space Required for Installing All Optional Components

In this exercise, you will calculate the disk space required to install every optional hardware component. While doing an actual Windows 95 installation (see Exercise 2.4), determine how many megabytes of additional hard disk space are required to install every component listed above and beyond the hard disk space required for the base Windows 95 operating system. Use the Reset button to return to the original preselected components.

If you add up all the greatest numbers in the Size in MB column of Table 2.3, the total for all the components listed is approximately 36MB.

Exercise 2.4: Windows 95 CD-ROM Setup

In this exercise, you will install Windows 95 on Computer 1 using a CD-ROM drive. This is a hands-on exercise that requires about 60 minutes. Walk through the following steps:

1. Reboot Computer 1, loading MS-DOS and Windows for Workgroups. Access the Windows 95 CD-ROM by selecting File | Run from Program Manager, and start the Windows 95 setup.exe program.

   A routine check of the system is done, and the Setup Wizard is prepared.

2. The software license appears. After reading it, tab or click the Yes button to continue.

3. The Setup Wizard appears to start collecting information about your computer. Click Next to continue.

4. When prompted for a location in which to install Windows 95, accept the default, which is C:\WINDOWS. Click Next to continue.

5. Windows 95 will prepare the directory, check for installed components, and check for available disk space.

continues

Exercise 2.4: Continued

6. Because you upgraded from Windows for Workgroups, you will be asked whether you want to save system files. With these files saved, you could easily uninstall Windows 95 if you wanted to. These files take up approximately 6MB of disk space. If you want to be able to cleanly uninstall Windows 95, as if it were another software application, click the Yes button and then click Next to continue.

7. Choose the type of installation; the default is Typical. Click Next to continue.

8. For User Information, enter your full name and the name of your organization or company. Click Next to continue.

9. For Product Identification, enter the product key code from the CD-ROM cover.

   Setup will analyze your computer, searching for all hardware devices available.

10. If asked to check for specific hardware such as a CD-ROM drive or sound cards, check the appropriate boxes, and then click Next to continue.

11. After hardware detection, a Getting Connected dialog box will appear. Do not select any of these components.

12. You will be prompted to install the default components, as determined by your setup option. Accept the defaults, and click Next to continue.

13. Verify your network configuration if prompted. For a stand-alone installation, you will not see these screens.

14. If asked to identify your computer and workgroup, enter the appropriate information. Ensure that the computer name is unique. Click Next to continue.

15. When asked whether you want to create a startup disk, accept the default of Yes, I want a startup disk. Click Next to continue.

16. The Setup Wizard begins copying files to your computer. Click Next to continue.

17. The copying process might take a while. Put in a startup disk floppy when prompted.

18. The Setup Wizard reappears to finish the Windows 95 installation on your computer. Click Finish to continue.

19. Windows 95 starts and prompts you for your name and password. The Control Panel, Start menu, and Help system will be configured.

20. When prompted for the time zone, click your approximate location on the world map, which helps select the correct time zone. Click Close when done.

21. If you have a printer, ignore this setting and continue.

22. The Welcome to Windows 95 screen appears. Click the buttons to take the Windows 95 tour and to see what's new in Windows 95.

The Windows 95 Setup program is very automated and modular. In most cases, very little information is required in order to install it.

Exercise 2.5: Windows 95 Server-Based Setup

This exercise should be treated as a network (or server-based) installation. Run this from the CD-ROM on Computer 1. This requires access to either a mapped, shared drive on Computer 2 or a new, separate directory on Computer 1 if you're using only one computer. You need up to 87MB of hard disk storage.

1. From Computer 1, with the CD-ROM drive, start Windows 95. On Computer 2, install both DOS and Windows for Workgroups. In this case, the server-based installation can be to either Computer 2, as a network shared drive, or to a Windows NT server or a Novell NetWare server.

continues

Exercise 2.5: Continued

For the purposes of this example, use Computer 2. If you have only one computer, install to a new directory.

2. Establish an Install directory share with full rights on Computer 2. If you're using a Windows NT server or a NetWare server, be sure to grant sufficient privileges or rights if required.

3. Run NETSETUP from the ADMIN\NETTOOLS\NETSETUP directory on Computer 1 from the Windows 95 CD-ROM. The server-based setup program can only be run from a computer that is already running Windows 95.

4. The Server Based Setup dialog box will appear. Click the Set Path button to specify the server path where the Windows 95 installation files will be installed. Click OK when done. If the server path was defined earlier, the button name is Change Path.

5. Click the Install button to start the installation.

6. You will see a series of dialog boxes. They will confirm the paths to install from and to. They will also specify how you can install Windows 95 from the server to a local hard drive as a shared copy or user's choice. Select user's choice for the purposes of this exercise. Click OK to continue.

7. Click Don't Create Setup Batch Scripts, because you will be doing this in the next exercise.

8. Enter the Product Identification number when prompted. Click OK to continue.

9. You will see a dialog box when the server-based setup is complete. Click OK, but don't close the window. You want to examine a batch file script in the next exercise.

The Windows 95 server-based setup program is simple and makes it easy to install Windows 95 on a server. With the Windows 95 installation files on a server, installations are much faster, because the files are stored on the server's hard disk, not on the CD-ROM (hard disks are much faster than CD-ROM drives).

Exercise 2.6: Windows 95 Batch File Creation

The following exercise walks you through creating a batch script file.

1. From Computer 1, with the CD-ROM drive, start Windows 95.
2. If you left the server-based Setup program running at the end of Exercise 2.5, go to step 2. However, if you're beginning anew, run NETSETUP from the ADMIN\NETTOOLS\NETSETUP directory on Computer 1, from the Windows 95 CD-ROM. The server-based Setup program can be run only from a computer already running Windows 95.
3. The Server Based Setup dialog box will appear. Click the Make Script button to specify that you want to create a batch script.
4. Select the MSBATCH.INF file from the server-based setup directory. A properties sheet will appear that lets you graphically create a batch script file for use in automating your Windows 95 installations.
5. Set a few values, save them by clicking OK, and then exit.
6. Start the Notepad application by choosing Start | Programs | Accessories | Notepad, and then open the text file MSBATCH.INF in your server-based setup directory. You will see how the information gathered in the preceding step is translated into options, fields, and values that the Windows 95 Setup program can read and understand.

Exercise 2.7: Removing Windows 95

The following exercise, which shows you how to remove Windows 95 from a computer, works properly only if you selected Save System Files during the Windows 95 installation. Otherwise, you need to follow a longer series of steps, as described in Chapter 6 of the *Windows 95 Resource Kit* under "Removing Windows 95 with Your Previous Operating System."

continues

Exercise 2.7: Continued

1. From Computer 1, place your Windows 95 startup disk in the floppy drive.
2. Select Start | Run. Type `a:\uninstal.exe` and press Enter.
3. In the Windows 95 Uninstall dialog box, click Yes to begin the uninstallation process.

   Windows 95 will then shut down, and the uninstallation will continue automatically.

Your previous configuration will be restored. When finally prompted, remove the Windows 95 startup disk from the floppy drive, and press Enter to reboot your computer.

1. From Computer 1, place your Windows 95 startup disk in the floppy drive.
2. Select Start | Run. Type `a:\uninstal.exe` and press Enter.
3. In the Windows 95 Uninstall dialog box, click Yes to begin the uninstallation process.

   Windows 95 will then shut down, and the uninstallation will continue automatically.

Your previous configuration will be restored. When finally prompted, remove the Windows 95 startup disk from the floppy drive, and press Enter to reboot your computer.

Exercise 2.7 will remove Windows 95 from the computer. To continue with the remaining exercises in this chapter, either do a standard Windows 95 installation to Computer 1, as outlined in Exercise 2.4, or a clean Windows 95 installation to Computer 1, as outlined in the next exercise.

Exercise 2.8: Windows 95 New Installation

Although in this exercise you will install a new copy of Windows 95 on the computer, the network administrator still has the arduous task of reinstalling all the applications. A better approach might be to create a clean MS-DOS and Windows 3.x image with all the applications already installed, download that image, and then upgrade the computer to Windows 95.

This exercise uses either the floppy disk or CD-ROM version of Windows 95 to do a clean installation. The following are the steps for doing an installation with the floppy disk version. If you removed Windows 95 in the preceding exercise, you should complete this exercise as well.

1. From Computer 1, boot with the Windows 95 startup disk, format the hard drive, and add the Windows 95 system files to the boot drive (`format c: /s`).
2. Insert disk 1 of the floppy version of the Windows 95 installation disks into the floppy drive and run setup.exe from the command prompt.
3. Complete the Windows 95 installation (refer to Exercise 2.4).

If you have only the CD-ROM version of Windows 95, you have to boot the computer with an earlier version of MS-DOS that has all the files required to access the CD-ROM drive. Or you can create a modified Windows 95 startup disk that adds the equivalent files to allow access to the CD-ROM drive. Here are the steps for doing an installation with the CD-ROM version:

4. From Computer 1, boot with either the Windows 95 startup disk or an equivalent MS-DOS boot disk. The boot files on the disk, CONFIG.SYS and AUTOEXEC.BAT, must be able to allow access to the CD-ROM drive. Format the hard drive and add the Windows 95 system files to the boot drive (`format c: /s`).

continues

Exercise 2.8: Continued

5. Insert the CD-ROM version of the Windows 95 installation disks into the CD-ROM drive and run setup.exe from the command prompt.

6. Complete the Windows 95 installation (refer to Exercise 2.4).

Exercise 2.9: Installing a Modem

In this exercise, you will install a modem. If you already have one installed, you can install another one. Even if you don't have a modem on your computer, Windows 95 will let you install one. This is how you do it:

1. Go to Control Panel and double-click Modems.

2. The modem properties dialog box appears. Click Add.

3. Select Don't detect my modem; I will select from a list.

4. Windows 95 will build a driver list and give you a selection of modems to choose from.

5. Select Standard modem type (300 bps) (that way, you know it is bogus). Click Next.

6. Now choose a COM port to assign to the modem.

7. Click Next. Windows will install the modem.

8. Click Finish and then close the wizard.

Exercise 2.10: Removing a Modem

In this exercise, you will remove the 300bps modem you installed in the preceding exercise.

1. Go to Control Panel and double-click System.

2. Select the Device Manager tab.

3. Click the plus sign beside the modem icon.
4. Select the Standard 300 bps (installed in Exercise 2.9).
5. Click the Remove button, and then click OK.
6. Click the × button.

Exercise 2.11: Installing a Printer

This exercise walks you through the process of installing a printer.

1. Select Add Printer from the Printer folder.
2. Click Next to add a printer.
3. Choose Local printer and click Next.
4. Choose the Apple LaserWriter and click Next.
5. Select LPT1 for the port.
6. Accept the default for the printer name.
7. If this is the first printer installed on the machine, it will be the default Windows printer. Otherwise, choose No.
8. Do not print a test page.
9. Click Finish.
10. Windows 95 now prompts you for installation files and installs the driver.
11. Choose Yes when asked if the test page printed.
12. To delete the printer, just highlight the icon and press the Delete key.
13. Windows 95 prompts you to remove unused files. Choose Yes.

Exercise 2.12: Backing Up a Single File

In this exercise, you will back up a single file to a floppy disk. If you have not already done so, add Windows 95 Backup by going to Control Panel and selecting Add/Remove Programs. (When Backup runs for the first time, it will create a full backup set. Do not run this set now.)

1. Start Windows 95 Backup. By default, it is located under Start | Programs | Accessories | System Tools.
2. Select the Backup tab.
3. Check a directory on the left side.
4. Clear all check marks from boxes on the right side.
5. Select one file from the right pane.
6. Click Next.
7. Insert a formatted floppy into the drive.
8. Select the drive from the left pane.
9. Click the Start Backup button.
10. Name the backup set.
11. Do not password-protect it.
12. The Backup will now run.

Review Questions

The following questions will test your knowledge of the information in this chapter.

1. Windows 95 provides compatibility with many of today's existing computers. Before installing Windows 95 on a computer, you should make sure that it has a processor that can run it. The lowest Intel processor recommended by Microsoft to run Windows 95 is ______.

   A. 80286

   B. 80386SX

   C. 80386DX

   D. 80486

   E. Pentium

2. Sharon uses a computer at work that runs Windows 95. Her computer at home doesn't have Windows 95 installed yet. She asks you how much Random Access Memory she needs in her computer to install Windows 95. You tell her the minimum amount of RAM that Windows 95 requires is ______.

   A. 2MB

   B. 4MB

   C. 8MB

   D. 14MB

   E. 16MB

3. Graphics Unlimited is upgrading five computers to Windows 95. The company must decide which media type to purchase to be able to upgrade all its computers. Which three of the following installation options are available for Windows 95?

   A. 5¼-inch floppy

   B. 3½-inch floppy

C. CD-ROM

D. Network

E. Optical disk

4. On a "minimal" computer, as defined by Microsoft, the performance of Windows 95 should be ______ and ______ using Windows 3.1 with the same hardware (choose two).

   A. worse than

   B. about the same as

   C. possibly faster than

   D. much faster than

   E. twice as fast as

5. When putting together a company report for upgrading to Windows 95, you must list the computers in the company that will not run Windows 95. Windows 95 will not run on which two of the following types of Intel 386 processors?

   A. 386SX (with 16-bit I/O buffers)

   B. 386DX B-Step processor

   C. 386DX Non-B-Step processor

   D. 386DX with ID 0303

   E. 386DX with ID other than 0303

6. The minimum amount of RAM recommended for running Microsoft Exchange Inbox, Microsoft Network, or multiple 32-bit Windows-based applications is ______.

   A. 2MB

   B. 4MB

   C. 8MB

   D. 14MB

   E. 16MB

7. Windows 95 uses swap files as virtual memory storage. As a rule of thumb, the amount of RAM on a Windows 95 computer and the amount of free space needed for a swap file should total at least ______.

   A. 2MB

   B. 4MB

   C. 8MB

   D. 14MB

   E. 16MB

8. Markus upgrades his MS-DOS computer to Windows 95. When installing over an MS-DOS-based operating system, Windows 95 will only install on a computer with an operating system equivalent to ______ or later.

   A. MS-DOS 3.2

   B. MS-DOS 3.3

   C. MS-DOS 4.0

   D. MS-DOS 5.0

   E. MS-DOS 6.0

9. You are manning a technical support phone line, and you receive a call asking about partitions supported by Windows 95. Which of the following two types of partitions does Windows 95 support?

   A. HPFS

   B. NTFS

   C. CDFS

   D. FAT

   E. Unformatted

10. Windows 95 provides different installation types. Which one of the following is not a Windows 95 Setup type of installation?

    A. Custom

    B. Compact

    C. Express

    D. Typical

    E. Portable

11. Tracy is running Windows NT and wants to install Windows 95 on the same computer. She also has MS-DOS, Windows 3.x, and OS/2 installed on the same computer in different partitions. The Windows 95 Setup program can be run from which two of the following places?

    A. From within OS/2

    B. From within Windows NT

    C. From within Windows

    D. From a Windows DOS box

    E. From DOS

12. The preferred method for running the Windows 95 Setup program is from within ______ and ______ (choose two).

    A. MS-DOS

    B. Windows 3.1x

    C. An MS-DOS window inside Windows

    D. Windows for Workgroups 3.x

    E. A bootable floppy

13. Steve runs several 32-bit applications at the same time under Windows 95. What is the name of the type of multitasking that Windows 95 uses?

    A. Cooperative

    B. Cohabitive

    C. Preemptive

    D. Presumptive

    E. Shared

14. You create a file in Windows 95 Explorer named Budget For This Year.XLS. This is a long filename. Long filename (LFN) support on a Windows 95 computer works because it uses the ______ file system.

    A. FAT

    B. HPFS

    C. NTFS

    D. CDFS

    E. VFAT

15. You are setting up Windows 95 in a school's computer lab, which doesn't have a CD-ROM drive available. You know there are extra files on the CD-ROM version of Windows 95, and you want to persuade the school administration to purchase a new CD-ROM drive. From the following list, choose the three differences in the Windows 95 upgrade between the floppy version of Windows 95 and the CD-ROM version.

    A. Windows Tour

    B. What's New

    C. Full online help

    D. Accessibility options

    E. Administrative extras

16. Windows 95 is a large program that includes more than 1,000 files. To squeeze these files onto 3½-inch floppy disks, Microsoft uses which of the following formats for most of the Windows 95 installation disks?

    A. FAT
    B. VFAT
    C. DMF
    D. CDFS
    E. NTFS

17. You are installing Windows 95 as a server-based setup from a computer that has Windows 95 installed. Running the _____ program (and parameters) does the Windows 95 Administrative Setup.

    A. `setup /a`
    B. `setup /n`
    C. `setup /as`
    D. NETSETUP
    E. Batch

18. A batch script file can be used in which three of the following Windows 95 installations?

    A. From the Windows 95 3½-inch floppy disks
    B. From CD-ROM
    C. From the network
    D. From the local hard drive
    E. From 5¼-inch floppy disks

19. A coworker sends you email telling you he has Windows 3.1 installed on his laptop at home, but he can't remember the laptop's hardware specifications. To help him, you tell him that the minimum hardware requirements for Windows 95 are ______ the minimum needed for Windows 3.1.

    A. lower than

    B. the same as

    C. higher than

    D. no different than

    E. approximately the same as

20. Not all processors available can run Windows 95. Windows 95 will run on the ______ processor.

    A. Intel 286

    B. Intel 386 and higher

    C. DEC Alpha

    D. PowerPC

    E. MIPS

21. The B1 error that can happen on a Windows 95 installation is the result of ______.

    A. step B1, hardware detection, generating an error on the second floppy drive

    B. the processor being an SX type, without a math coprocessor

    C. the processor being a 386 B1 stepping chip, which can generate random math errors, making it incompatible with Windows 95

    D. failure of the network configuration

    E. corruption of the boot sector

22. Lynn wants to upgrade to Windows 95, but she also occasionally needs to boot into MS-DOS (her existing operating system). The Windows 95 option to boot into the previous version of MS-DOS is available only if you're upgrading from which version of MS-DOS or better?

    A. MS-DOS 3.2

    B. MS-DOS 3.3

    C. MS-DOS 4.0

    D. MS-DOS 5.0

    E. MS-DOS 6.0

23. Before you begin upgrading the computers in your company, you send an email asking all users to check the version of MS-DOS on their computers and to report back to you their findings. To check the version of DOS on their computers, you tell them to execute the ______ command at the DOS prompt.

    A. `setver`

    B. `winver`

    C. `dosver`

    D. `ver`

    E. `getver`

24. Hard drive space is at a premium at the Cycle Shop. They want to upgrade to Windows 95, but they're not sure they have enough hard drive space to accommodate it. The approximate disk requirement for Windows 95 in a Typical setup upgrade of Windows is ______.

    A. 20MB

    B. 30MB

    C. 40MB

    D. 47MB

    E. 55MB

25. Adam starts Windows 95 from the command prompt and uses WIN.COM command switches to control the way Windows 95 starts. Which three of the following command switches can he use with the Windows 95 Setup program?

A. `/?`

B. `/B`

C. `/ID`

D. `/D`

E. `/IS`

26. The naming standards for ______ are all the same: limited to 15 characters, no embedded spaces, and can contain these special characters:

```
! @ # $ % ^ & ( ) - _ ' { } ~ .
```

A. User's full name

B. Default user's name

C. Computer name

D. Workgroup name

E. Computer description

27. Teresa chooses to keep program groups and system settings from her previous Windows 3.1 installation when upgrading to Windows 95. To migrate program groups and system settings when upgrading from Windows 3.x to Windows 95, which of the following should she do?

A. Upgrade into a new Windows 95 directory

B. Upgrade into an existing Windows directory

C. Copy group and initialization files into a new Windows 95 directory

D. Copy older DLL files into the new Windows 95 directory

E. Run GRPCONV to convert older program groups into folders

28. The Windows 95 Setup program will not run from Windows 3.0; instead, it wants to run from MS-DOS. How much conventional memory is required to run from MS-DOS?

    A. 370KB

    B. 420KB

    C. 470KB

    D. 512KB

    E. 640KB

29. Windows 95 performs four logical phases during the Windows 95 Setup routine. Which one of the following is not a logical phase in the Windows 95 installation?

    A. Startup and information gathering

    B. Hardware detection

    C. Software detection

    D. File copy

    E. Final system configuration

30. Barney is running the Windows 95 Setup program from MS-DOS. You know there are differences between starting Setup in DOS and starting it in Windows. Which three of the following are differences?

    A. ScanDisk running in the foreground rather than in the background

    B. Checking for Windows 3.0 versus checking for Windows 3.1 or better

    C. Checking for TSRs versus checking for TSRs and other running Windows programs

    D. System checks done in DOS versus Windows

    E. DOS graphical interface versus Windows graphical interface after starting in protected mode

31. You are prompted for the user name and company name during which part of Windows 95 Setup?

    A. Initial startup and Setup Wizard load
    B. Gathering user and computer information
    C. Copying Windows 95 files
    D. Restarting the computer and finishing Setup
    E. After Windows 95 is completely installed

32. The startup disk is used in case you experience problems with your Windows 95 installation. You are asked to remove the newly created startup disk during which part of Windows 95 Setup?

    A. Initial startup and Setup Wizard load
    B. Gathering user and computer information
    C. Copying Windows 95 files
    D. Restarting the computer and finishing Setup
    E. After Windows 95 is completely installed

33. TSRs are known to cause problems when you install Windows 95. You are asked to unload any detected TSRs during which part of Windows 95 Setup?

    A. Initial startup and Setup Wizard load
    B. Gathering user and computer information
    C. Copying Windows 95 files
    D. Restarting the computer and finishing Setup
    E. After Windows 95 is completely installed

34. The Time Zone option is used to set up your computer's clock and maintain proper settings during the spring and fall. You are asked to enter a time zone for the computer during which part of Windows 95 Setup?

A. Initial startup and Setup Wizard load

B. Gathering user and computer information

C. Copying Windows 95 files

D. Restarting the computer and finishing Setup

E. After Windows 95 is completely installed

35. You can ask to run the verify option for the computer during which part of Windows 95 Setup?

A. Initial startup and Setup Wizard load

B. Gathering user and computer information

C. Copying Windows 95 files

D. Restarting the computer and finishing Setup

E. After Windows 95 is completely installed

36. Tom is setting up Windows 95 on his laptop. He wants to use the Portable setup option, but he doesn't know which option is the default setup type. Which one of the following is the default?

A. Custom

B. Compact

C. Express

D. Typical

E. Portable

37. Windows 95 lets you create a startup disk to help you recover from problems. The startup disk contains all of the following files except_____.

A. IO.SYS

B. MSDOS.SYS

C. COMMAND.COM

D. CONFIG.SYS

E. REGEDIT.EXE

38. The startup disk, when created by the Windows 95 Setup program, contains 16 files and uses ______ of disk space.

    A. 640KB

    B. 948KB

    C. 1.0MB

    D. 1.20MB

    E. 1.44MB

39. During a training session, you are asked to describe the Windows 95 startup disk. Which two of the following statements are true?

    A. It can be created only during a Windows 95 installation.

    B. It needs a preformatted floppy disk at the start.

    C. It lets you boot to the Windows 95 command prompt.

    D. It includes CD-ROM drivers if needed.

    E. It lets you troubleshoot your Registry files.

40. Your boss is running Windows NT 4.0 with Service Pack 3 installed. His computer is configured with a single NTFS partition for security reasons. He has 400MB of free space and wants to be able to dual boot Windows 95 to run an old accounting package that is incompatible with Windows NT. He calls you in and asks you to fix this up while he goes to lunch—giving you exactly one hour. What do you tell him?

    A. No problem. In fact, if you wait 15 minutes, I will join you for lunch.

    B. No problem. However, you had better go ahead. I will join you in about 45 minutes.

C. It is impossible. It simply can't be done.

D. I want to get a good backup first, and then I will boot up off an MS-DOS disk and start the installation. But I'm afraid it will take me a couple of hours.

E. It would be easier to add a second drive and format it as FAT and then do the installation. But I still want to make sure I have a good backup and a current ERD. I can do it, but it will take me a couple of hours after we get the second drive.

41. Your boss has a just bought a new Pentium II 300MHz machine with 64MB of RAM and a 3.2GB hard drive. It came preloaded with Windows 95. The hard drive is divided into two partitions. He would like you to configure it to dual boot with Windows NT 4.0. What do you tell him?

    A. I hate to mess up a nice computer like that. Why don't you just get another machine with NT on it?

    B. I'm not sure NT will support a drive that is 3.2GB in size.

    C. No problem. I will move any data you might have on your second partition to the first partition. Then I will delete the second partition and format it as NTFS when I install NT 4.0. Of course, I will make a complete backup of your data first.

42. When installing a modem on a Windows 95 machine, you must always give it what piece of information?

    A. The maker of the modem

    B. The speed of the modem

    C. The name of the driver to use

    D. The COM port to use

    E. The number to turn off call waiting

43. Mike is installing a modem on his new Windows 95 machine. He tells you he is certain he has selected the correct modem, but it isn't working. What do you tell him?

    A. Get on the Internet and download a new driver.

    B. Try a different COM port.

    C. See if Windows 95 will autodetect it.

    D. Try a different computer.

    E. Try a different modem.

44. Janet is installing a new printer on her Windows 95 computer. She asks you what she must do to make sure that she will always print to that printer. What do you tell her?

    A. It will just go wherever it wants to go. I don't guarantee anything.

    B. Do nothing. The last printer installed is always the default.

    C. Make sure you select it prior to printing.

    D. Plug and Play will know where you want to print to.

    E. Make sure you select Set as default when you install the printer.

45. Beverly upgrades to Windows 95 but doesn't install the Microsoft Exchange component during the Windows 95 installation process. She asks you if she can install Exchange now that she has Windows 95 running. You tell her she can, but she will have to ______.

    A. restart the Windows 95 Setup program to add a component

    B. restart the Windows 95 Setup program in verify mode and then add the component

    C. use the Add/Remove Programs option in Control Panel

D. use the Install Components Wizard from My Computer

E. restart the Windows 95 Setup program from scratch and reinstall Windows 95

46. Log files are ASCII text files that you can use to help troubleshoot problems encountered during installation. Which of the following log files is not used during the Windows 95 installation?

    A. SETUPLOG.TXT

    B. HARDWARE.TXT

    C. DETLOG.TXT

    D. NETLOG.TXT

    E. BOOTLOG.TXT

47. Jack experiences problems with his laptop computer during the Windows 95 installation process, and he can't get Windows 95 to install. You advise him to examine which three of the following key files to troubleshoot the Windows 95 installation process?

    A. SETUPLOG.TXT

    B. HARDWARE.TXT

    C. DETLOG.TXT

    D. NETLOG.TXT

    E. BOOTLOG.TXT

48. You want to boot your computer and have the Windows 95 Startup menu display. Which function key lets you see the Startup menu when Windows 95 is first booting?

    A. F1

    B. F4

    C. F5

    D. F6

    E. F8

49. A device doesn't work when you boot Windows 95, so you decide to use the Safe Mode option when you boot Windows 95. In safe mode, Windows 95 only loads which three of the following device drivers?

    A. CD-ROM

    B. Mouse

    C. Keyboard

    D. Sound

    E. VGA

50. Your new boss asks you to recommend a backup strategy for his new Windows 95 machine. He creates lots of proposals for new business, and as a result, he has many Excel files and PowerPoint presentations (complete with animation and sound). What do you recommend?

    A. Put in a slave drive and use it for storage.

    B. Install Windows 95 Backup and archive to floppy disks.

    C. Install Windows 95 Backup and a tape backup device. Create a full system backup set, and run that once a week. During the week, run an incremental backup set to catch files that change daily.

    D. Tell him to just save the files to disk and to use the disks whenever he wants to save something.

    E. Tell him it is his computer, so he is responsible for coming up with his own backup strategy.

Review Answers

1. C
2. B
3. B, C, D
4. B, C
5. B, D
6. C
7. D
8. A
9. D, E
10. C
11. C, E
12. B, D
13. C
14. E
15. A, C, E
16. C
17. D
18. B, C, D
19. C
20. B
21. C
22. D

23. D
24. C
25. A, C, E
26. B, C, D
27. B
28. C
29. C
30. A, B, C
31. B
32. C
33. A
34. D
35. E
36. D
37. D
38. B
39. C, E
40. E
41. C
42. D
43. C
44. E
45. C

46. B
47. A, C, E
48. E
49. B, C, E
50. C

Answers to Test Yourself Questions at Beginning of Chapter

1. 80386DX. See "Identifying Appropriate Hardware Requirements for Installation."
2. She should choose to install Windows 95 over her existing Windows 3.11 for Workgroups directory.
3. Windows NT Workstation running NTFS (NT File System) provides file-level security.
4. IPX/SPX, NetBEUI, and TCP/IP are Plug and Play-enabled. Microsoft NetBEUI and IPX/SPX are installed by default.
5. User-level security.
6. MSBATCH.INF.
7. Startup and information gathering, hardware detection, file copy, and final system configuration.
8. Step-By-Step Confirmation.
9. NETSETUP.EXE. See "Set Up Files for Network Installation and Shared Use: Windows 95 Server-Based Setup."
10. SETUPLOG.TXT, DETLOG.TXT, and DETCRASH.LOG.

Chapter

Installation and Configuration, Part 2: Network Components

This chapter helps prepare you for the exam by covering the following objectives:

- Installation and configuration of the network components of a client computer and peer server
- Installation and configuration of network protocols, including the following:
    - NetBIOS Enhanced User Interface (NetBEUI)
    - Internet Packet Exchange/Sequenced Packet Exchange (IPX/SPX)
    - Transmission Control Protocol/Internet Protocol (TCP/IP)
    - Data Link Control (DLC)
    - Point-to-Point Tunneling Protocol/Virtual Private Networks (PPTP/VPN)
- Configuration of system services, including the following:
    - Browser
    - File and Print Sharing for Microsoft Networks
    - File and Print Sharing for NetWare Networks

Test Yourself! Before reading this chapter, test yourself to determine how much study time you will need to devote to this section.

1. Windows 95 includes networking features to make it easier for users to connect to existing networks or build a network from the ground up. Which three networking protocols included with Windows 95 are Plug and Play-enabled? Which two protocols are installed by Windows 95 by default?
2. Windows 95 supports share-level and user-level security. Suppose you want to set up Windows 95 on 10 workstations on a network to share printer and file resources, but you want to make sure that pass-through authentication is used to validate users who access these resources. Which type of security must you set up?
3. Steve is connecting his Windows 95 computer to a network running Novell NetWare. He wants to share files and a printer with other users. Can he do this? If so, what type of security must he use?
4. You configure a Windows 95 workstation to connect to a NetWare network. When installing Client for NetWare Networks, Windows 95 automatically installs a protocol. Which one? Can you change this to another protocol and still access the NetWare server?
5. Windows 95 is designed to run over a NetWare network, but there are some disadvantages to using Microsoft's Client for NetWare Networks. Name two.
6. Elizabeth sets up Windows 95 to connect to a Windows NT network. She wants to be able to share files and printers with other users on the network. What type of security must she install? Also, can she assign file-level rights?
7. As system administrator, you're bringing up the entire department on a single-server Windows NT network. For workstations, you will use the Windows 95 client. You also want to set up user-level security on the Windows 95 client. When you set up Windows NT, what should you remember to do to make sure that user-level security will work?

8. You receive a call while stationed at the company help desk. The caller says she is trying to save her long filenames to the NetWare server but the server doesn't support them. What do you have to do to make NetWare support long filenames?
9. UNC is supported by Windows 95. What does UNC stand for? What two items make up a UNC? Does UNC require a drive-letter assignment?
10. Chuck uses Network Neighborhood to view other computers on the network. What is the name of the list that stores the computers on a network?
11. As you configure the browse list on a NetWare network, you need to set up the option to have Windows 95 automatically determine whether the computer is needed as a browse server. What is the name of this property?
12. Name one advantage and one disadvantage of using user-level and share-level security.
13. Eugene creates a PowerPoint slide showing the Windows 95 networking architecture layers. He places a layer called Network Providers in the slide. Is this the name of a layer in the architecture? If so, what two other layers are adjacent to the Network Providers layer?
14. When installing TCP/IP, it is recommended that a default gateway be configured for the Windows 95 client. What does a gateway do?
15. What are the two minimum pieces of configuration information required for the TCP/IP protocol, and what are two other items that are nice to include?

Answers are located at the end of the chapter...

Windows 95 is a perfectly viable operating system for people who only want to use it in a stand-alone operation, either at home, in an office, or on the road. When you introduce it into a network, the dynamics of the operating system change greatly. In this chapter, you will look at the installation of the four major components of the network subsystem: protocols and adapters, client services, and server services. You will examine protocols, adapters, and the computer browser service in depth. You will examine the managing of resources in Chapter 4 "Configuring and Managing Resource Access," and client configurations in Chapter 5 "Integration and Operability." This chapter addresses its topics in the following order:

- Installation of all network components
- Configuration of network adapters
- Configuration of and differences between network protocols
- Configuration of the computer browser service
- Installation of the File and Print Sharing for Microsoft Networks service
- Installation of the File and Print Sharing for NetWare Networks service
- An introduction to accessing network resources using UNC path names
- An overview of the Windows 95 network model

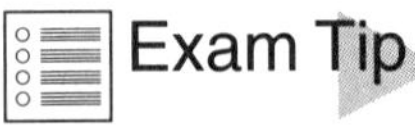

Here are some things you are likely to be tested on:

- Installation of network components that don't ship with the normal Windows 95 distribution files
- Differences between protocols, and when to use one protocol over another
- Causes and symptoms of browser failure
- Differences between the two major File and Print services

Installation of Network Components

The first time you're given access to the installation of network components is during the Windows 95 installation. After the hardware detection phase and the choice of additional Windows 95 components (only during a Custom setup), you will be prompted to complete the network information. The Windows 95 installation collects that information during two Windows 95 Setup Wizard steps. You are first prompted for the installation of other network components through the dialog box shown in Figure 3.1. After choosing the proper components, you are prompted for the computer and workgroup names, as shown in Figure 3.2. The proper configuration of a workgroup name for your network can greatly reduce the number of network browsing problems you experience. If you did not have a network card in your computer when you installed Windows 95, or you didn't have the correct drivers for your network card, you might also access all the network settings through the Network icon in Control Panel.

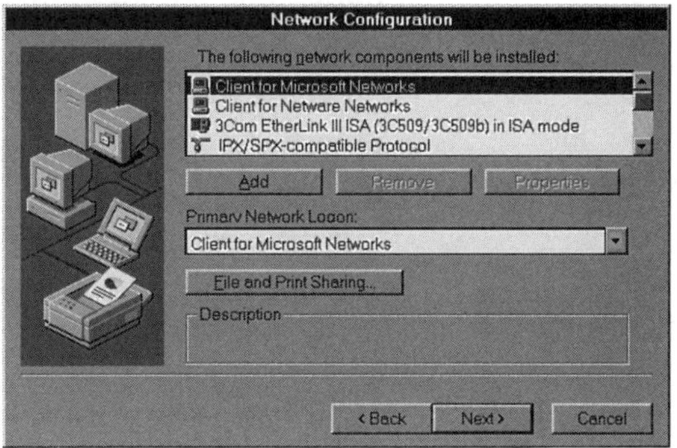

Figure 3.1

All network components can be installed during installation.

Much of the configuration of the network settings will be performed after the initial installation of Windows 95, due to the changing network environment in most workplaces. For example, most networks have to deal with the movement of computers, the replacement of network cards, and the addition or removal of servers and network protocols over the working life of the network. Since most of the configuration will be accomplished after the installation of Windows 95, this chapter deals with the configuration of the network components through the Network dialog box of Control Panel, shown in Figure 3.3. The Configuration tab lets you add, remove, and modify your network components. The four components that can be modified on this screen are as follows:

- Clients
- Adapters
- Protocols
- Services

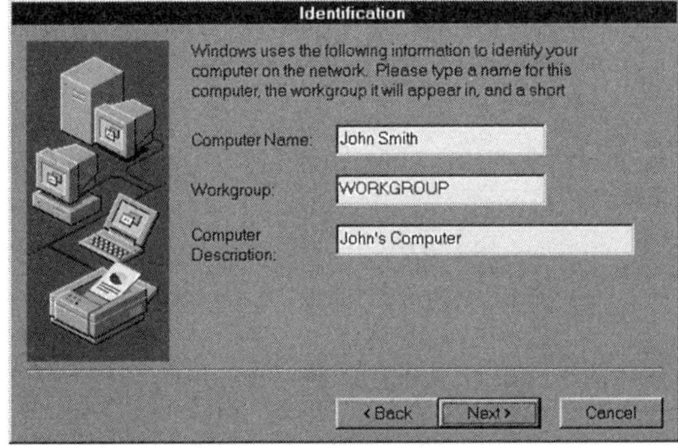

Figure 3.2 *The computer name and workgroup name may be assigned during the Windows 95 installation.*

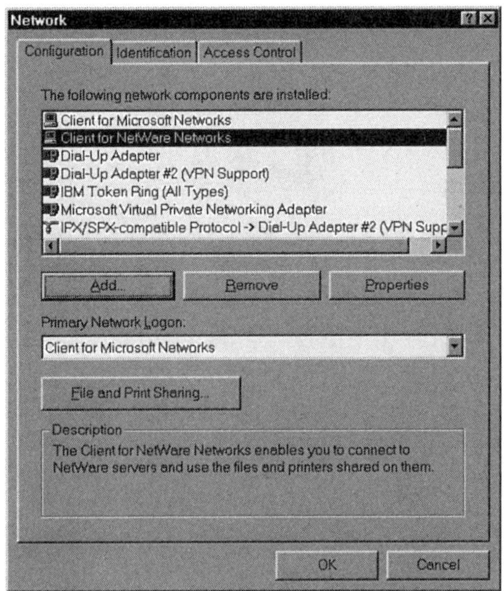

Figure 3.3 *The Network icon in Control Panel is used to modify the network components after installation.*

You can also configure which client will be your primary network logon and enable File and Print Sharing from the Configuration tab.

Installing Clients

The networking functionality built into Windows 95 allows a Windows 95 computer to be a client on a wide variety of networks. A Windows 95 client can run multiple network protocols, services, and clients at the same time and thus can be a client on many different networks at the same time.

Windows 95 includes software to support the following networks:

- Microsoft Windows NT
- Microsoft Windows 95
- Microsoft Windows for Workgroups 3.*x*
- Microsoft LAN Manager
- Novell NetWare version 3.11 and later
- Banyan VINES version 5.52 and later
- DEC Pathworks version 4.1 and later
- SunSoft PC-NFS version 5.0 and later

Even though Microsoft includes support for several 16-bit network clients, this doesn't include the client files. These files have to be installed from the disk supplied by the third-party vendor, as shown in Figure 3.4. The 16-bit network clients are from Banyan, Novell, DEC, and SunSoft. For most of these clients, Windows 95 doesn't support client installation after the installation of Windows 95; these clients should be installed before Windows 95. This won't be a problem for any computers that will be upgraded to Windows 95 from either MS-DOS or Windows for Workgroups, because the 16-bit network software will already be installed. This might require the installation of MS-DOS and the network software before the installation of Windows 95 if you're planning to install Windows 95 to a freshly formatted hard drive. If you want to install the client after Windows 95, you will have to manually install the client software from the third-party client installation disk.

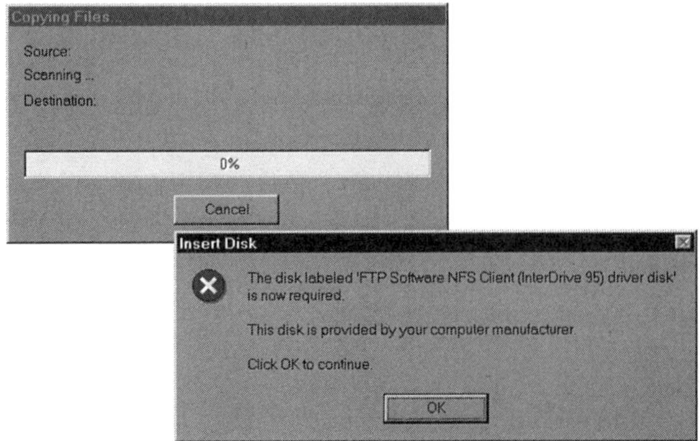

Figure 3.4

FTP Software's NFS Client is one of the clients that requires a manufacturer's disk during installation.

Windows 95 can have only one 16-bit network client installed at a time, but it can run multiple 32-bit clients. The 32-bit clients that come with Windows 95 are Microsoft Client for Windows Networks and Microsoft Client for NetWare Networks.

In addition, the modular architecture of Windows 95 allows Windows 95 components written by other network vendors to be installed. Many network vendors whose 16-bit network clients Windows 95 supports now have 32-bit network clients that can function in conjunction with the network components that ship with Windows 95.

To add a new network client, do the following:

1. Open the Network icon of Control Panel and choose the Configuration tab.
2. Click the Add button and select Client, as shown in Figure 3.5.
3. Click the Add button.
4. Select the manufacturer and client you want to install, as shown in Figure 3.6. If this is an updated or unlisted client, click the Have Disk button and provide the path to the OEMSETUP.INF file and choose the client. Click OK.

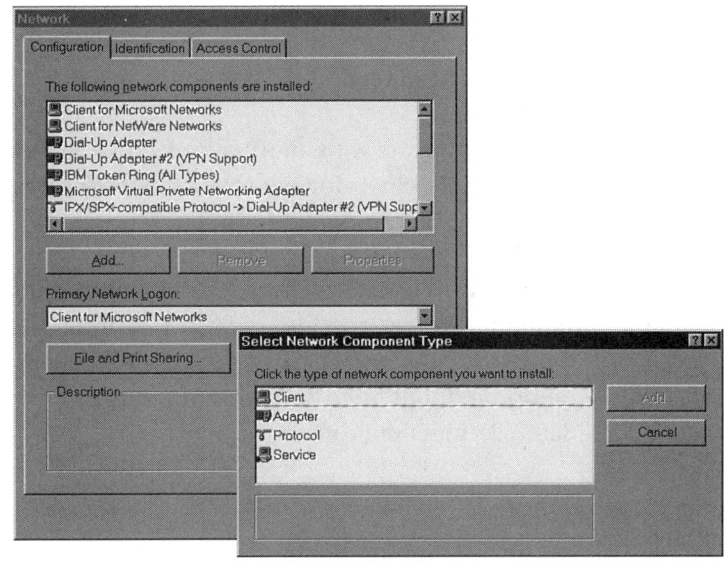

Figure 3.5

This Select Network Component Type dialog box lets you choose which component to add.

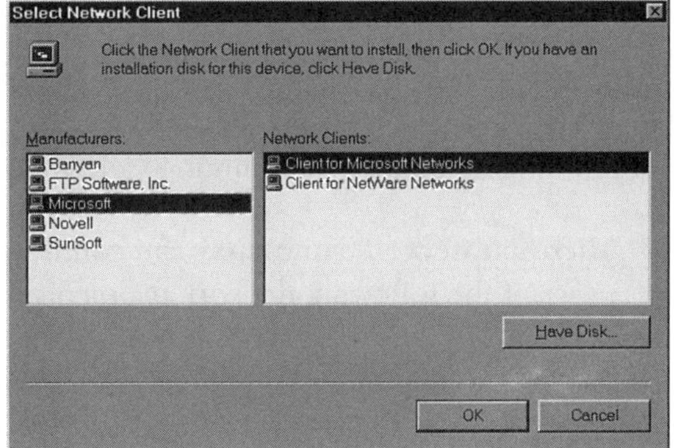

Figure 3.6

The Select Network Client dialog box lets you choose which type of client you want to install. Microsoft supplies two 32-bit clients.

5. After you click OK again, you might be prompted for the Windows 95 CD-ROM while the client files are copied to your hard drive.

Microsoft Networks

The Client for Microsoft Networks might be utilized if your network is made up of any of the following:

- Windows NT
- Windows 95

- Windows for Workgroups
- LAN Manager

To communicate with another computer, both computers must run a proper client for the other's server and must be using the same network protocol.

This client is one of the two 32-bit network clients that ship with Windows 95 (refer to Figure 3.6). Windows 95 can be used with the DOS real-mode clients using any of the network servers just mentioned, but Microsoft recommends that people use the updated 32-bit client due to these benefits:

- It can be installed with other 32-bit clients.
- It has full support for mapping, remapping, and browsing network resources.
- It frees up conventional memory in all Virtual DOS Machines before loading Windows 95.
- Faster 32-bit programming yields better network response.

Microsoft network computers can communicate using one or more of the following network protocols:

- Microsoft NetBEUI
- Microsoft TCP/IP
- Microsoft IPX/SPX-compatible (NWLINK)

A network protocol is a set of rules and conventions used by computers to exchange messages on a network. It is analogous to a language by which two computers communicate. The terms *network protocol, transport protocol,* and *protocol* are often used interchangeably.

NetWare Networks

Windows 95 integrates well into a NetWare network running Novell NetWare version 3.11 or higher. Microsoft includes with Windows 95 three options for communicating on a Novell network:

- Microsoft's 32-bit Client for NetWare Networks (refer to Figure 3.6)
- Novell NetWare Workstation Shell 3.*x* (NETX) (see Figure 3.7)
- Novell NetWare Workstation Shell 4.*x* (VLM) (see Figure 3.7)

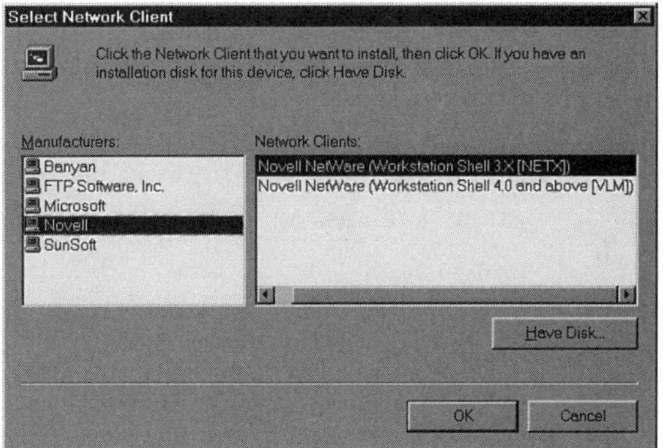

Figure 3.7

Microsoft supports two NetWare clients from Novell.

When you choose either of the clients supplied by Novell, you are prompted to insert the NETX or VLM client disk from your server client disks that shipped with your original server software. If you install the VLM client, you will be prompted to manually install the Workstation Shell 4.*x* software after completing the Windows 95 portion of the setup, as shown in Figure 3.8. Windows 95 requires that the VLM client be installed, but it won't perform the complete installation from within the Windows 95 client installation. For mixed NetWare 4.*x* (non-bindery mode) and Windows NT environments, Microsoft has a 32-bit Microsoft Service for NetWare Directory Services (NDS). It's available in the Windows 95 Service Pack 1, or you can download it from `http://www.microsoft.com/windows`.

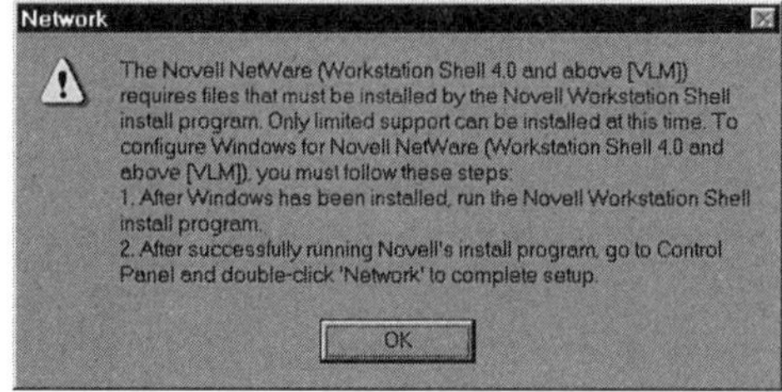

Figure 3.8

To install the VLM client, you have to manually install the workstation shell.

Here are some advantages of using the 32-bit Microsoft Client for NetWare Networks:

- It runs in protected-mode memory and thus doesn't use any conventional memory.
- Its architecture offers a 50 to 200 percent increase in network file I/O operations over the 16-bit versions running on Windows 3.*x*.
- It allows additional network clients to be used at the same time, such as the Microsoft Client for Microsoft Networks.

There are some disadvantages or limitations when running Windows 95 on a NetWare network:

- NetWare doesn't natively support long filenames. You must load the OS/2 Name Space (OS2.NAM) NetWare Loadable Module (NLM) in NetWare in order for long filenames to be supported on the network. This feature will only be challenged by the most diehard Windows 95 users. OS/2 Name Space filenames may be up to 254 characters, and Windows 95 supports filenames up to 255 characters. With IntraNetWare 4.11, the NLM has been changed to LONG.NAM and does support 255-character filenames. It replaces the OS2.NAM file.
- If you're running the real-mode ODI and VLM or NETX real-mode shell, performance might suffer because the real-mode NetWare driver uses RAM that MS-DOS applications could use.

- Administrators might perceive a lack of control because users can use Windows 95's Explorer and Network Neighborhood to access files without mapping network drive letters.
- Users of Windows 95 can direct jobs to print queues without capturing a printer port.
- Users can save drive mappings and print queue assignments as permanent and can reestablish them every time they log on to the network and start Windows 95.
- Users of Windows 95 can see whatever print queues the bindery or NDS provides them access to.
- Although administrators can limit what Windows 95 users see through the Network Neighborhood and Explorer, users still might be able to access programs, files, and directories by using the MS-DOS prompt or network mapping prompt if they know the Universal Naming Convention (UNC) of `\\server\volume and path`.

The Client for NetWare Networks can be used to access NetWare servers running NetWare 2.15 and above and NetWare 4.*x* servers using bindery emulation. The Client for NetWare Networks requires the IPX/SPX-compatible protocol, which is installed by default when the client is installed.

Although the 16-bit Novell NetWare clients don't offer all the advantages of the 32-bit client, a 16-bit NETX or VLM client is required if any of the following are used:

- NCP packet signature security (requires VLM)
- NetWare IP protocol (which doesn't use Microsoft's TCP/IP as it tunnels IPX/SPX through the IP protocol)
- Helper Terminate and Stay Resident (TSR) applications loaded from DOS (such as 3270 emulators)

- Custom Virtual Loadable Modules (VLMs) with functionality not provided by the Windows 95 components, such as Personal NetWare (PNW.VLM)
- Novell utilities such as NWADMIN and NETADMIN. Most of the DOS-based 3.*x* utilities will still work, such as SYSCON, RCONSOLE, and PCONSOLE.
- NetWare Directory Services (NDSs), although a separate Microsoft Service for NetWare Directory Services is now available
- IPX ODI protocol
- Monolithic IPX (IPX.COM) or ARCnet protocols

In addition to these clients, Novell has released a 32-bit NetWare client called IntraNetWare Client 2.2 for Windows 95, or Client 32 (see Figure 3.9). This client has been optimized to communicate with Novell IntraNetWare 4.11 servers and NDS. The IntraNetWare Client can utilize either NDIS (Network Device Interface Specification) network card drivers, which are a cross-industry standard, or ODI (Open Data-Link Interface) network card drivers, which are Novell-specific. By using the NDIS drivers, you will guarantee compatibility with other network clients.

Banyan VINES

For practice on this material, see Exercise 3.4.

Banyan VINES version 5.52 and later can be used with Windows 95. However, computers running only Banyan VINES can't use the browser services. For example, Banyan VINES computers aren't visible in Network Neighborhood.

> Windows 95 Banyan VINES computers must use NDIS network card drivers rather than monolithic network drivers. This allows the network to be bound to several protocols or clients.

Banyan now has several 32-bit clients that are designed to work with Windows 95. The latest client from Banyan is the Enterprise Client for Windows 95 version 8.02, shown in Figure 3.10. These clients support the following:

- Browsing network servers if the StreetTalk Directory Assistant (STDA) service is running on the network
- Compatible with other 32-bit network clients and can be installed with multiple clients
- UNC path names for all network services (see Figure 3.11)

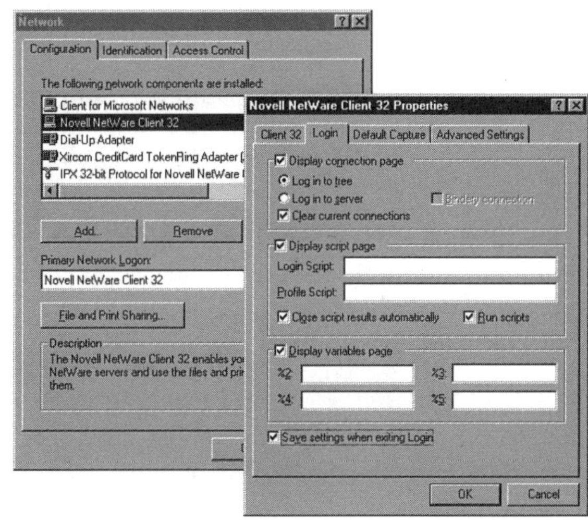

Figure 3.9

Novell's IntraNetWare Client 32 is another option as a client for Windows 95. It provides backward compatibility with NetWare 3.x servers, along with support for the NetWare 4.x NDS tree.

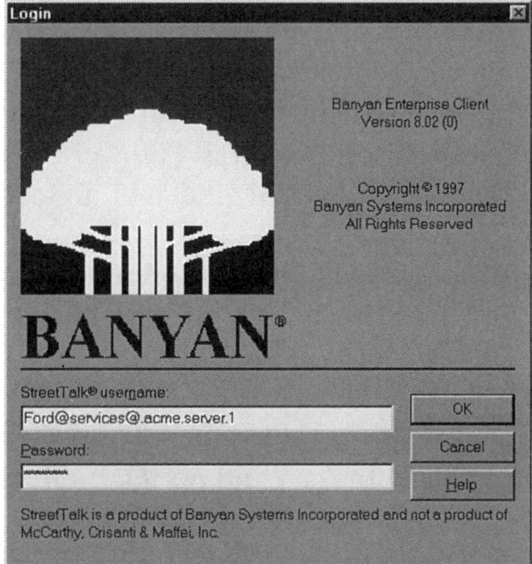

Figure 3.10

Banyan has released a new 32-bit network client to work with Windows 95.

You install the updated Banyan client by clicking the Have Disk button in the Select Network Client dialog box of the Network icon in Control Panel (see Figure 3.12).

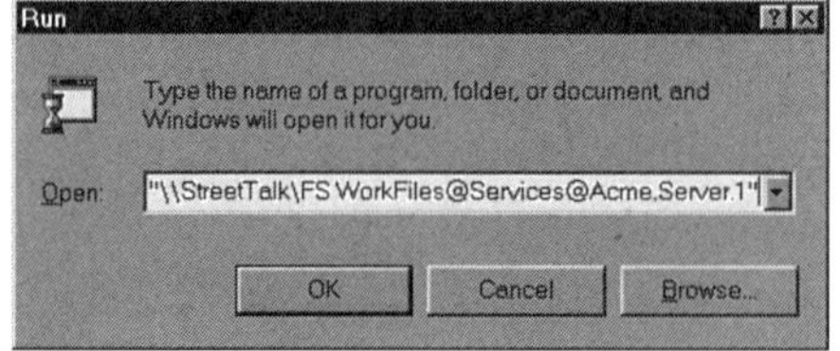

Figure 3.11

UNC path names are supported, but the format is slightly different from that of the Microsoft network client.

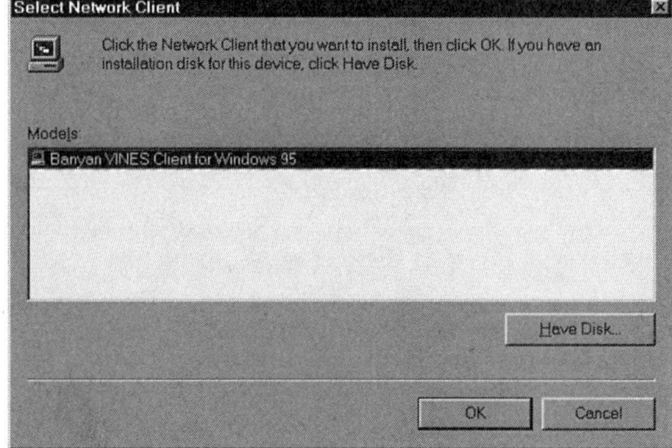

Figure 3.12

The new network client can be installed as an additional component through the Have Disk button.

DEC Pathworks

Digital Equipment Corporation (DEC) Pathworks is a LAN Manager-compatible protocol. The Pathworks 4.1, 5.0, and later protocols are included with Windows 95 for use with the Client for Microsoft Networks. Pathworks uses the STARTNET.BAT file, called from AUTOEXEC.BAT, to load the Pathworks drivers.

Windows 95 Pathworks computers can use the Microsoft NetBEUI, Microsoft TCP/IP, or DECnet protocols. DECnet isn't included with Windows 95.

Digital also now has a new 32-bit client called Digital Pathworks 32 version 7.0A for Windows 95. It offers the following benefits:

- Support for DECnet, LAT, and LAST network protocols
- Pathworks 32 Password Assistant, which allows for a unified logon with Windows 95 and Windows NT

- Pathworks 32 Print Services lets users share printers with other Pathworks computers

PC-NFS

SunSoft PC-NFS client and protocol support is included with Windows 95 for use on PC-NFS networks running version 5.0 or later. Computers running only PC-NFS can't use the browser service, nor are they visible when browsed from other computers.

Sun Microsystems had released a 32-bit version of its PC-NFS client called PC-NFS Pro. This client has now been updated in the form of a new 32-bit client called Solstice Network Client 3.1 Plus, which offers the following benefits:

- NFS 3 and NFS 2 client support over TCP/IP and UDP/IP
- NFS 2 server for peer-to-peer networking
- NIS+, NIS, and DNS support for enterprise-wide naming services
- Automounter from files, NIS, and NIS+
- Universal Naming Convention (UNC) support
- Unified Microsoft Windows and network login
- PCNFSD and LPR printer support to let users print directly to other network printers
- Full integration with the Microsoft TCP/IP stack and Network Neighborhood in Windows 95
- Ability to be managed by the DHCP and configuration capabilities of Solstice PC-Admin software
- LPD server allows a locally attached printer to be used by other PC or UNIX LPR clients
- SNMP support
- Support for long filenames and Network Neighborhood
- Automounter support

- Centralized administration and support for Microsoft Windows User Profiles and System Policies
- Uses Microsoft's TCP/IP protocol stack

Installing Adapters

Windows 95 includes drivers for many of the most popular network adapters. Additional network adapter drivers may be supplied by the network adapter vendor for use with Windows 95. Before you can install any other Windows 95 networking components, you must install a network adapter driver through the Network icon of Control Panel. If you don't have an actual network card in the computer, you can use the Microsoft Dial-Up Adapter driver, along with a compatible modem for network connectivity.

You configure network adapter card drivers by selecting the adapter from the Network icon of Control Panel and choosing Properties. If the network card supports the Plug and Play standard, Windows 95 can automatically configure the driver according to information the card provides to the Windows 95 operating system. Otherwise, the card should be configured according to the manufacturer's documentation.

To install a network adapter, follow these steps:

1. Open the Network icon in Control Panel and choose the Configuration tab.
2. Click the Add button and choose Adapter.
3. Click the Add button.
4. Choose the manufacturer and adapter you want to install, as shown in Figure 3.13. If it is an updated or unlisted adapter, click the Have Disk button, provide the path to the OEMSETUP.INF file, and choose the adapter you want. Then click OK.

Figure 3.13

Microsoft provides drivers for a wide range of network cards from most major card manufacturers.

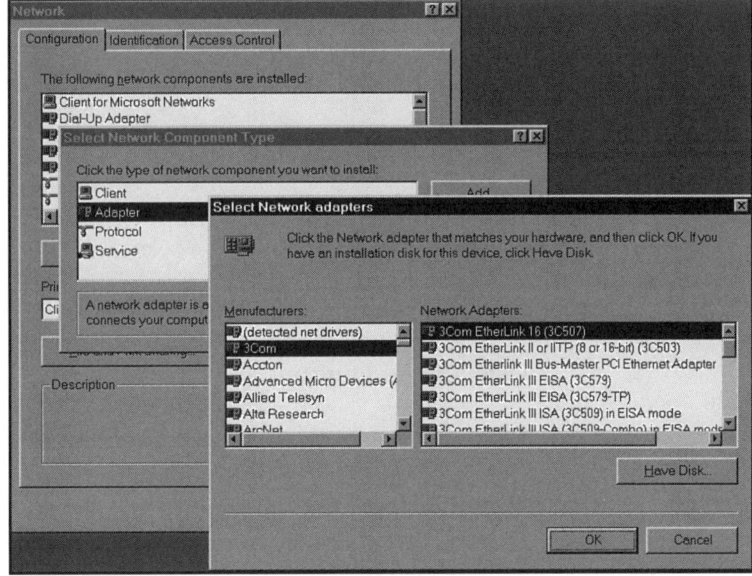

5. Click OK to close the Network dialog box. You might be prompted for the Windows 95 CD while the adapter files are copied to your hard drive.

Configuring network adapters, as well as some additional considerations, is covered later in this chapter.

Installing Protocols

Windows 95 supports many major protocols and ships with four. Some protocols have specific purposes, but others can be chosen by administrators for basic communication on your network. The four protocols that ship with the Windows 95 operating system are as follows:

- NetBEUI
- IPX/SPX-compatible
- TCP/IP
- Microsoft DLC

These four protocols will be discussed in depth later in this chapter. If you want to install any protocol other than these four, you will require software from the manufacturer of the protocol.

To install a network protocol, do the following:

1. Open the Network icon in Control Panel and choose the Configuration tab.
2. Click the Add button and choose Protocol.
3. Click the Add button.
4. Choose the manufacturer and protocol you want to install, as shown in Figure 3.14. If it is an updated or unlisted protocol, click the Have Disk button, provide the path to the OEMSETUP.INF file, and choose the protocol you want. Then click OK.

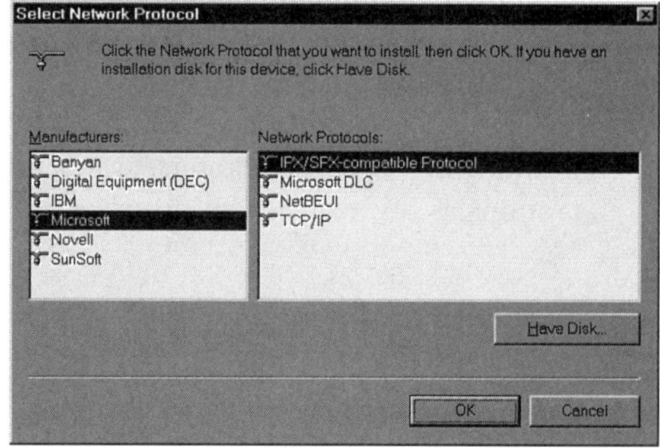

Figure 3.14

Support is included for other protocols, but the only protocols that ship with Windows 95 are found in the Microsoft section.

5. Click OK to close the dialog box. You might be prompted for the Windows 95 CD while the protocol files are copied to your hard drive.

Installing Services

Services are applications that execute in the background, similar to Terminate and Stay Resident (TSR) applications. Unlike TSRs, services load after Windows 95 boots. They often tend to offer additional network functionality in the form of a server application but can provide other capabilities, such as the Hewlett-Packard JetAdmin tool. The most-used service is File and Print Sharing for Microsoft Networks. To install a network service, follow these steps:

1. Open the Network icon in Control Panel and choose the Configuration tab.
2. Click the Add button and choose Service.
3. Click the Add button.
4. Choose the manufacturer and service you want to install, as shown in Figure 3.15. If it is an updated or unlisted service, click the Have Disk button, provide the path to the OEMSETUP.INF file, and choose the service you want. Then click OK.

Figure 3.15

Microsoft includes a variety of services from different manufacturers.

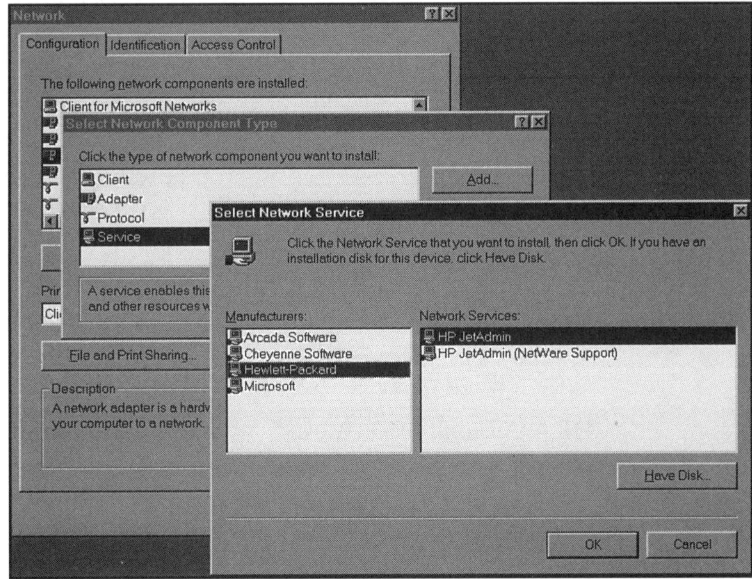

5. Click OK to close the dialog box. You might be prompted for the Windows 95 CD while the service files are copied to your hard drive.

> *Services* are applications that are started automatically after your network software is loaded and your logon screen is displayed. You do not have to log on in order for the services to start.

Table 3.1 describes the networking services included with Windows 95. You can add other services not included with Windows 95 by accessing the Network icon of Control Panel and clicking the Have Disk button.

Table 3.1

Networking Services Included with Windows 95

Service	Description
Arcadia Backup Exec Agent	Network file backup service to be used with Arcadia server backup software. This service lets local files be backed up on network servers.
Cheyenne ARCserve Agent	Network file backup service to be used with Cheyenne ARCserver backup software. Similar to Arcadia Backup Exec Agent.
Hewlett-Packard (HP) JetAdmin	Remote administration for HP JetDirect network interface printers.
HP JetAdmin for NetWare	Remote administration for HP JetDirect network interface printers on NetWare networks. This version of the service is geared toward working with the IPX/SPX-compatible protocol.
Microsoft File and Print Sharing for Microsoft Networks	File and printer sharing of local files on a Microsoft network.

Service	Description
Microsoft File and Print Sharing for NetWare Networks	File and printer sharing of local files on a NetWare network.
Microsoft Network Monitor Agent	Reports information to a remote network monitoring utility, such as Network Monitor, which comes with System Management Server (SMS).
Microsoft Remote Registry Editing Service	Allows the Registry to be administered or edited by another computer over your network.
Simple Network Management Protocol (SNMP) Agent	Reports information to, or allows your system to be monitored by, a third-party SNMP manager.

The Network Monitor Agent, Remote Registry Service, and SNMP Agent are found on the Windows 95 CD-ROM in the \ADMIN\NETTOOLS\NETMON, REMOTREGM, and SNMP directories.

Only one file and print sharing service can be installed on a computer at a time. If you install Microsoft File and Print Sharing for NetWare Networks, you will receive file and printer sharing capabilities for both NetWare and Microsoft networks.

Share as a verb means to allow others to access a resource. As a noun, it *is* a resource, such as a directory or print queue, that others can access.

Now that you have examined installing all the network components, you will take a look at configuring network adapters and protocols.

Configuration of Network Adapters

Proper configuration of network adapters is required to create and maintain network connectivity, a major concern for most people running Windows 95. Since every network card is different, you should consult the card's documentation to find out what settings are required. Network adapters can have some or all of their settings changed in two locations—either the Network icon of Control Panel or the Device Manager. These settings or properties usually include the following:

- Driver type
- Bindings
- Advanced configuration
- Resources

All of these settings are accessible through the Network icon of Control Panel. You can also access the resource's settings for the network card through the Device Manager tab of the System icon in Control Panel.

If you choose to access the settings on the network card through the Network icon of Control Panel, you must select the installed network card and then click the Properties button.

Choosing a Driver Type

Three driver types may be used: enhanced-mode (32-bit and 16-bit) NDIS, real-mode (16-bit) NDIS, and real-mode (16-bit) ODI (see Figure 3.16).

Whenever it is available, you should use the enhanced-mode NDIS driver, because it will load in protected memory, which frees up conventional memory for DOS sessions. If the drivers are 32-bit, they will also give you an added advantage of increased speed.

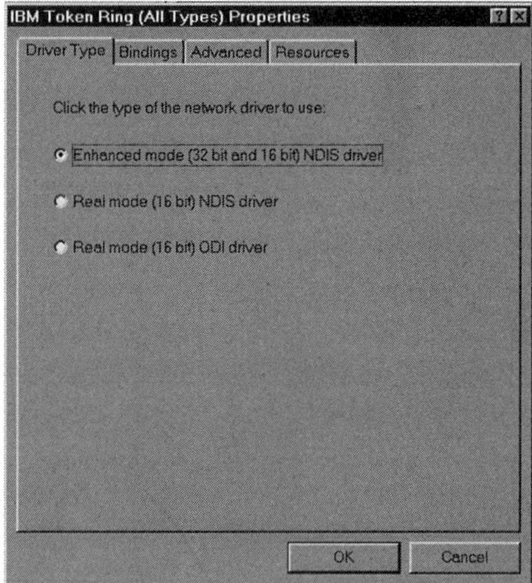

Figure 3.16

Choosing the driver type incorrectly can affect the system's overall network access.

16-bit drivers are a second choice. Two versions of 16-bit drivers are available. NDIS is a network driver specification developed by a consortium of Microsoft, Intel, and other computer vendors. It allows multiple protocols to be used independently on a network card. ODI is a similar network driver specification that was developed by Novell.

Configuring Bindings

If you think binding involves attaching two items together, you aren't wrong. The Bindings tab, shown in Figure 3.17, lists the connections to an adapter by various protocols. The Bindings tab always lists the items on the next level up in the Windows 95 network model (discussed later in this chapter). The Bindings tab lists all the protocols that are connected or "bound" to the adapter you're viewing. You can unbind the protocols by clearing the check boxes. In order to improve the overall speed of your computer's network access, you should unbind all unnecessary network protocols. If a protocol is installed on your computer but not bound to any adapters, you won't actually be using the protocol.

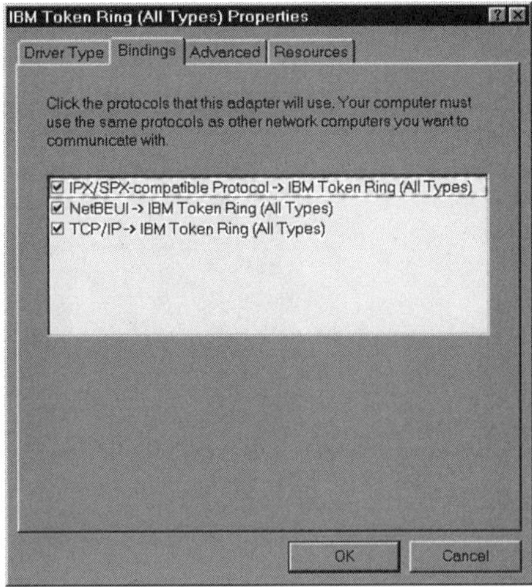

Figure 3.17

By making only necessary bindings, you can decrease the amount of time that it takes for your computer to establish a connection with a server.

Configuring Advanced Settings

The Advanced tab, shown in Figure 3.18, lists a series of advanced settings for the network card. This list of settings varies from one network card driver to another. This tab often includes settings such as the maximum transmission size for network packets and buffer settings for the network card. You shouldn't change the default values without consulting your network administrator or the card manufacturer, because a setting change might affect your network either positively or negatively.

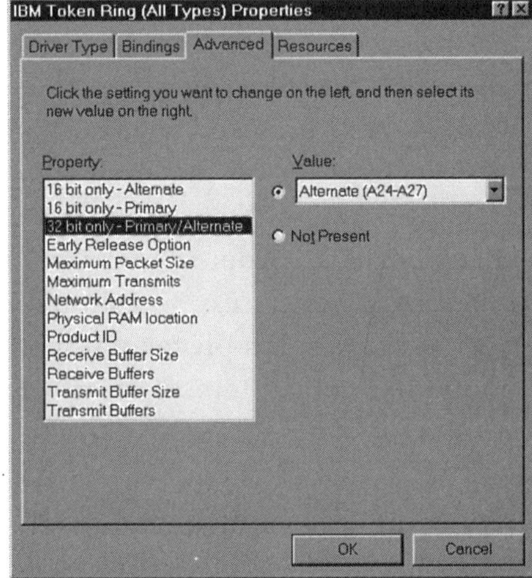

Figure 3.18

Many network adapters have advanced settings that can be modified to provide support of specific features.

Configuring Resources

Every network card occupies specific hardware resources on a computer. The Resources tab, shown in Figure 3.19, lets you see and—depending on your network card—change the resources being used by the network card. The resources used by the card include the IRQ and I/O address.

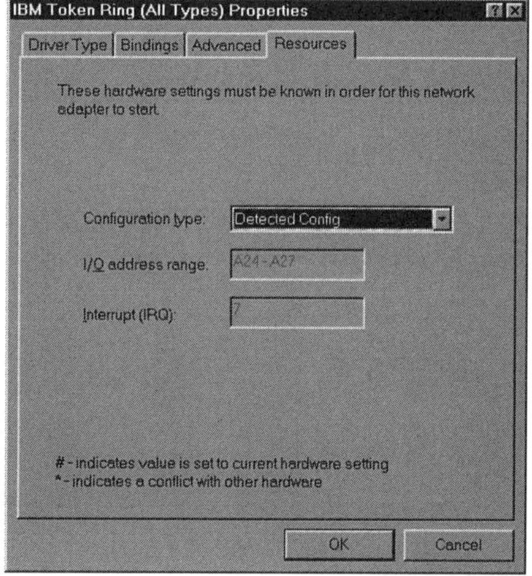

Figure 3.19

Hardware resources that Windows 95 reserves for the adapter may be modified. However, they might still have to be modified on the adapter itself.

Changes that are made to the network card's resources might alter the actual settings on the network card itself. However, not all network cards support these alterations by Windows 95. If you're using a network card that doesn't let Windows 95 modify the card's resources, the settings on the Resources tab will affect only the resources that Windows 95 expects the network card to have. If the settings aren't changed on the card itself, you will still have to change the settings on the card using whatever method is suggested by the manufacturer. Some cards will be changed through a configuration application, and others will require that changes be made to dip switches or jumper settings on the card.

Working with Device Manager

If the card doesn't let you change the settings in the Network icon of Control Panel, you might be able to change the settings on the

Device Manager tab of the System icon in Control Panel. Your network card should be located under the Network Adapters section. The settings can be changed in the Resources tab of the card's properties (see Figure 3.20). Not all network cards can be changed this way.

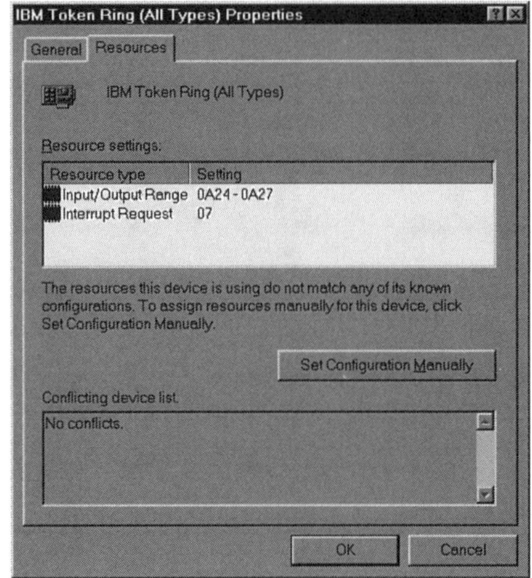

Figure 3.20

Sometimes Device Manager allows for a different view of resource configuration.

Device Manager will be discussed in depth in Chapter 7, "Troubleshooting."

Installing Plug and Play Cards

If a network interface card is Plug and Play-compliant, it can be automatically detected and configured with Windows 95. Simply plug the network card into the appropriate expansion slot and start Windows 95. The model of card will be detected, and the appropriate Windows 95 driver will be installed. Windows 95 then assigns an available interrupt request (IRQ) line and memory or I/O address range to the network card as appropriate and configures the card to use these settings. The administrator need only install the client and protocol software to be used with the network card.

Installing Legacy Cards

The term *legacy* refers to older cards in your system (not only network cards, but all expansion cards in your computer) that are not Plug and Play. Some legacy cards support software configuration for IRQ and I/O addresses, but many in this class only allow configuration changes by changing jumpers or dip switches. Since they are left over from days gone by, they don't always have support with 32-bit drivers; therefore, 16-bit (possibly real-mode) drivers might have to be used.

Dealing with Network Cards Not in Your Windows 95 Distribution

When working with very new network cards or very old legacy network cards, you might find that these cards aren't listed in the default distribution files that ship with Windows 95. When this happens, you have to work through the installation of the network card until you are prompted to choose a manufacturer and network card type. Instead of choosing a network card, click the Have Disk button and provide the path to the unlisted drivers.

If the network card that had been loaded is a Plug and Play card, the card might not be installed. Some Plug and Play cards that are not in the distribution files won't be installed until the next reboot. During the next boot, Windows 95 will identify the new card, since it now has drivers installed, and set the card up on the system through Plug and Play.

Configuration of and Differences Between Network Protocols

A network transport protocol is similar to a language that network computers use to communicate. In order for two computers to communicate, they must both speak the same language. In other words, they must both use the same network transport protocol. The following transport protocols are included with Windows 95:

- Microsoft NetBEUI
- Microsoft IPX/SPX-compatible (NWLINK)
- Microsoft TCP/IP
- Microsoft DLC
- Other third-party vendor transport protocols can be used by Windows 95.

The NetBEUI and IPX/SPX-compatible protocols are installed by default when a network adapter driver is installed.

If the Windows 95 computer needs to communicate with other computers, it must have the same protocol installed as the other computers. For example, if the other computers on the network are running DEC Pathworks 4.1, install that protocol on the Windows 95 computer. If a common protocol on the network hasn't yet been established, refer to the following sections for information on each protocol.

The following sections highlight the configuration options for each protocol. Please refer to the earlier section "Installing Protocols" for the procedure used to install protocols.

Unless you are required to use a third-party protocol to communicate with other computers, use one of the Microsoft protocols to take full advantage of the Windows 95 networking features. The third-party protocols provided often require extra components, licenses, and configuration.

There will be several test questions about the use of protocols within Windows 95. Remember that by default Windows 95 installs both Microsoft NetBEUI and IPX/SPX-compatible protocols. You might be tempted to choose the TCP/IP protocol stack for Microsoft networking, but the Microsoft default for Windows 95 is the NetBEUI protocol for Microsoft networks and the IPX/SPX-compatible protocol (also called NWLINK) for Novell networks. This differs from Windows NT, which defaults to TCP/IP. These three protocols are not the only protocols supported under Windows 95. Shipped with Windows 95 is support for Banyan VINES, DEC Pathworks, IBM DLC, Microsoft DLC, Novell IPX ODI, and SunSoft PC-NFS. Other protocols can also be added.

NetBIOS Extended User Interface (NetBEUI)

The NetBIOS Extended User Interface (NetBEUI) protocol is relatively easy to implement, because it doesn't require the configuration of additional network settings for each computer other than the computer name and domain or workgroup name.

The advantages of the NetBEUI protocol include the following:

- Communication is fast on smaller networks.
- Performance is dynamically self-tuned.
- The only configuration required is a NetBIOS computer name and a workgroup or domain name.

Besides the computer name and workgroup name, only two other settings can be changed (see Figure 3.21). These two settings are found on the Advanced tab of the Protocol to Adapter properties:

- Maximum Sessions identifies the maximum number of network sessions that your computer can keep track of. These include both inbound and outbound sessions.
- NCBS (Network Control Block Size) identifies the size or number of Network Control Blocks that Windows 95 will use. These blocks are used to transfer or carry NetBIOS information for the NetBEUI protocol.

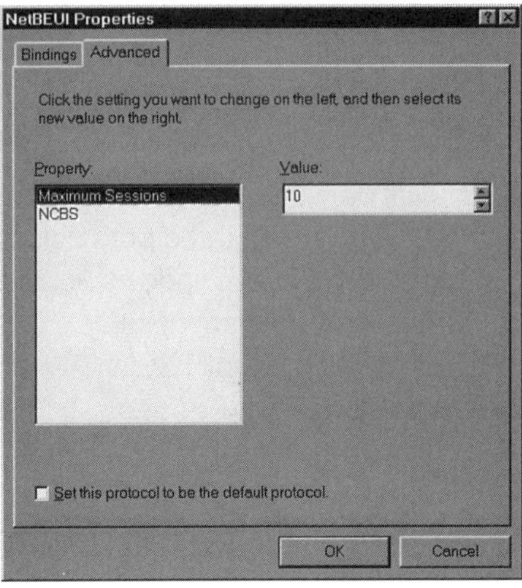

Figure 3.21
NetBEUI protocol advanced settings allow for only two options to configure the protocol.

Since these are the only two configuration settings that may be changed, NetBEUI is an easy protocol to configure. Even if you wanted to change other settings, you couldn't.

Bindings, like adapters, can be configured for each protocol. Protocols are bound to items on the next layer up in the Windows 95 network model. The next major layer above the protocols includes both clients and services, as shown in Figure 3.22.

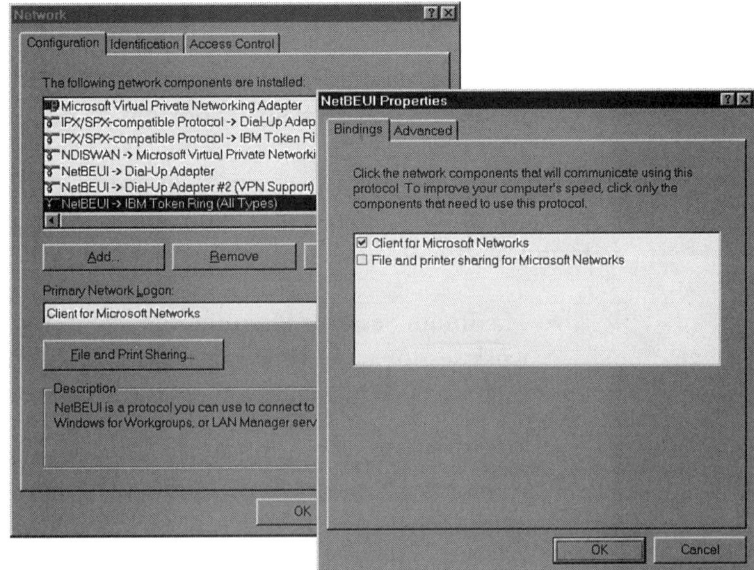

Figure 3.22
NetBEUI bindings allow you to disable clients or services for the protocol.

Bindings will be listed on the Bindings tab for any clients or services that can work using NetBEUI. Since the NetWare client requires the IPX/SPX-compatible protocol, it isn't listed on the Bindings tab for NetBEUI. As with bindings on the network card, any bindings that aren't used should be disabled.

IPX/SPX

The IPX/SPX protocol is a routable network protocol that was developed by Novell. IPX/SPX is a more complex protocol than NetBEUI. If you have multiple network segments on your network, you will require a routable protocol. The IPX/SPX protocol is required for communication with NetWare servers and has now become an industry standard protocol used by many network operating systems. IPX/SPX must be installed if the Client for NetWare Networks is used, although other protocols may also be installed at the same time. IPX/SPX is not required for the Client for Microsoft Networks, but it can be used as the primary or only protocol if you want a routable protocol. If IPX/SPX is used with the Client for Microsoft Networks, the optional NetBIOS support should be enabled.

IPX/SPX has a number of settings that can be adjusted on the Advanced tab of the IPX/SPX protocol, as shown in Figure 3.23:

- Force Even Length Packets is used for compatibility with older NetWare Ethernet drivers with monolithic protocol stacks and on some older IPX routers.

- Frame Type: IPX supports several variations on standard network packets. The different frame specifications are referred to by frame type. You can only talk to servers or clients that are using the same frame type as you. If a frame type isn't specified, Windows 95 will go with the detected frame type, or 802.2. Here are the other frame types you can choose from:

  802.2

  802.3

  ETHERNET II

ETHERNET_SNAP

Token_Ring

Token_Ring_Snap

- Maximum Connections allows you to set the maximum number of network sessions that Windows 95 will support.
- Maximum Sockets specifies the number of IPX Socket connections that can be made to or from the server. This is excluded from NetBIOS traffic.
- Network Address lets you change the network, hardware, or MAC address of your network card. This address is the basis of all communication on your network. Not all addresses typed in will be valid, and an invalid address will prevent you from communicating with other computers on your network. This should be changed only with extreme caution.
- Source Routing specifies the cache size to be used with source routing.

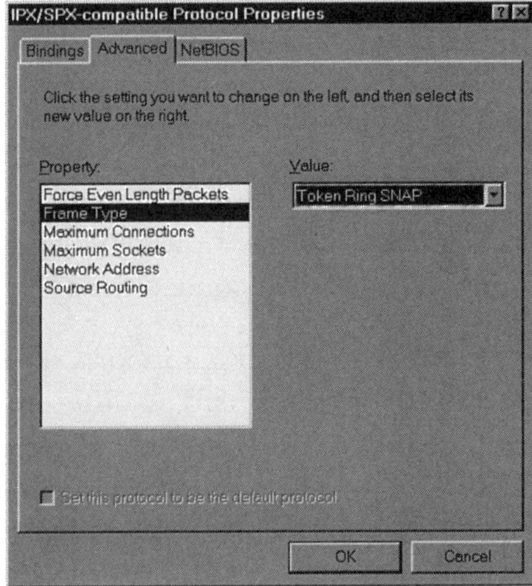

Figure 3.23

IPX/SPX-compatible protocol advanced settings let you modify several settings for the protocol.

With the number of settings that can be modified, and the loss of network connectivity if the settings are configured incorrectly, IPX/SPX is a more difficult protocol to work with on a network than NetBEUI.

NetBIOS is required in order for Microsoft network clients to communicate with Microsoft servers. NetBIOS is also used to create and maintain lists of servers on the network. By default, IPX/SPX doesn't use NetBIOS, but it can be enabled on the NetBIOS tab of the IPX/SPX protocol properties, as shown in Figure 3.24.

Figure 3.24

IPX/SPX-compatible protocol NetBIOS settings may be enabled or disabled.

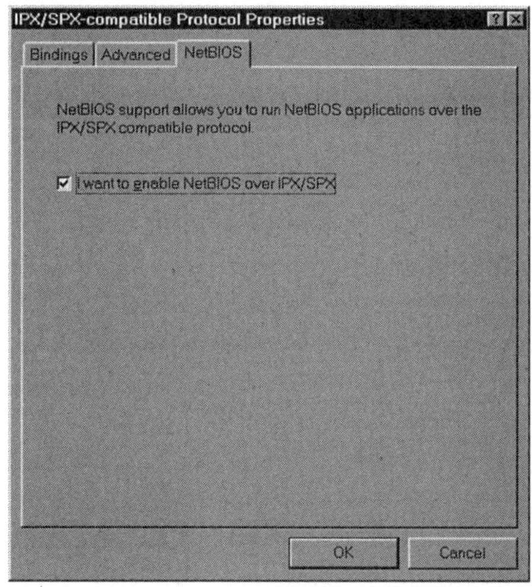

TCP/IP

Windows 95 comes with the Microsoft 32-bit TCP/IP protocol, related connectivity utilities, and an SNMP service.

To install the TCP/IP protocol on a Windows 95 computer, follow these steps:

1. Select Start, Settings, Control Panel.
2. Double-click the Network icon, and select the Configuration tab.
3. Click Add to open the Select Network Component Type dialog box.
4. Select Protocol and click Add to open the Select Network Protocol dialog box.

5. Select Microsoft from the Manufacturers list and TCP/IP from the Network Protocols list.

6. Click OK to return to the Network dialog box.

After you install TCP/IP on a Windows 95 computer, the tabbed TCP/IP Properties dialog box appears, from which you configure the appropriate values. To reconfigure TCP/IP, choose the Network icon from Control Panel to open the Network dialog box again.

To configure TCP/IP for Windows 95, follow these steps:

1. From the Network dialog box's Configuration tab, select TCP/IP and click Properties.

2. From the TCP/IP Properties sheet, select the IP Address tab. Select Obtain an IP address automatically if there is a Dynamic Host Configuration Protocol (DHCP) server on the network configured to supply this machine with an IP address. Otherwise, type the IP address and subnet mask in the spaces provided.

An incorrect IP address or subnet mask can cause communication problems with other TCP/IP nodes on the network. If an IP address is the same as another already on the network, this can cause either machine to hang. DHCP can help prevent duplicate addresses by automatically configuring TCP/IP on the client using parameters set on the DHCP server. The DHCP server keeps track of IP addresses it has assigned to clients and doesn't assign the same IP address to two different DHCP clients.

3. Each of the other tabs in the TCP/IP Properties sheet contains optional configuration information. For these tabs, enter the appropriate values as required. Click OK when you're done to restart the computer and initialize TCP/IP.

The other tabs of the TCP/IP Properties sheet, discussed in the following sections, contain optional TCP/IP configuration parameters.

Tip

It is highly recommended that you configure a default gateway for the Windows 95 client using the Gateway tab. The default gateway can help route TCP/IP messages to remote destinations.

IP Address

Every computer on a TCP/IP network is individually identified by a unique 32-bit address. This address is written using dotted decimal notation (see Figure 3.25). In addition to the IP address, you will also require a subnet mask. The subnet mask is used to determine if the people you are contacting are on your network segment or elsewhere.

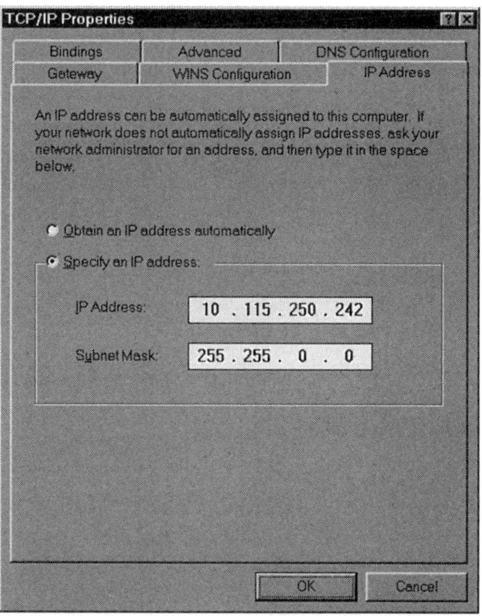

Figure 3.25

Every computer on your network requires an IP address specific to your network.

You receive these numbers from your network administrator. If your network administrator has created a server-to-host DHCP service, all you have to do is select the option Obtain an IP Address Automatically, and you will receive complete IP configuration from the server.

Gateway

When the route needed for an IP message to reach a destination is unknown, the message is forwarded to the default gateway. The default gateway is a router connected to other TCP/IP network segments. Messages are sent to this gateway when it isn't known which segment the destination is on. The Gateway tab, shown in Figure 3.26, contains the IP addresses of default gateways that can be used in the order they appear on the list.

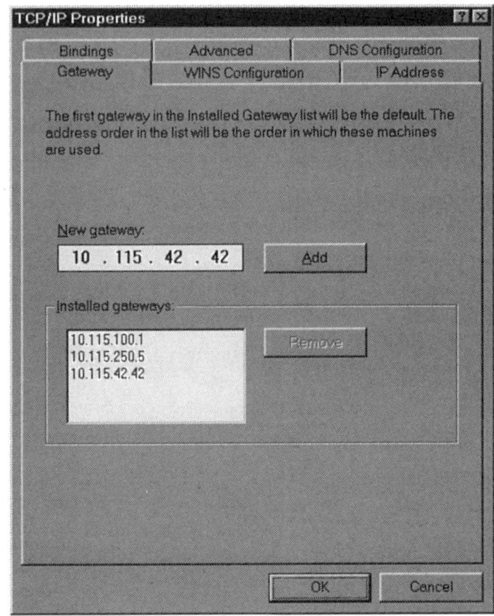

Figure 3.26

Gateways provide Windows 95 with paths off your network segment.

If the subnet mask determines that the address you are trying to reach is remote, your computer will send it to a gateway.

Only one gateway is used to route messages. If a gateway is unavailable (due to hardware problems, for example), the next gateway on the list is used. If that gateway doesn't respond, the next gateway is used. A second gateway is never used if the first one is available, even if the destination computer is unavailable or the message is undeliverable.

WINS Configuration

A Windows Internet Name Service (WINS) server can be used to register and resolve NetBIOS names to IP addresses. For example, if the Windows 95 computer wants to map a drive to the computer name SERVER3 on a remote TCP/IP network, it can query the WINS server to find out the IP address of SERVER3.

Communication using TCP/IP must always use IP addresses. Therefore, a WINS server or some other form of NetBIOS-name-to-IP-address resolution must be used if communication using NetBIOS names is required. The alternatives to using a WINS server include using a static LMHOSTS file in the *systemroot* directory, which contains NetBIOS-name-to-IP-address mappings. However, a WINS server is preferred, because NetBIOS names can be automatically and dynamically registered with the WINS server, which is much more flexible and accurate than an LMHOSTS file or some other method. All of the WINS configuration is completed in the WINS Configuration tab, shown in Figure 3.27.

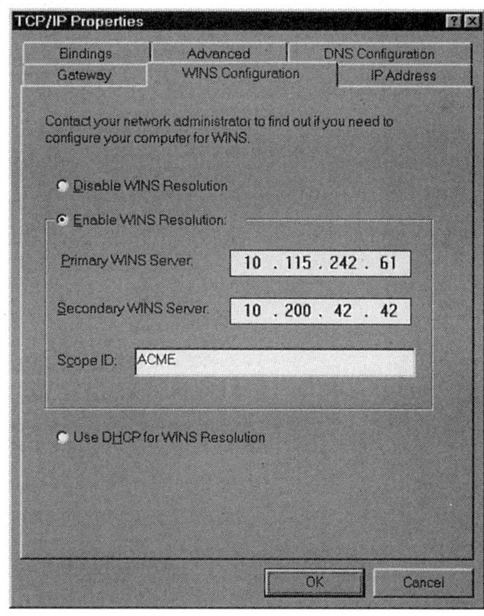

Figure 3.27

The WINS Configuration tab is used to configure information for NetBIOS name resolution.

The three choices of WINS configuration for a Windows 95 TCP/IP client are as follows:

- Enable WINS Resolution: If WINS resolution is enabled, you must enter the IP address of one or two WINS servers in the appropriate fields. If the primary WINS server is unavailable for some reason, TCP/IP accesses the secondary WINS server if one is configured.

- Disable WINS Resolution: If WINS is disabled, an alternative form of NetBIOS name resolution is required to resolve NetBIOS names to computer names for destinations on remote networks.
- Use DHCP for WINS Resolution: If DHCP has been enabled in the IP Address tab, you can select this option to use the WINS servers specified by the DHCP Server options.

The option Use DHCP for WINS Resolution doesn't mean that a DHCP server provides name resolution. This option is used when a DHCP server has been configured in order to advise the DHCP clients of the IP address(es) of the WINS server(s).

Do not fill in the Scope ID field on the WINS tab of the TCP/IP Properties sheet. This field is used to limit the number of computers a workstation can see on the network. For example, if a scope ID of ACME is applied, you will be able to contact only other computers that have a scope ID of ACME. You won't even be able to contact computers when the Scope ID field is left blank.

DNS Configuration

The Domain Name Service (DNS) provides address resolution for DNS host and domain names. Host names are used with Windows Sockets applications. The host name for a Windows-based computer is often the same as the computer name, but the domain name is usually something like `domain.company.com`. World Wide Web addresses often consist of DNS host names appended to the DNS domain name to form a Fully Qualified Domain Name, such as `www.microsoft.com`, where `www` is the host (computer) name and `microsoft.com` is the domain name. DNS options are configured on the DNS Configuration tab, as shown in Figure 3.28.

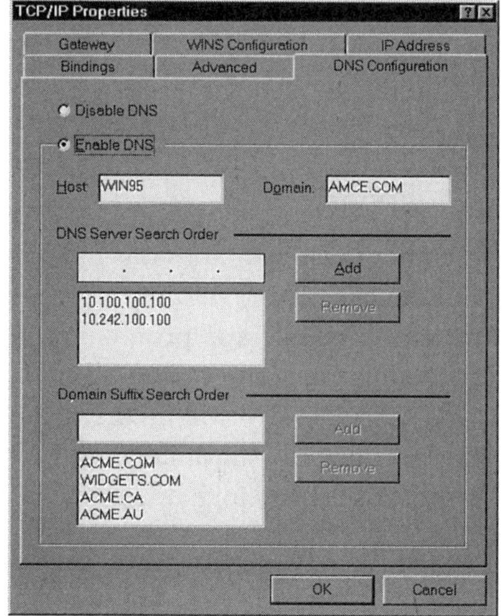

Figure 3.28

DNS configuration can be filled in by hand or configured through DHCP.

To access a computer using a DNS name over TCP/IP, the DNS name must be resolved to an IP address. This can be done using a static HOSTS file in the *systemroot* directory or by accessing a DNS server. The DNS server contains a database that is distributed over an internetwork. If a DNS server can't fully resolve a domain name to an IP address, it can pass the request on to another DNS server until the name is found and resolved.

The DNS Server Search Order list in the TCP/IP Properties sheet lists the order in which DNS servers will be queried for DNS name resolution. The Domain Suffix Search Order list shows the order in which domain names can be appended to a host name to try to resolve the resulting Fully Qualified Domain Name. For example, if the Domain Suffix Search Order list contains ACME.COM, and if the host name FRED can't be resolved, DNS then attempts to resolve the name FRED.ACME.COM. If that fails, DNS will attempt the resolve the host name with the next suffix on the list.

When DNS is enabled on a Windows 95 computer, it will set some internal Registry flags. However, if WINS is also providing DNS information, DNS is often disabled on the DNS Configuration tab. A trick to getting DNS to work correctly through WINS is to enable DNS with a valid host name and domain name, reboot, and then disable DNS.

Advanced

Use the Advanced tab, shown in Figure 3.29, to specify whether you want the TCP/IP protocol to be the default, or preferred, protocol. The default protocol is the first protocol used when attempting to connect to network resources. If the NetBEUI protocol is installed, it will be the default protocol. If most of the network resources you will be connecting to use TCP/IP, you can improve performance by setting TCP/IP to the default protocol.

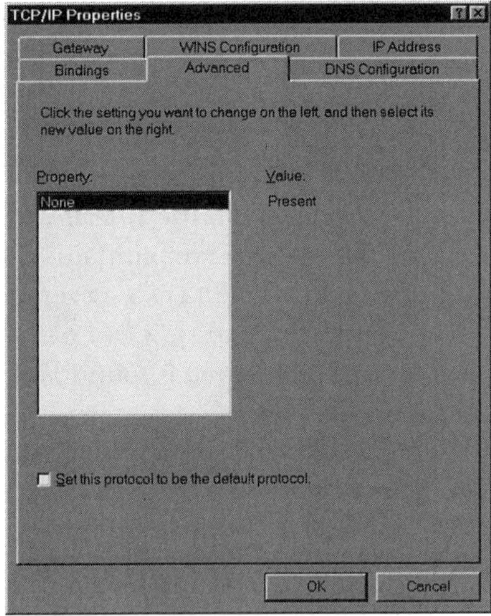

Figure 3.29

The only advanced setting for TCP/IP is the option to set it as the default protocol.

Bindings

The Bindings tab shows network components that can use the TCP/IP protocol. If a component has a check mark next to it, it will bind to TCP/IP and can then use the TCP/IP protocol for communication. To improve performance, remove the check marks from any components that do not require TCP/IP.

Data Link Control (DLC)

The other Microsoft-written network protocol included with Windows 95 is Microsoft DLC. However, this protocol is used only for communicating with certain network interface printers and mainframe systems. DLC is not used for peer-to-peer networking of Windows 95 computers. Due to DLC's limited use, you should consult the documentation for the items you are connecting to with DLC to determine the best settings for items listed on the Advanced tab, shown in Figure 3.30.

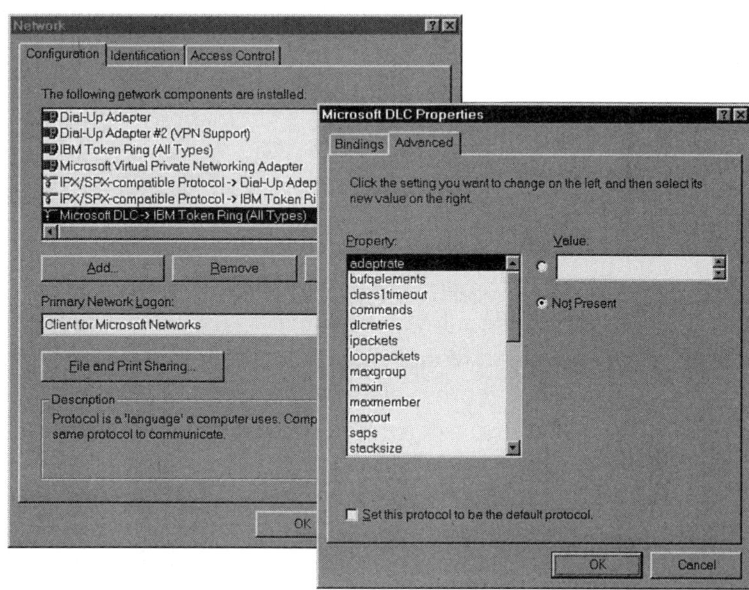

Figure 3.30

Advanced settings for Microsoft DLC allow for many configuration modifications.

PPTP/VPN

Point-to-Point Tunneling Protocol (PPTP) is a secure Wide Area Network (WAN) protocol that is starting to receive wide acceptance as a secure protocol over the Internet. PPTP lets you make a secure connection to your network from a remote location on the Internet. If you will have Internet connectivity on your network, you should consider installing PPTP on both your network servers and remote workstations. The protocol NDISWAN is a virtual protocol that doesn't exist. Instead, it is a modified version of TCP/IP that allows for carrying other packets in the data section of the IP packet. This virtual protocol receives a binding with an equally virtual Local Area Network (LAN) adapter—the Microsoft Virtual Private Networking (VPN) Adapter—as shown in Figure 3.31.

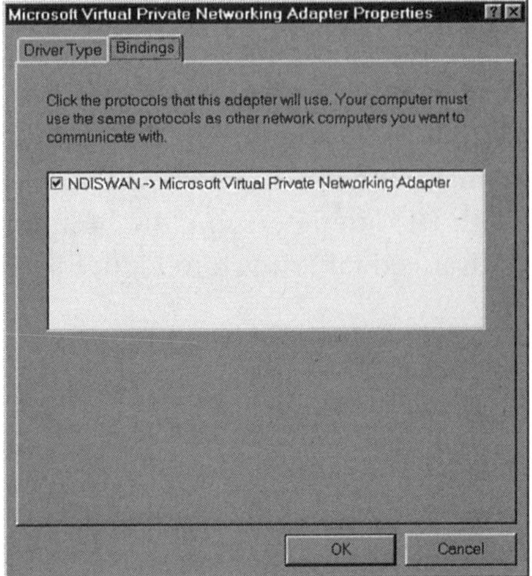

Figure 3.31

The Microsoft Virtual Private Networking Adapter is bound to the NDISWAN protocol. Both use TCP/IP for communication.

The Advanced tab on the VPN properties sheet (see Figure 3.32) allows for a log file (similar to the PPP or modem log files) to track and troubleshoot connections to remote servers. The Advanced settings also allow you to identify the physical media over which you will be running the PPTP connection.

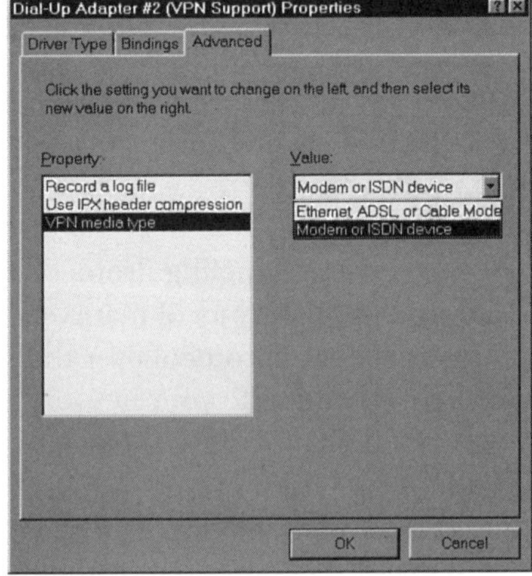

Figure 3.32

Dial-up Adapter #2 (VPN Support) advanced properties allow you to specify the log file creation and PPTP media types.

To effectively use PPTP and VPN, you need some or all of the following components installed (see Figure 3.33):

- Client for Microsoft Networks.
- Optional second client for use on remote LAN.
- Dial-up adapter if making the VPN connection through an Internet Service Provider (ISP).
- NDISWAN protocol installed for packet encapsulation.
- TCP/IP to act as a transport for the NDISWAN protocol.
- Optional second protocol to be used on the remote LAN. This would include NetBEUI or IPX/SPX if you will not be using TCP/IP on the remote LAN.

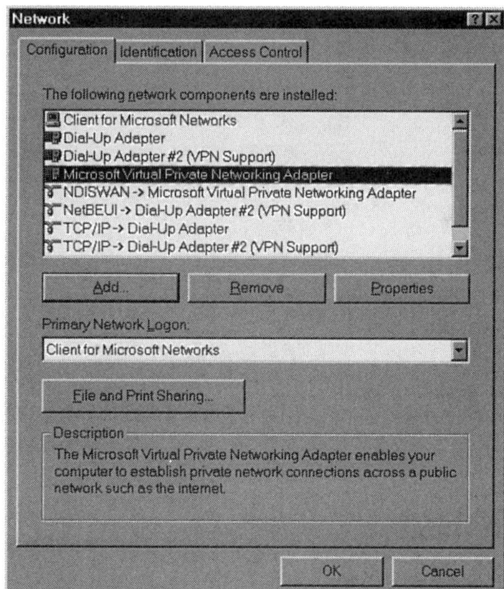

Figure 3.33

All the components that make up a PPTP Client configuration.

PPTP and VPN are available only if you have applied the WinSock 2 and Dial-up Networking updates to your installation of Windows 95. Both of these updates are available from Microsoft's Web site at `http://www.microsoft.com/windows`. The WinSock2 update has already been included in OSR2.

When creating the dial-up networking document to connect to your Remote Access Services server running PPTP, you will not specify a modem as a connection device, but the Microsoft VPN Adapter instead (see Figure 3.34). This connector will not dial a phone number. Instead, it will require the IP address of the network adapter on the RAS server (see Figure 3.35).

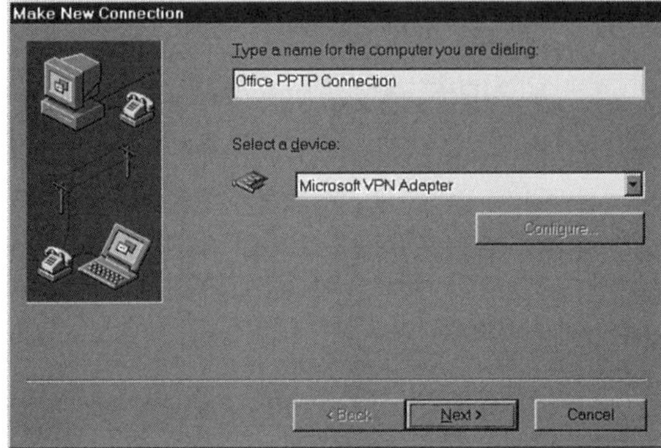

Figure 3.34

The Microsoft VPN Adapter takes the place of a modem during a PPTP connection.

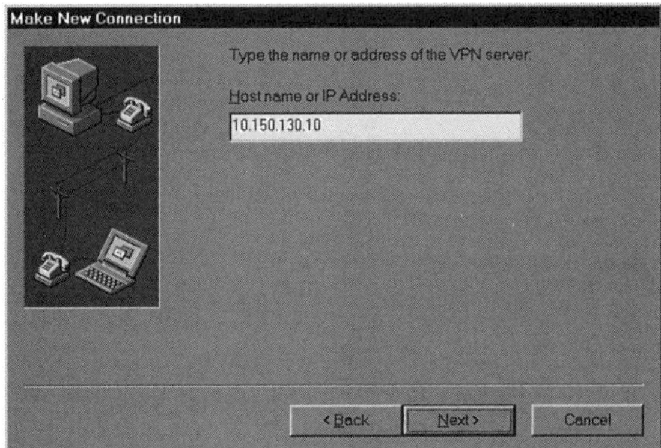

Figure 3.35

The VPN or PPTP connection has an IP address as a destination.

Before establishing a PPTP connection, you must first connect to a TCP/IP network. This may be a LAN connection or a dial-up connection to an ISP. After that connection is in place, you will open the PPTP dial-up connection (see Figure 3.36). This connection will have the IP address of the PPTP adapter on the RAS server as the destination. You will dial this virtual call, and it will keep your modem connected. After you dial, you have all the security on the transaction that you would have dialing the server directly.

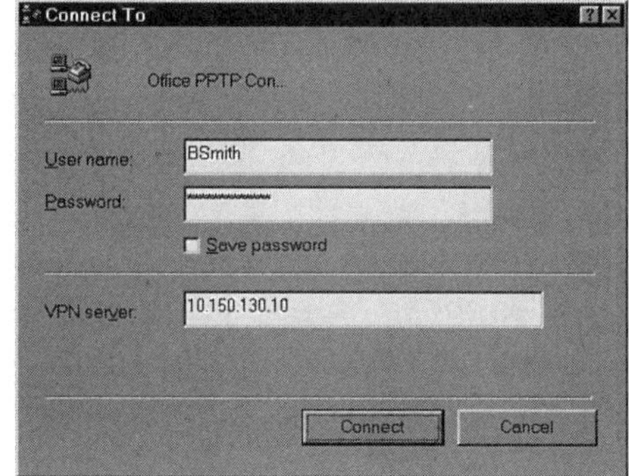

Figure 3.36

The dial-up connection leaves previous connections open.

For a comparison of the three basic network protocols, see Microsoft Knowledgebase article Q128233, "Comparison of Windows NT Network Protocols."

Configuration of the Computer Browser Service

As mentioned earlier, a Windows 95 computer can have more than one network client installed at a time. A single network wire may have multiple network protocols running on it. For example, if a network contains both Windows NT and Novell NetWare servers, the Windows 95 computer can run both the Client for Microsoft Networks and the Client for NetWare Networks. If the passwords are the same for the two networks, the unified logon feature of Windows 95 requires that the password be entered only once for both networks. Similarly, if the Windows password is the same as the network password, this password needs to be entered only once. If the passwords are not the same, they must be entered individually.

For practice on this material, refer to Exercise 3.1.

The password list file (PWL) is secured by each user's Windows 95 password. To cut down on the number of different passwords a user must track and maintain, some network administrators advocate the use of a blank Windows 95 password. However, using a blank Windows 95 password along with password caching can expose your user's network resources to unauthorized use. Blank Windows 95 passwords are not recommended.

The Password List Editor (PWLEDIT), shown in Figure 3.37, is used to edit a user's password list file. Use it to view the entries and remove specific password entries if you have problems using a cached password.

To install this tool on your local hard disk, use the following procedure:

1. Choose the Add/Remove Programs icon in Control Panel.
2. Select the Windows Setup tab.
3. Click the Have Disk button.
4. Install the ADMIN\APPTOOLS\PWLEDIT directory from a Windows 95 CD-ROM.

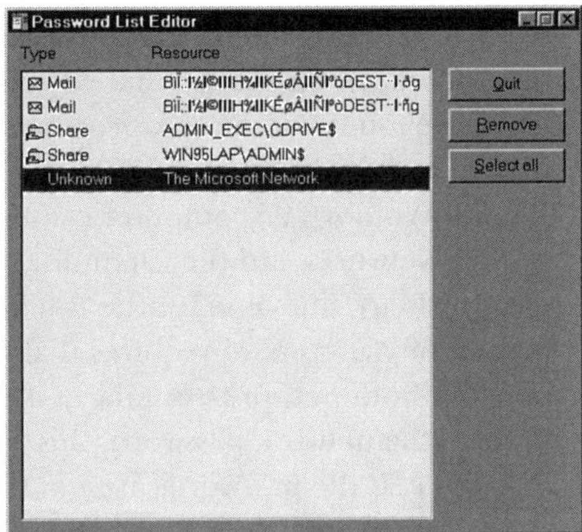

Figure 3.37

*The Password List Editor lets you delete saved passwords from the *.PWL file without deleting the entire file.*

Windows 95 also features *unified browsing,* in which all computers that can be browsed by Windows 95 are displayed together in the Network Neighborhood. For example, NetWare servers appear along with Windows-based computers in the Network Neighborhood if both Client for Microsoft Networks and Client for NetWare Networks are installed.

When users access the Network Neighborhood, they are viewing a list of computers on the network known as a *browse list.*

Microsoft and NetWare networks can use NetBIOS to distribute browse lists throughout a domain. The browse list contains all NetBIOS computers and shared resources in the domain; it is compiled by the master browser of the domain.

When the master browser has compiled the browse list, it distributes the list to the backup browsers. When a client requires access to the browse list, it obtains access from a backup browser so that the master browser doesn't become overloaded with requests from all the computers.

The decision about which computers are master and backup browsers is determined through browse elections. If a primary domain controller is present, that controller will always be the master browser. Each type of operating system in the network has a different potential to be a browser. Windows NT computers are more favored to be browsers than Windows 95 computers. If a computer is a preferred browser, it can be chosen to be a browser, depending on the operating system it is running and whether it has been manually configured to be a preferred browser.

When a network client needs to consult a browse list to browse the network, it contacts one of the backup browsers for a copy of the current browse list. The backup browsers periodically receive updated browse lists from the master browser to make sure that the browse lists remain current.

Normally, the browse lists are maintained and exchanged using local broadcasts. If the domain spans routers, however, extra steps are required to ensure that the browse lists are passed across the routers. Refer to your network protocol documentation if this is the case.

A Windows 95 computer can be configured to maintain or not maintain browse lists by configuring the File and Print Sharing service for either Microsoft or NetWare networks.

Configuring Browse Masters

Normally, you let the browser elections automatically determine which computers are the browsers. However, if you don't want the potential performance load on the Windows 95 computer that can result from browsing, you can configure the computer to never be a browser. In addition, you can set a particular computer, on which an extra network load would have little effect, to be a preferred browser.

The browser configuration is performed using the properties for the File and Print Sharing for Microsoft Networks service or the File and Print Sharing for NetWare Networks service.

Windows 95 computers make lousy browse masters simply because they don't share browse lists properly. You will achieve better browsing capability by placing NT-class computers on your networks to provide service as browse masters and domain browse masters. If your Windows 95 workgroup name happens to be the same as a Windows NT domain name, you will be able to receive even better, or what has been called "enhanced," browsing from the domain master browser.

Configuring Browse Master for Microsoft Networks

To access the browser configuration options for a computer running File and Print Sharing for Microsoft Networks, follow these steps:

1. Choose the Network icon in Control Panel and select the File and Print Sharing for Microsoft Networks service.
2. Click Properties and select the Browse Master property.
3. Choose one of the following options from the Value drop-down list (see Figure 3.38):
    - Select Automatic to have Windows 95 automatically determine whether the computer is needed as a browse server.

- Select Disabled to prevent the computer from maintaining browse lists for the network.
- To give the computer a higher weighting for the browse elections, select Enabled. This computer will then be preferred over other Windows 95 computers that have the Automatic value for the browse elections.

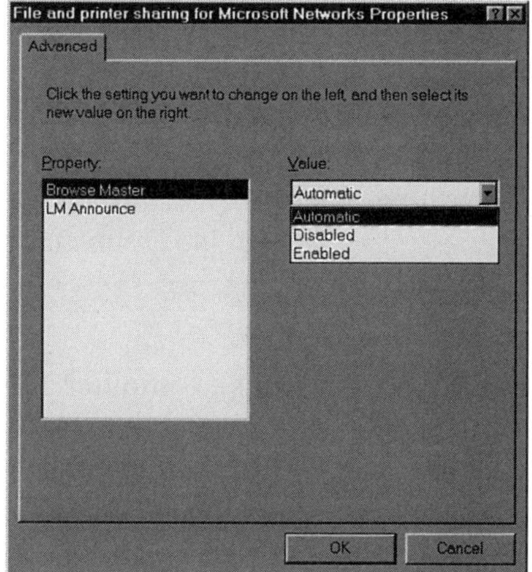

Figure 3.38

Browser options for File and Printer Sharing for Microsoft Networks Properties.

4. Click OK twice, and then restart the computer.

Configuring Browse Master for NetWare Networks

To access the browser configuration options for a computer running File and Print Sharing for NetWare Networks, follow these steps:

1. Choose the Network icon in Control Panel and select the File and Print Sharing for NetWare Networks service.
2. Click Properties and select the Workgroup Advertising property.

3. Choose one of the following options from the drop-down list (see Figure 3.39):

    - To have Windows 95 automatically determine if the computer is needed as a browse server, select Enabled: May Be Master.

    - To prevent the computer from maintaining browse lists for the network, select Enabled: Will Not Be Master.

The Enabled: Will Not Be Master option doesn't prevent the computer from browsing the network resources; it prevents the computer from maintaining a browse list for itself and other computers. Select the Disabled option to prevent the computer from using the browse service.

    - To give the computer a higher weighting for the browse elections, select Enabled: Preferred Master. This computer will then be preferred over other Windows 95 computers that have Automatic set for the Browse Master value for the browse elections.

    - To prevent the computer from using the browser service to browse network resources, select Disabled.

    - To allow the computer to send SAP broadcasts announcing its presence to real-mode NetWare clients, select the SAP Advertising property, and change the value to Enabled.

4. Click OK twice, and then restart the computer.

Selecting the Disabled option doesn't prevent the computer from browsing the network resources; it prevents the computer from maintaining a browse list for itself and other computers. As long as at least one computer on the network is a browser, other computers can use the browsing service.

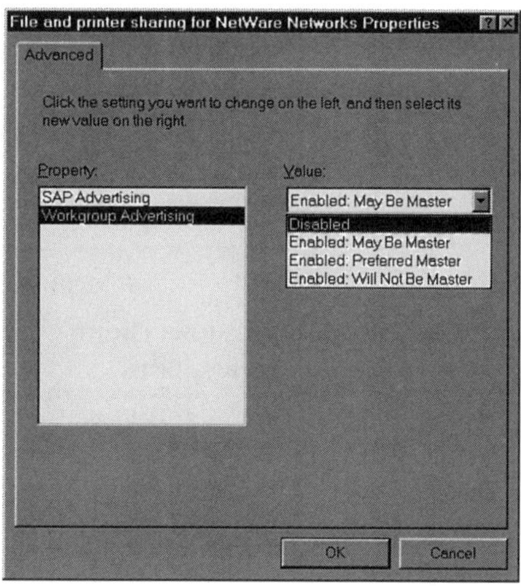

Figure 3.39

Browser options for File and Printer Sharing for NetWare Networks Properties.

Handling Browser Failures

A number of things can go wrong with the browser operations on a Microsoft network. If you are aware of the problems, it's easy to compensate for them. Table 3.2 lists some of the most common problems and solutions that will get you through the rough parts.

Table 3.2

Diagnosing Browser Problems

Problem	Solution
Computers appear on the browse list but are not accessible.	When a computer shuts down properly, it notifies the master browser, which removes the computer from the browse list. It may take up to 15 minutes for the master browser to let the backup browser know that the computer is gone. If a computer is shut down improperly, it must fail at three of its 12-minute announcements before the master browser

continues

Table 3.2 Continued

Problem	Solution
	removes the computer from the browser list. Wait, and it will fix itself, or reboot the master browser.
DOS clients and Windows clients receive different browse lists.	DOS browser clients don't know how to deal with backup browsers. Windows browser clients alway receive their server lists from the backup browser. Because the DOS client always gets its list from the master browser, it will be more current than the Windows list. Wait 15 minutes, and the lists should be the same. This is not a problem. The Windows clients try to reduce the workload on the master browser.
Windows 95 reports the error `Network unavailable` when attempting to browse the Network Neighborhood.	This will happen if there is no master browser for your workgroup. You should either change your workgroup name to match a workgroup that has a master browser or install File and Print Sharing and configure your workstation to maintain the browse list.
No other workgroups or domains are listed in the Network Neighborhood.	If your master browser has just started up, it will make workgroup announcements in addition to the default announcements

Problem	Solution
	every 15 minutes. This allows the master browser to show up on other work-group browse lists. However, it will have to wait until the other servers reach their 15-minute announcement period before it knows about other domains.

Most problems with the browse list will be solved on their own if you just wait. To be sure that you don't have a problem with network connectivity, choose Start, Run and type *server_name* for a known server that is currently running. If you are presented with a share list, you're on the network.

Installation of the File and Print Sharing for Microsoft Networks Service

For practice on this material, refer to Exercise 3.6.

To set up Windows 95 to use user-level security, you must have at least one Windows NT computer on your network. The Windows NT computer can be either a Windows NT Server, Windows NT Domain Controller, or Windows NT Workstation. All of these computers maintain a list of users that Windows 95 will use when applying access permissions. You also need to have Client for Microsoft Networks enabled. Then follow these steps:

1. Click Add in the Network Properties sheet to display the Select Network Component Type dialog box.
2. Select Service and click Add. The Select Network Service dialog box appears.
3. Select File and Print Sharing for Microsoft Networks and click OK. The service is added to the Network properties sheet.

4. Click the Access Control tab of the Network Properties sheet.
5. Choose the User-Level Access Control option.
6. In the Obtain List of Users and Groups From field, enter the name of the Windows NT computer or domain that contains the access account list for the user. This is the list that authenticates the user when he wants access to a resource.
7. Click OK. Insert the Windows 95 Setup CD-ROM or any disks Windows requests.
8. After the files for File and Print Sharing for Microsoft Networks are installed, Windows prompts you to shut down and restart Windows. Click Yes to do so. After Windows reboots, the client is set up to use the new service on a Windows NT network.

You can now set up folders and printers to be shared on the Windows 95 client computers. You can share a folder, for example, by opening Explorer in Windows 95, locating the folder you want to share, and right-clicking. Select Sharing from the context-sensitive menu and set up access rights as explained in Chapter 4, "Configuring and Managing Resource Access."

Installation of the File and Print Sharing for NetWare Networks Service

For practice on this material, refer to Exercise 3.2.

To allow directories and print queues to be shared with NetWare users, add the File and Print Sharing for NetWare Networks service in the Network icon in Control Panel. If the File and Print Sharing for Microsoft Networks service is already installed, remove that service first.

After File and Print Sharing for NetWare Networks is installed, enable sharing by choosing the appropriate File and Print Sharing options from the Network icon in Control Panel.

File and Print Sharing for NetWare Networks must use the User-level Access Control security model.

The computer name of the NetWare server that maintains the list of user accounts must be specified in the Access Control tab of the Network icon in Control Panel.

You can use user-level security when running Windows 95 on a NetWare network and you want to have peer services enabled for the Windows 95 clients. The user-level security available with NetWare networks is similar to user-level security with Microsoft networks. When using user-level security with NetWare networks, security authentication requests are handled using the pass-through security method. This type of security method passes the authentication requests to a NetWare server for authentication.

User-level security on NetWare is used to protect shared network resources by storing a list of users and groups who have access to a network resource. To gain access to a resource, a user must be on the access account list stored on the NetWare server bindery and then have the proper access rights for that resource. Administrators can set up access rights on a per-user or per-group basis. The rights that can be assigned to a user for a specific resource include read, write, create, delete, change attribute, directory search, and access control.

An example of setting up user-level security on a NetWare network is setting up the File and Print Sharing for NetWare Networks service. You can use this service to control access to a client computer's file and attached printer. File and Print Sharing for NetWare Networks is supported by NWSERVER.VXD, which requires NWREDIR.VXD to be installed and functioning.

Remember that File and Print Sharing for NetWare Networks can't run on the same machine on which you have File and Print Sharing for Microsoft Networks installed. You must remove the latter before installing the former.

The File and Print Sharing for NetWare Networks service is established in protected mode with NWSERVER.VXD, which is supported by NWSP.VXD. NWSP is the virtual device driver that handles the security for the Windows 95 client computer that shares its files and printers. Because File and Print Sharing for NetWare Networks depends on bindery security from the NetWare server, an additional function is necessary to read the NetWare server's bindery. This function is provided through the NWAB32.DLL file, which is responsible for reading the access account list from the NetWare server bindery.

Before you install the File and Print Sharing for NetWare Networks service, you should have the Client for NetWare Networks installed. You then open the Network Properties sheet again by double-clicking the Network icon in Control Panel. Next, follow these steps:

1. Click Add in the Network Properties sheet to open the Select Network Component Type dialog box.
2. Select Service and click Add. The Select Network Service dialog box appears.
3. Select File and Print Sharing for NetWare Networks and click OK. The service is added to the Network Properties sheet.
4. Click the Access Control tab of the Network Properties sheet.
5. Choose the User-level Access Control option.
6. In the Obtain List of Users and Groups From field, enter the name of the NetWare server that contains the access account list for the user. This is the list that authenticates the user when he wants access to a resource.
7. Click OK. Insert the Windows 95 Setup CD-ROM or any disks Windows requests.
8. After the files for File and Print Sharing for NetWare Networks are installed, Windows prompts you to shut down and restart Windows. Click Yes to do so. After Windows reboots, the client is set up to use the new service on a NetWare network.

Specifying the folders and printers to be shared on a client computer is done at the user level. To set up a folder as a shared resource, for example, the user opens Explorer, locates the folder to share, and right-clicks it. He selects Sharing from the context-sensitive menu and fills out the Sharing tab. You can learn more about sharing a folder in Chapter 4.

Understanding UNC Path Names

For practice on this material, refer to Exercise 3.5.

The Universal Naming Convention (UNC) is a standardized nomenclature for specifying a share name on a particular computer. The computer name is limited to 15 characters, and the share name is usually limited to 15 characters, depending on the network. Share names can be given to a print queue or a directory of files—for example, HP4 or WINAPPS.

The UNC uniquely specifies the path to the share name on a network. The UNC path takes the form of *server_name**resource_name* [*path*]. For example, the UNC path of the printer share HPLJ created on the server ADMIN_EXEC would be \\ADMIN_EXEC\HPLJ. Figure 3.40 shows the result of typing UNC path names at the Run command.

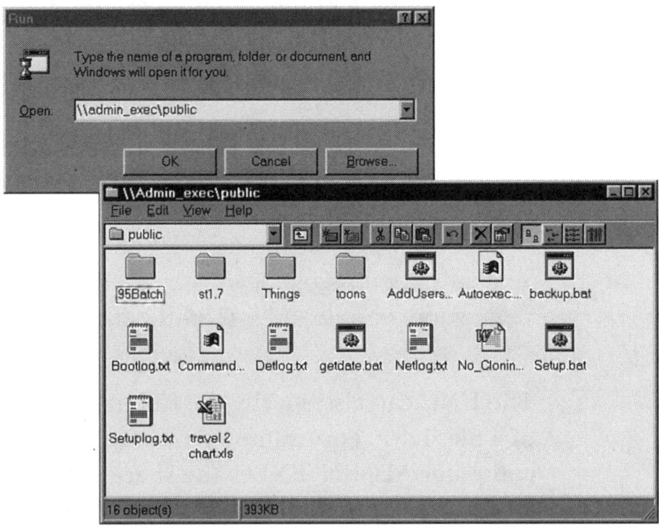

Figure 3.40

The UNC path name can be used to access resources from within the Windows environment. By typing a UNC path at the Run command, you can access any resource on your network.

UNC path names can be used from a command prompt to perform tasks that don't require mapped drive letters, as shown in Figure 3.41. Some executables and commands require a mapped drive letter to operate correctly—or at all. This problem will usually be reported as a DOS error that refers to disk access. If your UNC path has spaces in it, you must enclose the entire path in quotation marks, or Windows will treat the information after the space as parameters for the program before the space.

```
MS-DOS Prompt
Auto

C:\batch>dir \\admin_exec\public\st1.7\*.txt
 Directory of \\admin_exec\public\st1.7

LICENSE  TXT        27,789  08-11-97  5:17p LICENSE.TXT
RELN17   TXT        20,827  01-13-98 10:02a reln17.txt
RELNOTES TXT        20,825  08-11-97  4:16p RELNOTES.TXT
         3 file(s)         69,441 bytes
         0 dir(s)

C:\batch>copy \\admin_exec\public\st1.7\reln17.txt c:\batch\reln17.txt
        1 file(s) copied

C:\batch>ren \\admin_exec\public\st1.7\reln17.txt reln17a.txt
```

Figure 3.41

UNC path names also work from a command prompt. This avoids having to map drive letters to all network resources.

Note

A UNC name doesn't require a drive-letter assignment. Windows 95 takes full advantage of network connectivity using UNC names so that you can connect to a remote directory or printer share without having to map a drive letter to it. However, for MS-DOS-based applications that require that a drive letter or port be used, you can map a drive letter to a shared directory or a port to a shared printer.

The UNC can also specify the full path to a file in a subdirectory of a file share. For example, to share the entire C drive on the computer ADMIN_EXEC, the share name CDRIVE could be created for the root directory c:\. To specify the directory c:\windows\system using a UNC path with these share names, use \\ADMIN_EXEC\CDRIVE\windows\system.

Tip

Add a dollar sign ($) to the end of the share name to prevent the share name from being visible to another computer through a browser, such as Network Neighborhood. The share name CDRIVE$, for example, wouldn't be visible to users browsing the computer ADMIN_EXEC. Even though it isn't visible, users will still be able to access it by typing `\\ADMIN_EXEC\CDRIVE$` (see Figure 3.42). This follows the "out of sight, out of mind" rule: If people can't see the shared folder, they won't try to access it. You should still take all normal precautions to prevent other people from accessing these files by assigning passwords or access permissions to users.

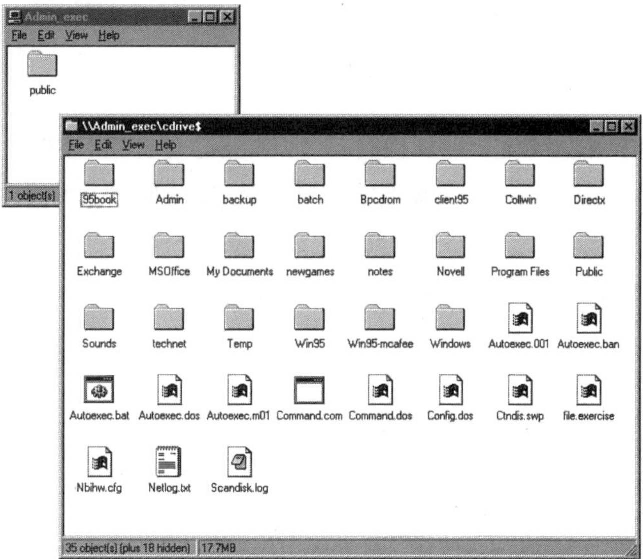

Figure 3.42

You can hide shared resources from a server's share list by adding a $ to the end of the share name. Anyone who knows the share name can still attempt access through the UNC name.

All Windows 95 functions support using a UNC name, including the Run option on the Start menu and the command prompt. NetWare servers, like Windows NT servers, can be accessed through a UNC name. Instead of using the share name, substitute the volume name to access a NetWare server.

> Share names in Windows 95 can be as long as the involved protocols and user interfaces will allow. However, NetBIOS names can be only 15 characters long and shouldn't contain spaces. Therefore, when establishing share names on your servers, keep them short, don't use spaces, and use 15 or fewer characters so that Windows 95 can view the names from within Network Neighborhood when browsing for network resources. Some network printers might require 14 or fewer characters.
>
> The actual folder name under Windows NT and Windows 95 can still be a long filename (LFN) of up to 255 characters. Only the share name needs to follow the guidelines just mentioned. For example, your TOPSECRET$ share can be on a folder named My Top Secret Projects.

How Everything Fits Together: The Windows 95 Network Model

For practice on this material, refer to Exercise 3.3.

Now that you have seen how to configure the different network components within Windows 95, you will examine how each component you have been working with fits into the larger Windows 95 Network model.

Windows 95 has a modular, layered architecture. Each layer needs to communicate directly only with the layers immediately above and below it. Therefore, a component of the architecture such as a network adapter driver needs to be compatible only with the layer adjacent to it—the device driver interface, in this case. Thus, only one version of the network adapter driver needs to be created, because the driver will work with any of the Windows 95-compatible transport protocols.

The modularity of the Windows 95 networking architecture means that components can be interchanged and new components added easily, as long as the component can communicate properly with the adjacent layers. This interoperability is made easier by the use of programming interfaces that are written by

Microsoft and that contain a standardized set of commands and procedures that the adjacent layers can use to intercommunicate.

Following are the layers of the Windows 95 networking architecture, starting from the topmost layer:

1. Application interface
2. Network providers
3. Installable File System (IFS) Manager
4. Redirectors and services
5. Transport Programming Interface
6. Transport driver protocols
7. Device driver interface

Application Interface

The application interface layer contains two interfaces that allow an application to access the Windows 95 networking services. The application interfaces contain a standardized set of commands and procedures that an application can use to communicate with the network provider. This lets a developer create an application that works with any Windows 95 network protocol, because the application needs to be able to communicate directly only with the application interfaces.

The two interfaces functioning at this layer are the Win32 Print Applicator Programming Interface (API) and the Win32 WinNet Interface. The Win32 Print API handles network printing-related functions. The Win32 WinNet Interface handles all other networking functions not performed by the Win32 Print API. In addition, the WinNet interface provides a high-level set of browsing APIs used to access resources, such as directories, printers, and other network resources.

Network Providers

The network providers include a more network-specific programming interface for access to networking services. Windows 95 ships with three network providers, but other third-party network providers written for Windows 95 can be incorporated into a third-party network protocol.

The network providers allow access to shared files and printers and provide browsing services. Here are the network providers included with Windows 95:

- Windows Network Provider/Print Provider
- NetWare Network Provider/Print Provider
- WinNet16

The Windows Network Provider/Print Provider is a 32-bit provider that supports networking products that use the Server Message Block (SMB) file-sharing protocol. It can be used by both WIN16 and WIN32 applications.

The NetWare Provider/Print Provider is a 32-bit provider for use with NetWare networks that use the NetWare Core Protocol (NCP) file-sharing service. The NetWare Provider/Print Provider can be accessed by both 16-bit and 32-bit applications on a NetWare network.

The WinNet16 network provider can be used for backward compatibility with older network applications that require it.

IFS Manager

Installable File Systems (IFSs) can be dynamically loaded into memory to handle files in Windows 95. Examples of Installable File Systems are the Compact Disk File System (CDFS) and the Virtual File Allocation Table (VFAT).

The IFS Manager handles communication between the various IFSs, the network provider, and the network redirectors and services. Each redirector and service is simply treated as an IFS even through it might refer to, or be referred to by, other file systems elsewhere on your network.

Redirectors and Services

At this layer, information passing between the application and transport protocol layers is processed and converted to the proper data format for the next layer. The redirectors and services residing at this layer each perform a specific function on the information.

Redirectors

The *redirector* or client maps network names used by an application to network device names to which the transport can send the information.

Windows 95 includes the following two redirectors:

- Microsoft Networking Redirector, used with SMB-based networks
- NetWare Networking Redirector, used with NCP-based networks

These redirectors or clients and their configuration are discussed in the earlier section "Installing Clients." That section details options for both the Microsoft Networks client and the NetWare Networks client.

Services

Networking *services* are individual dynamic link libraries (DLLs) or virtual device drivers (VxDs) that can be loaded into memory to provide certain networking services. These networking services are installed using the Add button on the Network icon in Control Panel.

Services are discussed in detail in the earlier section "Installing Services."

Transport Programming Interface

The *Transport Programming Interface* provides a standardized set of commands to let the network redirector and services send information to the underlying transport protocols. It is responsible for opening and maintaining sessions with the Transport Programming Interface on other computers on the network.

The Transport Programming Interface allows the services of the upper layers of the networking architecture to communicate with any of the Windows 95-compatible transport protocols, such as NetBEUI, TCP/IP, and IPX/SPX.

Windows 95 has two Transport Programming Interfaces:

- NetBIOS Interface: The Network Basic Input/Output System (NetBIOS) Interface allows NetBIOS names and commands to be passed to the transport protocol layer. Examples of NetBIOS names are computer names, share names, and workgroup names. Thus, when a Windows 95 computer connects to a computer named SERVER01 using the NetBEUI protocol, the NetBIOS interface passes instructions from the redirector to the NetBEUI protocol to start a connection with the NetBIOS computer named SERVER01. Windows 95 supports NetBIOS over all three of its major protocols.
- Windows Sockets Interface: The Windows Sockets Interface allows sockets-based applications to pass instructions back and forth to the transport protocols. Sockets are two-way communication paths between two computers. Sockets have traditionally been used with TCP/IP applications such as File Transfer Protocol (FTP), but they can be used with the IPX/SPX-compatible protocol as well.

Transport Protocols

The transport protocol is responsible for putting information in the correct format so that it can be understood by the network device to which the message is being sent.

A *transport protocol* essentially is a language that network devices use to communicate. In order for one network device, such as a computer, to communicate with another, both devices need to use the same transport protocol. In other words, they both need to speak the same language.

The following are the main communication protocols that are included with Windows 95:

- Microsoft NetBEUI
- Microsoft TCP/IP
- Microsoft IPX/SPX-compatible (NWLINK)
- Microsoft DLC

These protocols and additional Windows 95-compatible transport protocols can be installed using the Network icon in Control Panel.

Each of these protocols is discussed in depth in the earlier section "Installing Protocols."

Device Driver Interface

The *Device Driver Interface* handles communication between the transport protocol and the network card driver. This interface contains a standardized set of commands and procedures that the protocol and network card driver can use to communicate with each other. Because the protocol communicates directly only with the Device Driver Interface, it doesn't matter which network card driver is used, as long as it can understand the Device Driver Interface specifications. Therefore, a hardware vendor needs to develop only a single device driver that can be used with any Windows 95-compatible protocol.

The transport protocol and the device driver must be written to one of the three specifications supported by Windows 95:

- NDIS 3.1: This specification supports NDIS 3.x protected-mode drivers in addition to Plug and Play. Protected-mode drivers do not use conventional memory. An NDIS 3.x driver usually has a .VXD extension.
- NDIS 2: This specification is for real-mode drivers, which use conventional memory. NDIS 2 drivers usually have a .SYS or .DOS extension.
- Open Datalink Interface (ODI): Designed by Novell, ODI is similar to the NDIS 2 specification.

If your network adapter comes with only an NDIS 3.0 driver, contact the manufacturer for an updated driver. NDIS 3.x is a portable network-driver architecture designed to run on either Windows 95 or Windows NT computers.

Summary

This chapter has taken you through all the configuration options in the Network icon in Control Panel. You started with the network card and then dealt with the differences between 16-bit, 32-bit, NDIS, and ODI network card drivers.

With the network card installed, you then learned about the benefits and configuration of the different protocols included with Windows 95. Most of the material concerned the three basic protocols that can be used to communicate between Windows 95 computers: NetBEUI, IPX/SPX, and TCP/IP. Some of the protocol issues that were examined include NetBIOS and WinSock support. Other issues included routability and requirements by other network clients or services, such as the Client for NetWare Networks.

You then examined how the Microsoft Browser service works in order to maintain a list of servers on the network. You also saw that most problems with the browser service will be fixed automatically if you wait. With a list of servers on your network, you then looked at how to install File and Print Sharing services for both Microsoft and NetWare networks.

With the Clients and File and Print Sharing services installed, you saw how to access resources without mapping drive letters. This was accomplished through the Universal Naming Convention (UNC) names. This chapter concluded with an overview of the Windows 95 network model, which reviewed the topics covered in this chapter.

Chapter 4 deals with the management of resources, including those that are accessed through the File and Print Sharing services. Chapter 5 deals with additional configuration of the network clients.

Exercises

These exercises make the following assumptions about your Windows 95 installation and components:

- Your computer has a clean Windows 95 installation. If you are using a computer connected to a LAN, record all settings in the Network icon in Control Panel, and check with your LAN Administrator before proceeding.
- You are on some type of network, and you have a network card in your computer. If you don't, most of the exercises will work with the Microsoft dial-up adapter.
- You have a Windows NT Server installed on your network. A Novell NetWare server can be substituted for most of the exercises.

Exercise 3.1: Installing Network Components

This exercise takes you through the installation of several network components. You will install two network adapters and two protocols and configure your computer name.

1. Boot Windows 95 on your computer.
2. At the Windows 95 logon, log on as usual.
3. Select Start, Settings, Control Panel.
4. Select and open the Network icon.
5. You should see the Configuration tab by default. If you have a Plug and Play card whose drivers are included in Windows 95, you will already have the following items loaded:
    - Client for Microsoft Networks
    - Client for NetWare Networks
    - Your network card

- NetBEUI
- IPX/SPX-compatible protocol

If you have all of these items, skip to step 8.

6. To add your network card, click the Add button and select Adapter. Click the Add button again. (Check the documentation that came with your network card to see if there are any special setup requirements to make your card work with Windows 95.)

7. Locate the manufacturer of your network card in the manufacturers list, and the card model or type in the network device list. By default, Windows will install all of the software mentioned in step 5 when a network card is added.

8. Select Client for NetWare Networks and click the Remove button. Select IPX/SPX Compatible protocol and click Remove.

9. If Windows 95 didn't install all the client software for you, click the Add button, select a protocol, and click Add. Choose the NetBEUI protocol from Microsoft, and then click OK. Click the Add button again, select Client, and click Add. Choose the Client for Microsoft Networks, and then click OK.

10. Click the Add button, select Adapter, and click Add. Select the Dial-up Adapter from Microsoft, and then click OK. The Dial-up Adapter is used by Dial-up Networking as a modem interface. Click the Add button, select Protocol, and click Add. Select Microsoft's TCP/IP, and click OK. This will set up TCP/IP and the Dial-up Adapter for dialing to a TCP/IP network such as the Internet.

11. Select the Identification tab of the Network dialog box. Unless you changed this during the installation, it should have your name as the computer name and part of your company name as the workgroup name. Give your computer a single-word name of 15 or fewer characters. Set your workgroup

continues

Exercise 3.1: Continued

name to match the domain name of your Windows NT Server. Click the OK button to close this window.

12. Close the Network dialog box by clicking OK. Windows 95 will then attempt to copy the network software from the original installation media and prompt you to reboot the computer. Reboot.

After rebooting, you should receive no error messages from Windows 95 regarding your network card. If you do receive an error message, refer to the card manufacturer's documentation to resolve the error.

Exercise 3.2: Enabling User-Level Access Control

In this exercise, you will modify your access control settings. You will switch your computer from share-level control to user-level.

1. Select Start, Settings, Control Panel.
2. Select and open the Network icon in Control Panel.
3. Select the Access Control tab, and choose the User-level access control radio button. Type your domain name in the space provided. If you use a server name instead of the domain name, Windows 95 will change the setting for you when it connects to the server.
4. Click OK to close the Network dialog box. Windows 95 will prompt you to reboot. Reboot.

To see the effects of User-level access control, you must share a network resource. You will do so in Chapter 4.

Exercise 3.3: Connecting to Servers Using UNC Path Names

In this exercise, you will connect to a server and access a resource without mapping a drive letter to the resource. This exercise requires that there be files in your Windows NT server's NETLOGON share. The NETLOGON share is actually *win_root*\SYSTEM32\REPL\IMPORT\SCRIPTS on NT Server's local hard drive, where *win_root* is the WINDOWS directory, usually WINNT on Windows NT 4.0 servers.

1. Start Windows 95 and log on to your network. If you cancel the logon dialog, Windows 95 won't start your network client. This applies even if you aren't logging on to a domain.

2. Double-click the Network Neighborhood icon on your desktop. This should show you all the servers in your domain. If it doesn't, select the Entire Network icon and your Domain icon within.

3. Double-click your server. This will open a window listing all the shared resources on the server.

4. Double-click the NETLOGON directory to open it.

5. Close the NETLOGON directory while holding down the Shift key. This will close all the windows back to the desktop.

6. To access the same folder without opening the Network Neighborhood, select Start, Run, type `\\`*`server_name`*`\NETLOGON`, and click OK. The NETLOGON window should appear. Close the window.

7. To see the contents of the NETLOGON window from a command prompt, open a command prompt and type `DIR \\`*`server_name`*`\NETLOGON`.

Exercise 3.4 Installing the Client for NetWare Networks

In this exercise, you will install the NetWare client that is provided with Windows 95.

1. Select Start, Settings, Control Panel.

2. Select and open the Network icon.

3. Click the Add button, select Client, and click Add. Select Microsoft from the manufacturers list and Client for NetWare Networks from the Network Component list. Click OK to close the dialog.

continues

Exercise 3.4 Continued

4. Windows 95 should automatically install the IPX/SPX-compatible protocol for you. Confirm that your Primary Network Logon is still the Client for Microsoft Networks. Click OK to close the Network dialog box. Windows 95 will then attempt to copy the network software from the original installation media and prompt you to reboot the computer. Reboot.

After rebooting, you should see any NetWare servers that are on your network in the Network Neighborhood. If they don't appear, Windows 95 might have defaulted to the wrong IPX/SPX frame type. Windows 95 will always try to default the frame type to 802.2. If you aren't using 802.2 on your network, you can force Windows 95 to use the same frame type that you are using. To force Windows 95 to use a specific frame type, you have to choose it. In the Network dialog box, choose the Configuration tab, choose IPX/SPX-compatible Protocol, and select the Advanced tab.

Exercise 3.5: Installing the File and Print Services for Microsoft Networks

In this exercise, you will install the file and print services for Windows 95.

1. Select Start, Settings, Control Panel.

2. Select and open the Network icon.

3. You can install the File and Print Sharing services for your Primary Network Logon by clicking the File and Print Sharing button, placing checks in both check boxes, and clicking OK.

   The other way to install the file and print services is to click the Add button, choose Services, and click Add. Then select Microsoft as a manufacturer and File and Print Services for Microsoft Networks. Then close the dialog by clicking OK.

4. Close the Network dialog box by clicking OK. Windows 95 will then attempt to copy the network software from the original installation media and will prompt you to reboot the computer. Reboot.

After rebooting, you should see a Sharing option on the context menu when you click folders. Chapter 4 has exercises that illustrate the process of sharing and managing folders.

Exercise 3.6: Browsing the Network

This exercise examines some of the aspects of network browsing with Windows 95.

1. When opening the Network Neighborhood's Entire Network icon, you should see a complete list of domains and workgroups available on your network. This might mean that you see only your domain.

2. Change your workgroup name in the Network icon of Control Panel. If you aren't sure how to do this, consult Exercise 3.1, step 11. Change your workgroup name to MYGROUP and reboot.

3. Immediately after rebooting, go to the Network Neighborhood's Entire Network icon. You should see your workgroup only. If you get an error, you proceeded a little too fast.

4. Check the Entire Network icon on the Windows NT server machine. You should see your workgroup in the list at the server.

It might take as long as 15 minutes before the domain shows up on the Windows 95 computer. You have to wait for the next workgroup announcement. The Windows 95 computer (having just been made the master browser) announces immediately, but the domain will not make an announcement until its next scheduled cycle.

Review Questions

The following questions will test your knowledge of the information in this chapter.

1. You are responsible for connecting Windows 95 to a heterogeneous network. You're running a number of different network operating systems on this large network, and you want to be sure that Windows 95 is compatible with them. Windows 95 includes software to support which three of the following networks?

   A. Banyan VINES

   B. DEC Pathworks

   C. Novell NetWare

   D. Apple AppleShare

2. Jason installs a network adapter card on a computer running Windows 95. When he does this, Windows 95 automatically installs two protocols for this card. Which two protocols are installed by default when the first network adapter driver is installed?

   A. AppleTalk

   B. NetBEUI

   C. TCP/IP

   D. IPX/SPX-compatible

3. You want to install Windows 95 on a Novell NetWare network. Which two of the following are advantages of Microsoft Client for NetWare Networks as opposed to Novell's NETX workstation software?

   A. Microsoft Client for NetWare Networks lets you use TSR applications loaded from DOS.

   B. Microsoft Client for NetWare Networks runs in protected mode and thus doesn't use any conventional memory.

C. Microsoft Client for NetWare Networks allows additional network clients to be used at the same time.

D. Microsoft Client for NetWare Networks supports the ArcNet protocols.

4. In a training class you are teaching, you explain to end-users how to use UNC to access resources on the network. You provide this example to the class: What is the full UNC path for a file named test.bat in a directory named BATCH located in a share named PUBLIC on a server named FREDSPC? Select the correct answer.

   A. \\PUBLIC\BATCH\test.bat

   B. \\FREDSPC\BATCH\test.bat

   C. \\FREDSPC\PUBLIC\BATCH\test.bat

   D. None of these

5. In your office, you have a single network with multiple network protocols running on it. Because users might need to log on to several networks at boot time, you want to use the Unified Logon feature in Windows 95. To use Unified Logon, the ______ for all networks must be the same.

   A. Network operating systems

   B. Topologies

   C. Network protocols

   D. Passwords

6. Windows 95 has a modular, layered architecture. Which two of the following are interfaces functioning at the Windows 95 Application Interface layer?

   A. Win32 WinNet Applicator Programming Interface

   B. WinNet 16

   C. HP JetAdmin

   D. Win32 Print Applicator Programming Interface

7. Susan prepares for a presentation describing the Windows 95 network architecture. One of the bullet points is this: A _______ maps network names used by an application to a physical network device name. Fill in the blank.

   A. Device driver

   B. Redirector

   C. Requestor

   D. Transport interface

8. Which three of the following are layers in the Windows 95 networking architecture?

   A. Transport Programming Interface

   B. Internal File System Manager

   C. Device Driver Interface

   D. Network Providers

9. Isabel is configuring her Windows 95 computer with the TCP/IP protocol. As she fills out the properties for the protocol, she comes across a blank for the DNS entry. What does DNS stand for?

   A. Downloadable Network Share

   B. DOS-Node Server

   C. Domain Name Service

   D. Domain Network Server

10. You run a network with protocols that support NetBIOS. The ______ registers and resolves NetBIOS names to IP addresses.

   A. DNS Server

   B. IFS Manager

   C. Network Adapter Card

   D. WINS Server

11. Chuck is setting up a network to use user-level security. From the following list, choose the two places where the user list can be stored.

    A. Windows NT domain

    B. Windows 95 home directory

    C. NetWare bindery server

    D. Banyan VINES server

12. To access the Internet, you need to use Windows 95's Dial-up Adapter and associated software. From the following list, choose three items that you must have before setting up Windows 95 to access the Internet via a dial-up connection.

    A. ISP account

    B. Modem

    C. Gateway

    D. DNS information

13. While stationed at the company help desk, you receive a call from a user accessing the Internet. He asks what a fully qualified domain name is. From the following list, choose the item that would *not* meet this criteria.

    A. `www.microsoft.com`

    B. `www3.iquest.net`

    C. `www.microsoft_com`

    D. `www.mcp.com\newriders`

14. Name the protocol supported by Windows 95 that is used only for communicating with certain network interface printers and mainframe systems. (It isn't used for peer-to-peer networking of Windows 95 computers.)

   A. TCP/IP

   B. DLC

   C. IPX/SPX

   D. NetBIOS

15. You have Windows 95 installed on a computer connected to a network running only one network operating system (NOS). A user calls and says she can't browse network resources using Network Neighborhood. Which NOS could you be running that doesn't support browser services?

   A. Novell NetWare 3.12

   B. Banyan VINES

   C. Windows NT

   D. None of these

16. Stuart is attaching his Windows 95 computer to another Windows 95 computer using the Microsoft Network. He wants to provide access from one computer to the other so that each computer has access to files and printers on either machine. What must he do to enable this in Windows 95?

   A. Set up user-level security.

   B. Disable File and Print Sharing for Microsoft Networks.

   C. Set up share-level security.

   D. All of these.

17. You are asked to connect 10 Windows 95 computers to a Novell NetWare network. From the following list, choose the two components or features that Windows 95 has for NetWare networks.

    A. The capability to install File and Print Sharing for NetWare Networks with File and Print Sharing for Microsoft Networks

    B. Share-level support of File and Print Sharing for NetWare Networks

    C. IPX/SPX-compatible protocol

    D. 32-bit Client for NetWare Networks

18. As you instruct a user on how to configure a peer-to-peer network with five connected Windows 95 computers, you use the term "Windows 95 server" several times. After you finish, he asks you what a Windows 95 server is. What do you tell him?

    A. A computer that is the Primary Domain Controller (PDC) on the LAN

    B. A computer running Windows 95 that has the Enable Windows 95 Server Registry option turned on

    C. A Windows 95 computer that has the File and Print Sharing service enabled

    D. A computer running Windows 95 that performs as an application and database server for the LAN

19. Windows 95's modular architecture includes the Installable File System (IFS) Manager. The IFS Manager manages communication between which three of the following?

    A. The Miniport Driver

    B. The various Installable File Systems

    C. The Network Provider

    D. The network redirectors and services

20. Martina has been told that she can run multiple network clients under Windows 95, but she's having problems getting this feature to work on her system. She calls you and asks you to help her. What would be the best question to ask her to start diagnosing her problem?

    A. Do you have protocols for IPX/SPX set up?

    B. Is Windows 95 set up to handle user profiles?

    C. Is there a Primary Domain Controller (PDC) established on a Windows 95 Server?

    D. Are all the network clients 32-bit clients?

21. The naming standards for two of the following items are as follows: The name is limited to 15 characters, embedded spaces are not recommended, and it can contain these special characters:

    `! @ # $ % ^ & ( ) - _ ' { } ~ .`

    A. User's full name

    B. Default user's name

    C. Computer name

    D. Workgroup name

    E. Computer description

22. Windows 95 includes several networking protocols. Which three of the following networking protocols included with Windows 95 are Plug and Play enabled?

    A. Ethernet

    B. TCP/IP

    C. NetBEUI

    D. Token Ring

    E. IPX/SPX

23. You are asked to set up a standalone computer for several people to access at different times during the day. Which level of security would be used for a standalone computer with multiple users, each of whom has different Windows 95 preferences and Desktops?

    A. Windows 95 access control

    B. Unified logon process

    C. Windows 95 logon security

    D. Share-level security

    E. User-level security

24. Which level of security would be used to base the access rights to shared resources on the Windows 95 computer using a user accounts list stored on a Novell NetWare server?

    A. Windows 95 access control

    B. Unified logon process

    C. Windows 95 logon security

    D. Share-level security

    E. User-level security

25. Which level of security would be used to base the access rights to shared resources on the Windows 95 computer on a password-assigned basis?

    A. Windows 95 access control

    B. Unified logon process

    C. Windows 95 logon security

    D. Share-level security

    E. User-level security

Review Answers

1. A, B, C. Windows 95 does not ship with software that allows it to connect to an AppleShare network.

2. B, D. NetBEUI and IPX/SPX-compatible are the two protocols that are installed by default, to be used with the two default clients, Client for Microsoft Networks and Client for NetWare Networks.

3. B, C. Microsoft's client doesn't let you use TSRs that require the network to be loaded, nor does it provide support for ArcNet.

4. C. The format of the UNC path name is

   ```
   \\server\resource or share name\[path]\[filename]
   ```

5. D. To provide a unified logon, the user name and passwords for all clients must be the same.

6. A, D. WinNet 16 is used only with 16-bit real-mode drivers, and HP JetAdmin is a service.

7. B. The redirector is responsible for mapping names to physical devices.

8. A, C, D. Internal File System Manager is not part of the OSI model.

9. C. Domain Name Service.

10. D. Windows Internet Name Service is responsible for maintaining the NetBIOS-to-IP-address mapping table.

11. A, C. Windows NT domains and NetWare 3.x or bindery servers are the only locations where Windows 95 can retrieve the list of user names.

12. A, B, C. DNS information isn't required, but you will have to know the IP address of all the servers you want to visit.

13. C. `server.domain.root\[path]\[filename]` is the proper syntax of a fully qualified domain name.

14. B. DLC is not used for peer-to-peer networking in Windows 95.

15. B. The Banyan client that ships with Windows 95 doesn't support network browsing of Banyan VINES servers.

16. C. The File and Print Sharing service must be running, and the network doesn't have a valid security provider for user-level security.

17. C, D. Only one File and Print Sharing service can be installed at a time, and the NetWare File and Print Sharing service requires user-level access control.

18. C. Any computer that runs File and Print Sharing services can be considered a server.

19. B, C, D. The IFS Manager is a boundary layer between the Network Provider and the redirectors and services (as well as other Installable File Systems).

20. D. Many 16-bit and real-mode network clients require that no other clients be installed.

21. C, D. This restriction is for a NetBIOS name, and both the computer and workgroup names are NetBIOS names.

22. B, C, E. Token Ring and Ethernet are network topologies, not protocols.

23. A. There is no "true" security. Windows 95 will maintain a list of users who have logged into the system by creating a list of .PWL files in the Windows directory.

24. E. User-level security draws on a list of users that is stored on a server on your network.

25. D. Share-level security assigns passwords to resources as a means of controlling access.

Answers to Test Yourself Questions at Beginning of Chapter

1. IPX/SPX, NetBEUI, and TCP/IP are Plug and Play enabled. Microsoft NetBEUI and IPX/SPX are installed by default.
2. User-level security uses pass-through authentication.
3. Yes, he can do this, but he must install user-level security.
4. IPX/SPX. No, you can't change this. However, you can use additional protocols with this, but only IPX/SPX will be used to talk to the NetWare server.
5. Possible answers: Long filenames aren't supported by NetWare by default; OS/2 Name Space must be added; users of Windows 95 can reassign print queue assignments; administrators might feel a lack of control over resources because Windows 95's graphical user interface (GUI) makes it easy to change drive mappings.
6. User-level security. No, only directory-level rights can be set up under Windows 95.
7. Set up a primary domain on the Windows NT server.
8. Load OS/2 Name Space (OS2.NAM) on the server.
9. Universal Naming Convention. Computer name and share name. No drive-letter assignment is needed.
10. Browse list.
11. Enabled: May Be Master.
12. Advantage: User-level security requires the user to authenticate access against an account list stored on a Windows NT or NetWare server. Disadvantage: User-level security can be set up only on an NT or NetWare server. Advantage: Share-level security lets two networked Windows 95 workstations share resources using passwords. Disadvantage: The share-level password can be used by anyone to gain access. In other words, no authentication is needed to access the resource.
13. Yes. It is adjacent to the Application Interface and the IFS Manager.
14. Gateways help route TCP/IP messages to remote destinations.
15. Every computer requires at least an IP address and a subnet mask. If they have to cross network segments, they also must have a gateway address to reach the remote computers, and it is nice to give them the address of a DNS server to resolve the remote computer names to IP addresses.

Chapter 4

Configuring and Managing Resource Access

This chapter helps prepare you for the exam by covering the following objectives:

- Assign access permissions for shared folders. Methods include:
  - Passwords
  - User permissions
  - Group permissions
- Create, share, and monitor resources. Resources include:
  - File shares
  - Network printers
  - Shared fax modem
  - Unimodem/V
- Set up user environments using profiles and System policies
- Back up and restore data
- Manage hard disks. Tasks include:
  - Dealing with long filenames
  - Partitioning
  - Disk compression
- Establish application environments for Microsoft MS-DOS applications

Test Yourself! Before reading this chapter, test yourself to determine how much study time you will need to devote to this section.

1. Cindy calls you from marketing to tell you she just created a file in Microsoft Excel 95 and saved it with the long filename `Marketing Budget.XLS`. She copied the file to her laptop, which runs Windows 95, but the version of Excel on the laptop was released prior to Windows 95. She says she can't find the `Marketing Budget.XLS` file. What is one possible short filename you can tell her to look for?
2. You migrate to Windows 95 on a system that has a 1-GB hard drive. You want to compress part of the drive, but not all of it, to conserve space. What is the maximum size of a compressed volume using the Windows 95 DriveSpace program?
3. Jason is setting up a backup schedule for several of his machines. Name four storage media types supported by Windows 95. What utility is included with Windows 95 to help Jason back up his data?
4. Jennifer runs an MS-DOS-based application in Windows 95. She wants to take advantage of Windows 95 32-bit protected-mode driver support, preemptive multitasking, and increased conventional memory. Which mode should Jennifer run her DOS application in to use these features?
5. You are working at a help desk when you receive a call from a user. He is having difficulty running an MS-DOS application in a DOS virtual machine (VM). Although you can't provide specific reasons why his application isn't running, you can offer some general reasons why a DOS application might not run properly in Windows 95. Name two possible reasons why a DOS application might not run in a VM.
6. You're conducting a training session that teaches users how to run applications in Windows 95. You're asked to describe the way Windows 95 runs MS-DOS applications. What are the three ways MS-DOS applications can run in Windows 95?
7. Blake is migrating from Windows 3.1 to Windows 95. He wants to run MS-DOS applications in DOS mode under Windows 95. What are two disadvantages to running applications in DOS mode?

8. Taylor receives a general protection fault (GPF) when running a 32-bit application in Windows 95. She thought Windows 95 was exempt from GPFs. You explain to her that 32-bit applications do have GPFs, but they differ from 16-bit and DOS-based applications because they do not cause problems with other programs when you terminate them. Why is this?

9. A user says that a 16-bit application she is running in Windows 95 hangs. She doesn't know how to remedy the situation. What steps should she take to return the system to normal operations?

10. Sally likes to run multiple applications simultaneously in Windows 95. She has one 32-bit application running, one MS-DOS application running, and two 16-bit applications running. How many virtual machines is Windows 95 running? Explain.

11. As an administrator, you need to set up a training classroom. All student computers running Windows 95 on the network should have the same default setting. This default setting should be invoked each time the computer boots, regardless of any previous changes made by a user. Name two ways you can set up these computers to use a default setting at each boot-up.

12. A user asks how to modify her user profile. She's running a Windows 95 computer that is not connected to a network. What general steps should she take?

13. Jill wants to create two user profiles for her computer, one named WORK and the other named GAMES. How can she enable user profiles on her computer?

14. What is the default name of the System policy file used by Windows 95? Where is this file stored when a user is using share-level security? Where is this file stored when a user is working with user-level security?

15. Stan asks you to explain the System Policy Editor and why it is useful. Name two features of the System Policy Editor that help you administer Windows 95 workstations.

Answers are located at the end of the chapter...

Resources are items that provide information, that are of value, or that can be used or consumed. In Windows 95, resources include files and directories on your hard drive, printers, modems, processors, and memory. These objects can be utilized locally on your computer, or they can be utilized by others across your network. These resources can be configured in a number of ways to change how they operate, and they can be made available to other computers on your network.

This chapter examines how your computers operate, how they can be protected, and how their resources can be shared with others on your network. The topics discussed include the following:

- Methods for assigning access permissions to shared folders:
    - Passwords
    - User permissions
    - Group permissions
- Creating, sharing, and monitoring resources, including:
    - Remote file shares
    - Network printers
    - Shared fax modem
    - Unimodem/V devices
- Setting up user environments using profiles and System policies.
- Backing up and restoring data.
- Managing hard disks, which includes the following tasks:
    - Long filenames
    - Partitioning
    - Disk compression

- Establishing application environments for Microsoft MS-DOS applications.

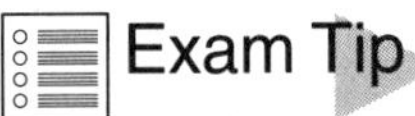

You are likely to be tested on the following:

- The difference between assigning access to resources when the computer is set to Share-level Access Control and when it is set to User-level Access Control
- The requirements that must be met to implement User-level Access Control
- The differences between implicit and explicit permissions on shared and not shared folders
- Granting access to folders using both the Microsoft File and Print Sharing service and the NetWare File and Print Sharing service
- Checking who is connected to your shared folders
- Using print spool settings to increase printing efficiency when printing over a network
- The requirements for sharing a fax modem
- The benefits of the Unimodem/V driver\
- How Roaming Profiles are implemented in both Windows NT and Novell NetWare environments
- Where System policy files should be stored and how they are created
- ypes of restrictions that can be implemented through System policies
- Benefits of implementing Hardware Profiles
- Types of media that BACKUP can use
- Benefits of disk compression
- Differences between FAT16 and FAT32
- Differences between DriveSpace and DriveSpace 3

continues

- Processes that corrupt or damage long filenames
- How Windows 95 uses virtual machines to provide stability for MS-DOS–based applications
- How to increase MS-DOS compatibility through modification of PIF settings

Assigning Access Permissions for Shared Folders

Later in this chapter, you will learn how to share folders and other resources. This section discusses the different types of security that can be implemented for shared resources. Assigned access permissions for shared resources can include the following:

- .Passwords
- User permissions
- Group permissions

Each of these security methods has a place on your network. The following sections examine them in more detail.

Passwords

Passwords are the simplest access control method. This method relies on each resource being assigned a password, which is then given to users requiring access. This method has several disadvantages (discussed later in this section), but it requires no additional services from the network.

To enable the password security method, you have to enable the Share-level Access Control in the Network control panel. This is the default setting for Windows 95. After the Share-level Access Control is enabled, any resource you want to present to the network gives you the opportunity to enter its password (see

Figure 4.1). For people to access this resource, you have to distribute the password to them.

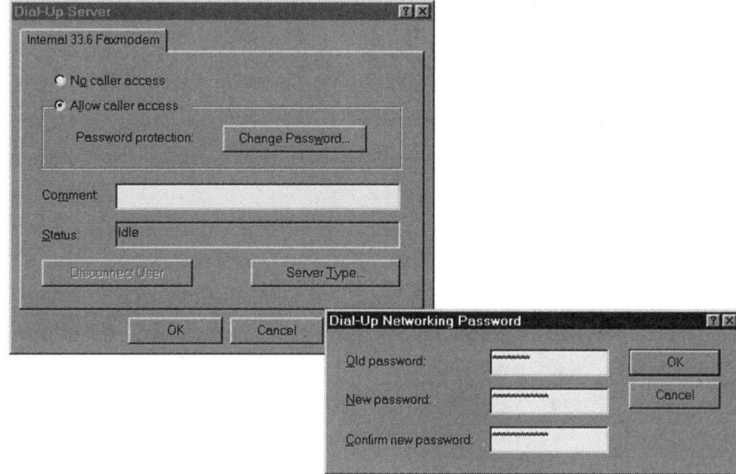

Figure 4.1

When implementing share-level security, passwords are assigned to resources.

The advantage of this security method is that it doesn't require other support devices elsewhere on the network. There are, however, two flaws with this security method. They are

- Distribution of passwords
- Maintaining control of passwords

The first disadvantage of this system is the distribution of passwords after they have been assigned. If you want other people to use this resource, you have to notify all the potential users. This notification process can be cumbersome on a large network.

The second disadvantage is maintaining control of passwords, or rather, maintaining control of access to resources. Even on a small network, the number of passwords to be remembered can quickly climb to an unmanageable level. Say you work in an office in which five employees each share five different resources from their computers. If your resources have only one password each, you have to remember and distribute the five passwords for your five resources. Five passwords are not unmanageable, but you also have up to 20 others to remember (five from each of the other four users sharing files). Remembering 25 passwords can quickly approach being unmanageable. These 25 passwords are generated from just five resources on five computers. Every user on the network that needs to access even half the resources must maintain a list of 12 passwords. Most users who need to remember this many passwords will keep them written down in a convenient place. This opens the door for a major breach in resource security.

This is the default method of security, and even though it is the easiest to implement, it also is the least secure. With just a little forethought and the commissioning of a few network resources, user permissions and group permissions can be implemented on your network, offering easier password distribution and greater security.

User Permissions

To implement user permissions, you first have to enable user-level security on your Windows 95 system. After this is accomplished, you will be able to share resources with individuals on your network according to each user's network name. This requires access to additional network services, but eventually it simplifies the entire process.

To enable user-level security, open the Network control panel and select the Access Control tab. When choosing User-level Access Control, you also have to supply the name of a security provider. The security provider can be any of the following:

- Microsoft Windows NT Domain
- Microsoft Windows NT Server
- Microsoft Windows NT Workstation
- Novell NetWare 3.x or 4.x Server

The security provider is responsible for supplying a list of users when you want to share a resource (see Figure 4.2). It also is responsible for verifying username and password pairs for Windows 95 when users attempt to access resources.

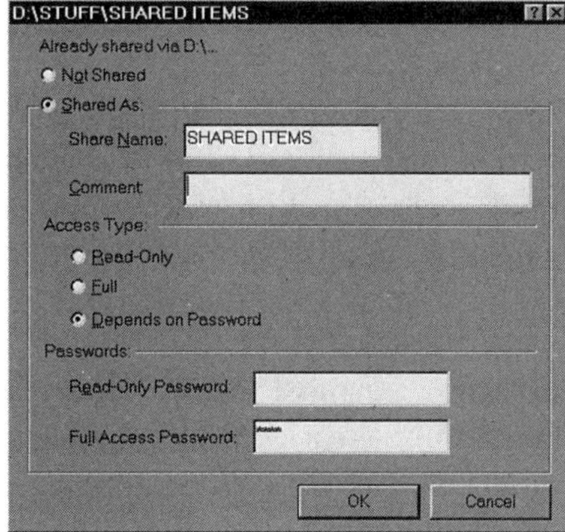

Figure 4.2

The security provider is responsible for supplying a list of users when sharing a resource.

When sharing resources, Windows 95 provides a list of users to whom you might grant access. You can select from the list which users you want to grant access to. These users don't need to provide any additional information before accessing the resource. When a user attempts to connect to the resource, the network client passes his network username and password to the Windows 95 computer he is connecting to. The Windows 95 computer then connects to its security provider and verifies the client's username and password. When the username and password are verified, the Windows 95 computer determines what level of access has been defined for that user.

This can be performed on a user-by-user basis or in groups, as discussed next.

Group Permissions

Implementing group permissions is similar to implementing user permissions. The first step is to enable user-level security on your Windows 95 system. After user-level security is enabled, you can share information with users on the network based on their group membership in your security provider.

All the security providers listed in the preceding section also support creating groups of users. Just as you can share with other users, you can share your resources and assign permissions to groups. When a client on the network attempts to connect with your Windows 95 computer, he provides his username and password. The Windows 95 computer then connects to its security provider and checks whether the user's name and password are valid. It also checks to what groups the user belongs. If the user is a member of any groups that have access to the resource, he will be granted access.

Both user permissions and group permissions provide an important benefit—ease of implementation. If your network has a computer that can act as a security provider, you no longer have to maintain a list of passwords, for your computer or for anyone else's. To access a resource on a computer, you only need to know your username and password on the security provider. This should be your only username and password for the network.

When you assign permissions for users to a directory, these permissions are termed Explicit. Each subdirectory automatically has the same permissions applied to it. For subdirectories, however, the permissions are called Implicit or Inherited.

These Explicit and Implicit permissions enable you to control access to your directory structure on a folder-by-folder basis.

Given the directory structure C:\DATA\MYFILES, you can share the DATA directory with a group of users and can grant them read access. The read permission you grant them at this level is Explicit. Let's say you do not want the users (with the exception of your user account) to have read access to MYFILES. Initially, the MYFILES directory has Implicit permissions that are the same as the DATA directory. In the Sharing tab of the folder properties, however, you are able to change the permission list without sharing the folder, thus changing the access to subfolder MYFILES.

Now that you have examined the security methods that can be implemented, you will learn how to apply this to shared resources.

Creating, Sharing, and Monitoring Resources (Remote Resources)

Several types of resources on your Windows 95 computer can be shared with others on your network. To you, these are local resources (on your computer); to other people on your network, however, they are remote resources (on the network). The types of access that can be granted to other users depend on both the type of resource and the type of access control on your computer. Most resources are monitored with different tools, depending on the type of resource.

Resources that can be shared with other users include the following:

- Files and directories (remote file shares)
- Printers (network printers)
- Fax modems (shared or network)
- Unimodem/V devices

Before sharing folders or printers, you have to enable the File and Print Sharing services on your Windows 95 computer. These services are installed through the Network control panel. (See Chapter 3, "Installation and Configuration, Part 2: Network Components," for more information about File and Print Sharing services.) Because each resource is different, you now will examine how to create, share, and monitor each resource one at a time.

Managing Shared Files and Directories or Remote File Shares

Files and directories are among the most common items shared on Windows 95 networks. (Printers, also commonly shared, are discussed in the next section.) In dealing with shared directories, the following items will be discussed:

- Creating directories
- Sharing directories
- Monitoring or managing directories

Three basic methods can be used to create a new directory or folder on your computer. Two of the methods utilize the graphical Windows environment; one uses the DOS command prompt. In the Windows 95 GUI, open the folder in which you want to create your new folder. You can either select File, New, Folder from the menus, or you can right-click a white area of the folder and select New, Folder (see Figure 4.3). Both of these methods create a folder with a box around the folder name. The folder name is selected; to give the folder a new name, just type a name and press Enter. If you prefer to create the new folder from a command prompt, you have a choice of two commands—`MKDIR` and the shorter `MD`. If you want to create the folder in your current directory, type the following:

```
MKDIR "MY NEW FOLDER"
```

When using Windows Explorer to work with folders, the menus at the top of the window are context sensitive. They change depending on which folder is selected in the left-hand or navigation frame of the Explorer window. New folders are created within the folder selected in the navigation frame.

If you prefer not to create the folder in the current directory, you can use `CD` or `CHDIR` to change the directory. Alternatively, you can type the full path to the directory you want to create, as in the following:

```
MKDIR "D:\MY FILES\MY NEW FOLDER"
```

If there are spaces in the folder name, enclose the entire path in quotation marks as shown here.

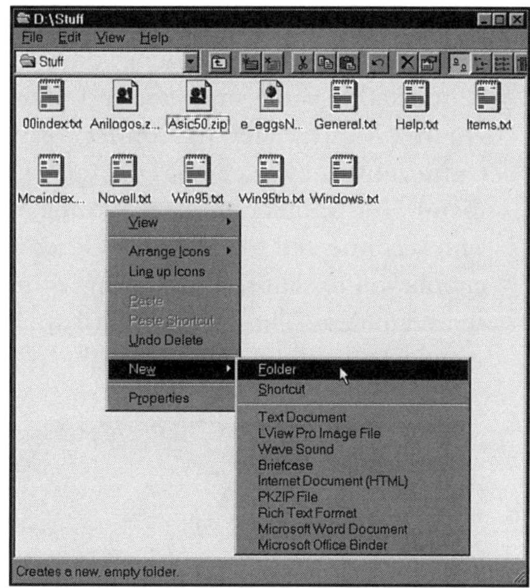

Figure 4.3

You can create a new folder by right-clicking the white area in an existing folder and selecting New, Folder.

Now that you have created a folder, you can share it by viewing the shared folder properties. You can access these properties using any of the following methods:

- Select the folder and choose Sharing from the File menu.
- Right-click the folder and choose Sharing from the context menu.
- Select the folder and choose Properties from the File menu, then select the Sharing tab.
- Right-click the folder and choose Properties from the context menu, then select the Sharing tab.

The Sharing tab enables you to assign the folder a share name. Although this name can differ from the name of the folder, it should be the same to avoid confusion. Depending on the type of access control implemented on your system, you are asked to provide either a password for the resource or a list of users allowed access to the resource.

After a folder is shared, you are not able to see who is or has been connected to your shared folders. To see who is currently connected to your shared folders, Microsoft provides Net Watcher with Windows 95. Net Watcher provides information about who is connected to your computer and what they are connected to (see Figure 4.4). The View by Connections option enables you to disconnect users by selecting Disconnect User from the Administer menu. Net Watcher also can provide a list of shared folders and who is connected to each one. Other features of Net Watcher enable you to share, stop sharing, or modify the properties of shared folders. These options are available from the Administer menu when you select View by Shared Folders (see Figure 4.5).

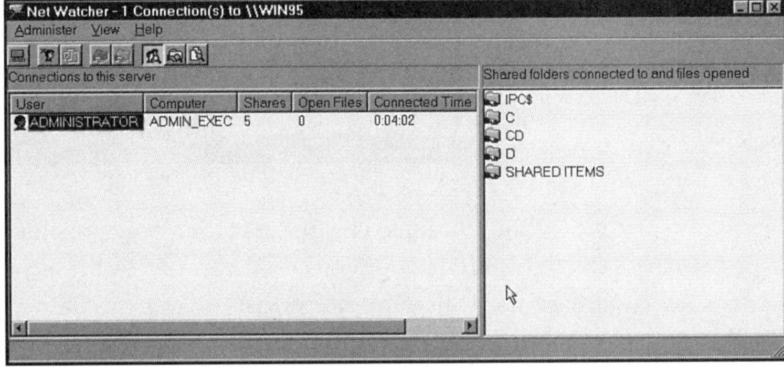

Figure 4.4

Net Watcher enables you to view users and the shared folders to which they are connected.

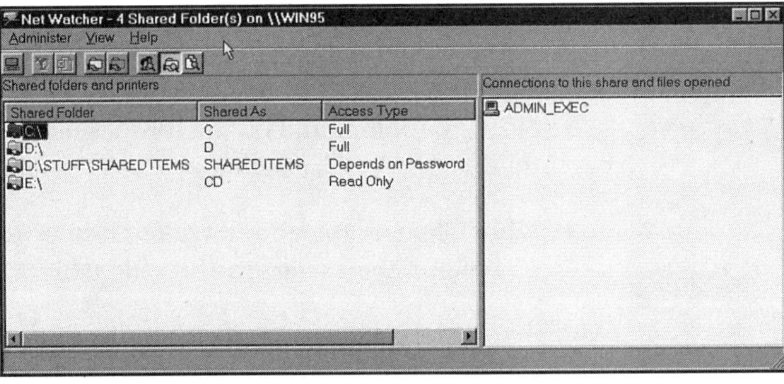

Figure 4.5

Net Watcher also enables you to share, stop sharing, or change the properties of your shared folders.

Other than Net Watcher, Microsoft does not provide utilities to see who is accessing your shared folders. This also is the only utility that can show you, in a glance, which folders are shared on your computer. Net Watcher is not able to manage shared printers; this must be done manually.

Managing Shared or Network Printers

Objective

Shared printers are on par with shared directories in Windows 95 computers. A printer is not provided for every user on the network, which makes it a perfect choice for sharing. This section examines the following:

- Creating printers
- Sharing printers
- Monitoring or managing printers

The easiest way to install a printer in Windows 95 is to plug it in and reboot. Windows 95 scans the printer port during every boot. If the printer is able to provide enough information, Windows 95 automatically installs its printer driver. If the printer is not identified by Windows 95, you can add it manually using the following steps:

1. Choose Printers from the Settings section of the Start menu.
2. In the Printers folder, double-click the Add Printer icon (see Figure 4.6).

Figure 4.6

The Add Printer icon is used to set up new printers on your computer.

3. Choose Local Printer and click Next.
4. Select your printer from the provided list, which includes most printer manufactures and types (see Figure 4.7). If your printer model is not listed, select Have Disk... to locate OEMSETUP.INF or the equivalent INF file for your new printer driver. Click Next to continue the installation.

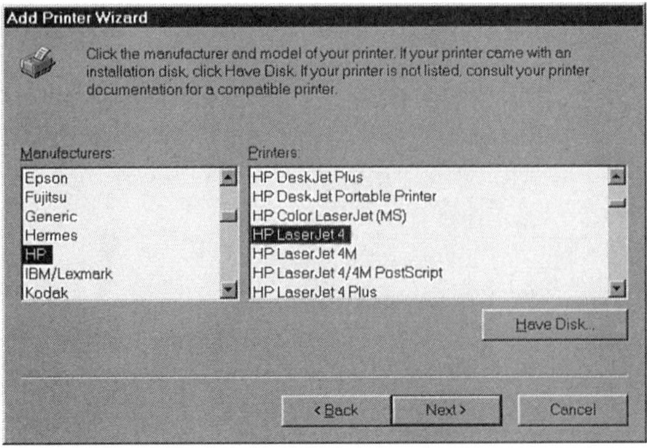

Figure 4.7

Choose the appropriate printer model from the list provided by Microsoft.

5. Select the Printer port you want to use and then click Next.
6. Choose a name for your printer. This name is the default name used when the printer is shared, but it does not have to be the name used to share the printer. Because most people tend to use the default name, the name given to your printer should be somewhat unique and descriptive. The name should help avoid confusion when people access your printer. Decide whether you want Windows 95 to use this printer as the default Windows printer. Click Next to continue.
7. Windows 95 finishes the printer installation and asks whether the test page printed properly.

After the printer is installed, you can share it by doing any of the following:

- Select the printer and choose Sharing from the File menu.
- Right-click the printer and choose Sharing from the context menu.
- Select the printer and choose Properties from the File menu, then select the Sharing tab.
- Right-click the printer and choose Properties from the context menu, then select the Sharing tab.

When the Share Printer window opens, it looks like one of the shared folders windows (for the User-level or Share-level Access Control), except it is geared to sharing printers (see Figure 4.8). You have the option to grant access to users or groups from the server or to assign a password to the printer. This window also enables you to assign a share or network name to your printer. Otherwise, it defaults to the local name you gave it.

When other Windows 95 computers first connect to your shared printer, they are required to install the drivers for it. Instead of prompting the user for the Windows 95 CD, the files are copied from a hidden Read-Only shared folder on your computer. The share is accessed through \\<server_name>\PRINTERS$ and is your <win_root>\SYSTEM folder.

Updating the printer driver on your computer does not force other users of your printer to automatically update their drivers. Anyone that has already set up your printer on their computer has to delete it and set it up again to get the updated printer drivers. This is only a problem for people who want to make use of features introduced in the new printer driver.

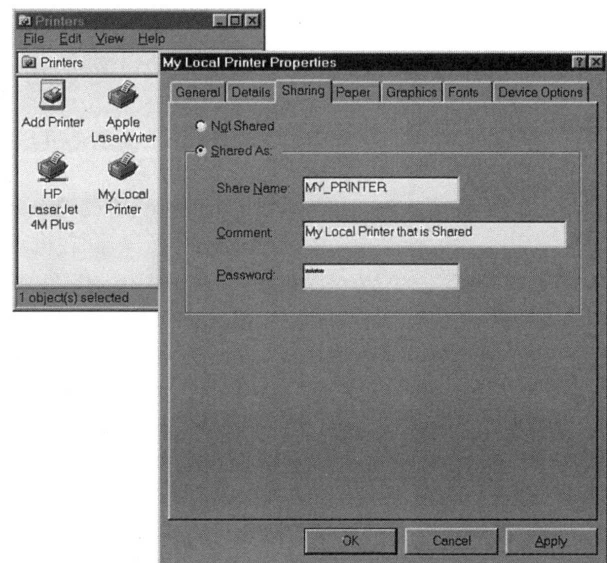

Figure 4.8

The dialog box for sharing a printer is similar to the dialog box for sharing a folder.

A printer can be managed through its icon in the Printers folder. When you double-click the printer's icon, it lists all the jobs that are spooled and waiting to be printed. At this point, you have the option to pause, cancel, or change the order of the print jobs (see Figure 4.9).

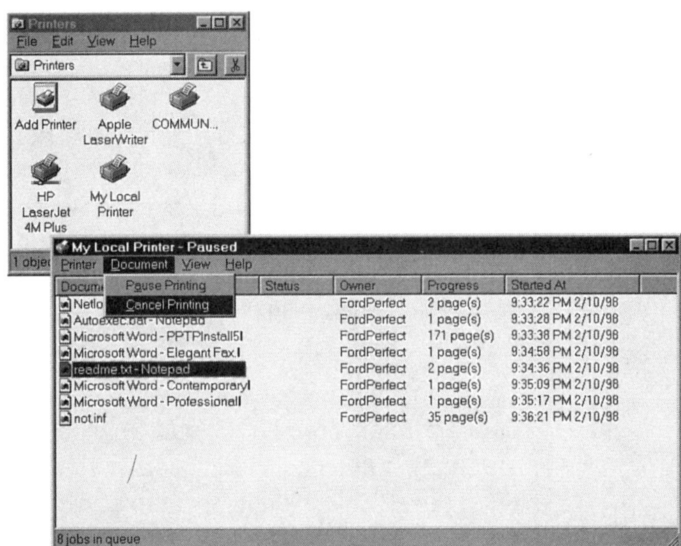

Figure 4.9

Management of print jobs is very intuitive.

Settings in the printer's Properties dialog box also affect printing performance. To view the Properties of your printer, right-click the printer's icon and select Properties. The Details tab contains a Spool Settings… button. Spool Settings options can help or can hamper the performance of the system (see Figure 4.10). Table 4.1 summarizes the options in the Spool Settings dialog box.

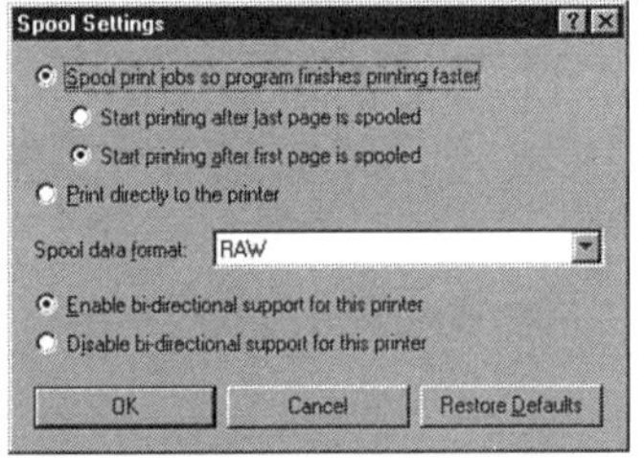

Figure 4.10

Proper spool settings can greatly improve the performance of your computer.

Table 4.1

Printer Spool Settings

Item	Description
Spool print jobs so program finishes printing faster	If you disable print spooling, your printer seems to take longer to print. Actually, the printer takes the same amount of time or less. Because it takes longer for the Printing dialog box to leave the screen, the user believes it has taken longer to print.
Start printing after last page is spooled	If you choose this setting, the total print time might increase, but the apparent print time de creases if many users print large print jobs. While one person is spooling a large print job, others on the network are able to spool and print their jobs.
Start printing after first page is spooled	If you chose this setting, large print jobs will tie up the printer from the time the first page is spooled until printing is finished. This does not prevent other, smaller jobs from being spooled. They are not able to print, however, until the larger job finishes.
Spool data format	If your network contains only Windows 95 computers and you are not using Windows NT for either servers or workstations, you might want to implement

continues

Table 4.1 Continued

Item	Description
	enhanced meta-file (EMF) spooling. A meta-file is a graphics file that is a representation of the print output for the application. It takes less time for the application to generate this file than to generate a RAW file. A RAW file contains data that has passed through the print processor and is completely rendered for the printer. The EMF file can be passed from the client to Windows 95 print server, and print processing can then be completed at the server.

Other than checking to see what jobs are in the print queue or are spooled on the printer, there is no way to see who is using your printer. For all print jobs that have been spooled, you can see who printed the job and at what time.

Although shared directories and shared printers have several properties that are similar, shared fax modems are very different, as you will see in the following section.

Managing Shared Fax Modem

Fax modems and separate phone lines are rare for users in offices. Many people, however, have come to rely on having these services at their desktop. Even though it's possible to share a fax modem, this is not as common as sharing printers. This section examines the following:

- Creating or setting up fax services
- Sharing your personal fax services
- Monitoring or managing fax services

Setting Up Fax Services

Before you can set up fax services, you have to create a Microsoft Mail postoffice. You can use the following steps to set up the postoffice:

1. Open the Add\Remove Programs control panel and select the Windows Setup tab.
2. Make sure Microsoft Mail Services (in the Details section of Microsoft Exchange) is checked and then click OK.

The retail version of Windows 95 ships with a universal inbox called Microsoft Exchange. This could be confusing for users of the Microsoft Exchange Server components of BackOffice because they have to reinstall the Exchange client. In OSR2, the universal inbox is called Windows Messaging to avoid confusion.

3. Close the Add\Remove Programs control panel. You might be prompted to insert the Windows 95 CD-ROM and to reboot your computer.
4. Open the new Microsoft Mail Postoffice control panel. You are given the option to either Administer an Existing Workgroup Postoffice or Create a New Workgroup Postoffice (see Figure 4.11). You should create a new postoffice.

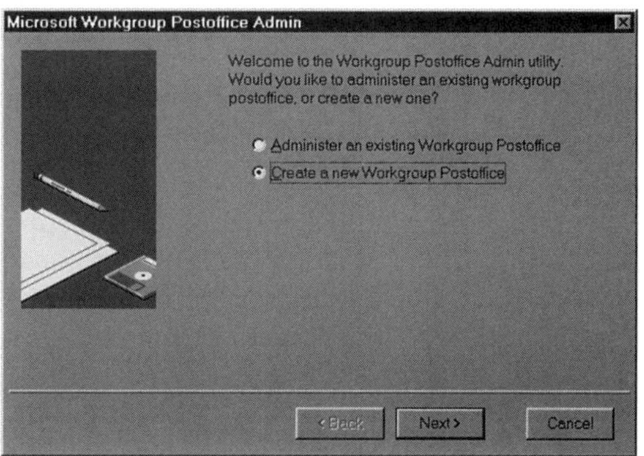

Figure 4.11

Whenever you open the Postoffice Administrator, you are asked about your intentions.

5. Your new postoffice is stored on your local hard drive. If you plan to use this postoffice for mail, you should share this directory so other users can send mail (see Figure 4.12).

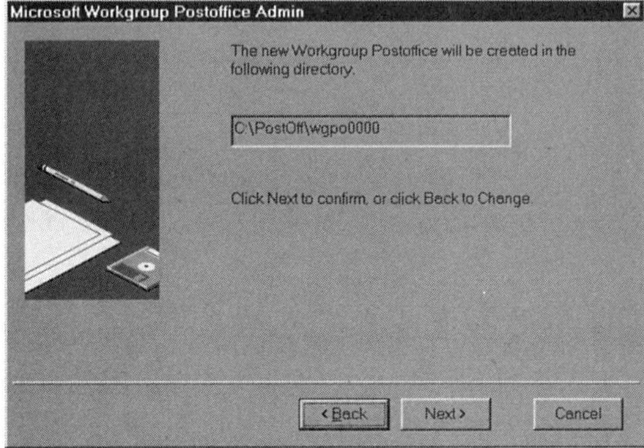

Figure 4.12

Because your postoffice is local, you have to share the folder for others to be able to use it.

6. The first user account on your mail server—even if it won't be used by anyone else—is for the postoffice administrator (see Figure 4.13). Be sure to remember the information you fill in here.

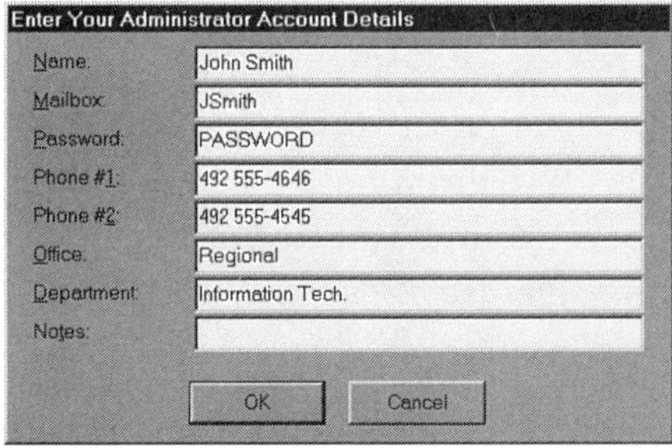

Figure 4.13

The person creating the postoffice automatically is the administrator.

Now that you have created a Microsoft Mail postoffice, you have to set up Microsoft Exchange to use the postoffice. You can launch Microsoft Exchange by selecting it from the Programs folder in the Start menu or by double-clicking the Inbox icon on the desktop.

When logging in to Microsoft Exchange, you need the location of your Workgroup Postoffice in addition to the login information you configured in the previous step (see Figure 4.14).

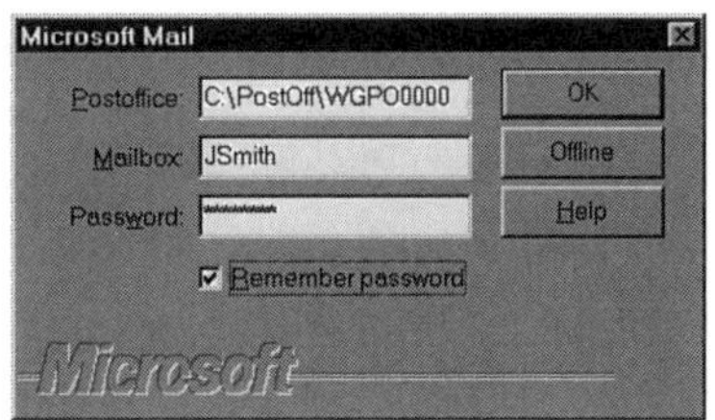

Figure 4.14

The Microsoft Mail service in Exchange needs to know which directory to use for mail.

This completes the steps required to create the Microsoft Mail Workgroup Postoffice used by the fax services.

Next you need to configure the fax services for the computer you are working on. The following steps enable you to set up fax services:

1. Open the Add\Remove Programs control panel and select the Windows Setup tab.
2. Make sure Microsoft Fax is checked and then click OK to close the control panel. You might be prompted to insert the Windows 95 CD-ROM and to reboot your computer.
3. Choose Start, Programs, Accessories, Fax, Compose New Fax. The first time you choose Compose New Fax, the Inbox Setup Wizard runs to configure the fax services.
4. Select your fax device from the list of installed fax modems (see Figure 4.15).
5. Configure your preferences for answering the phone to receive incoming faxes.
6. Type your personal information into the fax setup. This information is used for your fax cover pages (see Figure 4.16).
7. Choose the Default Dialing location for the fax services. A check box enables you to bypass this dialog box on all future faxes.
8. The next dialog box prompts you for a list of the new fax's intended recipients (see Figure 4.17).

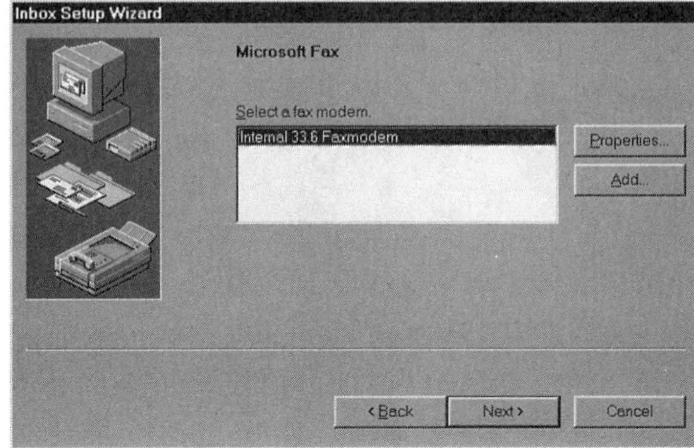

Figure 4.15

If multiple modems are installed, you have to choose one to use with the fax services.

Figure 4.16

Your personal information is collected for use with outgoing faxes.

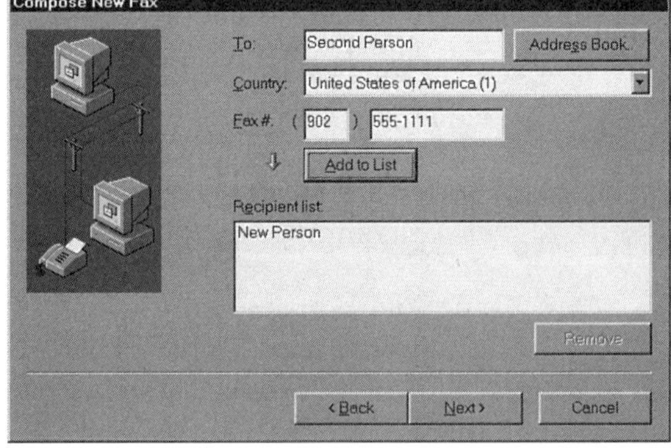

Figure 4.17

You have to build a list of people to receive the fax.

9. You can choose from a list of possible cover pages (see Figure 4.18). You also can use Microsoft's Cover Page Editor to create new cover pages. The Options... button enables you to schedule the fax to be sent later.

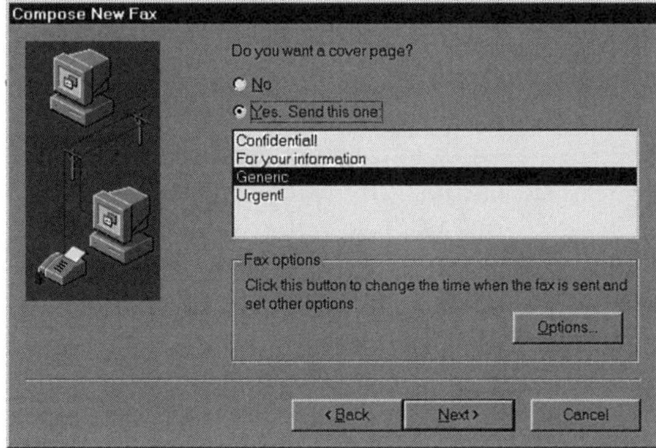

Figure 4.18

You can select a premade cover page or opt to build a new one.

10. You are almost finished with your first fax. You now can fill in the fax's subject line as well as the actual message (see Figure 4.19). Click Next and you can attach files from your hard drive to be sent with your fax as additional pages.

Figure 4.19

Your cover page message and subject line are collected to be inserted into the appropriate fields of the fax.

This completes the installation of the fax services. You also walked through sending a fax using Microsoft's Fax at Work service. Next you'll look at the most powerful feature of the service—sharing the fax modem.

Sharing the Fax Service

Now that the fax modem is set up on your computer, you can share it through the Exchange or Windows Messaging Inbox. The following steps describe how to share your fax service:

1. Right-click the Inbox icon on your desktop and choose Properties (or double-click the Inbox icon and choose Services... from the Tools menu).

2. Choose the Microsoft Fax service and click Properties. Select the Modem tab to configure sharing.

3. Check the Let other people on the network use my modem to send faxes option (see Figure 4.20). You are prompted for a drive to host the Shared Fax Service.

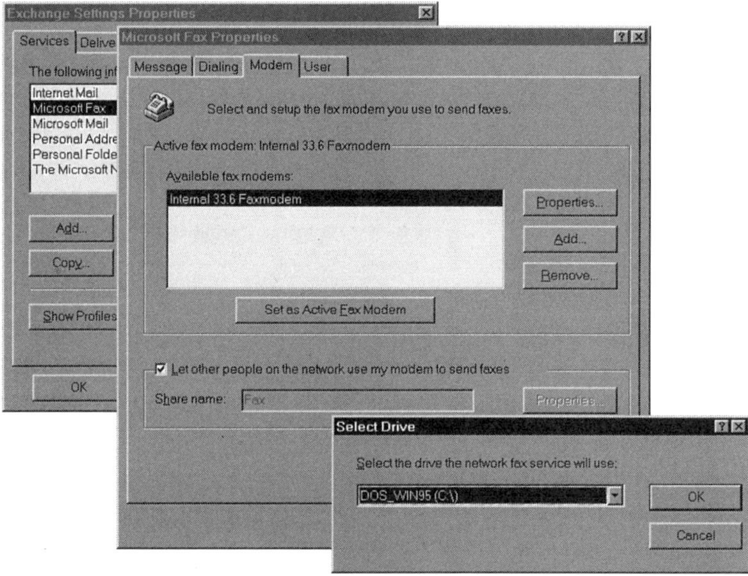

Figure 4.20

Sharing a fax modem is extremely easy.

4. The next dialog box you see is the same as the share options under the Properties button. It also is similar to the options you would see under a shared directory or a shared printer (see Figure 4.21). As with the other two resources, if the User-level Access Control has been set, you have the option of assigning access to a list of users rather than assigning passwords.

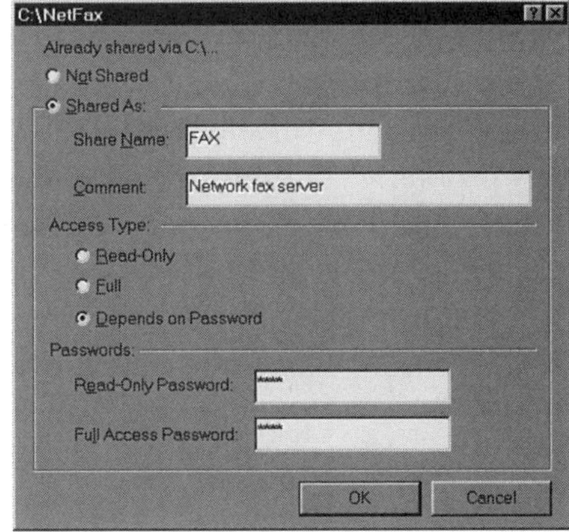

Figure 4.21

Shared access to a fax can be controlled by passwords.

5. Other users now can connect to the shared fax services by setting up an additional fax modem and selecting Network Fax Server. You then enter the UNC path to the fax service on the server (see Figure 4.22).

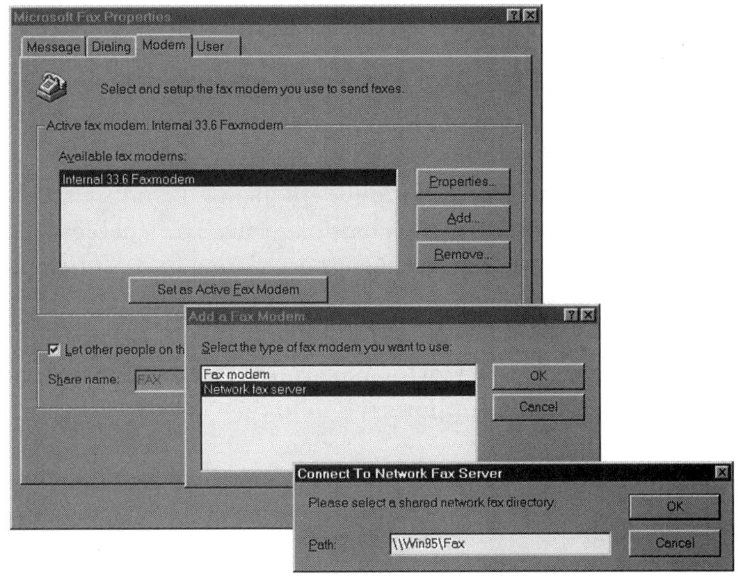

Figure 4.22

Attaching to a shared fax consists of adding it to the list of network fax servers and knowing the name of the fax server and the share.

This completes the installation of network fax services. Now that they are installed, you will learn how to monitor the services.

Monitoring Fax Services

You can monitor fax activity in Microsoft Exchange. Any faxes that have been sent will show up in the Sent Items folder. If there were any problems sending any of the faxes, you will see messages from the System Administrator in your Inbox. Each error message contains the subject and time of the fax and the name of any parties who did not receive it. The error message also contains a Send Again button. This is the only tool you can use to see what type of usage has taken place on your fax modem. If you use Microsoft Exchange for email in addition to faxing, the source of the messages in your Inbox can be confusing.

For more information about faxing from Windows 95, see Chapter 14 of the Windows 95 Reviewer Guide, "MS Exchange: E-Mail, Fax, and More." This guide is available on Microsoft's Web site or on Microsoft Technet.

Dealing with Unimodem/V Devices

The Unimodem/V driver enables shared fax services to operate over your network. Unimodem is short for universal modem and refers to the basic modem-driver components provided with Windows 95. Unimodem makes the entire modem-driver system in Windows 95 a modular one. This enables you to add multiple components that support dialing in or out, and it enables these components function without interfering with each other. Unimodem/V (Unimodem/Voice) was developed in November 1995 and was the next step in Unimodem technology. Unimodem/V supports the following:

- **Unimodem V Telephony Service Provider (TSP) and VxD.** The upgraded drivers.
- **Operator Agent.** A phone-answering agent that can route a call to the appropriate user.
- **Wave driver.** Support for some modems' WAV table.
- **Wave wrapper.** The basic WAV support for all other modems.

The advantages offered by the upgraded Unimodem driver deal specifically with support for modems with voice support.

You have examined the major resources that can be shared over a network, and you've learned how to manage those resources. As Windows 95 continues to develop, new resources will be able to be shared, and new tools will manage those resources. Next you will learn about user profiles.

Setting Up User Environments Through User Profiles

User profiles enable users to keep personalized settings on a computer. If the computer is used by multiple users, each user can have his own settings saved. These settings include items such as the following:

- Wallpaper and desktop settings
- Mouse tracking speed and button settings
- Desktop icons
- Start menu icons
- Application settings such as Microsoft Office 97

Not only can these individual settings be used for multiple users on a computer, in a network environment these settings can roam with the user (roaming user profiles).

The Windows 95 Registry is stored in two files on your local hard drive—USER.DAT and SYSTEM.DAT. SYSTEM.DAT stores all the hardware-specific information about your computer; USER.DAT stores all the user-specific information. Because USER.DAT is independent of your hardware, you can freely move your USER.DAT file from one computer to another. If you create a generic USER.DAT file on one computer, you can move that file to all other computers in your organization. Users can still modify their settings; this can place all users at the same starting point.

This section examines how user profiles are supported in Windows 95, both on stand-alone and networked computers. User profiles maintain individual USER.DAT files for each user on your computer.

User profiles are enabled through the User Profiles tab of the Password control panel. To enable user profiles, the correct choice is Users Can Customize Their Preferences and Desktop Settings. This option keeps a separate USER.DAT file for each user that logs on to the computer. The USER.DAT file for each user initially is copied from USER.DAT file in the Windows directory. Two additional settings can be included in each user profile—Include Desktop Icons and Network Neighborhood Contents in User Settings and Include Start Menu and Program Groups in User Settings. The latter option should be executed with care because applications installed by one user do not show up on the Start menu for others.

When working in a network environment, user profiles are copied to and from your servers as you log in and log out. This process enables the user profiles to move with a user from computer to computer. These profiles are referred to as *roaming user profiles.* The following criteria must be met to implement roaming user profiles:

- For Windows NT networks, your Windows 95 computer must be configured with the Log On To Windows NT Domain option enabled. This is configured in the Client for Microsoft Networks, on the Configuration tab of the Network control panel.
- Your Windows NT Domain Controller needs to have a Home directory configured for the user. This directory should be stored on a server.

The Windows 95 user profile automatically is copied from the local hard drive to the users' Home directory when the user logs out. If the profile becomes corrupted or unusable, log on as a different user and delete both the local and network-based copies of the profile. When a user logs in, profile existence is checked in the following order:

1. If there is a server copy, it is copied to the local hard drive.
2. If there is not a server copy, the local copy is used.
3. If there is not a local copy, a new copy is created from the default files in the Windows directory. This new local profile is copied to the server when the user logs out.

If you are implementing user profiles on a Novell NetWare network, the only difference is that the user profile is stored in the user's NetWare Mail directory. This directory within the SYS:MAIL directory is generated when the user account is created; it is assigned a random number as a directory name.

If you are having problems with user profiles, see Table 4.2 for possible solutions.

Table 4.2

Troubleshooting User Profiles

Problem	Solution
User profiles only are downloaded onto some computers; other computers only download part of the profile. The computers that do not take the entire profile leave out the desktop icons.	Make sure user profiles are enabled on all computers and that they have been set to include all the same settings, such as desktop icons and Start menu folders.
User profiles work on your current computer and are downloaded when you move to another computer. The settings, however, do not follow you back to your computer.	Check to see whether all your computers have the same system time. Windows 95 will not download a server-based profile if it has been saved with a future date. The date stamp placed on the file is the local date and time from the Windows 95 computer. On Windows NT networks, the `NET TIME` command can be used to synchronize time on all your computers.

continues

Table 4.2 Continued

Problem	Solution
Errors are generated when the profile is saved to the server when you log out of your computer; the profile does not function properly afterwards.	If you are using a Novell NetWare server, make sure OS2 name space or LONG name space has been enabled to support the long filenames used as part of the user's profile. If you are using a Windows NT server, make sure the user's home directory has not been compressed.

The next topic, System policies, relies on user profiles to maintain user settings.

Setting Up User Environments Through System Policies

The primary goal of System policies is to help reduce the total cost of ownership (TCO) for computers on your network. Each computer has hardware and software costs, and these costs are fixed. They also have a support cost, which often skyrockets over the lifespan of the computer. Much support time is spent fixing silly mistakes made by the operators of the computers. Some mistakes can be avoided with proper training, which increases the TCO. System polices reduce the TCO by limiting access to controls that can cause mistakes and by not requiring additional costs. This section examines five common problems that cost companies money in wasted support hours. The content of the list might vary from company to company. Whatever your problems are, however, careful policies can eliminate most of them. The following is the list of top support time-wasters:

1. Changes in video settings or the display adapter type that cause the display not to work

2. Changes to network settings (such as the removal of required protocols or clients) or the addition of conflicting components that cause network access to fail

3. Installation of unsupported or untested software that causes problems with required applications

4. Removal of required applications

5. Modification to or deletion of required configuration files such as CONFIG.SYS

System polices also can be used to create and enforce a custom environment for users. This environment can include wallpaper settings, color schemes, and auto-start applications. This enables you to have workstations that constantly reset themselves to the defined corporate standard as each user logs in. This system might require a few batch files to handle the deletion.

System policies enable you to automatically modify the USER.DAT and SYSTEM.DAT files on a destination computer when the user logs on to the network. If you want to apply policies to users based on the groups they belong to on their servers, each workstation needs a copy of the group policy files installed on the computer. If you want to create a new policy configuration file for your server, you have to use the System Policy Editor. To install the System Policy Editor, follow these steps:

1. In the Start menu, select Settings, Control Panel.

2. Open the Add/Remove Programs control panel.

3. Select the Windows Setup tab, and click the Have Disk... button.

4. From the Windows 95 CD-ROM, select the path <Windows_95_CD>\ADMIN\APPTOOLS\POLEDIT.

5. Enable the check boxes for both the Group Policies and System Policy Editor options, then click the Install button (see Figure 4.23).

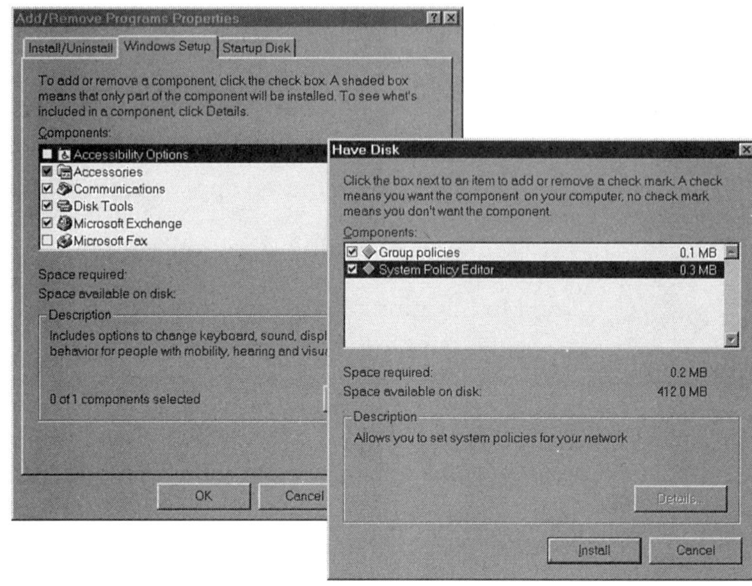

Figure 4.23

To install both components, you have to select both check boxes and click the Install button.

This installs the Group policies and the System Policy Editor on your computer. To create the System policy, you only have to install the System Policy Editor on the machine you will be using. If you plan to assign the policy to users based on the server groups they belong to, you have to install the Group policies on every machine on your network.

You can install the Group policy files on any computer using the following steps on each workstation that requires them:

1. In the Start menu, select Settings, Control Panel.
2. Open the Add/Remove Programs control panel.
3. Select the Windows Setup tab, and click the Have Disk... button.
4. From the Windows 95 CD-ROM, select the path <Windows_95_CD>\ADMIN\APPTOOLS\POLEDIT directory.

5. Enable the check box for the Group Policies option, then click the Install button.

This installs Group policies on your computer. With Group policies installed, your computer imports policy settings from the configuration file based on the server groups to which you belong. If you have not installed Group policies, you will ignore any group settings configuration file.

Depending on the type of network you use, Windows 95 expects the policy configuration file to be in a certain location. The locations are as follows:

- Windows NT Domain—in the NetLogon directory of the Domain Controllers, which is <win_root>\SYSTEM32\REPL\IMPORT\SCRIPTS\
- Novell Netware 3.x or 4.x Server—on the SYS volume in the PUBLIC directory

The name of the configuration file is CONFIG.POL. If you are creating policy files to be used with Windows NT 4.0 as well, the Windows NT policy file would be NTCONFIG.POL.

After the System Policy Editor is installed on your computer, you are able to create policy files. To launch the System Policy Editor, select it from the Start menu under Programs, Accessories, System Tools. It opens to a blank window. To create a new policy file, select New from the File menu. If you are working on a policy file, at least two icons should be visible—Default User and Default Computer.

When using the policy editor to make a policy file, each check box has three settings: on (checked), off (clear), and neutral (gray). Great care should be taken when creating policy files; changes implemented in a policy file are not always reversible.

The three settings for check boxes in the System Policy Editor (checked, clear, and gray) can be interpreted as follows:

A *checked* box represents the on position. It turns the setting on for all computers processing this policy. If the setting already was on, there will be no change; if the setting was off, however, it now will be turned on. Checking the Logon Banner option under Default Computer\Network\Logon, for example, turns the banner on for everyone.

A *clear* box represents the off position. It turns the setting off for all computers processing this policy. If the setting was on, it now will be set to the off position; if the value already was off, it will remain off.

A *gray* box is one you are going to leave alone. If the value currently is on, it will remain on; if the value currently is off, it will remain off. These values are neutral and will not change the settings. This is the default for all values in Default User and Default Computer.

An example of a change that is irreversible (if somewhat trivial) is the assignment of one wallpaper to all users. After the wallpaper has been assigned, you cannot return the users' computers to their original wallpaper. You have two options: clear the check box or gray the check box. A clear check box removes or turns off the wallpaper for all users. If they assign a new wallpaper while this policy is in effect, it also will be turned off at the next login. A gray check box leaves the wallpaper as it is but does not override any future changes the user makes.

The next sections discuss the settings that can be modified under the two icons in the policy file—Default User and Default Computer (or user settings and computer settings).

Changing the User Settings in the Policy File

This section examines the user settings that can be adjusted or enforced in a System policy. To access this information, you can double-click Default User in the System Policy Editor. The user settings are applied for each user regardless of which computer they have logged on to. The changes that are implemented are stored in the user's USER.DAT file. The following topics are covered:

- Control Panel settings
- Desktop settings
- File and Print Sharing settings
- Windows Explorer shell settings
- System restrictions

Control Panel Settings

Control Panel settings enable you to control or restrict access to most of the Control Panel applets. Microsoft's default Policy Template file targets the following Control Panel applets (see Figure 4.24), although others also can be included.

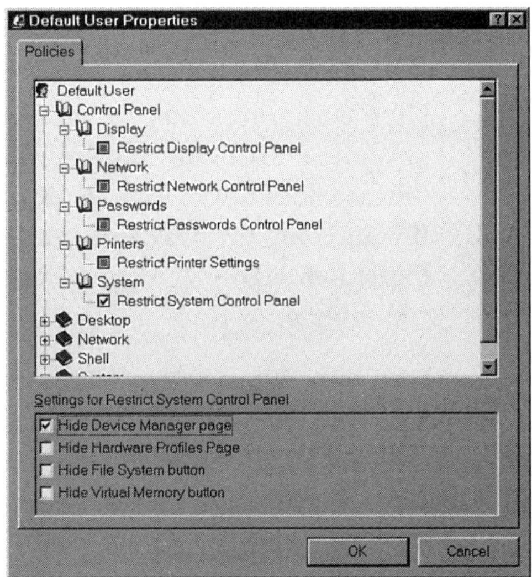

Figure 4.24

Control Panel settings affect only the major Control Panel applets.

Restrictions can be applied to the following Control Panel applets:

- Display
- Network
- Passwords
- Printers
- System

Next you'll examine the effect of each type of restriction.

Restricting the Display Control Panel

The restrictions for the Display control panel are

- **Disable Display Control Panel.** This setting disables all access to the Display control panel. It is useful if there is a justifiable reason for the user not to have access to any settings in the Display control panel. You might want to restrict access to the Wallpaper, Screen Saver, and Appearance tabs if your company has a corporate image policy and wants to enforce it. Restricting the Settings tab prevents users from setting screen resolutions and color-depth values beyond the capabilities of their monitor; these changes usually prompt a support call.
- **Hide Background Page.** This setting removes the Background tab from the Display control panel. Access to these settings does not tend to cause additional support problems. If your company has created a corporate wallpaper to be implemented on all workstations, this prevents users from changing it.
- **Hide Screen Saver Page.** This setting removes the Screen Saver tab from the Display control panel. Like the Background tab, access to these settings does not tend to cause support problems. If your company has created a corporate

screen saver, you might want to limit access to this tab. Limiting access to this tab also prevents users from disabling the Password Protect option.

- **Hide Appearance Page.** This setting removes the Appearance tab from the Display control panel. Having access to the color schemes can cause support problems. People with vision problems might require a special color scheme, but most users should be fine using the Windows default scheme. Limiting access to this tab prevents users from creating new color schemes such as the black-on-black color scheme—black menu bar, black menu text, black active window, black inactive windows, and so on.

- **Hide Settings Page.** This setting removes the Settings tab from the Display control panel. Access to this tab can cause many support problems. If a user decides to create a larger viewing area or greater color depth, the changes can be attempted on this tab. Windows 95 attempts to test the settings, but it is not always able to do so. Improperly configured display settings require a trip out to the offending workstation.

Restricting the Network Control Panel

The following settings enable you to modify restrictions to the Network control panel:

- **Disable Network Control Panel.** This setting prevents all access to the Network control panel. Most users do not require any access to the Network control panel. If you have a reason to limit access to the Network controls, do not disable them; rather, use the following settings to limit access.

- **Hide Identification Page.** This setting hides the Identification properties of the Network control panel. If you implement System policies, enabling users to change the name of their workstation provides an opportunity to bypass the System policy.

- **Hide Access Control Page.** This setting hides the Access Control (User-level versus Share-level) properties of the Network control panel. For network security on the File and Print Sharing service, you should implement User-level Access Control if your network supports it. Preventing users from changing back to the less secure Share-level Access Control is a must.

Restricting the Passwords Control Panel

Most require some access to the Passwords control panel. The following is a list of restrictions that can be applied:

- **Disable Passwords Control Panel.** This setting prevents all access to the Passwords control panel. Because access to this control panel is necessary to change the Windows password and many server passwords, this option is probably too severe for most environments.
- **Hide Change Passwords Page.** This setting hides the Change Passwords properties of the Passwords control panel. This prevents changing passwords, which might be necessary in your environment.
- **Hide Remote Administration Page.** This setting hides the Remote Administration properties of the Passwords control panel. Because Remote Administration leaves your computer open for full access to other users across the network, you do not want users configuring this option incorrectly. In user-level environments, Network Administrators (Domain Admins on Windows NT) automatically are added to the Remote Administration list. In denying access to this tab, you prevent the user from removing people from the administration list.
- **Hide User Profiles Page.** This setting hides the Profiles properties of the Passwords control panel. To properly implement System policies, user profiles must be enabled. If you hide this tab, users cannot turn user profiles off in an attempt to bypass security.

Restricting Printer Configuration

The following list describes the restrictions that can be placed on printers:

- **Hide General And Details Pages.** This setting hides the General and Details properties for the printer icons in the Printers folder. This prevents users from changing their drivers, assigned printer ports, and spool settings. It also prevents users from switching to printers you do not want them to use, such as a color printer that costs more per page.
- **Disable Deletion Of Printers.** This setting prevents the deletion of installed printers. This prevents you from having to repeatedly reinstall printers that have been deleted accidentally.
- **Disable Addition Of Printers.** This setting prevents the installation of printers. Some users attempt to do what they can without calling for help. If the wrong printer driver is selected for a printer, you can run into several printer problems that can be time-consuming to troubleshoot. You also can prevent users from adding the drivers that enable them to use a printer that is more expensive to operate.

Restricting the System Control Panel

The System control panel offers more dangers than most other control panels. The default policy template, however, does not include an option to disable this control panel entirely. The following is a list of restrictions that can be applied to this den of dangers:

- **Hide Device Manager Page.** This setting hides the Device Manager properties of the System control panel. With one quick press of the Delete key, users can accidentally remove required devices (or at least the drivers) from their workstations, including network cards, drive controllers, and keyboards. Even if devices are not completely deleted, settings on the devices might be modified to leave the devices in an unusable state. This is a big restriction.
- **Hide Hardware Profiles Page.** This setting hides the Hardware Profiles properties of the System control panel. This enables users to have several sets of device manager settings for different hardware configurations. In some cases, multiple hardware profiles are implemented to prevent users from

accessing certain devices at the same time, such as modems and network cards.

- **Hide File System Button.** This setting hides the File System button from the Performance properties in the System control panel. The File System button is used primarily for troubleshooting compatibility problems with older applications. Changes in settings should be made cautiously to prevent creating new problems and to prevent degradation in system performance.
- **Hide Virtual Memory Button.** This setting hides the Virtual Memory button from the Performance properties in the System control panel. Improper virtual memory settings can severely hamper system performance.

All these settings can be changed in the Control Panel section of the policy file.

Desktop Settings

The security side Desktop settings are fairly low. Many companies implement these settings to force users to comply with corporate-image standards. The following settings can be enforced:

- **Wallpaper Name.** Enables you to select a wallpaper for the user.
- **Tile Wallpaper.** Enables the wallpaper to be tiled instead of centered.
- **Color Scheme.** Set the color scheme for the user.

As previously mentioned, these settings can help enforce corporate-image standards by implementing specific color schemes and wallpapers. If the Display control panel has been restricted, users cannot change any of these settings. If users can access the Display control panel, they can change the settings. The settings reset to the corporate standards, however, the next time the user logs in. Because any changes made are lost at the next login, most users stop changing their settings because it's a losing battle. Administrators know if a user changes the settings, even though they are not permanent.

File and Print Sharing Settings

As discussed in Chapter 1, "Planning," File and Print Sharing might be a necessary evil that must be installed on workstations to enable Remote Administration. If this is the case, the following two policy entries enable you to keep the service installed but to remove all controls from users' hands. This enables the largest security risk to be controlled.

- **Disable File Sharing Controls.** Hides all the File Sharing Controls from Windows Explorer folder property sheets.
- **Disable Print Sharing Controls.** Hides all the Print Sharing Controls from Windows Explorer printer property sheets.

Windows Explorer Shell Settings

Windows Explorer is the default shell used by Windows 95. Policy Editor provides several security features for Windows Explorer in the form of custom folders (see Figure 4.25) and shell restrictions (see Figure 4.26).

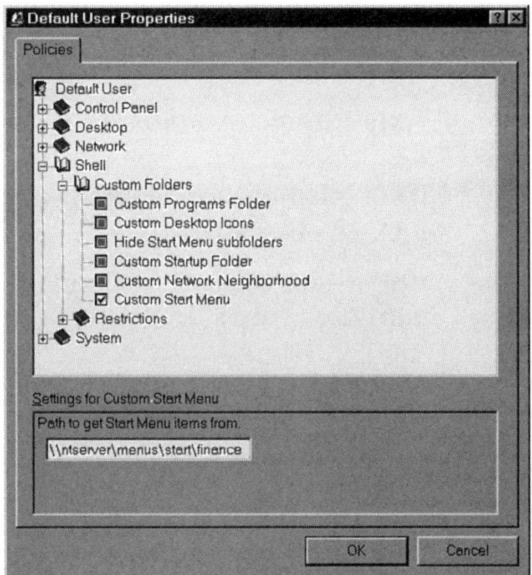

Figure 4.25

Custom Folders override the folders already in the Start menu.

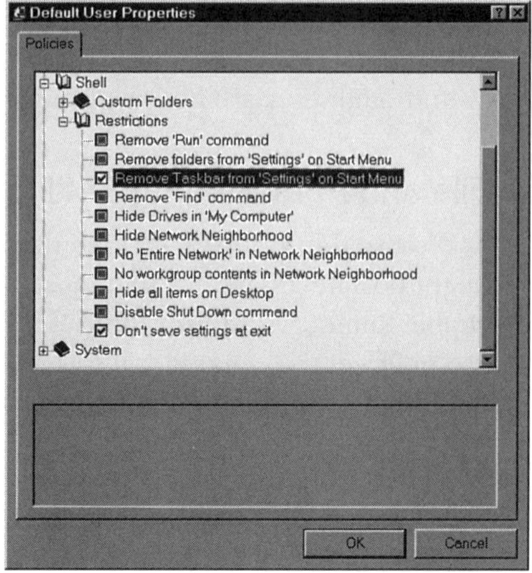

Figure 4.26

Shell Restrictions prevent users from accessing certain areas of the Explorer shell.

The settings for these two security features can be found in the following lists. The first list contains the custom folders that can be configured.

- **Custom Programs Folder.** This option enables you to specify an alternate location for a folder that contains the contents of the Programs directory. This folder should contain items or shortcuts you want to display in the Programs section of the Start menu. The folder can be stored locally on the workstation, or it can be located on a network drive and accessed through a UNC path such as:

  ```
  \\NTSERVER\MENUS\FINANCE\STARTMENU
  ```

  If you plan to use a centrally managed folder for any custom folders, make sure that all computers run applications off your servers and that any applications installed locally on the hard drives are stored using a common directory structure.

- **Custom Desktop Icons.** This option enables you to specify an alternate location for a folder that contains the contents of the Desktop directory. This folder should contain items or shortcuts you want to display on the desktops of the computers on your network.

- **Hide Start Menu Subfolders.** This option enables you to hide the default Start menu folders. If this option is not selected, users will see the normal Start menu folders.

If your policy uses a custom Start menu, Programs folder, or other custom folders, you have to turn on the Hide Start Menu Subfolders option. If you do not enable this option, users will not see the effect of your custom folders in their Start menu; they will see the normal Start menu. Enabling Hide Start Menu Subfolders is not an option, it is a requirement.

- **Custom Startup Folder.** This option enables you to specify an alternate location for a folder that contains the contents of the Startup directory. This folder should contain items or shortcuts that you want to start automatically when the desktop shell loads.
- **Custom Network Neighborhood.** This option enables you to specify an alternate location for a folder that contains the contents of Network Neighborhood. This folder should contain items or shortcuts you want to display in Network Neighborhood. This option prevents users from browsing the entire network for resources; instead, you provide a list of resources for them to use.
- **Custom Start Menu.** This option enables you to specify an alternate location for a folder that contains the contents of the Start Menu directory. This folder should contain items or shortcuts you want to display in the root of the Start menu. These items appear at the top of the Start menu.

In addition to custom folders, several restrictions can be applied to the user's desktop shell. The following list describes these restrictions:

- **Remove Run Command.** This option removes the Run command from the Start menu. This helps prevent users from running executables for which shortcuts are not provided in the Start menu.

- **Remove Folders From Settings On Start Menu.** This option hides the Printers and Control Panel folders from the Settings folder in the Start menu. It also removes the copies of these folders from the My Computer window.
- **Remove Taskbar From Settings On Start Menu.** This option hides Taskbar… from the Settings folder in the Start menu. It also disables the properties from the menu when you right-click the taskbar.
- **Remove Find Command.** This option removes the Find command from the Start menu. As with removing the Run command, this option helps prevent users from running other executables.
- **Hide Drives In My Computer.** This option removes all drive icons from My Computer.
- **Hide Network Neighborhood.** This option removes Network Neighborhood from the desktop.
- **No Entire Network in Network Neighborhood.** If you decide to leave Network Neighborhood on the desktop, you can hide the Entire Network icon to prevent network browsing outside the current workgroup.
- **No Workgroup Contents in Network Neighborhood.** If you choose to leave Network Neighborhood on the desktop, you can hide the current workgroup contents. This forces browsing resources through the Entire Network icon.
- **Hide All Items On Desktop.** This option removes all icons from the desktop, including both user- and OS-created icons.
- **Disable Shut Down Command.** This option removes Shut Down from the Start menu. Because the Shut Down dialog box also is used for logging out, this prevents the user from doing so. If you install Internet Explore 4.x's Shell Enhancements, Log On as a Different User is removed from the dialog box and a new Start Menu Logout command is added.

- **Don't Save Settings At Exit.** This option prevents desktop changes from being saved when exiting Windows. This includes any Explorer windows left open.

In addition to the desktop shell settings, additional restrictions are applied to other applications, as you will see in the next section.

System Restrictions

System restrictions are in place to prevent the user from escaping the Windows 95 graphical user interface (GUI) and the controlled environment (see Figure 4.27). If a user is allowed to close the Windows 95 GUI, none of the policy changes you have implemented (such as program restriction) will affect the user. All these restrictions are enforced by either the GUI or EXPLORER.EXE (the default shell). If the user is allowed to leave this environment, you lose control of the user. System restrictions are not limited to the shell itself but to the operating system.

- **Disable Registry Editing Tools.** This option prevents the use of any Registry editing tools on the system.

- **Only Run Allowed Windows Applications.** This option only enables the applications listed in the Show dialog box to run on the system (see Figure 4.28). The only exception is EXPLORER.EXE because it is required as a shell. This means you can prevent applications such as SETUP.EXE or INSTALL.EXE from running on computers.

- **Disable MS-DOS Prompt.** This option prevents the DOS prompt from being launched because no shell restrictions take effect in DOS.

- **Disable Single-Mode MS-DOS Applications.** This option prevents applications from running if they want to unload the Windows shell.

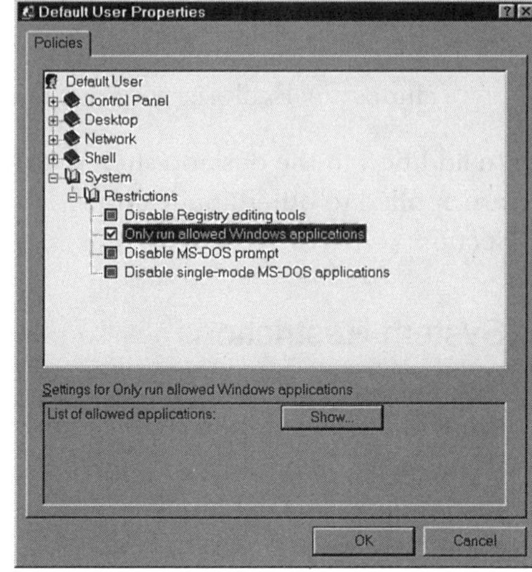

Figure 4.27

System restrictions are aimed at controlling applications that are executed.

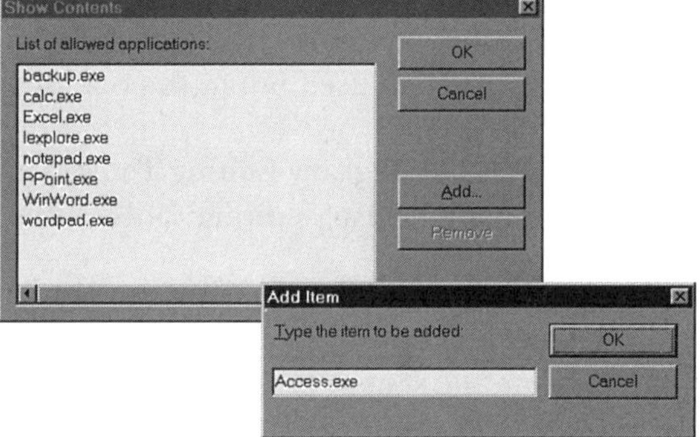

Figure 4.28

You can build an exclusive list of allowed applications on your network.

These are all the user settings that can be modified based on Microsoft's default template. Next you'll look at the sections or the template file that can be used to modify computer settings.

Changing Computer Settings in the Policy File

The next two lists examine the settings that can be adjusted or enforced in a computer section of a policy. To access this information, double-click Default Computer or Local Computer in the System Policy Editor (see Figure 4.29). The computer settings are applied to the computer regardless of which user has logged on.

The changes are stored in the computer's SYSTEM.DAT file. The two lists cover the following topics:

- Network settings
- System settings

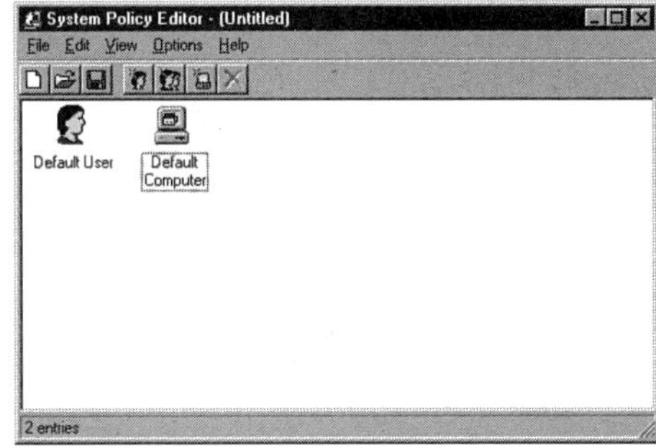

Figure 4.29

Initial policy files start with settings for Default Computer and Default User.

Network Settings

The network settings section of the computer policy covers configuration options for most of the Windows 95 network interface. The section is long, so it is covered in the following order:

- General Network settings
- Logon settings
- Microsoft Client for NetWare Networks
- Microsoft Client for Windows Networks
- Password
- Sharing
- Simple Network Management Protocol (SNMP)
- Update

Configuring General Network Settings

The first section deals with the following Network settings that have only a single configuration option:

- **Access Control.** This option enables you to specify User-level Access Control. When checked, it enables User-level Access Control with a security provider list in the Options section. You also must specify what type of network operating system the security provider is running. If cleared, then Share-level Access Control is enabled.
- **File and Print Sharing for NetWare Networks.** This option enables you to disable SAP advertising. This stops the server advertising protocol from being used for File and Print Sharing for NetWare networks. With this option turned off, your computer advertises itself in the same fashion as the NetWare servers on your network, which can lead to confusion for users.
- **Dial-Up Networking.** This option enables you to disable dial-in and stops dial-up server from working on this computer. This can turn out to be a preemptive strike. If the user is not running dial-up server, nothing happens; if the user installs dial-up server, it is disabled at the next restart and logon. The only way to re-enable dial-up server is to reinstall it. The change does not take effect until the next reboot, at which time dial-up server is disabled again.

Configuring Logon Settings

The Logon section enables you to set additional warnings and security on Windows 95. This is done through the following two settings:

- **Logon Banner.** You can set an option that causes a logon banner to display prior to presenting the Logon dialog box. This enables you to satisfy legal issues of informing unauthorized users of your system that they are not allowed. You are able to specify both a window title and a message.

- **Require Validation By Network For Windows Access.** This option forces users to validate their usernames and passwords before they can access the Windows 95 desktop. If this option is enabled, all desktop computers (and docked laptops) must be successfully logged in by a network server before the desktop shell will be loaded. This setting is not enforced for undocked laptops.

Configuring the Microsoft Client for NetWare Networks

Several configuration changes can be made for the Microsoft Client for NetWare Networks. These configurations are as follows:

- **Preferred Server.** This option specifies the name of your preferred NetWare server or the server on which your user account resides. If this option is left blank in your configuration, the closest server is used. This should yield an invalid user or password error.

- **Support Long Filenames.** This option enables Windows 95 to determine what to do when working with long filenames on your network. This option defines what level of support for long filenames your Novell NetWare server can handle. A value of 0 means there is no support for long filenames on your NetWare servers, 1 means there is support on NetWare servers version 3.12 and greater, and 2 means there is support if the NetWare server supports long filenames. A value of 2 can include NetWare 3.11 servers that have had a patch applied.

- **Search Mode.** This option enables you to set the NetWare search mode to a valid binary value between 0 and 7. For specific information about search modes, read the "Search Mode with Windows 95 on NetWare Networks" section of Chapter 9, "Windows 95 on NetWare Networks," in the *Windows 95 Resource Kit.*

- **Disable Automatic NetWare Login.** This option prevents Windows 95 from using the credentials of the Primary

Network Logon to authenticate the user on the NetWare network. This forces separate logins for each client installed on your computer, but it increases security by forcing the user to know all the passwords.

Configuring the Microsoft Client for Windows Networks

As with the NetWare client, many configuration changes can be implemented for the Microsoft Client for Windows Networks. These configurations are explained in the following list:

- **Log On To Windows NT.** This option enables the domain logon for Windows NT networks. If you leave the Domain Name field blank, the user is prompted for it during logon. If you fill in a name, the user can override the domain name during logon, but it reverts back to the one configured in the policy at the next logon.
- **Display Domain Logon Validation.** This option informs users whether they were logged on to the domain and what security level they were granted.
- **Disable Caching Of Domain Password.** This option disables the caching of the domain password in the local password list file (*.PWL).
- **Workgroup.** This option specifies a workgroup name for the computer.
- **Alternative Workgroup.** This option specifies a workgroup name to use for network browsing. If your workgroup does not have a computer running the Computer Browser service, you can use the browse list from another workgroup.

Configuring Password Settings

Configuring Password settings can greatly increase security on your computer. The following changes can be made to how Windows 95 works with passwords:

- **Hide Share Passwords With Asterisks.** This option applies to passwords listed in the Sharing tab of folder properties. The default value is on or hidden. If you disable this option, you can confirm the current password on forgotten shares without having to reset. Unfortunately, other people with access to your computer also can see the current passwords.

- **Disable Password Caching.** This option disables caching of network and other passwords in the local Password List file. If this option is enabled, the Quick Logon feature of the Microsoft network client cannot be used. Unfortunately, this option forces confirmation of a Windows password at every logon.
- **Require Alphanumeric Windows Password.** This option forces users to choose Windows passwords that are a combination of letters and numbers. This increases security by forcing users to have more complex Windows passwords.
- **Minimum Windows Password Length.** This option sets a minimum length for Windows passwords. This increases security because it prevents people from leaving their Windows password blank.

Configuring Sharing Settings

The Sharing settings apply to all File and Print Sharing on the computer. The options are as follows:

- **Disable File Sharing.** This option enables you to turn off File Sharing. This differs from the user policy setting Disable File Sharing Controls, which only hides the controls. This option actually stops the service.
- **Disable Print Sharing.** This option enables you to turn off Print Sharing. This differs from the user policy setting Disable Print Sharing Controls, which only hides the controls. This option actually stops the service.

Configuring Simple Network Management Protocol Settings

Many organizations currently do not implement Simple Network Management Protocol (SNMP) as a network management and monitoring tool. For companies that do, Windows 95's SNMP service can be configured using the following settings:

- **Communities.** This option enables you to specify the SMNP community names used by your computer. If not configured, Windows 95 uses the default community name "public."
- **Permitted Managers.** This option enables you to specify IP or IPX addresses of computers that are allowed make SMNP queries to the computer. By allowing only certain addresses to make queries, you limit the potential for security breaches.
- **Traps For Public Community.** This option specifies the IP or IPX address of the computer to which you will be sending Public Traps. By limiting the destinations, you ensure that the information is not being diverted for other uses.
- **Internet MIB (RFC 1156).** This option stores the computer's contact name and location as specified in the Internet MIB standards, which are detailed in RFC (Request For Comments) 1156.

Configuring Update Settings

The Update options enable you to move the active policy file to another location (one other than the default location). The following list describes the options for updates:

- **Remote Update.** This option sets the update method for future downloads of the System policy.
- **Update Mode.** This option can be either Automatic (for policies in the default location) or Manual (for policies stored in an alternate location).
- **Path For Manual Update.** This option requires a UNC path to the alternate location for the policy file. This enables certain computers to execute a different policy file than the rest.

- **Display Error Message.** This option enables the display of an error message if the policy is not available on the network when the user logs in.

- **Load-Balance.** This option is extremely important because it enables Windows 95 to process policy files from the Backup Domain Controller on a Windows NT network. If this option is disabled, Windows 95 only processes policy files from the Primary Domain Controller. This can cause slower logins and more network traffic.

This concludes the Network settings that can be configured as part of the policy file. The next section examines changes in the System settings.

System Settings

System settings enable you to configure basic options for Windows 95, including various methods of starting applications at boot time (see Figure 4.30). The following list describes these settings:

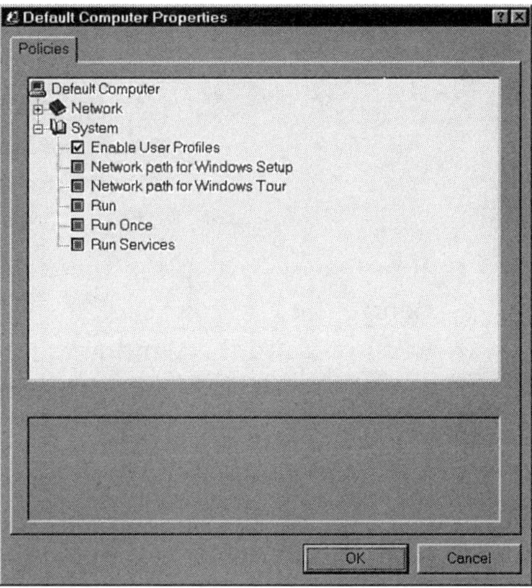

Figure 4.30

System settings enable you to configure startup commands for Windows 95.

- **Enable User Profiles.** This option enables user profiles. Before any settings in the User section of the system policy are enabled, user profiles must be turned on. This option turns user profiles on and keeps turning them back on if users turn them off.

- **Network Path For Windows Setup.** This option enables you to specify a UNC path to the network location of the Windows 95 Setup program. This location is used when Windows 95 needs to load new drives instead of prompting for the Windows 95 CD-ROM.
- **Run.** This option specifies a list of applications to run after the Windows shell loads (see Figure 4.31). This is similar to including items in the Startup folder or to adding Load or Run lines to WIN.INI. The list of applications is stored in the Registry in the HKEY_LOCAL_MACHINE\SOFTWARE\MICROSOFT\WINDOWS\CURRENTVERSION\RUN key. The applications are executed in order of Value Name.

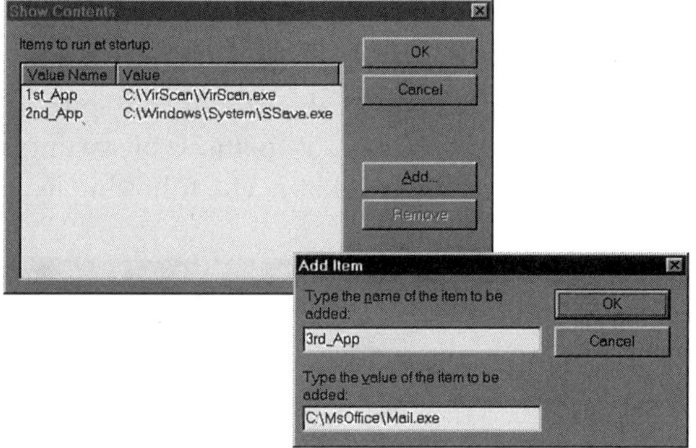

Figure 4.31

The Run section enables you to specify a list of applications to execute when Windows 95 starts.

- **Run Once.** This option specifies a list of applications to run before the Windows shell loads. These applications run one at a time, and the Windows shell will not load until the last application has finished. The list of applications is stored in the Registry in the HKEY_LOCAL_MACHINE\SOFTWARE\MICROSOFT\WINDOWS\CURRENTVERSION\RUNONCE key. After each application completes, its Registry entry is removed so it does not execute the next time Windows 95 loads. If you add these entries to the System policy, each time Windows 95 loads the policy (at each logon) it re-adds the entries to the Run Once key in the Registry.

- **Run Services.** This option specifies the list of applications to execute as services when Windows 95 loads. These applications start up first when Windows 95 loads. They execute when the Logon dialog box displays.

The Run, Run Once, and Run Services entries are similar. The difference lies in when and how they execute.

- **Services.** This option starts first and executes at the same time the user login screen appears. All services start, and you do not have to close or exit the services to continue.
- **Run Once.** These commands execute one at a time, in order, after the logon is complete. You have to exit each Run Once command before the next one is called. Services continue to run through this entire process.
- **Run.** These commands execute after all Run Once commands are finished and the desktop shell is loaded. These commands all execute at the same time. Services continue to run through this process.

This is a summary of all the items included in the default policy template that ships with Windows 95. The next section examines how to create individual policies for users, groups, and computers. These new policies enable you to apply the entries discussed for Default User and Default Computer to individual users, groups, and computers.

Creating Policies for Users, Groups, and Computers

When you create a policy file for a server, you have the option to add individual icons for each user or group of users from your server and icons for each computer on your network. To add additional entries to your policy, choose Add User..., Add Computer..., or Add Group... from the Edit menu. If your system is configured for User-level Access Control, you can browse a list of users, groups, and computers; otherwise, you have to type the name of the user, group, or computer.

Windows 95 follows a particular order when reading the policy file.

1. Windows 95 checks to see whether the user is a member of any groups it has entries for. If the user is a member of some groups, all groups he is a member of are processed in order of the group's priority.
2. Windows 95 then checks to see whether there is an entry for the user logging in. If there is an entry for the user, Windows 95 applies the changes for that user.
3. If there are no entries for that user or no groups are processed, the entry for Default User is applied.
4. After applying the user policy, Windows 95 applies a computer policy.
5. If there is an entry for your current computer name, it will be applied; otherwise, the entry for Default Computer is applied.

There is no way to create policies for groups of computers. All computers on the same domain or server use the same policy.

If some or all of the computers on the network are not processing the groups in the policy file, make sure Group policies were installed on the client computers following the procedure from the beginning of this section. If Group policies were not installed, clients should be processing the Default User policy. If this policy is not being implemented, check the location of the policy file and its structure. The priority of the groups is determined by their order in the Group Priority... dialog box under the Options menu. The list is processed from the bottom up; conflicting settings in the highest group override those from lower groups. Only policy entries for groups the user is a member of are applied.

Using Policy Template Files

The policy editor can be used as a second type of Registry Editor, but everything it knows about the Registry comes from the Policy Template file. The default template file is c:\WINDOWS\INF

\ADMIN.ADM. You can change the template by choosing Template... from the Options menu. The template file is a text file with a particular structure. The following list describes the keywords and their use within a policy file:

- **CLASS.** This is the largest section in the policy files. The class must be either User or Machine.
- **!! (two exclamation marks).** This identifies the next word as a variable or string that must be defined in the `STRINGS]` section at the end of the policy file.

  Strings are defined with the following structure:

  ```
  StringName="String value"
  ```

- **CATEGORY and END CATEGORY.** These keywords enclose each category in the policy editor structure. These are the expanding branches of the file and can be nested within each other as follows:

  ```
  CATEGORY !!CategoryOne
         CATEGORY !!CategoryTwo
           CATEGORY !!CategoryThree
           ...
           ...
           END CATEGORY ; CategoryThree
         END CATEGORY   ; CategoryTwo
      END CATEGORY      ; CategoryOne
  ```

- **KEYNAME.** Each category contains a KEYNAME or Registry key path that starts immediately after HKEY_LOCAL_MACHINE OR HKEY_CURRENT_USER. This determines where in the Registry changes should be made. The following is an example of a KEYNAME:

  ```
  KEYNAME System\CurrentControlSet\Services\Control\FileSystem
  ```

- **POLICY.** This is used to define the check boxes that are displayed.
- **VALUENAME.** This is the name of the Registry value you want to change. VALUENAME always is contained within a PART.

- **PART.** This defines individual items displayed in the Settings section of the Policy Editor at the bottom of the window. The following is an example of a PART statement:

  ```
  PART !!CPL_Display_Disable CHECKBOX
         VALUENAME NoDispCPL
  END PART
  ```

  PARTS can be of the following types:

  - **TEXT.** Used for display text. The following is an example of this PART type:

    ```
    PART !!NetworkTourPath_TIP TEXT END PART
    ```

  - **NUMERIC.** Used for values to be written to the Registry as REG_DWORD types. The following is an example of this PART type:

    ```
    PART !!SearchMode1 NUMERIC
           VALUENAME SearchMode
           MIN 0 MAX 7 DEFAULT 0
         END PART
    ```

  - **DROPDOWNLIST.** Used for list boxes and values. The following is an example of this PART type:

    ```
    PART !!MyPolicy DROPDOWNLIST
        VALUENAME ValueToBeChanged
          ITEMLIST
           NAME "One" VALUE NUMERIC 1
           NAME "Two" VALUE NUMERIC 2
           NAME "Three" VALUE NUMERIC 3
           NAME "Four" VALUE NUMERIC 4
          END ITEMLIST
    END PART
    ```

  - **COMBOBOX.** Used for list boxes with a text field that can be overridden. Suggestions in the drop-down list are in the following format:

    ```
    SUGGESTIONS
           Red Yellow Pink "Royal Blue"
    END SUGGESTIONS
    ```

- **EDITTEXT.** Used for string data to be written to the Registry with a type of REG_SZ.
- **REQUIRED.** Can be added to make data entry mandatory.
- **EXPANDABLETEXT.** Used for string data that includes replaceable strings such as %SYSTEMROOT%. This is stored in the Registry with a type of REG_EXPAND_SZ.
- **CHECKBOX.** Used for values set to 0 or 1. The following is an example of this:

```
PART !!DomainLogonConfirmation CHECKBOX
       KEYNAME Network\Logon
       VALUENAME DomainLogonMessage
END PART
```

PARTS can contain the following values:

- **MAXLEN.** Used to set a maximum length for typed strings.
- **MIN and MAX.** Used to set boundries on NUMERIC data types.
- **DEFAULT.** Used to set a default value for text or numeric data types.
- **DEFCHECKED.** Causes check boxes to be enabled by default.
- **VALUEON and VALUEOFF.** Similar to CHECKBOX, except this is used when ON and OFF values are not 1 and 0. The following is an example of this:

```
POLICY !!HideDrives
       VALUENAME "NoDrives"
       VALUEON NUMERIC 67108863      ; low 26 bits on
(1 bit per drive)
END POLICY
```

- **ACTIONLISTON and ACTIONLISTOFF.** Used to display alternating action lists if a check box is on or off.

If you want to know more about the structure of template files, read the *Windows 95 Resource Kit.*

You have seen how to configure an environment through both user profiles and System policies. Next, you'll learn how to modify hardware configurations through hardware profiles.

Working with Hardware Profiles

Hardware profiles can be used to maintain different hardware configurations for a single computer. They often are used for a laptop that has a docking station. A person can use a hardware profile with additional accessories when the laptop is docked, then use a separate profile when it is not docked. Hardware profiles also can be used on desktop computers to enable certain hardware components in groups. You can disable your network card, for example, when you want to use your modem; this follows the security rules on your network.

You always have at least one hardware profile, usually called Original Configuration. Additional profiles can be created by coping the Original Configuration. You can access hardware profiles on the Hardware Profiles tab of the System control panel (see Figure 4.32). To create a new profile, click Copy… . To rename an existing profile, click Rename… .

To configure different profiles, go to the Device Manager (see Figure 4.33). In the properties for each device, a small section at the bottom of the page lets you disable or enable the device in each hardware profile. This is useful if you do not want to load certain drivers while others are loaded. You might not want to load your network card driver, for example, if your modem driver has been loaded. This follows a security rule on your network. This rule can be implemented to prevent people from accessing your network by calling into your modem.

When deleting hardware profiles, you cannot delete your current profile. Regardless of which profile you use, your data remains the same. It is important to keep it safe by backing it up.

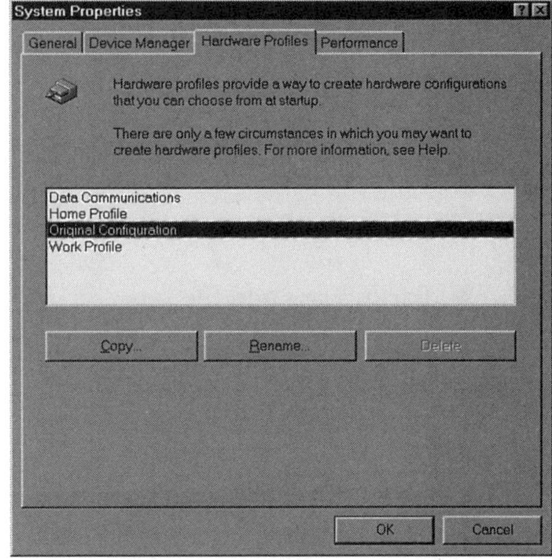

Figure 4.32

Hardware profiles are used to store different hardware configurations.

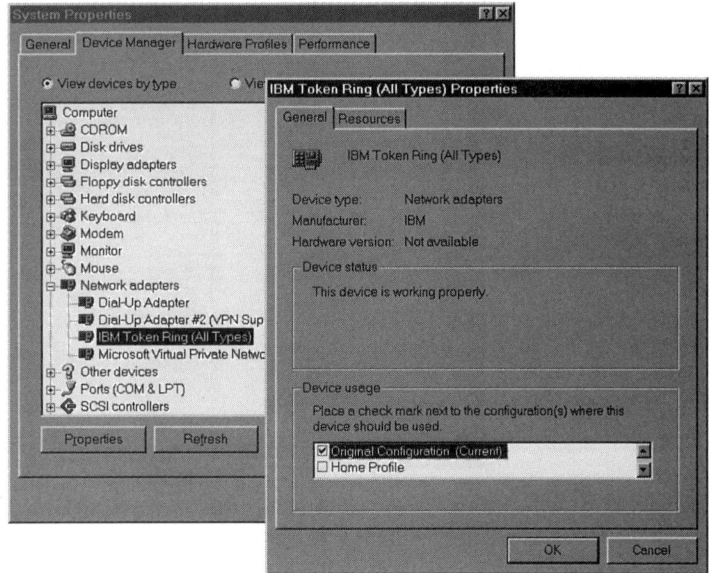

Figure 4.33

Device Manager is used to enable or disable hardware.

Backing Up and Restoring Data

To make sure system data is not lost due to power failures or other corruption, Windows 95 includes a Backup utility that enables users to make a copy of the data on their hard drives and to store it on alternate media. If the Backup utility is installed, you should be able to find it in the Start menu under Programs, Accessories,

System Tools, Backup (see Figure 4.34). You need to make several decisions regarding backup procedures. This section discusses the following topics:

- Backup destinations
- Backup types
- Backup sets and file sets
- Other features of Windows 95 Backup
- Restoring files from Backup

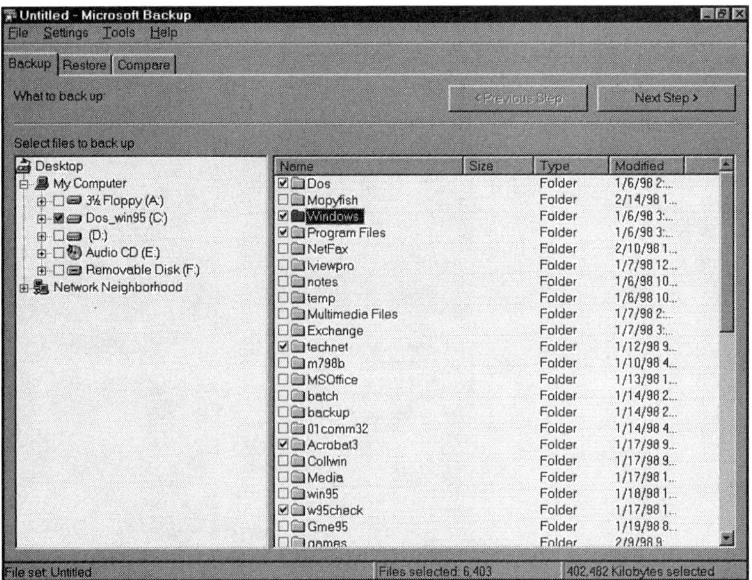

Figure 4.34

The Backup utility provided with Windows 95 is capable of maintaining complete backups of your system.

Learning the Different Backup Destinations

When making a backup copy of important data, you can use several different media types to store the copy. The Windows 95 Backup program supports the following four backup methods:

- Backing up to a tape drive
- Backing up to floppies

- Backing up to a hard drive
- Backing up to a network location

Backup to Tape

The capability to use tape drive backups is new in the Windows 95 version of Backup (previous MS-DOS versions supported only floppy backups). The tape media supported is Quarter-Inch Cartridge (QIC), which comes in various specifications. The supported tape drive specifications are as follows:

- QIC 40, QIC 80, and QIC 3010 tape drives connected through the primary floppy disk controller
- QIC 40, QIC 80, and QIC 3010 tape drives connected to a parallel port

SCSI tape backup units are not supported by Windows 95 Backup.

Windows 95 should be able to detect any supported tape drives automatically. If it cannot detect the tape drive, a message to that effect appears after starting Backup. A number of troubleshooting suggestions also are listed (see Figure 4.35).

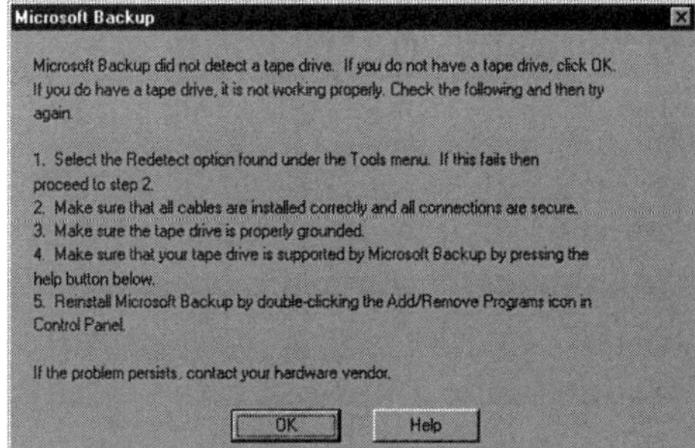

Figure 4.35

The Backup provided with Windows 95 can maintain a complete backup of your system.

Backup to Floppies

Floppies are the standard backup destination for both the MS-DOS and Windows 3.1 versions of Backup. Files are transferred from the local hard drive to a number of floppies.

Backup to Hard Drive

If you have a second hard drive on your computer, you can use a folder on this drive as a backup destination (see Figure 4.36). Although it's possible for the destination to be on the same drive, this does not give you any safety if the drive seizes or becomes corrupted. Backing up to a hard drive also eliminates the need for dozens of floppies.

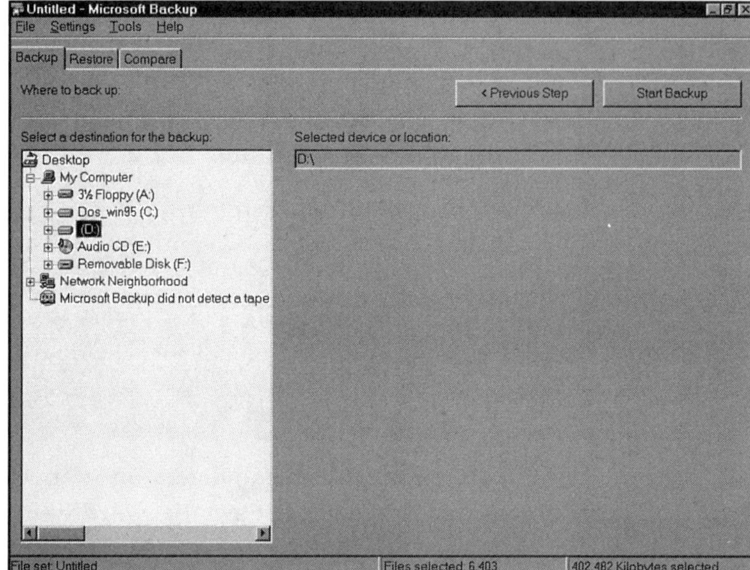

Figure 4.36

A second hard drive can be a fast, convenient backup location.

Backup to a Network Location

This type of backup enables the user to back up files to a remote location on the network. Backing up to a remote network location can be useful, for example, if a network administrator wants all users to back up their files to one central location on the network to simplify his management tasks. If you use a network location, make sure you have permission from your network administrator. Your administrator will make sure there's sufficient space to hold your backups, and he will monitor your disk usage.

Learning the Backup Types

Files can be backed up using either a full backup or an incremental backup. In a full backup, all selected files are backed up. An incremental backup copies only files that have changed since the last backup (full or incremental). The time/date stamp helps determine which files need to be backed up. Incremental backups typically are used to maintain archives without unnecessarily backing up files that have not changed since the last full or incremental backup. This conserves disk space at the backup destination. To restore the files, the full backup and all the incremental backups must be restored.

Learning the Backup Sets and File Sets

A *backup set* is a collection of files that have been backed up. A backup set is created during each backup procedure. It contains not only the actual files but the parameters set for the backup (for example, which file types to include). A *file set* is a list of files you want to back up. You can save file sets; you don't have to reselect the files every time you perform a backup.

Other Features of Windows 95 Backup

Exercise 4.3 demonstrates the use of the Windows 95 Backup utility. Make sure you have at least 6MB of free space on the C drive before you complete this exercise.

Windows 95 contains a number of additional features, including the following:

- It is possible to compare a backup set and the directory from which it was backed up to determine any differences between the two.
- LFNs are fully supported.
- It is possible to drag and drop backup sets onto a Backup icon to restore the set. You also can double-click the backup set icon to start the backup procedure. The backup program prompts you to confirm your actions.
- During a full-system backup, Windows 95 also backs up the Registry by copying it to a temporary file. When the backup set is restored, the Registry files are merged back into the existing Registry. Merging the Registry files back into the system eliminates errors caused by restoring to a computer with different hardware components.

- Backup enables the filtering of file types for inclusion or exclusion from a file set. File extensions can be excluded from backups using File Filter from the Settings menu.

MS-DOS 6.2 and Windows 3.1 backup sets cannot be restored using the Windows 95 Backup utility. This is due to incompatibility issues with LFNs in MS-DOS 6.2 and earlier.

Restoring Files from Backup

There are two times you'll definitely want to restore files: when you have lost a file or directory and when your entire hard drive has been lost or corrupted. In the latter situation, you have to install Windows 95 and then restore all your files. If you have lost or corrupt files, you only have to restore those files.

To restore files on your computer, you first launch the backup application. Select the Restore tab and locate your backup file (*.QIC). The Next Step > button opens a screen that enables you to select the individual files you want to restore. To select a file or folder to restore, place a check in front of it. To start the restore procedure, click Start Restore.

If there are any errors during the restore process, you are informed at the end and are asked if you want to view the error log. The log lists any files that were not restored and tells why Windows 95 was not able to restore them.

Backing up and restoring your data keeps it safe. In the short term, there are several things you can do to manage your drives.

Managing Hard Disks

This section discusses some of the basic features you can use to manage your hard disks. Tools such as Disk Defragmenter and ScanDisk are discussed in Chapter 6, "Monitoring and Optimization." This section covers the following features:

- Disk compression
- Partitioning
- Long filenames

This section covers disk management, not disk maintenance. Management involves planning and nonroutine tasks such as partitioning; maintenance involves routine tasks such as defragmentation.

Disk Compression

Windows 95 implements a form of disk compression known as *on-the-fly compression*. On-the-fly compression is so named because the compression/decompression process occurs automatically in the background and is transparent to the user. On-the-fly compression intercepts normal MS-DOS read/write calls and compresses the data before writing it to the hard disk. This enables the data to consume less space. When the data is read back, it automatically is uncompressed before being transferred to the application or process that requested it.

Disk compression, as implemented in Windows 95 (and in the version released with MS-DOS 6.x), consists of two processes. The first process, *token conversion*, replaces repetitive patterns in a given piece of data with a token, which takes up less space.

The second process, *sector allocation granularity*, changes the way data is stored on a hard drive by circumventing the large amounts of wasted space often created under a normal FAT file system. FAT file systems operate based on a cluster being the smallest traceable unit of measure. If the cluster size is 4KB, for example, and a 2KB file is stored in that cluster, 2KB are wasted. If 1,000 such files exist on a hard drive, 1,000×2 KB are wasted. With disk compression in place, the smallest allocation unit shrinks to one sector (or 512 bytes), which can greatly reduce the amount of wasted space on a drive. The two utilities that perform these actions are DoubleSpace and DriveSpace.

DoubleSpace and DriveSpace Structure

Microsoft first included disk compression with MS-DOS version 6.0, and the disk compression was called DoubleSpace. It later was re-released as DriveSpace in MS-DOS version 6.2. This new version contained some changes to the compression routines and a major new feature—the capability to uncompress a drive. The compression structure has since remained fairly consistent.

After disk compression is installed and the files are initially compressed, the files are stored in the Compressed Volume File (CVF). This actually is a large hidden file sitting on the physical drive C. When the system boots up, however, the CVF is assigned drive letter C. The physical C drive, which now contains only a few files because everything else is compressed inside the CVF, is assigned a higher drive letter, typically H. This higher-letter drive is called a host drive and is hidden from normal view by default. The process of switching the drive letters and making the CVF available for viewing in MS-DOS and Windows is called *mounting*. From this point on, any file operation is handled through the disk compression routines. These routines are responsible for compressing and uncompressing files as disk I/O requests are made by the operating system.

Advantages of Windows 95 Disk Compression

Windows 95 disk compression contains many features optimized specifically for Windows 95. The following are the main advantages of using Windows 95 disk compression:

- Disk compression is implemented with 32-bit code for better performance.
- It does not use any conventional memory.
- It is integrated with the operating system for ease of use and better performance.

When a floppy is compressed, the DriveSpace drivers only load when the floppy is in the drive. In general, DriveSpace drivers only load when compressed media (hard drive or floppy) is detected.

Further Notes on Windows 95 Disk Compression

Exercise 4.2 illustrates how disk compression can be used in Windows 95. Due to the considerable amount of time it takes to compress an entire hard drive, the exercise focuses on compressing a floppy disk.

The following information should be noted whenever a user is considering Windows 95 disk compression:

- Windows 95 is compatible with many third-party compression utilities such as Stacker versions 2.x, 3.x, and 4.x and all versions of SuperStor. These use real-mode compression, however; they take up conventional memory and are usually slower.
- The maximum size of a compressed volume is 512MB when using DriveSpace 2.0, which comes with Windows 95. If you use Microsoft Plus! or have Windows95 OSR2, both of which include DriveSpace 3.0, the maximum size of a compressed volume is 2GB. This size refers to the compressed size.
- The average compression ratio of a compressed volume is 2:1 (using DriveSpace 2.0). If you use Microsoft Plus! or OSR2, you can take advantage of DriveSpace 3.0, which improves the average compression ratio to approximately 2.4:1. Certain types of documents compress better than others.

DriveSpace enables you to set a compression ratio, which is used to report free space to the user. If you know you use your drive for files that do not compress much or that compress a lot, you might want to modify the compression ratio to get a more accurate reporting of free space. Files that are already compressed—such as JPEG or JPG, MPEG and ZIP—do not compress much if at all. Files that contain repetitive strings of text—such as a single page of type repeated 50 times in a document—compress fantastically. Most text or word

continues

processing documents compress well because people tend to use the same words throughout their documents. BMPs and other uncompressed graphics also compress well because they usually repeat color strings such as a white background (white, white, white, white, ...).

You might find that disk compression enhances, degrades, or leaves system performance at the same level. If you work on a system with large amounts of RAM (24–32MB) and have a slow hard drive with a fast CPU, you might notice disk compression improving system performance. With disk compression, you gain by reading smaller amounts of data (the compressed data) from the hard drive; you then must decompress that data in RAM. If the time spent decompressing the data is less than the time you would have spent reading the data, you get a performance increase. Most new computers have fast CPUs and more RAM. They also have fast hard drives, however, which lowers or reverses the speed benefit. On new computers, you likely will notice that the system performance decreases. It likewise will decrease on systems that are low on RAM or that have slow CPUs.

Effective use of compression can save a lot of space on your hard disk. Eventually, however, you will outgrow your current hard disk and decide to get a new one. In the next section, you learn how to prepare a hard drive for use.

Partitioning

Before a hard drive can be used in your computer, it has to be prepped with a partitioning utility. Most new hard drives are preformatted, but you might want to repartition the drive to meet your current needs. In Windows 95, the partitioning utility is FDISK.EXE (see Figure 4.37).

When dealing with drives over 540MB with OSR2, you have the option to enable large drive support. This enables partitions larger than 512MB to be formatted with FAT32. The following table provides differences between FAT16 and FAT32.

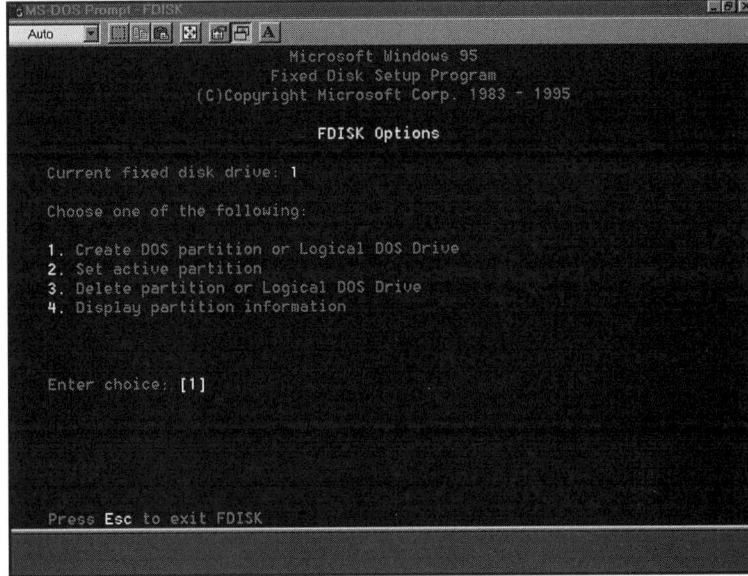

Figure 4.37

FDISK is used to create and delete partitions.

Table 4.3

Comparison Between FAT16 and FAT32

Description	FAT16	FAT32
Maximum partition size	2GB	2TB
Cluster size on a 2GB partition	32KB	4KB
Support for DriveSpace compression	Yes	No

In addition to these differences, the only operating system that can read FAT32 partitions after being installed is Windows 95 OSR2. The only way to remove a FAT32 partition is to delete it and create a new partition.

DOS and Windows 95 have some features in common when dealing with partitions. Both only allow the creation of one primary partition and one extended partition, which can hold as many logical drives as you want. Other operating systems sometimes allow the creation of multiple primary partitions. Windows 95 can read these multiple primary partitions, even though it cannot create them.

To create a partition, you first must launch FDISK.EXE. When FDISK is open, choose 1 to Create a DOS Partition or Logical DOS Drive. This option enables you to choose between a primary DOS partition, an extended DOS partition, or a logical drive(s) in the extended DOS partition. You only can create one primary partition and one extended partition on the drive. The extended partition is not usable unless you create logical drives within it. The primary partition is the bootable partition from which the computer loads the OS. The logical drives in the extended partition are not bootable; they only can be used for holding data.

If you used a product other than FDISK to create your partitions, you might end up with multiple primary partitions. Only one primary partition can be used to boot the computer. This one partition is the active partition.

FDISK knows how to identify primary partitions that are FAT16, FAT32, and OS/2's HPFS. Because NTFS and HPFS have similar structures, FDISK identifies NTFS partitions as HPFS. Windows 95 cannot read information off either NTFS or HPFS partitions. You can delete either of these partitions (NTFS or HPFS) by choosing option 3, Delete Partition or Logical DOS Drive, from the FDISK main menu and then choosing to delete the NON-DOS partition.

When choosing a size for a new partition, the smaller the partition, the smaller the cluster size. Each file saved to the hard drive has to use at least one cluster, regardless of the file's size. If you save a text file containing 20 characters of text to your hard drive, the text file should take up 20 bytes of space. If your hard drive has a cluster size of 16 KB, the file actually uses 16 KB of space. You can make the cluster size smaller by making the partition size smaller. This enables you to store less overall data on your hard drive, but it lessens the impact of lost space from large cluster sizes.

Understanding File System Support

To understand how Windows 95 supports long filenames, you need to understand how Windows 95 handles all file systems. This section looks at the Installable file system architecture.

Windows 95's modular design enables it to adapt to developing technologies. In this modular design, generic features of Windows 95 subsystems—such as networking, printing, and communications—are implemented into a universal component (for example, the universal printer driver). Functions that are specific to a type or brand of hardware or software are implemented in a type-specific driver (for example, the printer mini-driver for a Hewlett-Packard LaserJet). If a generic printing function is called by the operating system, it is handled by the universal printer driver; functions specific to an HP LaserJet are handled by the mini-driver.

Microsoft also uses a modular architecture for Windows 95 file systems. All I/O requests first are handled by a universal file-system manager. Instead of reengineering the operating system to implement compatibility with existing or future file-system structures, all that is necessary to accommodate a new file system type is a file-system driver that can communicate with the universal file-system driver and that can handle the unique functions of that file system.

The Windows 95 file systems are known as *installable* file systems because they can be loaded into and removed from the system memory as needed. This is another indication of the modularity of the Windows 95 file-system components.

File operations are handled by the installable file system (IFS) components of Windows 95. These components include the following:

- IFS Manager
- File-system drivers
- I/O Supervisor
- Volume Tracker
- Type-specific drivers
- Port drivers

IFS Manager

The IFS Manager analyzes incoming I/O requests from applications and other processes and determines which file-system driver can fulfill requests most effectively. When you install a new file-system driver, it registers itself with the IFS Manager. It informs the IFS Manager what types of I/O requests it can process. Note that the file-system driver does not need to know how to communicate with applications or other processes directly. It only needs to know how to communicate with the IFS Manager.

File-System Drivers

File-system drivers enable I/O requests to be sent to and from the installed file systems. Windows 95 includes support for the following file systems (although you can add others using third-party drivers):

- 32-bit virtual FAT (VFAT)
- 32-bit CD-ROM file system (CDFS)
- 32-bit network redirectors
- 16-bit FAT

The VFAT file-system driver (FSD) is the primary FSD for the system and cannot be disabled. It is responsible for all local hard disk I/O requests (including SCSI). This FSD gives Windows 95 a fully 32-bit virtualized MS-DOS FAT file system. Like all FSDs, VFAT supports long filenames (LFNs). (LFNs are discussed in more detail in the "Long Filenames" section later in this chapter.)

VFAT only is used for hard drives with 32-bit disk-access components installed. If a drive is accessed through real-mode drivers (for example, an Ontrack Disk Manager driver in CONFIG.SYS), the drive is accessed through MS-DOS compatibility mode and does not take advantage of the 32-bit VFAT.

In the case of SCSI drives, after the TSD for hard drives determines that a given I/O request is intended for a SCSI drive, a number of sublayers come into play. The TSD passes the request to either a SCSI translator for hard drives or one for CD-ROM drives. The translator is responsible for translating generic I/O commands into commands the SCSI bus can understand. These are known as SCSI command descriptor blocks.

The SCSI Manager then takes control and acts as the intermediary between the SCSI translator and the lowest layer—the miniport drivers, which are responsible for communicating with specific brands of SCSI adapters. There might be a specific miniport driver, for example, for all Adaptec SCSI controllers or for one particular product line.

Because data on a CD-ROM is stored and accessed differently than data on a hard drive, a separate FSD for CD-ROM file access is required. CDFS passes on the CD-ROM I/O request to a specific device driver based on one of the following four CD-ROM configurations:

- **IDE CD-ROM.** With this configuration, the CD-ROM typically is attached to the IDE hard drive controller of the computer. The I/O request is passed on to the ESDI_506.PDR port driver, which is the same driver used to communicate with IDE hard drives.
- **SCSI CD-ROM.** This type of CD-ROM is connected on the SCSI bus of the computer, along with any SCSI hard drives or other SCSI devices. It is supported through the various SCSI driver layers previously mentioned (see the section "VFAT File System Driver").
- **Proprietary CD-ROM controller.** This type of CD-ROM controller often is integrated on a sound card. Windows 95 currently ships with protected-mode drivers for proprietary controllers from Sony, Panasonic, and Mitsumi. Any other type of proprietary CD-ROM controller must be supported through protected-mode drivers from the OEM or through real-mode CD-ROM drivers until protected-mode drivers become available.

- **Real-mode CD-ROM drivers specified in CONFIG.SYS or AUTOEXEC.BAT.** All CD-ROM drives that do not fall into the preceding categories are supported by MS-DOS-based drivers specified in CONFIG.SYS or AUTOEXEC.BAT. The CD-ROM drive is said to be operating in MS-DOS compatibility mode.

Any hard drive or CD-ROM drive running in MS-DOS compatibility mode cannot take advantage of protected-mode caching. The MS-DOS disk cache Smartdrive must be used instead.

If the IFS Manager determines that an I/O request cannot be satisfied locally and that it likely is intended for a remote device, it attempts to pass the request to one of the 32-bit network FSDs (if any Windows 95 networking components have been installed). Chapter 5, "Integration and Operability," examines network redirectors in more detail.

Windows 95 includes support for the 16-bit FAT file system, which was used in MS-DOS and Windows 3.1. These operating systems used 16-bit, real-mode code to manage the 16-bit FAT and to read and write from the disk. In Windows 95, protected-mode drivers can be used to access the 16-bit FAT. MS-DOS file I/O access performance actually is increased in Windows 95 because the disk file system can be accessed from protected mode without dropping into real mode.

I/O Supervisor

The I/O Supervisor oversees all local I/O requests (as opposed to network-based requests). When the IFS Manager determines that a given I/O request can be fulfilled on the local computer, it passes the request to the I/O Supervisor. The I/O Supervisor's other duties include registering port and mini-drivers when a new device is installed and sending dynamic messages to drivers as necessary (for example, in the case of a Plug and Play event).

Volume Tracker

The Volume Tracker identifies and monitors removable media, such as CD-ROMs, floppies, and removable hard drives. It ensures that the correct media type is present and that it is not removed or inserted at the wrong time. The Volume Tracker enables CD-ROMs to autoexecute when inserted, for example, by polling the CD-ROM drive constantly for new insertions. When the Volume Tracker detects such an event, it scans the CD-ROM for a file called AUTORUN.INF. If it finds this file, it executes the commands in the file. The Volume Tracker also identifies disk geometry; it notes, for example, when a 1.44 MB floppy is removed and a 720 KB floppy is inserted.

Type-Specific Drivers

Type-specific drivers (TSDs) are intermediate to the I/O Supervisor and the physical device drivers (port drivers) that actually communicate with the hardware. TSDs are responsible for all functions associated with a particular type of hardware, such as CD-ROMs, floppy drives, or hard disks. A TSD for CD-ROM drives, for example, handles functions specific to CD-ROMs but not those specific to SCSI CD-ROMs.

Port Drivers

Port drivers, last in the chain of command, translate logical I/O requests (for example, "put this data on the CD-ROM") into physical requests (for example, "put these bytes on track 9, section 5 of the CD-ROM").

This completes the description of the Windows 95 file system architecture. The next section discusses how Windows 95 deals with long filenames.

Long Filenames

Windows 95 supports long filenames. In addition to its support of long filenames, you should be aware of the following:

- Rules for the construction of long and short filenames
- Long filename data structure

- Issues with long filenames
- Adding long filename support for Novell NetWare

Windows 95 supports descriptive filenames up to 255 characters, which includes blank spaces. A file's path can have up to 260 total characters. If both the path and the filename are specified, however, the total still can only be 260 characters. To remain backward-compatible with Windows 3.1 and DOS applications, Windows 95 automatically generates an 8.3-format short filename (known as the *alias*) for each LFN. The algorithm for the auto-generation of this short filename is as follows:

1. Remove any characters that are illegal in MS-DOS filenames, such as spaces.
2. For the eight-character name, take the first six remaining characters of the LFN, add a tilde character (~), and add an incremental number beginning with 1.

The number is added to ensure unique short filenames. Two files named November Sales Forecast and November Marketing Report, for example, would both auto-generate the character name Novemb~. To differentiate between them, one is named Novemb~1 and the other is named Novemb~2. If more than nine similar files exist, the first five characters are used, plus the tilde (~) and a two-digit number.

3. To create the three-character extension, take the first three remaining characters after the last period. If the long filename contains no period, the extension is omitted.

Long filenames preserve the case of characters, but they are not case sensitive. When you copy long filenames to floppy disks, they are preserved. The shorter 8.3 filenames also are not case sensitive, but they do not preserve the case of characters (see Table 4.4 for examples).

Table 4.4 shows how sample long filenames convert to short filenames. Each of the files in the table is assumed to be saved in the same folder; the files were created in the ordered shown.

Table 4.4

Converting Long Filenames to Short Filenames

Long Filename	Converted Short Filename
Fiscal Report Quarter 1.XLS	FISCAL~1.XLS
Fiscal Report Quarter 2.XLS	FISCAL~2.XLS
Fiscal Report Quarter 4.XLS	FISCAL~3.XLS
Employee Benefits 1997.DOC	EMPLOY~1.DOC
Employee Benefits 1998.DOC	EMPLOY~2.DOC
Taxes.Mdb	TAXES.MDB

Rules for the Construction of Long and Short Filenames

The following rules apply when creating a long filename and when generating a short filename alias:

- The symbols \ / : * ? " < > | are illegal in both long and short filenames.
- The symbols + , ; = [ ] are permitted in a long filename but not in a short filename alias.
- Lowercase characters in a long filename are converted to uppercase characters in a short filename alias.

Long Filename Data Structure

In a standard FAT-based operating system, the root directory of a hard disk can contain a maximum of 512 directory entries. In MS-DOS, each file or subdirectory typically takes up an entry. In the case of long filenames, however, each requires a minimum of two directory entries: one for the alias and one for every 13 characters of the long filename. A long filename with 79 characters, for example, requires seven entries (78/13=6, plus 1 for the alias).

It's important to remember this requirement for additional directory entries when dealing with LFNs in the root directory. This is because the MS-DOS limit of 512 entries in the root directory still applies. These entries get used up much more quickly with LFNs.

Issues with Long Filenames

When working in an environment that accepts both long and short filenames, you should be aware of the following issues:

- LFNs are active only when Windows 95 is running. Because they are integrated with the 32-bit file system native to Windows 95, LFNs are not visible, for example, when Command Prompt Only is selected from the Boot menu when the system boots. (LFNs are visible, however, from a DOS prompt inside Windows 95).

- When specifying LFNs with embedded spaces, you must enclose the name in double quotes, as in "MARKETING BUDGET WORKSHEET".

- Even if you do not add an extension to a file when you create it, the application you are using might automatically add an extension. (WordPad, for example, adds the extension `.doc` to any saved file by default.) Filenames enclosed in double quotes usually do not have the extension added.

- Using file utilities that are not long filename-aware (such as those in MS-DOS 6.x and earlier) to copy or rename a long filename destroys the long filename and leaves only the alias.

- If you are using a Windows 3.1 application and choose Save As (effectively renaming the file), the long filename is lost. If you choose Save, however, the long filename is preserved because the existing name is reused.

- Using a disk-repair utility that is not long filename-aware (such as MS-DOS 5.x ScanDisk or Norton Disk Doctor) on a volume containing LFNs might destroy the LFNs. The utility interprets the new long filename data structure as errors in the file system that must be corrected.

The file utilities SCANDISK.EXE, CHKDSK.EXE, and DEFRAG.EXE that shipped with MS-DOS 6.x do not harm long filenames on your hard drive.

- Windows 95 can read LFNs from an NTFS volume but only at a remote location (across a network). For security reasons pertaining to Windows NT, Windows 95 does not read local NTFS volumes at all.
- Windows 95 can read LFNs from a NetWare server but only at a remote location (across a network). The NetWare server needs to be running OS/2 Name Space to store LFNs using HPFS rules (not Windows rules) for the naming of the 8.3 alias.
- If you perform a search on a group of files, Windows 95 searches both the long filename and the alias for occurrences of the given search criteria.

If you need to remove long filenames from a disk, such as to run hard disk utilities released prior to Windows 95, run the LFNBK.EXE utility. (The DriveSpace utility included with Windows 95 is compatible with long filenames; you can use it to manage compressed disks that have been created with older versions of DriveSpace or DoubleSpace.) The LFNBK utility is located on the Windows 95 CD-ROM in the \ADMIN\APPTOOLS\LFNBACK folder. When the LFNBK utility runs at the command prompt with the `/B` switch, it renames each file with an alias. After running LFNBK and restarting Windows, the Start menu appears with its default settings rather than with your custom Start menu. You can restore your custom Start menu by restoring long filenames—run the LFNBK utility with the `/R` switch.

continues

Before running LFNBK, read the LFNBK.TXT file in the \ADMIN\APPTOOLS\LFNBACK folder on the CD-ROM. This text file explains how to use LFNBK and discusses the switches and other options you can use.

In Windows NT, you can tell the OS not to create any long filenames on a FAT partition by enabling the HKEY_LOCAL_MACHINE\System\CurrentControlSet\control\FileSystem Registry entry and by setting the Win31FileSystem value to 01. This Registry key also shows up in Windows 95, but it has no effect there. There is no way to force users in Windows 95 to limit themselves to an 8.3-character filename.

Adding Long Filename Support for Novell NetWare

When you run Windows 95 on a Novell NetWare volume, you must install a module called 0S2.NAM (the OS/2 Name Space feature) to activate long filenames. NetWare does not support long filenames by itself. To install the OS/2 Name Space feature, type the following at the file server console:

```
LOAD OS/2
ADD NAME SPACE OS/2 TO VOLUME volume_name
```

In the preceding command, the *volume_name* parameter should be replaced by the name of the volume on which you want Name Space to be added. You also need to add the following to the STARTUP.NCF configuration file:

```
LOAD OS/2
```

Novell NetWare 3.1x, 4.0, and 4.1 use OS/2 name space to support long filenames, although it actually supports only 254 characters. With the introduction of IntraNetWare 4.11, the name of the support file is now LONG.NLM, and it supports filenames up to 255 characters in length.

After you make these changes, shut down the server and bring it back up to make the OS/2 Name Space feature functional at the server. In general, the Name Space feature places additional memory burdens on your server; you will probably want to add more server RAM.

Now that you understand how long filenames work in Windows 95, the following section discusses how Windows 95 supports DOS applications.

Establishing Application Environments for Microsoft MS-DOS Applications

Before discussing configuration of MS-DOS application environments, you need some background on how Windows 95 supports all applications. This section discusses the following topics:

- Virtual Memory Manager
- Processor rings
- Virtual machines
- Configuring MS-DOS PIFs

Virtual Memory Manager

Windows 95 uses two types of memory: physical and virtual. Most users are familiar with the amount of RAM, or physical memory, on the computer. The minimum RAM requirement on a computer running Windows 95 is 4MB. The recommended amount of RAM is at least 8MB. Many experts even suggest 24MB of RAM for Windows 95. With Windows 95, the operating system uses all the available physical memory on the computer. You can overcome hardware memory limitations through the use of virtual memory.

The Windows 95 operating system uses a flat memory model, which leverages the Intel 386 (or greater) processor's capability to handle 32-bit addresses. This flat memory model provides a logical address-space range of up to 4GB. Although current computer hardware does not yet handle 4GB of physical memory, some file servers now can run with several GB of RAM. Virtual memory bridges the gap between physical memory and logical memory.

The 4GB of addressable space used as virtual memory in the flat memory model is implemented through the use of RAM and a swap file. The Windows 95 operating system performs memory management, called *demand paging*, in which code and data are moved in 4-KB pages between physical memory and the temporary Windows 95 swap file on the hard drive. The Virtual Memory Manager controls paging and maintains a page table. The page table keeps track of which pages are swapped to the hard drive, which remain in RAM, and to which system process or application they belong.

Application programs are allocated virtual memory address space, which is the set of addresses available for use by that program. Both 32-bit Windows and MS-DOS-based programs are allocated private virtual memory address space. All 16-bit Windows-based programs share a single virtual memory address space. Figure 4.38 shows how Windows 95 allocates the 4GB of virtual memory to each address space. Each process is allocated a unique virtual address space of 4GB. The upper 2GB are shared with the system; the lower 2GB are private to the application.

The virtual memory is allocated as follows:

- **0–640KB.** If not used for a virtual DOS machine (VDM), this memory is made available for any real-mode device drivers and terminate-and-stay-resident (TSR) programs.
- **0–1MB.** In a VDM, this memory range is allocated for the execution of MS-DOS programs. If 16-bit Windows applications are run, they run in this space in the system VM. The 16-bit Windows applications operate much as they do in Windows 3.1.
- **1MB–4MB.** This memory range usually is unused. Windows 95 does not use this space, nor do Windows 32-bit applications. If this memory is needed by 16-bit Windows applications, it is available.

- **2MB–2GB.** This memory range is allocated for 32-bit Windows applications and some 16-bit Windows applications. Each Windows 32-bit application has its own address space; Windows 16-bit applications all share a common address space.
- **2GB–3GB.** This memory range is allocated to run all core system service components, shared DLLs, and other shared objects. These components are available to all applications.
- **3GB–4GB.** This memory range is reserved for all Ring 0 components, such as the file management subsystem and the VMM subsystem. Any VxDs are loaded in this address space.

Virtual memory and addresses enable you to have more memory available than actually exists on the computer in physical RAM. The Windows 95 swap file implementation is much improved over that in Windows 3.1.

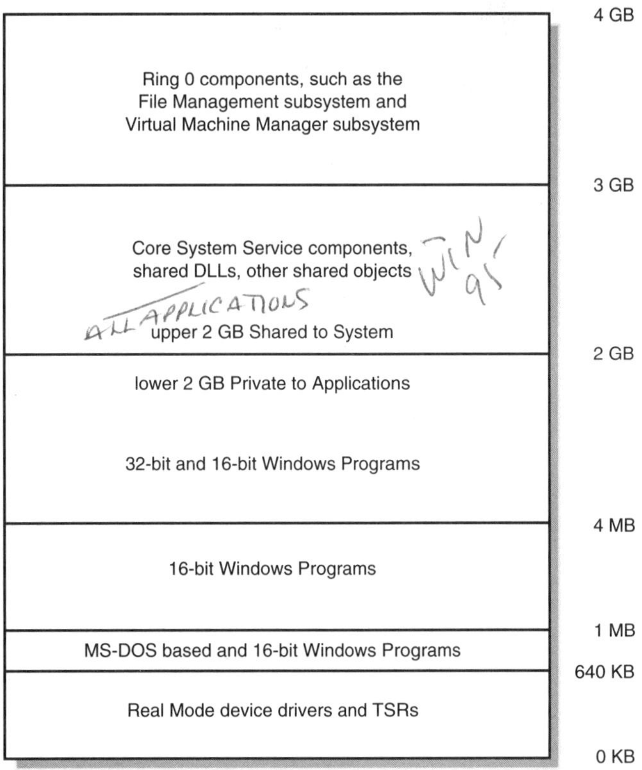

Figure 4.38

Virtual memory address space allocation.

With Windows 3.1, you can have either a temporary or permanent swap file. Windows 3.1 recommends how much hard disk memory to allocate to the swap file. If the hard-disk controller is compatible with 32-bit disk access, running 32-bit disk access will improve performance. A temporary swap file that does not need to be on contiguous hard disk space is created when Windows 3.1 starts. This same temporary swap file is released when the user exits Windows. Although a permanent, contiguous swap file provides better performance than a temporary swap file because it is a static file, hard disk space is not freed up when the user exits Windows.

In Windows 95, swap file configuration is much easier. The best features of both temporary and permanent swap files are combined through improved virtual memory algorithms and 32-bit access methods. By default, Windows 95 uses a dynamic swap file, which shrinks and grows based on the needs of the operating system and the available hard disk space. A permanent swap file has little benefit in Windows 95.

The best way to ensure swap file performance is to place the swap file on a hard disk with ample free space so the swap file can shrink or grow as required. If you have multiple hard drives, select the one with the fastest access time and the most free space.

Processor Rings

Windows 95 uses an Intel 386 (or better) processor to support multiple privilege levels for executable code. This means programs can run at one of four privilege levels. Privileges refer to how a program is allowed to interact with other programs, either at the same privilege level or at a different privilege level. Of the four levels, or *rings*, in the Intel 386 protection model, Windows 95 uses Rings 0 and 3. These rings provide different levels of protection and privileges. The lower the ring number, the higher the levels of protection and privileges.

Components of Windows 95 are divided between Ring 0 code and Ring 3 code. Each ring offers a different level of system protection. Ring 0 code is protected by the Intel processor architecture. It consists of low-level operating system services, such as the File Management subsystem and the Virtual Machine Manager subsystem. Ring 3 code is protected from other running processes by protection services provided in the operating system. Ring 3 code runs the system virtual machine and any virtual DOS machines.

Ring 0 components are protected by the processor architecture. The processor prevents a component's code from writing over another component's code. These Ring 0 components are the core elements of Windows 95. They can run all privileged operations including direct communication with hardware components. They have access to the entire operating system. One bad component in Ring 0 can bring down the entire system; therefore, every component in Ring 0 needs to be extremely reliable. All low-level Windows 95 core components run in Ring 0.

Ring 3 components have no processor protection; the operating system must provide protection for them. Ring 3 components cannot write to hardware components. They must communicate to a Ring 0 process to write to a hardware component. A bad application component in Ring 3 does not necessarily bring down the whole operating system. You usually can recover from any problems associated with a Ring 3 component by simply closing that component. Applications and noncritical system services of Windows 95 components run on Ring 3.

Understanding how the various components of an operating system fit together can be difficult. If you want to learn more about operating system components, the books *Windows 95 Resource Kit* and *Inside Windows 95* provide additional reference material. This section discusses only Windows 95 components.

Figure 4.39 shows you the Windows 95 components that run in both Ring 0 and Ring 3 of the Intel 386 protection model.

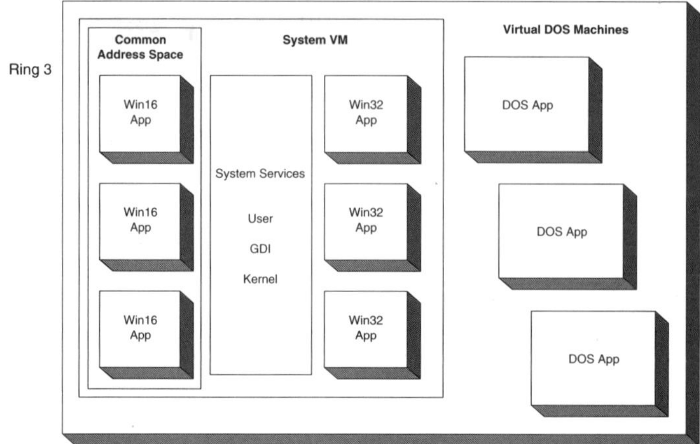

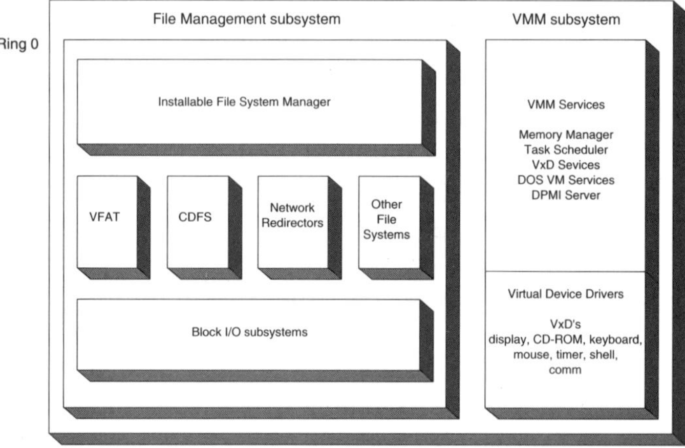

Figure 4.39

The Windows 95 system architecture.

Ring 3 hosts the virtual machines (VMs) in which MS-DOS, Windows 16-bit, and Windows 32-bit applications execute. The MS-DOS applications all run in separate VMs, known as Virtual DOS Machines (VDMs). All Windows applications, whether 16-bit or 32-bit, execute in the System VM. The System VM enables multiple concurrent applications to run. All Windows 32-bit applications are isolated in private address spaces, but all the active Windows 16-bit applications share a single address space. These applications are managed by the Virtual Machine Manager (VMM) in Ring 0. As a result, Windows 16-bit applications operate much as they do under Windows 3.1, in which they are cooperatively multitasked. Windows 32-bit and MS-DOS applications are preemptively multitasked. The central components of the

Windows graphical environment also run as system services. These include Kernel, GDI, and User.

Ring 0 hosts both the VMM subsystem and the File Management subsystem. The VMM subsystem provides the resources necessary for each application and system process running on the computer, including memory management and task scheduling. Virtual device drivers (VxDs) are 32-bit, protected-mode drivers that manage a system resource such as a hardware device or installed software. They enable more than one application to use the resource at the same time. The File Management subsystem features an Installable File System Manager that supports multiple file systems such as VFAT, CDFS, and Network redirectors. The Installable File System Manager also supports an open file-system architecture so future file systems can be added. The Block I/O subsystems are responsible for the interaction with the physical storage devices.

Much of the code in Windows 95, rather than 16-bit code, is either new 32-bit code or older Windows 3.x code rewritten as 32-bit code. Windows 95, however, is not completely a 32-bit operating system. Windows 95 strikes a balance between three requirements: delivering compatibility with existing applications and drivers, decreasing the size of the operating system to run on 4 MB of RAM, and offering improved system performance. To provide this balance, Windows 95 uses a combination of both 32-bit and 16-bit code.

Windows 95 employs 32-bit code wherever 32-bit code significantly improves performance without sacrificing application compatibility. Existing 16-bit code is retained where it is required to maintain compatibility or where 32-bit code increases memory requirements without significantly improving performance. All the I/O subsystems and device drivers in Windows 95, such as networking and file systems, are fully 32 bit. All memory management and scheduling components, such as Kernel and Virtual Memory Manager, are 32 bit as well. Figure 4.40 shows the relative distribution of 32-bit code versus 16-bit code in each of the Windows 95 system services. The sizes of the boxes in the figure illustrate the number of lines of code for each 16-bit and 32-bit version of the three system services files.

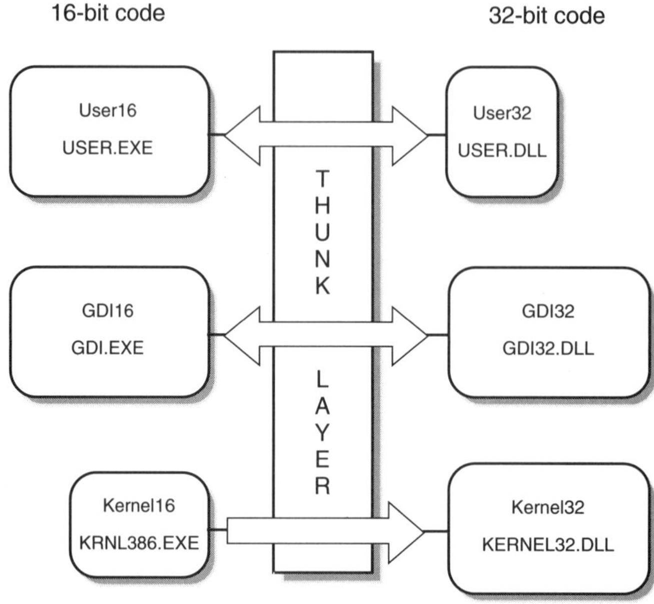

Figure 4.40

Ring 3 system services.

Three sets of files constitute the Windows 95 system services: the kernel, graphics device interface (GDI), and user interface files.

- **The kernel files (KRNL386.EXE and KERNEL32.DLL).** These files provide base operating system functions, including file I/O services, virtual memory management, application management, and task scheduling.
- **The GDI files (GDI.EXE and GDI32.DLL).** These files control the graphics operations that create images on the system display and other devices such as printers.
- **The user interface files (USER.EXE and USER32.DLL).** These files create and maintain windows on-screen and carry out all requests to create, move, size, or remove a window. The user interface files also handle requests regarding icons and other components of the user interface. They direct input to the appropriate application from the keyboard, mouse, and other input sources.

As illustrated, most of the system services provided by the operating system kernel are provided as 32-bit code. The remaining 16-bit code consists of hand-tuned assembly language, which delivers performance that rivals the 32-bit code. Many functions provided by the GDI have been moved to 32-bit code, including the spooler and printing subsystem, the font rasterizer, and the drawing operations performed by the graphics DIB engine. Roughly half of all GDI calls are handled in 32-bit code. The 16-bit code for GDI contains most of the drawing routines. Much of the window management user code still remains 16-bit to maintain Windows 16-bit application compatibility.

The Thunk Layer, shown in Figure 4.40, refers to the term thunking. This term describes how 16-bit code components communicate with their 32-bit code component counterparts. The thunking process translates memory addresses between 32-bit calls and 16-bit calls. A slight performance degradation occurs in the translation, but it is hardly noticeable.

Windows 95 provides 32-bit code to maximize the performance and reliability of the system. The 16-bit code balances the requirements for reducing operating system size while maintaining compatibility with existing applications and drivers.

Virtual Machines

All applications and dynamic link library (DLL) programs run in Ring 3. They execute in a virtual machine (VM), which looks like a separate computer from the application's perspective. A VM is an environment created by Windows 95 to simulate a complete computer. It contains all the resources available to a physical computer such as hard disk controllers and a timer. The VMM creates and maintains the virtual machine environments and provides each application with the necessary system resources to run the system.

The System VM runs the system services and all Windows 32-bit and 16-bit applications. The 16-bit Windows applications all run in a shared address space. Each 32-bit Windows application runs in its own private address space. Each MS-DOS application runs in its own separate VDM. The Virtual Machine Manager, in addition to creating and maintaining these virtual machines, provides the following key services:

- **Memory management.** The VMM controls the 4 GB of addressable virtual memory, paging from RAM to the hard disk, and performs memory address translation.
- **Task scheduling and multitasking.** The VMM allocates system resources and time to applications and other processes running on the computer.
- **MS-DOS mode support.** This is provided for MS-DOS applications that need exclusive access to system resources. This special mode of Windows 95 operations should not be confused with the VDM. It is a separate and exclusive MS-DOS operating environment that is discussed later in this chapter.

Understanding MS-DOS Program Information Files (PIFs)

A program information file (PIF) contains settings for establishing an MS-DOS environment for your MS-DOS application. This environment includes settings such as the amount of RAM the application has available to it. MS-DOS applications are 16-bit applications designed to work with MS-DOS version 6.x or earlier. Because these applications do not understand multitasking environments, it is necessary to simulate an MS-DOS environment for them to function properly. Windows 95 includes a number of improvements over Windows 3.x and Windows for Workgroups 3.x in handling MS-DOS applications. Windows 95 includes the following improvements:

- The capability to run in a window in most cases
- Better access to system resources because of the new 32-bit structure of the system resource stacks
- Improved support for sound devices
- Improved memory-protection schemes that enable you to isolate the MS-DOS system area to prevent it from being corrupted by misbehaving MS-DOS programs

- Support for scalable TrueType fonts in MS-DOS windows
- The capability to customize individual MS-DOS VMs with environment variables run from a batch file

The following additional information should be considered when using MS-DOS applications in Windows 95:

- Each executed MS-DOS application is assigned its own VM with separate virtualized device access and addressable memory space.
- The memory space created for an MS-DOS application mirrors that of a stand-alone DOS environment—640 KB of conventional memory, 384 KB of upper memory, and whatever extended or expanded memory is specified in the configuration settings of the MS-DOS session.
- Each MS-DOS application run in Windows 95 can execute only one thread at a time because MS-DOS does not support multithreading.

Note

MS-DOS applications cannot create threads of execution themselves. They generate MS-DOS hardware interrupts, which are intercepted by Windows 95 then translated into logical requests for executing a particular function.

- Each MS-DOS application has its own separate message queue to receive keyboard and mouse input.
- The APPS.INF file also contains configuration parameters for MS-DOS applications known to require them.

MS-DOS applications can be run in the following three modes:

- In an MS-DOS VM
- In MS-DOS mode after shutting down the Windows 95 GUI
- In MS-DOS mode outside of Windows 95 using parameters customized for the application

If Windows 95 detects that the application should be run in MS-DOS mode, it shuts down the Windows 95 GUI by default and runs the application in an environment similar to the one in which Command Prompt Only is selected from the Boot menu. The options on the shortcut Properties sheet for the MS-DOS application can be set to force the application to always run in MS-DOS mode or in a customized MS-DOS mode if necessary.

An application that does not require MS-DOS mode or is not configured to use it runs in an MS-DOS VM.

Several parameters can be configured to determine how an application runs in each of the preceding modes. These parameters are set through the Properties sheet of the application's shortcut and are described in the following sections.

MS-DOS Virtual Machine

MS-DOS VM mode should be used whenever possible because the application then can take advantage of 32-bit protected-mode driver support, preemptive multitasking, increased conventional memory, and other Windows 95 enhancements. All MS-DOS applications are set to run in an MS-DOS VM by default, whether they are executed by double-clicking the application from the Explorer or by typing the name of the file at a DOS prompt within Windows 95. If Windows 95 detects that the application must have exclusive use of the system resources and must run in MS-DOS mode, however, you are prompted to have Windows 95 automatically shut down the system and run the application in MS-DOS mode. Most applications should be able to function without incident in a VM. If an application functions, but not as well as it should, you can alter the configuration of the MS-DOS environment for that application.

Modifying PIF Settings

Numerous settings can be modified to facilitate the operation of MS-DOS programs. These settings can be configured in the properties of the application itself (see Figure 4.41) or in the properties of a shortcut to an application (see Figure 4.42). The settings are grouped into the following tabs on the Properties dialog box for the MS-DOS application:

- Program tab
- Font tab
- Memory tab
- Screen tab
- Misc tab

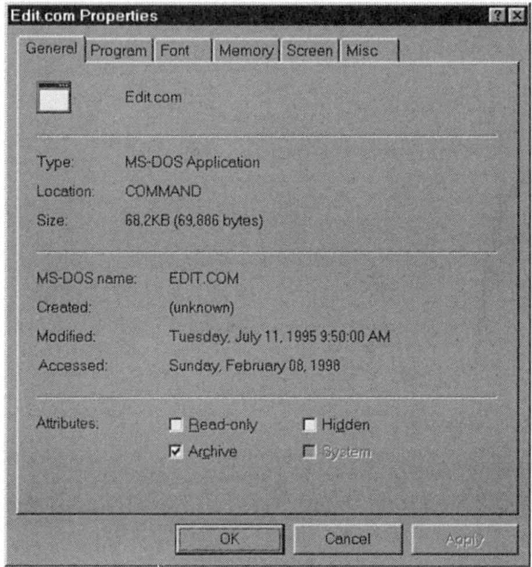

Figure 4.41

The properties of an application enable you to change the way the application executes.

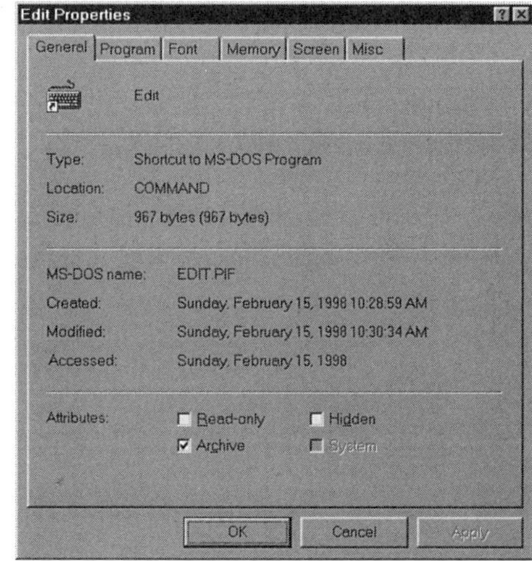

Figure 4.42

The properties of a PIF enable you to change the way the application executes.

The file extension on shortcuts to MS-DOS applications is `.pif`, unlike other shortcuts in Windows 95 that use `.lnk`. Each shortcut or PIF for an MS-DOS application can have its own settings so that multiple configurations can be set up in advance and enacted by double-clicking the shortcut (see Figure 4.43).

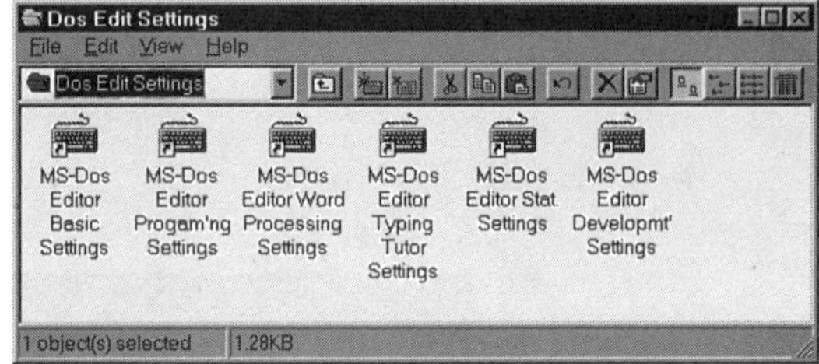

Figure 4.43

Multiple PIF's can be maintained for applications for different situations.

Program Tab

The Program tab includes settings that provide the location of files used to run the application as well as some other settings. The Advanced button on the Program tab is used to force the application to run in MS-DOS mode. Figure 4.44 displays the Program tab.

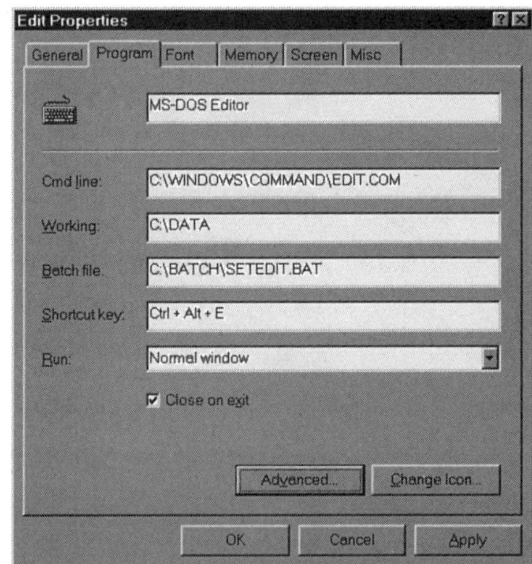

Figure 4.44

The Program tab of the MS-DOS Properties sheet.

The following list describes the parameters of the Program tab:

- **Cmd Line.** The path and filename of the MS-DOS program in question. Includes command-line parameters as permitted. The command line for the Edit command, for example, is C:\WINDOWS\COMMAND\EDIT.COM.

- **Working.** Indicates where data files should be stored if they are not in the directory in which the program resides. To save work in the MYWORK directory, for example, the working directory would be C:\MYWORK.

- **Batch File.** The name of a batch file that runs and loads any TSRs or specific environment variables that the program needs. You can specify DOSKEY, for example, to run before opening up a command prompt. If it is the only command you need to issue, DOSKEY.EXE could be your batch file.

- **Shortcut Key.** The key combination that can be used to run the program instead of clicking the shortcut icon.

Verify that the key combination you select is not in use by any other application. That application is no longer able to respond to that combination of keys after it is specified here.

- **Run.** Indicates whether to run the program in a normal window, minimized, or maximized.

- **Close on Exit.** If checked, the DOS VM window closes automatically when the application finishes processing. If not checked, the application finishes and includes the word Finished in the title bar of the application. It is useful to leave the window open after exiting if you want to see any error messages the application might generate when exiting.

Font Tab

This tab enables you to specify whether you want to use TrueType fonts, bitmap fonts, or both to display characters in the MS-DOS session. You also can choose from various font sizes and can

preview them before making a final selection. Figure 4.45 shows the Font tab.

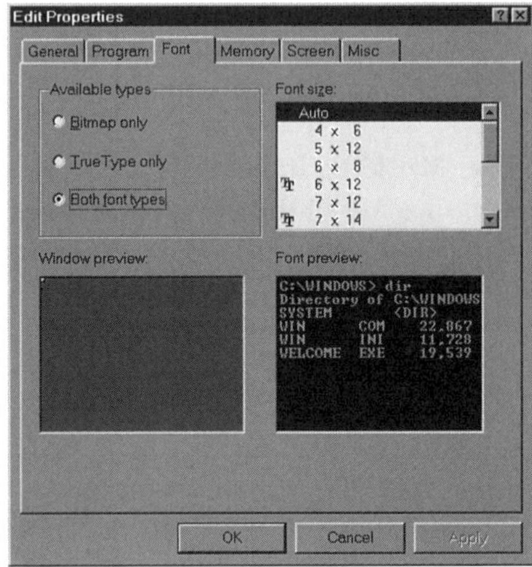

Figure 4.45

The Font tab of the MS-DOS Properties sheet.

If you leave the font size set to Auto, it is adjusted each time you resize the window of the MS-DOS application.

Memory Tab

In the Memory tab (see Figure 4.46), you can specify the type and quantity of memory the program needs in order to function. The four supported memory types are as follows:

- Conventional
- Expanded (EMS)
- Extended (XMS)
- DOS-protected mode (DPMI)

Windows 95 automatically allocates any memory the application needs when the application first requests it during operation. Some applications function better, however, if a fixed amount is allocated to them from the beginning. If the application queries the system for the amount of free memory before launching, it will fail to launch and you will have to specify the amount of memory on this tab. The conversation goes something like this:

Application:	Computer, how much memory is available for me to execute in?
Computer:	How much would you like?
Application (misunderstanding the response):	That is not enough.

Oddly enough, applications that do not check for an amount of free memory usually work at the automatic setting. The Initial Environment setting is used to specify additional environment memory for variables and other MS-DOS settings.

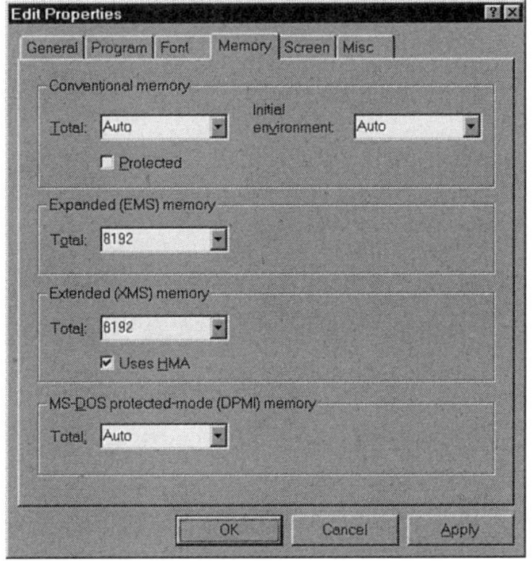

Figure 4.46

The Memory tab of the MS-DOS Properties sheet.

When many named variables are set within the AUTOEXEC.BAT file, the default environment memory can be used up rapidly. The lack of sufficient environment memory can prevent MS-DOS applications from running properly. In a real-world example, this lack of sufficient environment memory prevented the Microsoft System Management Server RUNSMS.BAT file from executing when booting an MS-DOS computer. The Memory tab settings in the Edit Properties dialog box can help correct these problems and meet the requirements of applications.

As previously mentioned, the Protected check box provides a higher level of security for the MS-DOS memory of this program by preventing it from being paged to disk. Some applications cannot be retrieved from the hard drive without stalling.

If multiple applications are launched, using the Protected check box to provide increased security can have a detrimental effect on overall system performance. If you include a statement in the CONFIG.SYS file that loads EMM386.EXE with the `noems` parameter, however, DOS protected-mode memory cannot be provided. Use the `RAM` parameter when loading EMM386.EXE in CONFIG.SYS, or use the `x=mmmm-nnnn` statement to allocate enough space in the upper memory area for Windows 95 to create an EMS page frame. See the *Windows 95 Resource Kit* for more details.

Screen Tab

The Screen tab contains settings that control how the application is displayed and how it uses video memory. Figure 4.47 shows the Screen tab.

The settings on the Screen tab include the following:

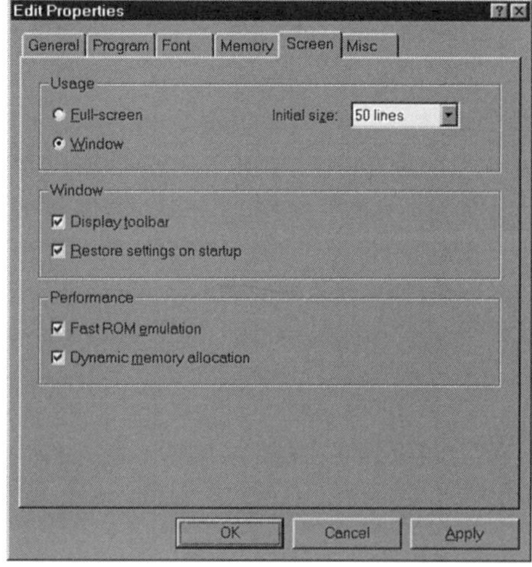

Figure 4.47

The Screen tab of the MS-DOS Properties sheet.

- **Usage.** This setting specifies in which video mode the program initially appears. The choices are Full-Screen (equivalent to what the program would look like in MS-DOS) or Window (a graphical mode simulation). Window displays the application in a window where it can coexist with other windowed applications. The initial width and height (in characters) also can be specified in the Initial Size field.

Not all applications respond to changes specified in the Initial Size field of the Screen tab. The MS-DOS Editor responds to any change in settings, but the Quick Basic 4.5 Editor, which resembles the MS-DOS Editor, ignores the settings and uses the default of 25 lines per screen.

- **Display Toolbar.** This setting is used to specify whether Windows 95 displays a toolbar at the top of a windowed MS-DOS session. The toolbar contains Cut, Paste, and Full Screen buttons among others. If you run the program full screen, the toolbar is not visible and this setting makes no difference.
- **Restore Settings on Startup.** When selected, this option restores all window settings (such as size, position, and so on) to what they were when the MS-DOS program was exited after it last ran. If this check box is not selected, the window uses the default MS-DOS window-positioning settings.
- **Fast ROM Emulation.** This setting enables screen updates to be accelerated by simulating video ROM drivers in protected mode. The video ROM instructions are copied into the faster RAM memory. If display problems occur, this option should be disabled.
- **Dynamic Memory Allocation.** This setting involves reserving video memory for the application when it switches between video and text mode This speeds up the operation.

Misc Tab

The Misc tab contains other miscellaneous settings for the application. Figure 4.48 shows a sample Misc tab for an MS-DOS application shortcut.

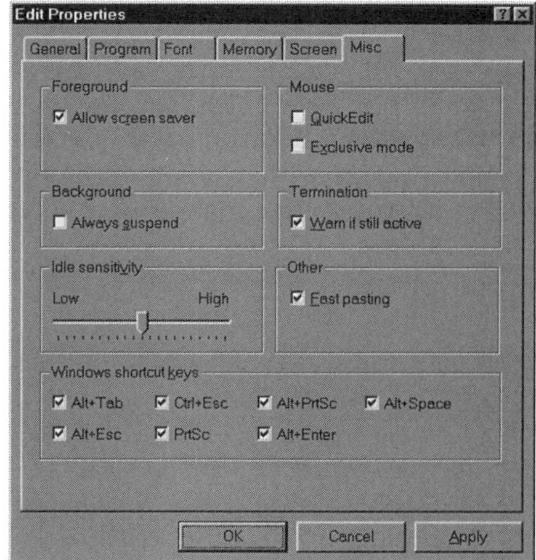

Figure 4.48

The Misc tab of the MS-DOS Properties sheet.

The following list describes the parameters of the Misc tab:

- **Allow Screen Saver.** If selected, this option enables any system screen saver to execute while the application is in the foreground. You should disable this feature for applications that are easily disrupted or that have a known problem with screen saver activity.
- **Always Suspend.** If selected, the application ceases execution when not in the foreground.
- **Idle Sensitivity.** This slide bar controls the amount of time the operating system waits before declaring the program to be inactive and suspending it.

Some applications do not appear to Windows 95 as being active; if the application is active, Windows 95 will not suspend it. If an application is stalling from being suspended, you should lower its idle sensitivity. Even if the application appears to be idle, Windows 95 still allocates processor time to it. Emulation programs for 3270-type terminals tend to suffer from this problem. When they are in the background, they only have to keep the network session open; if they are suspended, they drop the network session.

- **Quick Edit.** If selected, this option enables the user to highlight text in an MS-DOS window with the mouse. This feature should be disabled for applications that have their own DOS-based mouse support.
- **Exclusive Mode.** If selected, this option contains the mouse within the borders of the MS-DOS window. This enforces compatibility with programs that cannot track the mouse properly when it leaves the MS-DOS window. The mouse is still active in Windows applications, but you have to use Alt+Tab to switch to a Windows application.
- **Warn If Still Active.** If selected, this option warns users of potential data loss when they attempt to close an MS-DOS window without exiting the application.
- **Fast Pasting.** This option should be disabled if the application in question does not handle pasting from the Windows 95 Clipboard.
- **Windows Shortcut Keys.** Each check box enables or disables use of a Windows shortcut key combination within an application. This is useful if an application has a number of shortcut keys that overlap with those of Windows 95.

To force people to keep an application active until they exit it, you can set the application to run in full-screen mode on the Screen tab, then disable the following Windows shortcut keys: Alt+Tab, Ctrl+Esc, and Alt+Enter. This disables all the key combinations that enable a user to leave the application. The only event that can ruin this system is a Windows 95–generated error message. This causes the MS-DOS application to become minimized to display the Windows error message.

Determine When to Run Applications in MS-DOS Mode

Some MS-DOS applications are unable to run in an MS-DOS VM. The following are possible reasons:

- The application requires direct access to hardware, which is not permitted in a multitasking environment because of potential device conflicts. (This is the most common reason.)
- The application has incompatible memory requirements. The application does not like the way Windows 95 manages the 640 KB of conventional memory for the application (as a section of all the available memory). The application wants the actual memory below 640 KB to be used.
- The application's install program, for compatibility reasons, checks to see whether Windows is running and does not continue if Windows is detected.
- The application has video problems (usually with MS-DOS games) and does not want to draw the screen properly, either in a window or running full screen.

If any of these situations applies to the application in question, you might have to run the application in MS-DOS mode. MS-DOS mode can be configured using the Advanced… button on the Program tab of an MS-DOS PIF (see Figure 4.49).

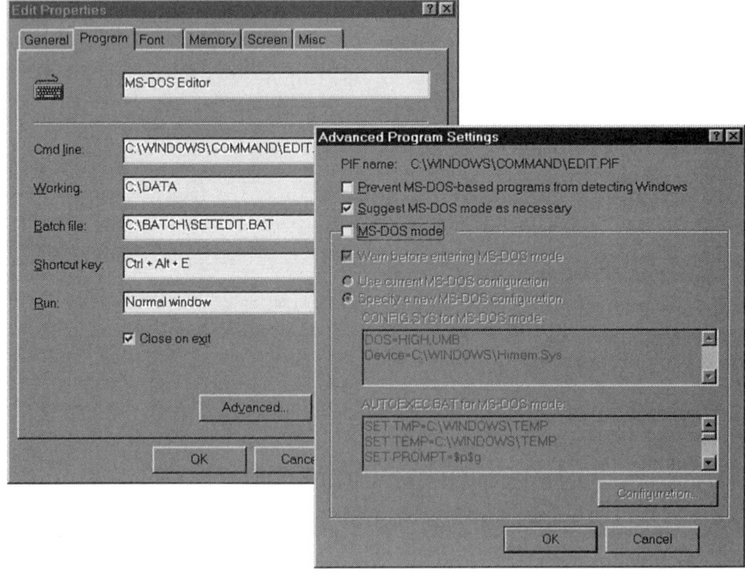

Figure 4.49

By default, MS-DOS is suggested based on the contents of APPS.INF.

Prior to using MS-DOS mode, you might want to try the Prevent MS-DOS-Based Programs From Detecting Windows option. With this option enabled, some applications that don't like to run in the Windows environment will execute. If you have programs that call Windows applications, however, you have to leave this option unselected.

In MS-DOS mode, Windows 95 unloads itself from memory, leaving the computer in a single-tasking MS-DOS-type of environment. All protected-mode support and drivers are removed. This permits the application to use only the CONFIG.SYS and AUTOEXEC.BAT parameters that were in effect at boot time before Windows 95 loaded. If the application needs a more particular configuration than that provided by default in the normal CONFIG.SYS and AUTOEXEC.BAT, you can create a customized MS-DOS environment for each application.

Customized MS-DOS Mode

If the application in question needs specific configuration parameters that differ significantly from those needed by most MS-DOS applications, you can create a customized CONFIG.SYS and AUTOEXEC.BAT that are swapped with the standard versions of these files when you double-click the application (see Figure 4.50). For the settings in these customized files to take effect, Windows 95 must reboot the computer.

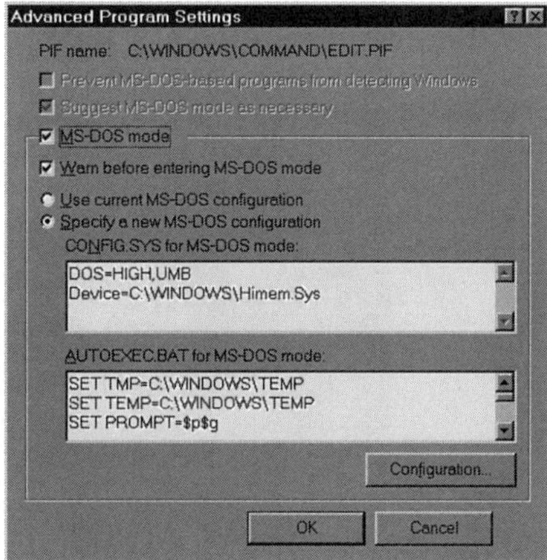

Figure 4.50

Custom configuration files require your computer to reboot.

When Windows 95 restarts the computer, it uses the customized configuration files and inserts a special command into CONFIG.SYS. The command reads `DOS=SINGLE` and indicates that this CONFIG.SYS and AUTOEXEC.BAT are to be used only once and that the system should return to the normal versions of these files when this application terminates.

For Windows 95 to remove this parameter from the CONFIG.SYS and to enable Windows 95 to reboot properly, the application must be exited in the normal fashion. If the application hangs or the computer is turned off without exiting, the parameter will not be removed. The system will boot back into the MS-DOS application directly. To remedy this problem, you can restart the application and exit properly, or you can press F8 during the boot process and choose to go to a command prompt only. Then you can manually edit the CONFIG.SYS to remove the `DOS=SINGLE` parameter.

Microsoft has provided a helper window to aid people with the creation of custom configuration files. You can enable this option by choosing the Configuration… button in the Advanced PIF settings (see Figure 4.51). Expanded Memory, Disk Cache, and Direct Disk Access are the three most common items people need to add to their configurations. DOSKEY is a useful option, but it's not usually required.

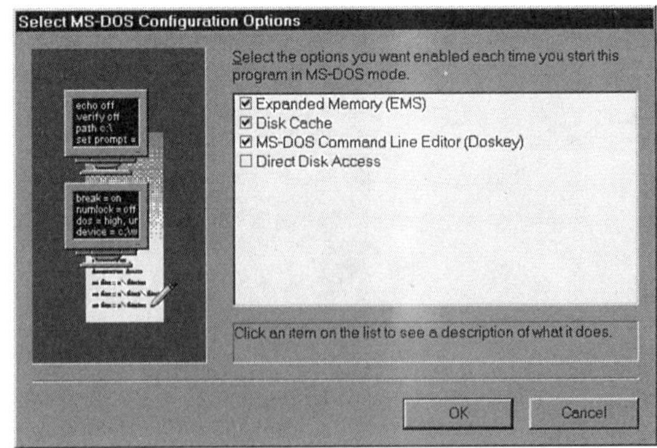

Figure 4.51

Creating custom configuration files is easier with the helper window provided by Windows 95.

Summary

The goal of this chapter was to teach you how to manage resources for both local and remote use. The chapter began by introducing the three different ways access permissions can be granted to users: by password, by network username, and by membership in network groups. You then learned where these access rights can be applied: file shares, printer shares, and fax modems. This chapter also discussed how to set up and share each of these resources, and it covered the changes made to the Unimodem driver since the original release of Windows 95.

To deal with access to local resources, you were shown how to create both a System policy that can be stored on your network and a policy template. Because System policies require user profiles to maintain user restrictions, this chapter also included information about how user profiles operate. You then learned the basics of the Windows 95 backup and restore procedure and how to manage your hard disk. The disk management discussion covered long filename support, disk partitioning, and disk compression. The chapter ended with an overview of how Windows 95 runs and supports all applications; it specifically discussed how to modify the environment for DOS applications. This information should prepare you for the Resource Management section of the Microsoft Certification Exam for Windows 95.

...cises

...cise 4.1: Creating and Using Long Filenames

Exercise 4.1 illustrates the creation and use of LFNs in Windows 95.

1. Choose Start, Programs, MS-DOS Prompt. A DOS window opens.
2. Type **C:** and press Enter to switch to the C drive.
3. Type **CD** \ and press Enter to switch to the root of the C drive.
4. Type **MD\LFNTEMP** and press Enter. A directory called LFNTEMP is created.
5. Type **CD\LFNTEMP** and press Enter. The current directory changes to LFNTEMP.
6. Type **DIR > "Directory Listing"** and press Enter to save the directory listing to a file. You are returned to a command prompt. (Note the quotations around the filename.)
7. Type **DIR** and press Enter. The alias for the file that was created is listed on the left; the LFN is on the right.
8. Type **DIR > "Directory Listing 2"** and press Enter. You are returned to a command prompt.
9. Type **DIR** and press Enter. The alias has been autonumbered sequentially, but the full name is preserved on the right.
10. Type **DIR >*DIRLIST** and press Enter. You receive a `File creation error` message because the * is illegal.
11. Shut down Windows 95. You now are in MS-DOS mode (no LFN support).
12. Type **CD\LFNTEMP** and press Enter. The current directory changes to LFNTEMP.

13. Type **DIR** and press Enter. LFNs no longer are displayed in the directory.

14. Type **COPY DIRECT~1 C:** and press Enter. The file created earlier is copied to the root of C.

15. Restart Windows 95 by typing **EXIT** and pressing Enter.

16. When Windows 95 is restarted, open a DOS window, and type **CD**, and press Enter. Then type **DIR** and press Enter. The file that was copied to the root no longer has an associated LFN (only the alias remains).

Exercise 4.2: Using Windows 95 Disk Compression

Exercise 4.2 illustrates how disk compression can be used in Windows 95. Because a considerable amount of time is involved in compressing an entire hard drive, this exercise focuses on compressing a floppy disk. The exercise requires a formatted floppy with at least 512 KB of free space.

1. Choose Start, Programs, Accessories, System Tools, DriveSpace. The DriveSpace menu opens.

2. Select the A drive and choose Drive, Compress. A window opens, showing the amount of free and used space before and after compression (estimated).

3. Click the Start button. As the drive is checked for errors, a status bar shows the progress of the compression procedure.

4. When the procedure is complete, click Close to return to the main DriveSpace window. (Note that drive A is now shown as compressed, and there is a host drive H for drive A.)

Exercise 4.3: Using the Windows 95 Backup Utility

Exercise 4.3 demonstrates how to use the Windows 95 Backup utility. Make sure you have at least 6 MB of free space on drive C before you complete this exercise.

continues

Exercise 4.3: Continued

1. Right-click the My Computer icon and choose Explore. The Exploring window opens.
2. From the list of drives, right-click C and choose Properties. The Properties sheet for drive C opens.
3. Click the Tools tab. From this tab, you can run ScanDisk, Backup, or the Disk Defragmenter.
4. Click the Backup Now button. The Microsoft Backup screen opens.
5. Click the plus sign (+) next to the C drive. The tree expands to show the subdirectories of drive C.
6. Click the plus sign next to the Windows subdirectory. The tree expands to show the subdirectories of Windows.
7. Click the plus sign next to the Media subdirectory. The tree expands to show the files in this subdirectory.
8. Click the check box next to Media. All the files in the Media subdirectory now are marked for backup.
9. Having selected the files for backup, click the Next Step button. You are prompted for a backup destination.
10. Click the icon for the A drive. This selects the root of A as the destination directory.
11. Click the Start Backup button. You are prompted for a backup set name.
12. Type **TEST** and press Enter. A status screen opens, showing the progress of the backup.
13. Click OK when the backup is complete. You are returned to the main Backup window.
14. Click the Restore tab. You are prompted to select a backup set to restore.

15. Click the icon for the A drive. The TEST backup set is displayed in the root of A.

16. Double-click the TEST backup set. You are prompted to select the files you want to restore.

17. Click three times in the check box next to TEST to select all the files in the backup set.

18. Choose Settings, Options. The Settings - Options dialog box opens.

19. Select the Restore tab, verify that Overwrite Files is selected under Advanced Options, and click OK. You are returned to the main Backup window.

20. Click the Start Restore button. A status screen shows the progress of the restore procedure.

21. When the restore procedure is complete, click OK twice to return to the main Backup window.

Exercise 4.4: Counting Virtual Machines

To illustrate the point about how Windows 95 manages virtual machines, Exercise 4.4 counts the number of virtual machines running on your Windows 95 computer.

1. From your computer, start Windows 95.

2. If you installed Windows 95 on your computer using the Typical Setup option, the System Monitor utility might not be installed because it's an optional component.

   To determine whether the System Monitor utility is installed, choose Start, Programs, Accessories, System Tools, then System Monitor. If System Monitor is not available, add it to your computer using the following steps:

   a. From the Start menu, choose Settings, Control Panel. From the Control Panel, double-click the Add/Remove Programs icon.

continues

Exercise 4.4: Continued

   b. Select the Windows Setup tab, double-click Accessories, then check the System Monitor option. Press Enter or click OK. Press Enter or click OK again to install the System Monitor.

3. From the Start menu, choose Programs, Accessories, System Tools, then System Monitor. The System Monitor utility displays key system information in a line-, bar-, or numeric-chart format.

4. Any items previously selected are displayed when the System Monitor utility starts. When you run the System Monitor utility for the first time, the Kernel Processor Usage (%) appears in a line chart.

5. You must remove all current items to finish this exercise. Highlight any items you want to remove, then select Remove Item from the Edit menu.

6. Choose Edit, Add Item to open the Add Item dialog box. From the Category list, click Kernel to display the list of Kernel items.

7. Choose Virtual Machines from the Item list. If you need an explanation of each item, click Explain. This shows the number of virtual machines present in the system. Press Enter or click OK to add Virtual Machines as a selection.

8. Choose View, Numeric Charts to obtain the number of virtual machines currently active. This value usually is 1 because the Windows 95 computer has just been started. It could be higher, however.

9. Open some Windows applications or the Windows Explorer. Has the number of virtual machines changed? The number of active virtual machines should not change when Windows programs are started.

10. Start an MS-DOS command prompt either by choosing Start, Run to open the Run dialog box or by choosing Start,

Programs, MS-DOS Prompt. Has the number of virtual machines changed? The number should change because each MS-DOS application starts another virtual machine.

11. Start a second MS-DOS command prompt and then a third. What happens to the number of virtual machines after you start each new MS-DOS command prompt? Each time another command prompt is started, the number of virtual machines should increase by 1. If the initial count was 1, then starting three MS-DOS command prompts should increase the number to 4.

12. Close the three new MS-DOS command prompts. How many virtual machines currently are active now? The count of virtual machines should be back to 1 (or whatever starting number you had in step 8).

    Based on what you know about virtual machines, explain why the count changes during the exercise.

    All the Windows 16-bit and 32-bit applications run in the same system virtual machine. Each MS-DOS application, however, runs in its own virtual DOS machine. Opening a new MS-DOS command prompt causes the virtual machine count to increase by 1.

13. When you finish viewing the System Monitor utility information, close the System Monitor.

Exercise 4.5: Configuring MS-DOS Applications

Exercise 4.5 demonstrates how to configure the various MS-DOS modes for a given application.

1. Right-click the My Computer icon and choose Explore. The Exploring window opens.

2. Click on the plus sign (+) next to the C drive. Subdirectories of the C drive appear.

3. Click on the plus sign next to the Windows subdirectory. The tree expands to show the subdirectories of Windows.

continues

Exercise 4.5: Continued

4. Right-click the COMMAND file in the right panel and choose Properties. The COMMAND.COM Properties sheet opens.
5. Click the Memory tab. The list of configurable memory settings appears.
6. Set the XMS memory parameter to 4096 and click OK. You return to the Explorer window.
7. Double-click the COMMAND file. An MS-DOS window opens.
8. Type **MEM** and press Enter from the command prompt. Note that the free XMS reads as 4096 KB.
9. Type **EXIT** and press Enter. You return to the Explorer window.
10. Go back to the Properties sheet of the COMMAND file, change the XMS memory parameter to 16384 KB, click OK, then double-click on the COMMAND file again. An MS-DOS window opens.
11. Type **MEM** and press Enter. The free XMS memory now reads 16384 KB.

Even if the amount of memory you assign exceeds the physical RAM of the computer, the parameter is accepted. The additional memory comes from the paging file system.

12. Type **EXIT** and press Enter. You return to the Explorer window.
13. Reset the XMS memory parameter to its original setting of Auto and click OK. You return to the Explorer window.
14. Click the Command folder. The files in the Command folder appear in the right panel of the Explorer window.

15. Right-click the EDIT file and choose Properties. The Properties sheet for the EDIT file opens.

16. Click the Program tab, then the Advanced button. The Advanced Program Settings window opens.

17. Click the MS-DOS Mode check box to enable use of standard MS-DOS mode support for this program. Some of the options below the MS-DOS Mode parameter become available.

18. Make sure Use Current MS-DOS Configuration is selected and click OK. You return to the Properties sheet. All other settings are disabled because this file now inherits all default MS-DOS settings.

19. Double-click the EDIT file and click Yes to continue. Windows 95 unloads, and the EDIT file executes.

20. Choose File, Open (or press Alt+F, O) to open a file for editing. Type **\CONFIG.SYS** as the filename and press Enter. The CONFIG.SYS file opens.

21. Note the contents of the file then press Alt+F, X to exit the program. Windows 95 restarts automatically.

22. When Windows 95 has restarted, go back to the Advanced Settings tab and specify a new MS-DOS configuration. CONFIG.SYS and AUTOEXEC.BAT for MS-DOS mode now are available and have default settings already in place.

23. Click the Configuration button. A wizard appears that helps you select which options you want active in your MS-DOS environment.

24. Expanded Memory should be deselected and Disk Cache should be selected; click OK three times to close all Properties sheets. You return to the Explorer window.

25. Double-click the EDIT file again and click Yes to continue. The system restarts and the EDIT program executes.

26. Choose File, Open to open a file for editing. Type **\CONFIG.SYS** as the filename and press Enter. The

continues

Exercise 4.5: Continued

CONFIG.SYS file appears for editing. (Note that `DOS=SINGLE` has been added to the file.)

27. Choose File, Open to open another file for editing. Type **\AUTOEXEC.BAT** as the filename and press Enter. The AUTOEXEC.BAT file appears for editing. (Note that a SmartDrive command has been added.)

28. Choose File, Exit (or press Alt+F, X) to exit the program, then press any key. The system restarts and Windows 95 loads normally.

29. Go back to the Properties sheet of the EDIT file and disable MS-DOS mode.

Exercise 4.6: Creating User Profiles

Exercise 4.6 demonstrates how to enable individual users to maintain user profiles.

1. From the Start menu, choose Settings, Control Panel. The Control Panel opens.

2. Double-click the Passwords icon. The Passwords Properties dialog box opens.

3. Select the User Profiles tab. By default, the All Users of This PC Use the Same Preferences and Desktop Settings option is selected.

4. Select the following options:

   Users Can Customize Their Preferences and Desktop Settings.

   Include Desktop Icons and Network Neighborhood Contents in User Settings.

   Include Start Menu and Program Groups in User Settings.

   Click OK. You are prompted to restart the computer.

5. Click OK to restart the computer.
6. Log on with the username **TESTPROFILE** and type **password** for the password. You will be prompted to verify the password by typing it again.

Do not press Enter after typing the username without first typing a password. If you press Enter with the password blank, you will not see the user logon screen when you next log on. If a blank password is used with a username, that user automatically is logged on. A different username cannot be used. To fix this situation, change the password to something other than blank using the Passwords control panel.

7. Confirm the password by typing it again. A message appears asking whether you want to save the user's settings in a user profile.
8. Click Yes to save the session's settings in a user profile. The default desktop is displayed.
9. Right-click the desktop and select Properties from the context menu. The Display Properties sheet appears.
10. Select a different wallpaper for the desktop and click OK. The new wallpaper is displayed.
11. Select Shut Down from the Start menu. The Shut Down Windows dialog box opens.
12. Select Close all programs and log on as a different user?, then click Yes. All programs close, and the Enter Windows Password logon screen appears.
13. Log on with a different username. The original default wallpaper or pattern appears on the desktop.

continues

Exercise 4.6: Continued

14. Log off, then log back on with the **TESTPROFILE** user name. The wallpaper that was selected for that profile appears on the desktop.

15. Log off, then log on with your normal username. The original settings are displayed.

16. Start Explorer and open the Windows 95 folder and the Profiles subfolder. The Profiles folder contains a subfolder for each profile created on the computer.

17. Examine the contents of each subfolder in the Profiles folder. You'll notice that a user.dat file was created for each profile. There also might be Start Menu, NetHood, Desktop, and Recent folders for each profile, depending on which options were selected in the User Profiles tab of the Passwords control panel applet.

Exercise 4.7: Installing the System Policy Editor

Exercise 4.7 demonstrates how to install the System Policy Editor.

1. From the Start menu, choose Settings, Control Panel. The Control Panel opens.

2. Double-click the Add/Remove Programs icon. The Add/Remove Programs Properties dialog box appears.

3. Select the Windows Setup tab and click Have Disk. The Install from Disk dialog box opens.

4. Click Browse and locate the \ADMIN\APPTOOLS\POLEDIT directory on the Windows 95 CD-ROM. The grouppol.inf and poledit.inf files are displayed.

5. Click OK twice, enable both Group Policies and System Policy Editor, then click Install. The files are copied to the hard drive, and the Start menu is updated.

6. From the Start menu, choose Programs, Accessories, System Tools, System Policy Editor. The System Policy Editor opens, and you are prompted for the template file to be used.

7. Select ADMIN.ADM as the template for creating policies. The System Policy Editor displays a blank window.

8. Close the System Policy Editor.

Exercise 4.8: Creating a System Policy

In Exercise 4.8, you create a simple System policy. You also set up a system so the policy overwrites the previous Registry setting for the specified workstation.

1. Start the System Policy Editor. The System Policy Editor opens, and you are prompted for the template file to be used.

2. Locate the \<*systemroot*>\INF\ADMIN.ADM file and click OK. The ADMIN.ADM template loads, and a blank System Policy window appears.

The INF directory is a hidden directory. To see this directory, choose Options from Explorer's View menu. On the View tab, select Show All Files.

3. Choose File, New File. The Default User and Default Computer icons appear.

4. Double-click the Default Computer icon. The Default Computer Properties sheet appears.

5. Click the plus sign (+) next to Network. The Network policy subkeys appear.

6. Click the plus sign next to Logon. The Network logon policy settings appear.

7. Click the check box next to Logon Banner until a check mark appears in the box. The Caption and Text fields appear.

continues

Exercise 4.8: Continued

8. Type **System Policies Test** in the Caption field, type **Welcome** in the Text field, and click OK. The Default User and Default Computer icons are displayed again.

9. Choose File, Save As and save the filename as CONFIG.POL in the <*systemroot*> directory.

10. This file now has to be copied to one of two locations. If you are using a Windows NT domain, the file must be copied to the NETLOGON directory of the server. If you are using a Novell NetWare server, the file must be placed in the SYS:PUBLIC directory.

The policy you create affects all users that log in to your server. If you are using a production server, create a computer entry in the policy file using Add Computer… from the Edit menu. Name this entry with your computer's name.

11. Choose Shut Down from the Start menu and select Close all programs and log on as a different user. Repeat this step. The first logon changes the HKEY_LOCAL_MACHINE section of the Registry; this is not visible until the second logon. Changes to HKEY_CURRENT_USER take effect immediately.

12. Log on to the computer. The Logon Banner specified in CONFIG.POL appears during logon.

13. Edit the policy file to reverse the Logon Banner options, then resave it to your server location.

14. Choose Shut Down from the Start menu and select Close all programs and log on as a different user. Repeat this step.

15. The Logon Banner should not appear during your second logon.

16. Delete the policy file from the server.

Review Questions

1. The ring architecture of Intel 386 processors provides different levels of protection and privileges. Windows 95 executes in which two of the following rings of the Intel 386 protection model? Select the two best answers.

   A. Ring 0

   B. Ring 1

   C. Ring 2

   D. Ring 3

   E. Ring 4

2. Windows 95 is an advanced operating system that takes advantage of the Intel ring architecture. To understand how Windows 95 uses the ring architecture, you need to understand the rings themselves. Which of the following rings of the Intel 386 protection model offers the most privileges, including direct communication with hardware components?

   A. Ring 0

   B. Ring 1

   C. Ring 2

   D. Ring 3

   E. Ring 4

3. You are asked to present an overview of the Windows 95 system architecture including rings. You draw a diagram that points out each ring and its protection level. Which of the following rings of the Intel 386 protection model offers no processor protection and relies on the operating system to provide this protection?

   A. Ring 0

   B. Ring 1

   C. Ring 2

   D. Ring 3

   E. Ring 4

4. In the diagram for the presentation in Question 3, you need to point out where applications run. In which of the following rings of the Intel 386 protection model do MS-DOS, Windows 16-bit, and Windows 32-bit applications run?

   A. Ring 0

   B. Ring 1

   C. Ring 2

   D. Ring 3

   E. Ring 4

5. Within its system services, Windows 95 uses a combination of 32-bit and 16-bit code to run applications. In which of the following rings of the Intel 386 protection model do system services run?

   A. Ring 0

   B. Ring 1

   C. Ring 2

   D. Ring 3

   E. Ring 4

6. Windows 95 runs applications in virtual machines. The Virtual Machine Manager is used to manage these applications. In which of the following rings of the Intel 386 protection model does the Virtual Machine Manager run?

   A. Ring 0

   B. Ring 1

   C. Ring 2

   D. Ring 3

   E. Ring 4

7. As system administrator, you need to set up each user's computer so users cannot start an MS-DOS prompt from within Windows 95. How can this be done?

   A. Using the System Policy Editor, open the Default User Properties sheet, click System, click Restrictions, then select the Disable MS-DOS Prompt check box.

   B. Using the System Policy Editor, open the Default User Properties sheet, click System, click Restrictions, then deselect the Enable MS-DOS Prompt check box.

   C. Using the System Policy Editor, open the Default User Properties sheet, click System, then select the MS-DOS Prompt check box.

   D. Using the System Policy Editor, open the Default User Properties sheet, click System, click Restrictions, then select the Disable Single-Mode MS-DOS Applications check box.

8. John runs several applications at once on his Windows 95 computer. Which of the following applications do not run in separate, private, virtual machines?

   A. Windows 32-bit applications

   B. Windows 16-bit applications

   C. MS-DOS applications

   D. All of the above

   E. None of the above

9. The Virtual Machine Manager provides several services, including memory management, task scheduling, and DOS-mode support. Every time you open an MS-DOS application, the number of virtual machines running under Windows 95 ______.

   A. decreases by two

   B. decreases by one

   C. stays the same

   D. increases by one

   E. increases by two

10. Windows 95 uses two types of memory: physical and virtual. Virtual memory comprises which of the following components? Select the two best answers.

    A. ROM

    B. RAM

    C. VMM

    D. A swap file

    E. A page table

11. Third-party developers can create file systems that extend Windows 95's capabilities. A key feature of Windows 95 that

makes this possible and that will enable Windows 95 to adapt easily to future technological developments is its ______.

   A. preemptive multitasking
   B. VCACHE cache subsystem
   C. modular design
   D. peer-to-peer networking support

12. You are responsible for training users on Windows 95's Installable File System (IFS). You create a diagram to display its different components. Which three of the following are components of the IFS?

   A. I/O Supervisor
   B. VFAT file system driver
   C. TSD Supervisor
   D. CDFS file system driver

13. On a diagram of the IFS, you point out the role for each of the components. Which of the following components is responsible for the insertion and removal of media?

   A. Drive Controller
   B. IFS Manager
   C. System Driver Supervisor
   D. Volume Tracker

14. Stephanie uses an older version of Windows and wants to know if she can use an older CD-ROM drive with Windows 95. You tell her yes, but you also tell her that a drive accessed through ______ cannot take advantage of the 32-bit VFAT.

   A. protected-mode drivers
   B. real-mode drivers
   C. virtual device drivers
   D. network redirector file system drivers

15. VCACHE is an upgrade of Smartdrive and is used for read-ahead and lazy-write (or write-behind) caching. VCACHE is used by all Windows 95 file system drivers except ______ file system drivers.

    A. CDFS

    B. VFAT

    C. network redirector

    D. SCSI

16. Brenda saves her Windows 95 files in long filename format. She asks you to explain how Windows 95 will save the files with short filenames. You tell her, for example, that the auto-generated alias for the long filename The Departmental Budget.wks is ______.

    A. THEDEPAR.~1

    B. THEDEP~1.WKS

    C. THEDEP~1

    D. BUDGET~1.WKS

17. A client asks how he can fit more data on his existing hard drive without adding another hard drive or storing files on a network. What Windows 95 disk utility should he use to compress the data on his hard drive?

    A. DoubleSpace

    B. DriveSpace

    C. Disk Defragmenter

    D. ScanDisk

18. As system administrator, you draft a purchase order to acquire tape backup devices. Windows 95 supports QIC tape systems but not universally. Which of the following tape backup systems is not supported by Windows 95?

    A. QIC 3010 through parallel port

    B. QIC 3010 through floppy disk controller

C. QIC 3010 through SCSI port

D. QIC 80 through floppy disk controller

19. When John runs Disk Compression in Windows 95, he calls asking you how files are compressed. You tell him that disk compression maximizes disk space in which two of the following?

A. Cluster conversion

B. Token conversion

C. ASCII collapse

D. Sector-allocation conversion

20. Your company runs Windows 95 with a NetWare server, but you experience problems with long filename support. A help-desk administrator tells you to install a specific feature in NetWare to enable long filename support. What is this feature?

A. Install OS/2 on the server.

B. Run an NLM released by Microsoft.

C. Install OS/2 Name Space.

D. NetWare cannot support Windows 95 long filenames.

21. Vanessa creates a file named Budget For Department. She wants to rename the file Budget For Marketing Team. Which of the following commands can be used at the command prompt to retain the long filename?

A. Type **RENAME Budget For Department TO Budget For Marketing Team**

B. Type **RENAME Budget For Department Budget For Marketing Team**

C. Type **REN Budget For Department Budget For Marketing Team**

D. Type **RENAME "Budget For Department" "Budget For Marketing Team"**

22. You are assigned a new department to administer. This department has a mixture of computers, including many MS-DOS and Windows 3.1 computers and some Windows 95 computers. Because this department frequently shares files and the file-naming conventions must remain consistent, you instruct your Windows 95 users to use short filenames at all times. To guarantee that these users do not create LFNs, you disable this feature using which Registry change? You make this change in the HKEY_LOCAL_MACHINE\System\CurrentControlSet\control\FileSystem.

    A. Set the Registry value **LongFileNames=** to **01**.

    B. Set the Registry value **Win31FileSystem=** to **01**.

    C. Set the Registry value **Win31FileSystem=** to **Yes.**

    D. Set the Registry value **ShortFileNames=** to **Yes**.

    E. None of the above. This cannot be done with Windows 95.

23. You are migrating to Windows 95 and will be upgrading many of your applications to 32-bit applications designed to run in Windows 95. You know that Windows 95 runs 32-bit applications differently from Windows 3.1 applications (16-bit applications). Every Windows 95 application is executed from within a specialized container called ______.

    A. an application box

    B. a virtual partition

    C. a task space

    D. a virtual machine

24. Jim is upgrading to Windows 95 and wants to be sure his existing computer can run it. Windows 95's multitasking feature requires an Intel processor to perform in two types of modes. Which two of the following are operating modes for Intel processors?

    A. Enhanced mode

    B. Protected mode

C. Fault mode

D. Real mode

25. Windows 95's protected-mode feature can regulate the behavior of multitasking process in two ways. One way is through graduated levels of processor privilege, commonly called rings. In the Intel ring protection scheme, Ring ______ allows complete control of the processor.

    A. 1

    B. 0

    C. 3

    D. 4

26. Typically, applications running in Windows 95 do so at a specific ring level. The operating system runs at a specific ring level as well. This way, applications cannot access critical system functions. Which of the following is true about rings?

    A. Most Windows 95 applications run in Ring 3.

    B. Most operating system components run in Ring 3.

    C. Windows 95 uses all Intel rings.

    D. Windows 95 uses only Rings 1, 2, and 3.

27. Linda is considering upgrading from Windows 3.x to Windows 95. She is not sure how to justify the upgrade based on application support because Windows 3.x, like Windows 95, supports multitasking. You explain the differences, however, between how 16-bit applications and 32-bit applications support multitasking. You tell her that WIN16 applications use ______ multitasking.

    A. fault-tolerant

    B. preemptive

    C. cooperative

    D. real-mode

28. It's important for users to understand how 16-bit applications are handled by Windows 95. Which of the following is true?

    A. WIN16 applications do not access the Registry.

    B. WIN16 applications do not use the System VM.

    C. WIN16 applications support multithreading.

    D. Each WIN16 application has its own message queue.

29. Leslie runs several MS-DOS applications in Windows 95. She wants to optimize how they run in Windows 95, and she wants to run 32-bit applications simultaneously with her DOS applications. You advise her that, if possible, it is best to run MS-DOS applications in ______.

    A. MS-DOS mode

    B. customized MS-DOS mode

    C. a WIN16 VM

    D. an MS-DOS VM

30. A user calls while you are manning a help desk. He asks how his MS-DOS program and Windows 95 will work together in MS-DOS mode. You tell him that, in MS-DOS mode, Windows 95 ______.

    A. unloads itself from memory

    B. remains in memory

    C. runs the application in protected mode

    D. can multithread multiple DOS sessions

31. You are a systems administrator in a company that migrated to Windows 95. Many users still use MS-DOS applications and must run them in Windows. Because of compatibility problems with older DOS applications, you customize the DOS-mode applications. What command is added to CONFIG.SYS when you run a customized MS-DOS–mode application?

A. `DOS=Custom`

B. `MODE=DOSCUST`

C. `DOS=CMODE`

D. `DOS=SINGLE`

32. For a PowerPoint presentation in front of the help-desk staff, you create a slide with a bullet point describing the Windows 95 System policy feature. What would be the appropriate ending to the sentence: A Windows 95 System policy ______.

    A. assigns priorities to applications accessing memory

    B. assigns priorities to users

    C. enables an administrator to set various Windows 95 Registry entries

    D. is a summary of configuration details

33. On the same PowerPoint slide as in the previous question, another bullet point explains the primary purpose of a Windows 95 System policy. From the following list, choose the correct ending for this statement: The primary purpose of a Windows 95 System policy is to ______.

    A. limit the capability of users to customize their environment

    B. increase the capability of users to customize their environment

    C. make the system run more efficiently

    D. make the system more adaptable

34. Billie modifies her user profile so that each time she starts Windows 95, a shortcut to her finance spreadsheet displays on the desktop. Which of the following cannot be done by setting user profiles?

    A. Displaying specific applications in the Start menu

    B. Customizing desktop settings such as colors and wallpaper

    C. Installing an application only for a specific user

    D. Displaying recently used documents in the Start menu's Documents folder

35. Michael administers a Windows NT network that has several Windows 95 workstations attached to the server. He stores user profiles for all workstations on the server to be downloaded during bootup. The user profiles can be updated by the users. To ensure that each profile is available from the server, where on the server are they stored?

    A. The user's home directory

    B. The user's C:\WINDOWS directory

    C. Any directory on the server to which the user has Read permissions

    D. None of the above

36. A user complains that settings she makes to her desktop are not saved each time she logs in to the network and starts Windows 95. Her computer is set up to download a user profile from the server and to enable her to save changes to it. What might be one of the reasons her settings are not saved properly?

    A. Her version of Windows 95 needs to be updated.

    B. Her workstation's time is not synchronized with the server's time.

C. She does not have the Remote Administration feature enabled.

D. All of the above.

37. In a training class you conduct for system administrators, you are asked why the Registry comprises two files. From the following list, what is the best answer to this question?

A. It makes editing configuration settings safer.

B. It separates user and system information so system policies and user profiles can be created.

C. It allows dynamic information from the hardware tree to be updated while user settings are idle.

D. It enables a user to copy USER.DAT from a floppy disk to a laptop while maintaining the same look and feel as his desktop computer.

Review Answers

1. A, D. Windows 95 executes programs in Ring 0 and Ring 3.

2. A. Ring 0 is the only processor ring with direct access to hardware. Ring 3 processes must go through Ring 0 to get to hardware.

3. D. Ring 0 has application processing protection built in, but Ring 3 requires the OS to provide protection.

4. D. All applications run in Ring 3; Ring 0 is reserved for the OS.

5. D. Most system services are applications and therefore run in Ring 3.

6. A. Ring 0 supports the Kernel, system drivers, and manager applications.

7. A. Selecting Disable MS-DOS Prompt prevents access to the MS-DOS prompt.

8. B. 16-bit Windows applications are the only applications that share memory address space. They do so for backward compatibility.

9. D. Each MS-DOS application runs in its own virtual machine.

10. B, D. Physical memory is RAM; virtual memory is space on your hard drive in the form of a swap file.

11. C. Windows 95 is extensible because it is so modular.

12. A, B, D. The TSD Supervisor is not part of the IFS.

13. D. The Volume Tracker tracks removable media.

14. B Only 32-bit protected-mode drivers are able to take advantage of 32-bit VFAT.

15. **A.** CDFS maintains a separate cache to increase the performance of the CD-ROM.

16. B. Windows 95 uses the first six valid characters, adds a tilde (~) and a number, then applies the extension for the file.

17. B. DriveSpace is the compression program included in Windows 95.

18. C. QIC 3010 SCSI drives are the only tape drives supported.

19. B, D. Token conversion and Sector-allocation conversion are the two ways space is saved.

20. C. Installing OS/2 name space enables you to store filenames up to 254 characters in length.

21. D. When working with long filenames from the command prompt, place the full path for a file inside quotation marks.

22. E. Even though the Registry exists, this feature does not work.

23. D. All 16-bit and 32-bit Windows applications share a common virtual machine.

24. B, D. The Intel processor can run in protected mode or real mode. Windows 95 uses real mode prior to the GUI starting up.

25. B. Ring 0 is the only ring that allows direct access to hardware.

26. A. Most Windows 95 applications run in Ring 3; Ring 0 is usually reserved for OS functions.

27. C. Windows 95 uses preemptive multitasking, which provides better scheduling of processor time than the cooperative multitasking used by 16-bit applications.

28. A. 16-bit applications store their settings in INI files; only 32-bit applications use the Registry.

29. D. To multitask MS-DOS applications and Windows applications, run the MS-DOS applications in an MS-DOS virtual machine.

30. A. When running applications in MS-DOS mode, Windows 95 is removed from memory.

31. D. DOS=SINGLE is added to CONFIG.SYS when running an MS-DOS application with custom CONFIG.SYS or AUTOEXEC.BAT settings.

32. C. System policies automatically edit the Registry on computers that process the policy.

33. A. System policies automatically configure an environment for users and prevent them from customizing many of the components of their environment.

34. C. User profiles enable users to maintain their personal settings, such as wallpaper, while maintaining custom Start menu settings.

35. A. User profiles are stored in the user's home directory on Windows NT networks.

36. B. Windows 95 checks the date stamp on the user profile and treats all profiles created in the future as invalid and ignores them.

37. B. Keeping the files separate allows for easier implementation of user profiles (just replacing the USER.DAT file) and System policies.

Answers to Test Yourself Questions at Beginning of Chapter

1. MARKET~1.XLS. This filename includes the first six valid characters followed by the tilde (~) and an incremental number.
2. 512 MB. Based on the default compression ratio of 2:1, the maximum size of the compressed volume will be 256 MB. This enables it to store 512 MB if the 2:1 ratio is achieved. 512 MB is the maximum size of the contents in any compressed-volume drive. If DriveSpace 3 is used, that limit is raised to 2 GB.
3. Jason can back up to a tape drive, a floppy disk(s), another hard drive, or a network location. He can use BACKUP.EXE.
4. MS-DOS virtual machine mode. If she runs the application in MS-DOS mode, she loses all these advantages.
5. Possible answers include the following: the application requires direct access to the hardware; the application has incompatible memory requirements; the application's installation program checks to see whether Windows is running and does not continue if Windows is detected; and the application has video requirements the DOS VM cannot support.
6. MS-DOS applications can run in Windows 95 in the following three ways: in an MS-DOS VM, in MS-DOS mode after shutting down the Windows 95 GUI, and in MS-DOS mode outside of Windows 95 using configuration files that are customized for the application.
7. Possible answers include the following: Windows 95 unloads itself, and the computer runs in a single-tasking MS-DOS environment; all protected-mode support and drivers are removed; and you might need to customize AUTOEXEC.BAT and CONFIG.SYS for each application.
8. 32-bit applications reside in their own separate address space, and each has a separate message queue.
9. Perform a local reboot by pressing Ctrl+Alt+Delete once. In the Close Program dialog box, select the offending process and click End Task.
10. Two. Windows 95 has one virtual machine running for both the Windows programs (the 16-bit and 32-bit applications), and it has one virtual machine running for the MS-DOS application.
11. Set a mandatory user profile that cannot be edited, or set a System policy that is downloaded to the computer each time the computer boots.
12. Make sure the Users Can Customize Their Preferences and Desktop Settings option is enabled on the User Profiles tab of the Passwords control panel. Advise the user to make any changes to the desktop, Start menu, and program groups. Shut down and reboot the system. After logging in, the new changes appear and are part of the user profile for that user.
13. Choose Start menu, Settings, Control Panel. Double-click on the Passwords icon in the Control Panel. Select the User Profile tab and click the Users Can Customize Their Preferences and Desktop Settings option.
14. CONFIG.POL. Regardless of the security level, if the policy file has been implemented on a Microsoft Windows NT network, the client must log on to the domain. The CONFIG.POL file should be in the NETLOGON share of the Domain Controllers. On a Novell NetWare network, the policy file should be in the SYS:PUBLIC directory.
15. It enables you to edit the Registry without using the Registry Editor. It also enables you to set default settings for a user or a group of users; these settings can affect the computer or user environment.

Chapter 5

Integration and Operability

This chapter helps you prepare for the exam by covering the following objectives:

- Configuring a Windows 95 computer as a client in a Windows NT network
- Configuring a Windows 95 computer as a client in a NetWare network
- Configuring a Windows 95 computer to access the Internet
- Configuring a client to use Dial-Up Networking for remote access

Test Yourself! Before reading this chapter, test yourself to determine how much study time you will need to devote to this section.

1. With Windows 95, what methods can you use to resolve NetBIOS names?
2. You configure a Windows 95 workstation to connect to a NetWare network. When installing Client for NetWare Networks, Windows 95 automatically installs a protocol. Which one? Can you change this to another protocol and still access the NetWare server? What other networking component might be useful when connecting to a NetWare network?
3. While setting up Windows 95 to access the Internet, you find that connections over TCP/IP by host don't work, but connections by IP number do. What could be wrong? What two methods can Windows 95 use to get the information necessary to resolve fully qualified domain names to IP addresses?
4. What are the advantages of share-level security? User-level security?
5. Jenny wants to gain access to the Internet, but her company doesn't have a dedicated line. Using Windows 95, how can she connect to the Internet?
6. Steve is connecting his Windows 95 computer to a network running Novell NetWare. He wants to share files and a printer with other users. Can he do this? If so, what type of security must he use?
7. The UNC is supported by Windows 95. What does UNC stand for? What two items make up a UNC? Does UNC require a drive-letter assignment?
8. When installing TCP/IP, it is recommended that a default gateway be configured for the Windows 95 client. What does a gateway do?
9. What does a master browser do? How is the browse list built?

Answers are located at the end of the chapter...

As a Windows 95 administrator, sooner or later you will be asked by your users to network machines together. This can be either a simple request to connect a single machine to an ISP for email and Internet access, or a huge project involving creating a departmental Local Area Network (LAN) and connecting it to your organization's Wide Area Network (WAN). Knowing Windows 95's capabilities and limitations can save you valuable time, and save your organization's budget, when such a moment finally arrives.

Understanding networking requires both a theoretical knowledge of how certain protocols and services are implemented in a particular operating system and a large amount of hands-on practice with that operating system. Without both, configuring and troubleshooting even the simplest network can be frustrating and time-consuming.

This chapter is designed to provide a quick introduction to Windows 95's network architecture and then give you hands-on practice configuring Windows 95 networking. No two networking environments are identical. The following text and exercises might be considered introductions and study guides: Each Windows 95 administrator must become familiar with his or her own unique network. The following topics are covered:

- Windows 95 layered networking, including network providers, protocols, NDIS, adapter drivers, and bindings
- Using Windows 95 in a Windows NT network, including workgroups and domains, working with UNC paths, protocols, browsing, and File and Print Sharing
- Using Windows 95 in a NetWare network, including configuring Windows 95 to access a NetWare bindery, configuring Windows 95 to access an NDS tree, File and Print Sharing for NetWare Networks, and configuring IPX/SPX

- Configuring Windows 95 to access the Internet (TCP/IP), including choosing manual configuration or DHCP, IP addressing, methods of name resolution, and troubleshooting TCP/IP
- Configuring Dial-Up Networking, including configuring DUN and PPP, setting up DUN to use Windows NT RAS, and enhancements with the DUN 1.2 upgrade

Windows 95 Layered Networking

Windows 95 has a networking architecture that is loosely based on industry-standard models for layered networking architectures. Two prominent reference models, the Open Systems Interconnect (OSI) model from the International Standards Organization (ISO) and the Institute of Electrical and Electronic Engineers (IEEE) 802 model, influenced the design of Windows 95 and Windows NT networking.

A thorough understanding of Windows 95 networking architecture will help you, as an administrator, understand each piece of the network "stack." When something goes wrong, this understanding is crucial for quick and accurate troubleshooting and interpretation of error messages.

In a layered architecture, each layer is responsible for a particular task or set of tasks. The OSI model describes data moving through the layers of the network architecture, each layer adding or removing information as the data is transferred. Each layer communicates only with the layers immediately above and below. This allows each layer to be written as a separate software component as long as it communicates correctly with its neighboring layers.

The Windows 95 modular architecture allows concurrent communications with several different networks using multiple protocols. A Windows 95 computer can have concurrent connections to a NetBEUI-based Windows NT network, an IPX/SPX NetWare network, and the TCP/IP-based Internet.

Figure 5.1 shows the layered components that make up the Windows 95 network model.

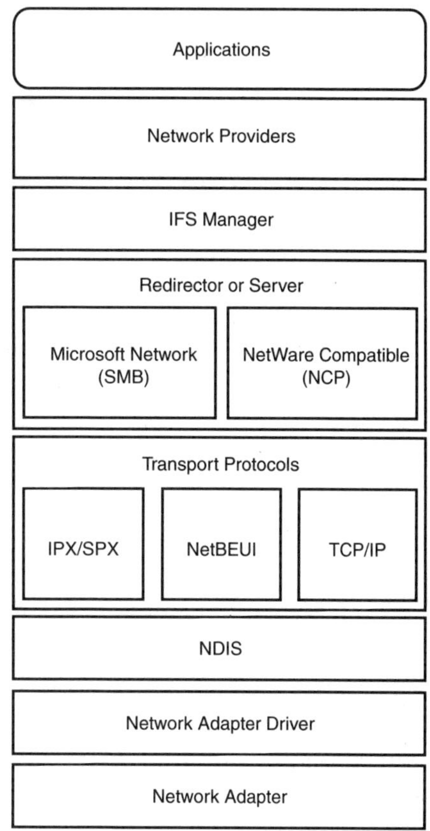

Figure 5.1

A layered networking model as implemented in Windows 95.

Network Providers

Windows 95 uses a modular network provider interface to allow multiple networks simultaneously. Each network provider interface accesses the multiple provider router, where features common to all networks are located, through the service provider interface, as shown in Figure 5.2.

One of the services that the network provider interface allows is the capability to allow users to access shared disk resources using the particular network's native server name syntax. If you want to access a Microsoft network's (SMB)-compatible shared resource, the UNC format of *\\servername\sharename* is recognized. Also, NetWare server syntax, *servername/volumename:directoryname*, can be used and correctly interpreted by Windows 95. The Windows 95 user interface and `net` command also support UNC names for connecting to NetWare resources.

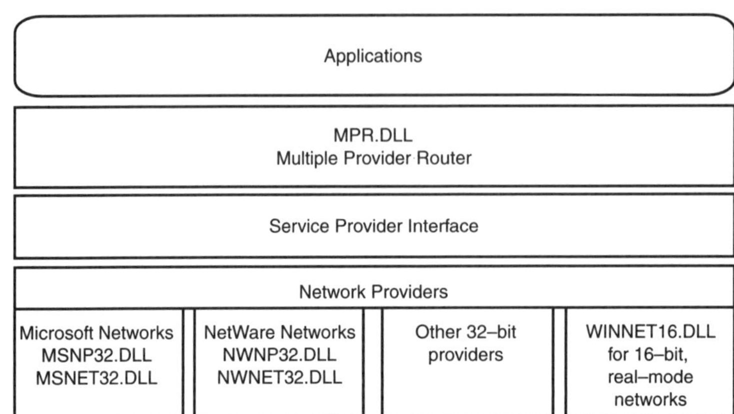

Figure 5.2

The open, modular network provider interface in Windows 95.

Redirectors and/or Servers

The redirector or server layer of the Windows 95 networking architecture corresponds roughly to the presentation layer of the OSI reference model. Whenever an application needs to send or receive data from a remote device, it sends a call to the redirector. Redirectors locate, open, read, write, and delete files, submit print jobs, and support application services such as mail slots and named pipes.

Protected-mode redirectors in Windows 95 are implemented as file system drivers. In order to determine whether a local or remote file system is needed, the redirectors are managed by the Installable File System (IFS) Manager. The IFS Manager controls file input/output transfers for all the supported file systems in Windows 95. Each request is formatted into a packet as it passes through the IFS Manager and redirector.

Microsoft Network Redirector

VREDIR.VXD is the redirector for the Client for Microsoft Networks. The data is reformatted into Server Messenger Block (SMB) packets as it passes through to the appropriate transport protocol.

NetWare Redirector

NWREDIR.VXD is the redirector for the Microsoft Client for NetWare Networks.

The data is reformatted into NetWare Core Protocol (NCP) packets as it passes through to the IPX/SPX-compatible transport protocol.

Peer Resource Sharing

Windows 95 at this layer of the networking model provides two peer resource-sharing server services:

- File and Print Sharing for Microsoft Networks supports SMB file sharing among resources.
- File and Print Sharing for NetWare Networks supports NCP resource sharing.

Share-level security is not supported if Windows 95 is configured to use File and Print Sharing for NetWare Networks. When planning to integrate a Windows 95 computer into a NetWare network, keep in mind that an account database on a NetWare server will have to be made available to the Windows 95 user.

Transport Protocols

Windows 95 includes support for NetBEUI, TCP/IP, and IPX/SPX-compatible transport protocols. All three protocols interact with the network adapter driver and network adapter hardware through the Network Device Interface Specification (NDIS) interface.

NetBEUI

NetBEUI, the NetBIOS framing protocol, is a protocol designed to have low-resource overhead. It features automatic configuration and installation. NetBEUI is designed for small LANs and supports only certain Microsoft-based clients. NetBEUI isn't routable. The NetBEUI module is NETBEUI.VXD.

Figure 5.3 shows the layered Windows 95 implementation of NetBEUI.

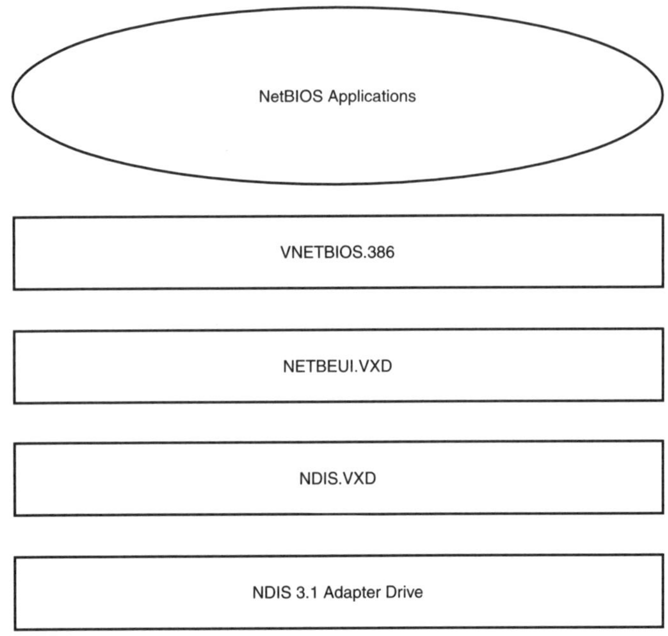

Figure 5.3

The Windows 95 architecture for the NetBEUI transport protocol.

TCP/IP

Transmission Control Protocol/Internet Protocol is a standard routable protocol for wide area networks, UNIX-based networks, and the Internet. The Windows 95 implementation of TCP/IP supports Windows Sockets or NetBIOS over TCP/IP (NetBT) connections.

Figure 5.4 shows the Windows 95 implementation of TCP/IP. Notice the separate interfaces for Sockets and NetBIOS applications.

IPX/SPX-Compatible Protocol

The IPX/SPX-compatible protocol from Novell lets Windows 95 communicate over an IPX network. Novell NetWare servers and other IPX routers can be used to transfer packets across LANs to access other IPX devices.

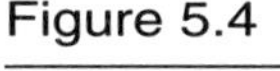

Figure 5.4

Windows 95 architecture for the TCP/IP transport protocol.

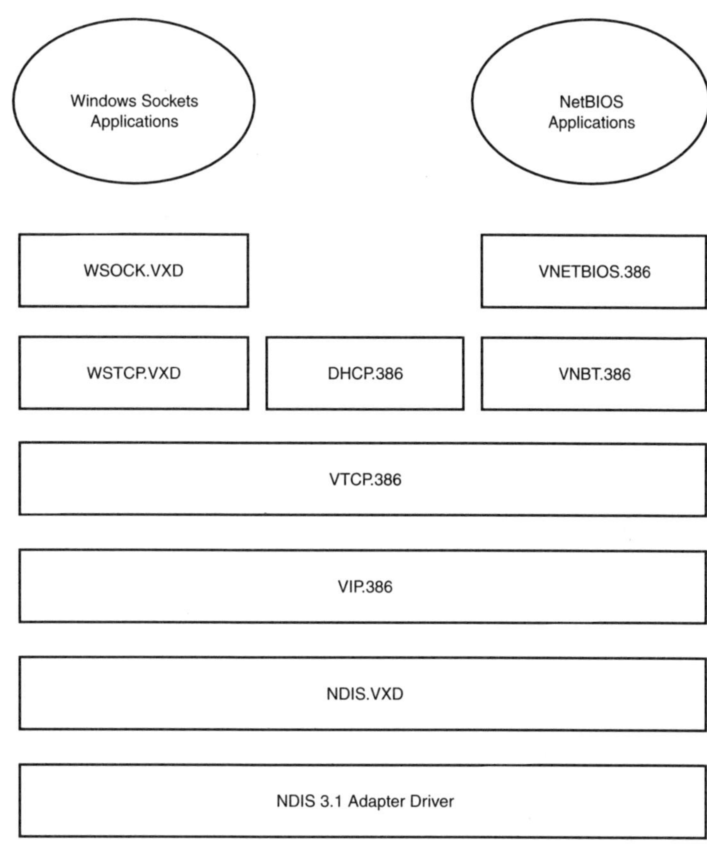

The Microsoft IPX/SPX-compatible protocol uses the NWNBLINK.VXD module to support NetBIOS and uses WSOCK.VXD to support Windows Sockets applications.

Figure 5.5 shows the Windows 95 implementation of the IPX/SPX-compatible protocol.

NDIS

Microsoft networking protocols communicate with network interface card (NIC) drivers using the Network Driver Interface Specification (NDIS). The NDIS interface layer provides basic services common to all networking protocols and provides a standard interface to which NIC adapter drivers can be written. The transport protocol uses the NDIS specification to send raw data packets over a network device and to receive notification of incoming packets received by the NIC. Windows 95 supports versions 2.x and 3.1 NDIS protocol and adapter drivers.

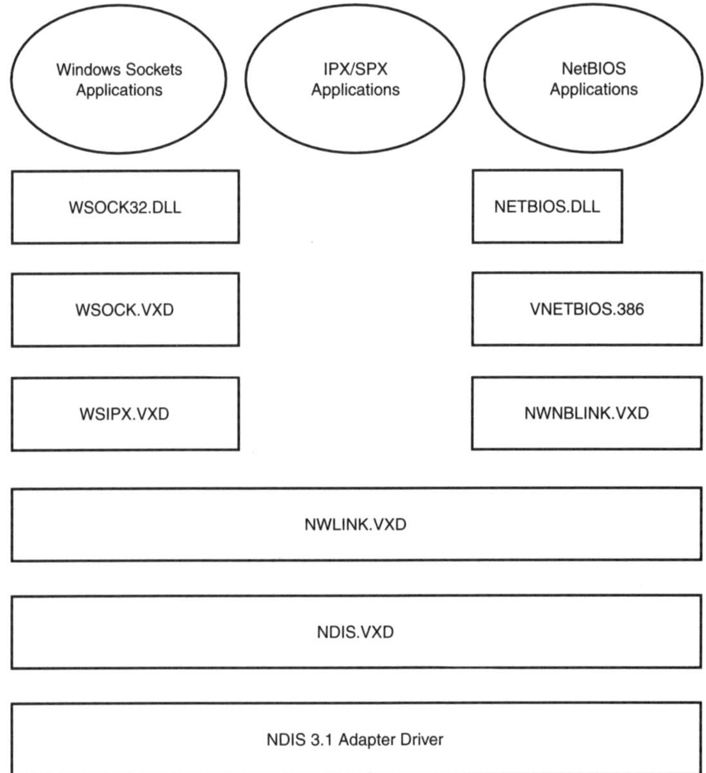

Figure 5.5

Windows 95 architecture for the IPX/SPX-compatible transport protocol.

NDIS allows a single adapter driver to be used for multiple protocols, eliminating the need to rewrite an adapter driver for each possible transport protocol and separating the transport protocols from the physical network media. NDIS 3.1 also incorporates Plug and Play features. This allows Plug and Play network adapters, such as PCMCIA network cards for laptops, to be inserted or swapped while the computer is running. If such an event occurs, the NDIS 3.1 protocols and drivers can automatically add or remove themselves from memory.

Network Adapter Drivers

Each network interface card (NIC) requires software, a network adapter driver, to control the NIC. Each adapter driver is written to work well with a specific NIC. Normally, adapter drivers are provided by the NIC manufacturer, but Windows 95 provides a large selection of drivers for many common NICs.

All Windows 95 network adapter drivers (and protocol settings) are configured using the Network control panel rather than editing text configuration files, as was common in Windows 3.x. Windows 95 stores these settings in the Registry.

Bindings

Bindings establish the relationship between transport protocols and network adapter drivers, allowing the protocols and NICs to communicate across the NDIS layer. Windows 95 automatically binds all configured transport protocols to all installed network adapters.

There are several reasons to break bindings between protocols and drivers. For example, a Windows 95 computer may have both an NIC and a dial-up adapter. The computer may access a LAN using NetBEUI and access the Internet via dial-up through an ISP. By default, TCP/IP will be bound to the NIC, even though the LAN doesn't use TCP/IP, and NetBEUI will be bound to the dial-up adapter. This can degrade network performance. By breaking the NIC-to-TCP/IP binding, Windows 95 can be forced to communicate over the LAN using only NetBEUI. Breaking the dial-up adapter-to-NetBEUI binding could clear up connection difficulties with the ISP's server.

Now that you have a grasp of the Windows 95 networking architecture, the following sections will focus on configuring Windows 95 networking in specific environments.

Using Windows 95 in a Windows NT Network

This section will focus on the Windows NT network components and concepts needed to integrate your Windows 95 workstation. Choosing between a workgroup or a domain, understanding UNC paths, and knowing how to configure your Windows 95 computer to participate in File and Print Sharing are all important parts of this integration.

Workgroups and Domains

When installing Windows 95 in a Windows NT environment, one of your first decisions is whether to join an existing domain or establish or join a workgroup.

The two main administrative architecture types of Windows NT network, workgroups and domains, each has advantages and disadvantages, and each is appropriate in a different networked environment.

Workgroups are used for small groups where there is no centralized security or server. If you're using TCP/IP or IPX, all workstations must reside on a single subnet. The number of workstations per workgroup should be kept low to reduce broadcast traffic on the network segment.

In a workgroup, each user is in full control of shared network resources on his or her workstation. This distributes the administrative load but requires a higher level of ability and responsibility on the part of each user. The lack of centralized resources makes enforcing security regulations very difficult.

Domains are used in complex environments to centralize security and administration. A domain requires at least one central server running Windows NT Server that serves as the domain controller and manages the security database. If using NetBEUI, all machines in a given domain must be in the same subnet. If using TCP/IP with IPX/SPX, domains may span multiple subnets, but this increases the difficulty of initial setup and configuration.

The domain model allows relatively easy centralized administration by a few specialists. Security regulations can be set from the central server, forcing users to operate within policy constraints. The initial cost of a domain is higher, due to the purchase of specialized server hardware and software. Depending on the workload, the domain controller can be used for additional central services.

Universal Naming Convention (UNC)

UNC paths are used to share resources in a Windows NT environment. This allows your Windows 95 workstation to take full advantage of Windows NT file, print, and application servers.

Microsoft's Universal Naming Convention (UNC) is a standardized nomenclature for specifying a share name on a particular computer. The NetBIOS computer name is limited to 15 characters, and the share name is usually limited to 15 characters, although share name length restrictions can vary, depending on the network protocol. Share names can be given to a print queue or a shared directory of files.

The UNC uniquely specifies the path to the share name on a network. The UNC path takes the form of *computername**sharename* [*optional path*]. For example, the UNC path of the printer share that LaserJet creates on Server1 would be \\Server1\LaserJet.

A UNC name doesn't require a drive-letter assignment. Windows 95 takes full advantage of network connectivity using UNC names so that you can connect to a remote directory or printer share without having to map a drive letter to it. However, for MS-DOS-based applications that require a drive letter or printer port to be used, you can map a drive letter to a shared directory or a port to a shared printer.

The UNC can also specify the full path to a file in a subdirectory of a file share. For example, to share the entire C: drive on the computer BIGBEN, you would do the following:

1. Right-click the C: drive.
2. Choose Sharing.
3. Click the Shared As radio button.
4. Type `CDRIVE` in the Share Name box.

The share name CDRIVE has now been created for the root directory c:\. To specify the directory c:\windows\system using a UNC path with these share names, use \\BIGBEN\CDRIVE\windows\system.

Adding a dollar sign ($) to the end of the share name creates what Windows NT calls an administrative share. The $ prevents the share name from being visible to another computer through a browser, such as Network Neighborhood. The share name TOPSECRET$, for example, wouldn't be visible to other computers browsing the computer. Only someone who knows the exact UNC path will be able to access the share.

All Windows 95 functions support using a UNC name, including the Run option on the Start menu and the command prompt. NetWare servers, like Windows NT servers, can be accessed through a UNC name. Instead of using the share name, substitute the volume name to access a NetWare server.

There are a couple of issues to be aware of when assigning shares:

- Share names in Windows 95 can be as long as the involved protocols and user interfaces will allow. However, NetBIOS names can be only 15 characters long and can't contain embedded spaces. Therefore, when establishing share names on your servers, keep them short, don't use spaces within the name, and use 15 or fewer total characters so that Windows 95 can view the names from within Network Neighborhood when browsing for network resources.
- Some older 16-bit Windows and DOS-based applications need mapped drives to access shared files or printers. If an older application is having connectivity problems or is

reporting that files are not found, the application might require a mapped drive or captured LPT port.

Binding the Client for Microsoft Networking to a Protocol

A Windows NT network can take advantage of any of the supported transport protocols. The Client for Microsoft Networks needs to be bound to the appropriate protocol, and the protocol needs to be configured.

To check the bindings, do the following:

1. Select Start | Settings | Control Panel, and choose the Network icon.
2. Double-click the adapter you want to check.
3. Select the Bindings tab.
4. Make sure there is a checkmark next to every protocol you want to use.

Bindings may be checked in the Adapter properties sheet, which can be accessed through the Network icon of Control Panel (see Figure 5.6).

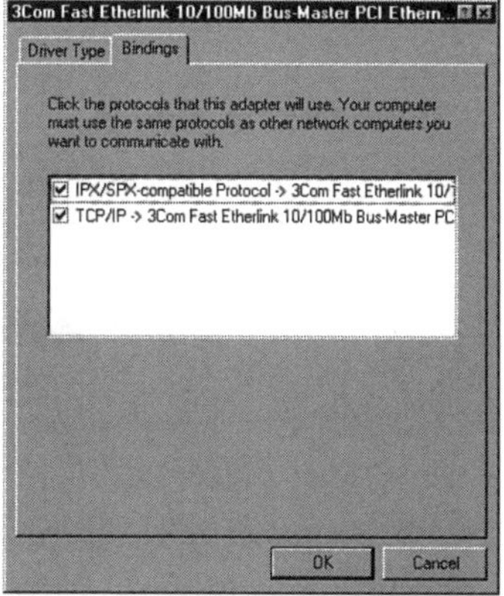

Figure 5.6

Checking protocol adapter bindings in Windows 95.

Browsing Services

The Windows 95 browsing service allows reduction of network traffic by maintaining a central list of all active servers in a workgroup. This list is kept current by having all active servers send a status message to a single computer, the master browser, on a regular basis. The master browser server updates the list as servers join and leave the local network section.

To minimize the network traffic going to the master browser, backup browsers can be designated to help with browse query requests. Usually there is one master or backup browser for every 15 computers in a given workgroup or domain.

In a Windows NT network, the Primary Domain Controller (PDC) serves as the domain master browser, collecting browse lists from the local master browsers. This centralized collection of browse lists allows an enterprisewide browsable network.

If no master browser is present for a workgroup, the first workstation that attempts to access a browse list will send out an election request to the remaining servers in the workgroup. This election request will cause a comparison of all the remaining servers to determine which is most suitable to be the new master browser.

In the Network icon of Control Panel, the Browse Master parameter in the Advanced properties sheet for File and Print Sharing for Microsoft Networks controls which computers can become master or backup master browsers (see Figure 5.7).

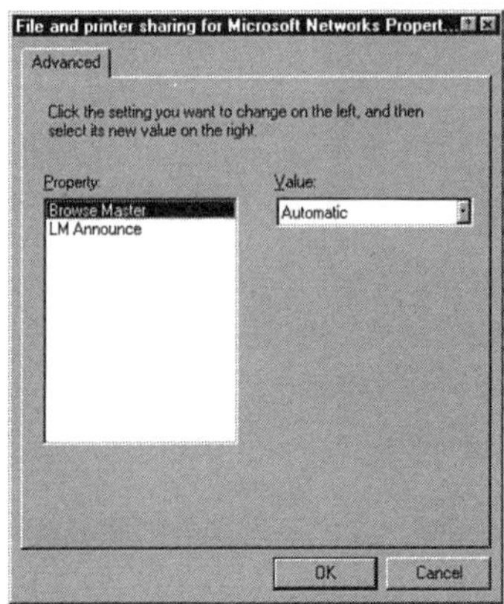

Figure 5.7

The Browse Master parameter set to Automatic.

If the Browse Master parameter is set to Automatic, the default, the Windows 95 computer can participate as a master browser. If the Browse Master parameter is set to Enable, the workstation will attempt to become a master browser. This might be desirable on a little-used computer that is always left on. Being the master browser does cost the master browser workstation or server a little in system resources. If the Browse Master parameter is set to Disable, the Windows 95 computer will never serve as master or backup browser. Remember that at least one computer in the workgroup must serve as master browser.

Configuring File and Print Sharing

Once you have your network set up, you'll want to share files or resources from your Windows 95 workstation. Depending on your network, you might want to assign passwords to each share, or you might want to use the account database on a server to assign permissions. The first task is to install a service to allow sharing.

To install File and Print Sharing for Microsoft Networks, do the following:

1. Select Start | Settings | Control Panel. Choose the Network icon to display the Network window, shown in Figure 5.8.

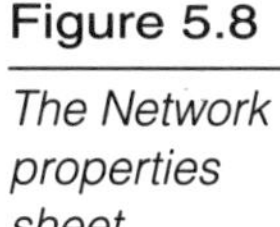

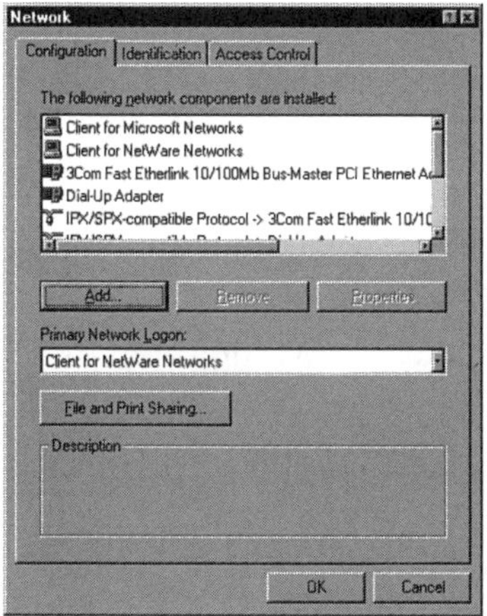

Figure 5.8

The Network properties sheet.

2. Click the Add button to open the Select Network Component Type dialog box, shown in Figure 5.9.

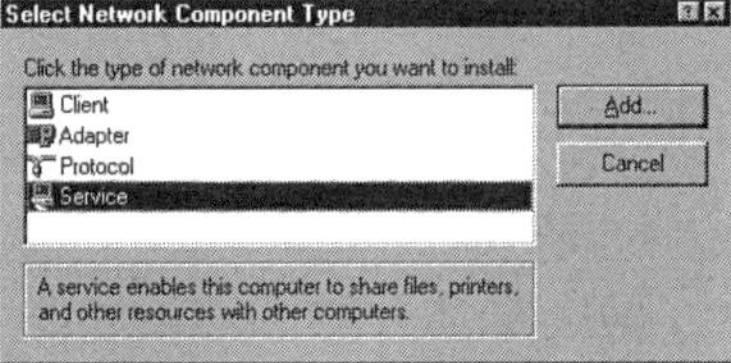

Figure 5.9

The Select Network Component Type dialog box.

3. Select Service and click the Add button. You see the Select Network Service dialog box, shown in Figure 5.10.

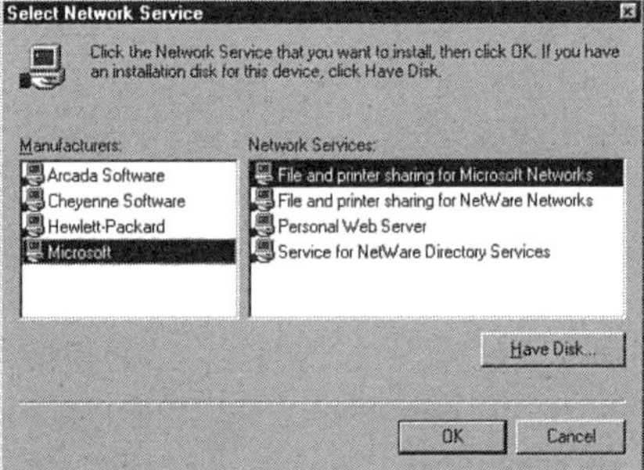

Figure 5.10

The Select Network Service dialog box.

4. From the Manufacturers list, select Microsoft. From the list of Network Services, select File and Printer Sharing for Microsoft Networks.

5. Click OK. File and Print Sharing for Microsoft Networks is added to your installed network components. When you click OK back on the Network properties sheet, the system updates and might prompt you for the location of required files.

6. Restart Windows 95.

Share-Level Security

There are two types of network share security in Windows 95: share-level and user-level.

Only one of these can be configured on a Windows 95 computer at a time.

Share-level security is easy to implement and maintain. Access to a resource is determined by a password assigned to the resource. Anyone who has access to your network by using the password may use the resource.

This requires users and administrators to remember a password for each resource. In complex networks, this can be difficult.

To set permissions on shares and printers, you use the Sharing tab of the Windows properties dialog box, shown in Figure 5.11.

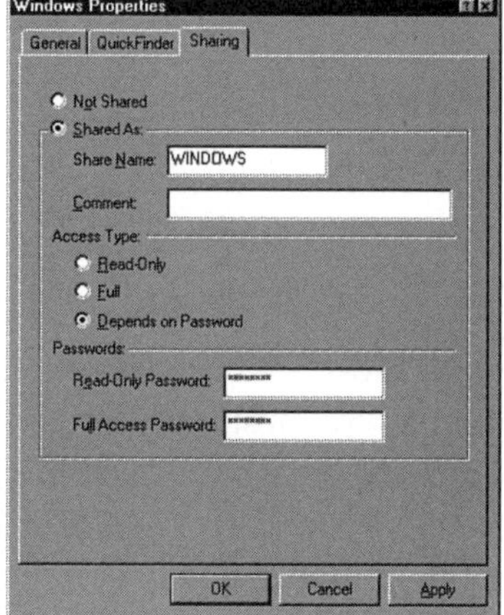

Figure 5.11

The Sharing properties dialog box for the Windows directory.

There are three levels of password-protected share-level security:

- Read-Only gives users access to a shared directory but prevents them from changing the contents.
- Full allows users to read and alter files.
- Depends on Password allows the type of access to be determined by the user's password. Different users can be given different passwords, depending on their access needs.

User-Level Security

User-level security requires a user database to reference logon attempts. Because Windows 95 doesn't have a user database, a server running Windows NT Workstation or Windows NT Server must be available. The name of the Windows NT computer must be configured in the Access Control tab of the Network icon of Control Panel, as shown in Figure 5.12.

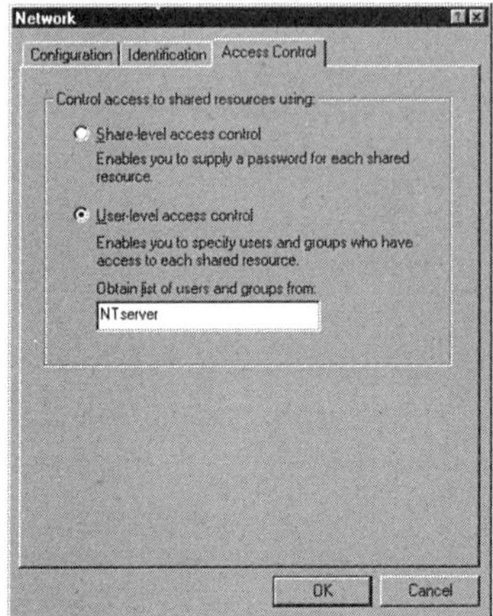

Figure 5.12

Configuring a Windows 95 computer to use a Windows NT server for user-level security.

When Windows 95 processes a request for access to a shared resource, the request is redirected over the network to the specified Windows NT machine that contains a user database. When sharing a file or resource, the Windows 95 administrator has three user-level options:

- Read Only allows users to access a shared directory but prevents them from editing files or changing contents.
- Full Access allows users to view and edit files.
- Custom is a specialized combination of individual privileges.

Figure 5.13 shows the Add Users sheet, accessed through the Sharing tab of a folder's properties.

Custom access lets you create an access level to a folder that consists of a combination of the following permissions:

- Read Files
- Write to Files
- Create Files and Folders

- Delete Files
- Change File Attributes
- List Files
- Change Access Control

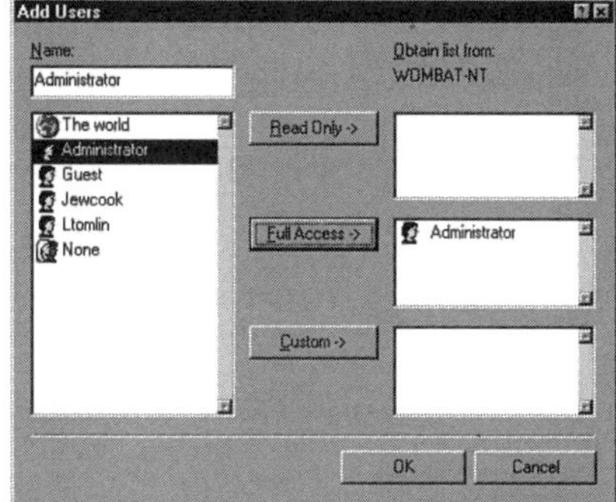

Figure 5.13

Granting administrators full access to the shared C: drive.

Figure 5.14 shows the Change Access Rights sheet being used to grant Read rights to the group The World.

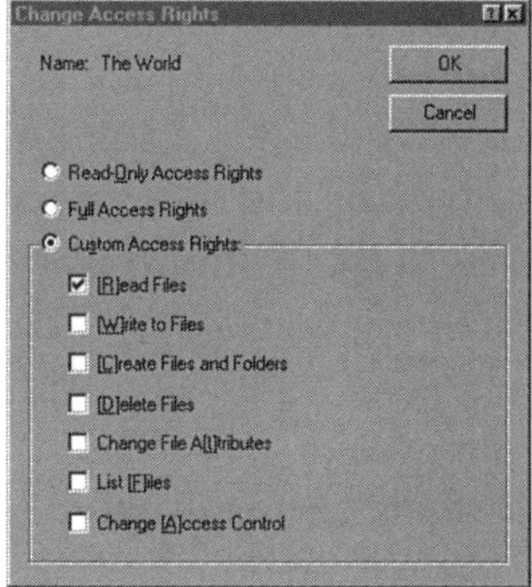

Figure 5.14

Granting The World Read rights to the Windows directory.

Configuring Windows 95 for a NetWare Network

Many existing LANs make use of Novell NetWare servers for application serving or File and Print Sharing, as well as for their directory database. Microsoft Windows 95 includes an IPX/SPX-compatible protocol that allows integration into existing NetWare LANs.

For interoperability with NetWare 2.x and 3.x networks and NetWare 4.x networks with servers using bindery emulation, the retail and OEM versions of Windows 95 include the following:

- The 32-bit Client for NetWare Networks, using the NWREDIR.VXD driver
- Support for older 16-bit NetWare clients
- A NetWare logon script processor
- The IPX/SPX-compatible protocol
- The IPX ODI protocol for compatibility with older NetWare networks
- The File and Print Sharing for NetWare Networks service

In later versions of Windows 95, the OSR2 release, or service-packed earlier versions, a NetWare Directory Services (NDS) service is also available. When assigned a valid user object and password, NDS allows Windows 95 computers to authenticate to a NetWare 4.x network and access shared resources.

The File and Print Sharing for NetWare Networks service allows Windows 95 to act as a peer-to-peer server on a NetWare network. This allows sharing of resources such as printers that might be attached to the Windows 95 computer.

Windows 95's ability to act as NetWare client or server allows gradual replacement of older NetWare workstations, avoiding the large expense of replacing all the workstations in a LAN at one time. Also, Windows 95's ability to use multiple network providers allows Windows 95 workstations to be integrated into mixed NetWare and Windows NT networks.

Configuring Windows 95 to Access a NetWare Bindery

To take advantage of the IPX/SPX-compatible protocol and allow connections to NetWare servers with binderies, your Windows 95 workstation can be configured with the Client for NetWare Networks.

To install the Client for NetWare Networks, follow these steps:

1. Select Start | Settings | Control Panel. Double-click the Network icon.

2. Click the Add button in the Network properties sheet. The Select Network Component Type dialog box appears.

3. Double-click Client. The Select Network Client dialog box appears, as shown in Figure 5.15.

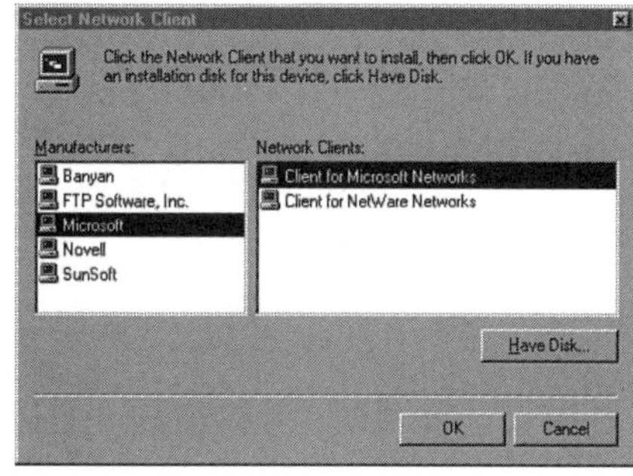

Figure 5.15

The Select Network Client dialog box, showing Microsoft's network clients.

4. From the Manufacturers list, choose Microsoft.

5. From the Network Clients column, choose Client for NetWare Networks.

6. Click OK. The Client for NetWare Networks will be installed.

7. On the Configuration tab of the Network sheet, double-click Client for NetWare Networks.

8. The Client for NetWare Networks properties sheet appears, as shown in Figure 5.16. Its options are as follows:

    - Preferred server: The NetWare server used for logon and authentication.

    - First network drive: The first drive that Windows 95 will allow to map to a network volume on a NetWare server.

Drives F through Z are allowed for NetWare, but this list might need to be altered, depending on your Windows 95 configuration.

- Enable logon script processing: Enables logon scripts. Logon scripts are often stored on the preferred NetWare server.

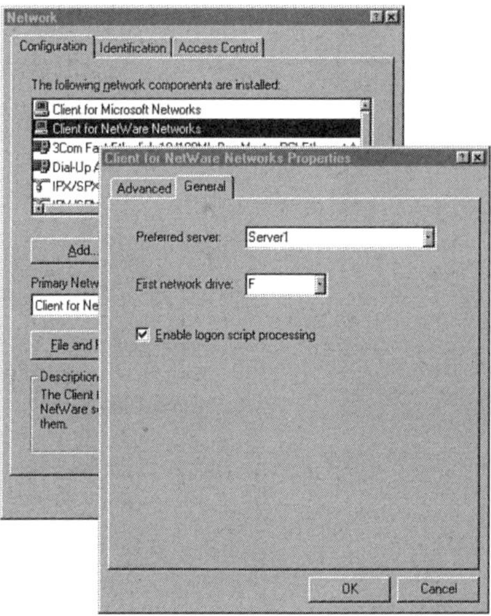

Figure 5.16

The Client for NetWare Networks properties sheet needs to be configured.

9. After you close the Network properties sheet, Windows 95 might ask you for the location of necessary files. You will need to restart in order to make the Client for NetWare Networks accessible.

Configuring Windows 95 to Access an NDS Tree

The OSR2 version of Windows 95 is provided with a NetWare Directory Services (NDS) service to allow access to NetWare 4.x NDS trees. Earlier versions of Windows 95 can run the NDS service if the Windows 95 version has been upgraded to at least service pack 1.

NDS is an X.500-compliant directory service that provides a hierarchical, distributed directory service. NDS allows an initial authentication to a particular NDS tree using a user object with associated password. This authentication can then be used, if the user object has sufficient permissions, to gain access to shared resources. This allows a single point of login for network services, reducing the number of possible forgotten passwords and usernames.

This service can be configured only on Windows 95 workstations that *already* have the IPX/SPX-compatible protocol and the Client for NetWare Networks installed.

To configure the Microsoft NDS client, follow these steps:

1. Select Start | Settings | Control Panel, and then double-click the Network icon.
2. Click the Add button in the Network properties sheet. The Select Network Component Type dialog box appears.
3. Double-click Service. The Select Network Service dialog box appears, as shown in Figure 5.17.

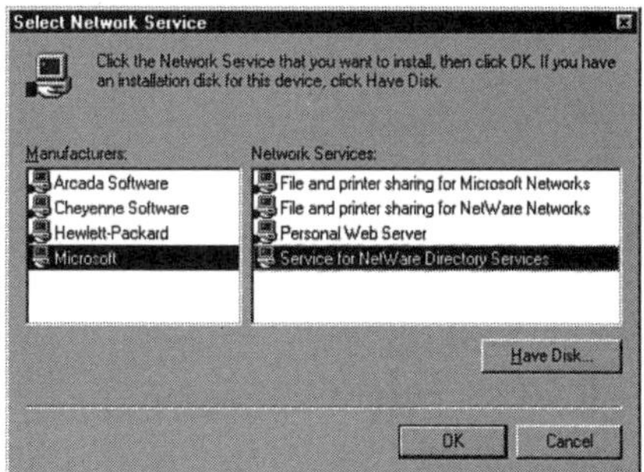

Figure 5.17

The Select Network Service dialog box.

4. In the Manufacturers column, choose Microsoft.
5. In the Network Services column, choose Service for NetWare Directory Services.
6. Click OK. The NetWare Directory Services service will be installed.
7. On the Configuration tab of the Network sheet, double-click NetWare Directory Services.

8. The Services for NetWare Directory Services properties sheet appears, as shown in Figure 5.18. You have the following options:

   - Preferred tree: This is the NDS tree where the user will access shared resources.
   - Workstation default context: The default context where the user's NDS user object can be found.

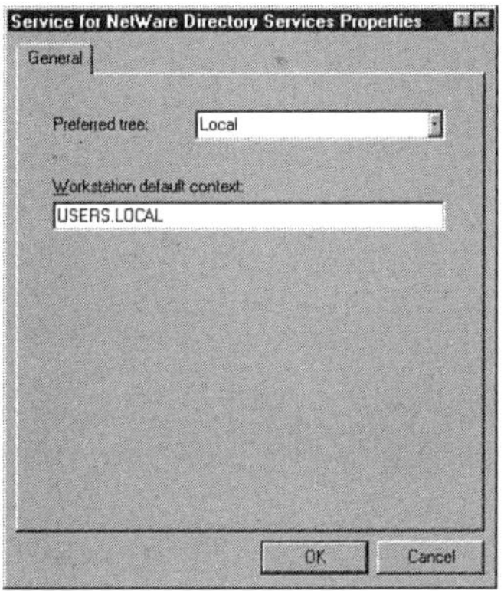

Figure 5.18

The NetWare Directory Services properties sheet.

9. After you close the Network properties sheet, Windows 95 might ask you for the location of necessary files. You will need to restart.

With Microsoft's NDS client, a user can log in to only one tree and context at a time. Changing your tree and context requires that Windows 95 be restarted. Also, the Windows 95 NDS user can't make a bindery connection to a NetWare server using a username or password different from his or her NDS user object.

File and Print Sharing for NetWare Networks

File and Print Sharing for NetWare Networks allows directories and printers to be shared with other NetWare users. There are two very important points to keep in mind when considering using File and Print Sharing for NetWare Networks:

- You can't have File and Print Sharing for NetWare Networks and File and Print Sharing for Microsoft Networks installed simultaneously. Only one can be configured on a particular Windows 95 workstation.
- File and Print Sharing for NetWare Networks must use the user-level security model. The account list must be on a NetWare server bindery or in the bindery context of a NetWare 4.x server using bindery emulation.

User-level security with NetWare networks is similar to user-level security for Microsoft networks. A server is queried anytime shared resource access is attempted. The username or group membership must be on the NetWare server's account list and must have the necessary rights to gain access to the resource.

File and Print Sharing for NetWare Networks can be set up as follows:

1. Select Start | Settings | Control Panel. Double-click the Network icon.
2. Click the Add button in the Network properties sheet. The Select Network Component Type dialog box appears.
3. Double-click Service. The Select Network Service dialog box appears.
4. From the Manufacturers column, choose Microsoft.
5. From the Network Services column, choose File and Print Sharing for NetWare Networks.
6. Click OK. The File and Print Sharing for NetWare Networks service will be installed in the Network properties sheet.
7. Choose the Access Control tab of the Network properties sheet.
8. Choose the User-level Access Control option.

9. Enter the name of the NetWare server that contains the account list in the Obtain List of Users and Groups From field.

10. Click OK. Windows 95 might ask for the location of needed files. It will prompt you to restart when it is done copying files.

When you share resources on a Windows 95 computer using File and Print Sharing for NetWare Networks, the share name associated with the shared directory becomes a volume name and can be designated using the Novell format of *server/volume:* or Microsoft's UNC of *\\server\volume.*

Windows 95 doesn't normally make a distinction between Microsoft shares and Novell volumes. Both appear as directories, also called folders, on the network to a Windows 95 computer.

You can use the `net` command from a DOS prompt to control connections to either type of network resource, using either Microsoft networking UNC paths or NetWare *server/volume* paths. This could be useful in the creation of batch files and login scripts.

To map the g: drive to the share cdrive on the server bigben, issue the following command from a DOS prompt:

```
net use g: \\bigben\cdrive
```

IPX/SPX Configuration

The IPX/SPX-compatible protocol is installed automatically when the Client for NetWare Networks is installed. You can also install this protocol to support different network clients, including the built-in Client for Microsoft Networks.

NetBIOS over IPX is also included with Windows 95. You can enable it by selecting the I want to enable NetBIOS over IPX/SPX check box in the IPX/SPX-compatible properties sheet.

Usually, the IPX/SPX-compatible protocol is self-configuring. By default, when a Windows 95 computer with IPX/SPX-compatible protocol is started, it determines by responses from routers which frame type is most prevalent on the local network. Network addresses are also determined automatically.

There are some unusual situations in which certain advanced IPX/SPX parameters need to be changed due to the configuration of your physical network. This is accomplished through the IPX/SPX-compatible Protocol properties sheet, shown in Figure 5.19. The important thing to know is that if IPX/SPX doesn't self-configure, it's because of your physical network design.

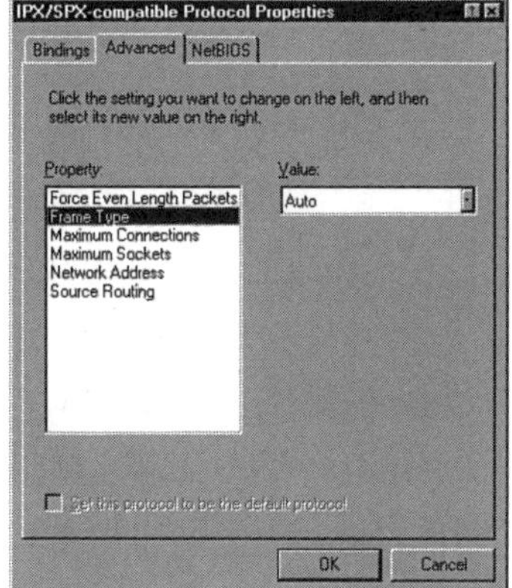

Figure 5.19

The Advanced tab of the IPX/SPX-compatible Protocol properties sheet.

In a mixed Windows NT and NetWare network, client-to-transport protocol bindings might need to be changed. This can improve your networking performance and can eliminate problems with older 16-bit network applications that might require a certain client-protocol configuration.

The best practice with bindings in a mixed environment is to have as few as possible. Don't keep the default binding between the Client for Microsoft Networks and the IPX/SPX-compatible protocol unless you actually need it. You can check IPX/SPX-compatible protocol bindings in the Binding tab of the IPX/SPX-compatible Protocol properties sheet.

Configuring Windows 95 to Access the Internet: TCP/IP

Windows 95 comes with the Microsoft 32-bit TCP/IP protocol, related utilities, and an SNMP client. TCP/IP gives Windows 95 an industry-standard, routable, enterprise-level networking protocol. TCP/IP is the transport protocol of the Internet. With TCP/IP, Windows 95 can access its rapidly growing resources.

To install the TCP/IP protocol on a Windows 95 computer, do the following:

1. Select Start | Settings | Control Panel, and then double-click the Network icon.
2. Click the Add button in the Network properties sheet. The Select Network Component Type dialog box appears.
3. Select Protocol and click Add to open the Select Network Protocol dialog box.
4. Select Microsoft from the Manufacturers list and TCP/IP from the Network Protocols list.
5. Click OK to return to the Network properties sheet.

After you install TCP/IP, the TCP/IP properties sheet will appear. There may be six or seven tabs on this sheet:

- IP Address
- Gateway
- DNS Configuration
- WINS Configuration
- NetBIOS
- Advanced
- Bindings

Which of the many settings you need to configure depends on your network configuration.

The following sections explain how to use each tab.

Choosing Manual or DHCP IP Configuration

The IP Address tab of the TCP/IP properties sheet, shown in Figure 5.20, has two radio buttons from which to choose.

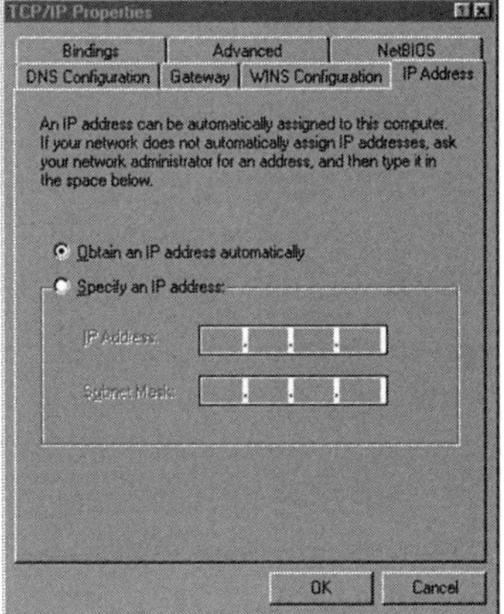

Figure 5.20

The IP Address sheet configured to use DHCP.

Dynamic Host Control Protocol (DHCP) allows automatic IP address assignment. DHCP is an open standard implemented by Microsoft in conjunction with the IETF and other vendors and is based on the older Bootp specifications.

When Windows 95 is configured as a DHCP client and then restarted, it broadcasts a message looking for a DHCP server. The DHCP server provides the client with an IP address to use for a predetermined length of time, the lease of the IP address. This lease, and other information passed from DHCP client to server, is configured by the server administrator.

A DHCP server can be configured to pass all the necessary IP address information to a DHCP client. This includes the IP address leased to the client, as well as the IP addresses of the default gateway, subnet mask, DNS servers, and WINS servers.

The centralized management of IP configuration, ensuring correct IP address assignments, is a large advantage of DHCP. In case of TCP/IP addressing errors, there is one centralized location to troubleshoot instead of trying to track down a single troublesome workstation. DHCP also allows for quicker TCP/IP setup by eliminating the need to enter up to 10 different 12-digit IP addresses.

An incorrect IP address can cause TCP/IP communication problems, not just with the misconfigured workstation, but also possibly with other machines. DHCP greatly reduces this problem by keeping track of which IP addresses it has leased and not leasing them to other workstations.

Understanding and Configuring IP Addressing

The current IP addressing scheme, version 4, uses a 32-bit number divided into four 8-bit octets. This results in four numbers, each in the range of 0 to 255, separated by periods.

For instance, the IP address of the `whitehouse.gov` server, 198.137.241.30, is expressed in four binary octets as

11000110.10001001.11110001.00011110

Each Internet-connected device has its own unique IP address, although numbers are starting to run short. Any other Internet-connected computer can contact your local workstation if the remote computer knows your IP address.

Since no computer can directly contact all the possible IP addresses on the Internet, intermediary devices called routers forward communications when your computer tries to communicate with a workstation not located on the local subnet. A TCP/IP data packet might pass through many routers, each one examining your data packet for address information, before reaching its destination.

Because humans have difficulty remembering lists of 12-digit numbers, friendly names are assigned to computers. Name services, provided by a Domain Name Service (DNS), a Windows

Internet Name Service (WINS), or both, must then be used to translate the friendly name back to an IP address.

Understanding Address Classes

Each TCP/IP device must have an IP address, but different organizations have very different IP addressing needs. A startup business might need only a handful of addresses, all at a single location. On the other hand, a multinational corporation might need many thousands of addresses located at a wide variety of locations.

Because of these issues, IP addresses are split into address classes depending on the total number of IP addresses an organization might need (see Table 5.1). Each address class has a different range of initial octets in its IP address. In order to participate on the Internet, organizations are assigned IP address ranges by InterNIC, a cooperative activity between the U.S. Government's National Science Foundation, AT&T, and Network Solutions, Inc. End users will then have their IP address assigned by an Internet Service Provider (ISP) or their organization's network administrator.

Table 5.1

IP Address Classes and Subnet Masks

Class	First Octet Range	Default Subnet Mask
Class A	1 to 126	255.0.0.0
Class B	128 to 191	255.255.0.0
Class C	192 to 223	255.255.255.0

A class A address is assigned all the IP addresses that start with a particular first octet as its domain. For instance, it might be assigned 120.0.0.0. This means that a class A address might have as many as 16,777,216 IP hosts.

A class B address is assigned the first two octets as its domain—for instance, 131.104.0.0. This would allow 65,536 hosts. Finally, a class C address is assigned the first three octets as its domain, such as 196.105.21.0. This allows a maximum of 256 hosts on a class C domain.

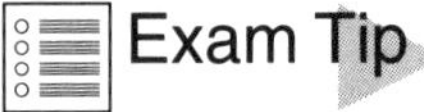

Although this information probably isn't emphasized very much on the exam, it's useful context information for the topic.

Subnet Masking

Along with the IP address, a subnet mask is required for every TCP/IP device. A subnet mask is used to determine if a destination address is located on the local subnet or on a remote network. Subnet masks can be configured by network administrators to reflect the organization's subnet and host needs and are usually consistent throughout a network segment.

On a multinetted segment, you can have a mix of subnet masks. This technique is sometimes used to prevent certain hosts from seeing other hosts. Also, you might want to explain earlier that hosts are different in the IP world. However, that type of setup can break some TCP/IP services, so it's generally not recommended.

To manually configure or change an IP address and subnet mask, do the following:

1. Select Start | Settings | Control Panel. Double-click the Network icon.
2. Double-click the TCP/IP protocol in the installed network components window.
3. Click the Specify an IP address radio button if Obtain an IP address automatically is enabled.
4. Fill in the IP address and subnet mask.
5. Click OK twice.
6. Windows 95 will restart using your new IP address information.

Configuring a Gateway

Once you have an IP address and subnet mask, your Windows 95 computer is ready to talk to other workstations on the local network, but it still has no way to reach a Wide Area Network or the Internet. A default gateway provides the connectivity to the rest of the networked world.

When your workstation tries to communicate with an IP address that isn't located on the local network, the message is forwarded to the default gateway. The default gateway is a router connected to other network segments and contains a table of IP information (called a routing table) that allows it to move your message closer to its final destination. Default gateway addresses can be provided by DHCP.

Multiple gateways can be configured to provide routing backup. If a gateway is unavailable, perhaps due to hardware failure, the next gateway on the list is used.

However, information packets are not sent to multiple gateways if the first is available. Even if the packet was later returned as undeliverable (for instance, if the default gateway's routing table has a bad entry), Windows 95 will try to resend the packet through the same default gateway. A single misconfigured or malfunctioning gateway can stop all communications from entering or leaving a particular network segment.

To configure a default gateway, do the following:

1. Select Start | Settings | Control Panel. Double-click the Network icon.
2. Double-click the TCP/IP protocol in the installed network components window.
3. Select the Gateway tab on the TCP/IP properties sheet, as shown in Figure 5.21.

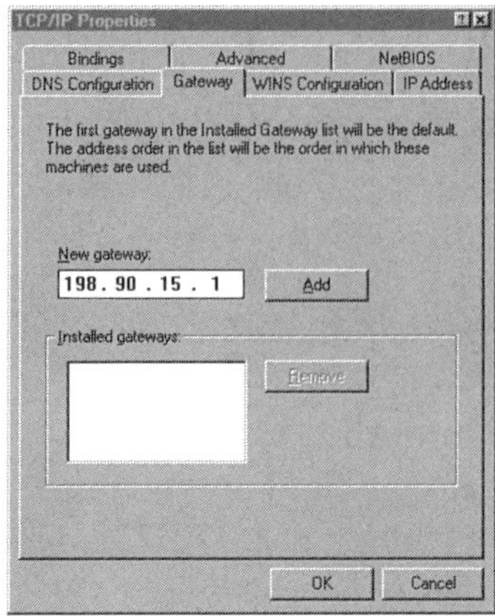

Figure 5.21

The Gateway tab of the TCP/IP properties sheet.

4. Enter your default gateway's IP address in the New gateway box.

5. Click Add. The new default gateway will appear in the Installed gateways window.

6. Click OK twice. Windows 95 will prompt you to restart with your new gateway information.

Using Name Resolution

Name resolution is the process of turning a host or computer name into an IP address. There are several ways to configure Windows 95 to attempt name resolution:

- Domain Name Service (DNS)
- Windows Internet Name Service (WINS)
- LMHosts file
- Hosts file
- Broadcasts

Configuring Windows 95 to Use DNS

The Domain Name System (DNS) is a hierarchical name space that provides a naming scheme for TCP/IP hosts. Historically, these hosts have been UNIX workstations and servers, but with the growing popularity of the Internet in the early 1990s, desktop computers needed easy access to DNS as well.

DNS provides a static, centrally administrated database for resolving domain names to IP addresses. A DNS server is typically a well-equipped UNIX server, but DNS services are also included with Windows NT Server.

A Fully Qualified DNS name consists of a host name appended to a domain name. For example, the host www would be appended to microsoft.com to give the Fully Qualified Domain Name `www.microsoft.com`. In order to participate on the Internet, organizations must register their domain names with InterNIC. InterNIC registers domain names based on the top-level domains listed in Table 5.2.

Table 5.2

Internet Top-Level Domain Names

Domain Name	Type of Organization
COM	Commercial organization
EDU	Educational institution
GOV	Government institution
MIL	Military group
NET	Network service provider
ORG	Other organizations, often nonprofit
Country code, such as JP for Japan	A country

Windows 95 can be configured to use DNS with the DNS Configuration tab on the TCP/IP properties sheet, shown in Figure 5.22.

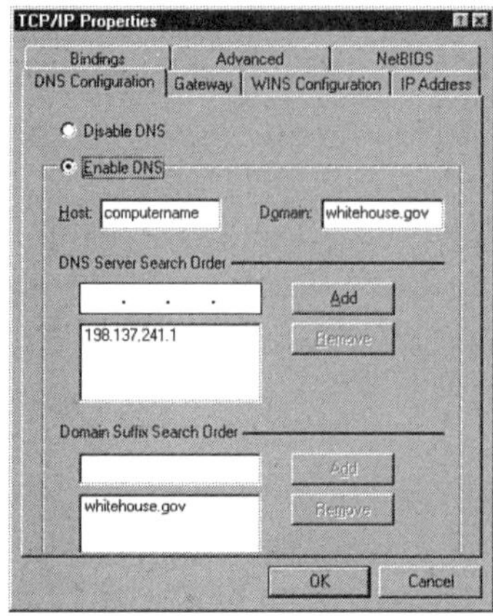

Figure 5.22

Enabling DNS through the TCP/IP properties sheet.

The Enable DNS fields on the DNS Configuration page allow Windows 95 to take advantage of several DNS services:

- Host is the local computer's registered DNS name.
- Domain is the organization's InterNIC registered domain name.
- DNS Server Search Order allows backup DNS servers to be configured in case the primary fails.
- Domain Suffix Search Order tells TCP/IP utilities what domains to append and search if only a hostname is given to the utility.

To configure a Windows 95 computer to use DNS, follow these steps:

1. Select Start | Settings | Control Panel. Double-click the Network icon.
2. Double-click the TCP/IP protocol in the installed network components window.
3. Select the Enable DNS radio button.
4. Enter your computer's registered name and domain in the appropriate fields.
5. Enter your primary DNS server's IP address in the DNS Server Search Order box, and click Add.

6. Repeat step 5 for each secondary DNS server.
7. As each is added, the DNS servers' IP addresses will appear in the DNS Server Search Order window.
8. Enter your primary domain in the Domain Suffix Search Order box, and click Add.
9. Repeat step 8 for secondary domains you might use often.
10. As each domain is added, it will appear in the Domain Suffix Search Order window.

Configuring Windows 95 to Use WINS

A Windows Internet Name Service (WINS) server allows centralized resolution and dynamic registration of NetBIOS names to IP addresses. When a new NetBIOS-capable device is first brought online, it attempts to broadcast its NetBIOS name and IP address to a WINS server. If a WINS server is found, the new device will automatically be registered and will almost immediately be available for name resolution.

WINS allows a Windows 95 user to use a human-friendly NetBIOS name in network utilities—for instance, using a UNC path to access a share. Then Windows 95 can query the WINS server to resolve the NetBIOS name to an IP address, allowing TCP/IP communication to take place.

It is important to keep in mind the differences between WINS and DNS:

- WINS uses a dynamic registration system. DNS relies on static tables.
- DNS resolves Fully Qualified Domain Names into IP addresses. WINS resolves NetBIOS computer names into IP addresses.
- DNS is a hierarchical system. WINS uses the flat NetBIOS name space.

Windows 95 is configured to use a WINS server through the WINS Configuration tab of the TCP/IP properties sheet, shown in Figure 5.23.

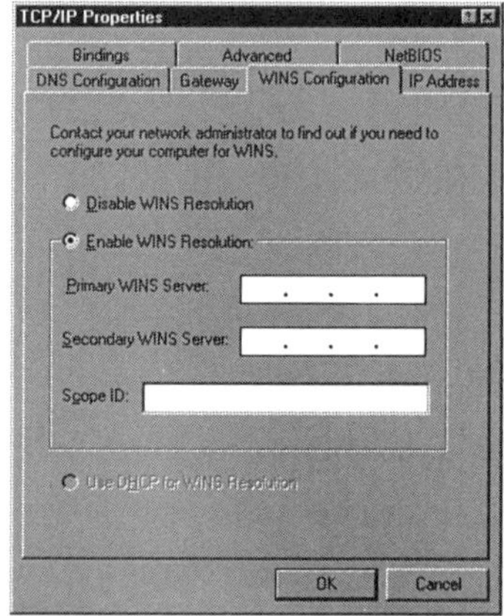

Figure 5.23

Enabling WINS through the TCP/IP properties sheet.

There are three choices of WINS configuration for a Windows 95 TCP/IP client:

- Disable WINS Resolution: If WINS is disabled, an alternative form of NetBIOS name resolution, such as an LMHosts file, is necessary.
- Enable WINS Resolution: If WINS resolution is enabled, the IP address of a primary WINS server is required. A secondary WINS server can be configured to provide backup.
- Use DHCP for WINS Resolution: If the Windows 95 client is using DHCP to configure IP numbers, you can select this option to use the WINS servers specified by the DHCP server.

Configuring Static Name Resolution: Hosts and LMHosts

If WINS or DNS is unavailable, the Hosts and LMHosts files provide local, static lists that allow name resolution:

- The Hosts file is used as a local DNS equivalent to resolve host names to IP numbers.
- The LMHosts file is used as a local WINS equivalent to resolve NetBIOS computer names to IP addresses.

Each of these files is a host table, a simple text list of name-to-IP address mappings. Sample versions of these files (LMHosts.sam and HOSTS.sam) are added to the Windows directory when Windows 95 TCP/IP is installed.

Maintaining an accurate host table on multiple workstations can be very difficult. Each change to the name registration would need to be propagated to each workstation. In an environment with even a modest amount of change, you can quickly be overwhelmed trying to keep track of which workstation's tables have what registrations.

Hosts and LMHosts files can be replicated from a central server to each workstation, but changes might require time to propagate to each workstation. While changes are taking place, incorrect information might be in use, causing incorrect name resolutions.

Broadcast Name Resolution

Computers running Microsoft TCP/IP can use broadcast name resolution. A NetBIOS-over-TCP/IP mode of operation involves the client computer making IP-level broadcasts to register its name by announcing it on the network. Each computer in a broadcast area is responsible for challenging attempts to register a duplicate name and for responding to name queries. Broadcasts are often filtered at routers, so relying on broadcasts across subnets might not be possible.

Troubleshooting Windows 95 TCP/IP

Common TCP/IP problems can be solved using Windows 95's built-in TCP/IP diagnostic utilities, which are listed in Table 5.3.

Table 5.3

Windows 95 TCP/IP Utilities

Utility	Description
WINIPCFG	Displays all TCP/IP addressing information, including DHCP lease status.
NetStat	Indicates network status.
Ping	Tests connections.
Route	Lets you configure a route.
Tracert	Checks and displays the route to a remote computer.
Nbtstat	Checks the state of NetBIOS-over-TCP/IP connections.
Arp	Checks the local ARP table.

The following sections list some common TCP/IP troubles that can be solved using the Windows 95 TCP/IP utilities.

Connection Difficulties or No Connection

1. From a DOS prompt, use WINIPCFG to make sure there are no errors in your TCP/IP configuration.
2. Ping 127.0.0.1, the loopback address, to check basic TCP/IP functionality.
3. Ping the IP address of your computer, your default gateway, and a remote host.
4. If your connection difficulty is only with a remote host, use tracert to determine where along the route the connection is failing.

Ping Verifies Connections, but Windows Explorer or UNC Path Names Fail

1. Verify that the correct remote host name was used.
2. Verify that the remote host uses NetBIOS.

3. Verify that your computer has correctly configured WINS server addresses or an LMHosts file. Check that the WINS server is functioning.

The IP Address Connects but Host Names Do Not

1. Verify the DNS settings with WINIPCFG, or check the DNS Configuration tab in the TCP/IP properties sheet.

2. Ping the DNS server to verify the connection.

3. Ping the remote computer, both by host name and IP address.

4. If you are using a Hosts file, verify that the host name and IP number of the computer are correct.

Setting Up Dial-Up Networking (DUN)

Unless you are connected to the Internet through a permanent connection at a company or organization, you probably will gain access through a commercial provider via a dial-up connection using a modem and regular telephone line. Windows 95 includes the Dial-Up Adapter, which you can set up to connect to an Internet Service Provider (ISP). You then bind this adapter to the TCP/IP protocol, dial into your ISP (using the Dial-Up Networking feature), and communicate over the Internet.

The following steps show you how to set up Windows 95 to access the Internet through a dial-up connection. Before you begin, you need to make sure the following requirements are met:

- A modem is installed and works properly with Windows 95.
- You have an Internet account set up with an ISP. You need a user name, IP information (see the section "TCP/IP" earlier in this chapter), telephone number of the ISP, password, email address, and DNS Server name. Your ISP can give you this information.

- Internet software is installed on your computer. The software can vary, but users usually have a WWW browser (such as Microsoft Internet Explorer), an email application, and a newsgroup reader. Windows 95 clients for the common TCP/IP communications utilities FTP and Telnet are included with the operating system.

After these requirements are met, follow these steps:

1. Select Start | Settings | Control Panel. Double-click the Network icon.
2. On the Configuration tab of the Network properties sheet, click the Add button. The Select Network Component Type dialog box appears.
3. Select Adapter and click the Add button. The Select Network Adapters dialog box appears.
4. Scroll down the Manufacturers list and choose Microsoft. This displays Dial-Up Adapter in the Network Adapters list.
5. Click OK. The Dial-Up Adapter component and a network protocol are added to the list of components shown on the Configuration tab. The default protocol added is NetBEUI. If you don't have the TCP/IP protocol installed yet, you'll need to add it as the protocol for Dial-Up Networking, as shown in the next steps.
6. Click the Add button on the Configuration tab of the Network Properties sheet and select Protocol from the Select Network Component Type dialog box.
7. Click Add again. The Select Network Protocol dialog box appears.
8. Select Microsoft from the Manufacturers list and choose the TCP/IP item from the Network Protocols list. Click OK. You return to the Configuration tab.
9. Select the TCP/IP Dial-Up Adapter component and click the Properties button. The TCP/IP Properties sheet appears.

10. On the IP Address tab, specify how your IP address is set up. If you have a dynamic IP address, choose the Obtain an IP Address Automatically option. If your ISP assigned a permanent IP to you, choose the Specify an IP Address option and fill in the IP Address field. If your ISP also assigned you a subnet mask, fill in the Subnet Mask field with that number.

See the earlier section "Configuring Windows 95 to Access the Internet: TCP/IP" for more information about TCP/IP.

11. Click the DNS Configuration tab to set the Domain Name Service information. Choose the Enable DNS option and fill in the options.

If your ISP uses DHCP, you might not need to manually configure DNS information.

The other tabs on the TCP/IP Properties sheet usually don't need to be filled out for most ISPs or networks. However, if your network uses the Windows Internet Naming Service (WINS) for the NetBIOS protocol, you need to obtain the primary and secondary (optional) WINS server address and scope ID and specify whether the server uses DHCP (Dynamic Host Configuration Protocol) for WINS resolution. This information needs to be entered on the WINS Configuration tab. You must obtain this information from your ISP network administrator.

12. Click OK to save your settings and to return to the Network property page. Click OK.

13. When prompted to restart Windows 95, click Yes to shut down and restart Windows 95.

Setting Up a DUN Connection and PPP

After Windows 95 restarts, you need to configure a Dial-Up Networking connection for the client computer. This is so you can actually dial out from your computer and connect to another computer that is attached to the Internet (this other computer is your ISP's computer). After you make a dial-up connection to the other computer, you become attached to the Internet and can communicate and navigate on it. You configure a dial-up connection by following these steps:

1. Double-click the My Computer icon on the client computer.
2. Double-click the Dial-Up Networking icon to display the Dial-Up Networking folder.
3. Double-click the Make New Connection icon to start the Make New Connection Wizard, shown in Figure 5.24. Enter a name for the connection in the Type a name for the computer you are dialing field, such as the name of your ISP.

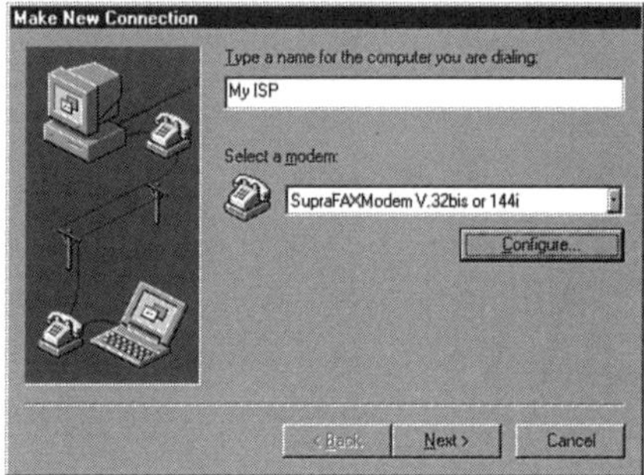

Figure 5.24

The Make New Connection Wizard showing a SupraFAX modem.

4. In the Select a modem drop-down list, choose the modem you want to use to dial out using the new Dial-Up Networking connection. Click the Next button.
5. In the Make New Connection screen, enter the area code and telephone number of the host computer. Click the Next button.
6. Click Finish to create a new Dial-Up Networking connection. A new icon for that connection is added to the Dial-Up Networking folder. See the section "Configuring DUN Options" for more on configuring DUN.

After you install DUN, you can dial into your ISP, establish an Internet connection, and start using Internet resources.

Setting Up DUN with Windows NT Remote Access Services

Windows NT has a built-in Remote Access Server (RAS) that allows Windows NT Workstation or Windows NT Server to act as a connection to a network. Windows NT Workstation allows only one inbound dial-in connection at a time, so it's not suitable as a large-scale gateway to your institutional network.

A RAS server can automatically provide a Windows 95 client with an IP address because the RAS server is configured with a reserved pool from which to draw. RAS can also allow NetBEUI or IPX/SPX-compatible connections.

Setting up DUN to dial into a RAS server is identical to the setup with any other PPP server, except that a RAS server can support Microsoft-encrypted logons. You may also log on to your Windows 95 machine with the correct username and password for a Windows NT domain you want to use. This information will be passed through the RAS server, giving you access to domain resources.

If using RAS and the DUN 1.2 upgrade, you might want to configure the Dial-Up Networking with DNS and WINS information to allow name resolution. Follow these steps:

1. In My Computer, go to Dial-Up Networking. Right-click the connection icon that you will use to dial into a RAS server.

2. Select Properties, and then select the Server Types tab.

3. If it isn't selected already, select the TCP/IP check box and then click the TCP/IP Settings button. The TCP/IP Settings dialog box, shown in Figure 5.25, appears.

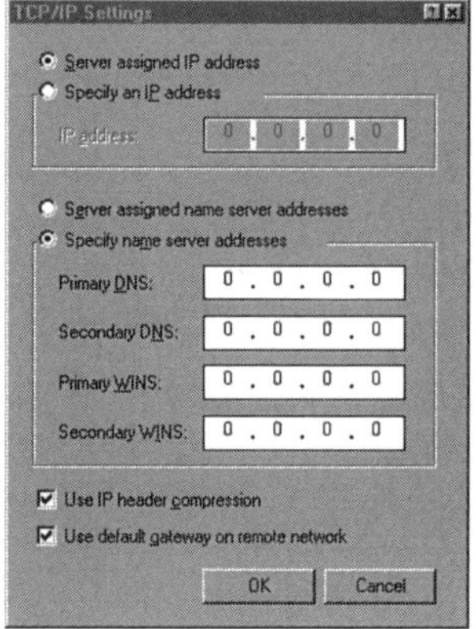

Figure 5.25

Configuring Dial-Up Networking with WINS and DNS information.

4. Select the Specify name server addresses radio button.

5. Fill in your DNS and WINS information.

Configuring DUN Options

Dial-Up Networking supports many configuration options and can be a client for several different dial-up servers. This flexibility allows Windows 95 to connect into most dial-up environments.

Windows 95 can be a client for a Windows NT RAS server, can use the Serial Line Internet Protocol (SLIP) or PPP line protocol, and can function with Novell NetWare Connect. Windows 95 can authenticate passwords using Password Authentication Protocol (PAP), Shiva Password Authentication Protocol (SPAP), and Microsoft's version of Challenge Handshake Authentication Protocol (CHAP). It also provides terminal dial-up window and scripting capabilities if none of the standard password authentication schemes are being used. DUN can use the following three network protocols:

- NetBEUI
- IPX/SPX-compatible
- TCP/IP

IPX/SPX-compatible and NetBEUI are automatically installed when the dial-up adapter is installed. TCP/IP has to be installed later. Configuration instructions for these protocols can be found earlier in this chapter.

NetBEUI, IPX/SPX-compatible, and TCP/IP are supported by DUN only in their 32-bit implementations as provided with Windows 95. For example, you can't use DUN with a real-mode IPX protocol, such as that provided by Novell and installed through a batch file.

Choosing Line Protocols

Line protocols are the means by which network protocols are transported over communication media for which they were not originally intended. The line protocol provides a *wrapping* for the network protocol packet that allows it to be transmitted over the unfamiliar media. When the line protocol packet reaches the dial-up server, the packet is *unwrapped*, and the normal network protocol packet is sent to the network.

The most common line protocol, and the default protocol that Windows 95 installs, is PPP. PPP was originally designed for the TCP/IP environment but is capable of transporting all three network protocols DUN supports and connecting to a wide variety of dial-up servers. PPP allows the following:

- Multiplexing of sessions across a single serial link, allowing multiple network applications to appear to communicate simultaneously
- Multiple network protocols to be transported simultaneously over a single link
- Software compression to increase throughput
- Automatic negotiation of addressing, allowing DHCP to assign a dynamic IP address to Windows 95
- Error detection

SLIP, an older line protocol, is not installed by default with Windows 95. It must be installed from the Windows 95 CD-ROM. SLIP has the following limitations:

- It doesn't support dynamic IP addressing.
- It doesn't support multiple protocols.
- It doesn't have error detection or correction.
- It doesn't have data compression support, although you can compress the IP header information.

To install SLIP from the Windows 95 CD-ROM, follow these steps:

1. Select Start | Settings | Control Panel.
2. Choose the Add/Remove Programs icon, choose the Windows Setup tab, and click the Have Disk button.
3. In the Install From Disk dialog box, type `d:\admin\apptools\dscript`, where `d:\` is the drive letter of your CD-ROM drive, and then click OK.

SLIP might not be available on all versions of the Windows 95 CD-ROM.

In the Select Network Service dialog box, choose UNIX Connection for Dial-Up Networking, and then click Install.

CSLIP, SLIP with IP header compression, and regular SLIP will all be visible in the Server Types dialog box

Windows 95 also provides support for the original RAS (Asynchronous BEUI) and NetWare Remote Networking (NRN) line protocols. As might be expected, these line protocols allow only their manufacturer's network protocols. RAS allows NetBEUI, and NRN allows IPX/SPX.

The Asynchronous BEUI RAS is not the same as the RAS included with Windows NT 3.51 and 4.0. Windows NT RAS supports PPP as its default line protocol.

Password Authentication Schemes

PPP supports several password authentication schemes, which are used by different servers and have different features. The DUN connection automatically negotiates which of the following authentication protocol schemes to use:

- Password Authentication Protocol (PAP) uses a two-way handshake to establish identity. This handshake occurs only when the link is originally established. Passwords are sent over the media in text format, offering no protection from playback attacks.
- Challenge Handshake Authentication Protocol (CHAP) periodically verifies the identity of the peer using a three-way handshake. CHAP provides protection from playback attack, and the password is never sent over the media, protecting against illicit snooping. Windows 95 and NT don't support ongoing challenges with CHAP, but they implement Microsoft's version of CHAP, MS-CHAP.
- Shiva Password Authentication Protocol (SPAP) offers encryption of PAP passwords and Novell NetWare bindery access for user account information.

A PPP server that doesn't support PAP or MS-CHAP might require that you use a terminal window to log on. Dial-Up Networking has an option that allows a terminal window to be displayed after dialing. Without PAP or CHAP, encrypted passwords can be used to improve security.

The Microsoft Plus! Pack for Windows 95 includes a scripting tool that can be used to automate dial-up to servers not supporting PAP or MS-CHAP.

To display a terminal window after dialing, do the following:

1. From My Computer, choose Dial-Up Networking, right-click the connection icon you created, and click Properties.

2. In the Properties dialog box, click the Configure button, and then choose the Options tab.

3. In the Options dialog box, check Bring up terminal window after dialing, and then click OK.

The options available show in the Dial-Up Networking properties sheet.

Configuring Network Protocols Through DUN

Three network protocols are supported by Windows 95 DUN: NetBEUI, IPX/SPX-compatible, and TCP/IP. These three protocols are configured through the Server Types properties sheet. NetBEUI and IPX/SPX-compatible are enabled and disabled through the provided check boxes. In order to increase the speed of your connection, it's a good idea to have only the necessary protocols enabled.

TCP/IP can be further configured through the TCP/IP Settings button.

The IP address the ISP assigns, plus DNS and WINS information, can be configured in the TCP/IP Settings properties sheet. This allows you to have multiple sets of IP address information—one for each DUN connection icon you have created.

There are also two other check boxes in the TCP/IP settings: one to allow higher throughput by enabling IP header compression, and one to use the default gateway on the remote network. IP header compression might not work with some dial-up servers and might need to be disabled if you experience connection difficulties.

Enhancements in the DUN 1.2 Upgrade

The Microsoft Dial-Up Networking 1.2 upgrade fixes bugs and replaces several parts of the original DUN.

The following features were added to the DUN 1.2 upgrade:

- Client support for PPTP
- Support for internal ISDN adapters
- Multilink capabilities
- Connection-time scripting

All of the improvements to Microsoft's DUN included in the OSR2 release of Windows 95 and the ISDN 1.1 Accelerator Pack are included in DUN 1.2.

The Microsoft Dial-Up Networking 1.2 upgrade client supports Point to Point Tunneling Protocol (PPTP). PPTP lets the Windows 95 user establish a Virtual Private Network (VPN) over the Internet. Your VPN connection allows PPTP to encapsulate its data stream in the PPP protocol and send the information over the public Internet. PPTP can encrypt the data, preventing anyone from easily accessing your sensitive information.

Summary

This chapter was meant to teach you, the Windows 95 administrator, how to configure networking for a variety of different environments. You should now be familiar with the following:

- Windows 95 networking architecture, including clients, services, and protocols
- Windows 95 protocols, especially IPX/SPX-compatible, NetBEUI, and TCP/IP, and when each is necessary
- File and Print Sharing

- Windows 95 TCP/IP utilities and functionality
- Windows 95 Dial-Up Networking

You should understand the role of each part of a network and how they work together to allow communication.

You should also be aware how each protocol and client interacts in a mixed environment through bindings of clients, protocols, and adapters. Know what works together and what doesn't.

Finally, become familiar with all the configuration settings by completing the following exercises and questions.

Exercises

Exercise 5.1: Configuring Windows 95 for a Microsoft Network

This exercise demonstrates the installation of three networking components by having you install the NetBEUI protocol, Client for Microsoft Networks, and an appropriate network adapter card driver.

1. Select Start | Settings | Control Panel.
2. Double-click the Network icon. The Network dialog box appears.
3. Before removing all the components (except the network adapter), write down the name of each component and any additional configuration information from the properties sheet(s) for each component. Double-click an item to display its properties sheet.
4. Remove all the components except the adapter card by selecting each item and clicking Remove. The adapter is displayed.
5. Click Add, select Client, and click Add. The manufacturers list is displayed.
6. Select Microsoft and Client for Microsoft Networks, and then click OK. The Client for Microsoft Networks is added, along with the NetBEUI and IPX/SPX-compatible protocols.
7. Select IPX/SPX-compatible protocol and click Remove. The client, adapter, and NetBEUI protocol remain.
8. Click OK and restart the computer.

Exercise 5.2: Using UNC Names

This exercise illustrates the use of a UNC name. For this exercise, you must be connected to a network and be able to browse file shares on other computers on the network.

1. Open Network Neighborhood from the Desktop. The other computers in your workgroup or domain are displayed.
2. Double-click another computer that contains a share to which you have access. The shares on that computer are displayed.
3. Write down the computer name and share name on a piece of paper.
4. Select Start | Programs | MS-DOS Prompt. A command prompt window opens.
5. Enter `DIR \\computername\sharename`, using the computer name and share name you wrote down. The directory listing from the remote network share is displayed.
6. Select Start | Run and then enter `\\computername`. You will see a list of accessible shares on a remote computer.

Exercise 5.3: Sharing a Directory Using Share-Level Security

In this exercise, you will create a directory share using share-level security.

1. Select Start | Settings | Control Panel.
2. Double-click the Network icon. The Network dialog box appears.
3. Select the Access Control tab and select Share-level access control.
4. Select the Configuration tab and click File and Print Sharing. The File and Print Sharing dialog box appears.
5. Select both the I want to be able to give others access to my files and the I want to be able to allow others to print to my

printer(s) check boxes to allow others to access your printers and files. Click OK. File and Print Sharing for Microsoft Networks is automatically installed.

6. Click OK and restart the computer.

7. Start Explorer and select a directory on your hard drive.

8. Right-click the selected directory and choose Sharing from the context-sensitive menu. The Sharing dialog box appears.

9. Type `TEST` for the Share Name and select an Access Type of Read-Only. Enter a password for read-only access and click OK. The sharing hand symbol replaces the folder symbol for the shared directory.

10. If you have another computer on the network, browse the first computer in Network Neighborhood to display the share name. The share name TEST is displayed under the appropriate computer name.

11. Double-click the share name TEST. You are prompted for the password.

12. Enter the password and click OK. The directory contents are displayed.

13. Try to copy a file to the local hard drive. The file read will be successful.

14. Try to delete a file in the shared directory. The file deletion will not be allowed.

Exercise 5.4: Sharing a Directory Using User-Level Security

This exercise shows you how to give a network user access to a directory share. For this exercise, you must be part of a domain that contains a server with a user accounts database. If the user accounts are on a NetWare server, you should install the Client for NetWare Networks, the IPX/SPX-compatible protocol, and File and Print Sharing for NetWare Networks.

continues

Exercise 5.4: Continued

1. Select Start | Settings | Control Panel.
2. Double-click the Network icon. The Network dialog box appears.
3. Select the Access Control tab and select User-level access control.
4. Type the name of the server with the user accounts database on it. Windows 95 attempts to access the Windows NT or NetWare server to obtain the users list.
5. Select the Configuration tab and click File and Print Sharing. The File and Print Sharing dialog box appears.
6. Select both the I want to be able to give others access to my files and the I want to be able to allow others to print to my printer(s) check boxes to allow others to access your printers and files. Click OK. File and Print Sharing for Microsoft Networks is automatically installed.
7. Click OK and restart the computer.
8. Start Explorer and select another directory on your hard drive. The new directory is highlighted in Explorer, but the directory from the preceding exercise is no longer shared due to the changed security model.
9. Right-click the selected directory and choose Sharing from the context-sensitive menu. The Sharing dialog box appears.
10. Type `TEST2` for the share name and give a user full access privileges by selecting the user and clicking Full Access. Click OK. The folder symbol for the shared directory is replaced with a folder being held by a hand.
11. Log on to another computer on the network using the user name to which you gave full access permissions. Locate the share name TEST2 in Explorer by browsing the entire network. The share name TEST2 is displayed under the appropriate computer name.

12. Double-click the share name TEST2. The directory contents appear.

13. Try to copy a file to the shared directory. The file write is allowed.

Exercise 5.5: Configuring Windows 95 for Use in a Windows NT Domain

In this exercise, you will configure a Windows 95 computer to participate in a Windows NT domain. If the Client for Microsoft Networks is not already installed, perform Exercise 5.1 before proceeding.

1. Select Start | Settings | Control Panel.

2. Double-click the Network icon. The Network dialog box appears.

3. Select Client for Microsoft Networks and click Properties. The Client for Microsoft Networks properties sheet appears.

4. Select Log on to Windows NT domain, enter the Windows NT domain name, and click OK. The Client for Microsoft Networks properties sheet again appears.

5. Select the Identification tab and type the Windows NT domain name in the Workgroup field.

6. Enter a computer name and an optional description in the other fields and click OK. You are prompted to restart the computer.

7. Restart the computer and log on to Windows 95 using your Windows NT domain account. If your domain password is the same as your Windows password, enter the password once.

Exercise 5.6: Configuring the Client for NetWare Networks

In this exercise, you will install and configure the Client for NetWare Networks. You must have a network adapter driver already installed in the Network icon of Control Panel.

continues

Exercise 5.6: Continued

1. Select Start | Settings | Control Panel. Double-click the Network icon.

2. Click Add, select Client, and click Add. The Manufacturers list is displayed.

3. Select Microsoft and Client for NetWare Networks and click OK. The Client for NetWare Networks and the IPX/SPX-compatible protocol are installed.

4. Select the Client for NetWare Networks and click Properties. The Client for NetWare Networks properties sheet appears.

5. Select the General tab and enter the name of the NetWare server that should process the logon in the Preferred Server field.

6. In the First Network Drive field, select the first drive letter to be available to be mapped by a NetWare login script and click OK twice. You are prompted to restart the computer.

7. Restart the computer and enter your NetWare user name at the unified logon screen. If your NetWare password is the same as your Windows password, you have to enter the password only once.

   If your NetWare password is different from your Windows password, change your NetWare password to your Windows password by entering the `SETPASS` command from the SYS/PUBLIC directory on the NetWare server.

Exercise 5.7: Configuring Dial-Up Networking

In this exercise you will configure Dial-Up Networking to access the Internet. This exercise assumes that you already have a modem and DUN installed.

1. Go to My Computer and choose Dial-Up Networking.

2. Double-click Make New Connection.

3. Select the modem to be used, and type a name to use for the connection settings. Click Next.
4. Type the phone number and country for the connection you want to make. Click Next.
5. Click Finish to exit. The Dial-Up Networking folder will now show an icon containing the new connection settings you created.
6. To change the network-related settings for the new connection, right-click the icon you created and choose Properties. The main properties sheet for the new connection appears.
7. Click Server Type to view the network settings. The Server Types Properties sheet appears.
8. Deselect the NetBEUI and IPX/SPX-compatible protocols, and click the TCP/IP Settings button. The current settings for TCP/IP appear.
9. Enter the appropriate setting for your ISP and click OK three times until all properties sheets are closed.
10. Double-click the connection icon you created. You are prompted for a username and password.
11. Type your username and password for your Internet account, and click the Connect button. Your modem should start dialing.

Review Questions

The following questions test your knowledge of the information in this chapter. For additional questions, see MCP Endeavor and the Microsoft Roadmap/Assessment Exam on the CD-ROM that accompanies this book.

1. You are responsible for connecting Windows 95 to a heterogeneous network. You're running a number of different network operating systems on this large network, and you want to be sure that Windows 95 is compatible with them. Windows 95 includes software to support which three of the following networks?

    A. TCP/IP

    B. NetBEUI

    C. Novell NetWare

    D. Apple AppleShare

2. Jason installs a network adapter card on a computer running Windows 95. When he does this, Windows 95 automatically installs two protocols for this card. Which two protocols are installed by default when the first network adapter driver is installed?

    A. AppleTalk

    B. NetBEUI

    C. TCP/IP

    D. IPX/SPX-compatible

3. You want to install Windows 95 on a Novell NetWare network that includes NetWare 4.x servers. Which two of the following network components might you need?

    A. Microsoft Client for NetWare Networks

    B. Microsoft NDS service

    C. File and Print Sharing for Microsoft Networks

D. NetBEUI protocol

E. TCP/IP protocol

4. In a training class you are teaching, you explain to end users how to use UNC to access resources on the network. You provide this example to the class: What is the full UNC path for a file named test.bat in a directory named BATCH located in a share named PUBLIC on a server named FREDSPC? Select the correct answer.

   A. \\PUBLIC\BATCH\test.bat

   B. \\FREDSPC\BATCH\test.bat

   C. \\FREDSPC\PUBLIC\BATCH\test.bat

   D. None of the above

5. Windows 95 has a modular, layered architecture. Which two of the following are interfaces functioning at the Windows 95 Application Interface layer?

   A. Win32 WinNet Interface

   B. WinNet 16

   C. HP JetAdmin

   D. Win32 Print Applicator Programming Interface

6. Susan prepares for a presentation describing the Windows 95 network architecture. One of the bullet points is this: A ______ maps network names used by an application to a physical network device name. Fill in the blank.

   A. device driver

   B. redirector

   C. requestor

   D. transport interface

7. Which three of the following are layers in the Windows 95 networking architecture?

   A. Transport Programming Interface
   B. Internal File System Manager
   C. Device Driver Interface
   D. Network Providers

8. Isabel is configuring her Windows 95 computer with the TCP/IP protocol. As she fills out the properties for the protocol, she comes across a blank for the DNS entry. What does DNS stand for?

   A. Downloadable Network Share
   B. DOS-Node Server
   C. Domain Name Service
   D. Domain Network Server

9. You run a network using NetBIOS. The ______ registers and resolves NetBIOS names to IP addresses.

   A. DNS Server
   B. IFS Manager
   C. Network Adapter Card
   D. WINS Server

10. Chuck is setting up a network to use user-level security. From the following list, choose the two places where the user list can be stored.

   A. Windows NT domain
   B. Windows 95 home directory
   C. NetWare bindery server
   D. Banyan VINES server

11. To access the Internet, you need to use Windows 95's Dial-Up Adapter and associated software. Choose two items from the following list that you must have before setting up Windows 95 to access the Internet via Dial-Up Networking.

    A. ISP account

    B. modem

    C. gateway information

    D. DNS information

12. While stationed at the company help desk, you receive a call from a user accessing the Internet. He asks what a fully qualified domain name is. From the following list, choose the item that would *not* meet this criteria.

    A. `www.microsoft.com`

    B. `www3.iquest.net`

    C. `www.microsoft_com`

    D. `www.mcp.com\newriders`

13. You are configuring TCP/IP on Windows 95 and have just put in the IP address 135.33.45.5. What is the default subnet mask?

    A. 255.0.0.0

    B. 255.255.0.0

    C. 255.255.255.0

    D. 255.255.255.255

14. You have Windows 95 installed on a computer connected to a network running only one network operating system (NOS). A user calls and says she can't browse network resources using Network Neighborhood. Which NOS could you be running that doesn't support browser services?

    A. Novell NetWare 3.12

    B. Banyan VINES

    C. Windows NT

    D. None of the above

15. Stuart is attaching his Windows 95 computer directly to another Windows 95 computer using Microsoft networking. He wants to provide access from one computer to the other so that each computer has access to files and printers on either machine. What must he do to enable this in Windows 95?

    A. Set up user-level security

    B. Install File and Print Sharing for Microsoft Networks on both computers

    C. Set up share-level security

    D. All of the above

16. You are asked to connect 10 Windows 95 computers to a Novell NetWare network. From the following list, choose the two components or features that Windows 95 has for NetWare networks.

    A. The capability to run File and Print Sharing for NetWare Networks with File and Print Sharing for Microsoft Networks

    B. Share-level security support of File and Print Sharing for NetWare Networks

    C. IPX/SPX-compatible protocol

    D. 32-bit Client for NetWare Networks

17. As you instruct a user on how to configure a peer-to-peer network with five connected Windows 95 computers, you use the term "Windows 95 server" several times. After you finish, he asks you what a Windows 95 server is. What do you tell him?

    A. A computer that is the Primary Domain Controller (PDC) on the LAN

    B. A computer running Windows 95 that has the Enable Windows 95 Server Registry option turned on

    C. A Windows 95 computer that has the File and Print Sharing Service enabled

    D. A computer running Windows 95 that performs as an application and database server for the LAN

18. Windows 95's modular architecture includes the Installable File System (IFS) Manager. The IFS Manager manages communication between which three of the following?

    A. The Miniport Driver

    B. The various Installable File Systems

    C. The Network Provider

    D. The network redirectors and services

19. Martina has been told that she can run multiple network clients under Windows 95, but she's having problems getting this feature to work on her system. She calls you and asks you to help her. What would be the best question to ask her to start diagnosing her problem?

    A. Does she have protocols for IPX/SPX set up?

    B. Is Windows 95 set up to handle user profiles?

    C. Is there a Primary Domain Controller (PDC) established on a Windows 95 Server?

    D. Are all the network clients 32-bit clients?

20. Which of the following two utilities are most useful in tracking down TCP/IP connection problems?

    A. Ping

    B. Arp

    C. WINIPCFG

    D. Netuse

21. You want to configure a dial-up connection to a server that allows simultaneous applications to be run using multiple network protocols. Assuming that the server is capable, what line protocol do you have to use to connect?

    A. SLIP

    B. NRN

    C. PPP

    D. RAS (Asynchronous NetBEUI)

22. Which of the following password authentication protocols protect against a playback-type attack and are supported by DUN?

    A. PAP

    B. CHAP

    C. MS-CHAP

    D. DUN terminal pop-up windows

Review Answers

1. A, B, C

2. B, D

3. A, B

4. D

5. A, D
6. B
7. A, C, D
8. C
9. D
10. A, C
11. A, B
12. C
13. B
14. B
15. B, C
16. C, D
17. C
18. B, C, D
19. D
20. A, C
21. C
22. B, C

Answers to Test Yourself Questions at Beginning of Chapter

1. WINS, the LMHosts file, and broadcasts are all capable of resolving NetBIOS names. See "Using Name Resolution."
2. IPX/SPX-compatible. No, this can't be changed to another protocol. Other possibly useful components include File and Print Sharing for NetWare Networks, and the Microsoft NDS service. See "Configuring Windows 95 for a NetWare Network."
3. Windows 95 might not be making a connection to a DNS server. This might be due to configuration or a network failure. If a Hosts file is being used, the information contained in it might be incorrect. DNS and Hosts are the two ways to resolve fully qualified domain names to IP addresses. See "Using Name Resolution."
4. Share-level security allows quicker setup of shares and sharing in a peer-to-peer network. User-level security allows centralized account management on a Windows NT or NetWare server, allows finer permission control, and allows groups to be assigned rights. See "Configuring File and Print Sharing."
5. Use the Dial-Up Networking feature of Windows 95; configure the Dial-Up Adapter for an Internet Service Provider (ISP); use a modem to dial into the ISP. See "Setting Up Dial-Up Networking (DUN)."
6. Yes, he can do this, but File and Print Sharing for NetWare Networks supports only user-level security. See "File and Print Sharing for NetWare Networks."
7. Universal Naming Convention. A UNC consists of a computer name and a share in the following syntax: *\\computer\share*. UNC does not require a drive-letter assignment. This would cause some 16-bit programs problems. See "Universal Naming Convention (UNC)."
8. Gateways allow TCP/IP messages to be routed to remote networks. Without a gateway, TCP/IP is limited to the local network segment. See "Configuring a Gateway."
9. A master browser is a workstation that is responsible for maintaining the list of workstations in the local workgroup on the local network segment. New computers announce themselves by broadcast to the local network, and the master browser retains and distributes this information. See "Browsing Services."

Chapter 6

Monitoring and Optimization

This chapter helps prepare you for the exam by covering the following objectives:

- Monitoring system performance using the following tools:
  - Net Watcher
  - System Monitor
- Tuning and optimizing the system using the following tools:
  - Disk Defragmenter
  - ScanDisk
  - Compression Utility

Test Yourself! Before reading this chapter, test yourself to determine how much study time you will need to devote to this section.

1. You're working on the help desk, and a user calls you. He says his computer is running very slowly and his hard drive is always busy. He says he thinks he should get his hard drive upgraded. How can you diagnose his problem?
2. On your home computer, you have been doing a lot of work with five new applications for one month. At the end of the month, you remove the applications from your computer, but the computer still runs slowly. What can you do to improve its performance?
3. You're working in Microsoft Word, and a document you have worked with in the past now appears to be corrupted when you open it. The first half of the document is fine, but the second half is gibberish. What can you do to prevent further corruption of your documents?
4. You're working on a laptop with a 500MB hard drive. You would like to get additional storage space through compression. What other features of your laptop should you consider before compressing your drive?
5. While shutting down your computer for the day, you get a message stating that three users are connected to your computer. What should you do?
6. You're about to store a large file on your computer. The instructions that came with the file state that the file must be copied to your drive and must not be fragmented during the process. You're in a hurry. What is the quickest way to ensure that this is possible?
7. You would like to know what type of response time you are getting from a file transfer session with your file server. What tool(s) would you use to do this?
8. You are about to copy three 200MB files to your computer. The data contained in them is critical. What steps can you take to ensure that the files will be readable after you copy them to your computer?

Answers are located at the end of the chapter...

If you want to get the best performance out of your automobile, you would never think of ignoring its needs. You would regularly take it in for oil changes and tune-ups, you would consider replacing or upgrading parts with higher-performance parts, and you would pamper it with any number of gifts to make its life better. The same rules apply to your computer and its hard drive. The unfortunate thing is that your computer is usually ignored unless something goes wrong (which is also true for some people and their automobiles).

This chapter looks at what you can do to maintain your computer and its hard drive to get the best performance possible. The topics that will be covered deal with monitoring, tuning, and optimizing your system. The tools you will use to monitor your system include Net Watcher for monitoring network connections and System Monitor for monitoring your overall system. The tools you will use to tune and optimize your system include Disk Defragmenter and ScanDisk for maintaining hard drive health and performance, and DriveSpace (Microsoft's compression utility) for managing compressed drives. These tools will be examined to show you how to diagnose and prevent system performance problems.

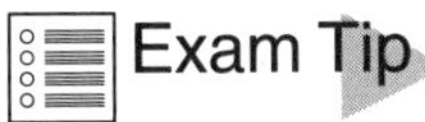

Here are some things you are likely to be tested on:

- How to find out who is connected to your computer over the network
- How to find out what resources people are using on your computer
- What type of information you can get from System Monitor
- The different ways you can view information about your system in System Monitor
- How to use System Monitor to view other computers
- The benefits of disk defragmentation
- Errors that can occur on your hard drive through normal use, such as cross-linked files, and how to fix them

continues

- The differences between ScanDisk and ScanDisk for Windows
- Situations in which disk compression might be useful

Monitoring System Performance

The only way you will ever know that you have a problem with your computer, short of a failure in the system, is to monitor its performance. The first topic in this chapter is how you can use both Net Watcher and System Monitor to track your computer's use and performance. Both of these tools can also monitor other computers on your network.

Using Net Watcher

Net Watcher was designed to allow you to see who is currently attached to your computer from other locations on your network. Net Watcher also lets you track open files, create new shared folders, and stop sharing folders. The number of people who have connected to your computer will adversely affect its performance. The more files that are accessed, the larger they are, and the length of time they are kept open, the more your computer will be affected.

Microsoft has not imposed file sharing limits on Windows 95, so technically you can have everyone on your network connect to your computer. If those people wanted to maintain a high level of activity on multiple files, you would quickly realize that Windows 95 wasn't designed for this type of file sharing. Windows 95's File and Print Sharing services are low-performance and were designed for low activity, rare access, or low numbers of users. Net Watcher lets you track some of the activity on your computer.

In examining the use of Net Watcher, you will see how to

- Connect to other computers
- Monitor shared folders

- Share folders
- Monitor users
- Monitor open files

The first topic is how to connect to another computer on your network with Net Watcher, after which you will see how Net Watcher can report on your system usage.

Connecting to Other Computers

Net Watcher may be used locally on your own computer to track user activity, or it may be used to view another computer on your network.

Before you can use Net Watcher to view another computer, you will have to be an administrator for that computer. This means that if that computer has implemented user-level access control, you have to be included on the Remote Administration tab of the Passwords icon of Control Panel. You may also be a member of a group that has been included on the Remote Administration list. If the other computer is using share-level access control, you will need to know the password that was used to set up remote administration. For more information on setting up remote administration, see Chapter 1, "Planning."

Once you are an administrator for the other computer, you will be able to access it either by its properties in Network Neighborhood (see Figure 6.1) or by selecting Administer | Select Server from Net Watcher. You will be able to do everything to the other computer that you could do to your own computer with Net Watcher.

One of the things that Net Watcher can do is report on what folders have been made available to network users.

Monitoring Shared Folders

Net Watcher can give you a list of shared folders that are currently available on your system. This is an extremely useful feature, because the folders that are shared could be buried under several layers of folders. Without Net Watcher, you would have to spend several hours searching for all the shared folder symbols (a hand holding a folder) on your hard drive.

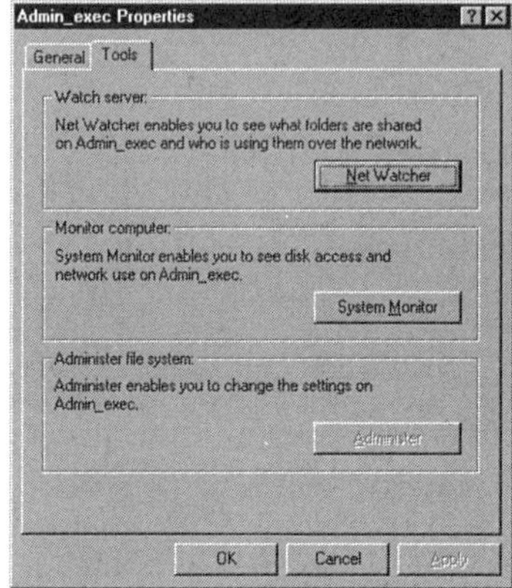

Figure 6.1

Net Watcher may be launched from the Tools tab of a computer's properties sheet in Network Neighborhood.

Not only does Net Watcher give you a list of shared folders, but it also tells you what the share name is and the access level granted to the folder (only when you select View | Details; see Figure 6.2). The usefulness of this screen is enhanced when you select one of your shared folders, because a list of connected computers appears in the right pane. This list of connected computers also shows any open files that are maintained by that computer.

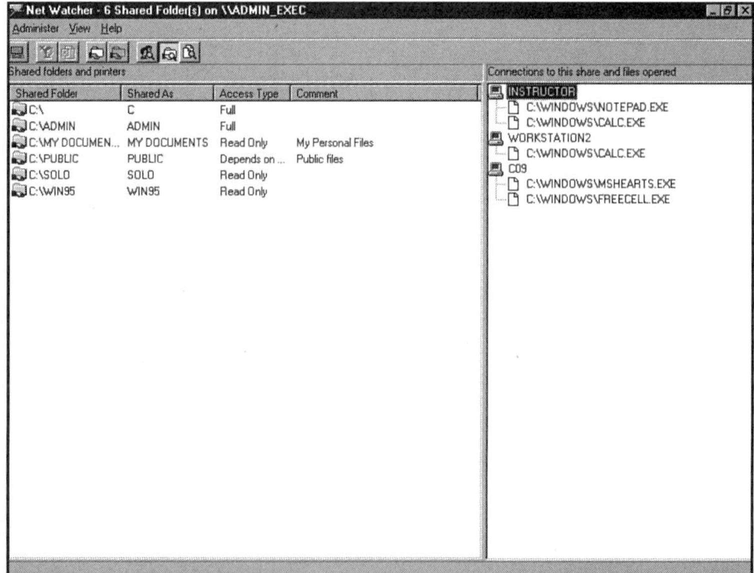

Figure 6.2

Net Watcher provides you with a list of shared folders, as well as who is accessing them.

> The Windows 95 definition of Open File might be misleading to some people. These are files that are currently open for read or write access. A file is open only if your computer tells the file system that it still needs access to the hard disk. If you open a document in a word processing program such as WordPad, WordPad tells the file system that it wants to open the file for read access. It reads the file and then closes the read session. According to the file system, the file is now closed, even though you're looking at the document on your screen in WordPad.

You should keep a watchful eye on the number of folders that are shared on your computer. Each shared folder uses a small amount of your computer's sharing resources, and an excessive number of shared folders will affect network performance. You should keep the number of shared folders below 10 for Windows 95.

In addition to monitoring shared folders, Net Watcher also lets you share folders and change the properties of shared folders.

Sharing Folders

Before you can change the settings for any shared folder, you have to switch to the shared folder view by selecting View | by Shared Folder. Net Watcher can control which folders are shared on the network. This is accomplished with the Administer menu. This menu lets you add a shared folder, stop sharing a folder, and change the shared folder properties.

To add a new shared folder, select Administer | Add Shared Folder. When you do this, you will be prompted for a path to the folder. You can either type in a path or click the Browse button. If you're sharing a folder on a computer through remote administration, you will be able to browse the resources through the hidden administrative drive shares such as C$ (see Figure 6.3). After choosing a directory to work with, you will see the standard Share Directory dialog box. Information on sharing directories was presented in Chapter 1 and in Chapter 4, "Configuring and Managing Resource Access."

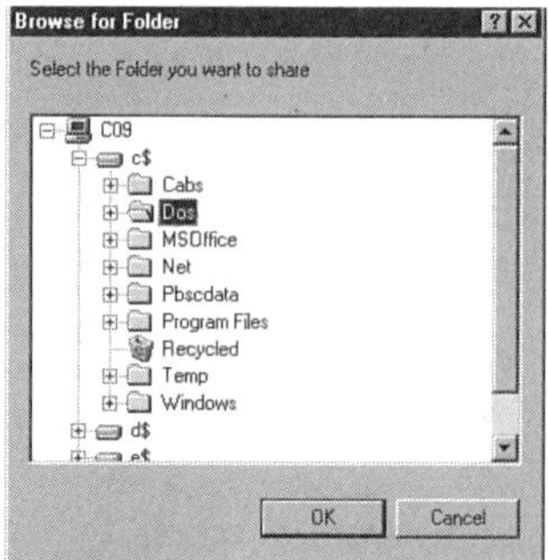

Figure 6.3

Net Watcher can browse through remote hard drives by accessing the administrative shares.

To change the properties of a shared folder, select the folder from the list of shared folders and then choose Administer | Shared Folder Properties. This brings up the sharing settings for that folder. You can change any of the settings, such as the allowed users or the share password, and then close the dialog by clicking OK.

To stop sharing a folder, select the shared folder from the list of shared folders and select Administer | Stop Sharing Folder. This will stop the folder from being shared with other people on the network.

In addition to monitoring the shared resources themselves, you can also monitor the system by connected user.

Monitoring Users

In order to monitor your system by connected users, select View | by Connections. When you switch to this view, you will see a list of users who are currently connected to your computer, as shown in Figure 6.4. In Details view, you also see the name of the computer that they are using to establish the connection and the number of shares and open files that they are accessing. The last two detail columns that are listed are Connected Time and Idle Time. When you select a user, you see the list of shared folders that that person is accessing, as well as the list of open files.

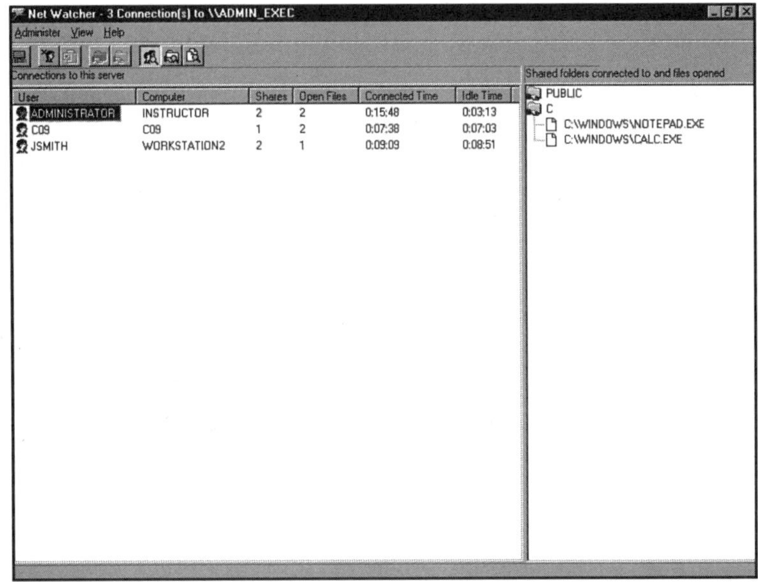

Figure 6.4

Net Watcher lets you track activity by user.

When using Net Watcher as a maintenance tool, you can examine the number of users who are connected to your computer and the number and types of files they are accessing. Windows 95 will suffer from a performance degradation if it must maintain a large number of idle open sessions. When viewing by connection in Net Watcher, you can track these sessions and close sessions that are nonessential.

To close a session, you need to disconnect the user by selecting the user and then selecting Administer | Disconnect User.

> If you change the permissions assigned to a user who is currently accessing a shared folder, the effect of those permissions won't be noticeable until the user disconnects and reconnects to the folder. To force the user to reauthenticate, you should manually disconnect him from using Net Watcher. If the user doesn't have any open files, he shouldn't notice the interruption and should automatically reconnect.

You have now examined your network usage by shared folder and by connected user. The third way you can monitor your network is by the files that are actually in use.

Monitoring Open Files

When users access files on your computer, they have to read or write the files from or to your hard drive. During the read and write processes, these files are open for either input or output. Some files that you work with, such as applications, will remain open for extended periods of time. Net Watcher will list all your open files when you select View | by Open Files.

When viewing open files, you will see who is accessing the files, what share name they are using, and the type of access they are using for the file (read or write), as shown in Figure 6.5. In a sharing environment, open files play a larger role in performance degradation than the number of connected users will.

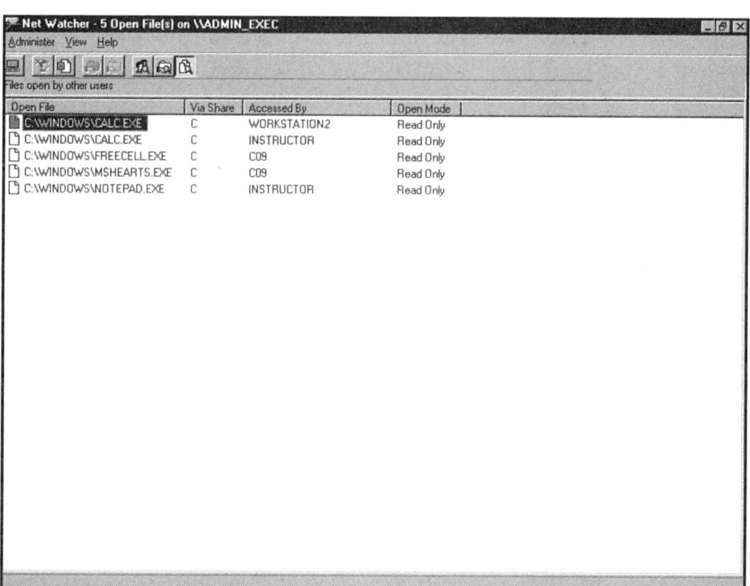

Figure 6.5

High activity on your computer is caused by open files, not connected users.

If you find that you have too many open files, and you think performance might be suffering, the only thing you can do is stop sharing. As long as you are sharing resources, other users will be able to open your files.

Net Watcher's main focus as an application is to let you see who is connecting to what resources on your computer. Its role in your computer's routine maintenance is to let you see what type of activity is currently occurring on your shared resources. This information helps you decide if you're sharing too many folders and should cut back in order to improve local performance. In order to determine how badly local performance is suffering, you can use System Monitor.

Using System Monitor

System Monitor tracks performance statistics about your computer and displays the information in three different chart formats. This information lets you see what areas of your computer are performing properly and which areas are performing marginally. System Monitor can be found under Start | Programs | Accessories | System Tools. In exploring the use of System Monitor as a maintenance tool, you will examine the following:

- How System Monitor gathers information
- How to remotely monitor a computer's performance
- The different ways to view information
- Adding objects to the monitor screen
- Key counters to watch in system maintenance

Seeing Where the Information Comes From

Your computer is constantly keeping track of a series of performance statistics, but it displays them only if you ask. The statistics are kept in the Registry in the `HKEY_DYN_DATA\PerfStats\StatData` key (see Figure 6.6). In this key, you will see a series of values such as `KERNEL\CPUUsage`, whose value is a hexadecimal number. This number is usually displayed as a decimal value in the System Monitor charts. Your Registry always keeps these performance statistics up-to-date for you.

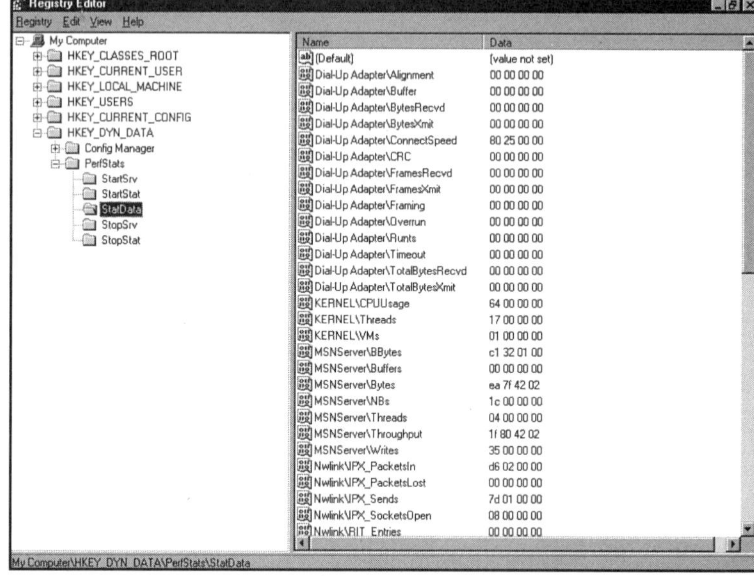

Figure 6.6

All the performance counters are stored in the Dynamic Data section of the Registry.

Running System Monitor Remotely

System Monitor may be used to monitor your own computer or another computer on your network. To monitor another computer on your network, you need to ensure that the following conditions have been met:

- You have administrative privileges on the target computer.
- The target computer is currently on the network.
- The target computer has been set for user-level access control.
- Both computers have the Remote Registry Editing service installed.

All of these requirements are actually the requirements for Remote Registry Editing. Because all the System Monitor counters are stored in the Registry, and because System Monitor simply reads the values of these counters from the Registry, in order to use System Monitor to monitor another computer on the network, you need to be able to read that Registry. To view the other computer, select File | Connect and type in the computer name of the computer to which you want to connect.

Viewing Information

There are three different ways to view the information in System Monitor: line charts, bar charts, and numeric charts. To switch between chart types, you use the View menu.

Line charts display an area graph for each counter you add to the System Monitor window. As you add more counters, System Monitor decreases the size of each graph to allow all the graphs to be displayed in a single window (see Figure 6.7). If you select one of the graphs, System Monitor shows you the name of the counter, as well as the last and peak values for the counter over the graph period. Line charts are great tools if you want to get a feel for how the values interrelate. For instance, when free memory decreases, disk access increases due to increased access to the swap file or page file. A line chart will demonstrate this visually. Line charts make tracking exact numbers somewhat more difficult, especially if you're tracking a large number of counters, because each chart will be very small.

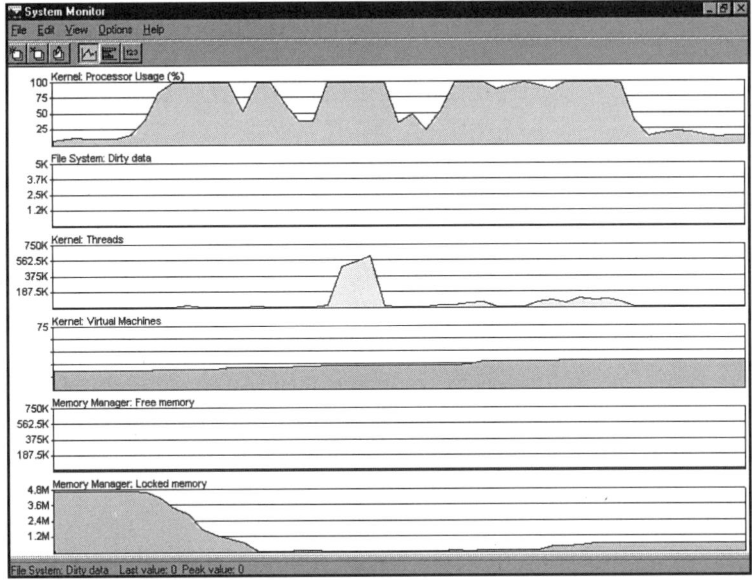

Figure 6.7

Line charts make examining relationships between counters easier.

Bar charts give you another way to view the data that is being collected. Bar charts display a moving bar on a horizontal scale, as shown in Figure 6.8. Whenever the value peaks, System Monitor leaves a marker on the scale until it reaches the seventh reading, at which time it decreases to the current value. The advantage of bar charts is that the numeric value of the counter is easier to read, and they allow you to see how the value has decreased over the last seven readings. This chart walks a fine line between line charts and numeric charts.

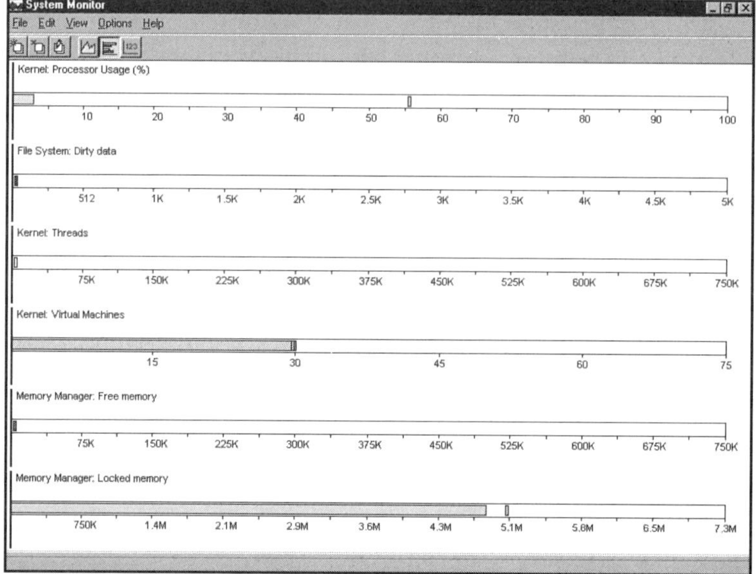

Figure 6.8

Bar charts make interpreting numbers much easier than when done with line charts.

Numeric charts let you have the greatest number of counters monitored at any given time, but with one large drawback. If you add enough counters, they aren't labeled (see Figure 6.9). With both of the previous charts, you saw the name of the counter and the line or bar. With the numeric chart, you are given a series of numbers with no labels. If you select one of the numbers, the status bar at the bottom of the window shows the name of the counter and the last and peak values. The advantage of this type of chart is that it is very easy to see the exact value of the counter.

As with most programs, each view has its strong points and its weaknesses. If you are familiar with all three of the views, you will be able to choose the view that will best allow you to get the information you need. You might even feel that the best way to gather your information is to switch between the different views while System Monitor is running. Doing this will let you draw on the best features of each view.

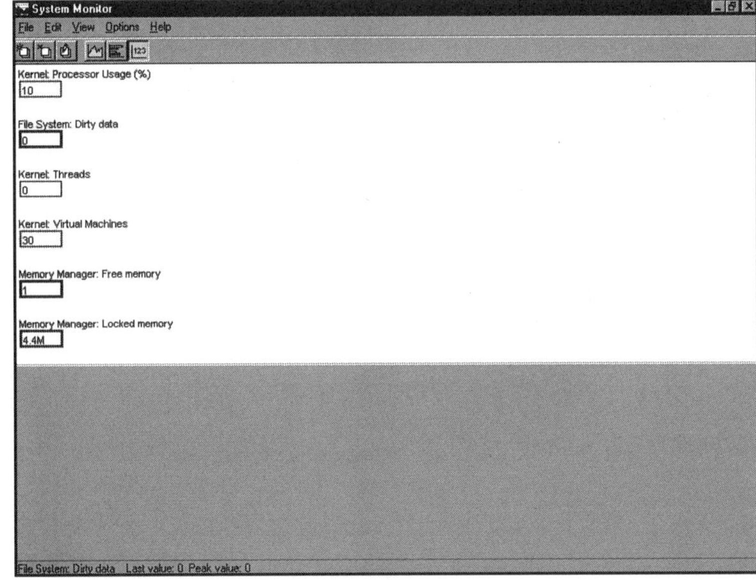

Figure 6.9

Numeric charts make getting the correct value easy, but you don't see the name of the counter.

Adding Counters to Be Monitored

The first time you open System Monitor, it will be charting the processor usage on a line chart. Any changes you make will automatically be saved for the next time you open System Monitor. These changes could be the selection of a different view or the addition of a counter to be monitored. To add a new counter for monitoring, select Edit | Add Item. You will see a screen that lets you select an item to be monitored from a specific category. If you're unsure what the counter is for, click the Explain button. You see the dialog box shown in Figure 6.10.

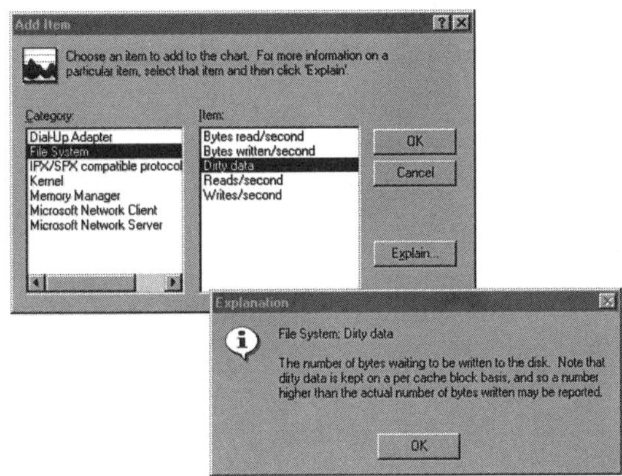

Figure 6.10

You can select new components to be monitored from a list of counters.

The Edit menu has two additional commands for your counters: Remove Item and Edit Item. When you select Remove Item, you will see a list of counters that you are currently tracking, and you have the option of removing one or more of them. Edit Item presents you with the same list of installed counters, and you may choose one of them to edit. When you edit a counter, you can change the color that is used to draw it and decide whether it should have a dynamic (Automatic) scale or a fixed scale (see Figure 6.11). This window displays the current top of the scale. If the scale is fixed, you can set the value of the top of the scale.

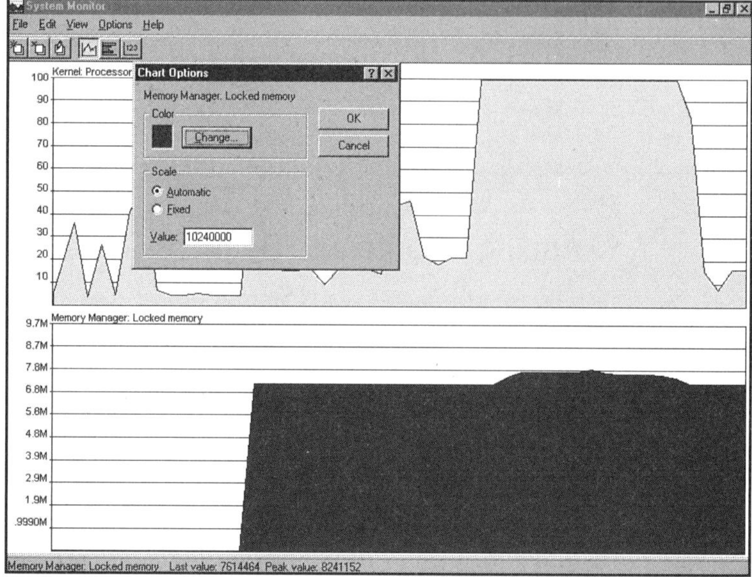

Figure 6.11

For readability, you might want to change to scales on your charts or assign different colors.

Key Counters to Watch in System Maintenance

If Microsoft didn't think counters were valuable, they wouldn't have added them to System Monitor. This doesn't mean that all the counters will always be valuable to you. In certain instances (for example, while trying to diagnose the reason for a performance loss), you might care about only a small number of counters. This section helps you identify how some of the counters may be used to monitor performance.

Counters from all areas will receive some attention in this section: Dial-Up Adapter, File System, IPX/SPX-compatible protocol,

Kernel, Memory Manager, Microsoft Network Client, and Microsoft Network Server. You will see why you might care about some of these counters and the types of performance problems you will be trying to diagnose.

Here are the counters in the Dial-Up Adapter category and why they are important:

- *Bytes Received/Second* gives you an idea of the rate of incoming data to your system. You will be able to take the rated speed of your modem and compare this value on extended reads to see if you are achieving speeds close to the registered limits.
- *Bytes Transmitted/Second* is the same as Bytes Received/Second, except that it works with transmitted data.
- *Connection Speed* reports the negotiated line speed between your modem and the target modem. If the speed is far below the speed that either modem supports, you might want to examine the line itself, because there might be an excessive amount of line noise.
- *CRC Errors* should not occur with any regularity. If these errors occur regularly, you should look at either a hardware failure or excessive line noise.

Most of the counters that affect Dial-Up Networking are installed when you add the Dial-Up Networking 1.2 system update.

When monitoring the File System, in addition to tracking reads and writes per second, you might want to track dirty data. Dirty data is sometimes referred to as lazy writes. It represents the number of bytes of data currently residing in RAM that are waiting to be written to disk. The actual number is the number of cache blocks waiting to be written, which might be higher than the number of bytes. The more dirty data on your system, the more efficient disk caching is. The drawback of this efficiency is that more data is volatile in the event of a power outage or system crash.

A key measure of the utilization of the IPX/SPX-compatible protocol on your computer and your network servers is the total number of open sockets. Each socket represents a file connection from your computer to the server. A higher-than-normal number of open sockets might indicate that the server or your computer isn't closing off the connections properly. This will eventually impede the performance of both the server and your computer.

When monitoring the Kernel, the most obvious counter to monitor is Processor Usage, which displays a percentage utilization of the processor. It's acceptable for the processor to experience small peaks (even as high as 100 percent) for brief periods of time. For this counter, performance problems would be indicated if the processor achieves and maintains a high level of utilization. An example of high utilization is 70 to 80 percent utilization for several minutes.

The Memory Manager is responsible for several key counters:

- *Disk Cache Size* is the total size of the disk cache for reading data from your hard drive. The larger the size of the disk cache, the faster and more productive disk reads are.
- *Free Memory* is the amount of free or available RAM on your system. If your RAM falls to too low a level, Windows 95 attempts to use the dynamic swap file.
- *Locked Memory* is memory that the operating system has deemed special. This memory is special because whatever else happens on the computer, this information is kept in RAM and is never sent to the page or swap file.
- *Page Faults* indicates that there is a problem accessing information that an application has stored in RAM. This isn't really a problem, but rather a signal to the rest of the operating system that the information has been swapped with physical RAM and is stored in the swap file on the computer's hard drive. When attempting to get that piece of information, the computer will do a quick check to see if it is in physical memory. If not, it generates a page fault. The page fault will trigger the loading of the information from the hard drive.

Page faults also apply to all applications that haven't been opened. For example, Windows 95 will check to see if the application that you are opening is in RAM yet. If not, it will generate a page fault and load the application. If your computer is suffering from an excessive number of page faults, you should be noticing very slow performance. Excessive page faults is a signal that too much information is being swapped to your hard drive. The best way to prevent information from being swapped to your hard drive is to add more RAM to the system.

- *Page-outs* is information that is written specifically to the Windows 95 swap file. The lower the number, the less you're using the swap file, and the more you're using RAM.
- *Swapfile in use* represents the amount of the swap file you are currently using.
- *Swapfile Size* is the current dynamic size of the swap file.

Microsoft Network Client System Monitor counters tend to focus on the speed of access across your network. They include the following:

- *Bytes Read/Second* is the number of raw bytes that are read by the network client per second. Compare this to the theoretical 100MBps or 12.5MBps for your network.
- *Bytes Written/Second* is similar to Bytes Read/Second, but it represents data sent to the server. If either of these numbers is too low, you might want to consider upgrading to a faster network card.
- *Sessions* is the number of network conversations you have open. If you aren't closing off network sessions properly, this number will continue to grow and will cause performance problems for both the server and your workstation. If you have sessions that are not being closed off properly, this is probably the result of a particular application. To find out which application is the problem, you will have to monitor the sessions while working with the various applications on your computer.

The Microsoft Client for NetWare Networks counters, like the Microsoft Network Client counters, focus on network access speed:

- *Dirty Bytes in Cache* is the number of bytes of data that have been cached by the redirector (network client) waiting to be written to the hard drive.
- *BURST and NCP packets dropped* are the number of packets that are lost in transit on the network.
- *Requests Pending* is the number of requests that your redirector wants to make but is waiting for the server to process.

When your computer is running File and Print Sharing Services for Windows Networks, it is a Microsoft Network Server. Here are some of the counters you might want to keep an eye on:

- *Bytes Read/sec* is the number of bytes of data that have been transferred to your computer from across the network. This is similar to the Bytes Read/sec on the client.
- *Bytes Written/sec* is the number of bytes that the server has transferred to clients on the network or written to the network.
- Memory represents the total amount of memory that the server services is using on your computer.
- *NBs* is the number of network buffers that have been allocated to handle talking to network clients. The more buffers, the faster the communication.
- *Server Threads* is the number of threads, or execution segments, that Windows 95 is executing for the File and Print Sharing services.

Microsoft shows the counters for the File and Print Sharing Services for NetWare Networks under the heading of Server. Here are some of the counters in this category you might want to track:

- *Bytes Throughput/Second* is the number of bytes of data that is handled by the File and Print Sharing service.

- *Cache Memory* is the amount of memory that is reserved to handle the server's burst buffers.
- *Packets Dropped* is the number of packets that are lost on the network.
- *Total Heap* tracks the total amount of memory that is used by the server.
- *Transactions/Second* records the total number of requests that the server responds to for the clients on the network.

If you notice that any of these counters have started reporting numbers that deviate from the norm, this might indicate a problem with performance. The only way you will know what is normal for you is to monitor the counters for a period of time when you think everything is working.

Now that you've seen Net Watcher and System Monitor as tools to monitor your system, next you will look at some of the tools you can use to tune or optimize your computer.

Tuning and Optimizing Your System

Extended use of your computer will eventually cause a number of small problems. These problems won't be visible on their own, but if not fixed or resolved, they will grow and become large problems. These problems can range from fragmented files to files with invalid dates to files that have overwritten portions of other files. You will see what some of these problems are and the utilities you can use to resolve or fix them. The next sections examine three utilities: Disk Defragmenter, ScanDisk, and the compression utility DriveSpace.

Using Disk Defragmenter

All hard drives, as a matter of course, eventually become fragmented. A fragmented drive has files on it that have been broken into pieces. The job of Disk Defragmenter is to reassemble each file into a single piece.

Files become fragmented through normal use of your hard drive. When your hard drive is new, it has no files. As you add a file, it is easy for Windows 95 to save the file in free space that is large enough to hold the entire file. As you delete files, you invariably leave holes in the used space. As you continue to work with your hard disk, the contiguous free space areas get smaller and smaller—even the little areas of free space that once held files. Every time you attempt to save a file to your hard disk, Windows 95 will attempt to write the file to the largest area of free space on your disk. However, there will quickly come a time when you attempt to write files that will not fit in the largest free areas. When this happens, Windows 95 writes part of the file in the largest area and leaves a pointer at the end of the file that indicates where the rest of the file is stored. The file is now fragmented.

As files are deleted, they leave holes in the used areas of the disk.

Now enter the defragmentation program. It slowly and methodically moves each file on your disk to a new location, thereby leaving a hole that can be used to move another file into. The program continues with this process, from the first sector of your hard disk to the last. As it moves through your disk, it slowly creates a block of free space that moves through your disk until it is at the end of the disk and the job is done.

The disk defragmentation program that is included with Windows 95 is Disk Defragmenter. It can be found under Start | Programs | Accessories | System Tools. When you open Disk Defragmenter, it asks you which drive you want to work with, as shown in Figure 6.12. Select the drive from the drop-down menu or choose All Hard Drives to defragment all drives in order.

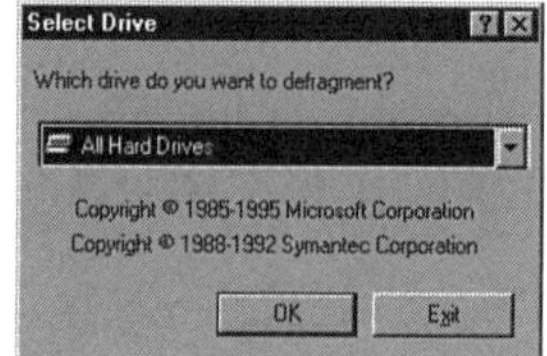

Figure 6.12

Choose the drive you want to defragment.

When you select a drive to defragment, you will see a dialog telling you how badly fragmented your drive is. If your drive is fragmented more than 10 to 20 percent, you probably have noticed a slowdown in performance. You will be able to start defragmentation or configure the advanced options.

Applying Advanced Options

The options under the Advanced button include settings to specify the defragmentation method, error checking, and the ability to save your settings (see Figure 6.13).

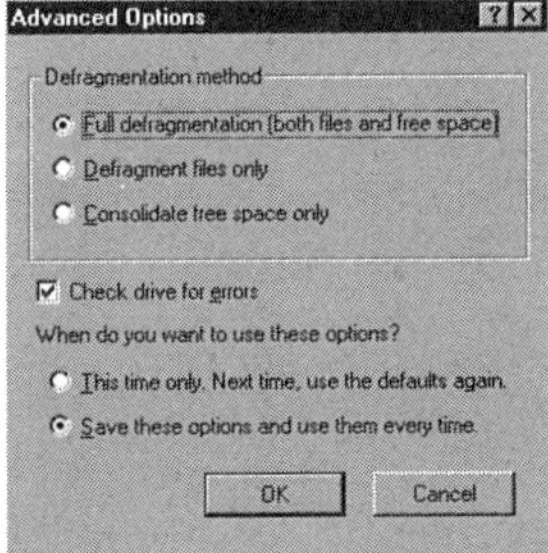

Figure 6.13

The advanced options let you choose a defragmentation method.

Disk Defragmenter lets you choose from the following defragmentation methods:

- *Full defragmentation* defragments the files and consolidates all the free space at the end of the drive. This method is the most thorough and therefore takes the most time to complete.
- *Defragment files only* completes its task much quicker than a full defragmentation without worrying about leaving the free space in a single block. Since the free space is not consolidated, new files that are saved to the disk will quickly become fragmented, causing performance problems for Windows 95.
- *Consolidate free space only* also completes its task much quicker than a full defragmentation without worrying about defragmenting any of your files. It moves the files only in such a

way as to consolidate your free space. There is actually a good chance that this process of moving your files will actually cause greater fragmentation of your current files. It will reduce the fragmentation of new files added to your drive, because they will have a large area of free space in which to be written.

In addition to the defragmentation method, you have the option of checking the drive for errors during the defragmentation process. The next topic in this chapter is ScanDisk. This option allows ScanDisk algorithms to check the areas of the drive that are being read from and written to. This provides a level of safety to the data that is being moved around. If you had just completed a full ScanDisk of the drive before defragmenting, you could make this check box blank. Otherwise, you should leave the check mark in the box. Prior to using any process that works with the data over your entire drive, you should run ScanDisk to ensure that the medium you are working with is free of errors.

To finish off the Advanced Options dialog box, Windows 95 asks when you want to use these options. Here are your choices:

- *This time only. Next time, use the defaults again:* This option discards your settings changes.
- *Save these options and use them every time:* This option preserves your settings changes for all future defragmentations.

After you have made your changes to the way Disk Defragmenter will perform the defragmentation, close the dialog by clicking OK. Now you only have to start the defragmentation process.

Watching What Is Happening

To start the defragmentation process, click the Start button in the Disk Defragmenter dialog box. The defragmenter will display a bar that indicates the progress of the defragmentation as a percentage, as shown in Figure 6.14. If you would like to see a more detailed description of what is going on, click Show Details.

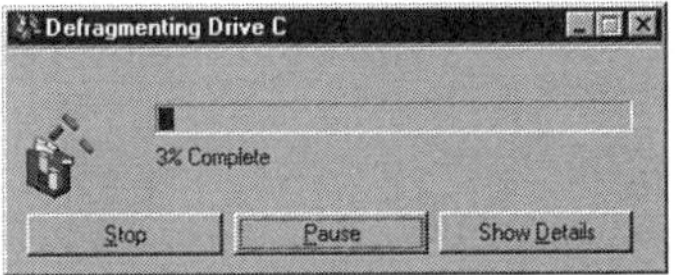

Figure 6.14

The default user interface is a status bar that indicates the overall defragmentation of your hard drive.

When you click Show Details, you see a large window that displays each cluster on your hard disk as a box, as shown in Figure 6.15. Each box is color-coded based on the type of data. This details window has four buttons:

- *Stop* stops the defragmentation process and lets you confirm your decision, select a different drive, or exit the program.
- *Pause* temporarily halts the defragmentation process until you click the Resume button.
- *Legend* displays the legend, which describes the color-coded boxes. This gives you better insight into what is happening on your hard drive.
- *Hide Details* switches you back to the summary of the defragmentation status.

With the details screen visible, you can watch Windows 95 move clusters of data from one section of your hard drive to another. You will see each read and write, and Windows 95 will move the view of the screen to keep pace with where it is performing the defragmentation. If you would like to see what type of data is represented by each color block, you can bring up the legend, which is as follows:

- *Optimized (defragmented) data* is data that has already been processed.
- *Data that will not be moved*: Windows 95 maintains some open files and knows of other files that applications don't want to see moved. These clusters are left in place.

- *Bad (damaged) area of the disk*: Windows 95 marks these clusters as damaged and won't use them to store any other data.

When Disk Defragmenter has completed its job, you should see some improvement in hard disk performance. The difference will be more noticeable on systems that were badly fragmented.

In order to keep your computer working at its highest performance level at all times, you should perform a full defragmentation once a month. If your hard drive doesn't have a large amount of free space, you might want to perform defragmentations more often. The less free space you have, the quicker it gets fragmented.

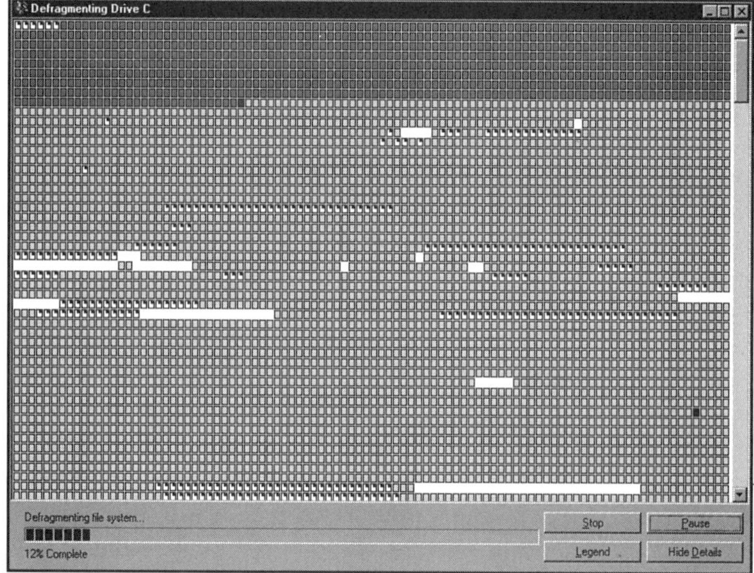

Figure 6.15

The details window gives you a better picture of what is happening to your hard drive during defragmentation.

To automate the defragmentation process, you can plan to implement the Microsoft System Agent, which is available in both the Windows 95 Plus pack and Windows 95 OSR2.

Before you defragment your hard drive or perform any task that works with large amounts of data on your hard drive, consider scanning your hard drive for errors with ScanDisk.

Using ScanDisk for Windows

ScanDisk is a variation of the MS-DOS utility for checking your hard drive for errors in the file and directory structure as well as errors with the actual medium. The utility now ships in two forms with Windows 95. SCANDSKW.EXE is designed to work within the Windows 95 GUI, and SCANDISK.EXE is a command-line version that is designed to be used when the Windows 95 GUI has not been loaded. This section will first examine the options that are available with ScanDisk for Windows and then the options that are available with ScanDisk. You will also see when you should use the command-line version instead of the Windows version.

To open ScanDisk for Windows, select Start | Programs | Accessories | System Tools | ScanDisk. You can choose a hard drive to scan, a type of scan, and whether you want to be notified of errors, as shown in Figure 6.16.

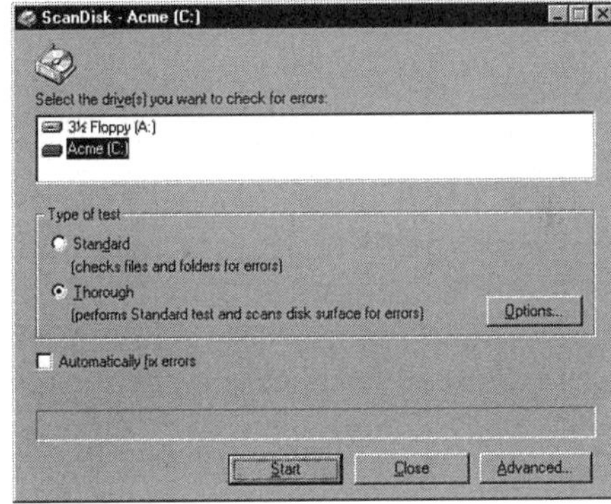

Figure 6.16

ScanDisk lets you choose the type of scan you want to perform.

Choosing a Scan Type

ScanDisk can perform two types of scans:

- The *standard* scan type performs a check on the file allocation table. This scan makes sure that the structure of the file allocation table is proper. This step is vital, because the file allocation table holds pointers to the start of every file on your hard drive. If you don't know where the files start, you won't be able to read them.

- The *thorough* scan type also performs a check of the file allocation table. After doing this, the thorough scan follows up with a surface scan. The surface scan accesses *every cluster* on your hard drive to ensure that each is functioning properly. If it finds any bad clusters, it attempts to move the data to a new area and map out the bad clusters on your hard drive. The thorough scan also checks each file for invalid information, such as invalid dates and names.

When conducting a thorough or surface scan, you may configure a few additional options by clicking the Options button (see Figure 6.17):

- *System and data areas* allows ScanDisk to scan both the boot sector and data areas of the drive. This is the default option.
- *System area only* checks only the boot sector and file allocation table areas of the hard disk. If there is an error in these areas of the disk, you probably will have to reformat or replace the damaged hard disk.
- *Data area only* will move the damaged data to a new area of the disk if the data hasn't been damaged to the point of being unreadable.
- *Do not perform write-testing* causes ScanDisk to read the contents of each sector of your hard drive, but ScanDisk doesn't write the data back to the disk to complete the verification of the hard drive's clusters. This operates on the assumption that if you can read the data from the disk, the disk must be working well enough to hold the data written to it. The actual process of writing the data back proves that the area of the disk works.
- *Do not repair bad sectors in hidden and system files* means that rather than attempting to recover the data and moving it to a new location on the hard drive, Windows 95 will leave it

where it is. Leaving the data damaged but in its original location prevents some programs that expect to find files in specific locations from working properly.

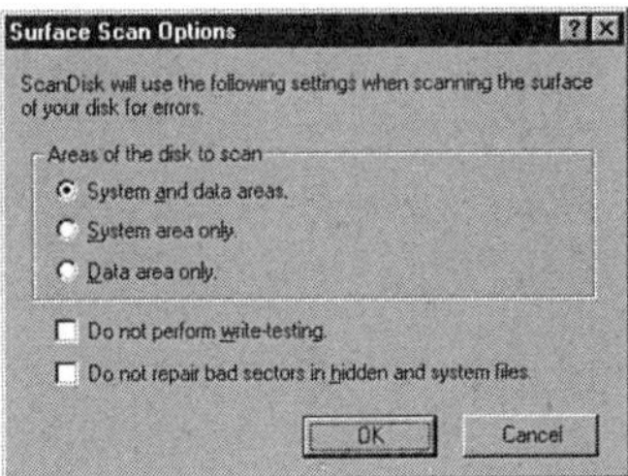

Figure 6.17

ScanDisk supports some additional options for thorough scans.

This concludes the configurations for all the surface scan options. If you don't want Windows 95 to prompt you about correcting each type of file that it might find, you might want to select the Automatically fix errors check box. When this option is selected, all errors encountered are fixed automatically. You shouldn't worry about the scans that are performed by ScanDisk; they won't hurt your data. They will, however, prevent data that is already damaged from further corrupting other data on your hard drive.

Applying Advanced Options

Regardless of the type of scan that ScanDisk performs, you may configure some advanced options by clicking the Advanced button, as shown in Figure 6.18:

- Display summary
- Lost file fragments
- Log file
- Check files for
- Cross-linked files
- Check host drive first

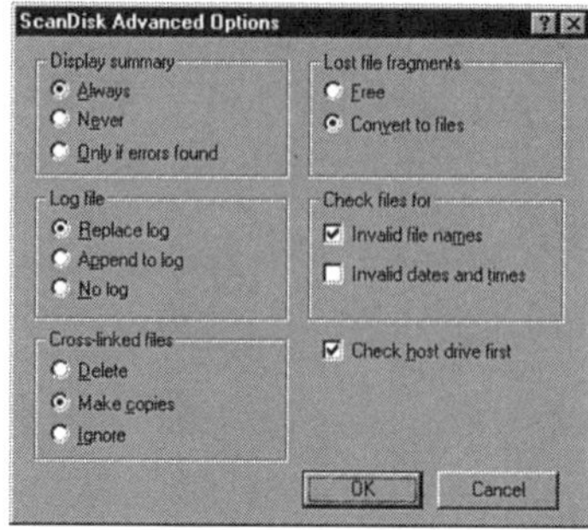

Figure 6.18

The Advanced Options dialog box lets you set options prior to the scan, which prevents ScanDisk from having to prompt you for options during the scan.

Displaying a Summary

ScanDisk may be configured to display a summary at the following times:

- Always display a ScanDisk summary
- Never display a ScanDisk summary
- Display a ScanDisk summary only if errors were found during the scan

Handling Lost File Fragments

Files are stored on a FAT (File Allocation Table) partition using a linked cluster directory structure. This means that the FAT stores the location of the first cluster of the file. The end of each cluster points to the beginning of the next cluster of files. Occasionally something goes wrong with this system, and in the middle of a file, a cluster in one file starts to point to a cluster used by another file. When this happens, the last clusters of the original file are left floating freely on the disk. These are lost file fragments. You may do one of the following things with lost file fragments:

- *Free (delete) the file fragments.* In most cases, you will not find any useful information in the file fragments, so you should delete them.

- *Convert to files* will cause all the file fragments to be saved in a folder on the root of your hard drive, and the files will be numbered sequentially (such as FILE0001).

Recording a Log File

These options let you configure how the log file will be managed on your computers. You have the following options:

- Replace the log each time ScanDisk is run
- Append to the log each time ScanDisk is run
- Bypass saving any log file at all

Checking File Settings

These options let you tell ScanDisk to check files for the following invalid settings:

- Invalid filenames, where the name might be corrupted through an error on the drive. ScanDisk lets you give the file a different name.
- Invalid dates and times causes ScanDisk to set the date and time for the file to today's current date and time. Some applications won't work with the file if the date and time are invalid.

Dealing with Cross-Linked Files

As mentioned a moment ago, sometimes the linked directory structure of files gets confused. When this happens, the files are referred to as cross-linked files. The file has two starting points that share a common ending point. In this case, it is possible that both files are now corrupted. You can do the following with cross-linked files:

- *Delete both files,* working on the assumption that both files are probably damaged.

- *Make copies of both of the potential files.* There is a chance that one of the files is still okay, and only the second file is corrupted.
- *Ignore these files* and deal with the error later.

These are the options that are possible with ScanDisk for Windows. Once the options have been chosen, you will be able to start the scan by clicking the Start button in the ScanDisk dialog box. To keep your drive healthy, it is wise to run a scan of your drive every time your computer freezes and requires you to reboot it. You should also run a scan of your drive prior to installing applications that will load files on the majority of your hard drive. In addition, it is wise to get in the habit of checking your drives once a month to prevent possible corruption of your data and keep your drives performing at peak efficiency.

Using SCANDISK.EXE (the Command-Line Version)

In addition to the Windows version of ScanDisk, Microsoft provides you with a command-line version of ScanDisk. It may be used outside of the Windows 95 GUI to fix errors in compressed drives, or when your system has been rebooted from a system hang. Windows 95 OSR2 runs this version of ScanDisk automatically in the event of a system hang.

Using the Compression Utility (DriveSpace)

Disk compression was discussed in Chapter 4. In that chapter, you saw that files are compressed on your drive into Compressed Volume Files (CVFs). The act of writing the file into a CVF forces you to run a compression algorithm. Running the compression algorithm costs time on your computer. If the level of compression that you receive shrinks the file sufficiently, the smaller file will take less time to write to your hard drive. If you don't receive a high compression level, the file will take the same amount of time to write to your hard drive, and the time taken to execute the compression algorithm was wasted on the computer.

In most cases, the only time compression will act as a performance-enhancing tool is if you have a hard drive with a slow access time and a fast processor with large amounts of RAM.

For more on using disk compression, see Exercise 4.2.

This concludes the discussion of monitoring and optimization. You examined the monitoring tools, Net Watcher and System Monitor, as well as the performance tools Disk Defragmenter, ScanDisk, and DriveSpace. You saw how to use Net Watcher to keep an eye on who was accessing your computer from elsewhere on your network and how to use System Monitor to examine performance counters on your computer. You saw how Disk Defragmenter can improve the performance of your hard drive by keeping your files in single units. You also saw how ScanDisk can keep your drive in good repair by diagnosing and fixing problems early. Finally, you examined situations in which DriveSpace can improve your computer's performance.

Exercises

The first three exercises will use Net Watcher to administer the shared resources on a computer. To complete these exercises, you will require two computers. The first computer must have File and Print Sharing installed, and the second computer will be used as a client to connect to a shared resource. You will also require a shared folder. If you don't have any shared folders, see Chapter 4 or complete Exercise 6.2.

Exercise 6.1: Using Net Watcher to Examine Your Shared Resources

This exercise uses Net Watcher to examine the shared folders on your computer.

1. On the computer that has File and Print Sharing installed, open the Net Watcher application by selecting Start | Programs | Accessories | System Tools | Net Watcher.
2. Select View | by Shared Folders. You should see all the shared folders on your computer.
3. Select one of your shared folders and choose Administer | Shared Folder Properties. This should leave you looking at the sharing properties of that folder. Examine the following entries:
   - Share Name
   - Comment
   - Access Type (only if you have implemented share-level access control)
   - User List and Access Rights (only if you have implemented user-level access control)
4. If you want to, you can change the settings on the shared folder. Click OK to close the Share Folder Properties window.
5. Select Administer | Exit.

Exercise 6.2: Using Net Watcher to Create a Shared Folder

This exercise uses Net Watcher to create a new shared folder on your computer.

1. On the computer where File and Print Sharing is installed, open the Net Watcher application by selecting Start | Programs | Accessories | System Tools | Net Watcher.
2. To see the folders already shared on your computer, select View | by Shared Folders. You must also be in this view to activate the sharing controls on the Administer menu.
3. To share a new folder, select Administer | Add Shared Folder. The dialog that appears prompts you to type in the path to the folder you want to share. You can also click the Browse button to browse for the folder you want to share. This will display a browse window starting from My Computer.

If you are sharing a folder on a remote computer, the browse window will start from your network computer name and show the list of shared resources on your computer, including the hidden administrative shares for each drive on your computer. For example, C$ is the share for the C: drive.

4. Select the Windows directory on the C: drive and then click OK to go back to the Enter Path dialog box. Click OK to finish the folder selection.
5. Configure the sharing properties for the Windows folder. Assign the folder a share name and a comment. If nothing else has the share name of Windows, you can leave the share name as Windows.

   If you're using share-level access control, assign read-only permissions and assign a password. You will be prompted to confirm that password when you leave this dialog.

continues

Exercise 6.2: Continued

If you're using user-level access control, you must assign a user from your server whom you want to have access to your Windows directory. Click the Add button and locate your user account on the server. Select the Read-only button to give yourself read access. Click OK to save the permitted users.

6. Click OK to close the Share Folder Properties window and finish sharing the Windows folder.
7. Select Administer | Exit.

Now you should test the access to your new folder. This also sets up a connected user for Exercise 6.3.

1. Go to your second computer.
2. Choose Start | Run.
3. Type the following:

```
"\\<your_first_computer_name>\<Windows_Folder_Share_Name>"
```

   The quotation marks are required if you have a space in either your computer name or the share name for the Windows directory.

4. Locate CALC.EXE and FREECELL.EXE in the Windows directory and launch them both.
5. Leave this computer and start Exercise 6.3 while sitting at the computer that has the shared Windows directory.

Exercise 6.3: Using Net Watcher to Monitor Access to a Shared Folder

This exercise uses Net Watcher to monitor access to a shared folder on your computer.

1. On the computer that has File and Print Sharing installed, open the Net Watcher application by selecting Start | Programs | Accessories | System Tools | Net Watcher.

2. Select View | by Open Files. You should now be looking at a list of the open files that are being accessed through shared folders. If the list is empty, complete the last five steps in Exercise 6.2. If you don't have any shared folders, complete all of Exercise 6.2.

3. Examine the list of open files. It should contain at least C:\WINDOWS\FREECELL.EXE and C:\WINDOWS\CALC.EXE. Both of these files should be opened via share *windows_share_name* and be opened for read access by your other computer's computer name.

4. Select View | by Connections. You should see a list of connected users and the names of the computers that they are using. Select your user name or your second computer name from the list. In the right pane of Net Watcher, you will see a list of the shared folders that have been accessed, along with the two open files.

5. To disconnect the other user, select him from the list and choose Administer | Disconnect User. You normally shouldn't do this when users have open files, because it might result in data loss for the user.

6. Select Administer | Exit.

Exercise 6.4: Using System Monitor to Diagnose a Local Machine

This exercise will have you track the number of counters on your computer during the launching of applications, to see the effect that they will have on your computer.

1. Open System Monitor by selecting Start | Programs | Accessories | System Tools | System Monitor.

2. Remove all of the current counters by selecting Edit | Remove Item, selecting all the counters, and clicking OK.

3. Select Edit | Add Item. Select Kernel from the Category list and Processor Usage (%) from the Item list. Hold down the Ctrl key and select Threads from the Item list. Click the OK button to add these two counters.

continues

Exercise 6.4: Continued

4. To add two additional counters, select Edit | Add Item. Select Memory Manager from the Category list and Free Memory from the Item list. Hold down the Ctrl key and select Page Faults from the Item list. Click the OK button to add these two counters.

5. Switch to Bar Chart view by selecting View | Bar Charts.

6. Wait for the counters to stabilize, and then record the following information:

   Kernel - Processor Usage (%): __________
   Kernel - Threads: __________
   Memory Manager - Free Memory: __________
   Memory Manager - Page Faults: __________

7. Open WordPad by selecting Start | Programs | Accessories. Record the following information for the peak values in System Monitor:

   Kernel - Processor Usage (%): __________
   Kernel - Threads: __________
   Memory Manager - Free Memory: __________
   Memory Manager - Page Faults: __________

8. What was the change in the counters? Record the changes in the counters in the following chart:

   Kernel - Processor Usage (%): __________
   Kernel - Threads: __________
   Memory Manager - Free Memory: __________
   Memory Manager - Page Faults: __________

9. What was the maximum reading for Processor Usage? Should this concern you?

10. Exit System Monitor by selecting File | Exit.

To answer the second question in step 9, high processor usage shouldn't concern you if it's high for only a short period of time. This is known as a spike.

Exercise 6.5: Using Disk Defragmenter

This exercise leads you through defragmenting your hard drive with options.

1. Close all your applications. Open Disk Defragmenter by selecting Start | Programs | Accessories | System Tools | Disk Defragmenter. (You can defragment your drive with applications open, but it will probably take longer.)
2. Choose the C: drive from the drop-down menu and click OK. You will be told of the current fragmentation status on your drive, and Disk Defragmenter will make a recommendation as to whether you should defragment your hard drive.
3. Click the Start button to start the defragmentation.
4. To view the actual movement of files, click the Show Details button.
5. Click the Legend button to see what the colored blocks represent.
6. Watch the processes. Exit Disk Defragmenter when it is finished.

Exercise 6.6: Using ScanDisk for Windows

This exercise leads you through the scanning of your computer's hard disk for errors.

1. Close all your applications. Open ScanDisk by selecting Start | Programs | Accessories | System Tools | ScanDisk. (You can scan your drive with applications open, but it will probably take longer.)
2. Select Thorough from the Type of Test section.

continues

Exercise 6.6: Continued

3. Click the Advanced button, and choose from the following options:
   - Display Summary: Always
   - Log File: Replace Log
   - Cross-linked Files: Make Copies
   - Lost File Fragments: Free
   - Check Files For: Invalid File Names
   - Check Files For: Invalid Dates and Times
   - If your drive is compressed, you should also select the Check host drive first checkbox.
4. After making your selections, click the OK button.
5. Make sure that you haven't selected the Automatically fix errors checkbox so that you will be able to see anything that is wrong with your drive. You might want to enable this option during routine scans of your hard drive, but if you do, you should check C:\SCANDISK.LOG for any errors.
6. Click the Start button to start the scan. If there are errors on your drive, you will be notified of them and given the option of fixing them.
7. When the scan is finished, click OK.

Review Questions

1. You are working on a support desk and you receive a call from a user whose computer has stopped responding. After the user presses Ctrl+Alt+Delete, the computer still isn't responding. You tell the user to press the Reset button. What should the user do when Windows 95 restarts?

   A. Run Disk Defragmenter, because the hanging of the computer has probably left fragmented files.

   B. Run ScanDisk, because the hanging of the computer might have left some corruption on the hard drive.

   C. Run System Monitor, because it will tell you what caused the hang.

   D. Run Net Watcher to see if anyone was connected to the computer when it hung.

2. Your computer has become sluggish. What can you do to try to improve its performance? Choose all that apply.

   A. Run ScanDisk to look for errors in the file system.

   B. Run Net Watcher to see if other people on your network have file sessions with your computer.

   C. Run Disk Defragmenter to defragment any files that require it.

   D. Run DiskCheck to look for any cross-linked files.

3. You're sitting at your desk doing paperwork, and your computer that is on the corporate LAN starts to have disk activity for an extended period of time. What could you check to see where the activity is coming from?

   A. ScanDisk

   B. Net Check

   C. System Meter

   D. Net Watcher

4. You open a document and find that it has been corrupted. You decide to run ScanDisk on your hard drive. When you do, what advanced settings should you set to attempt to find the missing data?

    A. Always display summary

    B. Replace log file

    C. Make copies of cross-linked files

    D. Convert lost file fragments to files

5. You want to run System Monitor to monitor another computer on your network. Which of the following is not a condition that is required to do this?

    A. Remote administration is enabled on the target computer.

    B. You are on the remote administration list.

    C. The target computer has System Monitor installed.

    D. The target computer has File and Print Sharing installed.

    E. Both computers have the Remote Registry Editing service installed.

6. Which of the following is not a factor that affects the performance of DriveSpace disk compression?

    A. The amount of RAM in the computer

    B. The speed of your network

    C. The speed of your hard drive

    D. The speed of your processor

Review Answers

1. B. When your computer hangs, you should run ScanDisk upon reboot to ensure that none of the data on your hard

drive has become corrupted. Windows 95 OSR2 is set up to do this for you by default.

2. A, B, C. DiskCheck is not a Windows 95 utility.

3. D. Since you are on a LAN, you could check Net Watcher to see if anyone has a connection with your computer. You could also run System Monitor, because it might lead you to where the activity is coming from.

4. D. Making copies of cross-linked files might prevent other files from becoming corrupted, but looking for lost file fragments might locate the missing section of the document.

5. C. The target computer doesn't need to have System Monitor installed, because the statistics are read directly from the Registry.

6. B. Your network speed, activity, and topology have no effect on the speed of disk compression.

Answers to Test Yourself Questions at Beginning of Chapter

1. If the system has been configured for remote system monitoring, you will be able to connect to his computer and check the performance statistics on his hard drive, free memory, and page faults. This will help you determine if the problem is his hard drive or excessive paging from limited RAM. See "Using System Monitor."
2. The addition, use, and removal of the five programs will likely have caused some level of fragmentation, especially if the hard drive was nearing its capacity. You should defragment the hard drive. See "Using Disk Defragmenter."
3. It's possible that this file has been the target of a cross-linked file. You could close the document without saving changes and then run ScanDisk. This document has been corrupted, but the other file in the cross-linked pair might be able to be rescued. See "Using ScanDisk for Windows."
4. You should also consider the amount of RAM on the system and the processor speed of the CPU. You will likely see a large decrease in performance if you're using a 486/66 with 8MB of RAM but notice little effect if you're using a Pentium 166 with 32MB of RAM. See "Using the Compression Utility (DriveSpace)."
5. You could use Net Watcher to examine your own computer to see who the connected users are and if they have open files. See "Using Net Watcher."
6. To consolidate free space quickly, run Disk Defragmenter with the advanced option of Consolidate free space only. See "Applying Advanced Options."
7. System Monitor can be used to monitor the Bytes Read/Second for the Microsoft Network Client. See "Key Counters to Watch in System Maintenance."
8. Use ScanDisk to run a thorough scan on your drive to ensure the integrity of the disk media and defragment the drive so that the files can be stored in contiguous space. See "Using ScanDisk for Windows."

Chapter 7

Troubleshooting

This chapter helps you prepare for the exam by covering the following objectives:

- Diagnosing and resolving installation failures
- Diagnosing and resolving boot process failures
- Diagnosing and resolving connectivity problems in a Microsoft environment and in a mixed Microsoft and NetWare environment. Tools include WinIPCfg, Net Watcher, and troubleshooting wizards.
- Diagnosing and resolving printing problems in a Microsoft environment and in a mixed Microsoft and NetWare environment
- Diagnosing and resolving file system problems
- Diagnosing and resolving resource access problems in a Microsoft environment and in a mixed Microsoft and NetWare environment
- Diagnosing and resolving hardware device and device driver problems. Tools include MSD and the Add New Hardware Wizard.
- Performing direct modification of the Registry as appropriate by using Regedit

Test Yourself! Before reading this chapter, test yourself to determine how much study time you will need to devote to this section.

1. Describe the six general steps to troubleshooting problems in Windows 95.
2. Windows 95 has many built-in tools you can use for troubleshooting connectivity issues. Name three of these utilities.
3. In such an environment as Windows 95, a need exists for careful management of the systems resources. When two processes request the use of a device at the exact same moment, how does Windows 95 arbitrate such requests?
4. You want to optimize the Windows 95 file system. What are two ways to maximize the use of 32-bit drivers under Windows 95?
5. As more and more companies migrate their technical resources to the Internet, locating new drivers and finding technical data on software products is increasingly easy. Name three sources Microsoft recommends for finding technical information.
6. By pressing the F8 key when Windows 95 boots, you can access the Boot menu. Name at least five of the options on this menu.
7. WIN.COM includes support for a number of error-isolation switches. These switches are as follows: f, m, n, s, v, x. Describe what each of these switches does.
8. If you are presented with the problem of not being able to print to a network printer from a Windows 95 computer, what are two possible solutions for correcting it?
9. This morning when you logged on to the network at work you saw some kind of DHCP error, but you did not think much about it. Now you are unable to access the Internet through the Proxy server. What utility would you use to make sure you in fact obtained an IP address this morning?
10. Windows 95 provides ways to optimize the file system. Name three ways you can ensure the highest file system performance.

Answers are located at the end of the chapter...

In a complex operating system environment, troubleshooting technical problems or optimizing for performance is never an exact science. Although the number of possible hardware and software combinations (and resulting conflicts and configuration issues) on any given computer is virtually limitless, you can narrow the scope of any problems that may arise and, with luck, isolate the offending component(s), whether internal or external to Windows 95. Often the problems are a combination of both internal and external factors. Troubleshooting is your bread and butter as a network administrator, or as a Microsoft Certified Systems Engineer. Your users or clients are not really interested in how many tests you have passed, or how many trade journals you read. They want to know, "Can you fix my computer…NOW!" To this end (and to prepare you to pass the Windows 95 exam), this chapter looks at troubleshooting.

This chapter examines the following topics:

- Installation failures
- Boot process failures
- Connectivity problems
- Printing problems
- File system problems
- Resource access problems
- Hardware device and driver problems
- Editing the Registry

General Troubleshooting Guidelines

You can follow a number of steps when attempting to isolate technical problems. Some are specific to Windows 95; others are just part of a logical approach to any problem:

1. Determine whether the problem is intermittent or occurs with regularity. If the problem is regular, your next step is to

look for patterns and what factors are common to each occurrence of the problem. If the problem is intermittent, it becomes more difficult to diagnose. You should note that, although a problem seems to occur randomly, it often is in fact occurring regularly—but the factors linking each occurrence may be very obscure. It is rare for computers to behave erratically for no apparent reason, except in the case of intermittent hardware failures, when the laws of physics are dictating system behavior.

2. Determine whether the problem began after a particular change was made to the configuration of the operating system, such as a driver update, the addition of a new modem, or a new video resolution setting. If this is the case, try to determine how the new configuration and the problem may be related.

3. Use binary logic to isolate one variable at a time in your search for the failing component. If the operating system is suspect, for example, turn off all its advanced features simultaneously. If the problem goes away, refine your search, turning the features back on one at a time until the problem reoccurs. If turning off all the features does not solve the problem, you can likely look elsewhere.

4. Determine as precisely as possible whether the problem seems to be clearly internal to Windows 95 or includes external software/hardware. Generally, installing Windows 95 on a new computer will not cause many problems, unless those problems are related to hardware incompatibilities. The situation always becomes more complex when an existing system's software and hardware are migrated to Windows 95, because Windows 95 is then likely to inherit any existing problems with the computer as well as some potential new problems (such as Windows 3.1 applications that do not work properly under Windows 95). The best example of this methodology is booting into Safe mode, because this disables many if not all special features, drivers, and software of the operating system. If the problem goes away in Safe mode, the problem probably is limited to a few key configuration parameters.

5. Determine whether sequence is important to the problem. Is it a matter of the order in which things happen in the operating system? This can point out conflicts between different applications, for example. Does one application fail only after another particular application has loaded?

6. Is this a known or common problem? Does it occur on other computers, or is it an isolated event? To find known problems, consult your available technical resources (see "Technical Resources for Troubleshooting Information") to learn potential solutions or to determine whether a known solution exists. Obviously, this is much easier to do if you can produce the problem on demand.

Troubleshooting Other Specific Scenarios

Although you cannot anticipate every potential problem that a system may encounter when Windows 95 is installed, certain courses of action are recommended for particular troubleshooting scenarios. Because every technical problem is in many ways unique to its operating environment, these suggestions are neither exhaustive nor guaranteed to work in the given situation. Table 7.1 shows some possible solutions for common problems. These solutions are intended to provide examples of applicable methodologies.

Table 7.1

Troubleshooting Examples

Problem	Possible Solution
Cannot print to a local printer.	Verify that the correct driver is installed, ensure that the printer's buffer is clear, and try printing directly to the LPT port from a DOS prompt.
Cannot print to a network printer.	Ensure that File and Printer Sharing is enabled at the remote computer; verify that you have correct network protocols configured.

continues

Table 7.1 Continued

Problem	Possible Solution
Print jobs are not spooling properly.	Disable spooling in the Properties sheet of the printer, which will indicate whether spooling is in fact the problem; verify that enough disk space is available to hold the spooled print jobs.
Print jobs are garbled.	Disable EMF spooling; check whether Windows 3.1 printer drivers are being used.
Fatal Exception errors and GPFs.	Try Safe mode; try a standard VGA driver; run ScanDisk with a full surface scan to check for corrupted files.
Message that communications port is already in use when attempting to use a terminal program.	Verify that no fax manager software is running in the background, waiting for calls, because this ties up the communications port.
A newly installed ISA device is not functioning.	Check the Device Manager for conflicts with existing devices (designated by a yellow exclamation mark).
CD-ROM drive is not listed as a drive in the Explorer or the Device Manager.	Most likely not a supported brand; install Real-mode driver support.
A device is malfunctioning; but when it is removed from Device Manager and redetected, the problem persists.	Edit the Registry, delete the associated key under HKLM\Enum\Root\, restart the computer, and run hardware detection again.

Troubleshooting Setup Problems

Troubleshooting setup issues is really a rather unique problem. Many of the normal troubleshooting techniques do not apply. Questions such as "When did it last work?" and "What has changed?" hardly seem appropriate. Instead, the questions become "Is it compatible?" and "What drivers do I use?"

Fortunately, the Windows 95 installation is usually successful, but on occasion problems do arise. These problems are often traceable to legacy hardware or poorly documented off-brand equipment. This section is directed toward helping you troubleshoot the Windows 95 installation process. Your key to successful troubleshooting is a thorough understanding of the different phases of the Setup program. You may want to review some of the material covered in Chapter 2, "Installation and Configuration, Part 1," under the section titled "Installation," if you are not completely fluent with this process.

In addition to knowledge of the setup process, you can use log files to guide your troubleshooting. The Windows 95 Setup program creates these log files (SETUPLOG.TXT and DETLOG.TXT) during hardware detection failure, and other files (NETLOG.TXT and BOOTLOG.TXT) as Windows 95 starts up the first time. The following list looks at these files in detail:

- **SETUPLOG.TXT.** This is an ASCII text file that contains the Windows 95 setup information created during installation. As Windows 95 is being installed, entries are written into this text file for each step in sequence. This file will show any error conditions encountered. It is used by the Windows 95 Setup program in case of setup failure, and you can use it to troubleshoot errors during the installation process.

  The Windows 95 Setup program uses the information contained within SETUPLOG.TXT to ensure that the Windows 95 Setup program does not fail twice on the same problem. When you restart the Windows 95 Setup program after a failure, the contents are reviewed to see which process started, but did not complete successfully. These processes are skipped, and the next process in sequence is run. The DETLOG.TXT and DETCRASH.LOG files, discussed next, are used to skip any hardware detection modules that failed.

Buried on the CD-ROM version of Windows 95 is a helpful program called LOGVIEW.EXE, which enables you to examine all the text files mentioned in this list in a manner similar to the

SYSEDIT.EXE program found in earlier versions of Windows. To find this program, look in the OTHER\MISC\LOGVIEW directory. The ability to have all these files readily accessible in an easy-to-read format greatly facilitates the troubleshooting process by enabling you to work with the logs at the same time.

SETUPLOG.TXT is stored as a hidden file on the computer's root directory. Information is added to this file in the same order as the installation process. If you need to determine what caused the Windows 95 Setup program to fail, look at the entries at the bottom of this file before restarting.

- **DETLOG.TXT.** This is an ASCII text file that contains a record of all devices found during the hardware detection phase of installation. If a device is found, the detected parameters are identified and recorded.

  Do not confuse this with DETCRASH.LOG! If the hardware detection phase should cause the computer to stall or lock up, a binary file named DETCRASH.LOG is created. Although DETLOG.TXT is an ASCII file for you to read, the Windows 95 Setup program reads the binary information in DETCRASH.LOG to determine what steps were successfully completed.

  DETLOG.TXT is stored as a hidden file on the computer's root directory. Information is added to this file in the same order as the hardware detection phase. If you need to determine what caused the Windows 95 Setup program to fail or lock up, look at the entries at the bottom of this file before restarting.

- **DETCRASH.LOG.** Do not confuse this with DETLOG.TXT! DETCRASH.LOG is a binary file that only exists during the hardware detection phase. It tracks the entire process in case of errors for the Windows 95 Setup program. You need to be aware of its existence, but you would use the DETLOG.TXT ASCII file to do any troubleshooting.

- **NETLOG.TXT.** This is an ASCII text file that contains a record of all detected network components found during installation. The network detection phase consists of four parts. These correspond with the four class types of network configuration: network clients, network protocols, network adapters, and network services (such as file and print sharing).

  This file is stored as a non-hidden file on the computer's root directory. Information is added to this file in the same order as the network detection phase. If you need to determine what caused the Windows 95 Setup program to not communicate across the network, look at the entries in this file. You will see where Windows 95 found the network adapter and identified which protocols, clients, and services to bind to the card. At the end of each line, you should see `OK`. If you see a line such as `Couldn't determine...`, or some other failure notice, you have found your problem.

- **BOOTLOG.TXT.** This is an ASCII text file that contains a record of the current startup process when starting Windows 95. When Windows 95 is started for the first time, this file is created automatically. This file records the Windows 95 components and drivers as they are loaded and initialized, and records the status of each step.

  The information in BOOTLOG.TXT is written in sequence during startup. You might need to examine it closely to determine which error occurred. The Windows 95 Resource Kit has a good description of the sections within this file. You also can create this file by pressing F8 during the Starting Windows 95 startup and then choosing menu option 2—Normal with a Boot Log.

  This file is stored as a hidden file on the computer's root directory. Information is added to this file during the Windows 95 startup process. If you need to determine what caused Windows 95 to fail or lock up, look at the entries within this file before restarting. The BOOTLOG.TXT seems to write everything twice. The first line will tell you something like `Loading VXD=...` and the next line will say something like `LoadSuccess VXD=...`. In troubleshooting, it is important to see what loaded successfully, as well as what loaded unsuccessfully. BOOTLOG.TXT provides that information.

The three key files used to troubleshoot the Windows 95 Setup process are the SETUPLOG.TXT, DETLOG.TXT, and BOOTLOG.TXT ASCII text files. If the machine I am working on does not have Logview installed, I find it helpful to open the logs in Notepad, and do a quick search for a word such as *fail* to get an idea as to what is loading and what is not loading properly.

Technical Resources for Troubleshooting Information

Countless sources of information exist to guide you in solving technical problems. They include the following:

- Online help
- Microsoft TechNet
- The Internet
- The Windows 95 Resource Kit
- Technical support by phone
- Hardware and software compatibility lists
- Online discussion forums

Online Help

The Online Help feature in Windows 95 contains a great deal of technical information, and it includes several interactive troubleshooting tools that can resolve many common problems. By accessing Help from the Start menu, the troubleshooting book on the contents menu provides instant access to nearly a dozen of these interactive tools. If you are troubleshooting a modem problem, for example, it takes you step by step through several different scenarios to aid in finding the problem.

Microsoft TechNet

Microsoft TechNet is a monthly subscription CD-ROM publication and is an invaluable tool that contains vast amounts of technical data on all Microsoft products, including electronic versions of various resource kits, driver updates, and databases of known problems. You can customize this tool by creating (and saving) custom queries to more easily find information when you need it. This is a resource you need to learn how to use before an emergency strikes. To aid you in this endeavor, read the articles on how to use TechNet in the TechNet news section.

The Internet

As more and more companies migrate their technical resources to the Internet, locating new drivers and finding technical data on software products is increasingly easy. It is rare that a hardware or software manufacturer is not accessible through the Internet. If new or updated drivers are required to resolve a problem, or sending a technical question through e-mail is applicable, the Internet is the first place to go. You can also find many Windows 95 discussion groups where technical questions can be posted. In addition to this, Microsoft maintains a UseNet server with numerous discussion groups that cover the entire range of Microsoft products, from the Access discussion group to the various Windows groups. You can find this server at `msnews.microsoft.com`.

The Windows 95 Resource Kit

This is the book that should have shipped with Windows 95. Although you can access the Resource Kit electronically either from Microsoft's WWW site or on the TechNet CD-ROM, reading large amounts of information from a book rather than from a computer screen is much easier. The support tools and utilities that come on the CD-ROM with the *Resource Kit* (such as the configuration Help file, enhanced print troubleshoot, and INF installer) are also available for download from Microsoft's WWW site.

Technical Support by Phone

If you are looking for help on a technical problem and you are in a situation in which intuition is more important than information, you may find contacting Microsoft Product Support directly by phone to be productive. Because support is generally charged on a per-incident basis, it is important to obtain a case number, and use the same number until the issue is resolved. In addition to an in-depth knowledge of the product, the technical representatives have access to a great deal of technical data that is not available to the consumer. Their phone number is 206-637-7098.

Hardware and Software Compatibility Lists

These lists, which are on the TechNet CD-ROM or can be downloaded from Microsoft's WWW site, contain all the hardware and software that have been tested and are known to work with Windows 95. (You may find notes on how to make them work better as well.) Although not all working products are listed, seeing a product on the list gives you affirmation that you should continue troubleshooting because the product is supposed to work with Windows 95.

Online Discussion Forums

If you have access to online services, you can get access to a number of very useful Windows 95-related discussion groups through news groups, mailing lists, and general forums. You can also usually contact Microsoft Product Support specialists and other professionals through these groups as well; Microsoft and other companies assign a certain number of technical support representatives to monitor the groups. To help you find the exact mailing list you need, check out the CataList, catalog of Listserv lists at `http://www.lsoft.com/lists/listref.html`.

Before you begin your troubleshooting activities, make sure you have a good boot disk for your previous OS (for example, Windows 3.1). This boot disk should have a basic AUTOEXEC.BAT and CONFIG.SYS, as well as any files needed to access files on your hard drive and on the CD-ROM. In addition to this disk, the Windows 95 Startup disk (created from Add/Remove programs in Control Panel) can come in handy as well. The Windows 95 Startup disk is a bootable disk that contains the tools necessary to diagnose and resolve many hard disk-related problems. You will need the disk with CD-ROM drivers, however, if you need access to any files not already on your hard drive.

Troubleshooting General Setup Issues

The first step in troubleshooting Windows 95 setup issues is to get back to basics. Most of the following items will aid you in preparing the hard drive to receive the Windows 95 files. When installation fails in the first stages of the Setup program, it is often attributed to these listed issues:

- Is a disk management utility installed? If it is, can you safely remove it? This might entail a BIOS upgrade (if available) and quite possibly require using FDISK and repartitioning the drive. If this is the case, do you have a good backup?
- Is the disk compressed with a third-party utility? If so, can you safely uncompress the drive?
- Does Setup hang during the ScanDisk phase of installation? (An application is considered to be hung if it is still running, but not responding to any messages from the system.) If Setup does hang during the ScanDisk phase, you can manually run ScanDisk, and force a thorough inspection of the drive prior to Windows 95 installation. If it passes, you may want to specify the /IS switch when calling the Windows 95 Setup routine. This will tell Setup to run CHKDSK.EXE to check for cross-linked files.
- Have you disabled virus protection? Remember it may be loading automatically from your previous OS, or it may be enabled in the computer's BIOS. Some anti-virus programs

prevent writing to the boot sector of the hard disk. If this is the case, Windows 95 Setup will either fail to install, or will not load correctly. To correct this situation, you must disable the virus protection. After Windows 95 is properly installed, you can re-enable virus protection.

- Have you turned off power management? At times power management can cause problems (particularly if your computer decides to take a nap during some long-winded phase of Windows 95 setup).
- Have you made certain your computer does not have a virus? Run a current anti-virus program and check for viruses after booting from a known clean disk.
- SmartDrive can cause problems with some SCSI hard disks. By default, during Windows 95 setup Smart Drive is loaded, but double buffering is turned off. To work around this situation, simply use the /c switch to run setup without SmartDrive.
- What is being loaded from the AUTOEXEC.BAT and CONFIG.SYS?
    1. Rename AUTOEXEC.BAT by typing the following from the command line: **ren c:\autoexec.bat autoexec.aaa**
    2. Rename CONFIG.SYS by typing the following from the command line: **ren c:\config.sys config.aaa**
    3. Restart the computer and run Windows 95 Setup again.

Troubleshooting Specific Setup Issues

In this section, you look at troubleshooting some specific Windows 95 setup issues. The problems listed are ones that crop up from time to time, and as a result provide a good approach from which to generalize a systematic approach to your troubleshooting issues. The first example examines the vexatious issue of dealing with a floppy installation of Windows 95.

Setup Hangs at Disk 2 During Installation

If you have removed all disk managers, virus protection, and prepared your hard drive prior to running Setup (refer to troubleshooting steps in the preceding section) and Setup hangs at disk 2, you are probably having trouble extracting the cab files for whatever reason. This section examines an approach to resolving this issue.

The Setup files (except for disk 1) are stored on what are called DMF (Distribution Media Format) disks. DMF disks allow Microsoft to hold more information than regular 1.44MB floppies (and therefore you have fewer disks to deal with); however, some computers have trouble reading them. To troubleshoot this, and to verify whether this is the problem, follow these steps:

1. Copy the extract.exe program from disk 1 to the root of drive C: by typing the following at a command prompt: **copy a:\extract.exe c:**

2. Create a temporary directory to expand the cab files into by typing the following at a command prompt: **md c:\w95tmp**

3. Insert disk 2 into drive A: and extract Precopy2.cab into your w95tmp directory by typing the following at a command prompt: **extract /e a:\precopy2.cab /l c:\w95tmp**

4. Type the following at a command prompt: **extract /e a:\win95_02.cab /l c:\w95tmp**

5. Switch to your w95tmp directory and verify the files copied correctly.

If you are able to extract the preceding two cab files into your w95tmp directory, you are able to read the DMF disk; unfortunately, however, you are going to have to manually extract the files prior to running Setup.

If you cannot extract the cab files, repeat the preceding steps at another computer to verify the integrity of the installation disks. If they are defective, you will need to have them replaced by Microsoft.

If you can extract them at another computer, you should check your machine for a virus with a current virus scanning package. If a virus is detected, you should scan your Windows 95 setup disks to ensure they have not been infected. If they were infected, you must replace them. If not, then after the virus is properly removed, you should be able to install Windows 95 from your distribution media.

If your machine does not have a virus, and you cannot read the DMF disks, but you were able to extract them onto another machine, you may have a hardware problem. Refer to Chapter 2 for more information on resolving hardware problems during Windows 95 setup.

Setup Hangs During Hardware Detection Phase

Windows 95 automatic detection of hardware during setup is *great* when it works—and most of the time it is beautiful. However, the complexity involved in trying to detect every conceivable card and piece of equipment that can be attached to a modern computer is incredible. This situation is compounded if the manufacturer did not strictly adhere to the Plug and Play specifications. As a result, if you have installed Windows 95 on multiple machines, you have probably encountered situations where Setup locked up the computer during the hardware detection phase. The first rule is *do not panic.* If you follow a good recovery procedure, you increase your chances for performing a successful installation of your new operating system. To recover from a hardware detection problem during setup, follow these steps:

1. Turn off the machine and wait 15–30 seconds to allow time for the machine to settle down. Do not press Ctrl+Alt+Delete or use the Reset button to restart the computer. You must turn the machine off by using the power switch.

2. Turn your computer back on, and run Setup again; this time choose Smart Recovery when prompted to do so.

3. If Windows 95 Setup continues to hang in the same place, you will need to go into Custom Setup when you are prompted.

> You may need to allow Windows 95 to attempt automatic hardware detection several times before giving up. Although it may seem the computer is lockingup at the same place, in fact it might not be the same thing causing the lockup each time. Setup remembers what it was doing the last time it locked up and it tries something else. Allow automatic hardware detection to do its job before choosing the manual route.

4. When prompted `Do you want Setup to look for all hardware devices?`, choose No, and modify the list.

5. From the Hardware Type dialog box, select Display, Floppy Disk Controller, Hard Disk Controller, Keyboard, and Mouse if appropriate.

6. If Setup continues to hang, run Setup again, and select a different combination of devices.

Setup Hangs After First Reboot

If Windows 95 Setup hangs after it has performed the first reboot, there is possibly a video conflict. To correct this problem, you need to try and start Windows 95 in Safe mode by following these steps:

1. Restart Windows 95, and press F8 when you see the `Starting Windows 95` message onscreen.

2. Choose Safe Mode from the menu.

3. After Windows 95 comes up in Safe mode, choose Display in Control Panel.

4. Select the Settings tab, and click on the Change Display Type button. See Figure 7.1.

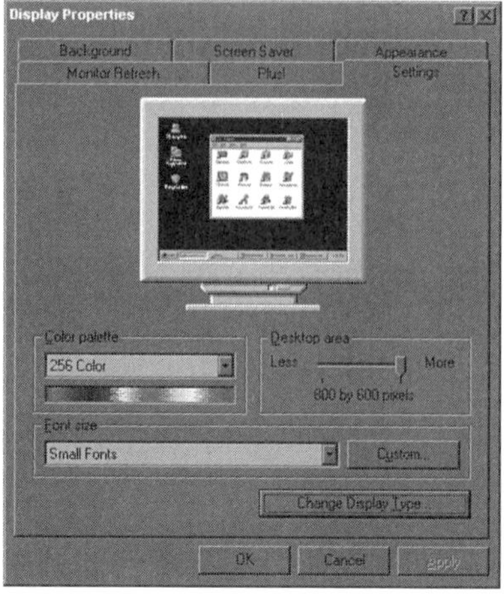

Figure 7.1

To correct video problems, press Change Display Type in the Display Properties box.

5. Click the Change Adapter Type button, and select the Show All Devices button near the bottom of the dialog box.

6. Double-click the Standard display types at the top of the list in the left panel.

7. Select the Standard Display Adapter (VGA) and click on OK. See Figure 7.2 below.

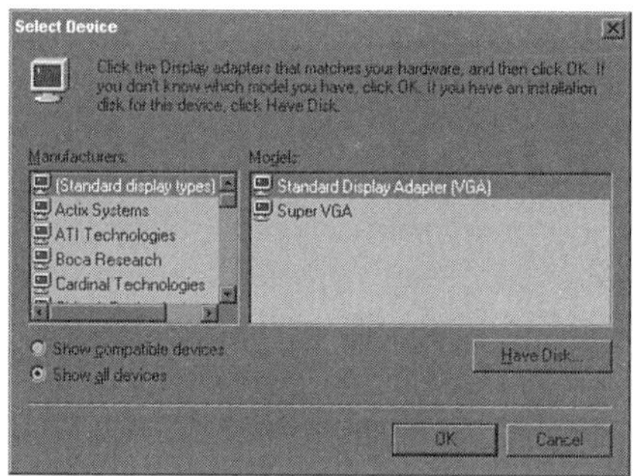

Figure 7.2

Display problems are often corrected by selecting a Standard VGA adapter.

8. Restart Windows.

This should enable Windows 95 to come up in a normal manner. After you have Windows 95 running in Normal mode, you can change your display adapter settings to maximize the capability of your particular video card and monitor.

After you install Windows 95, and have been using it for a while, it is common to run into boot problems when things go astray. To address these types of issues, it is helpful to have a plan of attack. This section helps you to develop a strategy for dealing with boot problems on Windows 95 machines.

Diagnose and Resolve Boot Process Failures

A large majority of the technical problems that arise under Windows 95 can be traced back to the configuration files and how these files control the boot process. Especially in upgrade situations, many settings that were necessary and that worked properly in a Windows 3.1 environment are either redundant or incompatible in a Windows 95 environment. Isolating which of these settings are redundant or incompatible with Windows 95 can be difficult. Windows 95 provides a number of tools and configuration parameters that can aid in this task:

- Safe Recovery mode of Setup
- The Boot menu
- The Verify install procedure
- The Startup disk
- WIN.COM switches

Safe Recovery Mode of Setup

To avoid having to restart the entire installation procedure in the event of a system crash or other mishap during setup, Windows 95 implements an automatic Safe Recovery mode. When the computer is restarted following the crash, and Setup is rerun, it may seem like you are going through the entire procedure again; in actuality, you are not. Setup verifies all the devices already in the Registry, and then skips those modules and the one that caused the crash. Safe Recovery mode then continues the detection process starting with the next module.

The Boot Menu

By pressing the F8 key when the `Starting Windows 95` message first appears, you can access the Boot menu, which provides a number of different modes in which Windows 95 can be booted. The menu options depend in part on what parameters are specified in the MSDOS.SYS file, but generally consist of the following:

- Normal mode
- Logged mode
- Safe mode
- Safe mode with network support
- Step-by-step confirmation
- Command-prompt-only mode
- Safe-mode command prompt
- Previous version of MS-DOS

Normal Mode

This is the normal operation mode of Windows 95. If you decide to complete the boot process to start Windows 95 under normal conditions, select this mode.

Logged Mode

When you select Logged mode, the entire boot process is logged to a file called BOOTLOG.TXT, which catalogs VxD initializations, driver loads, and various other boot-related events. In all other respects, the Logged mode will perform a normal boot procedure (of course, it will be a bit slower as it writes to the BOOTLOG.TXT file). BOOTLOG.TXT will normally be found in the root and can be loaded into Notepad as seen in Figure 7.3.

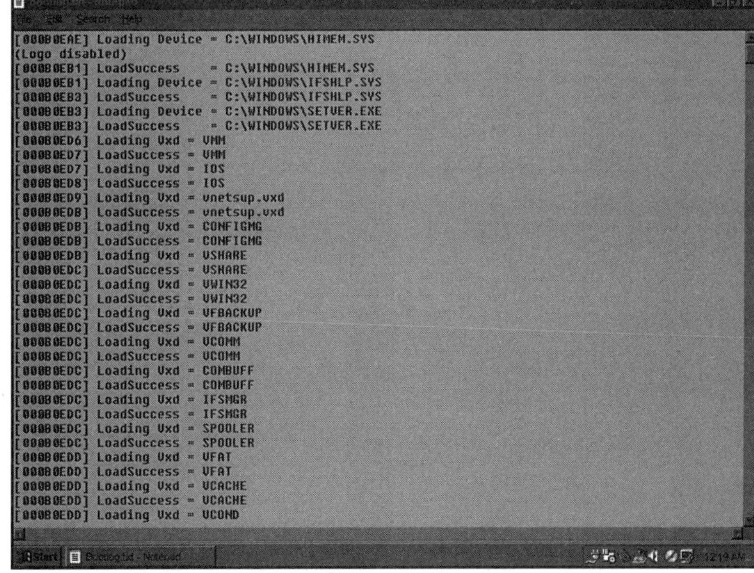

Figure 7.3

By loading BOOTLOG.TXT into Notepad, you can look for boot-up failures to aid your trouble-shooting endeavors.

Safe Mode

Safe mode is likely the single most important troubleshooting tool available in Windows 95. In this mode, a number of key Windows 95 components and settings are disabled, including the following:

- CONFIG.SYS and AUTOEXEC.BAT
- The [Boot] and [386Enh] sections of SYSTEM.INI
- The `Load=` and `Run=` parameters of WIN.INI
- The Startup group in Windows 95
- The Registry
- All device drivers except the keyboard, mouse, and standard VGA video driver

Disabling these items allows the separation of fundamental operating system problems from those caused by a combination of software factors. In a situation in which the display is not functioning properly in Normal mode, for example, if the problem does not appear in Safe mode, the problem probably is video driver–related and is not due to a defective video card.

Similarly, you can use Safe mode to troubleshoot scenarios such as the following:

- GPFs (General Protection Faults)
- Application hangs
- A hang during the boot process
- A blank screen at boot time

In some instances, you cannot use the Safe mode boot option because certain drivers in the CONFIG.SYS or AUTOEXEC.BAT are necessary for booting the system (such as partitioning software drivers). In these cases, you can boot to a Command-prompt-only mode (which processes CONFIG.SYS and AUTOEXEC.BAT) and then, using the command `WIN /d:m`, you can continue with the remainder of the Safe mode boot process.

Safe Mode with Network Support

This mode is similar to Safe mode, but enables Real-mode NetBEUI networking support. This mode also processes some Registry information needed to enable network support. This mode can be useful when the following problems occur:

- The computer hangs during a network operation.
- Network print operations fail.
- The computer is using a shared install of Windows 95 and requires access to the shared files, and networking in Normal mode is not functioning.

Step-by-Step Confirmation

This boot mode is similar to the F8 function of previous versions of MS-DOS; it permits the user to step through the various stages of the boot process and specify whether each should or should not be completed. This mode can be very useful when you are trying to isolate boot stages to determine which may be causing a given problem. You can also use it to view system responses to various parameters in CONFIG.SYS and AUTOEXEC.BAT, which otherwise are displayed far too quickly to read.

Command-Prompt-Only Mode

Command-prompt-only boot mode is similar to a normal boot of MS-DOS. Only CONFIG.SYS, AUTOEXEC.BAT, COMMAND.COM, and the Registry are processed (along with any necessary disk compression drivers). This mode is useful in troubleshooting problems running MS-DOS applications in a VM under Windows 95. If the application functions in this mode but not inside Windows 95, the problem is likely due to a compatibility issue. If the application does not function in Command-prompt-only mode, the problem is likely a configuration problem in CONFIG.SYS or AUTOEXEC.BAT, or the application may be corrupt.

Safe-Mode Command Prompt

This mode functions similarly to Command-prompt-only, except that CONFIG.SYS and AUTOEXEC.BAT are not processed (disk compression drivers are still loaded). This mode can be useful in situations in which even Safe mode does not function properly.

Previous Version of MS-DOS

Although the previous version of MS-DOS boot mode is not intended for troubleshooting, it can be used in situations in which particular MS-DOS–related functions worked in previous versions of MS-DOS but do not seem to function properly under Windows 95. This boot mode can be used to test that functionality in both environments. Of course, you can only boot to a previous version if you upgraded the computer from a previous version.

The Verify Install Procedure

If you suspect that some Windows 95 files or Registry information has become corrupted, you can have Windows 95 examine all installed components to determine whether this is the case and, if so, recopy or reconstitute the component. If Setup is rerun after installation, Windows 95 prompts the user as to whether installation should be rerun or components should be verified. If verification is chosen, the following occurs:

- A validity check is performed on all required files. If the check fails, the file is recopied from the Windows 95 installation media.
- The VMM32.VXD file is rebuilt.
- Incorrect Registry entries are overwritten.

The Startup Disk

You can create the Startup disk at installation time or later through the Add/Remove Programs option in the Control Panel as seen in Figure 7.4. The disk serves as an emergency boot disk should the operating system fail to load. The disk also contains FDISK, FORMAT, and several other MS-DOS–based file and disk utilities that may be useful in diagnosing and repairing system problems.

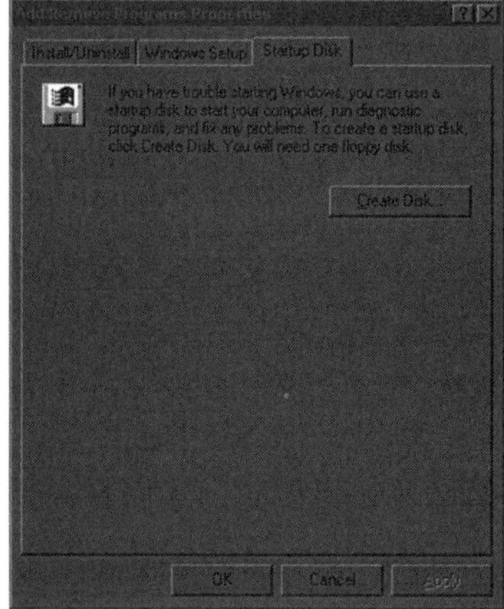

Figure 7.4

A Windows 95 Startup disk can be created at any time by going into Control Panel and choosing Add/Remove Programs.

When you install Windows 95 in a shared network situation, the Startup disk includes information for that shared environment. In this situation, the Startup disk can be a floppy disk, a remote-boot disk image on a server, or a local hard disk. It includes Real-mode software needed to start the computer and attaches it to the shared Windows folder on the server. It also includes a copy of the mini-Registry Windows 95 uses to start the computer.

WIN.COM Switches

WIN.COM includes support for a number of error-isolation switches. Although some are available from within Windows 95, you may have to specify them from the command prompt in situations in which Windows 95 fails to load. These switches are specified in the following format:

```
win /d:[f] [m] [n] [s] [v] [x]
```

The switches function as follows:

Switch	Function
[f]	Disables 32-bit file system drivers
[m]	Starts Windows 95 in Safe mode
[n]	Starts Windows 95 in Safe mode with networking
[s]	Excludes the ROM address space between FOOO and 1MB from use by Windows 95
[v]	Disables virtualization of hard disk interrupts
[x]	Disables use of upper memory by Windows 95

You can use these switches independently or together as part of a single command.

Diagnose and Resolve Connectivity Problems

Connectivity problems can be some of the more vexatious issues to resolve in Windows 95. Part of the difficulty lies in trying to determine where the problems are occurring. Which machine is having the problem? Is it computer A or computer B that is not talking, or listening? Is it a protocol problem, an application problem, or a hardware problem? As you can see, connectivity problems can quickly escalate out of control. Fortunately, Windows 95 has some good built-in tools to aid you in troubleshooting these issues.

Using WinIPCfg

With the increased utilization of TCP/IP, diagnosing and resolving connectivity problems based on this protocol are important skills. Fortunately, Microsoft has provided an extremely useful and easy-to-use tool to assist in exploring these issues (see Figure 7.5).

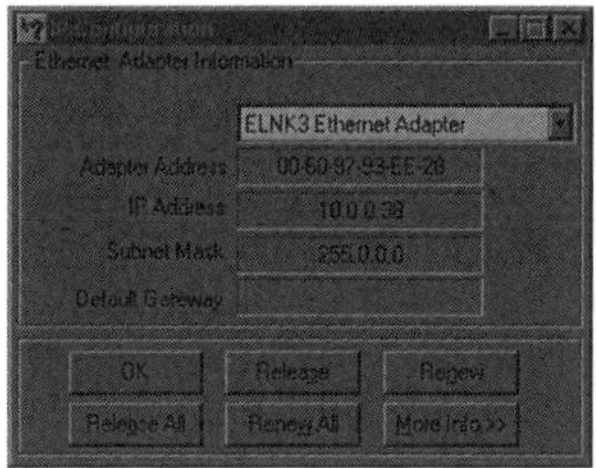

Figure 7.5

The compact view of WinIPCfg tells you your IP address and subnet mask at a glance.

WinIPCfg enables you to quickly view important troubleshooting information such as IP address, subnet mask, network adapter address, and default gateway (if assigned). If your IP address is being assigned by a DHCP server, the first item to check is whether an IP address has in fact been assigned to the machine. If the IP address box has 0.0.0.0 listed, you have not obtained an address and consequently cannot communicate with any other machine by using TCP/IP.

WinIPCfg is not dynamically updated while it is on your screen. If you wish to see current information, you must click on the OK button to close the box, and then run it again.

Now look at the different information that can be obtained through WinIPCfg.exe. The following list explains the settings and how to use them. Refer to Figure 7.5 to see where the information appears in the box.

1. The drop-down box lists the adapters configured in the machine. It might be an Ethernet adapter, modem, or other device with an IP address bound to it.

2. The adapter address in the case of an Ethernet card is a string of unique hexadecimal numbers that are hard coded into the device by the manufacturer. If the adapter is a modem, a bogus number is displayed in this box because a modem does not have such a number assigned to it.

3. The IP address is a set of four decimal-separated values bound to the preceding adapter to enable communication between machines using this protocol. This number is either statically assigned to the machine when the protocol was configured, or is dynamically allocated when the computer connects to the network.

4. The subnet mask is also either statically assigned when you manually configure TCP/IP or dynamically obtained when you connect to a network with the computer. A subnet mask tells the computer whether the address of another machine is on the same local network, or whether it is on a remote network. Every computer configured with TCP/IP *must* have a subnet mask assigned.

5. The default gateway tells the computer where to go to gain access to a remote network.

By clicking on the More Information button in WinIPCfg, you gain information about lease TTL and DHCP server and the like as shown in Figure 7.6. Refer to the figure as you read the following discussion about the use of these items:

1. The host name is the name your computer is identified by on the network. It is configured under Network Properties in Control Panel. This name must be unique to avoid conflict on the network.

2. The DNS Server block lists the IP address of the server that provides name resolution for your machine. This server keeps a list of IP addresses and domain names for the network. A DNS server enables you to send message traffic to frodo.com, for example, instead of having to type in the IP address for it. If you can connect to a machine by typing in the IP address, but not by typing in the domain name, you might take a look at your DNS Server settings.

3. The WINS Server blocks list the IP addresses of the primary and secondary WINS servers. In a routed Windows NT environment, a WINS server provides name resolution similar to the DNS server listed in item 2. It maintains a database of computer names and maps them to IP addresses. If you can connect to a machine by typing in the IP address, but not by typing in the machine name, you might take a look at your WINS Server settings.

4. If your IP address is handed out dynamically from a DHCP server, you will have lease information displayed in the two boxes near the bottom of the WinIPCfg box. When the server grants you an IP address for your machine, it also sets an expiration time for the address. This allows a greater number of computers to share a limited number of IP addresses. When one computer leaves the network, the address is still reserved for it until it is either released by the computer or expires due to age. It must be renewed prior to expiration; otherwise, the PC will drop off the network. If you are

experiencing sporadic connectivity using TCP/IP, it might be due to the settings for lease expiration. The lease duration might need to be adjusted on the server, depending on your particular situation.

5. The Release, Renew, Release All, and Renew All buttons (see Figure 7.6) are helpful in troubleshooting IP address leasing problems. You can release the address, reboot the machine, and see whether the machine picks the address back up. Also, you can attempt to renew the address and see whether you can obtain a renewal of your lease.

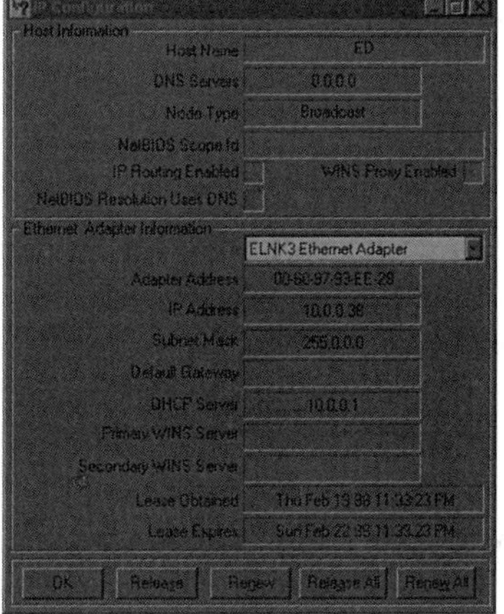

Figure 7.6

The expanded view of WinIPCfg enables you to release and renew your IP address.

Dial-Up Networking Problems

To troubleshoot Dial-Up Networking problems, the first places to start looking for the problem are in the Network Properties sheets for the Dial-Up Adapter, the Dial-Up Networking connection, the modem, and the application you want to use over the connection. This isolates your troubleshooting to the client computer. You then can start checking for problems that may be affecting the phone line connection such as a busy signal on the other end, a dead phone line, or the connection to the outgoing phone line. Finally, you can isolate the problem to the server-side computer. In this case, you may not have physical access to that computer and may need to rely on someone local to that computer to diagnose and fix any problems on the server.

Some of the problems you may encounter with Dial-Up Networking (DUN) include the following:

- **Modem problems.** Be sure your modem is installed properly to work with Windows 95. If the modem is external, make sure it is turned on. Also, be sure it is plugged in to the phone line.
- **Phone numbers.** Double-check the phone number you are dialing to be sure your modem is correctly dialing that number. If you need to dial a number for an outside line, be sure to enter it. If you have Call Waiting on your phone line, disable it. If you need to dial a long distance number, be sure the entire number, including 1 + area code, is being dialed. Also, make sure the number you are dialing is for a modem or fax modem.
- **Protocol issues.** Make sure the Dial-Up Adapter is configured to use the same protocol as the server-side computer. If, for example, you use DUN to connect one Windows 95 computer to another using the Dial-Up Networking Server software, use the same protocol, such as NetBEUI or IPX/SPX. Also, if you use TCP/IP to connect to the Internet, make sure your DNS, IP address, host names, and other configurations are correct. These values cannot be wrong by one character; they must be exact.
- **Access rights.** If you can connect to a remote server but cannot access user resources on that site, you may not have proper access privileges. Make sure you enter the correct password and that the server side is set up to allow you access to it.
- **Server problems.** A common problem with the Dial-Up Networking Server is that it is not enabled. Enable it by opening the Dial-Up Networking folder and choosing Connections, Dial-Up Server. Choose the Allow Caller Access option. Also, the computer on which the server software resides must be turned on, running Windows 95, and connected to a phone line.

- **Application problems.** If your application does not function properly over Dial-Up Networking, you may have a slow or bad connection or your application is not intended to function as remote-access software. Read the application's documentation to make sure it can operate as remote software, or contact its manufacturer for specific steps on making it work with Windows 95. Check whether it is an application problem by using the Windows 95 applet HyperTerminal. HyperTerminal is a bare-bones, no-frills communication program that seems to connect when no other program does. If you can connect with HyperTerminal, chances are you have a configuration problem with your application.

When you attempt to use an application that does not work with Windows 95 TAPI architecture and you have the Dial-Up Server enabled, your application will not be able to call out. If, for example, you use CompuServe WinCIM 2.01 or earlier software to dial CompuServe, you receive a `Cannot Initialize Port` message when Dial-Up Server is running. You may forget you have Dial-Up Server running in these cases. (Windows 95 does not display a message or indicator that it is on.) When this happens, you just disable the Dial-Up Server until you are finished using the application.

Using Net Watcher

You can use the Net Watcher utility to create or delete shared resources on remote computers, or monitor access to those resources (see Figure 7.7). Remember, however, that it is also an important tool for anyone troubleshooting connectivity problems in a networked environment.

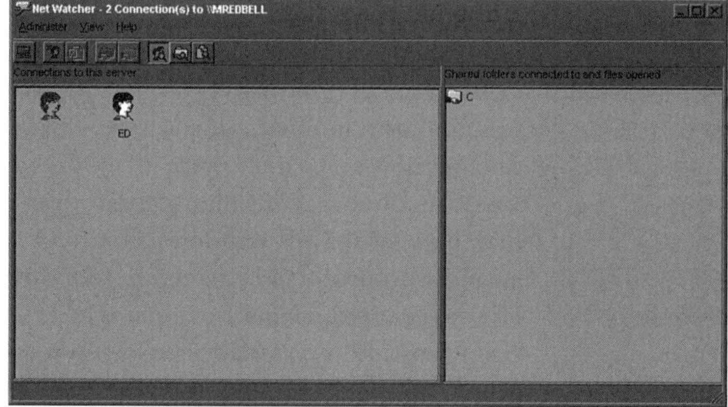

Figure 7.7

Net Watcher aids in connectivity trouble-shooting by graphically displaying shares and connections.

By using Net Watcher, you can see at a glance who can connect to a Windows 95 machine and who cannot. You can see what shares are created and who is utilizing what files. The following factors are important when considering remote administration using Net Watcher:

- The remote computer must have File and Printer Sharing enabled.
- You can access only remote systems that use the same security model you are using on your computer. (Share-level security computers cannot access user-level security computers.)
- You can connect only to remote systems that use the same type of file and printer sharing (Microsoft or NetWare).

If Remote Administration is enabled on the remote computer, Net Watcher is used to display the status of connections to shared folders. The features of Net Watcher enable an administrator to remotely perform the following tasks:

- Create a new, shared folder
- List the shared folders on a server
- Stop the sharing of a folder
- Show which users are connected to a shared folder

- Show how long a user has been connected to a shared folder and how long the user has been idle
- Disconnect users or close files opened by a user

Figure 7.8 shows an example of a Net Watcher display.

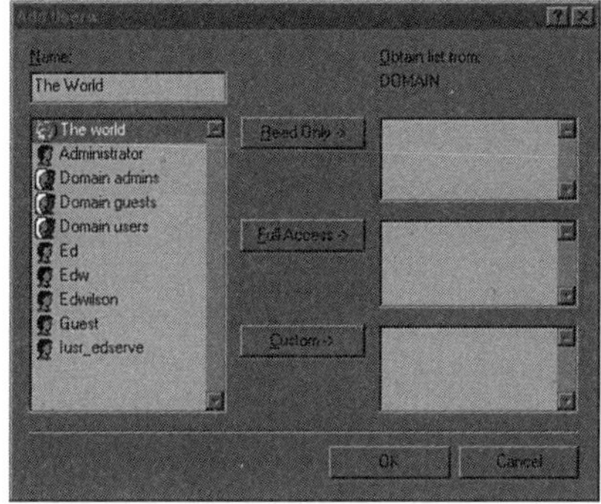

Figure 7.8

When remote administration is enabled, Net Watcher can manage shares on remote systems.

Net Watcher can also be accessed through the Network Neighborhood by right-clicking on a computer and choosing Properties from the context-sensitive menu. Choose Net Watcher from the Tools tab to view the shared folders and the users accessing those folders on the selected computer.

The following steps show how to monitor a remote computer using Net Watcher:

1. Start Net Watcher as previously described. You can also select the Start menu, and choose Programs, Accessories, System Tools, Net Watcher.
2. Choose Administer, Select Server. The Select Server dialog box appears.
3. Enter the name of the server (the remote computer) you want to view. Click the Browse button to see a list of the computers you can connect to.
4. Click on OK. A view of the remote computer appears in Net Watcher.

5. Click on the Show Users button to see the users connected to the selected computer. On the left you see the username, computer name, number of shares, number of open files, time of connection, and idle time. On the right, you see the shared folders that are connected to and the files that are opened.

6. Click on the Show Shared Folders button to see the names of the shared folders on the selected computer. On the left, you see the shared folder, the name it is shared as, the access type, and a comment associated with the folder. On the right, are the connections to the shared folder and the files that are opened.

7. Click on the Show Files button to see files that are opened by other users. You see the name of the file, which share it is using, who is accessing it, and what the open mode is.

8. Press F5 to refresh the display.

9. Choose Administer, Exit to exit Net Watcher.

Using System Monitor to Observe Performance

Windows 95 is equipped with a tool for monitoring various performance-related factors of the operating system environment. This tool is called the *System Monitor*. You can use it to provide real-time monitoring of system activities both locally and at remote computers, to determine the effect of configuration changes, and to identify potential system performance bottlenecks.

Performance information—such as the percentage of processor utilization, the number of programs currently running, or how many bytes of information are being written to a hard disk per second—can be displayed in one of three formats: as a bar chart, as a line chart, or as numbers. By observing this information over time as various operations are performed by the operating system or applications, you can see how a certain operation affects a given performance parameter and tune the system to minimize any negative effects on performance. For more information on System Monitor, refer to Chapter 6, "Monitoring and Optimization."

To monitor a remote computer, the owner of that computer must have enabled Remote Administration and have specified you as an authorized user. See more on monitoring a remote computer in Chapter 6.

The following are some guidelines for using System Monitor to identify technical problems or bottlenecks:

- Run System Monitor during normal activity at first, to get a sense of how certain values change when certain actions are performed.
- Identify which items in System Monitor are applicable to the problem (for example, monitor swap file size to determine whether more memory is needed in the system), and then set up specific tests.

Use System Resource Meter to Monitor System Performance

You can use the System Resource Meter utility to monitor dynamic changes in system resources. Many Windows 3.1 applications fail to release the resources allocated to them when they unload from memory, which causes the total system resource pool of the system to decrease. If you suspect an application of this behavior, it is advisable to activate the System Resource Meter and observe whether subsequently closing the suspected application restores the resources to their previous levels. If this is not the case, the application may not be releasing all its allocated resources back to the operating system.

Using the Troubleshooting Wizard

If, in spite of everything else, you still cannot connect to the network, there is still hope. Windows 95 has an in-depth Network Troubleshooter as shown in Figure 7.9. The Network Troubleshooter walks you through everything from logging on to the network to browsing the network.

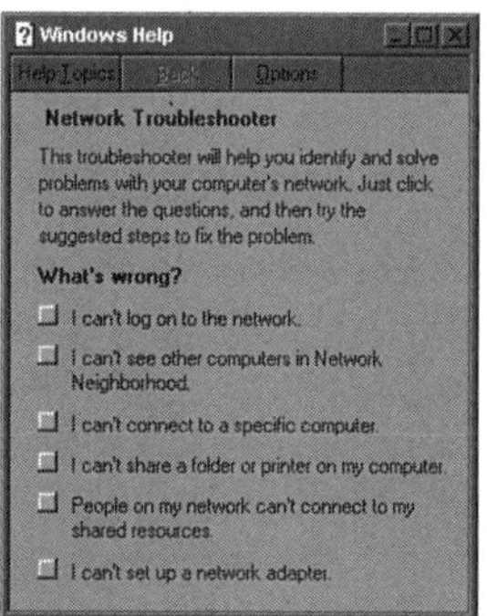

Figure 7.9

The Network Troubleshooter is an in-depth wizard that assists in resolving numerous connectivity issues.

Diagnose and Resolve Printing Problems

The main factor in ensuring print performance is spool settings. Windows 95 spools, by default, using a proprietary internal page description format called *Enhanced Metafile* (EMF), which is discussed in more detail in Chapter 2, "Installation and Configuration, Part 1." When printing across a network, the translation into EMF format, and ultimately into a printer-specific format called *raw*, is performed differently, depending on the operating system installed at the print server. If the print server has Windows 95 installed (which can interpret EMF format), most of the rendering of the print job from EMF format into raw format is done at the server. If the print server has any other operating system installed, the EMF and raw format rendering must be done at the client, which increases the client's processing load. When printing locally, both types of rendering are done at the local computer.

A second consideration in print performance is how quickly control is returned to the user after a print job is submitted. You can configure the print subsystem of Windows 95 to return control to the user after the first page of a print job is spooled or after the last page is spooled. This parameter can be configured from the Spool Settings dialog box (click on the Spool Settings button on the Details tab of the Properties sheet for the printer in question). Choosing to return control after the first page shortens wait time but increases printing time and consumes more disk space; the inverse is true if control is returned after the last page is spooled.

Troubleshooting Tips for Printing Problems

One way to remedy a printing problem is to use the Print Troubleshooter, which is available from the Windows 95 Help utility. You also can use the following guidelines to help clear up printer problems:

- Make sure the printer is turned on, full of paper, and is online.
- Check the printer cable and parallel port to make sure the printer is connected to the computer.
- Open the Printers folder, right-click on the printer, and choose Properties. Make sure the settings are correct for your printer.
- Turn off Metafile Spooling. It may not work properly for all printers.
- Make sure you have the latest printer driver installed. Sometimes reinstalling the same printer driver fixes the problem. Contact the printer manufacturer to obtain a new printer driver for Windows 95, if available.
- Download a PostScript error handler to the printer if the problem is with a PostScript printer.
- View your resources, such as free disk space and free memory. For each print job, you need some free disk space for temporary files to be stored. Likewise, free memory address space is needed to process the print job. Close an idle application to free up some memory, if necessary.

- Attempt to print to the printer from another application. A quick test is to open Notepad, create a line of text, and print the file. If this works, the original application that failed to print may need to be configured for printing. If this does not work, you may need to reinstall the printer.
- Print to a file; next, copy the file to a printer port to see whether the file prints to the printer. If this works, the problem is due to spooler or data transmission problems. If this does not work, the program or printer driver is at fault.
- Shut down and restart Windows 95. Similarly, turn the printer off for 15 seconds or so, and then turn it back on. Sometimes this clears memory buffers that at times get clogged with downloaded fonts on the computer and printer.
- If you cannot print a complex document, try removing some of the graphic elements in the document. In addition convert the fonts in the document to a printer-resident font such as Courier.

A good habit to develop is to document printer problems and distribute copies of the document to other users in your company or organization. Because most end users send a job to the printer sooner or later, the rate at which they experience printer problems far outweighs many other problems they encounter. Having a document that end users can refer to might decrease the number of support calls you get for printer problems.

Diagnose and Resolve File System Problems

The first step in resolving file system problems is to ensure that the computer is fully optimized and is using the proper drivers.

One of the main ways in which you can enhance performance and reliability in Windows 95 is by using 32-bit Protected-mode device drivers. These drivers are designed to work faster and more efficiently in relaying data than older 16-bit drivers. As manufacturers begin updating their product lines for Windows 95 compatibility, obtaining native Windows 95 drivers for most hardware devices will become easier. A Windows 3.1 driver or MS-DOS–based driver should be used only if no 32-bit driver ships with Windows 95 and the manufacturer has not yet developed one.

A number of ways exist to maximize the use of 32-bit drivers:

- Verify that the Performance tab in the My Computer Properties sheet shows all 32-bit components for the file system and for virtual memory (see Figure 7.10).

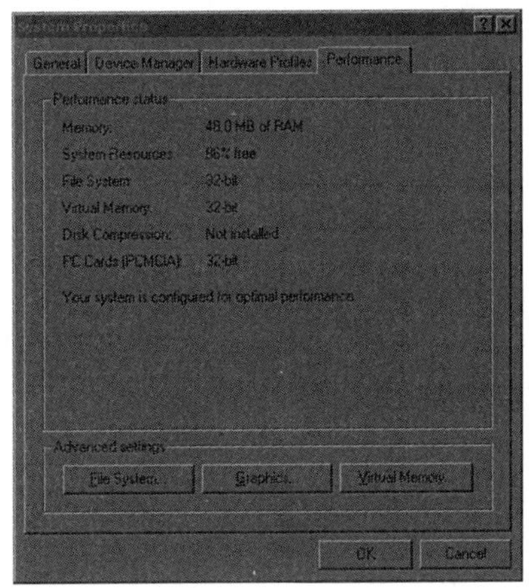

Figure 7.10

The Performance tab of system properties provides a convenient summary of crucial information.

- If you are using non-Microsoft disk compression, that compression is operating in Real mode (unless you have obtained a 32-bit compression driver since the release of Windows 95) and should be updated with a 32-bit driver from the manufacturer.

- Ensure that disk partitioning software is not being used. If a local hard drive employs nonstandard or software-based partitioning, it likely will not be able to function with the 32-bit file system drivers of Windows 95.

Optimizing the File System for Desktop Performance

You can take a number of actions to ensure the highest file system performance, including the following:

- Remove SHARE.EXE and SMARTDRV.EXE from the AUTOEXEC.BAT because these files are not needed in Windows 95 and needlessly take up memory.
- If the Performance tab of the My Computer Properties sheet indicates that the file system is not using 32-bit drivers, check the IOS.LOG to find the filename of the Real-mode driver that may be preventing the use of 32-bit file system drivers.
- Use Windows 95 Disk Defragmenter regularly to ensure that system performance does not degrade due to fragmentation of data on your hard drive.

Configuring the File System for Different Roles

Because computers can be optimized for different roles, including network performance, Windows 95 allows the configuration of certain performance-related file system parameters according to what role the computer is expected to play. Figure 7.11 shows the three possible configurations available under File System Properties. They are as follows:

- Desktop computer
- Mobile computer
- Network server

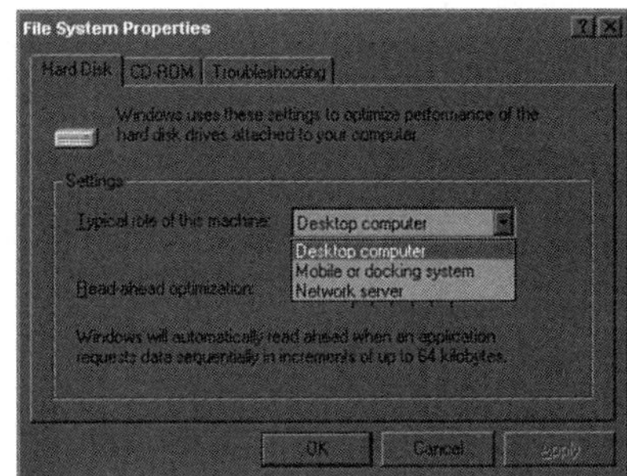

Figure 7.11

There are three possible file system configurations under File System Properties.

The following parameters in the Registry are keyed to these configurations:

- **PathCache.** The size of the cache VFAT uses to track most recently accessed folders. This affects performance by limiting the number of times the file system accesses the file allocation table to search for directory paths. The setting is 32 paths for a desktop, 16 for a laptop, and 64 for the server profile.
- **NameCache.** Stores the most recently accessed filenames. The setting is 8KB (or about 677 filenames) for a desktop, 4KB (or about 337 names) for a mobile system, and 16KB (or about 2,729 names) for a server profile.

The settings are calculated based on each configuration's needs. In the case of a network server, for example, due to its intensive file-processing needs, both the listed settings would be at their maximum to increase efficiency in retrieving files. It is important to note that the PathCache and the NameCache settings use memory from the general system heap. Also, if you have a low memory machine that is lightly utilized, you may consider using the mobile settings. Conversely, if you have a powerful machine and are heavily hitting the hard drive, you might consider using the network server profile.

If you encounter difficulty with any applications and you suspect the file system might be involved, you can disable a number of file system features by using the Performance tab of the My Computer Properties sheet to isolate the problem (see Figure 7.12, and refer back to Figure 7.10). Disabling any of these, however, will result in performance degradation:

- File sharing
- Long filename preservation for old programs
- Protected-mode hard disk interrupt handling
- Synchronous buffer commits
- 32-bit protected-mode disk drivers
- Write-behind caching

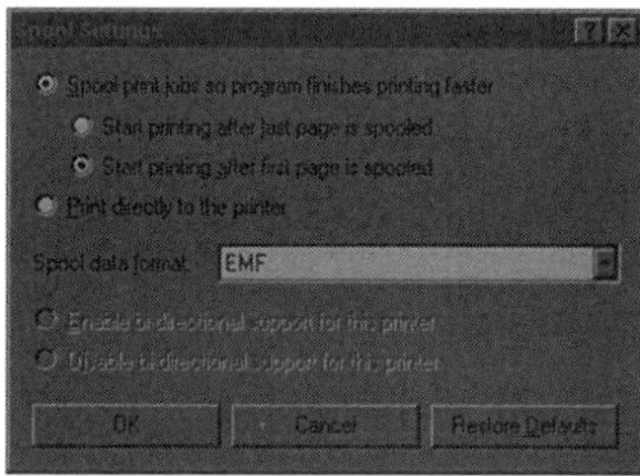

Figure 7.12

The Troubleshooting tab of File System Properties gives you six ways to isolate problems.

Disabling File Sharing

You can disable file sharing for applications that are incompatible with the way Windows 95 typically implements file sharing (use SHARE.EXE until the application is updated to support Windows 95 file sharing).

Disabling Long Filename Preservation for Old Programs

If an application requires the directory space used by LFNs in Windows 95, you might have to disable this support for older applications. However, if you turn this off here, you turn off the tunneling feature that preserves Long File Names for all old programs.

Disabling Protected-Mode Hard Disk Interrupt Handling

The Disable Protected-Mode Hard Disk Interrupt Handling option disables Windows 95's normal practice of intercepting all MS-DOS–level disk I/O requests and handling them with a 32-bit Protected-mode driver. Disk performance is degraded, but compatibility with older applications is enhanced.

Disabling Synchronous Buffer Commits

If you disable the Synchronous Buffer Commits, the Commit File API initiates a write of dirty buffers (uncommitted) to disk. However, it does not wait for the write to complete. This means the data may not be on the disk when the API returns.

It almost sounds as though you could get some extra performance by using this option, but that is not the case for most programs and in fact may cause file integrity problems for any programs that expect data to be committed to disk. You should use this option only when you are troubleshooting. It is also a good idea to check with tech support before using this option.

Disabling All 32-Bit Protected-Mode Disk Drivers

If a hard drive is experiencing problems reading or writing information while Windows 95 is running, you can disable all 32-bit disk drivers to enhance compatibility with older applications. Once again, disk performance is degraded.

Disabling Write-Behind Caching

The Disable Write-Behind Caching for All Drives option is useful when data integrity is crucial and you cannot risk losing data in the write-behind cache when a power failure occurs. Write-behind caching causes Windows to wait until idle time to write disk changes, which may be too late if a power failure occurs and all cache items are lost. When write-behind is disabled, all write operations are performed immediately. Yet again, performance likely will be degraded.

Diagnose and Resolve Resource Access Problems

A clear understanding of Windows 95 architecture is needed when troubleshooting resource allocation and access problems. Also, the following sections provide an overview of virtual machines, multitasking, process, and threads in Windows 95. You also learn about how WIN16-based applications multitask under Windows 95.

Multitasking: Preemptive and Cooperative

Windows 95 uses two types of multitasking, depending on the type of application involved: preemptive multitasking and cooperative multitasking. *Preemptive multitasking* involves dividing the processors capacity into time slices that are allocated according to the priority of the processes requiring them. Thus, one application processes for *x* number of milliseconds, and then may be interrupted by a process with a higher priority. However, periodically, all processes will get a bump up in priority to preclude them from becoming compute bound.

Cooperative multitasking also divides the processors time into slices, *but* is different in that it allows a given process to engage the processor until it voluntarily cedes its control to another process. The disadvantage of this type of multitasking is that a misbehaving application can monopolize the processor's time and effectively stop other processes from executing. Recognizing multitasking problems when they occur can save you from hours of frustration. If the computer seems to hang, for instance, you might suspect a hardware problem or a device conflict. But if you identify the misbehaving application, you might find a multitasking problem. If you are lucky, the software vendor will release an update to fix the problem you just diagnosed.

Multithreading

Multithreading is the capability of a process to create multiple threads, each having access to the memory space inhabited by its parent process. In this manner, the application can have two separate execution processes multitasked by the processor, creating the impression that the application is itself performing two tasks simultaneously. Word can repaginate a document and allow the user to type at the same time, for example. All multitasking is done at a thread level, with applications submitting either single or multiple threads, depending on the application type.

Virtual Machines

Windows 95 is capable of running three types of applications:

- MS-DOS 16-bit applications
- Windows 3.1 16-bit applications (also known as WIN16 applications)
- 32-bit Windows applications (also known as WIN32 applications; includes most Windows NT software)

Windows 95 can run these varying applications because of a number of architectural design factors, the most important being the idea of virtual machines (VMs). In a single-tasking, single-threaded environment such as MS-DOS, in which only one application at a time is requesting the operating systems resources, managing those resources is much easier. In an environment such as Windows 95, which is intended to manage multiple applications that might be operating simultaneously, a much greater need for careful management of the system's resources exists because the computer remains primarily a single-task machine (one processor equals one task at a time, no matter how fast it performs those tasks). In this single-task environment, two processes requesting the use of a device at the exact same moment would be very problematic. Clearly, a procedure in place to arbitrate such requests is necessary.

Windows 95 implements this procedure through VMs. One VM (called the System VM) is home to all 32-bit applications, and 16-bit Windows applications. But inside this Virtual Machine are two distinct memory spaces. The 32-bit applications run in one memory space, and the 16-bit Windows applications run in the other memory space. In this manner, Windows 95 can keep applications separate from each other as much as possible, thus minimizing the chance that they might not work together. Additionally, if a 16-bit Windows application should terminate unexpectedly, it is less likely to affect other applications. The second type of VM is the DOS VM. Because some applications (MS-DOS applications) were not designed to function in a multitasking environment, the operating system must deceive them into thinking they are the only process running on the computer (or they would fail to operate properly). For this reason, every DOS application run on a Windows 95 computer is run inside a separate VM. Therefore, if you are running three DOS applications on a Windows 95 computer, you will have three separate DOS VMs.

Hardware Virtualization

Another important component in the creation of VMs is hardware virtualization. Legacy MS-DOS, and (to a lesser extent) Windows 3.1 applications, often required direct access to the system hardware. This is something Windows 95 generally does not allow, which results in greater stability. To provide backward compatibility, the concept of hardware virtualization was created. By simulating the hardware environment in which the application is accustomed to running, all the devices are available when needed. This is implemented through software drivers called VxDs (Virtual Device Drivers). These VxDs are responsible for arbitrating requests (often simultaneous) from running processes and queuing them so they do not conflict with each other or cause the device in question to fail because it is trying to do two things at once.

Internal Messaging

A *message* is generated each time a key is pressed or the mouse is clicked, effectively asking an application to do something. In a single-tasking environment, there is no question which application the keyboard or mouse input is intended for. In a multitasking environment, a more complex system of determination and delivery is required. Because you can have multiple applications onscreen simultaneously, where the mouse is clicked or what window is active when a key is pressed determines which application the message is intended for. After the intended application is targeted, the message is placed in the appropriate message queue to be processed.

16-Bit Applications Resource Usage

WIN16 applications generally are those created for Windows 3.1. If possible, upgrade the application to a 32-bit version. If this is not feasible, however, you need to remember the following when troubleshooting WIN16 applications:

- Windows applications (including WIN32 applications) exist in the System Virtual Machine, which is a special VM designed to provide one hardware virtualization layer for all Windows software.
- Within this VM, WIN16 applications share a common address space. (This is necessary to maintain backward compatibility with the way Windows 3.1 applications are designed to interact.)
- WIN16 applications operate on a cooperative multitasking basis. (This also is due to the way applications were designed for Windows 3.1, which did not support preemptive multitasking.)

- A single message queue is used for all WIN16 applications.
- All WIN16 applications are single-threaded, because Windows 3.1 does not support multithreading.
- WIN16 applications generally load themselves into the virtualized space between 3GB and 4GB, and some also use a space between 0 and 4MB to be able to share data with other WIN16 applications.
- WIN16 applications do not access the Registry because they are designed to use INI files for their stored settings. However, Windows 95 can migrate certain settings from the INI files into the Registry. The WIN16 applications can continue to access and modify the INI files, and these modifications then can be migrated to the Registry.
- 16-bit applications are not designed to recognize or use LFNs because LFNs are not implemented in Windows 3.1.
- Whereas under Windows 3.1 system resource stacks are 64KB, these have been converted to 32-bit stacks in Windows 95, dramatically decreasing the likelihood of running out of system resources.

32-Bit Applications Resource Usage

Windows 95 is designed to support and best interact with 32-bit applications specifically designed for Windows 95 or for Windows NT. These applications are best suited to take advantage of the new architectural design features of Windows 95. These design features include the following:

- The capability to take advantage of Windows 95 flat 32-bit, 4GB memory address space. (WIN32 applications typically load into the 4MB to 2GB range of memory.)

- The capability to pass more information in a single 32-bit programming call than is possible with a single 16-bit programming call, thus increasing processing performance.
- The capability to submit multiple simultaneous threads for processing, allowing greater user productivity within the 32-bit application because the user does not need to wait for one task to finish to start another.
- The capability to take advantage of Windows 95 preemptive multitasking, which is more efficient and runs more smoothly than Windows 3.1 cooperative multitasking.
- More comprehensive protection from other applications because each WIN32 application is assigned its own separate address space that is not visible to other applications.
- A separate message queue for each thread in a WIN32 application, which prevents other applications from interfering with the receipt or processing of system messages.
- The capability to use the Registry to store all application settings on a generic or per-user basis.
- The capability of the application to uninstall itself more easily than previous application types, because all changes to the Registry can be tracked and rolled back in the case of uninstallation.

Predicting Application Problems

Although applications should normally run without interruption, situations do arise when, due to either programming errors or incompatibilities, applications cease to function properly. The two main problems that occur with applications are General Protection Faults and application hangs.

Recognize General Protection Faults and How They Are Caused

A General Protection Fault (GPF) typically is caused by an application that attempts to violate system integrity in one of a number of ways:

- By making a request to read or write to a memory address space owned by another application.
- By attempting to access the system hardware directly.
- By attempting to interact with a failing hardware driver. (Drivers operate at Ring 0, and so can seriously impact the operating system.)

The GPF is generated when the operating system shuts down an offending application to prevent a system integrity violation. How the offending application is specifically handled depends on its application type.

Because MS-DOS applications reside in their own VMs and have their own message queues, if they cause a GPF, a message is displayed and the application is terminated without impacting the rest of the operating system.

In the case of WIN16 applications, the procedure is somewhat more complex. Because WIN16 applications share both a common address space and a common message queue, when one application creates a GPF, all others are suspended until the offending application is terminated. After this is done, the remaining applications resume processing.

Finally, with 32-bit applications, the procedure is quite straightforward. Because 32-bit applications exist in their own separate address spaces, and each has a separate message queue, a GPF in one 32-bit application in no way impacts any other 16- or 32-bit programs. Only the offending program is terminated.

Choose the Appropriate Course of Action When an Application Fails

Much improved support exists in Windows 95 for a local reboot of the application in question, which permits the application to be terminated without impacting other currently running processes. A local reboot is performed by pressing Ctrl+Alt+Delete once, which opens a Close Program dialog box. Listed in this dialog box are all currently running tasks (including system processes not otherwise listed on the taskbar). You must then select a process (`Not Responding` usually is indicated in brackets next to the process name) and click on the End Task button. The operating system then attempts to terminate the process (which might take several seconds). Depending on the reason why the application is hung, you also might be presented with the option to wait a few seconds for the application to respond, and then to terminate the application if no response is received.

The following sections describe some considerations you should make when an application hangs, based on the application type:

- MS-DOS
- Windows 16-bit subsystem (WIN16)
- Windows 32-bit subsystem (WIN32)

MS-DOS Application

A normal local reboot as described previously should work on an MS-DOS session because the MS-DOS application exists in its own VM and has its own message queue; a hung MS-DOS session does not impact the operation of any other process. An MS-DOS session also can be terminated from the Properties sheet of the session if the session is in a window.

16-bit Windows Subsystem

As stated earlier, because WIN16 applications share a common memory address space and a common message queue, if a WIN16 process hangs while in the foreground, all other WIN16 processes cease to receive messages from the operating system and also appear to be hung.

This is due to a flag that is set for WIN16 processes, known as the *WIN16 mutex* (mutually exclusive). Because 16-bit code is considered non-reentrant (it cannot be used by more than one process at a time), a system must be in place to ensure that no two processes attempt to use the same piece of 16-bit code simultaneously. Under Windows 95, this is done by enforcing the rule that only the process that currently owns the rights to the WIN16 mutex can make requests to 16-bit API functions. When the given process is finished using the 16-bit code, it hands the mutex to the next process.

If an application hangs while it owns the WIN16 mutex, no other application can access 16-bit API functions. Thus, all 16-bit applications appear to be hung. In addition, any 32-bit application that requires the use, through thunking, of a 16-bit API function (such as writing to the screen) also appears to be hung. The application is still running but cannot make any updates to the screen, and thus appears to be inactive or unresponsive.

To remedy this situation, the 16-bit application that currently holds the mutex must be locally rebooted through the means described previously. After this is done, the mutex should be reset and available for use by other processes.

32-bit Windows Subsystem

Just testing to see whether you have been paying attention! A 32-bit application will not hang the system, because it will be preemptively multitasked. In other words, control will be taken away from a misbehaving WIN32 application even if it does not want to relinquish control.

Understanding Windows 95 Memory Paging

Windows 95 uses two types of memory: physical and virtual memory. The Windows 95 operating system uses a *flat memory model,* which leverages off the Intel 386 or greater processor's capability to handle 32-bit addresses. This flat memory model provides a logical address space range of up to 4GB. Although current computer hardware does not yet handle up to 4GB of physical memory, some file servers can now run with up to 1GB of RAM. Virtual memory bridges the gap between physical memory and logical memory.

The 4GB of addressable space used as virtual memory under the flat memory model is implemented through the use of both RAM and a swap file. The Windows 95 operating system performs memory management, called *demand paging*, whereby code and data are moved in 4KB pages between physical memory and the temporary Windows 95 swap file on the hard drive. The Virtual Memory Manager controls paging and maintains a page table. The *page table* tells which pages are swapped to the hard drive, and which remain in RAM, and to which system process or application they belong.

Application programs are allocated a virtual memory address space, which is the set of addresses available for use by that program. Both WIN32- and MS-DOS–based programs are allocated private virtual memory address space. All WIN16-based programs share a single, common virtual memory address space. Windows 95 allocates the 4 GB of virtual memory to each address space. Each process is allocated a unique virtual address space of 4GB. The upper 2 GB is shared with the system, whereas the lower 2GB is private to the application.

The virtual memory is allocated as follows:

- **0–640KB**. If not used for a Virtual DOS Machine (VDM), this memory is made available for any Real-mode device drivers and terminate-and-stay-resident (TSR) programs.
- **0–1MB**. In a VDM, this memory is used to execute MS-DOS programs. If a shared, common WIN16 VM is used, WIN16 applications operate much as they do under Windows 3.1.
- **1–4MB**. Normally, this memory is unused. Windows 95 does not use this space, nor do WIN32 applications. If this memory is needed by WIN16 applications, it is available.

- **2 MB–2GB**. This memory is used by WIN32 applications and some WIN16 applications. Each WIN32 application has its own address space, whereas WIN16 applications all share a common address space.
- **2–3GB**. This memory is used to run all Core System Service components, shared DLLs, and other shared objects. Those components are available to all applications.
- **3–4GB.** This memory is reserved for all Ring 0 components, such as the File Management subsystem and the Virtual Machine Manager (VMM) subsystem. Any VxDs are loaded in this address space.

Virtual memory and virtual addresses enable you to have more memory available to programs than actually exists on the computer in physical RAM. The Windows 95 swap file implementation is much improved over that from Windows 3.1.

With Windows 3.1, you can have either a temporary or permanent swap file. Windows 3.1 recommends how much hard disk memory to allocate to the swap file. If the hard-disk controller is compatible with 32-bit disk access, running 32-bit disk access will improve performance. A temporary swap file that does not need to be on contiguous hard disk space is created when Windows 3.1 starts. This same temporary swap file is released when the user exits Windows. Although a permanent, contiguous swap file provides better performance than a temporary swap file because it is a static file, hard disk space is not freed up when the user exits Windows.

In Windows 95, the swap file configuration is much easier. The best features of temporary and permanent swap files are combined through improved virtual memory algorithms and 32-bit access methods. By default, Windows 95 uses a dynamic swap file, which shrinks and grows based on the needs of the operating system and the available hard disk space. A permanent swap file has little benefit in Windows 95.

Using Microsoft Diagnostics (MSD)

When it comes to solving old problems such as IRQ conflicts and base memory addressing issues, sometimes the old tools still work the best. Remember MSD (Microsoft Diagnostics)? That friendly tool from Windows 3.x days is still around. MSD is not installed by default, but you can find it on the Windows 95 CD-ROM under \other\msd. MSD.exe is a rather small program, and you can copy it to your Windows directory from the CD-ROM so that it will be in your path and easier to access. Figure 7.13 shows all the categories MSD reports on.

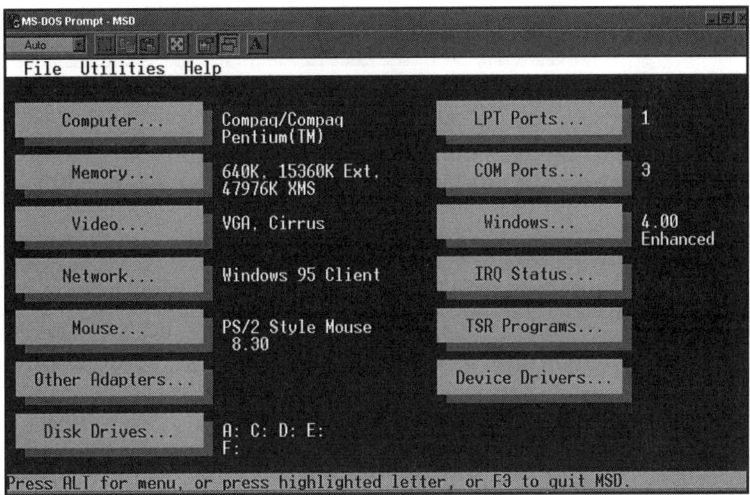

Figure 7.13

MSD provides detailed information in an easy-to-use format to aid in hardware configuration problems.

If you are installing a piece of legacy hardware and are getting conflicts, MSD can help (see Figure 7.14). MSD can provide extremely detailed memory map information, or IRQ listings—the kind of information needed when configuring legacy hardware. TSR programs, device drivers, and similar information are all easily available through the Microsoft Diagnostics software. One other very beneficial feature is its ability to produce hard-copy reports. To print reports, you choose Print Report from the File menu. At that point, you are presented with the chance to select which items to include in the report.

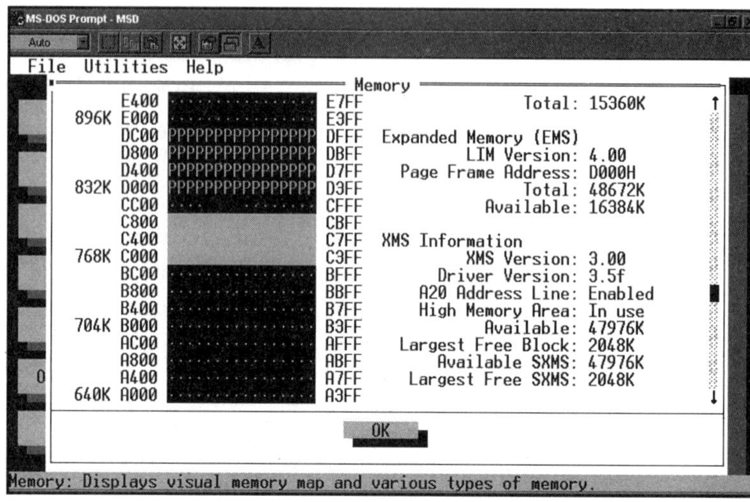

Figure 7.14

Memory mapping information is just one of the detail-level menus available from MSD.

Using the Add New Hardware Wizard

One of the really neat things about Windows 95 is the Add New Hardware Wizard. Anyone who has ever configured sound cards and the like under old Windows knows what a welcome relief the Hardware Wizard is. To run the Add New Hardware Wizard, just select the icon in Control Panel. The wizard begins, as shown in Figure 7.15, by asking whether you want to let Windows search for new hardware. You want to select Yes here if at all possible. The detection phase will normally last a few minutes, depending, of course, on the speed of the machine. After this phase is complete, Windows 95 either comes back and says it finished detecting hardware and prompts you to install software for it, or comes back and says it could not find new hardware and gives you the chance to specify what devices are in the system.

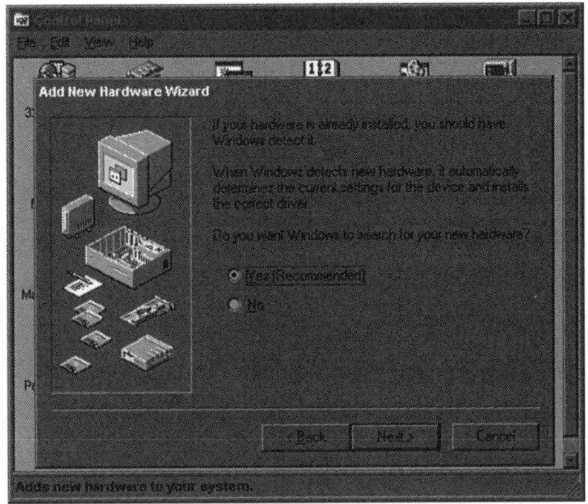

Figure 7.15

The Add New Hardware Wizard makes short work out of installing new hardware in Windows 95.

Perform Direct Modification of the Registry as Appropriate Using Regedit

The Registry in Windows 95 consists of two files that contain all essential configuration information. The two hidden and read-only files found in the Windows directory are User.dat and System.dat. Most changes required by users can be easily made by using Control Panel or some other Windows mechanism. With this in mind, it is extremely important to ensure that good backups of the Registry are made and caution is exercised when examining the Registry. One reason great care should be exercised when looking at the Registry is that changes are at times applied dynamically and prompts (such as `Are you sure you want to do this?`) are nonexistent.

The first thing you want to do prior to even looking at the Registry is to make a backup. Windows 95 comes with two very good (and easy to use) utilities to back up the Registry. They are both located on the Windows 95 CD-ROM in the \other\misc directory. The first is called CFGBACK, and the second is the ERU. You will use each of these in exercises later on in this chapter. There are, of course, other ways to back up the Registry. You can use the Windows 95 Backup utility, for instance, or you can just copy the User.dat and System.dat files that contain the Registry. One thing to be aware of is that on a Windows 95 machine which stores local profiles for different users, you will have a separate User.dat stored in the windows\profiles directory for each user of the machine. A good backup would take this into account.

Understanding the Windows Registry

The Windows Registry is essentially a database of configuration information about your computer. It is organized into groups of information that Microsoft calls *hives* (as in bee hives, believe it or not). By default, six of these hives are visible when you first open the Registry Editor. As you look at the screen, you will see the six default hives on the left side, and the values on the right side of the screen.

The Registry can be thought of as mimicking the directory structure of your hard disk. The root would be MY COMPUTER, and each of the hives would be directories. Under them would be the files (called keys), which contain the values.

These keys can contain three basic types of values: Dword, Binary, and String. *Dword* values are either decimal or hexadecimal. *Binary* values are the 0s and 1s type, and *String* values are alphabetic. This chapter looks at these in more detail later. Each of these values performs a specific function; if the Registry becomes corrupted, Windows 95 will not perform properly. It is vital, therefore, that you exercise caution when working with the Registry.

Figure 7.16 shows the REGEDIT when it first opens up. As you can see, six default keys are listed.

HKEY_CLASSES_ROOT

HKEY_CLASSES_ROOT is exactly the same as HKEY_LOCAL MACHINE\software\classes and it contains software registration and OLE (Object Linking and Embedding) information. It is broken out of the HKEY_ LOCAL_MACHINE subkey as an alias to provide backward compatibility with old Windows 3.1 programs. Take a look at Figure 7.17. This figure shows some of the things found in HKEY_CLASSES_ROOT.

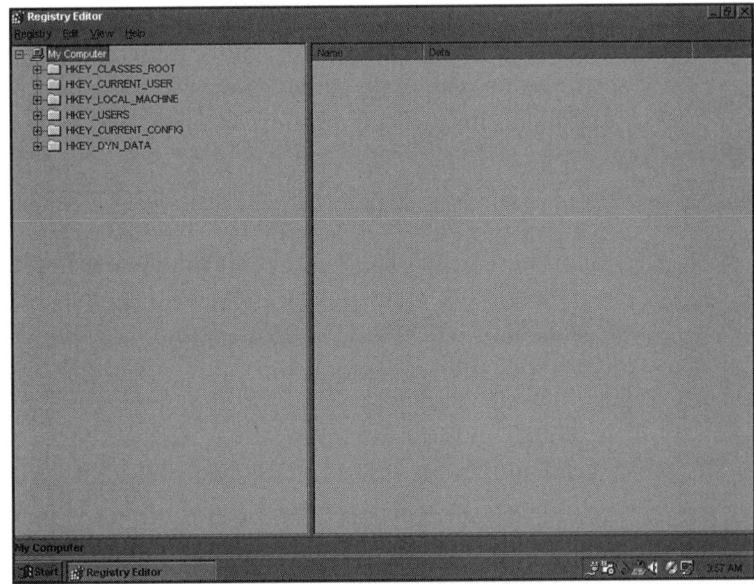

Figure 7.16

The Windows 95 Registry consists of six default keys that are shown in the left pane. These keys contain nearly all the configuration information required by your PC. As a result, great care should be exercised when viewing its contents.

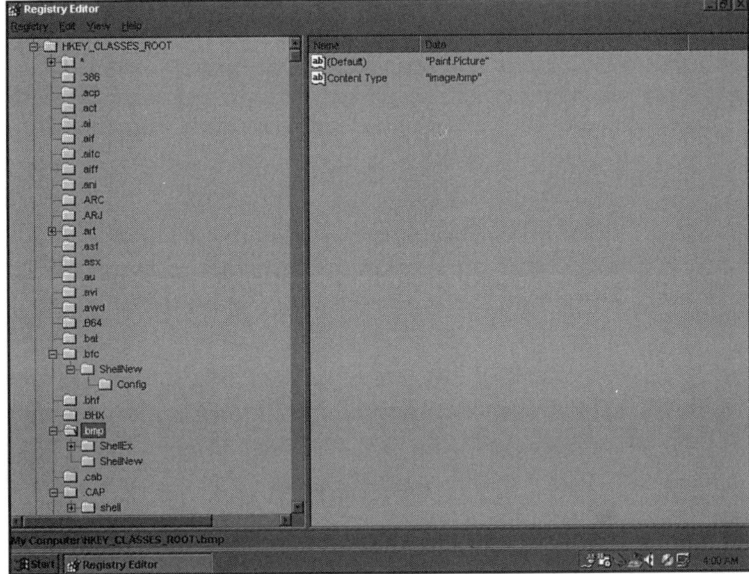

Figure 7.17

HKEY_CLASSES_ROOT contains OLE registration, file associations, and other information that tells Windows 95 how to react when you double-click or otherwise work with a file.

When you click on the plus sign (+) beside HKEY_CLASSES_ROOT, it will open up and give you a long listing of file extensions Windows 95 recognizes. Although many will just have default types associated with them (such as `.ani` will say it is an ani file), others will have much more information contained in their keys. You can easily tell this because if the key has a [+] beside the folder, subvalues are hiding underneath.

If you look at the `.bmp` key, you will see this extension is associated with paint.picture and it has the default type of image/bmp. If you were to scroll down the left side, you would find an entry for paint.picture and would see it is associated with the `.bmp` extension. This tells Windows 95 what to do when you double-click on a file with the `.bmp` extension.

When you install a new program, Setup will write information such as that previously discussed in HKEY_CLASSES_ROOT. This information also gets here when you work with file associations through Explorer. If you were in Explorer and selected View Folder Options, and then clicked on the File Types tab, you would be able to make changes to the keys here.

HKEY_CURRENT_USER

HKEY_CURRENT_USER contains information pulled from the HKEY_USERS key. In this way, Windows 95 can maintain profile information for many different users. When you log on, Windows 95 takes your logon name and associates it with a subkey in HKEY_USERS and copies the information into HKEY_CURRENT_USER. If you have not logged on to the particular machine previously, you are given the default profile (also stored in HKEY_USERS) and as you make changes, they are saved in your new settings. Your desktop configuration, sound schemes, and program preferences are all stored here.

HKEY_LOCAL_MACHINE

HKEY_LOCAL_MACHINE is the most extensive key in the Windows 95 Registry. HKEY_LOCAL_MACHINE\Software\Classes provides file extension registration information to the alias HKEY_CLASSES _ROOT, and HKEY_LOCAL_MACHINE\config feeds HKEY_CURRENT _CONFIG. When your computer starts up, it reads the HKEY_LOCAL _MACHINE \config key to match the current configuration. This enables you to have different hardware settings, depending on your application. If you have one hardware configuration where you connect to a network and another which is standalone, for example, these will be stored here and Windows 95 will know whether to load the Ethernet card drivers and restore persistent network drive connections.

If you install a Plug and Play device, it writes information into the HKEY_LOCAL_MACHINE key. If you use Add New Hardware from Control Panel, it writes information here as well. HKEY _LOCAL_MACHINE includes information about configuration, drivers, and network settings.

HKEY_USERS

HKEY_USERS stores the user's preferences for sound events, cursor settings, and more. It is also from where the HKEY _CURRENT_USER key is drawn. A default profile is stored here, which is given to users who have not yet stored their settings. There will be a subkey listed for each profile stored on the machine.

HKEY_CURRENT_CONFIG

HKEY_CURRENT_CONFIG is drawn from the HKEY_LOCAL _MACHINE\config and points to the current system configuration. Information on the display fonts and current screen resolution are stored here, as are any unique printer or fax settings.

HKEY_DYN_DATA

HKEY_DYN_DATA provides dynamic data that must be accessed quickly, and is therefore stored in RAM. This information comes from hardware devices that were detected when the machine started up, and the drivers associated with them. This information is pulled from RAM whenever you select this key in the Registry Editor, and consequently it is never out of date. Other information found here includes information for the bus enumerator, and performance statistics gleaned from various network components.

Deciding to Edit the Registry

Hopefully, you will not have to modify the Windows 95 Registry. However, occasions will arise when you will need to fire up Regedit and do battle with a wayward program or application. In general, you can make most of the normal modifications to the Registry through programs found in Control Panel, or other applications. In general, the following are occasions when you might have to make direct modifications:

- You removed a program or device from your computer, and the uninstall program did not go a good job, or the uninstall failed. In this instance, hopefully, you have some good information from the maker of the device, or the company that wrote the application. In this instance, you use the Find utility to search for specific words until you can remove vestiges of the old application.

- You need to make a change to enhance performance or fix a bug, and you read about the fix in the Microsoft Knowledge Base or TechNet. Occasionally Microsoft posts a bug fix that requires direct editing of the Registry. You should not make such changes, however, unless your machine is exhibiting the problems the fix is designed to correct. In these instances, it might be best to not fix something that is not broken.

- You want to change the behavior or enhance a feature of Windows 95, and there is no other way to make the modification without editing the Registry. A word of caution here: Be especially wary of Registry hacks that do not come from reputable sources. One can find thousands of neat tricks on the Internet, for example, but most of these have no place in a business/production environment.

Discriminate Resource Usage in Windows 3.1, Windows 95, and Windows NT

As you prepare for the Troubleshooting section of the exam, you need to be able to discriminate the resource usage in Windows 3.1, Windows 95, and Windows NT. You need a clear understanding of the Windows 95 system architecture. Chapter 5, "Integration and Operability," discusses the details of running applications under Windows 95. Table 7.2, however, compares and contrasts the memory usage of a Microsoft MS-DOS–based application, a WIN16 application, and a WIN32 application operating in Windows 95. Also, complete Exercise 7.2 at the end of the chapter to refresh your memory on how to count virtual machines using System Monitor.

Table 7.2

Comparing Memory Usage

Application	Memory Usage
MS-DOS	Each runs in a private Virtual DOS Machine (VDM). No message queue. Loaded in the lower 1MB of virtual memory.
Windows 16-bit	All run in a common address space and share a single message queue. Loaded in the lower 2GB of virtual memory.
Windows 32-bit	Each runs in a private address space, and each thread has its own message queue. Loaded in the 4MB to 2GB range of virtual memory.

Exercises

Exercise 7.1: Configuring and Using System Monitor

Exercise 7.1 demonstrates how to configure and use the System Monitor. This exercise assumes you have installed the System Monitor component through the Add/Remove Programs option in the Control Panel.

1. From the Start menu, choose Programs, Accessories, System Tools, System Monitor. The System Monitor window appears.
2. Choose Edit, Remove Item. Select any listed items and click on OK. The System Monitor window should not now contain tracked items.
3. On the View menu, verify that Line Charts is selected, and then choose Edit, Add Item. A list of system-related counter categories appears.
4. Select the Kernel category and the Processor Usage (%) item. Kernel: Processor Usage (%) now appears as a line chart.
5. Choose Options, Chart; increase the Update interval to 1 second; and click on OK. The chart now updates more frequently.
6. Choose View, Bar Chart. Kernel: Processor Usage (%) now appears as a bar chart.
7. Close the System Monitor. You return to the desktop.

Exercise 7.2: Counting Virtual Machines

To illustrate the point about how Windows 95 manages virtual machines, follow Exercise 7.2 to count the number of virtual machines running on your Windows 95 computer.

1. From your computer, start Windows 95.
2. If you installed Windows 95 on your computer with the Typical Setup option, the System Monitor program might not be installed because it is an optional component.

To determine whether the System Monitor utility program is installed, from the Start menu choose Programs, Accessories, System Tools, System Monitor. If System Monitor is not available, you must add it to your computer by following these steps:

a. From the Start menu, choose Settings, Control Panel. From the Control Panel program group, choose the Add/Remove Programs icon.

b. Click on the Windows Setup tab, double-click on Accessories, and select the System Monitor check box. Press Enter or click on OK. Press Enter or click on OK again to install the System Monitor.

3. From the Start menu, choose Programs, Accessories, System Tools, System Monitor. The System Monitor utility program displays key system information in a line chart, bar chart, or numeric chart format.

4. Any items previously selected are displayed when the System Monitor utility program starts. When you run the System Monitor utility program for the first time, the Kernel: Processor Usage (%) appears in a line chart.

5. You must remove all current items to run this exercise. Highlight any items you want to remove, and choose Edit, Remove Item.

6. Choose Edit, Add Item to open the Add Item dialog box. From the Category list, click on Kernel to display the list of Kernel items.

7. Choose Virtual Machines from the Item list. If you need an explanation of each item, choose Explain to see that this shows the number of virtual machines present in the system. Press Enter or click on OK to add the item Virtual Machines as a selection.

continues

Exercise 7.2: Continued

8. Choose View, Numeric Charts to obtain the number of virtual machines that currently are active. Normally, this value is 1 because the Windows 95 computer has just been started. It could be higher.

9. Open some Windows program applications or the Windows Explorer. Has the number of virtual machines changed? The number of active virtual machines should not change when Windows programs are started.

10. Start an MS-DOS command prompt by choosing Start, Run to open the Run dialog box, or choose Start, Programs, MS-DOS Prompt. Has the number of virtual machines changed? It should change because each MS-DOS application will start another virtual machine.

11. Start another MS-DOS command prompt, and then a third. What happens to the count of virtual machines after you start each new MS-DOS command prompt? Each time another MS-DOS command prompt is started, the number of virtual machines should increase by 1. If the initial count was 1, starting three MS-DOS command prompts increases the number to 4.

12. Close all three MS-DOS command prompts. How many virtual machines are currently active? The count of virtual machines should be back down to 1, or the starting number in step 8.

    Based on what you know about virtual machines, explain why the count changes during the exercise.

    All the Windows 16-bit and 32-bit applications run in a single system virtual machine. But each MS-DOS application runs in its own Virtual DOS Machine. Opening a new MS-DOS command prompt causes the virtual machine count to increase by 1.

13. When you finish viewing the System Monitor utility information, close the System Monitor.

Exercise 7.3: Rebuilding the Default Program Groups

Exercise 7.3 shows how to rebuild the default program groups. When you do this, you do not affect any new groups or shortcuts you have created.

1. From the Start menu, choose Run.
2. In the Open field of the Run dialog box, type **GRPCONV**.
3. Click on OK. The default program groups are rebuilt.

Exercise 7.4: Using Microsoft Configuration Backup

In this exercise, you use the Microsoft Configuration Backup utility to create a backup of the System Registry.

1. If the Configuration Backup utility is not already installed, copy it into a folder from the Windows 95 \other\misc folder. Cfgback does not have an installation routine, and consists of only two files: Cfgback.exe and Cfgback.hlp.
2. After you have it in a folder, double-click on the icon, and a screen will appear that tells you about the program. Click on Continue.
3. Another screen appears that tells you to select a unique name for your backup. Click on Continue.
4. A screen tells you whether your machine is set for multiple users, and then tells you that the user data will not be backed up.
5. After naming the backup, click on the Backup button. The program does the rest.

Exercise 7.5: Restoring the Registry Using Microsoft Configuration Backup

In this exercise, you restore the Registry settings you backed up in the preceding exercise.

1. Double-click on the CfgBack icon you created in the preceding exercise.
2. Click on Continue, until you get to the Select Backup Name screen.
3. Select the backup you made in the preceding exercise, and click on Restore. You may get a warning about restoring over a previous backup. (You can click on the Exit button if you do not want to risk it.)
4. When the backup is completed, you will be prompted to restart your machine.

Exercise 7.6 Using the Emergency Recovery Utility

In this exercise, you make a backup of your system files, using the ERU (Emergency Recovery Utility).

1. If you have not already done so, you need to copy the files from \other\misc to the Windows directory.
2. After you have done this, you can run the ERU by double-clicking on the icon.
3. Choose a destination for the files.
4. Click on Next.
5. A listing of files to be saved is presented. You can customize the list, if you wish, by pressing the Custom button and checking or unchecking files as desired.
6. Click on OK. The files copy to the location you selected.

Review Questions

The following questions will test your knowledge of the information in this chapter. For additional questions, see MCP Endeavor and the Microsoft Roadmap/Assessment exam on the CD-ROM that accompanies this book.

1. Your boss comes to you and asks whether you want to belong to Microsoft TechNet. What is Microsoft TechNet?

    A. A CompuServe forum

    B. An Internet forum

    C. A CD-ROM publication

    D. A users group

2. You set up Windows 95 on 10 computers in your company. You want to set up optimization and troubleshooting tools on all these computers. Which three of the following are Windows 95 optimization and troubleshooting tools?

    A. System Resource Monitor

    B. Net Watcher

    C. System Monitor

    D. System Resource Meter

3. Which two of the following statements are true?

    A. System Monitor cannot monitor a remote computer.

    B. A share-level computer cannot monitor a user-level computer using Net Watcher.

    C. System Monitor is located in System Tools in the Accessories group.

    D. System Monitor is located in the System Control Panel applet.

4. You want to optimize all printers connected to your Windows 95 computers. From what you know about Windows 95 printer support, what is the main factor in ensuring print performance?

   A. Spool settings

   B. Driver compatibility

   C. Queue management

   D. Font management

5. Frank prints several documents from the same application and wants to know how Windows 95 spooling affects his wait time. Choosing to return control after the first page is spooled ______ Frank's wait time.

   A. increases

   B. shortens

   C. doesn't change

   D. eliminates

6. While at the help desk, you receive a call from a user who wants to start Windows 95 from a Boot menu item. He doesn't know how to display the Boot menu. You tell him to press ______ while Windows 95 boots.

   A. Ctrl+Alt+Delete

   B. Alt+Tab

   C. F6

   D. F8

7. Which two of the following are disabled in Windows 95 Safe mode?

   A. A 256-color display driver

   B. Control Panel applets

   C. AUTOEXEC.BAT

   D. A non-Microsoft mouse

8. You create a troubleshooting document to circulate around the IT department. One of the issues is about error-isolation switches. Which of the following includes support for a number of error-isolation switches?

   A. BOOT.COM

   B. WINCHK.COM

   C. WIN.COM

   D. WIN95.COM

9. Abby wants to record her boot process to isolate problems with devices not setting correctly. If she uses the Logged mode to log the entire boot process, which file is created?

   A. BOOT.LOG

   B. BOOTLOG.TXT

   C. BOOT.TXT

   D. LOGBOOT.TXT

10. Pierre runs several types of applications under Windows 95, but is having problems with some of them. He asks you what types of applications Windows 95 can run. You tell him which of the following two?

    A. All OS/2 applications

    B. MS-DOS and 16-bit Windows applications

    C. 24-bit Windows applications

    D. 32-bit Windows applications (also known as WIN32 applications; includes most Windows NT software)

11. Windows 95 has many built-in tools that you can use for both optimizing and troubleshooting. Which two of the following are Windows 95 utilities?

    A. System Monitor

    B. System Resource Meter

C. Net Connector

D. Speed Disk

12. In an environment such as Windows 95, a need for careful management of the system's resources exists. When two processes request the use of a device at the exact same moment, what does Windows 95 use to arbitrate such requests?

    A. WIN95.COM

    B. Virtual memory

    C. Virtual Machine Manager

    D. None of these

13. When Peter attempts to use WinCIM 2.01 to dial into CompuServe, he receives an error telling him the port is already busy. He checks and no other applications are running. What could be causing this problem?

    A. Dial-Up Networking Server caller access is enabled.

    B. His modem is not plugged in.

    C. CompuServe's phone line is busy at the moment.

    D. Registry Editor is running.

14. After setting up Windows 95 on a shared networked server, you need to run the Startup disk for it. Where can the Startup files exist for this situation? Choose all that apply.

    A. On a floppy disk

    B. On a local hard drive

    C. On a remote-boot disk image on a server

    D. A and C only

15. You want to optimize the Windows 95 file system. Which two are ways to maximize the use of 32-bit drivers under Windows 95?

    A. Delete all TMP files on your system under Windows 95.

    B. Set the virtual memory settings on the Performance tab of the My Computer Properties sheet to 0% or disable it.

    C. Update any non-Microsoft disk compression to a 32-bit driver from the manufacturer.

    D. Verify that the Performance tab of the My Computer Properties sheet shows all 32-bit components for the file system and for virtual memory.

16. WIN.COM includes support for a number of error-isolation switches. What does the m switch do?

    A. Disables 32-bit file system drivers.

    B. Starts Windows 95 in Safe mode.

    C. Starts Windows 95 in Safe mode with network support.

    D. Excludes the ROM address space between F000 and 1MB from use by Windows 95.

17. Karen starts a print job to a local printer. The print job comes out garbled. What are two possible solutions to fixing this problem?

    A. Resend the print job until it comes out correctly.

    B. Check whether Windows 3.1 printer drivers are being used and update to Windows 95 drivers.

    C. Reduce font size on the document.

    D. Disable EMF spooling.

18. James is using an application that does not work with the Windows 95 TAPI architecture. He discovers that when he tries to use that application with an installed modem, he gets an error message telling him the requested port is still open. What could be causing this error message?

    A. The Dial-Up Server application is enabled on his system.

    B. The serial cable is not tightened to the serial port.

    C. The Enable-TAPI switch is turned on.

    D. None of these.

19. When diagnosing Dial-Up Networking (DUN) problems, you tend to concentrate on protocol issues. Pick the best reason why this is so.

    A. Because DUN cannot use the TCP/IP protocol.

    B. Because the Dial-Up Adapter automatically synchronizes protocols on the client and server sides.

    C. Because the Dial-Up Adapter needs to be configured to use the same protocol as the server-side computer.

    D. All of these.

20. Normally, memory in the 1–4MB range is not used by Windows 95. What is this memory range used for?

    A. MS-DOS applications that need it

    B. Networking applications running as 32-bit applications

    C. TSRs

    D. 16-bit applications that need it

Review Answers

1. C
2. B, C, D
3. B, C
4. A
5. B
6. D
7. A, C
8. C
9. B
10. B, D
11. A, B
12. C
13. A
14. A, B, C
15. C, D
16. B
17. B, D
18. A
19. C
20. D

Answers to Test Yourself Questions at Beginning of Chapter

1. You can follow a number of steps when attempting to isolate technical problems. Some are specific to Windows 95; others are just part of a logical approach to any problem. See the six general ones in "General Troubleshooting Guidelines."
2. System Monitor, Net Watcher, and WinipCfg. See "Diagnose and Resolve Connectivity Problems."
3. Virtual machines. See "Virtual Machines."
4. Update any non-Microsoft disk compression to a 32-bit driver from the manufacturer. And verify that the Performance tab in the My Computer Properties sheet shows all 32-bit components for the file system and for virtual memory. See "Diagnose and Resolve File System Problems."
5. Microsoft TechNet, the Internet, and Online Help. See "Resolve Problems Using Available Technical Resources."
6. Answers can include the following: Normal mode, Logged mode, Safe mode, Safe mode with network support, Step-by-step confirmation, Command-prompt-only mode, Safe mode command prompt, and Previous version of MS-DOS. See "The Boot Menu."
7. f: disables 32-bit file system drivers; m: starts Windows 95 in Safe mode; n: starts Windows 95 in Safe mode with network support; s: excludes the ROM address space between F000 and 1 MB from use by Windows 95; v: disables virtualization of hard disk interrupts; x: disables use of upper memory by Windows 95. See "WIN.COM Switches."
8. Ensure that File and Printer Sharing is enabled at the remote computer; verify that you have correct network protocols configured. See "Diagnose and Resolve Printing Problems."
9. WinIPCfg would be a good one to use in this situation. In addition to your IP address, it gives your default gateway and much more. See "Diagnose and Resolve Connectivity Problems."
10. Remove SHARE.EXE and SMARTDRV.EXE from AUTOEXEC.BAT; Check the IOS.LOG for any Real-mode drivers that might be causing Windows 95 not to use 32-bit file system drivers; Use Windows 95 Disk Defragmenter regularly. See "Diagnose and Resolve File System Problems."

Part 2
Exam Practice

1

Practice Exam

This practice exam is an amalgamation of some of the review questions and pre-chapter quizzes from the chapters within this book. They are arranged in random order and cover all the objectives. This exam tests whether you have learned what you are supposed to from within this book. If you did all the review questions from the chapters, these might look familiar to you. The practice exam uses new questions, also; these, too, are in random order. Answers are located at the end of the exam.

Practice Exam Begins

1. As more and more companies migrate their technical resources to the Internet, locating new drivers and finding technical data on software products is increasingly easy. Name three sources Microsoft recommends for finding technical information.

2. You migrate to Windows 95 on a system that has a 1 GB hard drive. You want to compress part of the drive, but not all of it, to conserve space. What is the maximum size of a compressed volume using the Windows 95 DriveSpace program?

3. Cindy encounters problems during the Windows 95 installation process and needs to troubleshoot the process. Name the three log files Windows 95 created when Cindy ran the Windows 95 Setup program.

4. Which two of the following would be disabled in Windows 95 Safe mode?

   A. A 256-color display driver

   B. Control Panel applets

   C. AUTOEXEC.BAT

   D. A non-Microsoft mouse

5. In a training class you conduct for system administrators, you are asked why the Registry comprises two files. From the following list, what is the best answer to this question?

   A. Makes editing configuration settings safer

   B. Separates user and system information, so Systems policies and user profiles can be created

   C. Allows dynamic information from the hardware tree to be updated while user settings are idle

   D. Enables a user to copy his USER.DAT from a floppy disk to a laptop and maintain the same look and feel as his desktop computer

6. The UNC is supported by Windows 95. What does UNC mean? What two items make up a UNC? Does UNC require a drive-letter assignment?

7. What is required to be on a computer that will be using File and Print Sharing for NetWare Networks?

8. You configure a Windows 95 workstation to connect to a NetWare network. When installing Client for NetWare Networks, Windows 95 automatically installs a protocol. Which protocol is this? Can you change this to another protocol and still access the NetWare server?

9. You configure a Windows 95 workstation to connect to a NetWare network. When installing Client for NetWare Networks, Windows 95 automatically installs a protocol. Which protocol is this? Can you change this to another protocol

and still access the NetWare server? What other networking component might be useful when connecting to a NetWare network?

10. A user asks how she can modify her user profile. She's running a Windows 95 computer that is not connected to a network. What are the general steps for doing this?

11. Beverly upgrades to Windows 95 but does not install the Microsoft Exchange component during the Windows 95 installation process. She asks you whether she can, now that she has Windows 95 running, install Exchange. You tell her she can, but she will have to ________ .

    A. Restart the Windows 95 Setup program again to add a component

    B. Restart the Windows 95 Setup program in Verify mode and then add the component

    C. Use the Add/Remove Programs option in Control Panel

    D. Use the Install Components Wizard from My Computer

    E. Restart the Windows 95 Setup program from scratch and reinstall Windows 95

12. Windows 95 is an advanced operating system that takes advantage of the Intel ring architecture. To understand how Windows 95 uses the ring architecture, you need to understand the rings themselves. Which one of the following rings of the Intel 386 protection model offers the most privileges, including direct communication with the hardware components?

    A. Ring 0

    B. Ring 1

    C. Ring 2

    D. Ring 3

    E. Ring 4

13. Which level of security would be used to base the access rights to shared resources on the Windows 95 computer on a password-assigned basis?

    A. Windows 95 access control

    B. Unified logon process

    C. Windows 95 logon security

    D. Share-level security

    E. User-level security

14. What are some of the factors that should be considered before moving a network over to Windows 95?

15. Stan asks you to define the System Policy Editor and explain why it is useful. Name two features of the System Policy Editor that help you administer Windows 95 workstations.

16. As you instruct a user on how to configure a peer-to-peer network with five Windows 95 computers connected together, you use the term "Windows 95 server" several times. After you finish, he asks you what a Windows 95 server is. What do you tell him?

    A. A computer that is the Primary Domain Controller (PDC) on the LAN

    B. A computer running Windows 95 that has the Enable Windows 95 Server Registry option turned on

    C. A Windows 95 computer that has the File and Printer Sharing Service enabled

    D. A computer running Windows 95 that performs as an application and database server for the LAN

17. As you configure the browse list on a NetWare network, you need to set up the option to have Windows 95 automatically determine whether the computer is needed as a browse server. What is the name of the property?

18. The ring architecture of Intel 386 processes provide different levels of protection and privileges. Windows 95 executes in which two of the following rings of the Intel 386 protection model?

    A. Ring 0

    B. Ring 1

    C. Ring 2

    D. Ring 3

    E. Ring 4

19. What does a master browser do? How is the browse list built?

20. Windows 95 provides ways to optimize the file system. Name three ways you can ensure the highest file system performance.

21. To access the Internet, you need to use Windows 95 Dial-Up Adapter and associated software. Pick three items from the following list that you must have before setting up Windows 95 to access the Internet via Dial-Up Networking.

    A. ISP account

    B. Modem

    C. Gateway information

    D. DNS information

22. Jason is setting up a backup schedule to back up several of his machines. What are four storage media types Windows 95 supports? Also, what is the name of the utility included with Windows 95 that Jason can use to back up his data?

23. You run a network with protocols that support NetBIOS. The registers and resolves NetBIOS names to IP addresses.

    A. DNS Server

    B. IFS Manager

    C. Network Adapter Card

    D. WINS Server

24. Jill uses a computer running Windows 3.11 for Workgroups, with several 16-bit applications installed. She has program groups set up for these applications. When she installs Windows 95, what is one way she can ensure that her application program groups are maintained?

25. When planning to deploy Windows 95 you should ________ . Choose all that apply.

    A. Check all CPU types and peripherals for compatibility

    B. Check all required business applications for compatibility

    C. Purchase installation licenses for Windows 95

    D. Check compatibility with current network servers

    E. Deploy across the company at once to shorten the transition period

    F. Book all employees into training for Windows 95 this month for next year's deployment

26. A user complains that the settings she made to her desktop are not saved each time she logs on to the network and starts Windows 95. You have her computer set up to download a user profile from the server and enable her to save changes to it. What might be one of the causes for her settings not to be saved properly?

A. Her version of Windows 95 needs to be updated.

B. Her workstation's time is not synchronized with the server's time.

C. She does not have the Remote Administration feature enabled.

D. All of these.

27. Which level of security would be used to base the access rights to shared resources on the Windows 95 computer using a user accounts list stored on a Novell NetWare Server?

    A. Windows 95 access control

    B. Unified logon process

    C. Windows 95 logon security

    D. Share-level security

    E. User-level security

28. Jenny wants to gain access to the Internet, but her company does not have a dedicated line to it. How can she, using Windows 95, connect to the Internet?

29. Which two of the following statements are true?

    A. System Monitor cannot monitor a remote computer.

    B. A share-level computer cannot monitor a user-level computer using Net Watcher.

    C. System Monitor is located in System Tools in the Accessories group.

    D. System Monitor is located in the System Control Panel applet.

30. Jennifer runs an MS-DOS–based application under Windows 95. She wants to take advantage of Windows 95 32-bit Protected-mode driver support, preemptive multitasking, and increased conventional memory. Which mode should Jennifer try to run her DOS application in to use these features?

31. When diagnosing Dial-Up Networking (DUN) problems, you tend to concentrate on protocol issues. Pick the best reason why this is so.

    A. Because DUN cannot use the TCP/IP protocol

    B. Because the Dial-Up Adapter automatically synchronizes protocols on the client and server sides

    C. Because the Dial-Up Adapter needs to be configured to use the same protocol as the server-side computer

    D. All of these

32. Your new boss, Don, asks you to recommend a backup strategy for his new Windows 95 machine. He creates a lot of proposals for new business, and as a result has many Excel files and PowerPoint presentations (complete with animation and sound). What do you recommend?

    A. Put in a slave drive, and use it for storage.

    B. Install Windows 95 Backup, and archive to floppy disk.

    C. Install Windows 95 backup, and a tape backup device. Create a full system backup set, and run that once a week. During the week, run an incremental backup set to catch files that change on a daily basis.

    D. Tell him to just save them to disk, and use them whenever he wants to save something.

    E. Tell him it is his computer; he is responsible for coming up with his own backup strategy.

33. Michael administers a Windows NT network that has several Windows 95 workstations attached to the server. He stores user profiles for all workstations on the server to be downloaded during bootup time. The user profiles can be updated by the users. To ensure that each profile is available from the server, where are they stored on the server?

    A. User's home directory

    B. User's C:\WINDOWS directory

    C. Any directory on the server to which the user has Read permission

    D. None of these

34. Windows 95 is being installed from a network server as a server-based setup. What is the name of the server-based setup program you must use to install Windows 95 source files on the network server?

35. You are asked to set up a standalone computer for several different people to access at different times during the day. Which level of security would be used for a standalone computer with multiple users, each of whom has different Windows 95 preferences and desktops?

    A. Windows 95 access control

    B. Unified logon process

    C. Windows 95 logon security

    D. Share-level security

    E. User-level security

36. What is the default name of the system policy file Windows 95 uses? Where is this file stored when a user is using share-level security? Where is this file stored when a user is using user-level security?

37. Eugene creates a PowerPoint slide showing the Windows 95 networking architecture layers. He places a layer called the Network Providers in the slide. Is this the name of a layer in the architecture? If so, what two other layers are adjacent to the Network Providers layer?

38. What are some tasks that can be accomplished through Remote Administration?

39. Name the protocol supported by Windows 95 that is used only for communicating with certain network interface printers and mainframe systems. It also is not used for peer-to-peer networking of Windows 95 computers.

    A. TCP/IP

    B. DLC

    C. IPX/SPX

    D. NetBIOS

40. You are asked to present an overview of the Windows 95 system architecture, including rings. You draw a diagram that points out each ring and its protection level. Which one of the following rings of the Intel 386 protection model offers no processor protection, but instead needs the operating system to provide processor protection?

    A. Ring 0

    B. Ring 1

    C. Ring 2

    D. Ring 3

    E. Ring 4

41. Which three of the following are layers in the Windows 95 networking architecture?

    A. Transport Programming Interface

    B. Internal File System Manager

    C. Device Driver Interface

    D. Network Providers

42. Normally, memory in the 1–4 MB range is not used by Windows 95. What is this memory range used for?

    A. MS-DOS applications that need it

    B. Networking applications running as 32-bit applications

    C. TSRs

    D. 16-bit applications that need it

43. Barney is running the Windows 95 Setup program from MS-DOS. You know there are differences running Setup from DOS and from Windows. Which three of the following are differences between starting the Windows 95 Setup program in MS-DOS versus starting it in Windows?

    A. ScanDisk running in the foreground rather than the background

    B. Searching for Windows version 3.0 versus checking Windows version 3.1 or better

    C. Checking for TSRs versus checking for TSRs and other Windows programs running

    D. System checks done in DOS versus Windows

    E. DOS graphical interface versus Windows graphical interface after starting Protected mode

44. Billie modifies her user profile so that each time she starts Windows 95, a shortcut to her finance spreadsheet displays on the desktop. Which of the following cannot be done by setting user profiles?

    A. Display specific applications in the Start menu.

    B. Customize desktop settings, such as colors and wallpaper.

    C. Install an application only for a specific user.

    D. Display recently used documents in the Start menu Documents folder.

45. Log files are ASCII text files you can use to help troubleshoot problems encountered during installation. Which one of the following log files is *not* used during the Windows 95 installation?

    A. SETUPLOG.TXT

    B. HARDWARE.TXT

    C. DETLOG.TXT

    D. NETLOG.TXT

    E. BOOTLOG.TXT

46. What is the name of the answer file for the Windows 95 setup executable?

47. Windows 95 supports share-level and user-level security. You want to set up Windows 95 on 10 workstations on a network to share printer and file resources, but you want to make sure pass-through authentication is used to validate users who access these resources. Which type of security must you set up?

48. You are working at a help desk when you receive a call from a user. He says he is having difficulty running an MS-DOS application in a DOS virtual machine (VM). You can't give him specific reasons for why his application isn't running, but you can give him some general reasons why a DOS application may not run properly under Windows 95. What are two reasons why a DOS application cannot run in a VM?

49. Isabel is configuring her Windows 95 computer with the TCP/IP protocol. As she fills out the properties for the protocol, she comes across a blank for the DNS entry. What does DNS stand for?

   A. Downloadable Network Share

   B. DOS-Node Server

   C. Domain Name Service

   D. Domain Network Server

50. After setting up Windows 95 on a shared networked server, you need to run the Startup disk for it. Where can the Startup files exist for this situation? Choose all that apply:

   A. On a floppy disk

   B. On a local hard drive

   C. On a remote-boot disk image on a server

   D. A and C only

51. Chuck uses Network Neighborhood to view other computers on the network. What is the name of the list that stores the computers on a network?

52. A coworker sends you e-mail telling you he has Windows 3.1 installed on his laptop at home, but cannot remember the laptop's hardware specifications. To help him, you tell him that the minimum hardware requirements for Windows 95 are _______ the minimum needed for Windows 3.1.

    A. Lower than

    B. The same as

    C. Higher than

    D. No different than

    E. Approximately the same as

53. Jill wants to create two user profiles for her computer, one named WORK and the other named GAMES. How does she enable user profiles on her computer?

54. Which of the following statements about Systems policies is *not* true?

    A. Systems policy files can be stored on local hard drives.

    B. Policy files can be stored on either NetWare server, or Windows NT Domain controllers.

    C. Policy files are created from template files.

    D. To fully implement policies, User Profiles must be enabled.

    E. The name that must be given to the default policy file is CONFIG.POL.

55. Adam starts Windows 95 from the command prompt and uses WIN.COM command switches to control the way Windows 95 starts. What three of the following command switches can Adam use with the Windows 95 Setup program?

    A. /?

    B. /B

C. /ID

D. /D

E. /IS

56. On the "minimal" computer, as defined by Microsoft, the performance of Windows 95 should be _______ or using Windows 3.1 with the same hardware. Choose two.

    A. Worse than

    B. About the same as

    C. Possibly improve over

    D. Much faster than

    E. Twice as fast as

57. In which of the following rings of the Intel 386 protection model do the MS-DOS, Windows 16-bit, and Windows 32-bit applications run?

    A. Ring 0

    B. Ring 1

    C. Ring 2

    D. Ring 3

    E. Ring 4

58. While stationed at the company help desk, you receive a call from a user accessing the Internet. He asks what a fully qualified domain name is. From the following list, pick the one that would *not* meet this criterion.

    A. www.microsoft.com

    B. www3.iquest.net

    C. www.microsoft_com

    D. www.mcp.com\newriders

59. The modular architecture of Windows 95 includes the Installable File Service (IFS) Manager. The IFS Manager manages communication between which three of the following?

    A. The miniport driver

    B. The various Installable File Systems

    C. The network provider

    D. The network redirectors and services

60. Describe the six general steps to troubleshooting problems in Windows 95.

61. Which of the following does *not* have to be enabled for Remote Registry Editing to be implemented?

    A. The Remote Registry Editing Service must be installed on both computers.

    B. File and Print Sharing must be installed on the target computer.

    C. Share-level security must be enabled.

    D. The editor must be on the target Remote Administration list.

62. What is the primary purpose of a Windows 95 Systems policy?

    A. Limit the ability of users to customize their environments

    B. Increase the ability of users to customize their environments

    C. Make the system run more efficiently

    D. Make the system more adaptable

63. While setting up Windows 95 to access the Internet, you find that connections over TCP/IP by host don't work, but connections by IP number do. What could be wrong? In what two ways can Windows 95 get the information necessary to resolve fully qualified domain names to IP addresses?

64. Missy has Windows 95 installed on her computer. When she boots her computer, it usually starts Windows 95. One day, however, Windows 95 fails to start and her computer displays the Startup menu. Name the Startup menu option Missy needs to select to start Windows and display each Startup file line by line.

65. Martina has been told that she can run multiple network clients under Windows 95, but is having problems getting this feature to work on her system. She calls you and asks you to help her. From the following list, what would be the best question to ask to start diagnosing her problem?

   A. Does she have protocols for IPX/SPX set up?

   B. Is Windows 95 set up to handle user profiles?

   C. Is there a Primary Domain Controller (PDC) established on a Windows 95 server?

   D. Are all the network clients 32-bit clients?

66. You're conducting a training session teaching other users how to run applications under Windows 95. You are asked to describe the way Windows 95 runs MS-DOS applications. What are the three ways MS-DOS applications can run under Windows 95?

67. The naming standards for _______ are all the same: limited to 15 characters, no embedded spaces, and can contain these special characters:

   ! @ # $ % & ( ) - _ ' { } ` .

   A. User's full name

   B. Default user's name

   C. Computer name

   D. Workgroup name

   E. Computer description

68. Windows 95 includes networking features to make it easier for users to connect to existing networks or to build a network from the ground up. Which three networking protocols included with Windows 95 are Plug and Play–enabled? Which two protocols are installed by default by Windows 95?

69. For a PowerPoint presentation in front of the help desk staff, you create a slide with a bullet point describing the Windows 95 System Policy feature. Select the response that best completes this sentence: A Windows 95 Systems policy ________ .

    A. Assigns priorities to applications accessing memory

    B. Assigns priorities to users

    C. Enables an administrator to set various Windows 95 Registry entries

    D. Is a summary of configuration details

70. You want to install Windows 95 on a Novell NetWare network that includes NetWare 4.x servers. Which two of the following network components might you need?

    A. Microsoft Client for NetWare Networks

    B. Microsoft NDS service

    C. File and Print Sharing for Microsoft Networks

    D. NetBEUI protocol

    E. TCP/IP protocol

71. The time zone option is used to set up your computer's clock and maintain proper settings during the spring and fall. You are asked to enter a time zone for the computer during which part of running the Windows 95 Setup program?

    A. Initial startup and Setup Wizard load

    B. Gathering user and computer information

    C. Copying Windows 95 files

D. Restarting the computer and finishing Setup

E. After Windows 95 is completely installed

72. You are responsible for connecting Windows 95 to a heterogeneous network. You're running a number of different network operating systems on this large network and want to be sure Windows 95 is compatible with them. Windows 95 includes software to support which three of the following networks?

    A. Banyan VINES

    B. DEC Pathworks

    C. Novell NetWare

    D. Apple AppleShare

73. As administrator you need to set up a training classroom so that all student computers running Windows 95 on a network have one default setting. Each time the computer is booted, you want this default setting to be invoked, regardless of any previous changes made by a user. Name two ways you can set up these computers to use a default setting at each bootup.

74. What file is replaced or copied for every user who maintains a user profile on a computer, and what directory is it stored in?

75. Elizabeth sets up Windows 95 to connect to a Windows NT network. She wants to be able to share files and printers with other users on the network. What type of security must she install? Also, can she assign file-level rights?

76. What are the advantages of share-level security? User-level security?

77. Lynn wants to upgrade to Windows 95, but also needs to boot into MS-DOS (her existing operating system) at times. The Windows 95 option to boot into the previous version of MS-DOS is available only if upgrading from which version of MS-DOS or better?

A. MS-DOS 3.2

B. MS-DOS 3.3

C. MS-DOS 4.0

D. MS-DOS 5.0

E. MS-DOS 6.0

78. Within its System Services, Windows 95 uses a combination of 32-bit and 16-bit code to run applications. In which of the following rings of the Intel 386 protection model do the System Services run?

    A. Ring 0

    B. Ring 1

    C. Ring 2

    D. Ring 3

    E. Ring 4

79. You have Windows 95 installed on a computer connected to a network running only one network operating system (NOS). A user calls and says she cannot browse network resources using Network Neighborhood. Which NOS could you be running that does not support browser services?

    A. Novell NetWare 3.12

    B. Banyan VINES

    C. Windows NT

    D. None of these

80. WIN.COM includes support for a number of error-isolation switches. What does the m switch do?

    A. Disables 32-bit file system drivers

    B. Starts Windows 95 in Safe mode

C. Starts Windows 95 in Safe mode with network support

D. Excludes the ROM address space between F000 and 1 MB from use by Windows 95

81. Mike is installing a modem on his new Windows 95 machine, and calls and tells you he is certain he has selected the correct modem, but it just is not working. What do you tell him?

A. Get on the Internet and download a new driver

B. Try a different COM port

C. See whether Windows 95 will autodetect it

D. Try a different computer

E. Try a different modem

82. You are a systems administrator in a company that migrated to Windows 95. Many users still use MS-DOS applications and must run them under Windows. Because of some compatibility problems with the older DOS applications, you customize the DOS-mode applications. What command is added to the CONFIG.SYS when you run a customized MS-DOS–mode application?

A. DOS=Custom

B. MODE=DOSCUST

C. DOS=CMODE

D. DOS=SINGLE

83. Teresa chooses to keep program groups and system settings from her previous Windows 3.1 installation when upgrading to Windows 95. To migrate program groups and system settings when upgrading from Windows 3.x to Windows 95, which of the following should Teresa do? Choose the best answer:

A. Upgrade into a new Windows 95 directory

B. Upgrade into an existing Windows directory

C. Copy group and initialization files into a new Windows 95 directory

D. Copy older DLL files into the new Windows 95 directory

E. Run GRPCONV to convert older program groups into folders

84. What are the two minimum pieces of configuration information required for the TCP/IP protocol, and what are two other items that are nice to include?

85. Which of the following questions should be considered before granting Internet access to users on the network? Select all that apply.

    A. Will they have local File and Print Sharing installed?

    B. Will the network have a firewall enabled?

    C. What network protocols will they have installed?

    D. Will they have dial-up or LAN access to the Internet?

    E. Which Web sites will they be accessing?

86. The Windows 95 installation process is modular. Name the four logical phases to the Windows 95 installation process.

87. Blake is migrating from Windows 3.1 to Windows 95. He wants to run MS-DOS applications in DOS mode under Windows 95. What are two disadvantages to running applications in DOS mode?

88. Which of the following utilities are most useful in tracking down TCP/IP connection problems?

    A. Ping

    B. Arp

    C. WINIPCFG

    D. Net use

89. You want to optimize the Windows 95 file system. What are two ways to maximize the use of 32-bit drivers under Windows 95?

90. You are installing Windows 95 on a computer that currently has MS-DOS 5.0 and Windows 3.1. What is the lowest Intel processor you can have in this computer to install Windows 95?

91. Windows 95 can run applications in Virtual Machine. The Virtual Machine Manager is used to manage these applications. In which of the following rings of the Intel 386 protection model does the Virtual Machine Manager run?

   A. Ring 0

   B. Ring 1

   C. Ring 2

   D. Ring 3

   E. Ring 4

92. A device is not working when you boot Windows 95, so you decide to run the Safe Mode option when you boot Windows 95. In Safe mode, Windows 95 loads which three of the following device drivers?

   A. CD-ROM

   B. Mouse

   C. Keyboard

   D. Sound

   E. VGA

93. Name one advantage and one disadvantage of using user-level security. Name one advantage and one disadvantage of using share-level security.

94. When opening the Network Neighborhood, what icons should you see?

95. You are asked to connect 10 Windows 95 computers to a Novell NetWare network. From the following list, pick the two components or features that Windows 95 has for NetWare networks.

    A. Capability to run File and Printer Sharing for NetWare with File and Printer Sharing with Microsoft Networks

    B. Share-level Security support of File and Printer Sharing for NetWare

    C. IPX/SPX-compatible protocol

    D. 32-bit Client for NetWare Networks

96. When Peter attempts to use WinCIM 2.01 to dial into CompuServe, he receives an error telling him the port is already busy. He finds that no other applications are running. What could be causing this problem?

    A. Dial-Up Networking Server caller access is enabled.

    B. His modem is not plugged in.

    C. CompuServe's phone line is busy at the moment.

    D. Registry Editor is running.

97. Windows 95 includes networking features to make it easier for users to connect to existing networks or to build a network from the ground up. Which three networking protocols included with Windows 95 are Plug and Play–enabled? Which two protocols are installed by default by Windows 95?

98. Sally likes to run multiple applications simultaneously under Windows 95. She has one 32-bit application running, one MS-DOS application running, and two 16-bit applications running. How many virtual machines is Windows 95 running? Explain.

99. Not all processors available can run Windows 95. Windows 95 will run on the ________ processor.

    A. Intel 286

    B. Intel 386 and higher

    C. DEC Alpha

    D. PowerPC

    E. MIPS

100. Windows 95 is designed to run over a NetWare network, but there are some disadvantages to using Microsoft's Client for NetWare. Name two.

101. User profiles provide a high level of security for a computer because ________ .

    A. They enforce Registry settings as users log on to networks.

    B. They are stored in network locations that users have no access to, making editing and changing them secure.

    C. They do provide security.

102. You have Windows 95 installed on a computer connected to a network running only one network operating system (NOS). A user calls and says she cannot browse network resources using Network Neighborhood. Which NOS could you be running that does not support browser services?

    A. Novell NetWare 3.12

    B. Banyan VINES

    C. Windows NT

    D. None of these

103. Windows 95 provides different installation types. Which one of the following is not a Windows 95 Setup type of installation?

A. Custom

B. Compact

C. Express

D. Typical

E. Portable

104. As system administrator, you set up each user's computer so that a user cannot start an MS-DOS prompt from within Windows 95. How can this be done?

A. Use the System Policy Editor, open the Default User Properties sheet, click on System, click on Restrictions, and select the Disable MS-DOS Prompt check box.

B. Use the System Policy Editor, open the Default User Properties sheet, click on System, click on Restrictions, and deselect the Enable MS-DOS Prompt check box.

C. Use the System Policy Editor, open the Default User Properties sheet, click on System, and select the MS-DOS Prompt check box.

D. Use the System Policy Editor, open the Default User Properties sheet, click on System, click on Restrictions, and select the Disable Single-Mode MS-DOS Applications check box.

105. Larry, a system administrator, must set up Windows 95 on 10 computers that are not connected to a network. He must perform a manual installation process on each machine, but he wants to automate the process as much as possible using a custom setup script. What is the name of the file on which Larry needs to base his setup scripts?

106. In a training class you are teaching, you explain to end users how to use UNC to access resources on the network. You provide this example to the class: What is the full UNC path for a file named test.bat in a directory named BATCH located in a share named PUBLIC on a server named FREDSPC? Select the correct answer.

   A. \\PUBLIC\BATCH\test.bat

   B. \\FREDSPC\BATCH\test.bat

   C. \\FREDSPC\PUBLIC\BATCH\test.bat

   D. None of these

107. You are presented with the problem of not being able to print to a network printer from a Windows 95 computer. What are two possible solutions for correcting it?

108. Susan prepares for a presentation describing the Windows 95 network architecture. One of the bullet points is this: A maps network names used by an application to a physical network device name. Pick the appropriate answer to fill in the blank.

   A. Device driver

   B. Redirector

   C. Requestor

   D. Transport interface

109. Steve runs several 32-bit applications at the same time under Windows 95. What is the name of the type of multitasking that Windows 95 uses?

   A. Cooperative

   B. Cohabitive

   C. Preemptive

   D. Presumptive

   E. Shared

110. A user calls you while you are manning a help desk. He asks how his MS-DOS program and Windows 95 will work together in MS-DOS mode. You tell him that in MS-DOS mode Windows 95________ .

   A. Unloads itself from memory

   B. Remains in memory

   C. Runs the application in Protected mode

   D. Can multithread multiple DOS sessions

111. The benefits of implementing user-level security include which of the following? Select all that apply.

   A. People connecting to the computer will each require a secure password. This password will be unique for each user.

   B. Passwords are validated at the Windows 95 computer.

   C. No additional information has to be given to users; their current network username and passwords are used to validate when connecting.

   D. Passwords are validated through a separate server.

112. Windows 95 includes several networking protocols. Which three of the following networking protocols included with Windows 95 are Plug and Play–enabled?

   A. Ethernet

   B. TCP/IP

   C. NetBEUI

   D. Token Ring

   E. IPX/SPX

113. Graphics Unlimited is upgrading five computers to Windows 95. The company must decide which media type to purchase

to be able to upgrade all its computers. Which three of the following installation options are available for Windows 95?

A. From 5.25-inch floppy

B. From 3.5-inch floppy

C. From CD-ROM

D. From the network

E. From optical disk

114. WIN.COM includes support for a number of error-isolation switches. These switches are as follows: f, m, n, s, v, x. Name what each of these switches does.

115. John runs several applications at once on his Windows 95 computer. Which of the following applications do not run in separate, private, virtual machines?

A. Windows 32-bit

B. Windows 16-bit

C. MS-DOS

D. All of these

E. None of these

116. You receive a call while stationed at the company help desk. The caller says she is trying to save her long filenames to the NetWare server but the server does not support them. What do you have to do to enable NetWare to support long filenames?

117. The Startup disk is used in case you experience problems with your Windows 95 installation. You are asked to remove the newly created Startup disk during which part of running the Windows 95 Setup program?

A. Initial startup and Setup Wizard load

B. Gathering user and computer information

C. Copying Windows 95 files

D. Restarting the computer and finishing Setup

E. After Windows 95 is completely installed

118. A user says that a 16-bit application she is running under Windows 95 hangs. She doesn't know what to do to remedy the situation. What are the steps she needs to take to return the system to normal operations?

119. A law office with 15 desktop computers are networked using Windows NT Server on one server. The partners want to ensure that their new operating system for the 15 desktop computers (either Windows 95 or Windows NT Workstation) provides file-level security. Which operating system should the law office adopt?

120. Steve is connecting his Windows 95 computer to a network running Novell NetWare. He wants to share files and a printer with other users. Can he do this? If so, what type of security must he use?

121. Remote Administration can be enabled:

A. On all computers on the network, regardless of whether they have File and Print Services.

B. Through the Passwords Control Panel

C. Through the Network Control Panel

D. Through the Remote Administration Control Panel

E. Only on computers using the Client for Microsoft Networks

122. Stuart is attaching his Windows 95 computer to another Windows 95 computer using the Microsoft Network. He wants to provide access from one computer to the other so that each computer has access to files and printers on either machine. What must he do to enable this in Windows 95?

A. Set up user-level security

B. Disable File and Printer Sharing for Microsoft Networks

C. Set up share-level security

D. All of these

123. Jason installs a network adapter card on a computer running Windows 95. When he does this, Windows 95 automatically installs two protocols for this card. Which two protocols are installed by default when the first network adapter driver is installed?

A. AppleTalk

B. NetBEUI

C. TCP/IP

D. IPX/SPX-compatible

124. The Virtual Machine Manager provides several services, including memory management, task scheduling, and DOS-mode support. Every time you open an MS-DOS application, the count of the number of virtual machines running under Windows 95 __________ .

A. Decreases by two

B. Decreases by one

C. Stays the same

D. Increases by one

E. Increases by two

125. During a training session, you are asked to describe the Startup disk. Which two of the following statements are true about the Windows 95 Startup disk?

A. It can be created only during a Windows 95 installation.

B. It needs a preformatted floppy disk at the start.

C. It enables you to boot to the Windows 95 command prompt.

D. It includes CD-ROM drivers, if needed.

E. It enables you to troubleshoot your Registry files.

126. You want to optimize the Windows 95 file system. Which two are ways to maximize the use of 32-bit drivers under Windows 95?

A. Delete all TMP files on your system under Windows 95.

B. Set the Virtual Memory settings on the Performance tab of the My Computer Properties sheet to 0% or disable it.

C. Update any non-Microsoft disk compression to a 32-bit driver from the manufacturer.

D. Verify that the Performance tab of the My Computer Properties sheet shows all 32-bit components for the file system and for virtual memory.

127. You are asked to connect 10 Windows 95 computers to a Novell NetWare network. From the following list, pick the two components or features that Windows 95 has for NetWare networks.

A. Capability to install File and Printer Sharing for NetWare with File and Printer Sharing with Microsoft Networks

B. Share-level support of File and Printer Sharing for NetWare

C. IPX/SPX-compatible protocol

D. 32-bit Client for NetWare Networks

128. Leslie has several MS-DOS applications she runs under Windows 95. She wants to optimize the way they run under

Windows 95, as well as run 32-bit applications simultaneously with her DOS applications. If possible, you advise her it is best to run MS-DOS applications in _______.

A. MS-DOS mode

B. Customized MS-DOS mode

C. A WIN16 VM

D. An MS-DOS VM

129. Windows 95 provides compatibility with many of today's existing computers. Before installing Windows 95 on a computer, make sure it has a processor that can run it. The lowest Intel processor recommended by Microsoft to run Windows 95 is _______.

A. 80286

B. 80386SX

C. 80386DX

D. 80486

E. Pentium

130. What is the name of the default template file that ships with the System Policy Editor, and what program do you use to edit the template file?

131. The preferred method for running the Windows 95 Setup program is from within _______ and _______.

A. MS-DOS

B. MS Windows 3.1x

C. An MS-DOS window inside Windows

D. MS Windows for Workgroups 3.x

E. A bootable floppy

132. With Windows 95, what methods can you use to resolve NetBIOS names?

133. Windows 95 supports share-level and user-level security. You want to set up Windows 95 on 10 workstations on a network to share printer and file resources, but you want to make sure pass-through authentication is used to validate users who access these resources. Which type of security must you set up?

134. Taylor receives a General Protection Fault (GPF) when running a 32-bit application under Windows 95. She thought Windows 95 was exempt from having these. You explain to her that 32-bit applications do have GPFs, but they differ from 16-bit and DOS-based applications because they do not cause problems with other programs when you terminate them. Why is this?

135. You want to optimize all printers connected to your Windows 95 computers. From what you know about Windows 95 printer support, what is the main factor in ensuring print performance?

    A. Spool settings

    B. Driver compatibility

    C. Queue management

    D. Font management

136. Jack experiences problems with his laptop computer during the Windows 95 installation process, and cannot get Windows 95 to install. You advise him to examine which three of the following key files to troubleshoot the Windows 95 installation process?

    A. SETUPLOG.TXT

    B. HARDWARE.TXT

C. DETLOG.TXT

D. NETLOG.TXT

E. BOOTLOG.TXT

137. Windows 95 uses two types of memory: physical and virtual. Virtual memory is comprised of which two of the following components?

A. ROM

B. RAM

C. VMM

D. A swap file

E. A page table

138. Sharon uses a computer at work that runs Windows 95. Her computer at home does not have Windows 95 installed yet; she asks you how much RAM she needs in her computer to install Windows 95. You tell her the minimum amount of RAM that Windows 95 requires is ________.

A. 2 MB

B. 4 MB

C. 8 MB

D. 14 MB

E. 16 MB

139. How must a computer be configured for Remote Registry Editing to take place?

140. While stationed at the company help desk, you receive a call from a user accessing the Internet. He asks what a fully qualified domain name is. From the following list, pick the one that would not meet this criterion.

   A. www.microsoft.com

   B. www3.iquest.net

   C. www.microsoft_com

   D. www.mcp.com\newriders

141. The naming standards for ________ are all the same: limited to 15 characters, embedded spaces are not recommended, and can contain these special characters:

   ! @ # $ % & ( ) - _ ' { } × .

   A. User's full name

   B. Default user's name

   C. Computer name

   D. Workgroup name

   E. Computer description

142. You are setting up Windows 95 in a school's computer lab, which does not have a CD-ROM drive available. You know there are extra files on the CD-ROM version of Windows 95 and want to persuade the school administration to purchase a new CD-ROM drive. From the following list, choose the three differences in the Windows 95 upgrade between the floppy version of Windows 95 and the CD-ROM version.

   A. Windows Tour

   B. What's New

   C. Full online help

   D. Accessibility options

   E. Administrative extras

143. It's important for your users to understand how 16-bit applications are handled by Windows 95. Which of the following is true?

   A. WIN16 applications do not access the Registry.

   B. WIN16 applications do not use the System VM.

   C. WIN16 applications support multithreading.

   D. Each WIN16 application has its own message queue.

144. Your boss Billy is running Windows NT 4.0 with Service Pack 3 installed. His computer is configured with a single NTFS partition for security reasons. He has 400 MB of free space, and wants to be able to dual boot Windows 95 to run an old accounting package that is incompatible with Windows NT. He calls you in and asks you to do it while he goes to lunch—that gives you exactly one hour. What do you tell him?

   A. No problem. In fact, if you wait 15 minutes, I will join you for lunch.

   B. No problem, however, you had better go ahead. I will join you in about 45 minutes.

   C. It is impossible. It cannot be done.

   D. I want to get a good backup first, and then I will boot up off of an MS-DOS disk, and start the installation. But I am afraid it will take me a couple of hours.

   E. It would be easier to add a second drive, and format it as FAT and then do the install. But, I still want to make sure I have a good backup, and a current ERD. I can do it, but it will take me a couple of hours after we get the second drive.

145. When installing TCP/IP, it is recommended that a default gateway be configured for the Windows 95 client. What does a gateway do?

146. What is the relationship between user profiles and Systems policies?

147. Linda is considering upgrading from Windows 3.x to Windows 95. She is not sure how to justify the upgrade based on application support because Windows 3.x, like Windows 95, supports multitasking. However, you explain the differences between how 16-bit applications and 32-bit applications support multitasking. You tell her that WIN16 applications use multitasking.

   A. Fault-tolerant

   B. Preemptive

   C. Cooperative

   D. Real-mode

148. Which three of the following are layers in the Windows 95 networking architecture?

   A. Transport Programming Interface

   B. Internal File System Manager

   C. Device Driver Interface

   D. Network Providers

149. By pressing the F8 key when Windows 95 boots, you can access the Boot menu. Name at least five of the options on this menu.

150. When putting together a company report for upgrading to Windows 95, you must list those computers in the company that will not run Windows 95. Windows 95 will not run on which two of the following types of Intel 386 processors?

   A. 386SX (with 16-bit I/O buffers)

   B. 386DX B-Step Processor

   C. 386DX Non-B-Step Processor

   D. 386DX with ID 0303

   E. 386DX with ID other than 0303

151. Third-party developers can create file systems that extend the capabilities of Windows 95. A key feature of Windows 95 that allows this and enables Windows 95 to adapt easily to future technological developments is its ________.

   A. Preemptive multitasking

   B. VCACHE cache subsystem

   C. Modular design

   D. Peer-to-peer networking support

152. When installing a modem on a Windows 95 machine, you must always give it what piece of information?

   A. The maker of the modem

   B. The speed of the modem

   C. The name of the driver to use

   D. The COM port to use

   E. The number to turn off Call Waiting

153. Martina has been told that she can run multiple network clients under Windows 95, but is having problems getting this feature to work on her system. She calls you and asks you to help her. From the following list, what would be the best question to ask to start diagnosing her problem?

   A. Does she have protocols for IPX/SPX set up?

   B. Is Windows 95 set up to handle user profiles?

   C. Is there a Primary Domain Controller (PDC) established on a Windows 95 Server?

   D. Are all the network clients 32-bit clients?

154. When installing TCP/IP, it is recommended that a default gateway be configured for the Windows 95 client. What does a gateway do?

155. In your office, you have a single network with multiple network protocols running on it. Because users may need to log on to several networks at boot time, you want to use the Unified Logon feature in Windows 95. To use Unified Logon, the ________ for all networks must be the same.

A. Network operating systems

B. Topologies

C. Network protocols

D. Passwords

156. In a training class you are teaching, you explain to end users how to use UNC to access resources on the network. You provide this example to the class: What is the full UNC path for a file named test.bat in a directory named BATCH located in a share named PUBLIC on a server named FREDSPC? Select the correct answer.

A. \\PUBLIC\BATCH\test.bat

B. \\FREDSPC\BATCH\test.bat

C. \\FREDSPC\PUBLIC\BATCH\test.bat

D. None of these

157. You are installing Windows 95 as a server-based setup from a computer that has Windows 95 installed. Running the ________ program (and parameters) does the Windows 95 Administrative Setup.

A. Setup /a

B. Setup /n

C. Setup /as

D. Netsetup

E. Batch

158. You are responsible for training users on the Windows 95 Installable File System (IFS). You create a diagram to display the different component of it. Which three of the following are components of the IFS?

    A. I/O Supervisor

    B. VFAT file system driver

    C. TSD Supervisor

    D. CDFS file system driver

159. Windows 95 enables you to create a Startup disk to help you recover from problems. The Startup disk contains all the following files *except* ______.

    A. IO.SYS

    B. MSDOS.SYS

    C. COMMAND.COM

    D. CONFIG.SYS

    E. REGEDIT.EXE

160. In an environment such as Windows 95, a need for careful management of the system's resources exists. When two processes request the use of a device at the exact same moment, how does Windows 95 arbitrate such requests?

161. You run a network using NetBIOS. The _______ registers and resolves NetBIOS names to IP addresses.

    A. DNS Server

    B. IFS Manager

    C. Network Adapter Card

    D. WINS Server

162. Windows 95 uses swap files as virtual memory storage. As a rule of thumb, the amount of RAM on a Windows 95 computer and the amount of free space needed for a swap file should total at least ________ .

    A. 2 MB

    B. 4 MB

    C. 8 MB

    D. 14 MB

    E. 16 MB

163. Typically, applications running under Windows 95 do so at a specific Ring level. The operating system runs at a specific Ring level as well. This way, applications do not have access to critical system functions. Which of the following is true about rings?

    A. Most Windows 95 applications run in Ring 3.

    B. Most operating system components run in Ring 3.

    C. Windows 95 uses all Intel rings.

    D. Windows 95 uses only Rings 1, 2, and 3.

164. Stuart is attaching his Windows 95 computer directly to another Windows 95 computer using Microsoft Networking. He wants to provide access from one computer to the other so that each computer has access to files and printers on either machine. Which of the following must he do to enable this in Windows 95? Choose all that apply:

    A. Set up user-level security

    B. Install File and Printer Sharing for Microsoft Networks on both computers

    C. Set up share-level security

    D. All of these

165. Do all servers support long filenames? If not, what types of servers do not?

166. The modular architecture of Windows 95 includes the Installable File Service (IFS) Manager. The IFS Manager manages communication between which three of the following answers?

A. The miniport driver

B. The various Installable File Systems

C. The network provider

D. The network redirectors and services

167. You are responsible for connecting Windows 95 to a heterogeneous network. You're running a number of different network operating systems on this large network and want to be sure Windows 95 is compatible with them. Windows 95 includes software to support which three of the following networks?

A. Banyan VINES

B. DEC Pathworks

C. Novell NetWare

D. Apple AppleShare

168. James is using an application that does not work with the Windows 95 TAPI architecture. He discovers that when he tries to use that application with an installed modem, he gets an error message telling him the requested port is still open. What could be causing this error message?

A. The Dial-Up Server application is enabled on his system.

B. The serial cable is not tightened to the serial port.

C. The Enable-TAPI switch is turned on.

D. None of these.

169. On a diagram showing the IFS, you point out the role for each of the components. Which one of the following components is responsible for the insertion and removal of media?

    A. Drive Controller

    B. IFS Manager

    C. System Driver Supervisor

    D. Volume Tracker

170. A batch script file can be used in which three of the following Windows 95 installations?

    A. From the Windows 95 3.5-inch floppy disks

    B. From CD-ROM

    C. From the network

    D. From thc local hard drive

    E. From 5.25-inch floppy disk

171. As system administrator, you're bringing up the entire department on a single-server Windows NT network. For workstations, you're going to use the Windows 95 Client. You also want to set up user-level security on the Windows 95 Client. When you set up Windows NT, what should you remember to do to make sure user-level security will work?

172. You are prompted for username and company name during which part of running the Windows 95 Setup program?

    A. Initial startup and Setup Wizard load

    B. Gathering user and computer information

    C. Copying Windows 95 files

    D. Restarting the computer and finishing Setup

    E. After Windows 95 is completely installed

173. You are configuring TCP/IP on Windows 95 and have just put in the IP address 135.33.45.5. What is the default subnet mask?

    A. 255.0.0.0

    B. 255.255.0.0

    C. 255.255.255.0

    D. 255.255.255.255

174. The minimum amount of RAM recommended for running Microsoft Exchange Inbox, Microsoft Network, or multiple 32-bit Windows-based applications is ________ .

    A. 2 MB

    B. 4 MB

    C. 8 MB

    D. 14 MB

    E. 16 MB

175. UNC is supported by Windows 95. What does UNC mean? What two items make up a UNC? Does UNC require a drive-letter assignment?

176. Stephanie is using an older version of Windows and wants to know whether she can use an older CD-ROM drive with Windows 95. You tell her yes. However, you tell her that a drive accessed through ______ cannot take advantage of the 32-bit VFAT.

    A. Protected-mode drivers

    B. Real-mode drivers

    C. Virtual device drivers

    D. Network redirector file system drivers

177. Windows 95 performs four logical phases during the Windows 95 Setup routine. Which one of the following is not a logical phase in the Windows 95 installation?

    A. Startup and information gathering

    B. Hardware detection

    C. Software detection

    D. File copy

    E. Final system configuration

178. Windows 95 has many built-in tools you can use for both optimizing and troubleshooting. Which two of the following are Windows 95 utilities?

    A. System Monitor

    B. System Resource Meter

    C. Net Connector

    D. Speed Disk

179. Tom is setting up Windows 95 on his laptop. He wants to use the Portable setup option, but doesn't know which option is the default setup type. Which one of the following is the default Windows 95 setup type of installation?

    A. Custom

    B. Compact

    C. Express

    D. Typical

    E. Portable

180. VCACHE is an upgrade to Smartdrive and is used for read-ahead and lazy-write (or write-behind) caching. VCACHE is

used by all Windows 95 file system drivers except _______ file system drivers.

A. CDFS

B. VFAT

C. Network redirector

D. SCSI

181. Marcus upgrades his MS-DOS computer to Windows 95. When installing over an MS-DOS–based operating system, Windows 95 will only install on a computer with an operating system equivalent to _______ or better.

A. MS-DOS 3.2

B. MS-DOS 3.3

C. MS-DOS 4.0

D. MS-DOS 5.0

E. MS-DOS 6.0

182. Windows 95 has a modular, layered architecture. Which two of the following are interfaces functioning at the Windows 95 Application Interface layer?

A. Win32 WinNet Interface

B. WinNet 16

C. HP JetAdmin

D. Win32 Print Applicator Programming Interface

183. The Windows 95 Protected Mode feature has the capability to regulate the behavior of multitasking process in two ways. One way is through graduated levels of processor privilege, commonly called Rings. In the Intel ring protection scheme, Ring _____ allows complete control of the processor.

A. 1

B. 0

C. 3

D. 4

184. You want to boot your computer and have the Windows 95 Startup menu display. Which Function key enables you to see the Startup menu when Windows 95 is first booting?

A. F1

B. F4

C. F5

D. F6

E. F8

185. You want to install Windows 95 on a Novell NetWare network. Which two of the following are advantages of Microsoft Client for NetWare Networks as opposed to Novell's NETX workstation software?

A. Microsoft Client for NetWare Networks enables you to use TSR applications loaded from DOS.

B. Microsoft Client for NetWare Networks runs in Protected mode and thus does not use any conventional memory.

C. Microsoft Client for NetWare Networks allows additional network clients to be used at the same time.

D. Microsoft Client for NetWare Networks supports the ArcNet protocols.

186. Before you begin upgrading the computers in your company, you send an e-mail asking all users to check the version of MS-DOS on their computers and to report back to you their

findings. To check the version of DOS on their computers, you tell them to execute the _______ command at the DOS prompt.

A. Setver

B. Winver

C. Dosver

D. Ver

E. Getver

187. Brenda saves her files under Windows 95 in long filename format. She asks you to explain how Windows 95 will save the file as a short filename. You tell her, for example, that the auto-generated alias for the long filename The Departmental Budget.wks is _______.

A. THEDEPAR.~1

B. THEDEP~1.WKS

C. THEDEP~1

D. BUDGET~1.WKS

188. Janet is installing a new printer on her Windows 95 computer. She calls and asks you what she has to do to make sure whenever she prints she will go to that printer. What do you tell her?

A. It will just go wherever it wants to go. I do not guarantee anything.

B. Do nothing; the last printer installed is always the default.

C. Make sure you select it prior to printing.

D. Plug and Play will know it is where you want to print.

E. Make sure you select Set as Default when installing the printer.

189. Chuck is setting up a network to use user-level security. From the following list, pick the two places where the user list can be stored.

   A. Windows NT domain

   B. Windows 95 home directory

   C. NetWare binary server

   D. Banyan VINES server

190. TSRs are known to cause problems when you install Windows 95. You are asked to unload any detected TSRs during which part of running the Windows 95 Setup program?

   A. Initial startup and Setup Wizard load

   B. Gathering user and computer information

   C. Copying Windows 95 files

   D. Restarting the computer and finishing Setup

   E. After Windows 95 is completely installed

191. Karen starts a print job to a local printer. The print job comes out garbled. What are two possible solutions to fixing this problem?

   A. Resend the print job until it comes out correctly

   B. Check whether Windows 3.1 printer drivers are being used and update to Windows 95 drivers

   C. Reduce font size on the document

   D. Disable EMF spooling

192. A client asks how he can fit more data on his existing hard drive without adding another hard drive or storing files on a network. What Windows 95 disk utility should he use to compress the data on his hard drive?

A. DoubleSpace

B. DriveSpace

C. Disk Defragmenter

D. ScanDisk

193. You are manning a technical support phone line and receive a call asking about partitions supported by Windows 95. Which two of the following two types of partitions does Windows 95 support?

A. HPFS

B. NTFS

C. CDFS

D. FAT

E. Unformatted

194. Steve is connecting his Windows 95 computer to a network running Novell NetWare. He wants to share files and a printer with other users. Can he do this? If so, what type of security must he use?

195. As system administrator, you draft a purchase order to acquire tape backup devices. Windows 95 supports QIC tape systems, but not universally. Which of the following tape backup systems is *not* supported by Windows 95?

A. QIC 3010 through parallel port

B. QIC 3010 through floppy disk controller

C. QIC 3010 through SCSI port

D. QIC 80 through floppy disk controller

196. Jim is upgrading to Windows 95 and wants to be sure his existing computer can run Windows 95. The Windows 95 Multitasking feature requires an Intel processor to perform in two types of modes. Which two of the following are operating modes for Intel processors?

   A. Enhanced mode

   B. Protected mode

   C. Fault mode

   D. Real mode

197. You can ask to run the verify option for the computer during which part of running the Windows 95 Setup program?

   A. Initial startup and Setup Wizard load

   B. Gathering user and computer information

   C. Copying Windows 95 files

   D. Restarting the computer and finishing Setup

   E. After Windows 95 is completely installed

198. Susan prepares for a presentation describing the Windows 95 network architecture. One of the bullet points is this: A maps network names used by an application to a physical network device name. Pick the appropriate answer to fill in the blank.

   A. Device driver

   B. Redirector

   C. Requestor

   D. Transport interface

199. The Windows 95 Setup program will not run from Windows 3.0, but instead wants to run from MS-DOS. How much conventional memory is required to run from MS-DOS?

A. 370 KB

B. 420 KB

C. 470 KB

D. 512 KB

E. 640 KB

200. Windows 95 has a modular, layered architecture. Which two of the following are interfaces functioning at the Windows 95 Application Interface layer?

A. Win32 WinNet Applicator Programming Interface

B. WinNet 16

C. HP JetAdmin

D. Win32 Print Applicator Programming Interface

201. Pierre runs several types of applications under Windows 95, but is having problems with some of them. He asks you what types of applications Windows 95 can run. You tell him which of the following two?

A. All OS/2 applications

B. MS-DOS and 16-bit Windows applications

C. 24-bit Windows applications

D. 32-bit Windows applications (also known as WIN32 applications; includes most Windows NT software)

202. Tracy is running Windows NT and wants to install Windows 95 on the same computer. She also has MS-DOS, Windows 3.x, and OS/2 installed on the same computer in different partitions. The Windows 95 Setup program can be run from which two of the following places?

A. Within OS/2

B. Within Windows NT

C. From within Windows

D. From a Windows DOS box

E. From DOS

203. When John runs Disk Compression under Windows 95, he calls asking you how files are compressed. You tell him which two of the following are ways in which disk compression maximizes disk space?

A. Cluster conversion

B. Token conversion

C. ASCII collapse

D. Sector allocation conversion

204. The Startup disk, when created by the Windows 95 Setup program, contains 16 files and uses _______ of disk space?

A. 640 KB

B. 948 KB

C. 1.0 MB

D. 1.20 MB

E. 1.44 MB

205. Windows 95 has many built-in tools you can use for both optimizing and troubleshooting. Name four of these utilities.

206. You are migrating to Windows 95 and will be upgrading many of your applications to 32-bit applications designed to run under Windows 95. You know that Windows 95 runs 32-bit applications differently than Windows 3.1 applications (16-bit applications). Every Windows 95 application is executed from within a specialized container called _______ .

A. An application box

B. A virtual partition

C. A task space

D. A virtual machine

207. Your boss, Jim, has just bought a new Pentium II 300 MHz machine with 64 MB of RAM and a 3.2 GB hard drive. It came preloaded with Windows 95. The hard drive is divided into two partitions. He would like you to configure it to dual boot with Windows NT 4.0. What do you tell him?

A. I hate to mess up a nice computer like that. Why don't you just go and get you another machine with NT on it?

B. I'm not sure NT will support a drive that is 3.2 GB in size.

C. No problem. I will move any data you might have on your second partition to the first partition. Then I will delete the second partition, and format it as NTFS when I install NT 4.0 on it. Of course, I will make a complete backup of your data first.

208. Chuck is setting up a network to use user-level security. From the following list, pick the two places where the user list can be stored.

A. Windows NT domain

B. Windows 95 home directory

C. NetWare binary server

D. Banyan VINES server

209. Discuss the function of the System Monitor.

210. You create a file in Windows 95 Explorer named Budget For This Year.XLS. This is a long filename. Long File Name (LFN) support on a Windows 95 computer works because it uses the _____ file system.

A. FAT

B. HPFS

C. NTFS

D. CDFS

E. VFAT

211. In such an environment as Windows 95, a need for careful management of the system's resources exists. When two processes request the use of a device at the exact same moment, what does Windows 95 use to arbitrate such requests?

   A. WIN95.COM

   B. Virtual memory

   C. Virtual Machine Manager

   D. Nonc of these

212. Isabel is configuring her Windows 95 computer with the TCP/IP protocol. As she fills out the properties for the protocol, she comes across a blank for the DNS entry. What does DNS stand for?

   A. Downloadable Network Share

   B. DOS-Node Server

   C. Domain Name Service

   D. Domain Network Server

213. Your company runs Windows 95 with a NetWare server, but you experience problems with the long filename support. A help desk administrator tells you to install a specific feature under NetWare to enable long filename support. What is this feature?

   A. Install OS/2 on the server.

   B. Run an NLM released by Microsoft.

C. Install OS/2 Name Space.

D. NetWare cannot support Windows 95 long filenames.

214. Abby wants to record her boot process to isolate problems with devices not setting correctly. If she uses the Logged mode to log the entire boot process, which file is created?

A. BOOT.LOG

B. BOOTLOG.TXT

C. BOOT.TXT

D. LOGBOOT.TXT

215. Hard drive space is at a premium at the Cycle Shop Company. They want to upgrade to Windows 95, but they're not sure they have enough hard drive space to accommodate it. The approximate disk requirements for Windows 95 in a Typical Setup upgrade of Windows is ______.

A. 20 MB

B. 30 MB

C. 40 MB

D. 47 MB

E. 55 MB

216. You create a troubleshooting document to circulate around the IT department. One of the issues is about error-isolation switches. Which of the following includes support for a number of error-isolation switches?

A. BOOT.COM

B. WINCHK.COM

C. WIN.COM

D. WIN95.COM

217. To access the Internet, you need to use the Windows 95 Dial-Up Adapter and associated software. Pick three items from the following list that you must have before setting up Windows 95 to access the Internet via a dial-up connection.

    A. ISP account

    B. Modem

    C. Gateway

    D. DNS information

218. At the help desk, you receive a call from a user who wants to start Windows 95 from a Boot menu item. He doesn't know how to display the Boot menu. You tell him to press ________ while Windows 95 boots.

    A. Ctrl+Alt+Delete

    B. Alt+Tab

    C. F6

    D. F8

219. The B1 error that can happen on a Windows 95 installation is the result of ________ .

    A. Step B1, hardware detection, generating an error on the second floppy drive

    B. The processor being an SX type, without a math coprocessor

    C. The processor being a 386 B1 stepping chip, which can generate random math errors, making it incompatible with Windows 95

    D. Failure of the network configuration

    E. Corruption of the boot sector

220. As you instruct a user on how to configure a peer-to-peer network with five Windows 95 computers connected together, you use the term "Windows 95 server" several times. After you finish, he asks you what a Windows 95 server is. What do you tell him?

   A. A computer that is the Primary Domain Controller (PDC) on the LAN

   B. A computer running Windows 95 that has the Enable Windows 95 Server Registry option turned on

   C. A Windows 95 computer that has the File and Printer Sharing Service enabled

   D. A computer running Windows 95 that performs as an application and database server for the LAN

221. Vanessa creates a file named Budget For Department. She wants to rename the file to Budget For Marketing Team. Which of the following commands can she use at the command prompt and retain the long filename?

   A. Type **RENAME Budget For Department TO Budget For Marketing Team**

   B. Type **RENAME Budget For Department Budget For Marketing Team**

   C. Type **REN Budget For Department Budget For Marketing Team**

   D. Type **RENAME "Budget For Department" "Budget For Marketing Team"**

222. You set up Windows 95 on 10 computers in your company. You want to set up optimization and troubleshooting tools on all these computers. Which three of the following are Windows 95 optimization and troubleshooting tools?

   A. System Resource Monitor

   B. Net Watcher

C. System Monitor

D. System Resource Meter

223. Jason installs a network adapter card on a computer running Windows 95. When he does this, Windows 95 automatically installs two protocols for this card. Which two protocols are installed by default when the first network adapter driver is installed?

A. AppleTalk

B. NetBEUI

C. TCP/IP

D. IPX/SPX-compatible

224. You are assigned a new department to administer. This department has a mixture of computers, including many MS-DOS and Windows 3.1 computers and some Windows 95 computers. Because this department shares files a great deal and the file naming conventions must remain consistent, you instruct your Windows 95 users to use short filenames at all times. To guarantee that these users do not create LFNs, you disable this feature using which Registry change? You make this change in the HKEY_LOCAL_MACHINE\System\CurrentControlSet\control\FileSystem.

A. Set the Registry value LongFileNames= to **01**.

B. Set the Registry value Win31FileSystem= to **01.**

C. Set the Registry value Win31FileSystem= to **Yes**.

D. Set the Registry value ShortFileNames= to **Yes**.

E. None of these. This cannot be done with Windows 95.

225. Your boss comes to you and asks whether you want to belong to Microsoft TechNet. What is Microsoft TechNet?

A. A CompuServe forum

B. An Internet forum

C. A CD-ROM publication

D. A users group

226. Windows 95 is a large program and includes many files (more than 1,000 files). To squeeze these files on the 3.5-inch floppy disks, Microsoft uses which of the following formats for most of the Windows 95 installation disks?

A. FAT

B. VFAT

C. DMF

D. CDFS

E. NTFS

227. Frank prints several documents from the same application and wants to know how Windows 95 spooling affects his wait time. Choosing to return control after the first page is spooled ______ Frank's wait time.

A. Increases

B. Shortens

C. Doesn't change

D. Eliminates

228. Cindy calls you from marketing and tells you she just created a file in Microsoft Excel 95 and saved it as a long filename called Marketing Budget.XLS. She copies the file to her laptop, which also run Windows 95, but the version of Excel on the laptop was released prior to Windows 95. She says she can't find the Marketing Budget.XLS file. What is one possible short filename you tell her to look for?

Practice Exam 1 Answers

1. Microsoft TechNet, the Internet, and Online Help.

2. 512 MB. Based on the default compression ratio of 2:1, the maximum size of the compressed volume will be 256 MB. This will allow it to store 512 MB if the 2:1 ratio is achieved. 512 MB is the maximum size of the contents in any compressed volume drive. If DriveSpace 3 is used, that limit is raised to 2 GB.

3. SETUPLOG.TXT, DETLOG.TXT, and DETCRASH.LOG.

4. A C

5. B, keeping the files separate allows for an easier implementation of User Profiles (just replacing the USER.DAT file) and Systems policies.

6. Universal Naming Convention. A UNC consists of a computer name and a share in the following syntax: *\\computer\share.* UNC does not require a drive-letter assignment; this will cause problems for some 16-bit programs.

7. To use File and Print Sharing for NetWare Networks, you must have the IPX/SPX-compatible protocol, the Microsoft Client for NetWare Networks, and User-level Access Control enabled.

8. IPX/SPX. No, you cannot change this. You can, however, use additional protocols with this, but only IPX/SPX will be used to talk to the NetWare server.

9. IPX/SPX-compatible. No, this cannot be changed to another protocol. Other possibly useful components include File and Print Sharing for NetWare and the Microsoft NDS service.

10. Make sure the Users Can Customize Their Preferences and Desktop Settings option is checked. This option can be enabled on the User Profiles tab of the Passwords Control Panel. Next, advise the user to make any changes to the desktop,

Start menu, and program groups. Shut down and reboot the system. After logging on, the new changes will appear and will be part of the user profile for that user.

11. C

12. A, Ring 0 is the only processor ring that has direct access to hardware; Ring 3 processes must go through Ring 0 to get to the hardware.

13. D, Share-level security assigns passwords to resources as a means of controlling access.

14. Current hardware and software in operation, network OS, knowledge level of employees and training requirements, need for new OS, and configuration of services.

15. Enables you to edit the Registry without using the Registry Editor. Enables you to set default settings for a user or group of users. These settings may affect the computer or user environment.

16. C

17. The Enabled: May Be Master setting.

18. A D, Windows 95 executes programs in Ring 0 and Ring 3.

19. A master browser is a workstation responsible for maintaining the list of workstations in the local workgroup on the local network segment. New computers announce themselves by broadcast to the local network; the master browser retains and distributes this information.

20. Remove SHARE.EXE and SMARTDRV.EXE from AUTOEXEC.BAT; check the IOS.LOG for any Real-mode drivers that might be causing Windows 95 not to use 32-bit file system drivers; use the Windows 95 Disk Defragmenter regularly.

21. A B C

22. Jason can back up to a tape drive, a floppy disk(s), another hard drive, or a network location. He can use BACKUP.EXE.

23. D, Windows Internet Name Service is responsible for maintaining the NetBIOS to IP Address mapping table.

24. Jill should choose to install Windows 95 over her existing Windows 3.11 for Workgroups directory.

25. A B C D. Windows 95 training should be planned to coincide with the deployment so that there is very little overlap between the two. Your deployment should be careful, with, a test deployment on a small group of machines. When the system is considered to be stable, Windows 95 should be deployed across the network at a rate that ensures trouble-free operations for all concerned.

26. B, Windows 95 checks the date stamp on the user profile and treats all profiles that were created in the "future" as invalid, and ignores them.

27. E, User-level security draws on a list of users stored on a server on your network.

28. Use the Dial-Up Networking feature in Windows 95; configure the Dial-Up Adapter for an Internet service provider (ISP); use a modem to dial into the ISP.

29. B C

30. MS-DOS Virtual Machine mode. If she runs the application in MS-DOS mode, she will lose all these advantages.

31. C

32. C

33. A, User profiles are stored in the user's home directory on Windows NT networks.

34. NETSETUP.EXE.

35. A, There is no "true" security. Windows 95 will maintain of list of users who have logged on to the system by creating a list of PWL files in the Windows directory.

36. CONFIG.POL. Regardless of the level of security, if the policy file has been implemented on a Microsoft Windows 95 network, the client must log on to the Domain, and the CONFIG.POL file should be in the NETLOGON share of the Domain Controllers. On a Novell NetWare network, the policy file should be located in the SYS:PUBLIC directory.

37. Yes, and it is adjacent to the Application Interface and the IFS Manager.

38. Remote Administration can read and write to any hard drive through hidden drive shares, as well as controlling shared resources on the remote machine.

39. B, DLC is not used for peer-to-peer networking in Windows 95.

40. D, Ring 0 has application processing protection built in, but Ring 3 requires the OS to provide protection.

41. A C D

42. D

43. A B C

44. C, User profiles enable users to maintain their personal settings such as wallpaper settings, and also enable them to maintain custom Start menu settings.

45. B

46. Any answer files created for the Windows 95 installation have an extension of INF. If not specified in the setup command, Windows 95 will look for and use MSBATCH.INF in the Setup directory.

47. User-level security.

48. Possible answers include the following: The application requires direct access to the hardware; the application has incompatible memory requirements; the application's

installation program checks to see whether Windows is running and will not continue if Windows is detected; and the application has video requirements that the DOS VM cannot support.

49. C

50. A B C

51. Browse list

52. C

53. In the Start menu, choose Settings, Control Panel, and double-click on the Passwords icon. Click on the User Profile tab and click on the Users Can Customize Their Preferences and Desktop Settings option.

54. A, Systems policies must be stored on a network drive. By default, the location will be the NETLOGON share on Windows NT Domain controllers, and the SYS:PUBLIC directory on Novell NetWare servers. User profiles are used to restrict access on a user-by-user basis.

55. A C E

56. B C

57. D, All applications run in Ring 3; Ring 0 is reserved for the OS.

58. C, <server.domain.root>\[path]\[filename] is the proper syntax of a fully qualified domain name.

59. B C D

60. You can follow a number of steps when attempting to isolate technical problems. Some are specific to Windows 95; others are just part of a logical approach to any problem.

61. C, The computer must be set up to use user-level security.

62. A, Systems policies both automatically configure an environment for users and prevent them from customizing many of the components of their environments.

63. Windows 95 might not be making a connection to a DNS server. This might be due to configuration or a network failure. If using a HOSTS file, the information contained in the HOSTS file might be incorrect. DNS and HOSTS are the two ways to resolve fully qualified domain names to IP addresses.

64. Step-by-Step Confirmation.

65. D

66. In an MS-DOS VM, in MS-DOS mode after shutting down the Windows 95 GUI, and in MS-DOS mode outside of Windows 95 using configuration files customized for the application.

67. B C D

68. IPX/SPX, NetBEUI, and TCP/IP are Plug and Play–enabled. Microsoft NetBEUI and IPX/SPX are installed by default.

69. C, Systems policies automatically edit the Registry on the computers that process the policy.

70. A B

71. D

72. A B C, Windows 95 does not ship with software that allows it to connect to an AppleShare network.

73. Set a mandatory user profile that cannot be edited. Set a system policy that is downloaded to the computer each time the computer boots.

74. USER.DAT, which maintains user settings, is copied and individually maintained for each user on the computer in <win_root>\PROFILES\<user_name>\.

75. User-level security. No, only directory-level rights can be set up under Windows 95.

76. Share-level security allows quicker setup of shares and sharing in a peer-to-peer network. User-level security allows centralized account management on a Windows NT or NetWare server, allows finer permission control, and allows groups to be assigned rights.

77. D

78. D, Most system services are application, and would therefore run in Ring 3.

79. B, The Banyan client that ships with Windows 95 does not support network browsing of Banyan VINES Servers.

80. B

81. C

82. D, DOS=SINGLE is added to the CONFIG.SYS file when running an MS-DOS application with custom CONFIG.SYS or AUTOEXEC.BAT settings.

83. B

84. Every computer requires at least an IP address and subnet mask. If they have to cross network segments, they will also need to have a gateway address to reach the remote computers, and it is nice to give them the address of a DNS server to resolve the remote computer names to IP addresses.

85. A B D, File and Print Sharing is okay to install if you have a firewall to separate your clients from the servers they are attempting to access. If you grant dial-up access, you will not have a firewall; this leaves those individual computers open to attack.

86. Startup and information gathering, hardware detection, file copy, and final system configuration. See "Installation Process."

87. Possible answers include the following: Windows 95 unloads itself and the computer runs in a single-tasking, MS-DOS environment; all Protected-mode support and drivers are

removed; and you may need to customize AUTOEXEC.BAT and CONFIG.SYS for each application.

88. A C

89. Update any non-Microsoft disk compression to a 32-bit driver from the manufacturer. Verify that the Performance tab in the My Computer Properties sheet shows all 32-bit components for the file system and for virtual memory.

90. 80386DX.

91. A, Ring 0 supports the kernel, system drivers, and manager applications.

92. B C E

93. Advantage: User-level requires user to authenticate access against an account list stored on a Windows NT or NetWare server. Disadvantage: User-level security can be set up only on an NT or NetWare server. Advantage: Share-level security enables two Windows 95 workstations networked together to share resources using passwords. Disadvantage: Share-level password can be used by anyone to gain access; that is, no authentication is needed to access resource.

94. You should see any servers that are part of your current workgroup and the Entire Network icon.

95. C D

96. A

97. IPX/SPX, NetBEUI, and TCP/IP are Plug and Play–enabled. Microsoft NetBEUI and IPX/SPX are installed by default.

98. Two. Windows 95 has one virtual machine running for both the Windows programs (the 16-bit and 32-bit applications), and one virtual machine running for the MS-DOS application.

99. B

100. Possible answers: Long filenames are not supported by NetWare by default; OS/2 Name Space must be added; users of Windows 95 can reassign print queue assignments; administrators may feel a lack of control over resources because the Windows 95 graphical user interface (GUI) makes it easy to change drive mappings.

101. C, Systems policies provide security. User profiles maintain user settings, but do nothing to prevent the user from modifying the system.

102. B

103. C

104. A, Selecting Disable MS-DOS Prompt prevents access to the MS-DOS prompt.

105. MSBATCH.INF.

106. C, The format of the UNC pathname is \\<server>\<resource or share name>\[path]\[filename].

107. Ensure that File and Printer Sharing is enabled at the remote computer; verify that you have correct network protocols configured.

108. B, The requestor is responsible for mapping names to physical devices.

109. C

110. A, When running applications in MS-DOS mode, Windows 95 is removed from memory.

111. C D, Users do not require additional information before connecting to the Windows 95 computer, and their user credentials are verified against a security provider configured at the Windows 95 computer. The security provider may be Windows NT Workstation, Windows NT Server, Windows NT Domain, or Novell NetWare Server.

112. B C E, Token Ring and Ethernet are network topologies, not protocols.

113. B C D

114. f: disables 32-bit file system drivers; m: starts Windows 95 in Safe mode; n: starts Windows 95 in Safe mode with network support; s: excludes the ROM address space between F000 and 1 MB from use by Windows 95; v: disables virtualization of hard disk interrupts; x: disables use of upper memory by Windows 95.

115. B, 16-bit Windows applications are the only applications that share a memory address space, and they do this for backward compatibility.

116. Load OS/2 Name Server Space (OS2.NAM) on the server.

117. C

118. Perform a local reboot by pressing Ctrl+Alt+Delete once. In the Close Program dialog box, select the offending process, and click on the End Task button.

119. Windows NT Workstation running NTFS (NT File System) provides file-level security.

120. Yes, he can do this, but File and Print Sharing for NetWare Networks supports only user-level security.

121. B, Remote administration is enabled on the Remote Administration tab. File and Print Sharing is required for remote administration to function.

122. C, the File and Print Sharing service must be running, and the network does not have a valid security provider for user-level security.

123. B D

124. D, Each MS-DOS application runs in its own virtual machine.

125. C E

126. C D

127. C D, only one File and Print Sharing service can be installed at a time, and the NetWare File and Print Sharing service requires user-level access control.

128. D, To multitask MS-DOS applications and Windows applications, you will run the MS-DOS applications in an MS-DOS virtual machine.

129. C

130. ADMIN.ADM is the template file for System Policy Editor. It is a text file, so can be edited by NOTEPAD.EXE.

131. B D

132. WINS, an LMHosts file, and broadcasts are all capable of resolving NetBIOS names.

133. User-level security uses pass-through authentication.

134. 32-bit applications reside in their own separate address space and each has a separate message queue.

135. A

136. A C E

137. B D, Physical memory is RAM and virtual memory is space on your hard drive in the form of a swap file.

138. B

139. To employ Remote Registry Editing, both computers (the Editor and Target), must have File and Print Sharing installed, Remote Administration enabled, and the Remote Registry Editing Service installed; be enabled for user-level access control; and have the Editor on the Remote Administration list.

140. C

141. C D, The restriction is for NetBIOS name, and both the computer and workgroup names are NetBIOS names.

142. A C E

143. A, 16-bit applications store their settings in INI files; only 32 bit applications use the Registry.

144. E

145. Gateways help route TCP/IP messages to remote destinations.

146. User profiles are used to maintain user settings. Multiple user profiles can be maintained on one computer. Systems policies enforce specific desktop settings for users. Systems polices make use of user profiles to enforce their settings.

147. C, Windows 95 uses preemptive multitasking, which provides better scheduling of processor time than the cooperative multitasking used by 16-bit applications.

148. A C D, Internal File System Manager is not part of the OSI model.

149. Answers can include the following: Normal mode, Logged mode, Safe mode, Safe mode with network support, Step-by-step confirmation, Command-prompt-only mode, Safe mode command prompt, and Previous version of MS-DOS.

150. B D

151. C, Windows 95 is extensible because it is so modular.

152. D

153. D, Many 16-bit and Real-mode network clients require that no other clients be installed.

154. Gateways allow TCP/IP messages to be routed to remote networks. Without a gateway, TCP/IP is limited to the local network segment.

155. D, To provide a unified logon, the username and passwords for all clients must be the same.

156. D

157. D

158. A B D, The TSD Supervisor is not part of the IFS.

159. D

160. Virtual machines.

161. D

162. D

163. A, Most Windows 95 applications run in Ring 3; Ring 0 is usually reserved for OS functions.

164. B C

165. No, Windows NT Servers, Novell NetWare 3.11 (patched), Novell NetWare 3.12 and 4.x with OS/2 name space, Novell NetWare 4.11 with Long Name space, and Banyan VINES 7.0 all support long filenames.

166. B C D, The IFS Manager is a boundary layer between the network provider and the redirectors and services (as well as other Installable File Systems).

167. A B C

168. A

169. D, The Volume Tracker tracks removable media.

170. B C D

171. Set up a primary domain on the Windows NT Server.

172. B

173. B

174. C

175. Universal Naming Convention. Computer name and share name. No drive-letter assignment is needed.

176. B, Only 32-bit–protected mode drivers are able to take advantage of the 32-bit VFAT.

177. C

178. A B

179. D

180. A, CDFS maintains a separate cache to increase the performance of the CD-ROM.

181. A

182. A D

183. B, Ring 0 is the only ring that allows direct access to hardware.

184. E

185. B C, Microsoft's Client does not allow you to use TSRs that require the network to be loaded, nor does it provide support for ArcNet.

186. D

187. B, Windows 95 uses the first six valid characters, adds a tilde (~) and a number, and then applies the extension for the file.

188. E

189. A C

190. A

191. B D

192. B, DriveSpace is the compression program included in Windows 95.

193. D E

194. Yes, he can do this, but he must install user-level security.

195. C, QIC 3010 SCSI drives are the only tape drives supported.

196. B D, The Intel processor can run in Protected mode or Real mode. Windows 95 would use Real mode prior to the GUI starting up.

197. E

198. B

199. C

200. A D, WinNet 16 is used only with 16-bit Real mode drivers, and HP JetAdmin is a service.

201. B D

202. C E

203. B D, Token Conversion and Sector Allocation Conversion are the two ways that space is saved.

204. B

205. System Monitor, Net Watcher, System Resource Meter, and ScanDisk.

206. D, All 16-bit and 32-bit Windows applications share a common virtual machine.

207. C

208. A C

209. System Monitor provides real-time monitoring of system activities both locally and at remote computers, to determine the effect of configuration changes and to identify potential system performance bottlenecks.

210. E

211. C

212. C, Domain Name Service.

213. C, Installing OS/2 Name Space will enable you to store filenames up to 254 characters in length.

214. B

215. C

216. C

217. A B C, DNS information is not required, but you will have to know the IP address of all the servers that you wish to visit.

218. D

219. C

220. C, Any computer that runs File and Print Sharing services is considered to be a server.

221. D, When working with long filenames from the command prompt, place the full path for a file inside of quotation marks.

222. B C D

223. B D, NetBEUI and IPX/SPX-compatible are the two protocols installed by default, to be used with the two default clients: Client for Microsoft Networks, and Client for NetWare Networks.

224. E, Even though the Registry exists, this feature does not work.

225. C

226. C

227. B

228. MARKET~1.XLS. The first six valid characters followed by the ~ and an incremental number.

Practice Exam 2

This exam is a set of 115 questions. Each objective on the exam is covered by at least one question—most by two or three. The answers at the end include explanations.

1. You are acting as a consultant for a college MIS department. For security and administration reasons, the college has decided to install Windows 95 as a shared copy to run over the network. Which of the following scenarios are correct for this assignment? Choose all that apply.

   A. On a computer with a hard drive, with system files stored on and running from the server

   B. On a computer with only a floppy disk drive, booting from a floppy, with the system files stored on and running from the server

   C. On a computer with only a floppy disk drive, booting from a floppy, with the system files stored on and running from a shared Windows 95 CD-ROM

   D. From a NetWare server that supports diskless workstations and a RIPL boot to a startup disk image stored on the file server, then using system files stored on and running from the file server

2. By default, where are computer-specific policies downloaded from Windows NT servers?

   A. NETLOGON

   B. SYSTEM

   C. PROFILES

   D. None of the above

3. The Windows 95 print server to which you are connecting isn't printing properly. You try to reinstall the print driver on the print server, but you can't find the proper options. Why?

   A. The printer is offline.

   B. The print server is offline.

   C. The administrator is working at that computer.

   D. Only the administrator can remotely administer a print server.

4. How much conventional memory is allocated to an MS-DOS application VM?

   A. 640 KB

   B. 64 KB

   C. 384 KB

   D. 1024 KB

5. ScanDisk can detect files that have become ______.

   A. fragmented

   B. cross-clustered

   C. cross-linked

   D. compressed

6. You have installed Windows 95 on all the PCs in your NetWare environment. Which protocol should you use?

   A. IPX/SPX

   B. TCP/IP

   C. NetBEUI

   D. DLC

7. Rochelle picked up a used Sound Blaster 16 card at a flea market, but now she can't get Windows 95 to identify it. She calls you for help. What do you tell her?

   A. This is legacy hardware and therefore isn't compatible with Windows 95.

   B. If Windows 95 says it found new hardware when it boots up, click Have Disk and then load the drivers. Reboot the machine, and it will work.

   C. Start the Add New Hardware wizard from Control Panel. Tell it to automatically detect installed hardware. If it identifies the card, great. If not, tell it to show all devices, and then select the card from the list.

   D. Are you sure you got the card seated properly in the machine?

8. You are dual-booting between Windows 95 and Windows NT. Whenever you boot into Windows 95, you can't see all your Windows NT partitions. Why?

   A. Windows NT can't access FAT32 partitions.

   B. Windows 95 can't access NTFS partitions.

   C. You need to open Disk Administrator so that Windows NT can write a signature to Disk 0 so that Windows NT can access the FAT table on the disk(s).

   D. Windows NT can't read FAT partitions.

9. As system administrator, you draft a purchase order to acquire tape backup devices. Windows 95 supports QIC tape systems, but not universally. Which of the following tape backup systems is not supported by Windows 95?

   A. QIC 3010 through parallel port

   B. QIC 3010 through floppy disk controller

   C. QIC 3010 through SCSI port

   D. QIC 80 through floppy disk controller

10. Participating in an NT domain has what effect on logon scripts of Windows 95 machines?

    A. Logon scripts are not needed.

    B. Logon scripts are ignored.

    C. Logon scripts can be processed.

    D. Logon scripts are mandatory.

11. Ellen complains that recently her applications seem to take much longer to read and write to files on her hard disk. Which disk-management tool would you use to address this problem?

    A. Disk Defragmenter

    B. ScanDisk

    C. DriveSpace

    D. Backup

12. As a network administrator, you choose to implement roving user profiles using Windows 95 and Novell NetWare. Where should you place the user profiles on the NetWare server?

    A. SYS:SYSTEM

    B. SYS:PUBLIC

C. The user's home directory

D. Mail user_ID directory

13. Greg wanted to increase the performance of his dual-speed CD-ROM drive by setting the CD-ROM as a quad speed in the CD-ROM Settings tab of the File System Properties dialog box. He notices, however, that the system is even slower than it was before he made the change. Why?

    A. Changing the setting set the cache size to 0.

    B. He doesn't have enough RAM to support the new setting.

    C. Windows 95 detected that the CD-ROM is not a quad speed.

    D. None of the above.

14. In which directory on Novell NetWare servers can you find computer policies?

    A. SYS:SYSTEM

    B. SYS:MAIL\USER_ID

    C. LOGIN

    D. SYS:PUBLIC

15. Which protocol should be used to connect Windows 95 to the Internet?

    A. PPP

    B. NetBIOS

    C. NetBEUI

    D. TCP/IP

16. You decide to remove user profiles from your Windows 95 computer. Upon removing user profiles, what state does the computer return to after it is restarted?

    A. The computer returns to the last profile used on the machine before profiles were removed.

    B. The machine returns to the system profile.

    C. After restarting the computer, you must configure a new profile.

    D. The computer returns to the default user profile in place at the time user profiles were enabled.

17. Of the following, which are valid troubleshooting aids to help during Startup? Choose all that apply.

    A. Safe recovery

    B. Windows 95 startup disk

    C. Installed components verification

    D. win.com switches

18. To see computers that aren't in your workgroup, you can do which of the following?

    A. Double-click Network Neighborhood.

    B. Right-click Network Neighborhood.

    C. Double-click Entire Network.

    D. Right-click Entire Network.

19. To allow a dial-up client computer to access file and print capabilities when connecting to a dial-up server, which of the following components must be installed on the server?

    A. Point to Point Protocol

    B. File and Print Sharing services

C. Allow Caller Access option

D. Briefcase

20. Which of the following is not available on the properties sheet for an MS-DOS application?

A. Program tab

B. Display tab

C. Memory tab

D. Screen tab

21. What file keeps passwords on a Windows 95 machine?

A. system.dat

B. user.dat

C. .pwl

D. pass.ini

22. You suspect that an excessive amount of network traffic is consuming the available bandwidth on your network. You think the culprit is a file-copying process between two computers running Windows 95. What remote administration tool provides graphical measurements of network traffic?

A. System Monitor

B. Net Watcher

C. Registry Editor

D. None of the above

23. You are about to upgrade to Windows 95 from Windows for Workgroups. What must you do to migrate your program groups and user settings? Choose the best answer.

    A. Install Windows 95 in a different directory than Windows 3.1.

    B. Install Windows 95 in the same directory as Windows 3.1.

    C. Run the Setup program with the `/s` switch.

    D. After installation, run the grpconv.exe program.

24. You are storing user profiles on a Windows NT server. You want to let users access the same desktop settings from anywhere on the network, but you don't want them to be able to change the settings from session to session. Where must you store the user profile information on the Windows NT server, and what should the file be named?

    A. NETLOGON directory, USER.DAT

    B. NETLOGON directory, USER.MAN

    C. User's home directory, USER.MAN

    D. User's home directory, USER.DAT

25. As a system administrator, you use the Net Watcher utility to monitor shares in your Windows 95 workgroup. You would like to be able to monitor network shares using Network Neighborhood. Is this possible using Net Watcher?

    A. Yes

    B. No

    C. Only with the Network Neighborhood Registry parameter manually configured

    D. Only when the computers are not in your workgroup

26. How do you make a new Dial-Up Networking connection for a newly configured client computer?

    A. Open Network Neighborhood and make a new Dial-Up Networking connection.

    B. Open Dial-Up Networking and choose Connection | Connect.

    C. Double-click the Make New Connection icon in Dial-Up Networking.

    D. Right-click the Network Neighborhood icon and choose Map Network Drive.

27. If user profiles are enabled on a Windows 95 computer, where in the Registry is the user's information copied at logon?

    A. HKEY_LOCAL_MACHINE

    B. HKEY_DYN_DATA

    C. HKEY_USERS

    D. HKEY_CURRENT_USER

28. A user can print from a Windows 32-bit application but can't print from an MS-DOS application. What should you do to enable printing?

    A. Reinstall the print driver.

    B. Redirect the print job to a network printer.

    C. Enable spooling for MS-DOS applications.

    D. Capture the printer port in the printer's Properties dialog box.

29. Jill creates a shared directory called twocool$ on her Windows 95 computer. She then informs her department that they can begin using the directory to store new project files. Immediately, she is bombarded by complaints that the share can't be found. She runs the network troubleshooter wizard and confirms that File and Print Sharing is enabled and that it's configured correctly. She is about to start checking the wiring when the problem dawns on her. What do you think it was?

    A. Incompatible protocols.

    B. Browsing was turned off.

    C. You are not allowed to have a $ in a share name.

    D. A $ on the end of a share name makes it invisible.

30. You and a colleague are about to install Windows 95 to more than 100 PCs. What is the best type of installation to accomplish this?

    A. Automated

    B. Manual

    C. Custom

    D. NetSetup

31. You are installing a new printer and are prompted for the location of the files. What path should you enter?

    A. *systemroot*\SYSTEM\PRINTERS

    B. *systemroot*\SYSTEM

    C. The location of the Windows 95 CD-ROM

    D. *systemroot*\PRINTERS

32. You log on to two Windows 95 computers. On your network you have implemented roving user profiles on your Windows NT server. You make different changes to the settings on both computers you are currently logged into. You then log out of both Windows 95 computers. The next time you log on to the network, which user profile will be downloaded to the workstation?

    A. The profile contained on the server in the NETLOGON directory

    B. The profile with the most recent time stamp

    C. Your original user profile

    D. The default user profile

33. Using Net Watcher, what must you have enabled to allow remote administration?

    A. User-level security

    B. Domain authentication

    C. File and Print Sharing

    D. None of the above

34. You have installed Windows 95 but continually receive error messages reporting bad or missing files. What should you do?

    A. Reinstall Windows 95.

    B. Always use Safe mode.

    C. Run Setup's verification of installed components option.

    D. Use the Emergency Repair Disk.

35. You have installed Windows 95 on all the PCs in your NetWare environment. You used IPX/SPX as your first choice, but many of the Windows 95 machines can't see your NetWare 3 servers. What do you suspect is the problem?

    A. You didn't configure the IPX/SPX frame type correctly.

    B. SAP isn't enabled.

    C. You haven't specified the preferred server in the IPX/SPX setup.

    D. The users don't have access to the servers.

36. What file does Windows 95 create so that it can recover from hardware detection crashes?

    A. setuplog.txt

    B. setup.log

    C. detcrash.log

    D. detlog.txt

37. Participating in an NT domain allows a Windows 95 computer to use what level of security?

    A. Group level

    B. User level

    C. Share level

    D. Resource level

38. You would like to create a mandatory user profile to be used by all members of your organization. How might you configure such a profile?

A. Enable user profiles on a Windows 95 computer. Make the changes you want and save the desktop. Rename the created USER.DAT file USER.MAN and place the file in your users' home directories on your Windows NT server.

B. Enable user profiles on a Windows 95 computer. Make the changes you want and save the desktop. Rename the created USER.DA0 file USER.DAT and place the file in your users' home directories on your Windows NT server.

C. Enable user profiles on a Windows 95 computer. Make the changes you want and save the desktop. Rename the created SYSTEM.DAT file USER.MAN and place the file in your users' home directories on your Windows NT server.

D. Enable user profiles on a Windows 95 computer. Make the changes you want and save the desktop. Rename the created SYSTEM.DAT file SYSTEM.MAN and place the file in your users' home directories on your Windows NT server.

39. What file does Windows 95 create that contains a log of network information found during setup?

    A. net.log

    B. netlog.txt

    C. netinst.log

    D. There is no such file.

40. You want to dual boot between Windows 95 and Windows for Workgroups for a help desk environment that must support both operating systems. How can you do this?

    A. You can't dual boot between Windows 95 and Windows for Workgroups.

    B. You must create a Windows 95 startup disk and a Windows startup disk and boot from that startup disk whenever you want to boot to Windows 95 or Windows for Workgroups.

    C. You must install Windows 95 in a different directory than Windows for Workgroups.

    D. You must have two partitions. Install Windows 95 on the second partition.

41. Participating in an NT domain has what effect on logon scripts of Windows 95 machines?

    A. Logon scripts are not needed.

    B. Logon scripts are ignored.

    C. Logon scripts can be processed.

    D. Logon scripts are mandatory.

42. Why would you want to remove a printer driver for an existing printer?

    A. The printer needs to be serviced.

    B. The printer is out of paper and you don't want people sending print jobs until there is more paper.

    C. Printers can't be removed.

    D. To troubleshoot a printing problem.

43. You want to boot Windows 95 in Safe mode. How can you do this?

    A. Select Start | Shutdown and Restart in Safe mode.

    B. Press F8 when the message `Starting Windows 95` appears, and then select Safe mode.

    C. Choose Shutdown and Restart while holding down the Shift key.

    D. You can't force Windows 95 to go into Safe mode. It will automatically detect when there's a problem and reboot in Safe mode.

44. Which of the following operating systems can upgrade to Windows 95? Choose all that apply.

    A. MS-DOS 5

    B. Windows 3.x

    C. OS/2 1.0

    D. MS-DOS 2.x

45. In what two ways does Windows 95 support connecting to the Internet?

    A. Through a UNIX server

    B. Through a dial-up connection

    C. Through a permanent connection

    D. Through LAN Server

46. When a new user logs on to a Windows 95 computer that has user profiles enabled, a copy of what profile is loaded for the new user?

    A. DEFAULT

    B. SYSTEM

    C. USER.DAT

    D. USER.MAN

47. Loretta's modem was working fine until she loaded Microsoft Fax. Since then, she has been unable to use MS-DOS-based and Win16-based applications, but Windows 95 modem applications seem to be working fine. What could be the problem?

    A. The modem is not configured properly.

    B. She is using the wrong file transfer protocol.

    C. Microsoft Fax is waiting for incoming calls.

    D. She is using the wrong COM port.

48. Which of the following describes a peer workgroup?

    A. Windows-based computers that are not part of a Windows NT domain.

    B. Windows-based computers that are part of a Windows NT domain.

    C. Windows-based computers running NetBEUI.

    D. Non-Windows-based computers that are part of a Windows NT domain.

49. Leah finds that she is running out of disk space on her C drive. Which disk-management tool should she use?

    A. ScanDisk

    B. DriveSpace

    C. Disk Defragmenter

    D. Backup

50. Alice is having trouble connecting to the Internet on her stand-alone desktop Windows 95 computer. When you type WinIPCfg at a command prompt, the IP address is listed as 0.0.0.0. What is the first thing you tell Alice?

    A. You obviously have typed in an incorrect URL.

    B. Your modem is bad. I can sell you a new one, but they are really expensive.

    C. You don't have an IP address. We need to look at your TCP/IP settings and make sure you have checked Obtain an IP address automatically.

    D. Have you ever been able to connect to the Internet with this computer?

51. Cheryl is running Windows 95 Backup. She wants to select an appropriate backup destination. Which of the following can she choose?

    A. A Windows NT Server share

    B. A Novell NetWare volume

    C. A 1.44 MB floppy drive

    D. A SCSI tape backup unit

52. By default, Windows 95 installs which two protocols?

    A. NetBEUI

    B. IPX/SPX

    C. TCP/IP

    D. DLC

53. When printing many files to a printer, Gary complains that it takes too long for the print jobs to spool and return control to the application. What should he do to speed up the process?

    A. Free additional disk space on his computer.

    B. Set the jobs to print directly to the printer.

    C. Set the spool option to print after the last page is spooled.

    D. Set the spool option to print after the first page is spooled.

54. If user profiles are enabled on a Windows 95 computer, where in the Registry is the user's information copied at logon?

    A. `HKEY_LOCAL_MACHINE`

    B. `HKEY_DYN_DATA`

    C. `HKEY_USERS`

    D. `HKEY_CURRENT_USER`

55. Which Registry key contains the information for Plug and Play configuration?

    A. `HKEY_DYN_DATA`

    B. `HKEY_CLASSES_ROOT`

    C. `HKEY_CURRENT_USER`

D. `HKEY_LOCAL_MACHINE`

E. `HKEY_USERS`

56. You want to monitor more than one computer concurrently using System Monitor. What action must you take?

    A. You can connect to the desired computers by starting multiple instances of System Monitor.

    B. To connect to more than one computer, you need to select multiple computers using the File menu.

    C. You can view only one computer at a time using System Monitor.

    D. When selecting multiple computers, hold down the Ctrl key.

57. Workgroups must use what level of security?

    A. Group level

    B. User level

    C. Share level

    D. Resource level

58. Why can't Windows 95 Backup restore MS-DOS Backup sets?

    A. Windows 95 Backup can't mount MS-DOS drives.

    B. There are incompatibility issues with long filenames in MS-DOS 6.2 and earlier.

    C. Windows 95 and MS-DOS use different File Allocation Tables.

    D. MS-DOS Backup sets do not contain the Windows 95 Registry.

59. You want to change the name of your computer on the network. How can you do this?

    A. Right-click My Computer and choose Change Name.

    B. Right-click My Computer, choose Properties, and then choose Identification.

    C. Right-click Network Neighborhood and choose Change Name.

    D. Right-click Network Neighborhood, choose Properties, and then choose Identification.

60. Which two features affect 16-bit Windows applications?

    A. Disabling file sharing

    B. Disabling write-behind caching

    C. Disabling long filename preservation for old programs

    D. None of the above

61. Janine runs an MS-DOS application that displays important information to the screen when it exits. She can't read this information, however, because the application's window closes as soon as it exits. How can she prevent this from happening?

    A. Check Full Screen on the Screen tab of the application's properties sheet.

    B. Specify a shortcut key on the Program tab of the application's properties sheet.

    C. Uncheck Close on Exit on the Program tab of the application's properties sheet.

    D. Run the application in protected mode.

62. You have downloaded a new driver for your printer. What do you do first?

   A. Go to the Details tab on the properties sheet of the printer that is to be upgraded, and click New Driver to install the upgrade.

   B. Delete the printer and then install the new printer driver.

   C. Add a new printer with the new driver and then delete the old printer.

   D. Printer drivers can't be upgraded.

63. C. W. creates a shared directory called mycooldocs on his Windows 95 computer. He then informs his department that they can begin using the directory to store new work procedures. Immediately, he is bombarded by complaints that the share is inaccessible. C. W. opens Net Watcher and can see several users listed. He dismisses the complaints with "They don't know how to use a computer." Was C. W. hasty in his judgment? If so, what would you check?

   A. He was correct. If they connect to the computer, they can connect to the share. The complaints were from users who don't know how to properly browse a network.

   B. He was a bit hasty. I would first make sure I had set the LM Announce option under File and Print sharing for Microsoft Networks.

   C. He was a bit hasty. I would first make sure I had set the custom share attribute File Scan to let them browse the files in the shared directory.

   D. He was a bit hasty. I would first make sure I had granted them permission to access the share.

64. Support is available for NetWare clients using which two software packages?

    A. NETX

    B. VLMs

    C. WinNet

    D. NetBIOS

65. Jack wants to configure a Windows 95 computer to participate in a peer-to-peer workgroup. What information must he provide? Select all correct answers.

    A. Computer name

    B. Workgroup name

    C. IP address

    D. Default gateway

66. Jill sets up the Windows 95 Dial-Up Networking feature so that she can dial into a Windows NT 3.5 server. Which of the following is accessible through this connection?

    A. Microsoft-based servers, such as Windows NT, Windows for Workgroups, and LAN Manager running NetBEUI

    B. Novell NetWare servers running IPX/SPX on the Windows NT network

    C. The Internet via the Windows NT Internet gateway

    D. All of the above

67. A Win16-based application can't access the modem, but your MS-DOS-based and Windows 95-based applications can. How can you fix this problem?

    A. Increase the COMxBUFFER setting in the [386Enh] section of SYSTEM.INI.

    B. Make sure that the communications driver for Windows 3.1-based applications is COMM.DRV in the SYSTEM.INI file.

    C. Disable call waiting.

    D. Decrease the baud rate for the modem.

68. Which of the following is not a file for the Windows 95 Registry?

    A. SYSTEM.DA0

    B. SYSTEM.DAT

    C. USER.DAT

    D. CONFIG.POL

69. You are using the System Monitor to monitor memory usage statistics. Which of the following choices does the Memory Manager report values for?

    A. Allocated memory

    B. Disk cache size

    C. Free memory

    D. Virtual machines

    E. Bytes read/second

70. What are attributes of system policies? Choose all that apply.

    A. They let users' environments follow them wherever they log on.

    B. They control what users are allowed to do.

    C. They can control the users' environment.

    D. They can control activities on individual computers.

71. Kelly uses DriveSpace 2.0 to compress her hard disk. She wants to know where her files have been stored. What do you tell her?

    A. They are stored in a hidden file called a CVF, or Compressed Volume File.

    B. They have been moved to another disk, called a CVF disk.

    C. They have been moved to drive H:.

    D. They have been replaced by tokens.

72. A Windows 95 computer can be configured to maintain or not maintain browse lists by configuring which of the following?

    A. The File and Print Sharing service

    B. The share-level security tab

    C. The LMHOSTS file

    D. The Network Neighborhood properties

73. Which applications do not support long filenames?

    A. MS-DOS applications

    B. Windows 16-bit applications

    C. Windows 32-bit applications

    D. All of the above

74. You have just installed Windows 95 and you suspect that Windows 95 didn't detect your sound card because it doesn't show up in Device Manager. What file does Windows 95 create that records all devices found during Setup?

    A. setuplog.txt

    B. setup.txt

    C. detlog.txt

    D. detcrash.log

75. When a user profile is created, where is the user-specific information stored?

    A. %systemroot%\Profiles\

    B. %systemroot%\System\Profiles\

    C. %systemroot%\UserProfiles\

    D. %systemroot%\Config\Profiles\

76. Which tools let you remotely administer computers on your network?

    A. Registry Editor

    B. System Policy Editor

    C. Net Watcher

    D. Explorer

77. Which of the following is *not* a benefit of DriveSpace Compression?

    A. DriveSpace is integrated into the operating system.

    B. DriveSpace uses no conventional memory.

    C. DriveSpace uses all 32-bit code.

    D. DriveSpace drivers stay loaded at all times.

78. You are having trouble with your Windows 95 machine and have used the verification of installed components option. What crucial element of Windows 95 will be rebuilt during this process?

    A. vmm32.vxd

    B. system.dat

    C. user.dat

79. You and a colleague are using system policies for your Windows 95 users, but they don't seem to be working. You think they are being saved in the wrong location. Where on a Windows NT server are logon scripts saved?

    A. C:\nt_root\logon

    B. C:\nt_root\system32\

    C. C:\nt_root\system32\repl\import

    D. C:\nt_root\system32\repl\import\scripts

80. In addition to File and Print Sharing, what must be set up in order for a Windows 95 system to share a printer?

    A. Nothing

    B. Configuration files

    C. The appropriate printer drivers

    D. The administrator account

81. A user tried to print a memo, but the print job didn't reach the desired printer. No print errors were displayed, and the job isn't listed in the print queue. What is the most likely cause?

    A. The wrong print driver was installed.

    B. The user isn't logged on to the network.

C. The print job was sent to another printer.

D. The printer was paused.

82. Participating in an NT domain allows a Windows 95 computer to use what level of security?

A. Group level

B. User level

C. Share level

D. Resource level

83. Unless user profiles have been enabled in Windows 95, all users use which profile when using the workstation?

A. SYSTEM

B. USRPROF

C. DEFAULT

D. None of the above

84. Which program file in Windows 95 can save and restore the Windows 95 Registry?

A. REGIBACK.EXE

B. BACKUP.EXE

C. CFGREG.EXE

D. GFGBACK.EXE

E. CFGBACK.EXE

85. You and a colleague are using system policies for your Windows 95 users. They don't seem to be working, however. You think they are being saved in the wrong location. Where on a NetWare server are logon scripts saved?

    A. The user's home directories

    B. The user's Mail id

    C. SYS:PUBLIC

    D. SYS:LOGON

86. What protocol does Microsoft use to interact with the default protocol used by NetWare 3.x?

    A. NetBIOS

    B. NWLink

    C. IPX/SPX

    D. NetBEUI

87. You have implemented roving user profiles on your network, but your users complain that when they log in to other Windows 95 computers, they don't get their user profile information. What could be the cause of this problem?

    A. User profiles aren't enabled on the computers the users are accessing.

    B. The users in question aren't members of your Windows NT domain and can't access information on the NT server.

    C. The network users don't have rights to the NETLOGON directory located on the Windows NT server.

    D. The users have accidentally deleted their profile information.

88. You are a consultant to a small financial group. Because of the size of their LAN and their budget, you have opted to use only Windows 95 as their network OS. What is the best protocol to use at this time?

    A. IPX/SPX

    B. TCP/IP

    C. DLC

    D. NetBEUI

89. A client asks how he can fit more data on his existing hard drive without adding another hard drive or storing files on a network. Which Windows 95 disk utility should he use to compress the data on his hard drive?

    A. DoubleSpace

    B. DriveSpace

    C. Disk Defragmenter

    D. ScanDisk

90. The help desk has suggested that you reinstall your print driver. What should you do?

    A. Remove the print driver and then reinstall it.

    B. Remove the print driver, reboot the computer, and then reinstall the driver.

    C. Reboot the computer and then reinstall the driver.

    D. Reboot the printer and then reinstall the driver.

91. This is a scenario question. First you must review the situation, and then you should review the objectives. Following that is a proposed solution. You must choose the best evaluation of that solution. Note that Questions 92 and 93 deal with the same scenario.

SITUATION:

The Accounting group has 20 Excel spreadsheets that they swap back and forth on a regular basis. Until now, they had been saving the files to floppy disks and laying them on each other's desks. However, the "Accounting disks" finally began to wear out, and the accountants decided that there had to be a better way. One of the accountants, Fred, created a share on his hard drive and placed all the spreadsheets in it. But now it seems that everyone in the company can get into the files. To make matters worse, someone printed the spreadsheet that had all the payroll information and posted it on a bulletin board. Now the Accounting group is blaming you for not securing the network. Your boss told you in no uncertain terms to rectify the situation before you go home.

When you ask Fred what he did, he said he accepted all the defaults. However, he goes on to explain that there are three distinct functions in the Accounting group: Accounts Payable, Accounts Receivable, and Payroll. The objectives listed next are the ones that Fred tried to accomplish for these groups. To meet the demands of your boss and to regain the respect of your peers, you must achieve the same objectives.

MAJOR OBJECTIVES:

- Each Accounting function group must have complete access to its respective spreadsheets.
- Each Accounting function group should not have access to the spreadsheets that belong to the other groups.

MINOR OBJECTIVES:

- The Department head wants to be able to look at all of the spreadsheets from time to time.
- Under no circumstances should anyone outside of Accounting have access to any of the Accounting spreadsheets.
- The group has made it clear that they do not want to "put up with a bunch of passwords."

PROPOSED SOLUTION:

Tell Fred to go back to using floppy disks.

EVALUATION OF PROPOSED SOLUTION (choose the best answer):

A. The proposed solution meets all objectives and is outstanding.

B. The proposed solution meets all of the major objectives and most of the minor objectives and is very good.

C. The proposed solution meets only one of the major objectives and all of the minor objectives and is good.

D. The proposed solution meets none of the major objectives and all of the minor objectives but is adequate.

E. The proposed solution meets none of the major objectives and only some of the minor objectives and is not adequate.

F. The proposed solution meets none of the major objectives and none of the minor objectives and is likely to get you fired.

92. This question uses the same scenario and objectives as Question 91. Evaluate the proposed solution and choose the best answer.

PROPOSED SOLUTION:

Share the Accounting directory as actshare. Configure share-level security on all client workstations in the Accounting department. Select Depends on password for actshare, and set both read-only passwords and full-access passwords for the new share. Once this is done, inform the users of their new passwords.

EVALUATION OF PROPOSED SOLUTION:

A. The proposed solution meets all objectives and is outstanding.

B. The proposed solution meets all of the major objectives and most of the minor objectives and is very good.

C. The proposed solution meets only one of the major objectives and all of the minor objectives and is good.

D. The proposed solution meets none of the major objectives and all of the minor objectives but is adequate.

E. The proposed solution meets none of the major objectives and only some of the minor objectives and is not adequate.

F. The proposed solution meets none of the major objectives and none of the minor objectives and is likely to get you fired.

93. This question uses the same scenario and objectives as Questions 91 and 92. Evaluate the proposed solution and choose the best answer.

PROPOSED SOLUTION:

Create three directories on the server. Place all the Excel spreadsheets for Accounts Receivable in one directory. Place the spreadsheets for Accounts Payable and Payroll in their own separate directories. Create four groups on the server: ar, ap, py, and depthd. Grant full-access rights to each group for its respective directory. Do not grant rights to anyone else other than the depthd group. Grant read rights to all three directories for the depthd group.

EVALUATION OF PROPOSED SOLUTION:

A. The proposed solution meets all objectives and is outstanding.

B. The proposed solution meets all of the major objectives and most of the minor objectives and is very good.

C. The proposed solution meets only one of the major objectives and all of the minor objectives and is good.

D. The proposed solution meets none of the major objectives and all of the minor objectives but is adequate.

E. The proposed solution meets none of the major objectives and only some of the minor objectives and is not adequate.

F. The proposed solution meets none of the major objectives and none of the minor objectives and is likely to get you fired.

94. All other factors being equal, which of the following machines on a network would most likely be the master browser?

A. Windows 95 Workstation

B. Windows NT Workstation

C. Windows NT Server

D. Windows for Workgroups Workstation

95. Windows 95 allows communication scripts that are compliant with what standard?

    A. PPP

    B. SLIP

    C. TCP

    D. IPX/SPX

96. In which file does Windows 95 store specific user profile information?

    A. SYSTEM.DAT

    B. CONFIG.POL

    C. USER.DA0

    D. USER.DAT

97. What course of action would you recommend to a coworker if his MS-DOS-based application can't access the modem, but all Windows-based applications can?

    A. Adjust the IRQ setting in the MS-DOS-based application.

    B. Adjust the IRQ setting for the modem COM port.

    C. Reinstall the MS-DOS-based application.

    D. Set the modem to a higher baud rate in the Modem settings in Control Panel.

98. In what location on a Windows NT server must you place the USER.DAT or USER.MAN file to allow automatic downloading to Windows 95 computers when users log in?

    A. The Windows NT NETLOGON directory

    B. The Windows NT import\scripts directory

C. The user's home directory

D. None of the above

99. In order for users on a network to send and receive fax messages on a shared fax modem, what two requirements must be met?

A. The Automatic Routing option should be set so that messages are automatically forwarded to the appropriate user on the network.

B. On the computer that has the shared fax modem, Exchange must be running at all times.

C. Microsoft Fax must be running at all times.

D. The Let other people on the network use my modem to send faxes option should be set on the computer that has the fax modem.

100. You have just recently enabled user profiles on your network. You decide to use roving mandatory user profiles and place the appropriate USER.DAT file in the NETLOGON directory of your Windows NT server. You note, however, that when you log in to a Windows 95 computer that has user profiles enabled, your profile information is not downloaded to the workstation. What steps must you take to correct this problem and complete your implementation of user profiles?

A. Rename the USER.DAT file USER.MAN.

B. Share the NETLOGON directory as EVERYONE read access.

C. Rename the USER.DAT file USER.MAN and place the file in the user's home directory.

D. Rename the USER.DAT file USER.MAN and place the file in the user's mail user_id directory.

101. You and a colleague have decided to use the automated routing method of installing Windows 95. What are your choices with this method? Choose all that apply.

    A. Login scripts that automatically run Setup when a user logs into a file server or domain.

    B. Microsoft SMS, or another network management software package, to do a push installation.

    C. Use e-mail to send users an .inf file that starts Setup when they double-click the file.

    D. Use sysdiff.exe to clone images of Windows 95 PCs and download them to other PCs.

102. What information is contained in every backup set, in addition to the files that were backed up?

    A. The path to the Windows 95 Backup program

    B. The Windows 95 Registry

    C. The parameters that were set for the backup session

    D. The name of the last full backup set

103. A backup set that includes only files that have changed since the last full backup is called what?

    A. A partial backup

    B. An incremental backup

    C. An incomplete backup

    D. An archive backup

104. What is the default protocol used by NetWare 3.x?

    A. NetBIOS

    B. NWLink

C. IPX/SPX

D. NetBEUI

105. What types of remote access servers can a Windows 95 client connect to?

A. NetWare Connect

B. Any UNIX server that runs SLIP or PPP

C. Windows NT Workstation

D. MS-DOS-based server

106. You have installed Windows 95 on your PC, and you want to view information about the Setup process. What file does Windows 95 create that logs all Setup information?

A. setuplog.txt

B. setup.log

C. instlog.txt

D. detect.log

107. Which drivers are loaded when you reboot into Safe mode? Choose all that apply.

A. Network cards

B. Super VGA

C. Printer drivers

D. Mouse

108. Long filenames are preserved for older applications using which technique?

    A. LFN conversion

    B. Thunking

    C. Tunneling

    D. Thonking

109. When new users log on to a Windows 95 computer that has user profiles enabled, a copy of what profile is loaded for the new user?

    A. DEFAULT

    B. SYSTEM

    C. USER.DAT

    D. USER.MAN

110. When possible, which of the following client packages should be used?

    A. NETX

    B. VLMs

    C. 32-bit Client for NetWare Networks

    D. NetBIOS

111. Jack wants to use Net Watcher to view connections to his local computer. He wants to see the users connected to your computer. Which toolbar button do you click to allow this?

    A. View Users

    B. Show Connected Users

    C. View Connected Users

    D. Show Users

112. You want to install Windows 95 on your computer that is running Windows for Workgroups. What must you do to preserve your current setting for Windows 95?

   A. Back up all system files.

   B. Back up your config.sys and autoexec.bat files.

   C. Specify that Windows 95 should be installed in the same directory as Windows for Workgroups.

   D. Specify that Windows 95 should be installed in a different directory than Windows for Workgroups.

113. A user needs to restore the Registry on her computer. She has already removed the attributes on her files. What is the next step she needs to perform in order to complete the process of restoring the Registry?

   A. Copy USER.DA0 to USER.DAT and then copy SYSTEM.DA0 to SYSTEM.DAT.

   B. Delete USER.DAT and SYSTEM.DAT. Windows 95 will restore the Registry when it is rebooted.

   C. Rename USER.DA0 to USER.DAT, and then rename SYSTEM.DA0 SYSTEM.DAT.

   D. Delete USER.DA0 and SYSTEM.DA0. Windows 95 will restore the Registry when it is rebooted.

114. Where is the Add New Hardware wizard located in Windows 95?

   A. Taskbar

   B. My Computer

   C. The Start menu

   D. Control Panel

115. You want to monitor more than one computer concurrently using the System Monitor. What action must you take?

   A. You can connect to the desired computers by starting multiple instances of the System Monitor.

   B. To connect to more than one computer, you need to select multiple computers using the File menu.

   C. You can view only one computer at a time using the System Monitor.

   D. When selecting multiple computers, hold down the Ctrl key.

Answers and Explanations

1. A, B, D. C is not a realistic option. To run Windows 95 as a shared installation, the 95 source files must be on a hard disk, not a CD-ROM.

2. A. NETLOGON is the default location for the config.pol file in Windows NT for computers using user-level security.

3. D. Unless a user is given special permission, he can't change the drivers on a remote server.

4. A. The initial VM environment for MS-DOS applications is allocated 640 KB of conventional memory and 384 KB of upper memory.

5. C. ScanDisk can detect cross-linked files.

6. A. IPX/SPX is the protocol typically used by NetWare.

7. B, C, D. If the card isn't seated properly, Windows 95 won't detect it. When Windows 95 recognizes new hardware, it tries to find a driver. If it doesn't find one, or it can't tell what driver this is, often you can click the Have Disk button. Another thing you could tell her to do is to just run the Add New Hardware wizard. If Windows 95 can't find anything, you can tell it to show all devices and then manually select the device.

8. B. NTFS is accessible only by Windows NT.

9. C. SCSI tape devices are not supported by Windows 95 backup.

10. C. Windows 95 can process Windows NT logon scripts during logon.

11. A. Slow file access is a symptom of fragmentation. She should run Disk Defragmenter.

12. D. In NetWare, a user's profile is pulled from his mail user_id directory.

13. B. Changing the CD-ROM setting increases the amount of cache available to the CD-ROM. This can negatively affect system performance if RAM is limited.

14. D. Computer policies must be located in this directory in order to be implemented.

15. D. You use Windows 95's TCP/IP networking protocol to connect to the Internet.

16. D. The default profile is used when profiles are not enabled.

17. A, B, C, D. All options are correct.

18. C. Double-clicking Network Neighborhood will display all the resources on a network.

19. B, C. To access file and print capabilities on a dial-up server, you must install File and Print Sharing services in the Network icon of Control Panel and enable the Allow Caller Access option.

20. B. You configure display properties for an MS-DOS application from the Screen tab of the application shortcut icon's properties sheet.

21. C. Passwords are kept in the *.pwl file, where * represents the user's name.

22. A. System Monitor allows monitoring of the file system, such as bytes read per second or bytes written per second, to discover what is consuming bandwidth.

23. A. Install Windows 95 in a different directory than Windows 3.1.

24. C. In Windows NT, a user's profile is pulled from his home directory. The .man extension prevents changes from being written to his profile.

25. A. To get to Net Watcher through Network Neighborhood, right-click the computer.

26. C. You can make a new Dial-Up Networking connection by opening Dial-Up Networking and choosing the Make New Connection icon. The Make New Connection wizard will open.

27. D. Information in user.dat is used to create this key.

28. D. Most MS-DOS applications require the printer to be physically attached to a printer port. You can do this by capturing the printer port in the Details tab of the printer's Properties dialog box.

29. D. If you put a $ on the end of a share name, this makes it a hidden share.

30. A. By automating the installation process, administrators can save time and customize the installation.

31. C. The files are located with the original installation files.

32. B. The machine that logs out last will overwrite the profile information that is in the user's home directory.

33. C. File and Print sharing must be enabled, because you are dealing with network shares.

34. C. Through Setup you can run a verification that will ensure that Windows 95's system files are in working order. If they are found to be damaged or missing, Setup will reinstall the appropriate files.

35. A. The frame type used by NetWare servers must be consistent with the frame type used by the Windows 95 machines.

36. C. detcrash.log is a binary file that lets Setup evaluate what phase of hardware detection caused the machine to crash. This file exists only during installation.

37. B. When a Windows 95 computer participates in a domain, it can use user-level security to share and access resources on a per-user account basis.

38. A. The .man extension makes the profile mandatory, not allowing users to change their settings.

39. B. netlog.txt records all information about network components during the installation phase.

40. C. You must install Windows 95 in a different directory than Windows for Workgroups.

41. C. Windows 95 can process Windows NT logon scripts during logon.

42. D. Sometimes different drivers interfere with each other. Remove all drivers and then add them again, one at a time, noting any problems.

43. B

44. A, B

45. B, C

46. A. The default is used for new users. Any changes made to the settings will remain for that particular user in the future.

47. C. If MS-DOS-based and Windows 3.1-based applications are unable to access the modem, but Windows 95-based applications can, you should make sure that Microsoft Exchange Remote Mail, Microsoft Fax, and Dial-Up Networking are not waiting for incoming calls. If they are, older applications can't access the modem.

48. A

49. B. DriveSpace can compress the data on the drive, making more disk space available.

50. D. Did it ever work? This is one of the most basic questions to ask. She isn't getting an IP address, but does she need to specify one (her ISP would tell her), or does she need to select Obtain automatically in the IP Configuration tab? You don't want to start changing things until you know for sure what it is supposed to be.

51. A, B, C. Network locations and floppy disks are valid backup locations. Windows 95 Backup does not support SCSI tape devices.

52. A, B

53. D. Setting the spool option to print after the first page has spooled lets the printer print while the other pages are spooling. This is enabled by default.

54. D. Information in user.dat is used to create this key.

55. A. `HKEY_DYN_DATA` is a dynamic configuration table used by Plug and Play devices.

56. A. In System Monitor, when you select File | Connect, you may enter only one computer name. To look at more than one computer, you must start more than one instance of System Monitor.

57. C. Workgroups must use share-level security because the clients do not access a central Windows NT or NetWare accounts database.

58. B. Windows 95 Backup is not compatible with the MS-DOS Backup program.

59. D

60. A, C. Disabling file sharing and long filename preservation can affect older 16-bit applications. Long filenames are not supported under most 16-bit applications, and Windows 95 file sharing might not be compatible with older 16-bit applications.

61. C. If Close on Exit is checked, the VM for the MS-DOS application is closed as soon as the application exits.

62. A. You will be prompted to replace the existing files.

63. D. C.W. created a share but didn't give anyone permission to it. If you don't give permission to a share, people can't use it. Now, admittedly, he would have received error messages, but he was in a hurry.

64. A, B. Windows 95 provides support for 16-bit Novell NetWare clients, either NETX or VLMs.

65. A, B. To configure a Windows 95 computer to participate in a peer-to-peer workgroup, you need to specify only the computer name and workgroup name.

66. D. Windows NT 3.5 Server supports PPP, RAS, and SLIP clients.

67. B. Some applications replace this driver for various reasons.

68. A

69. A, B, C. All three are items from the category named Memory Manager.

70. B, C, D. Profiles can be managed through system policies, provided that the security has been configured to support roaming user profiles.

71. A

72. A

73. A, B. MS-DOS and most Windows 16-bit applications do not support long filenames.

74. C

75. A

76. A, B, C

77. D. DriveSpace drivers are loaded only when compressed media is detected and mounted.

78. A

79. D. System policies are saved on the NT Primary Domain Controller at \nt_root\system32\repl\import\scripts.

80. C. Without the right printer driver, printing won't work.

81. C. The wrong printer was probably selected as the default printer. Ensure that the desired printer is selected.

82. B. When a Windows 95 computer participates in a domain, it can use user-level security to share and access resources on a per-user account basis.

83. C. All logins use the default profile unless user profiles are turned on.

84. E. The CFGBACK.EXE file, found on the Windows 95 CD-ROM, can back up and restore the Registry.

85. C. System policies are saved on the NetWare server in SYS:PUBLIC.

86. B. NWLink is Microsoft's IPX/SPX-compatible protocol.

87. A. Profiles have not been enabled under Control Panel | Passwords | User Profiles.

88. D. NetBEUI is a small, fast protocol that is not routable.

89. B. DriveSpace is the Windows 95 utility that performs disk compression.

90. B. It is always a good practice to reboot the computer when you remove and then reinstall a service or device.

91. E. Laying floppy disks on desks is not a secure method. If they were kept locked up, you would have good physical security. However, this doesn't allow for file sharing in an expeditious manner. The only minor objective this solution might conceivably meet would be not having to remember passwords.

92. E. By sharing one directory with share-level security, you can't control access to the other groups' files. If they have the read password, users can read all the files in the share. There is no way to fine-tune controlled access to the files. In addition, this would require keeping track of extra passwords.

93. A. By configuring user-level security and creating specific directories for the files for each function, you now have a controllable solution. In addition, you can easily administer the solution in the future. If group membership changes,

you simply remove or add a person to the appropriate group on the server. Extra passwords are avoided because access is granted based on server group membership, not different passwords.

94. C. Windows NT computers are more favored to be browsers than Windows 95 computers.

95. B

96. D. This is the component of the Registry that contains user information.

97. A, B. If your MS-DOS-based applications can't access the modem, but all Windows-based applications can, try adjusting the IRQ setting in the MS-DOS-based application according to the application's documentation. If this setting can't be adjusted, adjust the IRQ setting for the modem COM port.

98. C. In Windows NT, the user profile file must be placed in the user's home directory.

99. B, D. Because Exchange is in charge of sending and receiving fax messages, it must be running at all times. You enable fax sharing with the Let other people on the network use my modem to send faxes option, located on the Modem tab of the Microsoft Fax properties sheet.

100. C. The file must have the .man extension and be located in the user's home directory.

101. A, B. C and D are not realistic options. Through login scripts, an .inf file could be initiated that would run the 95 Setup program before the user could continue with another process. Microsoft SMS is capable of completing a push installation.

102. C

103. B

104. C. IPX/SPX is the default protocol used by most versions of NetWare.

105. A, B, C. A dial-up client running the appropriate connection protocol can connect to many types of remote access servers, including Windows 95 dial-up server, Windows NT Workstation, Windows NT 3.1 or later, Windows for Workgroups 3.11, NetWare Connect, Shiva LanRover and other dial-up routers, and any UNIX server that runs SLIP or PPP.

106. A. setuplog.txt records information about the installation process.

107. D. Of all the possible answers, mouse is the only valid choice. Network cards, Super VGA, and printer drivers are not required for the operation of Windows 95, so they are not loaded with Safe mode.

108. C

109. A. The default is used for new users. Any changes made to the settings will remain in effect for that particular user in the future.

110. C. Where possible, the 32-bit Client for NetWare Networks is recommended for interoperability with NetWare networks.

111. D. Show Users will show the user name, computer name, connection time, open files, idle time, and number of shares he is using.

112. C. Install Windows 95 in the same directory as Windows for Workgroups.

113. A. Be careful to do this operation correctly. You copy USER.DA0 to USER.DAT, and then copy SYSTEM.DA0 to SYSTEM.DAT.

114. D

115. A. In System Monitor, when you select File | Connect, you may enter only one computer name. To look at more than one computer, you must start more than one instance of System Monitor.

Part 3

Appendixes

Appendix

70-064 Exam Hints

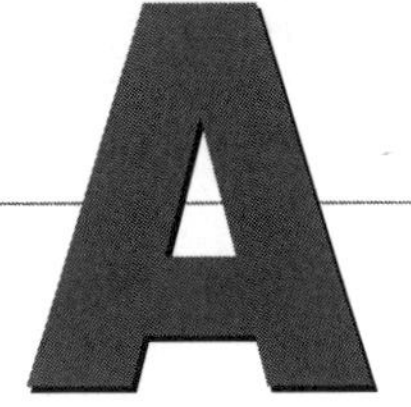

By now, you have studied the entire book, and are preparing to take the Windows 95 exam. Selecting the correct solution to a given situation often comes down to eliminating the obviously wrong choices, and then picking the right one from what is left. These exam tips will help you weed through some of the distracter answers you will see when you sit for your certification test. Rather than give you a bunch of facts you've read elsewhere in this book, this appendix reflects some of the author's experience in the beta exam—some things you need to know. The information is categorized by objective. Note that this is not a substitution for studying the rest of the book and working on a Windows 95 machine. It is to help you focus your studies.

Planning

Develop an appropriate implementation model for specific requirements in a Microsoft environment and a mixed Microsoft and NetWare environment. Considerations include the following:

- Choosing a workgroup configuration or logging on to an existing domain

Make sure you know the effect of the workgroup name on browsing and joining a domain. It is also important to know the different ways you can log on to an existing domain (that is, quick logon, and logon and restore connections).

Develop a security strategy in a Microsoft environment and a mixed Microsoft and NetWare environment. Strategies include the following:

- System policies

Make absolutely certain you have installed and configured system policies on a Windows 95 machine. This area is crucial for passing this exam. Know what effect checking a box, clearing a box, and leaving a box gray has on the policy. This can get somewhat confusing if you forget that a gray (does not matter) selection will not change what is currently in effect on the machine. Be very familiar with the kinds of things you can enforce from system policies (such as forcing a logon to a network).

- User profiles

User profiles are stored in different locations on a NetWare server, rather than on a Windows NT Server. NetWare stores profiles in the user's mail directory.

- File and printer sharing

You can install only one file and printer sharing per computer. For instance, if you have Client for Microsoft Networks and Client for NetWare Networks, you can install file and printer sharing for either Microsoft or NetWare, but not both. Additionally, if you do not have file and printer sharing installed, then your machine will not be able to share resident files or locally attached printers with other computers in the workgroup or domain.

Installation and Configuration

This objective is one of the main ones covered on the exam. In general, make sure you know how much space Windows 95 will require for a typical installation, a compact installation, and a portable installation. Of course, the custom installation option of Setup will allow more individualized control. (Refer to the tables in Chapter 2 for a quick refresher on these items.)

Install Windows 95. Installation options include the following:

- ▶ Automated Windows setup

Make sure you know what an MSBATCH.INF is, when you would use one, and what options can be specified with it. NETSETUP is also important. When you run NETSETUP, you can create a default script. Note that NETSETUP can only create a script. You cannot use NETSETUP to edit an existing script—to do that you must use a text editor (such as Notepad). NETSETUP also gives you the opportunity to allow (or disallow) user interaction. Make absolutely certain you know how to combine NETSETUP with Policies to achieve very specific setup configurations. This item shows up several times in scenario questions! (Microsoft goes into a good bit of detail on this objective. If it makes you nervous, you might want to review this section in Chapter 2.)

- ▶ New

Relatively straightforward—just remember that the hard disk needs an active partition. It also must be formatted with system files placed in it before you can install Windows 95.

- ▶ Upgrade

You can upgrade over Windows 3.1, Windows for Workgroups 3.11, and various versions of DOS as well as OS/2 (there are some specific questions so refer back to Chapter 2 and make sure you are comfortable with how this is done.) It is intuitively obvious, however, that you cannot upgrade programs like UNIX. Make sure you understand how to maintain program groups and related issues when upgrading as well.

- ▶ Uninstall

If you install Windows 95 (referring to UPGRADE, not new installation) into a separate directory, then you can use the uninstall routine later. If you install into the same directory (the default action), you cannot use the uninstall routine.

- Dual-boot combination with Microsoft Windows NT

The easiest way to do this is to install Windows 95 first, and then install Windows NT. There are a few "gotchas" to be aware of, though. Windows 95 will not work on an NTFS partition, and Windows NT will not work on FAT32. Also, Windows NT will not work if you use Windows 95 disk compression.

Install and configure the network components of a client computer and server in a Microsoft environment and a mixed Microsoft and NetWare environment.

You have two choices here: client for Microsoft, or client for NetWare. Just make sure you are comfortable with all the tabs and check boxes when you are configuring the clients. You may want to brush up on things like selecting the preferred server, and logging on to an NT domain. Do you know how to process login scripts? If you are not sure, then you might consider looking at Chapter 3 again.

Install and configure network protocols in a Microsoft environment and a mixed Microsoft and NetWare environment.

Protocols are hit pretty hard on the exam, both directly and indirectly. Some are general knowledge questions to ensure that you have a basic understanding of protocols, but the more particular questions require you to resolve poorly configured protocols. In general, make absolutely certain you know what each protocol is used for, and the advantages and disadvantages of each. If you need to brush up on these, review Chapter 3. Now, take a look at some of the more specific protocol issues on the exam:

- NetBEUI

NetBEUI is small and fast, but is not routable! This means it will not go across a router. Also, be aware that an NT Server with two Ethernet cards in it is acting as a router.

- IPX/SPX-compatible Protocol

IPX/SPX is used in NetWare environments. The Windows NT equivalent is NWLink. It is fast and routable. Make certain you know what SAP advertising is and when it is used. Do you know how to enable NetBIOS over IPX? What about frame types? IPX/SPX keeps on showing up in questions. If you are not comfortable with it, you really need to go back to Chapter 3 and brush up on it. When exam day rolls around, you will be glad you did.

- TCP/IP

TCP/IP is hit really hard. It seems as if they ask all kinds of questions here. Know what kind of information a DHCP server can give out. Know about default gateways, and subnet masks (they might show you a screen shot of a TCP/IP properties box—if they do, study it carefully). Make sure you know about DNS servers and WINS servers. A good background here will aid you in the troubleshooting scenario questions.

- Microsoft DLC

Basically, all you need to know is what it is used for (that is, some HP printers, connectivity to mainframes, and at times AS-400s).

- PPTP/VPN

Just know what it is and when it is used. This area is not hit very heavily on the exam. (Hey, don't be disappointed. They can't ask everything.)

Install and configure hardware devices in a Microsoft environment and a mixed Microsoft and NetWare environment. Hardware devices include the following:

- Modems

Are you familiar with the Add Modem Wizard? It seems that Microsoft is really proud of it. Make sure you know what it does, what it asks for, and how you use it. If you are unfamiliar with it, there are some screen shots in Chapter 2, as well as some exercises to walk you through using it. In addition to using the wizard, make sure you are familiar with the modem settings because they show up in some of the scenario questions.

- Printers

Printing is always an important topic, both in real life and on exams. Adding a new printer is nothing compared to configuring it. Make sure you are familiar with all the different properties you can have for printers. Make absolutely certain you are familiar with all the spool settings (look them over and know what each one does). Know the difference between RAW and EMF spooling. Know about bidirectional support and what kind of printer cable is needed (you need an IEEE 1284-compliant cable). Know about PCL and PS. To do point and print on a Windows NT server, you install the drivers for the Windows 95 machine on the server. If this is a little confusing, then look over the printer section in Chapter 2.

Configure system services. Services include the following:

- Browser

For browsing, make sure you know how to configure a browse master (under File and Print services for Microsoft Networks). In addition, this is where the SAP advertising comes in under File and Print services for NetWare. Remember that you cannot have both File and Print services on the same computer. In addition, if you have RPC Print Provider, then you cannot have File and Print services for NetWare installed. If you want to browse a Microsoft Network, you can use Network Neighborhood or you can use the Net View command from a command prompt.

Install and configure backup hardware and software. Hardware and software include the following:

- Tape drives

Remember that Windows 95 backup does not work with SCSI drives or QIC Wide drives. It does work with QIC 40, 80, and 3010 (but not 3020 drives). If you have properly installed a compatible tape drive, then Windows 95 will automatically detect the drive. If you change drives, you can select Redetect tape drive from the Tools menu if needed.

- The Backup application

You can back up your data to tape, floppy, or a networked drive. In addition to this, you can back up a networked drive if you want. Make sure you understand the difference between a full backup, and an incremental backup. If you are a little fuzzy on some of the nuances, you may want to look over the Backup section of Chapter 2.

Configuring and Managing Resource Access

Assign access permissions for shared folders in a Microsoft environment and a mixed Microsoft and NetWare environment. Methods include the following:

- Passwords

Passwords are changed by using the Password applet in Control Panel. If you are in a NetWare environment, then you have to go to a command prompt and type **SETPASS**.

- User permissions

Make sure you understand how User permissions are set, where they come from, and how they are changed.

- Group permissions

Here you need to know the effect of multiple group memberships. Know what happens if you single out one user for NO ACCESS, even if he has been granted access through membership in another group. If it sounds confusing, then you might want to look at Chapter 4 again.

Create, share, and monitor resources. Resources include the following:

- Remote

Remember that you have to be running USER Level Access Control to install and configure many of the Remote management tools.

- Network printers

Most of this was already covered in Printers in general. Just make sure you remember about RPC Printer and how you would manage a Network Printer remotely.

- Shared fax modem

Make sure you know how you would share a fax modem.

- Unimodem/V

Make sure you understand the Unimodem driver and how it is applied in Windows 95. Know how the .INF file is modified by vendor-specific settings.

Set up user environments by using user profiles and system policies.

This area is hit pretty hard on the exam. Make sure you know about NETLOGON and what is stored there. Know about logon scripts and home directories—what they do and when they are used. Make absolutely certain you know how to configure user profiles and system policies—this crops up in both general knowledge questions and in scenario questions. These are cause-and-effect kinds of things. For instance: You want to do A, B, and C. You do D, E, and F. Did you actually achieve A, B, and C, or maybe only B and C? Some of these questions actually take up two screens, and you have to scroll back and forth. You need to know this section well or time will slip away from you! If you need a little refresher, look back over Chapter 4. Finally, don't forget about roaming profiles: Know where they are stored, how they are configured, and when you would use one.

Back up data and restore data.

The beta exam had only a few questions on this objective; see the previous hints above under configuring Tape drives and the Backup application.

Manage hard disks. Tasks include the following:

- Disk compression

Make sure you understand how to create a compressed drive and how to move around the amount of space on the Host drive. Remember, you cannot compress a drive and expect Windows NT to run on it.

- Partitioning

You use FDISK to create and manage partitions on a drive. Make sure you understand about extended DOS partitions, Primary DOS partitions, and active partitions. This knowledge will be good for a couple of extra points on the exam.

Establish application environments for Microsoft MS-DOS® applications.

Make sure you are familiar with the different ways you can configure a DOS application to run in Windows 95. Know the differences between suggest DOS mode and DOS mode. Know how to configure memory and what happens when you run full screen as opposed to in a Window. You do not edit PIF files anymore.

Integration and Interoperability

Configure a Windows 95 computer as a client computer in a Windows NT network.

See the previous notes under configuring network components of a client computer.

Configure a Windows 95 computer as a client computer in a NetWare network.

See the previous notes under configuring network components of a client computer.

Configure a Windows 95 computer to access the Internet.

This is basically a combination of Configuring Dial–Up Networking and TCP/IP.

For specific information, refer to Chapter 5 for a brush-up on configuring clients in other networks.

Configure a client computer to use Dial-Up Networking for remote access in a Microsoft environment and a mixed Microsoft and NetWare environment.

Here, again, it is mostly a matter of getting Dial-Up Networking installed properly, setting up the modem properly, and binding the appropriate protocols. It can get complicated, but mercifully is not hit too hard on the exam. Remember, if you do not have a modem installed, and you try to configure Dial-up Networking, it *will* take you through the Add Modem Wizard first. Also, remember in Windows NT, Dial-Up Networking is called RAS (Remote Access Service). If you feel you need more study in this area, look at Chapter 5 or in the configuring modems section in Chapter 2.

Monitoring and Optimization

Monitor system performance. Tools include the following:

- Net Watcher

Know the requirements to install and use Net Watcher. Make sure you have a good feel for the kind of information you can obtain here.

- System Monitor

You do not need to know what every single counter is in System Monitor, but you do need to experiment with it, and have a really good feel for the kinds of information you can get from it. If you need a overview of this tool, look over Chapter 6.

Tune and optimize the system in a Microsoft environment and a mixed Microsoft and NetWare environment. Tools include the following:

- Disk Defragmenter

Know when you would run the Disk Defragmenter and why. You also need to remember that there are different ways to run the Disk Defragmenter, such as Full Defragmentation, Defragment Files, and Consolidate Free Space Only. Make sure you have a good feel for when you would use each option.

- ScanDisk

Do you know what kinds of errors ScanDisk will detect and correct? If not, you might want to look over Chapter 5.

- DriveSpace

See the earlier comments on DriveSpace.

Troubleshooting

Many of the Troubleshooting items have already been covered. On the exam, questions seem to fall into multiple objectives. This is particularly true of the scenario questions. Although there are a few general knowledge questions, the majority are couched in some kind of troubleshooting genre.

Diagnose and Resolve Installation Failures

Make sure you know about the different files a Windows 95 setup creates. Know which ones you can read and use for diagnostics, and which ones Windows 95 reserves for its own use. Pay particular attention if the installation is an upgrade: Where was the old installation and where did you install the new files? Remember that Windows 95 does not need Share and SmartDrive. Make sure you look at old configuration files very carefully. If you need some more help with this area, look at Chapter 7.

Diagnose and Resolve Boot Process Failures

You'll see only a few basic types of bootup issues with a Windows 95 machine, including virus, hardware, and Registry problems. Make sure you know the symptoms of each. In addition to these items, if you know how to use Safe Mode to get the machine back up and running, then you have this objective well in hand. If not, you might want to refer to Chapter 7.

Diagnose and resolve connectivity problems in a Microsoft environment and a mixed Microsoft and NetWare environment. Tools include the following:

- WinIPCfg

Make sure you are familiar with the information you obtain from WinIPCfg. Couple this with the information from the TCP/IP section and you will do well here.

- Net Watcher

With Net Watcher, it is important to know what you can do with it, and what you cannot do with it. Make sure you understand the requirements for running Net Watcher.

- Troubleshooting wizards

The troubleshooting wizards are not covered in very much detail. You basically need to know that they are available and how you would use them.

Diagnose and resolve printing problems in a Microsoft environment and a mixed Microsoft and NetWare environment.

See the earlier discussion on printing under configuring printers.

Diagnose and resolve file system problems.

Refer to the discussions on ScanDisk and Disk Defragmenter.

Diagnose and resolve resource access problems in a Microsoft environment and a mixed Microsoft and NetWare environment.

This was covered in the section on configuring clients and protocols.

Diagnose and resolve hardware device and device driver problems. Tools include the following:

- Add Hardware Wizard

You cannot use the Add Hardware Wizard to remove hardware, but you can remove a device in Device Manager, reboot the machine, and then run the Add Hardware Wizard to correct configuration problems. In addition to this, you can use Device Manager (under system in Control Panel) to identify and resolve IRQ problems, in a fashion similar to that of MSD in old Windows 3.x. You need to remember, however, that device information is not available under Safe Mode because many of the drivers are not loaded. You can use Safe Mode, though, to make changes to a display setting or to add a missing driver that is keeping Windows 95 from booting. If you need assistance with this objective, refer to Chapter 7.

Perform direct modification of the Registry as appropriate by using Regedit.

Make sure you know that Regedit is used to edit the Registry in Windows 95. It is also important to know how to back up the Registry. For instance, you can export a key, copy the USER.DAT and SYSTEM.DAT files, or use CFGBCK. However, are these the only ways to back up the Registry? If you are unsure, refer to the section on the Registry in Chapter 7. If you couple this with a general knowledge of the six keys (regarding what is contained in each key) and you know how to use Remote Registry Editor, then you will do fine on this part of the exam.

Summary

Here's hoping you do well on the exam. Hopefully, this book and this appendix, as well as your experience actually working with Windows 95 (a must), will have appropriately prepared you. If you feel you need more exam-type practice, you are encouraged to take the practice exams located before this appendix and pick up a copy of Macmillan Publishing's *Windows 95 TestPrep* for exam 70-064. It is basically a workbook with tons of questions by objective and some practice exams. Also, make sure you spend some time using the TestPrep test engine included on the CD-ROM that comes with this book. Study hard and good luck!

Appendix B

Glossary

32-bit operating system architecture—The 32-bit, protected-mode subsystems built into Windows 95 are more crash resistant. A bad application, whether 16-bit or 32-bit, is less likely to stop the operating system.

A

Active fax modem—The fax modem that is used to send and receive faxes. It can be a modem connected to the user's computer or a shared fax modem on the network.

Add/Remove Programs—A Control Panel applet used to add and remove programs, install additional Windows 95 components, and create a Windows 95 StartUp disk.

Address Resolution Protocol (ARP)—Used to map IP addresses to the MAC address layer of a NIC.

ADMIN.ADM—A system policy template used to define system policies.

Algorithm—A formula for performing a certain calculation. Windows 95 uses a particular algorithm to calculate an 8.3 alias for a long filename.

Alias—The 8.3 name associated with long filenames, so that long filenames are accessible through DOS and Windows 3.x.

Application Program Interface (API)—Provides all applications with a common means of interacting with an application.

Archive—A stored copy of data files that is kept up to date over time.

Arrange Icons—Leads to another menu that enables the contents to be sorted alphabetically by name, size, type, or modification date.

Attributes—Properties of a file that indicate whether the file is a Hidden, Read-Only, or System file.

B

B1 error—This message appears when the user runs the installation program and the processor type is a stepping processor that is not supported under Windows 95.

Background—Use the Background tab to establish settings for the screen's background pattern and wallpaper.

Backup set—A backed-up copy of data files along with the preferences that were set up for that backup session.

Bad clusters—Clusters on a hard disk that reside in an area where the surface magnetic media is defective.

Bad sectors—Sectors of the media that cannot hold a magnetic charge due to normal wear or physical damage.

Baseline—A snapshot of the performance settings for a computer during its normal day-to-day functions. It represents an average use of the computer and is used for comparisons.

BATCH.EXE—A Windows-based program called Batch Setup makes it easy to create custom scripts.

Bindery—NetWare's database of users and resources that is a means by which items are bound or linked.

Bindings—The process of associating a protocol with a network card or a service.

Bitmap (BMP)—Bitmap file is the standard Windows bitmap format.

Boot menu—A displayed text screen listing StartUp options when F8 is pressed during Windows 95 StartUp.

BOOTLOG.TXT—An ASCII text file that contains a record of the current StartUp process when starting Windows 95, including components and drivers.

Bottlenecks—Areas that can slow down a computer's performance by creating a queue where processes or functions must wait to be processed or executed.

Briefcase—When the user updates files by using Briefcase, Windows 95 automatically replaces unmodified files with modified files. If both files have changed, Windows 95 calls the appropriate application (if available) to merge the disparate files.

Browse master—The master browse server is responsible for maintaining the master list of workgroups, domains, and computers in a given workgroup.

Browsing—Seeing what computers and resources are available across the network.

Bus enumerator—A software driver that communicates with the devices attached to a particular type of bus architecture.

C

Caching—The process of storing disk information in memory for faster access. Windows 95 can store information to be written to disk in memory and write it to disk at a later time when the system is not busy.

Cancel—To delete a print job from the queue.

CFGBACK.EXE—A Configuration Backup utility that can save and restore up to nine configurations of a Windows 95 Registry.

Chain—A series of clusters that make up a file. The first cluster in a chain contains a pointer to the location of the second, which contains a pointer to the location of the third, and so on.

Challenge—Handshake Authentication Protocol (CHAP)—Periodically verifies the identity of the peer, using a three-way handshake. The authenticator sends a challenge message to the peer, which responds with a value using a one-way encryption. The authenticator then checks this response and, if the values match, the authentication is acknowledged; otherwise, the connection is ended.

Cluster—A grouping of sectors that is the minimum amount of disk space that can be allocated to a file.

Cold-docking—A style of docking that requires the laptop to be turned off before it can be removed from or inserted into a docking station.

Command-line switches—Adds flexibility to the way a window or folder is viewed.

Compact—The option for users who have extremely limited disk space. Installs only the minimum files required to run Windows 95.

Compressed drive—Files that have been compressed are stored in a Compressed Volume File (CVF), which is assigned a drive letter. This drive letter refers to the compressed drive.

Compressed Volume File (CVF)—The CVF contains the contents of a compressed drive.

CompuServe—An online information service that offers email messaging, forums, and access to the Internet.

CONFIG.POL—The policy file that contains policy information related to the system user settings, created with the System Policy Editor and which must be placed in the default location. Registry information in the CONFIG.POL file can overwrite any existing information in the computer's Registry when downloaded.

Configuration Manager—The Windows 95 component that is in charge of the entire Plug and Play configuration process.

Consolidate—To move together; Windows 95 can consolidate free space on a hard disk by moving all data together to the front of the disk.

Contiguous space—An uninterrupted stream of disk clusters. Files that occupy sequential clusters on a disk without empty clusters are said to reside in contiguous space.

Cooperative multitasking—Cooperative multitasking requires the application to periodically check the message queue and cooperatively release control of the system to other applications that are running. In a cooperatively multitasked environment, one application generally maintains control of the CPU until the application has completed its task. Once the task is completed, the CPU is released to the next application awaiting access to the CPU.

Corruption—Errors in the file system that result in unreadable data.

Cross-linked—If file A has a cluster with some data and a pointer to cluster 12, and file B has a cluster that also points to cluster 12, these files are said to be cross-linked.

Cross-linked files—When two or more files share the same sector on the storage media.

Custom installation—The option for users who want to select applications and network components to be installed, and confirm the configuration settings for devices.

Customized MS-DOS mode—MS-DOS mode can be customized so that an application can make use of specific system parameter settings that differ from those needed by most other MS-DOS applications.

D

DBLSPACE—This Windows 95 SetUp program replaces the old DOS file compression program.

DEBUG.EXE—A utility used to evaluate binary files during troubleshooting.

Deferred printing—The capability to print to a print queue even if the printer is currently unavailable.

Degradation—System performance loss due to less than optimal conditions on the hard disk.

Destination—The intended location for the backed-up files.

Details—Shows the contents of the folder as a detailed list. The detailed list contains the name, size, type, and date of the most recent modification.

DETCRASH.LOG—A binary file that exists only during the hardware detection phase.

DETLOG.TXT—An ASCII text file that contains a record of all devices found during the hardware detection phase of installation.

Device—A physical component on a computer, such as the printer, mouse, monitor, and so on.

Device conflicts—Conflicts can occur if applications access hardware directly. For this reason, direct access is not allowed under Windows 95. Direct access to hardware is only supported in MS-DOS mode.

Device driver—A configuration file that specifies the settings for a hardware component.

Device Manager—Part of the System applet that enables the user to view and edit hardware settings.

Dialing Properties—A utility that has been integrated with Phone Dialer, HyperTerminal, Dial-Up Networking, and other communications applications created for Windows 95.

Dial-Up Networking—A service used for remote access to network services such as file and printer sharing, electronic mail, scheduling, and SQL database access. It provides remote networking for telecommuters, mobile workers, and system administrators who monitor and manage servers at multiple branch offices.

Dial-Up Networking Client—A remote computer configured to access a Windows 95 dial-up server or other remote access servers. With Dial-Up Networking, the dial-up client running the appropriate connection protocol can connect to many types of remote access servers, including the following: Windows 95 Dial-Up Server, Windows NT Workstation, Windows NT 3.1 or later, Windows for Workgroups 3.11, NetWare Connect, Shiva LanRover and other dial-up routers, and any UNIX server that runs SLIP or PPP.

Dial-Up Scripting—A scripting application can be used by Dial-Up Networking for connecting to remote servers using SLIP. With this application installed, a user can associate an existing dial-in connection with a text file (script) to be run after the modem dials the remote server.

Direct access—Direct access to system hardware is not available under Windows 95. If an MS-DOS application requires this, it must be run in MS-DOS mode.

Direct Cable Connection—With Direct Cable Connection, the user can establish a direct serial or parallel cable connection between two computers so that the resources of the computer designated as the host can be shared. If the host is connected to a network, the guest computer can also access the network.

Directory entry—Each file in a FAT file system has an entry in the Directory entry table that points to the location of the file. Files with long filenames require additional Directory entries.

Disk cache—The disk cache is a memory on the hard drive that stores data to be written to the disk until the computer is less busy and able to write the data to the disk.

Disk Defragmenter—A Windows 95 utility that defragments the user's files so they are read from and written to in a more efficient and faster way.

Disk errors—Hard drives can contain defects in the surface magnetic media that result in loss of the data that the operating system attempts to store there. These areas are referred to as disk errors.

Distribution Media Format (DMF)—Enables more data to be stored on one disk.

Dithering—Controls how colors are blended for the output on a color printer.

Docking station—A desktop base unit into which a laptop computer can be inserted for the purpose of taking advantage of additional hardware devices (such as a monitor, a printer, or a network).

Domain controller—The server that keeps the master account database.

DriveSpace—Compresses the data on the computer's hard disk to make more space on the disk.

DRVSPACE.BIN—The driver that supports compressed drives under Windows 95.

Dual boot—The capability to boot between two or more operating systems on the same machine.

Dynamic Memory Access (DMA) channel—A channel that enables peripherals to access portions of the computer's RAM directly.

E

Elections—Choosing which computer will become the browse master.

End task—When an application is hung, the user can select its name in the Close Programs dialog box and click the End Task button to terminate the program.

Enhanced Industry Standard Architecture (EISA)—A bus designed by non-IBM companies in the late 1980s. It offers the same features as MCA. The bus supports 32-bit edge adapter cards, which are configured through software. To integrate with Plug and Play, an EISA bus enumerator must be present.

Enhanced Metafile (EMF)—A printer-independent printing format with most of the processing of the print job to RAW format occurring in the background.

Enumeration—The process by which each device is examined and assigned an ID that will be used to identify it.

Error control—Used to boost file transfer speeds by eliminating errors caused by noise on the telephone line. This feature is available on most new modems.

Error correction—ScanDisk is a Windows 95 disk management tool that can correct certain errors in the FAT file system.

ERU.EXE—Emergency Recovery Utility saves key Windows 95 files to either a floppy drive, a local drive, or a network drive.

Exclusive use—If an MS-DOS application must have exclusive use of system resources and cannot share them, it must be run in MS-DOS mode.

Explorer—Runs the Desktop, and the Start menu launches programs. It is also the main file-management program.

Extended Capabilities Port (ECP)—Enables Windows 95 to use data compression at both the computer and the printer if they are both compliant.

Extension—The three characters following the period in an 8.3 format filename.

F

FAT32—The file system provided by OEMs through the OSR2 release of Windows 95. Accessible only through Windows 95 OSR2.

Fax modem—A device attached to a computer that can send and receive text and images through telephone lines. It offers the functionality of a fax machine except that all documents are electronic.

FDISK—A utility used to create and delete partitions, mark drives as active, and retrieve disk configuration information.

File Allocation Table (FAT)—The file system used by MS-DOS and Windows 95.

File and print sharing services—Enable a Windows 95 machine to share resources on a network.

File set—A saved list of files to be backed up or restored.

File synchronization—Windows 95 provides a set of OLE interfaces that enable applications to bind reconciliation handlers to it, track the contents of Briefcase, and define the outcome of any reconciliation on a class-by-class basis.

File system integrity—Indicates that the file system is free of errors from lost clusters or cross-linked files.

Filtering—The process of specifying certain files for inclusion or exclusion from a backup set.

Flat memory—Unlike MS-DOS, which had conventional and extended memory, Windows 95 memory is linear with no breaks.

Forum—A discussion group in which a user can read information posted by other people regarding a specific subject. Additional ideas can be posted to the forum for other people to read and comment on.

Fragmentation—A situation in which the clusters that make up a file are spread across a wide area of the disk.

Full backup—A complete backup of all the files on a Windows 95 system, including the Registry files.

G

Gateway—When the network uses a gateway to communicate with a host computer, the client computer running Windows 95 communicates with the gateway computer just as it does with any other computer on the network. The gateway computer translates requests from the client into a form that can be understood by the host, then communicates with the host and returns the information to the client.

General Protection Fault (GPF)—Occurs when an application attempts to violate the integrity of the system by performing an illegal operation.

Graphical User Interface (GUI)—A generic term in the context of how an operating system is displayed.

GROUPPOL.DLL—The dynamic link library or application extension that must be present on Windows 95 computers for support to group policy files.

GRPCONV.EXE—The utility used to convert *.grp files into the Windows 95 Program menu when Windows 95 is installed in its own directory.

H

Hardware Compatibility List (HCL)—A list of hardware made available by Microsoft that has been demonstrated to be compatible with Windows 95.

Hardware profile—A named configuration of the hardware devices used in a system.

Hardware tree—A list, created from entries in the Windows Registry, of all the hardware devices installed on a computer.

High Performance File System (HPFS)—A file system, originally developed for IBM's OS/2, that supports long filenames.

HIMEM.SYS—Enables access to High Memory Area (HMA). Loads and runs the real-mode Memory Manager.

Host drive—The physical drive on which a CVF is stored. This drive is assigned a higher drive letter, typically H.

HOSTS—The file for mapping host names to IP addresses.

Hot-docking—A style of docking that enables the laptop to be inserted into or removed from the docking station while running at full power.

Hung—Applications that have stopped responding to the system are said to be hung.

I-J-K

IFSHLP.SYS—Installable File System (IFS) Helper, which loads device drivers that enable Windows 95 to make calls to the file system.

Illegal characters—Reserved characters used by the operating system that are not allowed in filenames.

Image Color Matching (ICM)—A technology that was developed by a number of industry leaders to get the video display to match the colors being printed.

Implicit connection—An implicit connection is a feature of Dial-Up Networking that remembers network connections in the event that the user tries to access a resource from a network when he is not connected.

Inbox—A built-in universal inbox used to send, receive, and organize email, hold a user's received messages, and fax items from online services.

Inbox icon—An icon on the Desktop that launches the Exchange program.

Incremental backup—A partial backup of a disk that includes only the files that have changed since the last full backup.

Industry Standard Architecture (ISA)—The bus design of the 1984 IBM PC/AT computer. The bus supports the original 8-bit or 16-bit edge adapter cards, configured through the use of jumper pins and dip switches.

Inefficient—When files on a hard disk become badly fragmented, it takes much more mechanical activity of the disk and slows performance. This type of disk activity is inefficient. Disk Defragmenter is a Windows 95 tool that addresses this.

INF files—These are files that define what is needed for a particular application or operating system.

INI files—These files are text-based, are limited to 64 KB in size, and use APIs that allow only simple get/write operations. WIN16 applications use INI files to store their configuration information. They cannot access the Windows 95 Registry.

Install program—Certain MS-DOS applications use an install program that detects whether they are running in a multitasking environment. If the applications are running in a multitasking environment, they shut themselves down. In this case, they must be run in MS-DOS mode.

Installable File System (IFS)—A file system with which the operating system can work.

Integrated Drive Electronics (IDE)—A standard for communication with hard drives and CD-ROM drives that is not Plug and Play.

Internet—A global network of computers used to exchange information.

Internet Mail—An information service supported by Exchange that sends and receives email over the Internet.

Internet Service Provider (ISP)—A company that provides Internet access or Internet presence to individuals, businesses, and other groups for a monthly fee.

Interrupt—The process by which a hardware device communicates with the system CPU. Windows 95 traps these messages and passes them to the appropriate driver for handling.

Interrupt Request (IRQ) line—A communication line that peripherals use to notify a software process that a hardware event has occurred.

I/O port—The Input/Output port is an area of the computer's memory that peripherals use to execute input and output functions.

IPX/SPX—A routeable protocol used primarily in Novell NetWare networks.

L

Legacy components—Devices and BIOS that were not designed with the Plug and Play technology.

Legacy hardware—Older computers and hardware devices that do not support Plug and Play.

Legend—A color-coded guide that Disk Defragmenter provides to define the graphical representation of its operation.

List—Displays the contents of a folder as a list.

LMHOSTS—A file for mapping NetBIOS names to IP addresses.

Local installation—Accomplished by installing Windows 95 on the local hard drive.

Local reboot—The process of terminating a stalled application without affecting the system or other applications. Pressing Ctrl+Alt+Del once while Windows 95 is running brings up a Close Program dialog box where you can select an application to terminate.

Long filenames—Windows 95 allows up to 255 characters in a filename and 258 characters maximum for both the path and filename.

Loss of data—Loss of data can occur due to power failure, hard drive failure, or other errors. Windows 95 Backup is a tool that addresses this problem.

Lost clusters—When two files are cross-linked, it means that one of the files has a pointer to the wrong cluster. The cluster to which it was supposed to point, and all subsequent clusters in the file, are no longer referenced by any file. These are lost clusters.

M

Mail and Fax—An applet in the Control Panel that enables a user to add information services, modify information service settings, and create and modify profiles.

Mailbox—A place where electronic messages (incoming, outgoing, pending, and deleted) are stored for a particular user. MAILBOX.PST is stored on the user's hard drive.

Memory region—A portion of the computer's memory that a device reserves for its own use.

Memory space—The region of memory into which an application is loaded.

Message queue—Applications use the message queue to pass messages between the application and the processor. Each MS-DOS and Windows 32-bit application has its own unique message queue, and Windows 16-bit applications share a common message queue.

MicroChannel Architecture (MCA)—A bus architecture originally developed by IBM for its PS/2 computers. To integrate with Plug and Play, a MCA bus enumerator must be present.

Microsoft Fax—An applet included with Windows 95 that enables a computer's fax modem to send and receive faxes.

Microsoft Mail Information Service—A messaging system that enables users to send and receive mail on a network.

Microsoft Mail Postoffice—An applet in the Control Panel that enables an administrator to create a Workgroup Postoffice, create mailboxes, reset passwords, and perform other Postoffice management.

Minidriver—The printer-specific code that the manufacturer provides.

Mounting—The process of assigning drive letters and making a CVF available for viewing.

MSBATCH.INF—The default batch script filename for automating the Windows 95 installation process.

MS-DOS mode—An environment in which the Windows 95 GUI unloads itself from memory and grants a single MS-DOS application exclusive use of system resources.

MSPSERV—The Microsoft Print Agent for NetWare networks that enables a Windows 95 print server to despool print jobs at a NetWare print server.

Multipurpose Internet Mail Extensions (MIME)—A message format for outgoing messages that maintains attached files if the recipient is also using MIME.

Multitasking—The capability of a computer to process more than one thread at a time. This is done by dividing the processor's time into slices and enabling each thread to access the processor for a specific amount of time. Windows 95 uses cooperative multitasking as well as preemptive multitasking.

My Briefcase—Represents a briefcase object that contains files and folders the user wants to keep current.

My Computer—Represents the computer object and loosely corresponds to the File Manager in the previous version of Windows. It is a folder that gives the user quick access to the entire computer.

N

Name space—Software that enables a Novell NetWare file system to support filenames and file formats used by another operating system's native file systems.

NetBEUI NetBIOS (Network Basic Input/Output System) Extended User Interface—A local area network transport protocol provided with Windows 95 and used in LAN environments. It is small, fast, and not routeable.

NETLOG.TXT—An ASCII text file that contains a record of all detected network components found during installation.

NETSETUP.EXE—A server-based setup program that enables the user to install source files and create machine directories for a shared network installation.

NetWare Core Protocol (NCP)—A client protocol for NetWare 3.x services.

Network adapter—A hardware device used to attach one computer to another to form a network.

Network client software—The software that Windows 95 uses to communicate over the network with other computers and the network server.

Network fax server—A fax modem that has been shared so that other users on the network can use it to send and receive faxes.

Network Neighborhood—A new concept in Windows 95 that the computers in the user's workgroup or any NetWare servers to which the user is connected.

Network Protocol—The language a network uses so that all computers connected to that network can communicate with each other.

New Technology File System (NTFS)—The file system provided by Windows NT that provides local security and is accessible only through NT. It also supports long filenames.

Notification Area—The area on the Taskbar where you can see status information.

Novell's DR-DOS—Novell's version of DOS. This operating system is no longer being developed.

NT Boot Loader (NTLDR)—A built-in multiboot capability in Windows.

NT Hardware Compatibility List (HCL)—This list refers to all hardware tested to operate with Windows NT. Available from Microsoft at `www.microsoft.com`.

NWLink—Microsoft's IPX/SPX-compatible protocol.

O

Object Link Extensions (OLE)—This information is stored in HKEY_LOCAL_ MACHINE\SOFTWARE\Classes. Shortcuts in Windows 95 are OLE links. OLE enables the user to share data between OLE-compliant applications.

Offending application—An application that has attempted to violate system integrity in some way.

Online help—Help regarding the current task that the user can access by selecting the Help menu or by pressing F1.

On-the-fly—A process that occurs automatically. Windows 95 compression/decompression is on-the-fly because it occurs automatically and is transparent to the user.

Orphan file—A copied file that does not have a master file with which to synchronize. This could be due to the original file being deleted or the file being created inside Briefcase.

Orphaned clusters—Another name for lost clusters.

OSI Reference Model—A seven-layer architecture that standardizes levels of service and types of interaction for computers exchanging information through a communications network. It is used to describe the flow of data between the physical connection to the network and the end-user program.

P

Path—The fully specified location of a file including all subdirectories between a file and the root directory of the drive on which the file is stored.

Pause—To stop printing a document or stop the entire printer.

PC-DOS—IBM's version of DOS.

PCX—This format has become the de facto graphics file standard.

Performance—Overall performance of the system can be improved with proper use of Windows 95 disk Management Tools—Disk Defragmenter, ScanDisk, DriveSpace, and Backup.

Peripheral Component Interconnect (PCI)—A standard bus architecture that is compatible with Plug and Play. It is being promoted as the logical successor to VL. It enables high-speed connections to peripheral hardware devices.

Personal Computer Memory Card International Association (PCMCIA)—A specification that supports the key features of Plug and Play.

PING—Used to verify that an IP address can be reached.

Plug and Play (PnP)—The goal of Plug and Play is to enable changes to be made to the computer's configuration without requiring active intervention by the user.

Point and Print—The capability to point to a printer that is shared on the network and print to it.

Pointer—A piece of information in a file cluster that indicates the location of the next cluster in the chain.

Point-to-Point Protocol (PPP)—An industry standard that is part of Windows 95 Dial-Up Networking. It ensures interoperability with remote access software from other vendors.

POLEDIT.EXE—The System Policy Editor executable file. Computer, User, and Group System policies are created using the System Policy Editor.

Portable—The recommended option for mobile users with portable computers. Installs the appropriate set of files for a portable computer. This includes installing Briefcase for file synchronization and the supporting software for direct cable connections to exchange files.

PostScript—PostScript is a device-independent page description language used commonly when printing graphics. This type of print code does not require rendering because it already has all the code provided.

Power failure—Power failure can result in loss of data. Run Windows 95 Backup at regular intervals to prevent loss of valuable data files.

Preemptive multitasking—In preemptive multitasking, applications are allocated time slices or periods of execution time in which the application has access to the CPU. These time slices are managed in part based on the applications' thread priority levels.

Prevention—It's always best to try to prevent problems from happening. Regular use of Windows 95 disk management tools can prevent many known problems with hard disks and the FAT file system.

Primary Scheduler—A component of the task scheduler responsible for evaluating all thread priorities and allocating time slices of execution for threads. If two or more threads have the same priority, they're stacked. Each stacked thread is granted a time slice of execution in sequence until no threads have the same priority.

Process—A process performs a specific function and is comprised of an executable program, a memory address space, system resources, and at least one thread to perform the function.

Profile—A collection of settings (Start menu, network connections, shortcuts, Desktop icons, and screen colors) that specifies which information services are configured for a particular user and defines what types of connections to use for each service.

Program Groups—A collection of executables or files in Windows 3.x and Windows 95.

PROGRAM.EXE—Program Manager is included as an optional interface at installation time for Windows 95. This enables a user to maintain the same interface as in Windows 3.1.

Properties—The properties of the environment in which an application runs can be modified and customized under Windows 95.

Properties sheet—An object's properties (settings and parameters) are found on this sheet.

Protected mode—A processor operating mode in which memory address space assigned to a process can be protected from other processes. Windows 95 32-bit drivers are protected-mode drivers.

Protected-mode drivers—Protected-mode drivers are 32-bit drivers that store configuration information in the Windows 95 Registry. These devices are dynamically loaded in Windows 95 when they are needed and release their allocated memory when unloaded, thereby increasing the amount of memory available to the system. MS-DOS applications can take advantage of these drivers if they run in a VM.

Protocol—The language a computer speaks on the network and a defined standard for how to perform an operation.

PSERVER—The DOS equivalent of MSPSERV, which must be run from a dedicated DOS computer to run the NetWare print service.

Q

Quarter Inch Cartridge (QIC)—The Tape backup specification that is supported by Windows 95 Backup.

Queue—The documents waiting to be printed.

Queue Management Services (QMS)—An API that Microsoft Print Agent for NetWare Networks uses for queue services.

R

RAW—This is the code that is native to the printer. When a document is sent to the printer, it must be rendered to this format. RAW printing is a printer-dependent format with the processing occurring in the foreground.

Real-mode drivers—Real-mode drivers are 16-bit drivers that were designed for Microsoft Windows 3.x. Real-mode drivers are implemented in AUTOEXEC.BAT or CONFIG.SYS. These drivers were loaded during boot-up and tend to use more memory than their respective 32-bit drivers.

Recycle Bin—Represents a trash-bin object. Any folders and files the user deletes are automatically moved to this folder.

Reentrant code—Reentrant code can be accessed by multiple applications at the same time, whereas non-reentrant code can be accessed by only one application at a time.

Refresh—Refreshes the contents of the folder. Any changes made in a folder may not always be shown immediately. Refresh updates the display.

REGEDIT.EXE—The Registry Editor executable file, which is used to view and change the contents of the Windows 95 Registry.

Registry—A database in which Windows 95 stores configuration information for hardware and software.

REGSERVE.EXE—The Microsoft Remote Registry Service executable file.

Remote Access Server (RAS)—A computer that is accessed remotely by modem and runs administrative software and controls access to all or part of the network and its resources.

Remote computer—Any Windows 95 computer that the user can physically connect to using network cabling or Dial-Up Networking.

Resolution—The number of dots per inch (dpi) used for printing scalable fonts and graphics.

Resource arbitrator—A Windows 95 component that is responsible for keeping track of resource allocation to the installed devices on a computer. Each major resource type has an arbitrator.

Restore—The process of retrieving files from a backup set and copying them back to their original location.

Resume—To continue printing a document or have the printer continue printing all documents.

Ring 0—The most protected and privileged ring in the Intel chip architecture. Ring 0 enjoys hardware-level protection services and contains system-level components such as virtual device drivers.

Ring 3—The third ring in the Intel architecture, which has software-level protection services and is used by Windows 95 for running all applications.

RLE—A compressed bitmap graphics format.

Roving User Profiles—User profiles available on a network. These files are located in the home directory of users in a Windows NT domain, or in the users' mail\user_id directory on a NetWare server.

Run—Enables the user to launch applications directly from the Start Menu.

S

Safe mode—A method of starting Windows 95 when the system is having trouble. When the user starts Windows 95 in the Safe mode, only the mouse, keyboard, and VGA device drivers are loaded.

Salvaged data—Data from a file that can be recovered after the file has become cross-linked.

ScanDisk—A Windows 95 utility that checks and fixes data errors and physical surface problems in files and folders on the user's hard disk.

Script—Typically, an .inf file that works as an "engine" to "assemble" executables, operating systems, drivers, and so on.

Secondary scheduler—A component of the task scheduler responsible for priority inheritance boosting and for adjusting the priority of threads over time to smooth the execution of programs.

Sector—A unit of space on a floppy or hard disk.

Separator page—A header page that is printed before each document to indicate whose print job it is and other specific information.

Serial Line Internet Protocol (SLIP)—An industry standard that can be used with Windows 95 Dial-Up Networking to ensure interoperability with remote-access software from other vendors.

Server Message Block (SMB)—A protocol developed by IBM for networking.

Server-based setup—The process of loading the source files on a server so that Windows 95 can be installed across the network.

SETUPLOG.TXT—An ASCII text file that contains the Windows 95 Setup information created during installation.

SETVER.EXE—Included for compatibility reasons. Some MS-DOS applications require specific versions of MS-DOS to be running. This TSR-type device responds to those applications that query for version number by responding directly from an internal table.

Share-level access—The processes of protecting network resources through passwords only.

Share-level access control—In share-level access control, the user assigns a password to a specific resource. Depending on the password used, a user may have Read-Only or Full Control.

Share-level security—Rights based on the access that users have to a resource.

Shared fax modem—A fax modem to which a user has given permission to other users on the network to send and receive faxes.

Shared installation—Accomplished by installing Windows 95 on a server and then running the OS across the network.

Shiva Password Authentication Protocol (SPAP)—SPAP offers encryption of PAP passwords and Novell NetWare bindery access for user account information. When Windows 95 is set up for user-level security using a NetWare server account list, this is the security type used for remote access clients.

Shortcut—An icon created for an application which points to the location of the executable file and contains properties that tailor the application's environment.

Shut down—Offers the user the choice to shut down, restart, restart in MS-DOS mode, close all programs and, if the user is on a network, to log on as a different user.

Simple Mail Transfer Protocol (SMTP)—An ASCII message format that is commonly used for mail sent on the Internet.

Single-tasking—When running in MS-DOS mode, the system becomes single-tasking, enabling only one application to be run at a time.

Small Computer Standard Interface (SCSI)—A bus architecture that can chain a number of devices on one cable.

Software compression—Software compression specifies that the computer will try to compress information before sending it. Compression will occur only if the computer to which the user is connecting is using a compatible compression program.

Spool—This is the act of rendering a document to be printed. The RAW code is kept on disk and then sent to the printer.

Stacker—A disk-compression product sold by STAC Electronics, Inc. Windows 95 is compatible with this product, but it cannot use protected-mode drivers to access Stacker drives and is consequently slower in performance.

Stacks—System resource stacks under Windows 95 are now 32-bit, decreasing the likelihood of running out of system resources.

Stall—An application is said to be stalled when it does not check its message queue. As a result, the application stops working.

Standard mode—One of the operating modes for ScanDisk in which it does not scan the physical surface of the disk for defects.

Start menu—The component of Windows 95 that provides fast access to various components of Windows 95, including applications.

StartUp disk—A floppy disk created in the Add/Remove programs applet or during installation. Used to boot Windows 95 into a non-GUI mode for emergency repair.

Status bar—A message bar at the bottom of the Windows Explorer. This bar displays information about the various parts and functions of a Windows Explorer session.

Status information—The items located in the Notification Area appear as small icons for programs running in the background.

Storage media—The particular type of storage used for a backup. Windows 95 backup supports floppy disks, hard disks, and QIC tapes as storage media.

Subnet—Division of the network into smaller networks.

Subnet Mask—The means by which networks are divided.

Supervisor—The highest-authority account on a NetWare network.

Suspended—When a WIN16 application creates a GPF, all other WIN16 applications are suspended until the offending application is shut down.

Swap file—The swap file is used by Windows 95 to provide Virtual Memory by swapping pages from RAM to the swap file.

Switches—Parameters specified at the end of the command that modify the way the command is executed. Each program file supports different switches.

Symptom—A careful analysis of problem symptoms can lead to the selection of the appropriate tool for problem resolution.

System integrity—Windows 95 maintains system integrity by separating application memory address space and processor privilege, and by virtualizing hardware devices.

System policies—Files used to control a user's environment and restrict privileges based on users, groups, or computers.

System Policy Editor—Use the System Policy Editor to create system policy users, groups of users, and computers.

System Virtual Machine—The Virtual Machine in which all 16-bit and 32-bit Windows applications run. The 16-bit applications share a common address space within the System Virtual Machine, and 32-bit applications each maintain separate address spaces.

SYSTEM.DAT—One of two files that make up the Registry, this is the Registry file that contains the hardware and computer- specific settings for a workstation. By default, this file is located in the Windows SYSTEM directory. SYSTEM.DAT contains machine-specific data.

T

Taskbar—A list of all active programs created by maintaining a title button for each active program.

TechNet—A CD-ROM available by subscription from Microsoft technical information and updates to Microsoft products.

Telephone Application Programming Interface (TAPI)—Arbitrates among applications that want to share the same communications ports and devices.

Terminated—Applications that attempt to violate system integrity are terminated to protect the system and other applications running concurrently.

Third party—Refers to manufacturers other than the manufacturer of the specific application or hardware.

Thread—The smallest unit of executable code contained in an application. 32-bit applications may have multiple threads executing concurrently.

Through mode—One of the operating modes for ScanDisk in which it scans the physical surface of the disk for defects.

Thunking—The process of translating a 16-bit API call to a 32-bit API, call and vice versa.

Token—A small piece of code used to represent longer, repetitive bit patterns in a data file.

Toolbar—The Toolbar provides a fast way to access menu items in Windows Explorer.

Tools—Windows 95 provides several tools, or utilities, for managing disk resources.

Transmission Control Protocol/Internet Protocol (TCP/IP)—A routeable protocol used to access the Internet, provide functionality in WANs, and access UNIX resources.

TSR—Terminate and Stay Resident programs can be activated each time an application is started by specifying them in a batch file on the application's shortcut Properties sheet.

Typical installation? or configuration?—The default option, which Microsoft recommends for most users with desktop computers.

U

Unidriver—The universal driver is the code that Microsoft provides that works with most printers. The manufacturer then supply only a small amount of code that is specific to the printer.

Unified Logon—The capability to connect to all resources after a single logon.

UNINSTAL.EXE—A utility used to remove Windows 95 from a computer.

Universal Naming Convention (UNC)—Refers to a standard way of referencing an object on another computer on a network.

USER.DAT— The file that contains user configuration settings used to implement user profiles either locally or on a network. One of two files that make up the Registry.

User-level access—The process of protecting network resources through users' logon accounts.

User-level access control—In user-level access control, specific users are given rights to a specific resource. A network server (NetWare or Microsoft) is required as a security provider, which provides a list of authorized users.

User-level security—Security based on rights assigned to a specific user.

USER.MAN—The file that contains user configuration settings used to implement mandatory user profiles on a network.

Utility—A tool for maintenance and problem resolution. Windows 95 provides four disk-management utilities: Disk Defragmenter, ScanDisk, DriveSpace, and Backup.

UUENCODE—A message format for incoming and outgoing messages that converts attached binary files into text format before they are sent over the Internet.

V

Video Electronics Standards Association (VESA)—A high-speed bus architecture that is not Plug and Play.

Video problems—Certain MS-DOS games experience video problems running under Windows 95. In this case, they should be run in MS-DOS mode.

Virtual DOS Machine (VDM)—The virtual machine created for each MS-DOS application running. Each MS-DOS application executed creates another VDM.

Virtual Machine (VM)—Applications in Windows 95 are designed to be run in a Virtual Machine that provides the application access to memory, resources, and the use of hardware using virtual drivers.

Virtual Machine Manager (VMM)—The VMM subsystem provides the resources needed for each application and system process running on the computer, including memory management and task scheduling.

Virtual memory—A combination of physical RAM and hard disk space that provides more memory than is installed on the computer.

W-X-Y-Z

Warm-docking—A style of docking that enables the laptop to be inserted into or removed from the docking station while in a suspended state.

WIN16 MUTEX—The flag set for WIN16 processes when they make requests to 16-bit API functions. This prevents other WIN16 applications from attempting to use the same code simultaneously.

Windows Internet Naming Service (WINS)—Automatic NetBIOS resolution service.

Windows 95 Registry—Stored in two files: the SYSTEM.DAT file and the USER.DAT file.

Windows 95 Taskbar—Provides quick access to all active programs by maintaining a set of buttons that represent the programs' title boxes.

WINIPCFG—Microsoft's utility used to retrieve IP information about a host.

WINNT32.EXE—The 32-bit Windows version of the Windows NT SetUp program.

WINREG.DLL—The application extension used by the Microsoft Remote Registry Service executable file. The default location for the file is the %systemroot%/system folder. This file must be present on all machines for the Remote Registry Service to function.

Wizard—A type of utility developed by Microsoft to make it easier for the average user to set up his computer and software.

Workgroup Postoffice—A folder that temporarily stores messages for members of a workgroup until users request delivery of their messages.

World Wide Web—A network of servers that uses hypertext links to find and access files. A browser enables users to view documents on servers around the world without having to manually type each location.

Write-behind caching—Also known as lazy writes, it is the process of storing data in cache until the processor can write the data to disk.

Appendix

Overview of the Certification Process

You must pass rigorous certification exams to become a Microsoft Certified Professional. These certification exams provide a valid and reliable measure of your technical proficiency and expertise. The closed-book exams are developed in consultation with computer industry professionals who have on-the-job experience with Microsoft products in the workplace. These exams are conducted by an independent organization—Sylvan Prometric—at more than 1,200 Authorized Prometric Testing Centers around the world.

Currently Microsoft offers six types of certification, based on specific areas of expertise:

- **Microsoft Certified Professional (MCP).** Qualified to provide installation, configuration, and support for users of at least one Microsoft desktop operating system, such as Windows NT Workstation. In addition, candidates can take elective exams to develop areas of specialization. MCP is considered the initial or first level of expertise leading to a premium certification.
- **Microsoft Certified Professional+Internet (MCP+Internet).** Qualified to plan security, install and configure server products, manage server resources, extend service to run CGI scripts or ISAPI scripts, monitor and analyze performance, and troubleshoot problems.
- **Microsoft Certified Systems Engineer (MCSE).** Qualified to effectively plan, implement, maintain, and support

information systems with Microsoft Windows NT and other Microsoft advanced systems and workgroup products, such as Microsoft Office and Microsoft BackOffice. MCSE is a second level of expertise.

- **Microsoft Certified Systems Engineer+Internet (MCSE+Internet).** Qualified in the core MCSE areas, plus qualified to enhance, deploy, and manage sophisticated intranet and Internet solutions that include a browser, proxy server, host servers, database, and messaging and commerce components. In addition, an MCSE + Internet–certified professional is able to manage and analyze Web sites.
- **Microsoft Certified Solution Developer (MCSD).** Qualified to design and develop custom business solutions by using Microsoft development tools, technologies, and platforms, including Microsoft Office and Microsoft BackOffice. MCSD is a second level of expertise.
- **Microsoft Certified Trainer (MCT).** Instructionally and technically qualified by Microsoft to deliver Microsoft Education courses at Microsoft-authorized sites. An MCT must be employed by a Microsoft Solution Provider Authorized Technical Education Center or a Microsoft Authorized Academic Training site.

For up-to-date information about each type of certification, visit the Microsoft Training and Certification World Wide Web site at **http://www.microsoft.com/train_cert**. You must have an Internet account and a WWW browser to access this information. You also can call the following sources:

- Microsoft Certified Professional Program: 800-636-7544
- Sylvan Prometric Testing Centers: 800-755-EXAM
- Microsoft Online Institute (MOLI): 800-449-9333

How to Become a Microsoft Certified Professional (MCP)

Becoming an MCP requires you to pass one operating system exam. The following list shows the names and exam numbers of all the operating systems from which you can choose to qualify for your MCP certification:

- Implementing and Supporting Microsoft Windows 95, #70-063*
- Implementing and Supporting Microsoft Windows 95, #70-064
- Implementing and Supporting Microsoft Windows NT Workstation 4.02, #70-073
- Implementing and Supporting Microsoft Windows NT Workstation 3.51, #70-042
- Implementing and Supporting Microsoft Windows NT Server 4.0, #70-067
- Implementing and Supporting Microsoft Windows NT Server 3.51, #70-043
- Microsoft Windows for Workgroups 3.11-Desktop, #70-048*
- Microsoft Windows 3.1, #70-030*
- Microsoft Windows Architecture I, #70-160
- Microsoft Windows Architecture II, #70-161

* Exams marked with an asterisk are scheduled to be retired. Check the Microsoft Training and Certification World Wide Web site at **http://www.microsoft.com/train_cert** for details.

How to Become a Microsoft Certified Professional+Internet (MCP+Internet)

Becoming an MCP with a specialty in Internet technology requires you to pass the following three exams:

- Internetworking Microsoft TCP/IP on Microsoft Windows NT 4.0, #70-059
- Implementing and Supporting Microsoft Windows NT Server 4.0, #70-067
- Implementing and Supporting Microsoft Internet Information Server 3.0 and Microsoft Index Server 1.1, #70-077

  OR Implementing and Supporting Microsoft Internet Information Server 4.0, #70-087

How to Become a Microsoft Certified Systems Engineer (MCSE)

MCSE candidates must pass four operating system exams and two elective exams. The MCSE certification path is divided into two tracks: the Windows NT 3.51 track and the Windows NT 4.0 track.

The exams included in this software product span the core requirements for the Windows NT 4.0 track only.

The following lists show the core requirements (four operating system exams) for the Windows NT 3.51 and 4.0 tracks, and the elective courses (two exams) you can choose from for either track.

The four Windows NT 3.51 Track Core Requirements for MCSE certification are as follows:

- Implementing and Supporting Microsoft Windows NT Server 3.51, #70-043

- Implementing and Supporting Microsoft Windows NT Workstation 3.51, #70-042
- Networking Essentials, #70-058
- Microsoft Windows 3.1, #70-030*

  OR Microsoft Windows for Workgroups 3.11, #70-048*

  OR Implementing and Supporting Microsoft Windows 95, #70-063*

  OR Implementing and Supporting Microsoft Windows 95, #70-064

The four Windows NT 4.0 Track Core Requirements for MCSE certification are as follows:

- Implementing and Supporting Microsoft Windows NT Server 4.0, #70-067
- Implementing and Supporting Microsoft Windows NT Server 4.0 in the Enterprise, #70-068
- Networking Essentials, #70-058
- Microsoft Windows 3.1, #70-030*

  OR Microsoft Windows for Workgroups 3.11, #70-048*

  OR Implementing and Supporting Microsoft Windows 95, #70-063*

  OR Implementing and Supporting Microsoft Windows 95, #70-064

  OR Implementing and Supporting Microsoft Windows NT Workstation 4.0, #70-073

For either the Windows NT 3.51 and or the 4.0 track, you must pass two of the following elective exams for MCSE certification:

- Implementing and Supporting Microsoft SNA Server 3.0, #70-013

  OR Implementing and Supporting Microsoft SNA Server 4.0, #70-085

- Implementing and Supporting Microsoft Systems Management Server 1.0, #70-014*

  OR Implementing and Supporting Microsoft Systems Management Server 1.2, #70-018

  OR Implementing and Supporting Microsoft Systems Management Server 1.2, #70-086

- Microsoft SQL Server 4.2 Database Implementation, #70-021

  OR Implementing a Database Design on Microsoft SQL Server 6.5, #70-027

  OR Implementing a Database Design on Microsoft SQL Server 7.0, #70-029

- Microsoft SQL Server 4.2 Database Administration for Microsoft Windows NT, #70-022

  OR System Administration for Microsoft SQL Server 6.5, #70-026

  OR System Administration for Microsoft SQL Server 7.0, #70-028

- Microsoft Mail for PC Networks 3.2-Enterprise, #70-037

- Internetworking with Microsoft TCP/IP on Microsoft Windows NT (3.5-3.51), #70-053

  OR Internetworking with Microsoft TCP/IP on Microsoft Windows NT 4.0, #70-059

- Implementing and Supporting Microsoft Exchange Server 4.0, #70-075*

  OR Implementing and Supporting Microsoft Exchange Server 5.0, #70-076

OR Implementing and Supporting Microsoft Exchange Server 5.5, #70-081

- Implementing and Supporting Microsoft Internet Information Server 3.0 and Microsoft Index Server 1.1, #70-077

  OR Implementing and Supporting Microsoft Internet Information Server 4.0, #70-087

- Implementing and Supporting Microsoft Internet Explorer 4.0 by Using the Internet Explorer Resource Kit, #70-079

How to Become a Microsoft Certified Systems Engineer+Internet (MCSE+Internet)

MCSE+Internet candidates must pass seven operating system exams and two elective exams.

The following lists show the core requirements and the elective courses (two exams). The seven MCSE+Internet core exams required for certification are as follows:

- Networking Essentials, #70-058
- Internetworking with Microsoft TCP/IP on Microsoft Windows NT 4.0, #70-059
- Implementing and Supporting Microsoft Windows 95, #70-063

  OR Implementing and Supporting Microsoft Windows NT Workstation 4.0, #70-073

- Implementing and Supporting Microsoft Windows NT Server 4.0, #70-067
- Implementing and Supporting Microsoft Windows NT Server 4.0 in the Enterprise, #70-068

- Implementing and Supporting Microsoft Internet Information Server 3.0 and Microsoft Index Server 1.1, #70-077

  OR Implementing and Supporting Microsoft Internet Information Server 4.0, #70-087

- Implementing and Supporting Microsoft Internet Explorer 4.0 by Using the Internet Explorer Resource Kit, #70-079

You must also pass two of the following elective exams:

- System Administration for Microsoft SQL Server 6.5, #70-026
- Implementing a Database Design on Microsoft SQL Server 6.5, #70-027
- Implementing and Supporting Microsoft Exchange Server 5.0, #70-076

  OR Implementing and Supporting Microsoft Exchange Server 5.5, #70-081

- Implementing and Supporting Microsoft Proxy Server 1.0, #70-078

  OR Implementing and Supporting Microsoft Proxy Server 2.0, #70-088

How to Become a Microsoft Certified Solution Developer (MCSD)

MCSD candidates must pass two core technology exams and two elective exams. The following lists show the required technology exams, plus the elective exams that apply toward becoming an MCSD.

You must pass the following two core technology exams to qualify for MCSD certification:

- Microsoft Windows Architecture I, #70-160
- Microsoft Windows Architecture II, #70-161

You must also pass two of the following elective exams to become an MCSD:

- Microsoft SQL Server 4.2 Database Implementation, #70-021

  OR Implementing a Database Design on Microsoft SQL Server 6.5, #70-027

  OR Implementing a Database Design on Microsoft SQL Server 7.0, #70-029
- Developing Applications with C++ Using the Microsoft Foundation Class Library, #70-024
- Microsoft Visual Basic 3.0 for Windows-Application Development, #70-050

  OR Programming with Microsoft Visual Basic 4.0, #70-065

  OR Developing Applications with Microsoft Visual Basic 5.0, #70-165
- Microsoft Access 2.0 for Windows-Application Development, #70-051

  OR Microsoft Access for Windows 95 and the Microsoft Access Development Toolkit, #70-069
- Developing Applications with Microsoft Excel 5.0 Using Visual Basic for Applications, #70-052
- Programming in Microsoft Visual FoxPro 3.0 for Windows, #70-054
- Implementing OLE in Microsoft Foundation Class Applications, #70-025

How to Become a Microsoft Certified Trainer (MCT)

To understand the requirements and process for becoming a Microsoft Certified Trainer (MCT), you must obtain the Microsoft

Certified Trainer Guide document (MCTGUIDE.DOC) from the following WWW site:

http://www.microsoft.com/train_cert/download.htm

On this page, click on the hyperlink MCT GUIDE (mctguide.doc) (117k). If your WWW browser can display DOC files (Word for Windows native file format), the MCT Guide appears in your browser window. Otherwise, you need to download it and open it in Word for Windows or Windows 95 WordPad. The MCT Guide explains in detail the following four-step process to becoming an MCT:

1. Complete and mail a Microsoft Certified Trainer application to Microsoft. You must include proof of your skills for presenting instructional material. The options for doing so are described in the MCT Guide.

2. Obtain and study the Microsoft Trainer Kit for the Microsoft Official Curricula (MOC) course(s) for which you want to be certified. Microsoft Trainer Kits can be ordered by calling 800-688-0496 in North America. Other regions should review the MCT Guide for information about how to order a Trainer Kit.

3. Pass the Microsoft certification exam for the product for which you want to be certified to teach.

4. Attend the Microsoft Official Curriculum (MOC) course for the course for which you want to be certified. This must be done so you can understand how the course is structured, how labs are completed, and how the course flows.

Consider the preceding steps a general overview of the MCT certification process. The precise steps that you need to take are described in detail in the MCTGUIDE.DOC file on the WWW site mentioned previously. Do not misconstrue the preceding steps as the actual process you must take.

If you are interested in becoming an MCT, you can receive more information by visiting the Microsoft Certified Training (MCT) WWW site at **http://www.microsoft.com/train_cert/mctint.htm**; or call 800-688-0496.

Appendix D

Study Tips

Self-study involves any method that you employ to learn a given topic, with the most popular being third-party books, such as the one you hold in your hand. Before you begin to study for a certification exam, you should know exactly what Microsoft expects you to learn.

Pay close attention to the objectives posted for the exam. The entire set of objectives is listed in the introduction to this book. The relevant subset of objectives also appears at the beginning of each chapter. The objectives can always be found on the WWW site at **http://www.microsoft.com/train_cert**. As well, you should notice at the beginning of the book a handy tear-out card with an objective matrix that lists each objective and the page you can turn to for information on that objective.

Another thing to think about is this: Humans vary in their learning styles. Some people are visual learners, others are textual, and still others learn best from aural sources. However, there are some basic principles of learning that apply to everyone. For example, students who take notes on lectures have better recall on exam day—even if they did not study the notes later—because they encoded the information as well as decoded it—they processed it in a deeper, more active fashion than those who simply listened to the lecture.

Hence, use the study techniques that you know work for you, but also take advantage of more general principles of learning. For example, if you are a visual learner, pay special attention to the figures provided in this book. Also create your own visual cues by doing things like diagramming processes and relationships.

A general principle of learning that you might take advantage of has to do with studying the organization and the details of information separately. Cognitive learning research has demonstrated that if you attempt to focus on learning just the organization of the information, followed by a focus on learning just the specific details, you will retain the information better than if you attempt to take in all of the information at once. Use your study materials to prepare a detailed outline of the material on the exam. Study it first by learning the organization of the material. Then, in your next pass through the outline, focus on memorizing and understanding the detail. Trying to do both at once only leads to the two types of information interfering with your overall learning.

Finally, follow common-sense practices in your studying as well. Some of these studying strategies are as follows:

- Study in bright light to reduce fatigue and depression.
- Establish a regular study schedule and stick as closely to it as possible.
- Turn off all forms of distraction, including radios and televisions; or try studying in a quiet room.
- Always study in the same place so your materials are always readily at hand.
- Take short (approximately 15-minute) breaks every two to three hours or so. Studies have proven that your brain assimilates information better when these rest periods are taken.

Testing Yourself

Before taking the actual exam, verify that you are ready to do so by testing yourself many times in a variety of ways. Within this book are questions at the beginning and end of each chapter. On the accompanying CD-ROM is an electronic test engine that emulates the actual Microsoft exam and enables you to test your knowledge of the subject areas. Use this repeatedly until you are consistently scoring in the 90 percent range (or better).

Repeatedly testing yourself means, of course, that you can't start studying five days before the exam begins. You will need to give yourself plenty of time to read, practice, and allow for testing yourself several times.

The New Riders' TestPrep electronic testing engine, we believe, is the best test preparation tool on the market, unparalleled by most other engines. TestPrep is described in detail in Appendix F, "All About TestPrep."

Hints and Tips for Doing Your Best on the Tests

When you go to take the actual exam, be prepared. Arrive early and be ready to show two forms of identification. Expect wordy questions. Although you have approximately 60 minutes to take the exam, you must answer all questions. This may sound like ample time, but remember that many of the questions can involve lengthy word problems, exhibits that must be referred to, and, more recently, even simulations. Your approximately 60 minutes of exam time can be consumed very quickly.

Approximately 85 percent of the candidates taking their first Microsoft exam fail it. They fail not so much because they are unprepared and lack the knowledge they need, but because they don't know what to expect and are immediately intimidated by the wordiness of the questions and the ambiguity they feel is implied in the answers.

Things to Watch For

When you take the exam, read very carefully! Make sure that you read the whole question and understand just what the question requires, and take notice of the number of correct choices you need to make. Remember that some questions require that you select a single correct answer; other questions have more than one correct answer. Radial buttons next to the answer choices indicate that the answers are mutually exclusive—there is just one correct answer. On the other hand, check boxes indicate that the answers are not mutually exclusive and there are multiple correct answers.

Again, read the questions fully. With lengthy questions, the last sentence often dramatically changes the scenario. When taking the exam, you are given pencils and two sheets of paper. If you are uncertain of what the question requires, map out the scenario on the paper until you have it clear in your mind. You must turn in the scrap paper at the end of the exam.

Choosing the Right Answer

Adopt a strategy for evaluating possible answers. Eliminate those answers that are impossible or implausible. Carefully evaluate those that remain. Be careful: Some answers are true statements as they stand on their own, but in the context of the question, might not make sense as correct answers. The answers must match or relate to the question before they can serve as correct choices.

Marking Answers for Return

You can mark questions on the actual exam and refer back to them later. If you encounter a wordy question that will take a long time to read and decipher, mark it and return to it when you have completed the rest of the exam. This will help prevent you from wasting time on it and running out of time on the exam.

Changing Answers

The rule of thumb here is *don't*! If you have read the question carefully and completely, and you felt like you knew the right answer, you probably did. Don't second-guess yourself! If, as you check your answers, one stands out as clearly marked incorrectly, however, of course you should change it in that instance. But if you are at all unsure, go with your first impression.

Attaching Notes to Test Questions

At the conclusion of the exam, before the grading takes place, you are given the opportunity to attach a message to any one question. If you feel that a question was too ambiguous, or tested on knowledge you do not need to know to work with the product, take this opportunity to state your case. Unheard of is the instance in which Microsoft changes a test score as a result of an attached message. However, it never hurts to try—and it helps to vent your frustration before blowing the proverbial 50-amp fuse.

Good luck!

Appendix

What's on the CD-ROM?

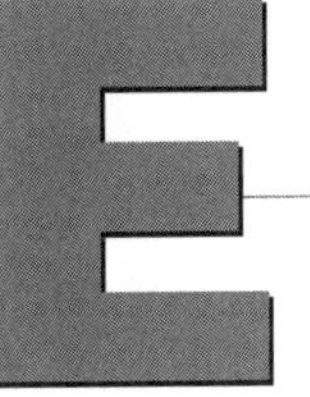

This appendix is a brief rundown of what you'll find on the CD-ROM that comes with this book. For a more detailed description of the newly developed TestPrep test engine, exclusive to Macmillan Computer Publishing, please see Appendix F, "All About TestPrep."

TestPrep

TestPrep is a new test engine developed exclusively for Macmillan Computer Publishing. It is, we believe, the best test engine available because it closely emulates the actual Microsoft exam, and enables you to check your score by category, which helps you determine what topics you need to study further. Before running the TestPrep software, be sure to read CDROM.hlp (in the root directory of the CD-ROM) for late-breaking news on TestPrep features. For a complete description of the benefits of TestPrep, please see Appendix F.

Exclusive Electronic Version of Text

Also contained on the CD-ROM is the electronic version of this book. You can use this version to help you search for terms or areas that you need to study. The electronic version comes complete with all figures as they appear in the book.

Copyright Information and Disclaimer

Appendix F

All About TestPrep

The TestPrep software on the CD-ROM accompanying this book enables you to test your Windows 95 knowledge in a manner similar to that employed by the actual Microsoft exam. Actually, three applications are included: Practice Exams, Study Cards, and Flash Cards. Practice Exams provides simulated multiple-choice tests. Study Cards provides the same sorts of questions (but enables you to control the number and types of questions) and provides immediate feedback to you. This format enables you to learn from your testing and control the topics on which you want to be tested. Flash Cards provides this same sort of feedback and allows the same sort of control but requires short answer or essay answers to questions; you are not prompted with multiple-choice selections or cued as to the number of correct answers to provide.

Although it is possible to maximize the TestPrep applications, the default is for them to run in smaller mode so you can refer to your Windows 95 desktop while answering questions. TestPrep uses a unique randomization process to ensure that each time you run the programs, you get a different sequence of questions; this enhances your learning and helps prevent you from merely memorizing the expected answers over time without reading the question each and every time.

Question Presentation

TestPrep Practice Exams and Study Cards emulate the actual Microsoft "Implementing and Supporting Windows 95" exam (70-064), in that radial (circle) buttons are used to signify a single correct choice, whereas check boxes (squares) are used to indicate multiple correct answers.

Scoring

The TestPrep Practice Exam Score Report uses actual numbers from the "Implementing and Supporting Windows 95" exam.

Index

Symbols

A

B

C

D

E

F

G

H

I-J

K

L

N

O

R

S

U

V

W-Z

Licensing Agreement

By opening this package, you are agreeing to be bound by the following:

This software product is copyrighted, and all rights are reserved by the publisher and author. You are licensed to use this software on a single computer. You may copy and/or modify the software as needed to facilitate your use of it on a single computer. Making copies of the software for any other purpose is a violation of the United States copyright laws.

This software is sold *as is* without warranty of any kind, either expressed or implied, including but not limited to the implied warranties of merchantability and fitness for a particular purpose. Neither the publisher nor its dealers or distributors assumes any liability for any alleged or actual damages arising from the use of this program. (Some states do not allow for the exclusion of implied warranties, so the exclusion may not apply to you.)